D0398138

THE
South
IN
MODERN
AMERICA

The

New American Nation Series

EDITED BY

HENRY STEELE COMMAGER

AND

RICHARD B. MORRIS

THE

South

IN

MODERN AMERICA

A REGION AT ODDS

Dewey W. Grantham

HarperCollins*Publishers*

THE SOUTH IN MODERN AMERICA. Copyright © 1994 by Dewey W. Grantham. All rights reserved. Printed in the United States of America. No part of this book may be used or, reproduced in any manner whatsoever without written permission except in the case of brief quotations embodied in critical articles and reviews. For information address HarperCollins Publishers, Inc., 10 East 53rd Street, New York, NY 10022.

HarperCollins books may be purchased for educational, business, or sales promotional use. For information please write: Special Markets Department, HarperCollins Publishers, Inc., 10 East 53rd Street, New York, NY 10022.

FIRST EDITION

Designed by Alma Hochhauser Orenstein

LIBRARY OF CONGRESS CATALOG CARD NUMBER 93-45928
ISBN 0-06-016773-4

94 95 96 97 98 CC/HC 10 9 8 7 6 5 4 3 2 1

For J. Isaac Copeland

Contents

Illustrations follow pages *138, 202,* and *266.*

Tables, Maps, and Graphs

Acknowledgments

This study could not have been written without the help of many other people, including a host of scholars and writers whose books and articles I have used. I am indebted as well to a large number of archivists and librarians, especially for the skillful and cheerful assistance given me at the Jean and Alexander Heard Library of Vanderbilt University, the Manuscript Division of the Library of Congress, the Southern Historical Collection at the University of North Carolina, the Woodruff Library, Atlanta University Center, and the libraries at Clemson University, Emory University, the University of Georgia, and the University of Tennessee, Knoxville.

I am grateful to my colleague Jacque Voegeli for reading this study in manuscript and providing me with a penetrating and extremely useful critique of the work. I have also profited from the thoughtful evaluation of the manuscript by a reader (anonymous to me) for the publisher. I wish to thank Hugh Van Dusen of HarperCollins for his continuing interest in the undertaking and for his many helpful suggestions. The editorial skill and efficiency of Stephanie Gunning and Pamela LaBarbiera at HarperCollins facilitated the process of publication and made this a better book. Henry Steele Commager and Richard B. Morris, editors of the New American Nation Series, helped sustain the project with advice and encouragement.

Among many others who helped me with this book, I am particularly obligated to Robert G. Spinney, an able and resourceful research assistant and the creator of the tables I have included based on public opinion polls. I also want to thank Miles K. Goosens and Bruce Harvey for their research assistance. My son, Wesley Grantham, generously gave me the benefit of his knowledge of computer science and word processing. Another son, Clinton Grantham, and his wife, Gayle Grantham, helped me prepare some of the maps and tables. My fellow townsman John Egerton aided my search for illustrations and helped me in other ways as well. Three other people gave me valuable assistance in locating photographs and cartoons: Donald A. Ritchie of the U.S. Senate Historical

Office; Richard A. Shrader of the Southern Historical Collection, University of North Carolina at Chapel Hill; and Paul F. Wells of the Center for Popular Music, Middle Tennessee State University. Gary Gore, Director of Publications and Design at Vanderbilt University, gave me expert advice on the reproduction of photographs and maps. I am grateful to my colleagues in the Department of History at Vanderbilt for the stimulating and supportive environment they have created there, and to the department's staff members for their many acts of assistance and their unfailing good humor.

The publication of this book gives me an opportunity to express my great appreciation to the National Endowment for the Humanities, which awarded me a senior research fellowship for 1986–87, and to the Holland N. McTyeire professorship at Vanderbilt for indispensable research support. I am also indebted to Professor John L. Gordon, Jr., and his colleagues at the University of Richmond for providing me with a marvelous place to work on this project in its final stages and for recommending my appointment as Douglas Southall Freeman Professor of History in the spring of 1993.

I can never repay my wife, Virginia Burleson Grantham, for her contributions to my work on this venture and for all she does to give meaning to my life.

Isaac Copeland, former director of the Southern Historical Collection and professor of history emeritus at the University of North Carolina at Chapel Hill, has spent much of his life in the pursuit of southern history: as student and teacher, librarian and collector of manuscript materials, facilitator of research and writing, and adviser of historians and other scholars. His extraordinary professional and personal qualities have made him a rare and unforgettable figure in the realm of southern history. He is, for the members of my family and for countless other people, a warm and valued friend. It is a special pleasure to dedicate this volume to him.

Introduction

In the twentieth century, as in the nineteenth, the South has been the region most sharply at odds with the rest of the nation. No other part of the United States has projected such a clear-cut sectional image. Although the most spectacular period of sectional conflict came to an end with the close of Reconstruction, sectionalism has been a powerful and a recurring force in the national experience since that time. The Republican party, for instance, continued for a long time to invoke the bloody shirt in northern political campaigns, just as southern Democrats continued to make political use of epithets like "Radical Reconstruction" and "black domination." This harsh rhetoric gradually became less strident as the nation moved out of the shadow of war and Reconstruction and into the sunlight of sectional reconciliation, the promise of a New South, and an interregional understanding on the treatment of black southerners. But conflict and hostility between North and South remained a conspicuous feature of American life.*

At the end of Reconstruction, the South stood out as the nation's poorest, most isolated, and most distinctive section. It was less industrialized, less diversified, and less literate than other parts of the country. Its per capita income was barely half that of the national average. The great majority of southerners were farmers "caught in the trap of low productivity, poverty, and despair."[1] The southern states began to industrialize and urbanize more rapidly in the 1880s, but at the turn of the century only 18 percent of their work force was employed

---

*The *South* in this study is defined as the eleven ex-Confederate states plus Kentucky and Oklahoma. The *North* is defined as the rest of the country, although the context will show that it frequently refers more specifically to the Northeast and Midwest. While the terms *section* and *region* are used interchangeably, contemporary preference for the first in the period before the 1920s and for the second since then is usually followed. In the 1930s, the so-called regionalists sought to distinguish between the two terms.

1. Gilbert C. Fite, "The Agricultural Trap in the South," *Agricultural History* 60 (Fall 1986): 38–50 (quotation on p. 38).

in nonagricultural pursuits. The section was essentially a colonial appendage of the North. Though the South shared in the nation's prosperity during the early part of the new century and its economy became more diversified, it was still a poor stepchild in a well-to-do American family.

This study of American regionalism focuses on the modern South and its interaction with the rest of the nation. The study is concerned with four major themes. The first is sectional conflict—in Congress, in national elections, in the struggle for economic advantage, in the media, and in the interregional dialogue between northerners and southerners. At bottom this conflict reflected the divergent interests of the two sections, and more generally those of the country's fast-growing "core" and its less developed agricultural "periphery" to the south and west. Issues such as the tariff, the banking system, federal fiscal policy, and the regulation of railroads and other corporate activities divided Americans along sectional lines. The quest for federal appropriations frequently assumed a sectional dimension. So, too, did intensely fought battles over the prohibition of alcoholic beverages, the protection of industrial labor, and the movement for woman suffrage. Meanwhile, national elections revealed a sectional cast, and in the Democratic party North and South contended for dominance, first in the Wilson era and the 1920s and subsequently, as the locus of power shifted away from the South, in the 1940s and 1950s. In the 1950s and 1960s, the nation found itself locked in a great struggle over civil rights for African Americans, the most searing sectional conflict since Reconstruction. By the 1970s, the rise of the Sunbelt and the decline of the industrial Northeast and Midwest had resulted in another economic contest between North and South.

Interregional conflict also encompassed a rhetorical and symbolic clash—in the use of damning words, stereotypes, and images. North and South, C. Vann Woodward has observed, "served each other as inexhaustible objects of invidious comparison in the old game of regional polemics." Each region provided the other with a scapegoat for "domestic embarrassments and burdens of guilt."[2] Northern censure of the South's "peculiar" institutions was matched by southern suspicion and condemnation of "outside meddling and coercion." In the 1920s, Henry L. Mencken, the most satirical of the northern commentators, summed up the cultural and political barrenness of the benighted Southland: "Fundamentalism, Ku Kluxry, lynchings, hog wallow politics—these are the things that always occur to a northerner when he thinks of the South."[3] The southern image in the northern mind embodied the idea of a section stubbornly dissenting from—and sometimes defying—the nation's progressive achievements and ideals. The South was perceived, with varying degrees of concern, as a national problem, a problem associated with Jim Crow, mob violence, reactionary politics, and economic failure.

A second important theme in this study is the part played by compromise

2. C. Vann Woodward, *American Counterpoint: Slavery and Racism in the North–South Dialogue* (Boston, 1971), pp. 6–7.

3. Quoted in George B. Tindall, "Business Progressivism: Southern Politics in the Twenties," *South Atlantic Quarterly* 62 (Winter 1963): 92.

and accommodation in the relationship between North and South. Northerners and southerners had much in common, including their racial attitudes and a preference for local control within the federal system, and neither region was ever united in opposing the other. It was possible to reach an accommodation on most sectional issues. In spite of southern apprehensions, in the years after Reconstruction the victorious North made few efforts to intervene in the South, much less to refashion the section in its own image. Political parties, business organizations, and other institutions worked to resolve regional differences. Thus compromise and the negotiation of working agreements have played a vital role in the interaction of North and South in the twentieth century.

This suggests a related aspect of the relationship between the sections. Despite its subordinate place in the nation, the South has always been part of a national system characterized by an intricate and often subtle process of regional interaction. Indeed, southerners have played an instrumental role in shaping modern American history. The South, in Carl N. Degler's words, has been a "co-creator of the nation's history."[4] One example is the powerful influence exerted by southern congressional leaders, most memorably in the administrations of Woodrow Wilson and Franklin D. Roosevelt. Another illustration is southern support of defense and international policies, which did much to determine the U.S. position in foreign affairs after 1917. One thinks, too, of the South's long and determined resistance to racial change, and how that affected the course of American history. In more recent years, the South's political and religious conservatism laid the basis for increasing Republican strength in the region, while contributing significantly to that party's tilt to the right and its succession of presidential victories. Southern ideological influence has grown conspicuously in recent decades. The historian Bruce J. Schulman remarks that "The South has passed on much to other regions—a fondness for high technology, a craving for defense industry, a suspicion of unions, a divided economy, an antipathy to welfare, an uneasy accommodation between black urban leaders and white business conservatives."[5]

Sectional conflict was sometimes followed by compromise and accommodation, which in turn often contributed to regional convergence, another emphasis in this study. In the 1880s adherents of the New South creed believed that, by emulating the dynamic North, southerners could develop their economy, introduce an era of prosperity, and modernize their social institutions. For a time many southerners even subscribed to the myth of a New South making rapid advances and on the verge of a great regional triumph. But the enormous regional inequalities in economic conditions and institutional effectiveness convinced thoughtful southerners of their section's continuing subordination in the nation. To be sure, the South changed over the years, diversifying its economy and improving its schools and public services. Yet it continued to lag far behind

4. Carl N. Degler, "Thesis, Antithesis, Synthesis: The South, the North, and the Nation," *Journal of Southern History* 53 (February 1987): 3–18 (quotation on p. 6).

5. Bruce J. Schulman, *From Cotton Belt to Sunbelt: Federal Policy, Economic Development, and the Transformation of the South, 1938–1980* (New York, 1991), p. 218.

other regions. During the depression-ridden 1930s, the sociologist Arthur F. Raper characterized the South as a land of "depleted soil, shoddy livestock, inadequate farm equipment, crude agricultural practices, crippled institutions, [and] a defeated and impoverished people."[6] In 1938 Franklin D. Roosevelt described the region as "the Nation's No. 1 economic problem." The *Report on Economic Conditions of the South* in the same year, sponsored by the Roosevelt administration, asserted that "The paradox of the South is that while it is blessed by Nature with immense wealth, its people as a whole are the poorest in the country."[7]

Nevertheless, a process of regional convergence had been under way for a long time. Its pace quickened after the 1930s. The Great Depression dealt a severe blow to the region's agricultural economy, and the farm policies of the New Deal and the stimulus of the Second World War brought a drastic restructuring of southern agriculture—the movement of millions of tenant farmers off the land, the mechanization of production, and the emergence of a more capital-intensive and efficient system. Since World War II, the South has enjoyed an expansive economy, impressive urbanization, unprecedented prosperity, and new institutions and social services. Its per capita income is not far below the national average. Many of the old landmarks of southern distinctiveness have disappeared. The Second Reconstruction was responsible for far-reaching changes, including the dismantling of legal segregation, the reentry of black southerners into politics, and a fundamental reorientation of racial attitudes and behavior. Political affairs have been transformed and a two-party system has developed. Meanwhile, the dramatic transformation of the region began to evoke the image of a superior South superseding a decaying and vulnerable North, what one scholar describes as a South assuming "a curious new role in American life—the nation's second chance, a relatively unspoiled land whose cities are new and sparkling and whose people retain the mythical innocence and simplicity of an earlier America."[8]

All of this seemed to represent the "Americanization" of the South. As John Egerton has noted, "The South is no longer simply a colony of the nation, an inferior region, a stepchild; it is now rushing to rejoin the Union, and in the process it is becoming indistinguishable from the North and East and West." This convergence left Egerton with some doubts and reservations. He referred to "deep divisions along race and class lines, an obsession with growth and acquisition and consumption, a headlong rush to the cities and the suburbs, diminution and waste of natural resources, institutional malfunctioning, abuse of political and economic power, increasing depersonalization, and a steady erosion of the sense of place, of community, of belonging."[9]

6. Quoted in Numan V. Bartley, ed., *The Evolution of Southern Culture* (Athens, Ga., 1988), p. ix.
7. National Economic Council, *Report on Economic Conditions of the South* (Washington, D.C., 1938), p. 8.
8. Fred Hobson, *Tell About the South: The Southern Rage to Explain* (Baton Rouge, La., 1983), p. 14.
9. John Egerton, *The Americanization of Dixie: The Southernization of America* (New York, 1974), pp. xix–xx.

If the South was becoming more Americanized, the rest of the nation seemed to be undergoing a process of "Southernization." There were many manifestations of this development. It was evident, for example, in the millions of black and white southerners who moved into northern cities and in the tendency of the North to look to the South for the roots of its problems. It was also apparent in the growing interest outside the South in things southern—ranging from country music to the Southern Literary Renaissance. In addition, it reflected a different outlook on the part of many northerners. "Having failed for the first time to win at war, having found poverty and racism alive and menacing in its own house," Egerton writes, "the North . . . has lately shown itself to be more and more like the South in the political, racial, social, and religious inclinations of its collective majority."[10]

Regional convergence has not caused the South to disappear as an organic entity, not, at least, in the minds of most southerners. The South remains the nation's most distinctive region, most notably perhaps in a cultural sense. This constitutes the fourth major theme of this study. The persistence of an identifiable and pervasive regional culture is evident in the South's religious life, in its "subculture of violence," in its emphasis on family and place, and in the explosion of literary talent it has witnessed since the 1920s. Southerners—particularly white southerners—seem to be as conscious of their regional identity and as loyal to the traditions and values of their culture as many other ethnic groups in the United States.

This study attempts to bring these themes together in a comprehensive historical inquiry into the relationship between the North and the South in modern America and to tell the story of the southern experience since the late-nineteenth century within the larger setting of our national history. The project is based on the extensive literature on the South produced by historians, social scientists, journalists, and literary specialists. Though essentially a synthesis, it seeks to provide a broad interpretation of the North-South relationship from the 1880s to the present. The work begins with a consideration of the circumstances and conditions that set the South apart from other sections in the post-Reconstruction years and in subsequent chapters follows the evolving position of the region in the nation. It analyzes the continuing sectional conflict involving the modern South and discusses the national implications of that conflict. It reveals that, while the interaction of North and South on some issues reflected a sharp division along sectional lines, it frequently mirrored internal differences within the two sections that encouraged interregional understanding and accommodation of various kinds. The narrative describes the slow convergence in the status, behavior, and thinking of southerners and other Americans in the twentieth century, as well as the persistence of a distinctive southern culture. It suggests how regional interaction helped shape modern American history. The study will perhaps throw some light on the way southerners have di-

10. *Ibid.*, p. xix.

vided their loyalties between region and nation, on the character and extent of regional unity in the United States, and on how the nation has responded to challenges from regional and subregional groups and interests. Finally, this book may offer a useful perspective for the interpretation of the American as well as the southern past.

THE
South
IN
MODERN
AMERICA

CHAPTER I

In the Shadow of Reconstruction

WHEN the Reconstruction of the American South was formally abandoned in the spring of 1877, a new stage arrived in the sectional conflict of the nineteenth century. The intense North-South antagonism of earlier years gave way to a greater measure of intersectional compromise and accommodation. But despite the moderating influences of the new era, sectionalism remained a powerful theme in American life, both in national politics and in the public affairs of states and localities. The consciousness of northerners and southerners was still infused with the dramatic and tragic experiences of the recent past, and politics inevitably reflected these recollections and predilections. Yet there was more to it than that. Northerners and southerners were separated by substantial economic and cultural differences, and these differences were expressed in state and national politics. The Populist revolt and the realignment of the major political parties in the 1890s brought this post-Reconstruction period to an end, replacing its turbulence and uncertainty with a more stable and predictable political order. The new order, however, was strongly conditioned by the politics of sectionalism.

By the mid-1870s, Republican leaders had begun to consider, in the words of one scholar, the idea "of dropping the carpetbagger and the Southern Negro and changing from a policy of military interference to one of nonintervention in the South."[1] Whatever the terms involved in the Compromise of 1877, southern conservatives acquiesced in the election of Rutherford B. Hayes in exchange for his pledge to remove the last federal troops protecting Republican state governments in the South, to restore "home rule" to the region, and to support federal expenditures for internal improvements in the southern states. Hayes believed that the policy of military interference in the South had frus-

1. Vincent P. DeSantis, "Rutherford B. Hayes and the Removal of the Troops and the End of Reconstruction," in *Region, Race, and Reconstruction: Essays in Honor of C. Vann Woodward*, ed. J. Morgan Kousser and James M. McPherson (New York, 1982), p. 439.

I

trated prospects for Republican success in the region. He was also convinced, as one historian has written, that "a complete reconciliation between the North and South was necessary for the moral and material prosperity of the South as well as for that of the nation as a whole."[2] The Compromise of 1877 suggested that the new administration—and by implication the North—had abandoned the concept of federal intervention in the South.

In the years that followed, a number of developments seemed to confirm the intersectional accord embodied in the Compromise of 1877. President Hayes and most of his successors displayed a keen sensibility in dealing with the South. The conservative Democrats who controlled the various southern states spoke of protecting the political rights of blacks, while advocating industrialization, outside investments, and sectional reconciliation. Meanwhile federal policy, including several Supreme Court decisions, and northern opinion revealed a weakening commitment to African-American equality. Nevertheless, many of the old abolitionists and racial reformers in the North remained optimistic, in part because they looked expectantly toward a new South of progress and reconciliation.

The rapprochement between North and South proved much less thorough than many contemporaries had hoped. Hayes's policy of reconciliation, launched with such fanfare in 1877, soon fell victim to the resistance of congressional Republicans to southern demands for federal appointments and economic assistance, while southern congressional support of free silver and other radical western proposals strained the region's relations with the president. Sectional themes reappeared in the elections of 1878, and the "southern question" remained important in national politics during the 1880s. Although the North's desire to transform the South lessened following the end of Reconstruction, southerners were still fearful of "Yankeefication," and they continued to define themselves in opposition to their old sectional enemies.[3]

For their part, most northerners regarded themselves as essentially different from their regional counterparts. They were inclined to feel morally superior to southerners and to see themselves as successful, progressive, and providentially favored. A majority was identified with the Republican party—the party of the Union, of Abraham Lincoln, of Emancipation. While they might have lost interest in "regenerating" the South and might applaud the reconciliation of the Blue and the Gray, most northerners continued to think of the South in terms of racial brutality, reactionary politics, poverty, and a backward economy. These pejorative images were put to good use, as George B. Tindall has remarked, in "the Republican outrage mills and bloody shirt political campaigns" of the post-Reconstruction years.[4] In the meantime, the rituals of the Grand Army of the Republic, the writings and oratory devoted to the war for the Union, and

2. *Ibid.*, p. 437. In the essay cited above, Vincent P. DeSantis surveys the historiography of the Compromise of 1877, beginning with the seminal study by C. Vann Woodward, *Reunion and Reaction: The Compromise of 1877 and the End of Reconstruction* (Boston, 1951).

3. See Richard N. Current, *Northernizing the South* (Athens, Ga., 1983), for a discussion of these fears.

4. George Brown Tindall, *The Ethnic Southerners* (Baton Rouge, La., 1976), p. 28.

the growth of the Lincoln legend kept alive and fresh the vision of northern valor and sacrifice during the war of the 1860s.

Southerners in the late-nineteenth century were no doubt even more self-conscious about their sectional identity than were northerners. History and mythology reinforced this self-consciousness. "The idea that the Southern people are a peculiar people," an Atlanta minister observed early in the twentieth century, "has been impressed on us all our lives. From the dawn of his intelligence the Southern boy is bred to the sentiment that the Southerner is a separate and distinct sort of man, especially different from the Northerner, and that the distinction is one of which he should be proud."[5] War and Reconstruction, the Virginia historian Philip Alexander Bruce wrote at about the same time, "served only to strengthen the homogeneity of the people of the Southern States, not only by practically barring out or discouraging all foreign immigration, but also by welding the native whites into the most perfect oneness for the preservation of all that they cherished."[6] Despite the divisions and enmities that contributed to the failure of the Confederacy, the war itself increased the social solidarity of the South's white inhabitants. As Wilbur J. Cash put it long afterward: "Out of that ordeal by fire the masses had brought, not only a great body of memories in common with the master class, but a deep affection for these captains, a profound trust in them, a pride which was inextricably intertwined with the commoners' pride in themselves."[7] The war experience—and the idealization of it in later years—bolstered the position of the Redeemers, the conservative Democrats who dominated the region's politics for a generation after the end of Reconstruction.

The fervent oratory of Confederate heroes like General John B. Gordon of Georgia, the flood of memoirs and military accounts by southern writers, the activities of the United Confederate Veterans and the United Daughters of the Confederacy, the pervasive raising of monuments to the Confederate dead, and the identification of the southern cause with the saintly figure of Robert E. Lee, all contributed to the vibrant myth of the Lost Cause. According to this legend, a valiant South fought to the end against enormous odds to maintain the "southern way of life." In the hands of the mythmakers, one historian remarks, "All Confederates automatically became virtuous, all were defenders of the rights of states and individuals, all were segregationists, all steadfast, all patriotic."[8] As Paul M. Gaston notes in his study of the New South creed, myths, whatever the degree of their validity, usually serve a social function, for they are "combinations of images and symbols that reflect a people's way of perceiving truth."[9] Charles Reagan Wilson has suggested that by linking Confederate images with religious values southerners created a kind of civil religion: "Each

5. John E. White, "The True and the False in Southern Life," *South Atlantic Quarterly* 5 (April 1906): 97.

6. Philip Alexander Bruce, *The Rise of the New South* (Philadelphia, 1905), p. 5.

7. W. J. Cash, *The Mind of the South* (New York, 1941), p. 111.

8. Frank E. Vandiver, "The Confederate Myth," *Southwest Review* 46 (Summer 1961): 199–204 (quotation on p. 200).

9. Paul M. Gaston, *The New South Creed: A Study in Southern Mythmaking* (New York, 1970), p. 9.

Lost Cause ritual and organization was tangible evidence that Southerners had made a religion out of their history." Yet even those who took the lead in celebrating the Confederate tradition usually advocated sectional reconciliation and supported the idea of the New South.[10] Most white southerners hoped to perpetuate a regional culture based on religion and tradition.

Other myths also helped raise the spirits of southerners in the late-nineteenth century. An idealized and romanticized picture of the antebellum South, for example, brought to mind an earlier time of southern strength, success, and virtue. But the alleged excesses of Radical Reconstruction proved more immediately useful to the Redeemers, who invoked the horrors of military occupation, Republican malfeasance, and black domination as a means of unifying white southerners. Reconstruction was pictured as an era of fraud and corruption, sectional vindictiveness, and exorbitant taxes, a time that must never be allowed to recur. This mythology became a powerful factor in shaping southern politics during the next half-century. In every presidential election, an authority on southern rural newspapers has written, "the angers of Reconstruction were to be stirred anew." Issues that related to the South "were examined to determine to what extent they were tinctured with the philosophy of radical Reconstruction and Yankee machination."[11]

Southern distinctiveness rested on more solid foundations than matters of mind and spirit, as critical as they were in creating a sectional self-consciousness among white southerners. The South was also set apart by economic, social, and cultural pecularities. In contrast to the rapidly changing Northeast and Midwest, the region below the Potomac and the Ohio was overwhelmingly agricultural and rural. It was also poor, at least by American standards, and its population was characterized by high fertility, extensive illiteracy, lack of industrial and vocational skills, and growing landlessness. Unlike the North, the South attracted few immigrants; its population was largely confined to millions of indigenous whites and blacks, whose relationship was governed by a slowly hardening code based on caste and color. Between the Civil War and the First World War, the number of black southerners more than doubled, and a great majority of the nation's African Americans lived in the southern states. As late as 1910, they made up 35 percent of the population in the ex-Confederate states, almost half that of the Deep South, and a majority of the inhabitants of Mississippi and South Carolina. The South was a land of Protestantism, intense religiosity, and, among the section's dominant sects, conservative orthodoxy. Its social and religious landscape contrasted with that of other parts of the country, where the impact of massive immigration and increasing secularization was producing a very different and more diversified society and culture.

None of these regional disparities was more striking than the economic contrasts. The southern economy revolved around a few staple crops, preeminently

10. Charles Reagan Wilson, *Baptized in Blood: The Religion of the Lost Cause, 1865–1920* (Athens, Ga., 1980), p. 36; Gaines M. Foster, *Ghosts of the Confederacy: Defeat, the Lost Cause, and the Emergence of the New South, 1865 to 1913* (New York, 1987), pp. 6, 103.

11. Thomas D. Clark, *The Southern Country Editor* (Indianapolis, 1948), p. 171.

cotton. The section's agriculture was increasingly commercialized in the late-nineteenth century, a trend that was encouraged by the penetration of the railroad into the hinterland and the rise of a new merchant class in the countryside and small towns. It resulted in the loss of land and independence by many small farmers and the growth of institutions such as sharecropping and the crop lien system. The South's industries in this period were primarily based on the extracting and processing of raw materials: lumber and timber, tobacco, cotton textiles, coal and iron, and the like. These industries were concentrated in low-wage, low-skill sectors, and they were heavily dependent on imported machinery and technology. In the 1880s, when the Northeast and the Midwest were making impressive strides in industrialization and urbanization, the South's per capita wealth was slightly more than one-third that of the rest of the country. The region's per capita income was 51 percent of the national average.[12]

Part of this can be attributed to the enormous material and human losses the section suffered during the Civil War. In addition, many contemporary southerners blamed their region's plight on the dominant position of the victorious North in the national economy—on their tributary role as producers of agricultural and unfinished products, on the one hand, and as consumers of industrial and finished products from the North, on the other. "The South was a 'colonial economy,'" the economist Gavin Wright observes, "because at every point Southerners had to deal with the large and often oblivious economic colossus to

PERSONAL INCOME PER CAPITA AS A PERCENTAGE OF THE U.S. AVERAGE, 1840–1950, BY REGION

Region	1840	1860	1880	1900	1920	1930	1940	1950
United States	100%	100%	100%	100%	100%	100%	100%	100%
Northeast	135	139	141	137	132	138	124	115
New England	132	143	141	134	124	129	121	109
Middle Atlantic	136	137	141	139	134	140	124	116
North-central	68	68	98	103	100	101	103	106
East	67	69	102	106	108	111	112	112
West	75	66	90	97	87	82	84	94
South	76	72	51	51	62	55	65	73
South Atlantic	70	65	45	45	59	56	69	74
East south-central	73	68	51	49	52	48	55	62
West south-central	144	115	60	61	72	61	70	80
West	—	—	190	163	122	115	125	114
Mountain	—	—	168	139	100	83	92	96
Pacific	—	—	204	163	135	130	138	121

SOURCE: Richard A. Easterlin, "Regional Economic Trends, 1840–1950," in *American Economic History*, ed. Seymour E. Harris (New York: McGraw-Hill, 1961), p. 28.

12. C. Vann Woodward, *Origins of the New South, 1877–1913* (Baton Rouge, La., 1951), pp. 175–234, 318–19.

the North."[13] Northern ownership and control of southern industries and natural resources were an important aspect of the southern economy in the late-
nineteenth century, and between 1880 and 1920 a steady decline occurred in
the fraction of nonagricultural wealth in the region owned by home-state residents. Outside capital entered the South, but it was not accompanied or quickly
followed by an inflow of people, either bankers and businessmen or farmers and
laborers. One reason was that the labor markets of the South, "a low-wage region in a high-wage country," were largely isolated from national and international labor markets.[14] Wright argues that this was the defining feature of the
southern economy. The South constituted a separate regional labor market,
outside the scope of the national and international labor markets of the time.[15]
This is a persuasive interpretation, and one that points up the isolation of the
southern population, the South's distinctive demographic patterns, and the
dominance of its major commodity—cotton—in the regional economy.

Nevertheless, the 1880s represented a decade of economic growth for the
South. Encouraged by some improvement in prices, southern farmers expanded production of their major cash crops, bringing in new acreage, using
more commercial fertilizers, and making their operations more labor-intensive.
They also talked about more efficient methods, agricultural diversification, and
other solutions to the "farm problem." But the most highly publicized economic gains of the 1880s took place in the South's nonagricultural industries—
in the extension of the railroad network, the growth of lumber and mining, the
development of iron and tobacco, and especially in the rise of cotton textiles.
The mills were small and scattered and generally lacking in capital, but the
southern cotton textile industry made impressive progress during the decade of
the 1880s—capital, labor, and machinery increased dramatically. The number
of spindles tripled. Although the South lagged far behind the North in industrialization, its industries grew during this period at a pace about equal to that in
other parts of the country. Southern industry "touched the lives of a million
people."[16] Urbanization also increased noticeably in the South, and a burst of
town building took place in many parts of the region. Thousands of new villages—settled places with populations below 2,500—and hundreds of towns
with larger populations came into being between 1880 and 1910. By 1900,
about one of every six southerners lived in a village or town. Southern cities,
according to a recent study, "were the nerve centers of a changing economy

13. Gavin Wright, *Old South, New South: Revolutions in the Southern Economy Since the Civil War* (New York, 1986), p. vii.

14. *Ibid.*, pp. 12, 63. See also Woodward, *Origins of the New South*, pp. 114–23.

15. Wright, *Old South, New South*, p. 7.

16. Edward L. Ayers, *The Promise of the New South: Life After Reconstruction* (New York, 1992), p. 105. Southern textile production increased 18.6 percent in the 1880s, 17.6 percent in the 1890s, and 13.8 percent during the first decade of the twentieth century. The rates of growth for New England, where the industry was fully developed, were 2.5, 1.9, and 1.9 percent for the three decades. Jack Blicksilver, *Cotton Manufacturing in the Southeast: An Historical Analysis* (Atlanta, Ga., 1959), pp. 1, 37. See also Wright, *Old South, New South*, pp. 124–46, and Nancy Frances Kane, *Textiles in Transition: Technology, Wages, and Industry Relocation in the U.S. Textile Industry, 1880–1930* (New York, 1988), pp. 9–35.

and culture that penetrated the rural hinterland and remade the South in the decades following the Civil War."[17]

The South's economic revival in the 1880s, particularly the progress of the campaign to launch new textile mills, seemed to justify the arguments of those who were advocating a New South. They envisaged a South transformed by southern leadership and enterprise. The region would benefit from northern capital and technology, but it would not abandon its most cherished traditions. The New South creed, writes Paul Gaston, "bespoke harmonious reconciliation of sectional differences, racial peace, and a new economic and social order based on industry and scientific, diversified agriculture—all of which would lead, eventually, to the South's dominance in the reunited nation."[18] Richard H. Edmonds, one of the New South spokesmen, wrote of "the vast, illimitable future of this glorious sunny South."[19] Edmonds and other New South advocates described a new El Dorado of industrial growth and economic diversification based on the South's abundant resources, plentiful labor, and salubrious climate. It was a cheerful and optimistic doctrine.

This New South brought a sympathetic response from northern observers, along with some indication of concern over potential southern competition for New England textile mills. Despite their desire for reconciliation between North and South and their quest for outside investments, the New South promoters sometimes complained that northern businessmen and politicians were

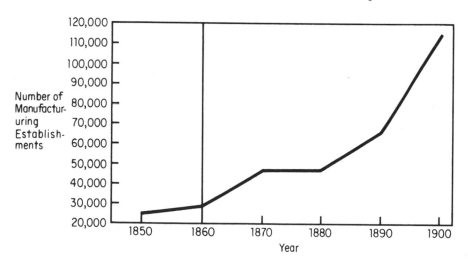

Number of Manufacturing Establishments in All Southern States, 1850–1900. SOURCE: Gavin Wright, *Old South, New South: Revolutions in the Southern Economy Since the Civil War* (New York: Basic Books, 1986), p. 44.

17. Don H. Doyle, *New Men, New Cities, New South: Atlanta, Nashville, Charleston, Mobile, 1860–1910* (Chapel Hill, N.C., 1990), p. xiii. See also Ayers, *The Promise of the New South*, p. 55.

18. Gaston, *The New South Creed*, p. 7.

19. Quoted in *ibid.*, p. l. See also Woodward, *Origins of the New South*, pp. 142–74, and Herbert Collins, "The Idea of Cotton Textile Industry in the South, 1870–1900," *North Carolina Historical Review* 34 (July 1957): 358–92.

trying to impede the industrial development of the South. In fact, southern textiles in the late-nineteenth century did pose a serious challenge to the prosperity
of the New England industry, and many northern business and political leaders
exerted themselves to retard the growth of industry in the South.[20] In urging
national reconciliation, the southerners were not endorsing "a surrender of
southern will to northern superiority." The New South spokesmen, Gaston remarks, "resented any suggestion that the South they were creating was a product of foreign or outside elements." It was "southern brains, and southern enterprise, and southern energy and courage" that had "inaugurated and
sustained the booming development of southern soil and resources," according
to Henry W. Grady of the Atlanta *Constitution*.[21]

For all the talk of a New South based on industrialization and diversification,
the region's political economy remained fundamentally different from that of
the Northeast and Midwest. "The historical events surrounding the Civil War
and Reconstruction, the preservation of segregation and its associated political
implications, and a continued dependence on a largely agricultural, cash crop
economy," one student of sectionalism has said, "produced a South whose distinctiveness within the American nation was matched by its political cohesion in
opposition to northern interests."[22] The Democratic party was the political vehicle for the waging of this opposition. In the North, as the political scientist
V. O. Key, Jr., has noted, "the hegemony of the Republican party rested on the
skillful maintenance of a combination of manufacturers, industrial workers, and
farmers. The protective tariff, opposed by the South, provided a common bond
for manufacturers and workers in protected industries."[23]

Congress inevitably became the center for the resolution of policy differences
between North and South. Following Reconstruction, Democrats quickly captured most of the South's congressional seats. These southern Democrats soon
outnumbered their party colleagues from other sections, constituting a large
and generally united "section-party bloc." The election of Democrat Grover
Cleveland as president in 1884 confirmed the growing belief of white southerners that the South had a political future within the Union. Southern newspapers
agreed that the Democratic return to power had "swept away all sectional distinctions," "brought the South back into the Union," and given it "the opportunity of impressing itself upon the national policy."[24] Yet in the 1880s a large
majority of southern congressmen had served in the Confederate army or gov-

20. Patrick J. Hearden, "New England's Reaction to the New South," *South Atlantic Quarterly* 75
(Summer 1976): 371–88; Blicksilver, *Cotton Manufacturing in the Southeast*, pp. 18–19.

21. Paul M. Gaston, "The New South," in *Writing Southern History: Essays in Historiography in
Honor of Fletcher M. Green*, ed. Arthur S. Link and Rembert W. Patrick (Baton Rouge, La., 1965), p.
322 (first quotation); Gaston, *The New South Creed*, p. 98 (second and third quotations). See also
Harold D. Mixon, "Henry Grady as a Persuasive Strategist," in Waldo W. Braden, ed., *Oratory in
the New South* (Baton Rouge, La., 1979), pp. 74–116, and W. Stuart Towns, "Atticus G. Haygood:
Neglected Advocate of Reconciliation and a New South," *Southern Studies* 26 (Spring 1987): 28–40.

22. Richard Franklin Bensel, *Sectionalism and American Political Development, 1880–1980* (Madison,
Wis., 1984), p. 12.

23. V. O. Key, Jr., *Politics, Parties, and Pressure Groups* (New York: 1964), p. 234.

24. Quoted in Paul H. Buck, *The Road to Reunion, 1865–1900* (Boston, 1937), p. 270.

ernment, a fact that provoked a Republican charge of "Rebel Brigadiers" seeking to gain control of the Union.[25] While southern Democrats usually went along with their party's northeastern leaders in presidential nominating contests, the region's congressmen consistently aligned themselves with western Democrats on most important issues in Congress.[26]

Not surprisingly, southern congressmen presented a united front against legislative proposals designed to protect black people and sought to undermine federal efforts to guarantee the right to vote. The southerners were usually supported in this endeavor by Democratic lawmakers from other parts of the country. A measure introduced in 1883 by Senator Henry W. Blair of New Hampshire, authorizing federal aid to education on the basis of illiteracy, would have allocated the bulk of the appropriations to southern states, for the benefit of black and white children. The bill was considered for several years in the 1880s before being abandoned by Republican leaders. Though initially supported by many southern politicians, the proposal aroused mounting suspicion among the region's spokesmen, who voiced constitutional objections but were probably primarily concerned over racial considerations.[27] Representative Henry Cabot Lodge of Massachusetts introduced a much more threatening measure in the Fifty-first Congress (1889–1891). This so-called Lodge Force bill, apparently intended to help the Republicans strengthen their control of the federal government by recapturing certain marginal areas in the South, would have authorized federal supervision of elections in the southern states. It aroused bitter protest in the South. After a fiercely partisan—and sectional—debate, the bill was passed by the House of Representatives in 1890. But the Senate failed to pass the measure, in part because of pressure from northern business interests anxious to maintain economic stability in the South.[28] In 1893, when the Democrats regained control of Congress and the presidency, the last surviving federal election enforcement act was repealed.

Southerners in the post-Reconstruction period were inclined to see the nation's currency, revenue, and tariff policies as a sectional system that drained income from their pockets while enhancing the profits of northern commercial and industrial interests. The congressional votes on virtually all important economic issues between the mid-1870s and the end of the century assumed a distinctly sectional character. The South's congressional delegations usually joined

25. Carl V. Harris, "Right Fork or Left Fork? The Section–Party Alignments of Southern Democrats in Congress, 1873–1897," *Journal of Southern History* 42 (November 1976): 471. See also Foster, *Ghosts of the Confederacy*, p. 63.

26. See Harris, "Right Fork or Left Fork?" pp. 471–506, for an illuminating analysis of congressional votes in the late nineteenth century. Also see Terry L. Seip, *The South Returns to Congress: Men, Economic Measures, and Intersectional Relationships, 1868–1879* (Baton Rouge, La., 1983), pp. 136–268, and James Tice Moore, "Redeemers Reconsidered: Change and Continuity in the Democratic South, 1870–1900," *Journal of Southern History* 44 (August 1978): 357–78.

27. Woodward, *Origins of the New South*, pp. 63–64; Allen J. Going, "The South and the Blair Bill," *Mississippi Valley Historical Review* 44 (September 1957): 267–90; Daniel W. Crofts, "The Black Response to the Blair Education Bill," *Journal of Southern History* 37 (February 1971): 41–65.

28. Bensel, *Sectionalism and American Political Development*, pp. 76–77; Harris, "Right Fork or Left Fork?" pp. 476–78.

with western Democrats (and sometimes western Republicans) in supporting lower tariff rates, silver coinage and easy money, and a more expansive and decentralized national banking system. They advocated a national income tax and a revision of the revenue system so as to shift the tax burden away from the South and West. Southern representatives and senators consistently urged the appropriation of federal funds for river and harbor improvement in their districts and states. They supported federal regulation of railroads in the South—railroads that were largely owned in the Northeast but were vital in developing areas like their own.[29]

Richard F. Bensel's analysis of votes in the House of Representatives in the 1880s and 1890s reveals the dominance of what he describes as "the northeastern-midwestern core" in a continuing struggle with the southern periphery and mountain West for control of "the national state apparatus." A vivid illustration of this political sectionalism is provided by the conflict involving the protective tariff, the revenue system, and pensions for Union veterans. The nation's high tariff policy, which subsidized the rapid industrialization of the Northeast and Midwest, helped create a national surplus, part of which was distributed in the form of pensions for northern soldiers who had fought in the Civil War. Southerners, along with many westerners, looked on high tariffs as a discriminatory instrument that raised the prices of the manufactured goods they bought, increased the profits of northern industrialists, and weakened the foreign markets for their major agricultural products. The surplus resulting from the customs duties stood in the way of revenue measures that would have been more equitable to the South and West. It also encouraged northern Republicans to pursue a generous pension policy as a means of reducing the surplus and countering demands for tariff revision. The national pension system excluded Confederate veterans, of course. When Grover Cleveland became president in 1885, he vetoed hundreds of private pension bills that extended the generous coverage of the basic pension system, often on flimsy grounds. Claims agents and the Grand Army of the Republic condemned the Democratic president as a "mere tool of the South."[30]

Southern congressmen were for the most part staunch supporters of tariff reduction. In the 1880s the Democrats intensified their argument that lower tariffs would ease the flow of agricultural exports, as well as encourage economic expansion overseas. To be sure, some southern industrialists endorsed the prevailing policy of protectionism, and southern congressmen from tobacco-growing and sugar-producing areas, fearing foreign competition, were not always reliable defenders of the party position. But in general southerners could be counted on to vote for tariff reduction. Not a single southern senator voted against Cleveland's ill-fated reciprocal trade treaty with Great Britain in 1888—and not a single senator from New England voted for it. There was some evidence of a sectional division within the Democratic party on the tariff issue, since protectionist Democrats usually came from northern states. On the

29. Harris, "Right Fork or Left Fork?" pp. 489–505.
30. Bensel, *Sectionalism and American Political Development*, pp. 60–88 (quotation on p. 66).

other hand, the Republican platform of 1896 denounced the Wilson-Gorman Tariff of 1894, a Democratic measure that did little to reduce rates, as "sectional."[31]

The national party system during this period was a product of the sectional crisis of the 1850s and 1860s. It was essentially a bipolar system, with northern and southern poles. The two major parties were more competitive than might be assumed. Outside the South ethnocultural conflict separated Republicans from Democrats along pietist versus anti-pietist lines. Although the Republican party, as the party of Lincoln, Union, and Emancipation, had a decided advantage in northern and western states, it was less competitive in the border states. The Democrats won their share of local and state elections in the 1870s and 1880s, and in 1874 they gained a majority of the seats in the U.S. House of Representatives. They controlled the House in seven of the next nine Congresses, won a majority of the Senate seats in 1878 and 1892, and captured the presidency in 1884 and 1892. The situation was not conducive to complacency among Republican leaders. In the South, meanwhile, the Democrats were dominant but far from secure. Below the presidential level, which became solidly Democratic as early as 1880, the South was not yet a one-party section, even though the trend was clearly in that direction. The political landscape was shifting and uncertain.

Politics in the southern states from the end of Reconstruction to the early 1890s was controlled by the Redeemers. The original architects of the "Solid South," they made an important contribution to the evolving politics of the South in the late nineteenth and early twentieth centuries. The Redeemers—or Bourbon Democrats—regarded themselves as the "natural leaders" of the South, and indeed by the late 1870s most of the section's traditional social and economic leaders, including many men of Whiggish persuasion, were identified with the Democratic party. The bulwark of the Redeemers' political control was the black belt that stretched across the lower South, and planters constituted a major faction in the politics of the various states, though not always the dominant one. But if planters exerted a controlling influence in the politics of the post-Reconstruction South, they were forced to share political power with a rising group of business-oriented politicians. Railroad and bondholding interests were closely identified with the Bourbon governments, and the New South emphasis on industrialization, economic diversification, and northern investments was warmly endorsed by the dominant political leaders in most southern states.[32]

While proclaiming themselves the guardians of fiscal integrity and a political climate favorable to economic developers, the Redeemers repudiated much of the Reconstruction debt in the southern states, took part in efforts to regulate

31. Tom E. Terrill, *The Tariff, Politics, and American Foreign Policy, 1874–1901* (Westport, Conn., 1973), pp. 11, 80, 90–140, 184–98, 210–11; Edward W. Chester, *Sectionalism, Politics, and American Diplomacy* (Metuchen, N.J., 1975), p. 124; Arthur M. Schlesinger, Jr., and Fred L. Israel, eds., *History of American Presidential Elections, 1789–1968*, vol. 2 (New York, 1971), p. 1832.

32. Woodward, *Origins of the New South*, pp. 1–22, 51–74; Dewey W. Grantham, *The Life & Death of the Solid South: A Political History* (Lexington, Ky., 1988), pp. 1–14.

railroads and other corporations, and supported appropriations for some state services, particularly to benefit farmers. If the new state constitutions whose drafting and adoption they spearheaded emphasized retrenchment in spending and low ceilings on taxation, they also included restrictions on state aid to private enterprises. According to one analyst of congressional voting patterns in the late-nineteenth century, the Redeemer congressmen "enjoyed an enormous political luxury: on major national economic issues they found essential agreement among most economic interest groups within their constituency." Although conservatives in the southern statehouses may have opposed the interests of small farmers on issues such as state debts and taxes, legislative apportionment, lien statutes, and stock laws, their counterparts in Congress, "dealing with the currency, the banking system, the tariff, the internal revenue, the development of waterways, and the regulation of monopolies, were often able to foster southern consensus by voting the common interests of southern farmers, planters, and businessmen."[33]

Having redeemed their individual states, the Bourbon leaders worked hard to maintain white unity and to perpetuate their control. While their tactics varied from state to state, their leadership tended to be oligarchical and conservative. In every southern state a relatively small number of popular leaders dominated the Democratic party, determined the acceptable candidates, and decided upon the issues. The oligarchies managed to secure control of the party organization in their respective states and make sure that their lieutenants and friends were in charge of the election machinery. The concentration of authority in the hands of governors and legislators enabled these state leaders to appoint important local officials in every county. While Redeemer control depended on the popularity of Democratic leaders with white voters, it also rested upon working alliances between state and local leaders. The latter were often part of what some contemporaries disparagingly called courthouse "cliques" or "rings." These influential local politicians looked after the interests of the party hierarchy in their towns and counties, particularly the operation of the election system and the selection of local officeholders, including members of the state legislature. Bourbonism was reinforced by an assortment of clever techniques and sharp practices: gerrymandering legislative districts, discriminatory apportionment of seats in party conventions, intricate registration and election laws, and use of fraud and intimidation at the polls. Although small farmers and workers found it difficult to protect their economic and class interests in politics, many of them voted for conservative Democratic leaders. White yeomen in southern Appalachia generally supported the Republican party, as did most blacks throughout the South who continued to vote. The region's exploitative economic and social structure—increasing farm tenancy, a pervasive credit system that authorized merchants to provide farmers with supplies in return for a lien on the future crop, and the growth of textile villages and mining towns— debilitated the political role of more and more small farmers and laborers.

Even so, the Democratic South was not yet secure; it continued to encounter

opposition from the Republican party and dissident Democrats. Although every southern state supported the Democratic presidential ticket in 1880, Republican strength in the region was still a factor of some consequence until the end of the century. In ten ex-Confederate states in the early 1880s, between a third and a half of all votes cast in statewide elections typically went to Republican and independent candidates. A substantial part of this non-Democratic vote was cast by white Republicans or third-party supporters.[34] Those southerners who belonged to the Grand Old Party in the post-Reconstruction years were largely of two very different and often mutually antagonistic types: the freedmen, who for the most part lived in the low country, and the white inhabitants of the mountainous areas. This Republican coalition of blacks and whites was a formidable political consideration in the late-nineteenth-century South, particularly in the upper part of the region. The party dominated local elections in southwestern Virginia, western North Carolina, East Tennessee, and eastern Kentucky. But the place of blacks in the party was a divisive issue in the southern GOP, and one that Republican leaders were never able to resolve satisfactorily. "The Republican strategy," one authority concludes, "became one of offering their black following just enough to ensure their continued support while emphasizing issues that would attract greater numbers of white voters."[35]

The persistence of southern Republicanism after 1876 can be attributed in part to GOP efforts at the national level to win support below the Potomac. In an age of close elections, Republican leaders looked to the South for help in strengthening their control of the national government and possibly enabling their party to become a genuinely national organization. Despite the return of "home rule" and Democratic control, there seemed to be some chance in the 1880s that interparty competition would continue in the southern states. In the presidential election of 1880, for example, a majority of the black adult males in nine of the eleven ex-Confederate states cast their ballots. The percentage of all adult males voting in presidential elections in the South between 1876 and 1896 was as high as 65 and never lower than 56 percent.[36] The problem was the incipient consolidation of the Solid South and the Republican need for a formula that would make the minority party more competitive and respectable. The "southern question" was widely discussed in the North during the 1880s. Had the Republicans succeeded, they might have changed the course of politics in the South and the nation. From this success, Vincent P. DeSantis suggests, "would have come new political alignments, new policies, and probably the end of Democratic supremacy and one party politics in the South."[37]

Seeing the cleavages that divided southern Democrats and recognizing the failure of their own Reconstruction policies, Republicans approached the

34. J. Morgan Kousser, *The Shaping of Southern Politics: Suffrage Restriction and the Establishment of the One-Party South, 1880–1910* (New Haven, 1974), pp. 27–28.

35. Gordon B. McKinney, "Southern Mountain Republicans and the Negro, 1865–1900," *Journal of Southern History* 41 (November 1975): 493–94.

36. Kousser, *The Shaping of Southern Politics*, pp. 12–15.

37. Vincent P. DeSantis, *Republicans Face the Southern Question—The New Departure Years, 1877–1897* (Baltimore, Md., 1959), p. 13.

southern question in a growing mood of experimentation. Seeking to attract white southerners, Republican strategists alternately tried to win the support of conservatives, old-line Whigs, and industrial-minded men, on the one hand, and the less affluent, independent, and even radical elements, on the other. They made use of federal patronage and urged cooperation between local Republicans and Democratic insurgents. Republican leaders promised that their protectionist policy would facilitate southern industrialization. At other times, as in the GOP platform of 1892, they denounced "the continued inhuman outrages perpetrated upon American citizens for political reasons in certain Southern States of the Union."[38] Rutherford B. Hayes appealed to southern conservatives on the basis of economic assistance, patronage, and a conciliatory approach to race problems.[39] James A. Garfield and Chester A. Arthur sought to bolster their party in the South by cooperating with agrarian radicals and independents. Benjamin Harrison, who assumed office in 1889 when his party had control of both Congress and the presidency for the first time since Reconstruction, eventually supported a new resort to radical intervention in the South. In four years, one historian has written, Harrison "recapitulated the whole schizophrenic history of southern strategies. He tried everything again, and again nothing worked."[40] That was not quite the end; in the agrarian upheaval of the 1890s, Republican leaders tried to work out successful coalitions with Populists and dissident Democrats.

None of these approaches to the southern question proved successful. The most spectacular Republican attempts to perfect a coalition politics—in Virginia early in the 1880s and in North Carolina in the 1890s—provoked bitter conflict and recrimination, and in the long run diminished the party's strength in the region. In Virginia Democratic insurgents who called themselves Readjusters controlled the state government in the first part of the 1880s. They carried through a reform program, repudiated part of the state debt, and finally entered into an electoral coalition with Virginia Republicans. But in 1883 the movement was turned back by the Democrats, who conducted an incendiary racist campaign in an effort to regain power. These episodes revealed the immensity of the obstacles confronting the Republicans. Their party lacked leaders, newspapers, and money in the southern states, and its ranks were torn by recurrent factionalism involving personal rivalry and strife between "black and tan" and "lily-white" groups.[41]

Republicans also encountered fraud and intimidation, as well as discriminatory election officials and harshly punitive election laws. Five southern states

38. Terrill, *The Tariff, Politics, and American Foreign Policy*, pp. 11, 138–39, 189; Schlesinger and Israel, eds., *History of American Presidential Elections*, vol. 2, pp. 1591, 1739 (quotation).

39. Vincent P. DeSantis, "President Hayes's Southern Policy," *Journal of Southern History* 21 (November 1955): 476–94. For an authoritative treatment of Republicans and the "southern question" in the late nineteenth century, see DeSantis, *Republicans Face the Southern Question*. See also Stanley P. Hirshson, *Farewell to the Bloody Shirt: Northern Republicans and the Southern Negro, 1877–1893* (Bloomington, Ind., 1962).

40. George Brown Tindall, *The Disruption of the Solid South* (Athens, Ga., 1972), p. 15.

41. For the Republicans as southern dissenters, see Carl N. Degler, *The Other South: Southern Dissenters in the Nineteenth Century* (New York, 1974), pp. 264–315.

enacted new poll tax, registration, secret ballot, and other restrictive voting laws between 1889 and 1893. These measures took a heavy toll on black and white voters. Under the circumstances, it was virtually impossible for Republicans to formulate a policy on the national level that would appeal to the enemies of the Redeemers in the South and at the same time satisfy powerful GOP interests outside the region. Thus the overtures President Arthur made to southern independents with radical ideas proved disquieting to orthodox Republicans. Changing sentiment in the North, reflecting the drift away from Reconstruction idealism, as well as the strong influence of business elements in the Republican party, doomed Harrison's attempt to secure passage of the Lodge Force bill. And to complicate matters still further, the very threat of such legislation became an effective weapon in the hands of those who championed white supremacy and a Solid South.

A far more serious challenge to Democratic dominance in the South came with the farmers' revolt and a powerful third party. Driven to radical protest and political action by a long period of agricultural depression and a feeling of public discrimination and neglect, southern farmers embraced the People's party in growing numbers during the early 1890s. Their insurgency threatened the whole structure of Democratic control in the South. The Populists, as they were called, entertained some radical ideas; they hoped to effect an alliance between the South and the West, to attract urban workers as well as farmers, and to bring blacks into their political coalition. They were also prepared to cooperate with Republicans, as they did in capturing control of the state government of North Carolina in 1894 and 1896. "No single idea or policy drove the Populist movement," Edward L. Ayers observes, "only a general insistence that the government pursue actions more equitable for the majority of citizens, become more open in its actions, and be willing to go beyond shibboleths."[42] The Populist crusade swept through the southern countryside in the early 1890s, striking fear in the ranks of the Democrats and causing them to employ desperate countermeasures. For a moment much of the South seemed to stand on the threshold of a political revolution in which a combination of upcountry dwellers, black and white farmers, and industrial workers might overcome the entrenched black-belt planters and their business allies and reverse the political trends of recent years.

Populism was both a manifestation of and a threat to sectionalism in late-nineteenth-century American politics. Southern agrarians resented the rising cities, expanding industry, and New South orientation of the conservative Democrats. By challenging the supremacy of the Democratic South, populism went against the grain of the sectional alignment in southern politics, including the concept of white solidarity and the desirability of a one-party system. Ironically, the Populists themselves were eventually caught in a cruel dilemma.

42. Ayers, *The Promise of the New South*, p. 266. See also Woodward, *Origins of the New South*, pp. 253–63; Robert C. McMath, Jr., *Populist Vanguard: A History of the Southern Farmers' Alliance* (Chapel Hill, N.C., 1975); Lawrence Goodwyn, *Democratic Promise: The Populist Moment in America* (New York, 1976), pp. 177–272; and Degler, *The Other South*, pp. 316–71.

When the party decided to support William Jennings Bryan in 1896, its members found themselves backing a Democrat for president while simultaneously cooperating with Republicans at the state and local levels in parts of the South.

In some respects, however, populism was itself a sectional phenomenon. The movement was largely the product of the South and the West. Much of the radicalism associated with it was indigenous to the South, and the movement probably had its greatest strength in that region. It owed much of its success to the National Farmers' Alliance and Industrial Union. Originating in Texas, the Farmers' Alliance spread rapidly through the South in the late 1880s, pulling other farm groups and thousands of unaffiliated farmers into its ranks. By 1890 over a million southerners were members of the Alliance. It was particularly successful in areas that had been settled after the Civil War. The movement also attracted black farmers, who organized their own locals and eventually formed the Colored Farmers' National Alliance. The principal source of the Alliances' popularity was their promise of direct economic relief, especially through cooperative programs, and the sense of community fostered by local chapters and activities. It was the Southern Alliance, as it was known, that formulated the economic and political ideas that were soon identified with the People's party and populism.[43]

These radical ideas were critical of the conservative political control in the South and West, whether exercised by Democrats or Republicans. But they emphasized the sectional disparities that characterized the nation's political economy and the concentration of economic power and political influence in the Northeast. In the eyes of southern Populists—and many southern Democrats—tight money, a centralized and inadequate banking system, a protective tariff, high railroad rates, rising land prices, and spreading industrial and financial monopolies were centered in the North and East. The agrarian radicals of the South and West increasingly blamed their troubles on the Northeast and its "unfair" advantages. Like absentee ownership, sectional dependency, and lagging economic development, the most threatening economic conditions were manifestations of a northern imperium as contrasted with a southern and western "colonial" status in the national economy. Thus populism was, in part at least, a "revolt against the East."[44]

This revolt revived the old debate over what Vann Woodward has termed "the sectional diplomacy" of the South—over whether the southern states should align themselves in national politics with the Northeast or the West.[45] When the New Yorker Grover Cleveland won the presidency a second time in 1892, most Democratic leaders in the South were predisposed to support his administration. But this soon changed. Following the onset of the depression in 1893, Cleveland launched what one scholar describes as "a financial program of contraction that the mass of Southern people regarded as legislation to enrich

43. McMath, *Populist Vanguard*, pp. 64–76, 90–157; Goodwyn, *Democratic Promise*, pp. 110–76; Ayers, *The Promise of the New South*, pp. 214–48.

44. Woodward, *Origins of the New South*, pp. 264–90. See also Samuel P. Hays, *The Response to Industrialism, 1885–1914* (Chicago, 1957), pp. 116–39.

45. Woodward, *Origins of the New South*, p. 235.

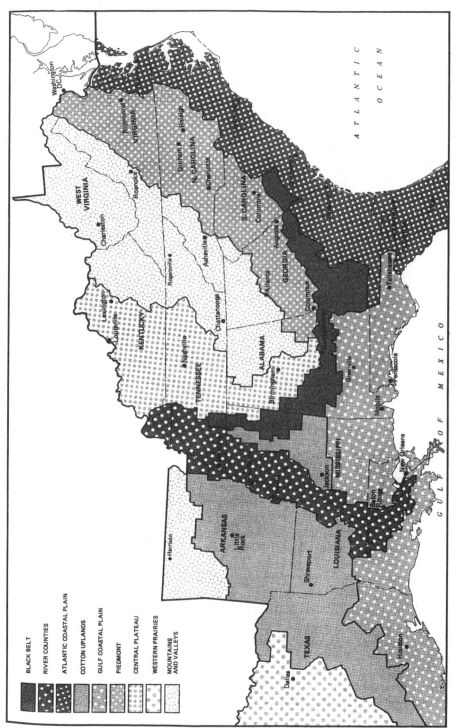

The Subregions of the New South. SOURCE: Edward L. Ayers, *The Promise of the New South: Life After Reconstruction* (New York: Oxford University Press, 1992), p. 5. Reprinted by permission.

the creditor section at their expense and depress them to the level of a colonial dependency."[46] The administration's financial orthodoxy and lack of understanding of the agrarian unrest bolstered populism in the South and provoked mounting criticism from the region's Democrats. By 1896 the opposition to the president's policies had captured the Democratic party in almost every southern state and, to the consternation of People's party leaders, had taken over a large part of the Populist platform, including the free and unlimited coinage of silver. Reform leaders such as James S. Hogg of Texas and Benjamin R. Tillman of South Carolina refused to leave the Democratic party, and their demands for change improved the reputation of their party. Southern Democrats helped place William Jennings Bryan at the head of their party's national ticket. Northern newspapers declared that the Democratic party had been taken over by "demagogues," "anarchists," "socialists," "communists," "agitators," and "Jacobins."[47]

The Populists, particularly those in the South, found themselves in a difficult position. There was, in fact, no way out for the People's party. It could not resist the pressure to endorse Bryan, and the failure of the Nebraskan's valiant campaign soon brought an end to the third party everywhere. In the South the majority party managed to overcome its challengers by appealing for white supremacy in the face of black power in politics, by fraudulent electoral practices, and by taking over part of the Populist platform and rhetoric. Although the silver Democrats carried every southern state except Kentucky for Bryan, the attempted fusion of Populists and Democrats in the national election encountered strong opposition, and many members of the majority party fought the third party with every means at their disposal. In the states where they were most successful—Georgia, Alabama, North Carolina, Arkansas, and Texas—the Populists tended to attract support in counties that concentrated on the production of cotton but where the land was poor or relatively unimproved. In most states, especially in the Deep South, the higher the proportion of blacks in a county, the less likely the People's party was to win, in part because opportunities for electoral fraud and intimidation were greater in areas of high black density and also because whites in such subregions were under enormous pressure to maintain political unity against Negro majorities or near-majorities.[48] While the Populists soon disappeared, their espousal of positive governmental action, business regulation, and political democracy left its mark on the South. The third party's emphasis on monetary inflation and credit needs, marketing reforms, minimum prices and acreage controls, and better farming methods helped shape southern politics in the twentieth century.

The political upheaval of the 1890s, the Cleveland administration's inability to deal effectively with the debilitating economic crisis, and the climactic presidential election of 1896 produced a great realignment of the nation's political

46. *Ibid.*, p. 272.
47. James L. Sundquist, *Dynamics of the Party System: Alignment and Realignment of Political Parties in the United States*, rev. ed. (Washington, D.C., 1983), p. 156.
48. Ayers, *The Promise of the New South*, pp. 278–82.

parties. The hard-fought campaign of 1896 emphasized economic concerns that cut across the traditional sectional issues of slavery, war, and Reconstruction. Republicans made the most of these issues, overpowering Democrats in the Northeast and Midwest. Though not strictly an agrarian-industrial conflict, the election, in the words of one historian, "came closer to a contest between classes, economic interests, and sections than any other campaign in the late nineteenth century."[49] "The Republican party's domination of national partisan politics," another scholar has noted, "reflected the concentration of people and economic power in the northeastern-midwestern states, and it consolidated the transfer of political power to northern financial-industrial elites that had begun in the 1850s."[50] The election of 1896, ushering in a new party system, settled the question of whether northern and eastern industrial interests or southern and western agricultural and mining interests would be victorious.[51]

Still, the old sectional loyalties had not lost their potency. In the South "the Civil War pattern" was hardly disturbed at all. Much of the Populist constituency in other sections returned to its original Republican support. "Northern Democrats," one scholar writes, "could become Republicans without too great an emotional and psychological strain, but silver Republicans could not bring themselves to become Democrats."[52] Indeed, in some respects "the system of 1896" represented the most sectional party alignment in American history. The sectional implications of the realignment are suggested in an essay by Robert Kelley:

> Through William Jennings Bryan the Populist creed now captured the Democratic party and transformed it into a Southern and Western party. New England had always distrusted both the South and the West; inflationism ran directly against the interests of the consuming masses in the Northeastern and Middle Western cities; the ethnic minorities distrusted Bryan's pietism and agrarianism; and in consequence the Democratic party, which formerly had been strong in the Northeast and Middle West, shriveled in those regions. Urban ethnic groups surged toward the Republicans, who during the depression preached even more enthusiastically their traditional message that the government should actively intervene in and stimulate the economy. At the same time, William McKinley damped down the prohibitionist and nativist elements in his party so as no longer to offend the German Protestants.[53]

49. Gilbert C. Fite, "Election of 1896," in Schlesinger and Israel, eds., *History of American Presidential Elections*, vol. 2, p. 1825.

50. Numan V. Bartley, "The South and Sectionalism in American Politics," *Journal of Politics* 38 (August 1976): 254.

51. For the realignment of the 1890s, see Walter Dean Burnham, *Critical Elections and the Mainsprings of American Politics* (New York, 1970), pp. 71–90; Sundquist, *Dynamics of the Party System*, pp. 134–69; and Paul Kleppner, "From Ethnoreligious Conflict to 'Social Harmony': Coalitional and Party Transformations in the 1890s," in *Emerging Coalitions in American Politics*, ed. Seymour Martin Lipset (San Francisco, 1978), pp. 49–52.

52. Sundquist, *Dynamics of the Party System*, p. 169.

53. Robert Kelley, "Ideology and Political Culture from Jefferson to Nixon," *American Historical Review* 82 (June 1977): 548.

Except for the South, the border states, and the mountain areas of the West, the Democratic party was reduced to the status of "a forlorn and noncompetitive minority."[54] So paramount were the Republicans following the realignment of the 1890s that much of the North and West was scarcely less subject to one-party politics than was the South. In fact, the American political universe that took shape at the turn of the century reflected a pronounced sectional alignment that "eventually separated the Southern and Western agrarians and transformed the most industrially advanced region of the country into a bulwark of industrial Republicanism."[55] At the same time, the political upheaval of the 1890s left southern Democrats in a stronger position than ever before. With the exception of a few Republican enclaves in the mountains of the upper South, Democratic supremacy in the region could scarcely have been greater during the decades that followed. Thus the realignment of the 1890s transformed the Republicans into the nation's majority party, ended the GOP's serious interest in southern politics, and removed the last institutional obstacle to the Solid South.

Democratic leaders in the South moved quickly following the political crisis of the 1890s to prevent a recurrence of the Populist revolt and to strengthen their control of state and local governments. They moved on two, somewhat contradictory, fronts. First, they sought to lure all disaffected white men back into the Democratic party. Democratic leaders began to liberalize party rules by introducing statewide primary elections and the direct election of U.S. senators. These innovations were in part a legacy of populism, and they were related to the Bryanization of the Democratic party in the South and to the persisting demand in the region for political reform. Second, the Democrats were able to settle the "race problem" to their own satisfaction and with the acquiescence of other parts of the country. This racial settlement completed the process begun two decades earlier of undermining the African American's political influence and legal position; it effectively institutionalized white supremacy in the southern states through disfranchisement and legal segregation. With the collapse of Populist hopes and with the memory of white factions bidding for black votes fresh in the minds of white southerners, Democrats managed to secure the adoption of a series of drastic disfranchisement measures. Eight of the southern states approved constitutional provisions, featuring literacy tests and poll tax requirements, as a means of depriving black citizens of the ballot. Disfranchisement was accompanied and followed by a wave of segregation laws designed to keep blacks "in their place."[56]

Disfranchisement advocates, recognizing an issue that would rally white southerners and, some supporters argued, even challenge conservative party bosses, worked energetically and with mounting confidence to complete the

54. Kleppner, "From Ethnoreligious Conflict to 'Social Harmony,' " p. 45.

55. Walter Dean Burnham, "The Changing Shape of the American Political Universe," *American Political Science Review* 59 (March 1965): 25.

56. For the details of disfranchisement and the "racial settlement," see Kousser, *The Shaping of Southern Politics*, pp. 139–223, and Jack Temple Kirby, *Darkness at the Dawning: Race and Reform in the Progressive South* (Philadelphia, 1972).

task. A campaign to call a constitutional convention in Mississippi was successful in 1890, and a new document was drafted to replace the Radical Recontruction constitution of 1868. The constitution of 1890 included a number of franchise provisions: a literacy test, cumulative poll tax, long residence requirement, registration four months before an election, and disqualification for a list of crimes. An alternative to the literacy requirement was devised for illiterate white men—the ability to "understand" and give a "reasonable interpretation" of any section of the constitution. In 1895 South Carolina followed Mississippi's course by adopting disfranchisement clauses as part of its new constitution. Louisiana, which resorted to constitutional disfranchisement in 1898, invented the "grandfather clause" as a temporary alternative to the literacy requirement. This provision exempted from the literacy test those who were entitled to vote on January 1, 1867, together with their sons and grandsons. North Carolina, Alabama, Virginia, and Georgia took similar action during the next few years. Oklahoma, in 1910, was the last state to adopt constitutional disfranchisement. Although the other southern states refrained from amending their constitutions to disfranchise black voters, all of them except Kentucky approved restrictive measures in one form or another. The white primary was also an effective suffrage-restriction weapon. In the early years of the twentieth century, most of the Democratic state committees and conventions in the region introduced statewide primaries that excluded blacks.

The intense struggle within the party of Redemption during the 1890s soon weakened the position of blacks in southern politics and made them a scapegoat in the aftermath of the agrarian revolt. As might have been expected, the regular Democrats, particularly in the black belts, were the principal architects of disfranchisement, which they saw as a means of striking at the Republican party as well as discouraging third-party ventures in the future. Some Democratic leaders may have supported suffrage restriction because it promised to deprive illiterate white men of the ballot and thus of any part in party politics. In a number of states, such as Virginia, Democratic opponents of entrenched party organizations apparently hoped that disfranchisement would undermine the power of the ruling political factions. Some agrarian reformers and ex-Populists such as Thomas E. Watson in Georgia became champions of Negro disfranchisement. Men like Watson, dispirited, often disillusioned, and sometimes embittered over the failure of their Populist dreams, turned on blacks with a vengeance. In this atmosphere the dwindling number of Republicans and Populists proved to be the most steadfast supporters of universal manhood suffrage and fair election laws.

Many white southerners undoubtedly believed that removing blacks from politics would end the political corruption of the 1890s and enable whites to deal constructively with substantive issues. Indeed, contemporary white southerners were inclined to view disfranchisement as a necessary step, even a reform, but the "race question" continued to supply politicians with an issue that aroused the average white man even more powerfully than economic and class exhortations. It should be noted that strong sentiment existed in the North for the use of educational requirements and secret ballot laws as a means of "purifying" the northern electorate, limiting the political rights of immigrants, and striking at the base of urban bosses. While many northerners complained about the excesses of disfranchisement in the South, the inhabitants of other regions were surprisingly tolerant and even supportive of suffrage restriction in the South.[57]

By the end of the century, American politics had moved out of the shadow of Reconstruction. New issues, reflecting the nation's economic and urban transformation following the war, had assumed center stage. The failure of populism opened the way to the triumph of the Solid South. Disfranchisement and the introduction of the Democratic primary enhanced the region's white solidarity and laid the foundation for the one-party system. Meanwhile, the realignment of the U.S. party system in the 1890s introduced a new sectional polarity in national politics and changed the role of the South in the Democratic party and in the nation's public life.

57. Kousser, *The Shaping of Southern Politics*, pp. 51–53, 57.

CHAPTER 2

The Easing of Sectional Tensions

T HE climactic developments of the 1890s paved the way for a relaxation of intersectional hostility and a new understanding between North and South. By the turn of the century, the "southern question" had become less ominous, and the nation's most wayward section seemed to be assuming a happier role in American life. Freed from the economic depression and political turmoil of the 1890s, Americans faced the new century in a buoyant mood. The triumphant war with Spain had precipitated an outpouring of patriotism and a satisfying display of national unity. Southerners shared in the optimistic outlook. They responded, as one historian has remarked, "with customary impetuosity to the upsurge of martial spirit and put aside sectional grievances."[1] The region's economic outlook had brightened, Democratic solidarity was assured, and the "race problem" was yielding to disfranchisement and new segregation laws. Some southerners were turning with a new hopefulness to the possibility of establishing a genuine educational system in their states and localities; others soon began to promote "reform" in a variety of other areas. "Sectional America," a contemporary wrote in 1905, "has now become a nation in the full, rich meaning of the word; and the New South and the New North are made up of the men and women who understand the significance of this tremendous growth and are determined to think and act in the light of it."[2]

By the mid-1890s, Wilbur J. Cash wrote long afterward, the South was "once more one with the North so far as standing shoulder to shoulder with it against any outside foe was concerned."[3] This heightened sense of nationalism among southerners owed a great deal to the spirit of goodwill and tolerance displayed in the commemoration of Blue and Gray heroism. Memorial Day in the North became an agency of reconciliation, expressions of fraternity became

1. C. Vann Woodward, *Origins of the New South, 1877–1913* (Baton Rouge, La., 1951), p. 369.
2. Hamilton Wright Mabie, "The New North," *South Atlantic Quarterly* 4 (April 1905): 111.
3. W. J. Cash, *The Mind of the South* (New York, 1941), p. 183.

characteristic of veterans' organizations, battlefields such as Chickamauga and Chattanooga were dedicated as national parks, and Robert E. Lee, the "incarnation of the Confederate cause," became a revered figure in the national pantheon.[4] *Outlook* magazine devoted an entire issue to Lee's career in 1906. In a typical comment the editor praised the Virginian's "stainless life" and declared that "the nation has a hero to place beside her greatest."[5] The South's new patriotism found enthusiastic expression in the Spanish-American War of 1898. The region became a staging area for the assault on Cuba; two Confederate heroes—Fitzhugh Lee and Joseph "Fightin' Joe" Wheeler—were appointed major generals of volunteers; and southerners generally gave unstinting support to the war. The conflict presented southerners with an opportunity not only to free Cuba and extend American influence abroad but also to free themselves from northern suspicions of their loyalty and to demonstrate southern honor.[6]

Many southern newspapers echoed the sentiment of the Richmond *Times*, which proudly proclaimed that "upon any battlefield of the war Confederate veterans and their sons will be seen upholding the national honor and guarding the country's safety with all the steadiness and resolution that characterized them in the early sixties."[7] Newspapers and magazines throughout the country applauded the new harmony, declaring that "the foes of bygone days were friends." As Richard N. Current has remarked, "By the early 1900s, Southernism had managed to identify itself with Americanism."[8] The South's sense of vindication was increased when the North, acting through the federal government, made two highly symbolic gestures in the interest of sectional harmony. Early in the century, Congress provided that the government should henceforth care for the graves of the Confederate dead, and it ordered the return of captured Confederate flags to the South.[9]

Southerners revealed their nationalism not only by rallying around the flag but also by appealing to the imagination and sympathy of northerners in numerous, less striking ways. The oratory of Henry W. Grady and other New South spokesmen in the 1880s had elicited a favorable response in other regions. In an eloquent address to the New England Society of New York in 1886, Grady spoke of a South "of slavery and secession" having been replaced by a South "of union and freedom."[10] The New South creed seemed to envisage a section that was becoming increasingly less *southern* and more *American*. Southern expatriates like Walter Hines Page, mediating between North and South, emphasized the basic similarities between the two regions. By the end of the century, northern philanthropists were broadening their support of southern

    4. Paul H. Buck, *The Road to Reunion, 1865–1900* (Boston, 1937), pp. 236–62.

    5. Thomas L. Connelly and Barbara L. Bellows, *God and General Longstreet: The Lost Cause and the Southern Mind* (Baton Rouge, La., 1982), p. 82. Also see Thomas L. Connelly, *The Marble Man: Robert E. Lee and His Image in American Society* (New York, 1977), pp. 99–122.

    6. Gaines M. Foster, *Ghosts of the Confederacy: Defeat, the Lost Cause, and the Emergence of the New South, 1865 to 1913* (New York, 1987), pp. 148, 153.

    7. Quoted in Buck, *The Road to Reunion*, p. 306.

    8. *Ibid.*, p. 307; Richard N. Current, *Northernizing the South* (Athens, Ga., 1983), p. 92.

    9. Foster, *Ghosts of the Confederacy*, pp. 153–54, 156, 159.

    10. Paul M. Gaston, *The New South Creed: A Study in Southern Mythmaking* (New York, 1970), p. 87.

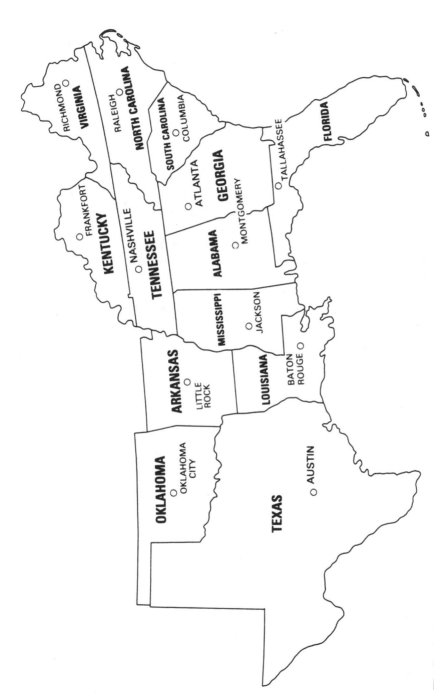

The South. Source: Dewey W. Grantham, *The Life & Death of the Solid South: A Political History* (Lexington: University Press of Kentucky, 1988), p. 30.

projects to include such endeavors as the improvement of public education for white children, vocational schools, and medical and welfare programs as well as black training and uplift.

There were signs that thoughtful southerners had become more concerned about their region's contributions to national life. Thus, when Edwin A. Alderman, president of Tulane University, was invited to deliver the Commemoration Day address at Johns Hopkins University in 1903, he decided to speak on the South's role in shaping the national character. He solicited suggestions from some twenty intellectuals, among them Henry Adams, Thomas Nelson Page, Albert Shaw, William P. Trent, Frederick Jackson Turner, and Woodrow Wilson. Those who responded identified a wide range of southern contributions: statesmanship in the early republic, Jeffersonian democracy, the emphasis on individual liberty, Jacksonian democracy, an upper class of striking virtues, the spirit of romanticism, the genius of oratory, and so on. Alderman used these suggestions in his address. He disclaimed any sectional purpose, asserting that "sectionalism as a creed, or as a philosophy, or as a passion, has passed out of our life." His objective, he insisted, was the "re-nationalization" of his region. He praised the southerners' feeling that their "section has something high and precious and distinctive in manhood and leadership to contribute to American civilization."[11]

Meanwhile, the romance of the Old South and the Confederacy as well as the exotic character of southern life attracted the interest of many northerners, who were charmed by the "local color" and black dialect in the stories and novels of southern writers. Among the more prominent of these authors were George Washington Cable and Grace King of Louisiana, Joel Chandler Harris of Georgia, Thomas Nelson Page of Virginia, and a group of younger writers that included James Lane Allen, Charles Waddell Chesnutt, Kate Chopin, John Fox, Jr., Ellen Glasgow, Sutton E. Griggs, and Ruth McEnery Stuart. These authors of fiction, one historian notes, "wrote less of public events than of conflicts over sexual identity, religious faith, the meaning of race, the experience of one's generation, the volatile changes in the class order, the meaning of industrialization." They tended to see themselves as "mediators between a genteel readership and a South that often refused to conform to standards of Northern gentility."[12] A Virginia professor of literature noted with pleasure in 1898 that "the great Northern magazines" had generously opened their columns to the contributions of southern writers, who, he said, were currently accorded "as ready a hearing in Boston and New York as in any city south of Mason and Dixon's line." The South's literary revival of the 1880s and 1890s helped bring a transition in other parts of the nation from "a critical attitude to a complete

11. Edwin Anderson Alderman, "Abstract of an Address Delivered on Commemoration Day, February 23, 1903," *Johns Hopkins University Circular* 22 (April 1903): 43–45 (quotations); Robert Bush, "Dr. Alderman's Symposium on the South," *Mississippi Quarterly* 27 (Winter 1973–1974): 3–19.

12. Edward L. Ayers, *The Promise of the New South: Life After Reconstruction* (New York, 1992), pp. 339–72, 537 (quotation on p. 339).

espousal of the tradition of a South of heroism and beauty. . . ."[13] Before long, leading historians of the sectional conflict such as James Ford Rhodes, John W. Burgess, and William A. Dunning—all northern born—were portraying the South during Reconstruction in a much more favorable light than had earlier writers. "Clearly," one historian has recently written, "in things of the imagination at least, the North was being quite thoroughly Southernized."[14]

The economic upturn in the late 1890s also seemed to allay sectional antagonism. Populism no longer posed a threat to North-South cooperation, and most governors and other state officials in the South were responsive to the conservative prescriptions for economic development and diversification. The South, too, was affected by the "nationalization of business," and every phase of southern industry testified to "the interlocking dependence of economic activity."[15] During the early years of the new century the quickening pace of economic development—increasing industrialization, economic growth of the region's cities, and rising agricultural prices—was widely interpreted as the precursor of the South's economic transformation and triumph. Its recent manufacturing growth seemed "as remarkable an industrial romance as the rise of New England."[16] "Nowhere on this continent," the president of Trinity College, in Durham, North Carolina, declared in 1909, "will you hear a finer note of nationalism than you will hear in the humming wheels of a Carolina cotton mill."[17] Southern industrialization, another contemporary proclaimed, was "one of the mighty agents for our intellectual and moral freedom."[18]

Despite the optimistic expectations of its leaders, the South failed to improve its economic position relative to that of the Northeast and Midwest. Within the national economy, the region's percentage of manufacturing establishments, capital, and value of manufactures in 1900 was about the same as in 1860. Its per capita income in 1900 was only 51 percent of the national average, unchanged from 1880. Progress was no doubt limited by the South's dependence on other regions for capital resources, technical skills, and manufactured goods. "Like republics below the Rio Grande," C. Vann Woodward has written, "the South was limited largely to the role of a producer of raw materials, a tributary of industrial powers, an economy dominated by absentee owners."[19] In many ways, another historian has observed, "the South in 1900 was like an under-

13. C. Alphonso Smith, "The Possibilities of the South in Literature," *Sewanee Review* 6 (July 1898): 303 (first quotation); Buck, *The Road to Reunion*, p. 229 (second quotation). See also Louis J. Budd and others, "The Forgotten Decades of Southern Writing, 1890–1920," *Mississippi Quarterly* 21 (Fall 1968): 275–90, and several essays in *The History of Southern Literature*, ed. Louis D. Rubin, Jr., et al. (Baton Rouge, La., 1985), pp. 199–232.

14. Current, *Northernizing the South*, p. 95. See also Nina Silber, *The Romance of Reunion: Northerners and the South, 1865–1900* (Chapel Hill, N.C., 1993).

15. Buck, *The Road to Reunion*, pp. 300–301.

16. Douglas Southall Freeman, "Fifty Years from the Ashes," *Harper's Weekly* 61 (August 14, 1915): 154.

17. John Carlisle Kilgo, "The Democracy and Fraternity of American Industrialism," *South Atlantic Quarterly* 8 (October 1909): 339.

18. John E. White, "The True and the False in Southern Life," *South Atlantic Quarterly* 5 (April 1906): 109.

19. Woodward, *Origins of the New South*, p. 311.

developed colony that looked north for credit and ideas, and northern investors eagerly extracted southern resources."[20] By 1900, for example, three-fourths of the South's railroad mileage, outside of Texas, were controlled by five corporations, all of which were dominated by northern bankers. In 1907 the region's largest and most promising firm in the steel industry—the Tennessee Coal, Iron and Railroad Company—was acquired by the United States Steel Corporation. The South remained overwhelmingly agricultural and rural, and its urban economy was essentially commercial.

Cotton, which was cultivated in a broad belt stretching from the Carolinas to Texas, dominated the regional economy. Other cash crops, predominantly tobacco, rice, and sugar cane, were all characterized by narrow geographical limits. Cotton, as Gavin Wright notes, defined the opportunities and dictated the pace of economic life below the Potomac. "When southern cotton prices drop," the agricultural editor Clarence Poe remarked in 1904, "every man feels the blow; when cotton prices advance, every industry throbs with vigor."[21] In the meantime, self-sufficiency steadily declined among southern farmers, the average size of farms in the region drifted downward, and the rate of tenancy surged upward in the 1890s. Southern industries, except for textiles and lumber, were small. Most of them produced a limited range of cheap, standardized, low-skill commodities that required relatively little processing and added relatively little value to the section's raw materials. Capital was scarce, and southern manufacturers were dependent on imported technology. Both industry and agriculture were less mechanized and more labor-intensive in the South than in the North. Southern wages were low compared with those in other regions, and the southern labor market was isolated.[22]

Nevertheless, the South experienced a period of unaccustomed prosperity in the years after 1900. The demand for cotton on the world market accelerated at the turn of the century, increasing at a rate of about 3.5 percent a year over the following fifteen years. Cotton prices rose from five cents a pound in 1898 to more than twelve cents in 1903. New records for the value of the cotton crop were set in 1909, 1910, and 1913. The demand for other southern staples also increased. The region's industries, led by cotton textiles, made solid gains in the new century. The textile industry was especially dynamic. In Georgia, one of the four southeastern Piedmont states in which the industry was concentrated, the number of active spindles increased more than threefold between 1900 and 1922. By 1909 the Southeast boasted 1,208 cotton mills, and by 1915 the South had over 40 percent of the nation's spindles.[23] While the census of 1900 revealed that the South was only 15 percent urban, its cities were growing and its

20. Pete Daniel, *Breaking the Land: The Transformation of Cotton, Tobacco, and Rice Cultures since 1880* (Urbana, Ill., 1985), p. xiii.

21. Quoted in Gavin Wright, *Old South, New South: Revolutions in the Southern Economy Since the Civil War* (New York, 1986), p. 59.

22. See the discussion of this point and other aspects of the southern economy in Wright, *Old South, New South*, pp. 81–197.

23. Jack Blicksilver, *Cotton Manufacturing in the Southeast: An Historical Analysis* (Atlanta, 1959), pp. 37, 50–52.

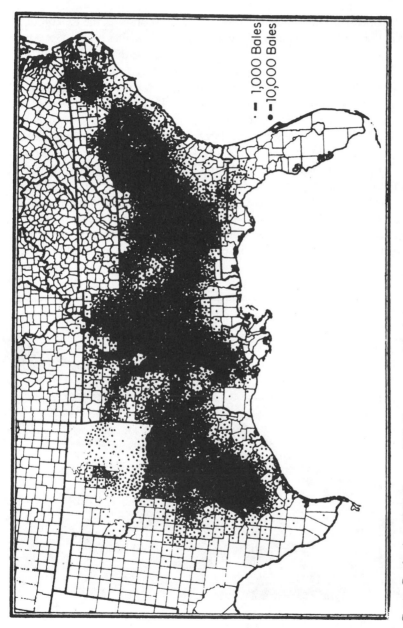

Cotton Production, 1899. SOURCE: U.S. Department of Agriculture, *Atlas of American Agriculture*, part 5, sec. A (Washington, D.C.: Government Printing Office, 1918), p. 17.

1,000 Bales
10,000 Bales

economy was slowly becoming more diversified. The labor market became more competitive during the early part of the century, wages rose for blacks and whites, and economic opportunities expanded, particularly for middle-class and professional people.

Another factor in the easing of intersectional tensions was the emergence by the turn of the century of a national consensus among whites on the "race problem." There were many manifestations of this broad understanding, but its essential elements were the implicit assumption that the southern states would be free to handle the issue of race relations within their borders and that the North would adopt a "hands-off" attitude in response. This racial consensus encouraged the reconciliation of North and South.

Two developments in the southern states raised doubts in the minds of some white Americans about this reconciliation. One was the repressive conditions and harsh treatment that became the daily lot of millions of black southerners under the new racial dispensation. The other was the spread of a virulent and extreme racism through the region. The broad sweep of disfranchisement and legal segregation vividly demonstrated the African American's second-class status. As one scholar has written, "Once effectively stripped of their Fifteenth Amendment rights, blacks were driven from public office, refused equality

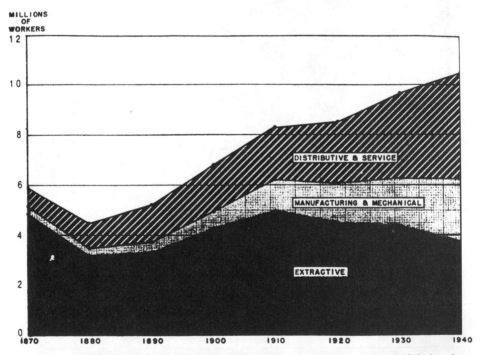

The Changing Occupational Distribution: The Trend in the Number of Gainful Workers by Three Major Occupational Groups, Southeast, 1870–1940. SOURCE: Rupert B. Vance, in collaboration with Nadia Danilevsky, *All These People: The Nation's Human Resources in the South* (Chapel Hill: University of North Carolina Press, 1945), p. 151.

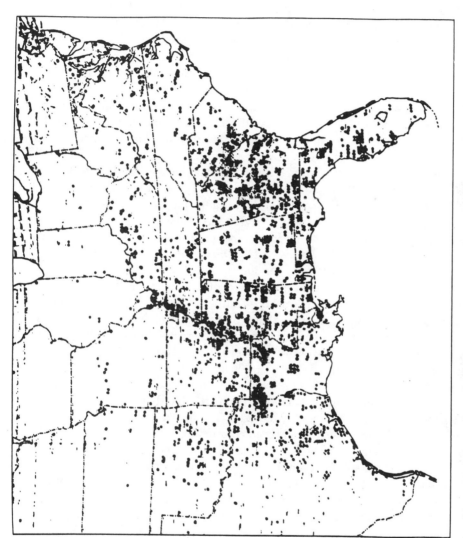

Lynchings, 1900–1930. SOURCE: *The South for New Southerners*, ed. Paul D. Escott and David R. Goldfield (Chapel Hill: University of North Carolina Press, 1991), p. 23.

under the law, excluded from places of accommodation and amusement, and denied the public services for which they were taxed."[24] It was generally understood that, in the exercise of police protection and the functioning of the courts, blacks could not expect the same treatment as that given whites. In addition, the resort to extralegal violence against blacks was widespread and notorious. More than 1,700 black southerners were lynched between 1889 and 1909. Several race riots early in the twentieth century—from Wilmington, North Carolina, in 1898 to Atlanta, Georgia, in 1906—pointed up the inflammatory atmosphere and the savagery inflicted on Negroes in a region preoccupied with the race question.[25] Although African Americans received some benefits from the return of prosperity early in the new century, a great many of them suffered the plight, along with millions of landless white farmers, of being caught in a worsening system of tenancy. Meanwhile, southern black people were systematically denied their rightful share of the newly authorized funds for public education and given few of the South's other public services.

Southern white thinking on race was strongly influenced by the rise of what has been called the "Radical mentality" in the 1890s. It flourished between 1897 and 1907, and it remained powerful until the First World War. "Radicalism," according to Joel Williamson, "envisioned a 'new' Negro, freed from the necessarily very tight bonds of slavery and retrogressing rapidly toward his natural state of savagery and bestiality."[26] The Darwinian concepts of racial degeneracy and extinction provided a "scientific" basis for Radicalism and other anti-Negro propaganda around the turn of the century. Energetically promoted by southern leaders such as Benjamin R. Tillman of South Carolina, James K. Vardaman of Mississippi, Thomas Dixon of North Carolina, and Rebecca Felton of Georgia, this form of white racism exerted great influence at the popular level. One reason was the work of southerners like Rebecca Felton, who became increasingly concerned in the 1890s about what she believed to be the mounting attacks of black men on white women. Felton belonged to a prominent family, had been intimately involved in her husband's political career as an independent Democrat, was a Methodist lay leader, was an advocate of women's rights, and wrote a widely read column for the Atlanta *Journal*. A bold and purposeful activist, she launched a personal campaign on the lecture platform and in her newspaper column, calling on good men to do their duty—and if necessary to lynch the "drunken, ravening human beasts." Felton identified the race problem with the cultural constraints that imprisoned white women and the double standard enjoyed by white men in the South. She "was in the vanguard of a Radical element that revolutionized popular white thought in the South about black people during the turn of the century decades."[27]

24. Neil R. McMillen, *Dark Journey: Black Mississippians in the Age of Jim Crow* (Urbana, Ill., 1989), p. 71.

25. Ayers, *The Promise of the New South*, p. 495; Joel Williamson, *The Crucible of Race: Black-White Relations in the American South Since Emancipation* (New York, 1984), pp. 180–223.

26. Williamson, *The Crucible of Race*, p. 6.

27. *Ibid.*, pp. 124–30, 303 (quotations on pp. 128 and 130). See also George M. Fredrickson, *The Black Image in the White Mind: The Debate on Afro-American Character and Destiny, 1817–1914* (New

The erosion of the North's once-strong commitment to racial justice and black uplift was reflected in the pronouncements and policies of the nation's chief executives. President William McKinley, eager to muster support for the war with Spain and for American overseas expansion, made a point of appealing to southern sensibilities. On a trip through the South in the spring of 1901, McKinley was given a warm reception. In his remarks to southern audiences, the president avoided the race question and dwelt on the theme of reconciliation between North and South.[28] McKinley's immediate successors, Theodore Roosevelt and William Howard Taft, also sought to attract the cooperation and goodwill of southern whites. None of the three Republican presidents made any effort to challenge the political and racial hegemony of white southerners. Indeed, the "lily-white" movement to deny blacks a significant role in the Republican party continued to gain ground while Republicans occupied the White House, though not always with presidential approval.

Although the Republicans controlled Congress for a decade and a half after 1894, that branch of the federal government was equally reluctant to intervene in the South. Despite occasional Republican protests against disfranchisement in the various southern states, most GOP congressmen accepted suffrage restriction in the South as a fait accompli. There was, however, one area in which Republican lawmakers showed a disposition to act against southern disfranchisers, and that was in settling contested elections in the House of Representatives. In the Fifty-fourth Congress (1895–1897), no fewer than thirty-one House seats were contested, most of these challenges arising out of alleged irregularities in southern congressional elections. Eleven challenges were successful, with the Republicans gaining nine seats.[29] But contested elections declined during the first years of the twentieth century, as the Democrats strengthened their control of the one-party system in the southern states. Following the completion of the census of 1900, Representative Edgar D. Crumpacker, an Indiana Republican, tried unsuccessfully to force the reapportionment of the South's congressional seats in accordance with the Fourteenth Amendment clause that stipulates a reduction of representation in proportion to the denial of the ballot to adult males. Similar efforts at reapportionment in later years proved equally fruitless. Federalism was too ingrained even in Republican members for them to undertake such a radical step. Meanwhile, southern congressmen regularly introduced legislation to repeal the Fifteenth Amendment and the representation section of the Fourteenth.

White southerners were also encouraged by the U.S. Supreme Court, which

York, 1971), p. 256, and John W. Cell, *The Highest Stage of White Supremacy: The Origins of Segregation in South Africa and the American South* (Cambridge, England, 1982), pp. 257–63.

28. Richard B. Sherman, *The Republican Party and Black America: From McKinley to Hoover, 1896–1933* (Charlottesville, Va., 1973), pp. 1–22.

29. Richard Franklin Bensel, *Sectionalism and American Political Development, 1880–1980* (Madison, Wis., 1984), pp. 84–85. In earlier years (1877–1893), the Justice Department had also brought a significant number of election prosecutions in the South. See Robert M. Goldman, *"A Free Ballot and a Fair Count": The Department of Justice and the Enforcement of Voting Rights in the South, 1877–1893* (New York, 1990).

undermined the Reconstruction guarantees to the freedmen in a series of cases in the last quarter of the nineteenth century. In *Plessy* v. *Ferguson* (1896), the court upheld a Louisiana statute requiring separate railroad coaches for blacks and whites by proclaiming the "separate but equal" accommodations rule. In *Williams* v. *Mississippi* (1898), the tribunal gave its stamp of approval to Mississippi's disfranchisement plan, and in *Giles* v. *Harris* (1903), the court held in an Alabama case that suffrage provisions, however unfairly administered, were beyond the reach of the federal courts. The equal protection of the laws, the privileges and immunities clause, and other federal guarantees to citizens throughout the nation had been largely nullified by a conservative court.

Northerners in general seemed to have grown tired of the struggle for racial justice. Southern ideas appeared to be making their way northward. A *New York Times* editorial in 1903 conceded that "practically the whole country" had acquiesced in the "southern solution" to the race problem, since "there was no other possible settlement."[30] Even former abolitionists had become disheartened as the status of African Americans worsened in the 1890s and as reform sentiment lost ground in the press, the courts, and other branches of the national government. Northerners with a special interest in the well-being of southern blacks turned increasingly to the idea of industrial education and manual training, an approach that elicited strong support from the northern business community. In 1896 the Republican party dropped its earlier demand for legislative and executive action to guarantee a free ballot and fair elections in the South. This retreat reflected the discouraging situation in the South as well as the popularity of scientific racism and the nation's sudden acquisition of an overseas empire inhabited by dark-skinned and supposedly inferior people. "As America shouldered the White Man's Burden," Woodward observes, "she took up at the same time many Southern attitudes on the subject of race."[31] The perception that the "close and harmonious alliance" forged between the North and South by the war had placed upon black Americans "a larger measure of eternal vigilance" seemed to find support in the nation's postwar imperialist policies. A racialist rationale emerged to undergird the new imperialism, made more popular and more plausible because it was associated with an ideology of moderation and the concept of "the white man's burden."[32]

Writing in the *Atlantic Monthly* in 1901, the historian William A. Dunning analyzed what he called "The Undoing of Reconstruction." He asserted that public opinion in the North had recognized that "its views as to the political capacity of the blacks had been irrational," and that northerners were not dis-

30. *New York Times*, 6 January 1903, quoted in Willard B. Gatewood, Jr., *Black Americans and the White Man's Burden, 1898–1903* (Urbana, Ill., 1975), p. 294.

31. C. Vann Woodward, *The Strange Career of Jim Crow*, 3d rev. ed. (New York, 1974), pp. 67–109 (quotation on p. 72). See also James M. McPherson, *The Abolitionist Legacy: From Reconstruction to the NAACP* (Princeton, N.J., 1975), pp. 299–367.

32. Gatewood, *Black Americans and the White Man's Burden*, p. 222 (quotations); Fredrickson, *The Black Image in the White Mind*, p. 308.

posed to undertake "a new crusade in favor of negro equality."[33] In an editorial in the same issue, the magazine's editors acknowledged that white southerners were "doubtless right in believing that open, avowed suppression of the negro vote—if that vote is to be eliminated—is better for all concerned than a scheme of fraud and chicanery." They thought the South was "justified in the inference that the country is now willing, for one reason or another, to give her a chance to show her real temper."[34] Many other northern journals expressed similar views. *Outlook* declared that "whatever injustice there is in the Southern suffrage laws lies in their provisions for admitting to the suffrage white men who are not competent to exercise it, not in excluding negroes who are competent to exercise it. . . ."[35] Indeed, if properly enforced, the permanent provisions of the new constitutions would prove "beneficent to the negro as well as to the white man," since they had made it "impossible in the future for ignorant, shiftless, and corrupt negroes to misrepresent their race in political action."[36] "Let the qualifications for the suffrage be what the separate States see fit to make them," admonished the *Nation*, "only let them be impartially and honestly applied."[37]

Reflecting on his participation in the approaching dedication of the Robert Gould Shaw monument in Boston, the psychologist and philosopher William James concluded in 1897 that it was "no longer necessary to keep flourishing the old conventional sentimentalisms about the war, and . . . that the daily civic virtues which save countries from getting into civil war are more precious to the world than the martial ones that save them after they get in."[38] Many other northerners agreed. Charles Francis Adams, Jr., who moved from a position of "muted idealism" to one of "repentant idealism" and occasional "fervent racism," complained in 1913 that northern "theorists and abstractionists" had completely disregarded "fundamental, scientific facts" in an effort to believe that all men were essentially the same under similar conditions.[39] Albert Bushnell Hart, a Harvard University professor and the son of an Ohio abolitionist, observed in 1910 that "the North as a section is weary of the negro question . . . it is disappointed in the progress of the race both in the South and in the North . . . and less inclined than at any time during forty years to any active interference in Southern relations."[40]

Still, northern neo-abolitionists and other reformers had not lost all hope of racial progress. Many of them were encouraged by the southern educational

33. William A. Dunning, "The Undoing of Reconstruction," *Atlantic Monthly* 88 (October 1901): 447.

34. "Reconstruction and Disfranchisement," *Atlantic Monthly* 88 (October 1901): 436.

35. "Negro Suffrage in the South," *Outlook* 74 (June 13, 1903): 402.

36. "Suffrage Limitations in the South," *Outlook* 76 (March 12, 1904): 634.

37. "The Caste Notion of Suffrage," *Nation* 77 (September 3, 1903): 182.

38. William James to Booker T. Washington, April 16, 1897, in *The Booker T. Washington Papers*, ed. Louis R. Harlan et al., vol. 4 (Urbana, Ill., 1975), p. 272.

39. L. Moody Simms, Jr., "Charles Francis Adams, Jr., and the Negro Question," *New England Quarterly* 41 (September 1968): 436–38. Also see Paul C. Nagel, "Reconstruction, Adams Style," *Journal of Southern History* 52 (February 1986): 3–18.

40. Albert Bushnell Hart, *The Southern South* (New York, 1910), p. 74.

crusade early in the century. Yet such optimism as they could muster was based on their faith in gradualism, education, and the goodwill of southern whites.[41] Some of them had begun to search for a new and more militant strategy, but in the meantime their hopes rested in the leadership of Booker T. Washington, whose emphasis on self-help, economic accumulation, industrial education, and middle-class virtues appealed to northerners and southerners alike. Washington identified himself with the South, renounced northern intervention, reminded white southerners of his race's "fidelity and love" during the Civil War, and referred to the white man in the South as the black man's best friend. The Tuskegee educator seemed to be more interested in industrial education and economic opportunity than in political rights and privileges, and he agreed that property and educational qualifications were desirable for the franchise. He asked only for "justice" and an end to sectional differences and racial animosities. These, combined with material prosperity, would bring a new era to "our beloved South." To his own people he preached "a gospel of conservatism, patience, and material progress."[42] Washington's famous address at the Atlanta Exposition of 1895 brought a favorable response from northerners. A Chicago editorial declared, "He has done more for the improvement of the negro in the South than has been accomplished by all the political agitators. . . . The possession of a vote does not always insure respect, but the possession of a good character, a good home and a little money reserve always insures respect. . . ." The editor concluded by asserting: "If every southern state had such an institution as that at Tuskegee, Alabama, presided over by such a man as Professor Washington, the race question would settle itself in ten years."[43]

Washington was an intersectional ambassador of extraordinary influence. He fostered sectional reconciliation by promoting the cooperation of northern philanthropists and southern educational reformers, business interests from the two regions, and conservative economic elements from North and South. The conciliatory and gradualist philosophy that emanated from Tuskegee dominated the thinking of most black Americans from the mid-1890s until Washington's death in 1915. It also won widespread white approval, North and South. It was no accident that the well-known muckraker Ray Stannard Baker relied heavily upon the Tuskegee principal when he traveled through the South gathering information for *Following the Color Line* (1908). While Baker did not neglect the brutality and injustice in the South's treatment of black people, he clearly shared the outlook of Booker Washington. He took pains to emphasize a "quiet,

41. McPherson, *The Abolitionist Legacy,* pp. 299–367; Williamson, *The Crucible of Race,* pp. 327–40.

42. Washington "sought out the very type of men whom Southern whites were trying to interest in the development of Southern industry. He thus identified himself with the Eastern affiliations of the conservative South." Woodward, *Origins of the New South,* pp. 356–59 (quotation on p. 358). See also August Meier, *Negro Thought in America, 1880–1915: Racial Ideologies in the Age of Booker T. Washington* (Ann Arbor, 1963), pp. 100–18; Louis R. Harlan, *Booker T. Washington: The Making of a Black Leader, 1856–1901* (New York, 1972), pp. 204–28; and August Meier and Elliott Rudwick, *From Plantation to Ghetto,* rev. ed. (New York, 1970), pp. 202–203.

43. *Chicago Inter-Ocean,* quoted in Rayford W. Logan, *The Betrayal of the Negro: From Rutherford B. Hayes to Woodrow Wilson* (New York, 1965), p. 285.

constructive movement" among white southerners for the amelioration of the "Negro problem." Baker called it the "new southern statesmanship."[44] Yet Washington's gradualism was already under attack in the North, and the organization of the National Association for the Advancement of Colored People in 1910 represented a more militant approach to the problem of racial injustice.[45]

A delegate to the Alabama disfranchisement convention of 1901 declared, in calling attention to recent U.S. involvement in Cuba, Hawaii, and the Philippines, that "this is not a sectional issue, the race problem is no longer confined to the States of the South, [and] we have the sympathy instead of the hostility of the North."[46] Even so, southern leaders were not altogether sure of northern sentiment. "Censorious and intemperate criticism from the North, however well-meaning," warned the Alabama moderate Edgar Gardner Murphy, "can only embarrass the leadership of the real moral forces of the South, can only intensify and solidify the forces of prejudice and postpone the arousal of the fullest sense of local responsibility." Murphy went on to say, "There is not a day in which the actual status of the negro in Alabama does not show progress, progress through his own efforts, progress through the kindly cooperation of his white neighbors."[47] Southern leaders frequently addressed northern audiences on the burdens and challenges of the omnipresent race problem. If the avenues to "division and hate and blood and carnage, outrages and lynchings and violence and mobs" had been opened up through Negro suffrage, ex-governor William J. Northen of Georgia asked the Congregational Club of Boston in 1899, whose sin was it? "Not the sin of the South, but the sin of the North."[48] Some southerners sought to build up a positive image of white people—a kind of white soul—and even to promote the doctrine of *whiteness* throughout the country. As Williamson has pointed out, they "poured great energies into the effort to propagandize the gospel of whiteness and to realize its genius."[49]

Southern white writers also tried to convince the North by dramatizing the section's racial burden. One of the most prominent of the South's creative writers in the early-twentieth century was the North Carolinian Thomas Dixon. He brought together most of the themes that were represented in what one scholar has called "the myth of southern history." These concepts, which found expression in *The Leopard's Spots* (1903) and other novels, included reconciliation and union of North and South; the idea that the South's suffering and humiliation made it unique as a section and contributed to its strength of character; the notion that the burden of the past and of the African American gave white southerners a compensatory guidance and inspiration for the future; and the

44. Ray Stannard Baker, *Following the Color Line: American Negro Citizenship in the Progressive Era* (New York, 1964), pp. 271–91.
45. McPherson, *The Abolitionist Legacy*, pp. 368–93.
46. Quoted in Woodward, *Origins of the New South*, pp. 325–26.
47. Edgar Gardner Murphy to the editor of the *New York Evening Post*, 2 May 1903, Murphy Papers, Southern Historical Collection, University of North Carolina.
48. Quoted in Claude N. Nolen, *The Negro's Image in the South: The Anatomy of White Supremacy* (Lexington, Ky., 1967), p. 92. For southern racial missionaries in the North, see Williamson, *The Crucible of Race*, pp. 327–40.
49. Williamson, *The Crucible of Race*, pp. 414–58 (quotation on p. 414).

idea of a southern mission to eliminate the black man from politics and society and to preserve the nation's racial purity.[50] Dixon's use of the past suggested a new role for the South in American life. At the time the North Carolinian was writing, southern white attitudes on race appproximated national attitudes, and he enjoyed some success in creating a synthesis.

Thomas Dixon's greatest influence came later, when one of his novels was made into the motion picture *Birth of a Nation*. Meanwhile, more moderate southern interpreters such as Edgar Gardner Murphy and Booker T. Washington helped create a northern consensus in favor of white supremacy, law and order, social harmony, and rule by a benevolent elite. The consensus was not perfect, and white Americans differed in their views as to the best approach to the race problem. By 1910 a vocal minority had gone over to the militant position of William E. B. Du Bois and the recently organized National Association for the Advancement of Colored People. White southerners were themselves divided by an ongoing conflict between extreme racists and more moderate accommodationists. The position of the latter was widely approved outside the South. According to George M. Fredrickson, the views of the southern accommodationists helped establish a new national consensus of "enlightened" and "liberal" opinion on the race question. In the context of progressivism and imperialism, Fredrickson writes, "an ideal approximating a benevolent internal colonialism came to dominate national thinking about the race question." It was ironic that the southern moderates "lost the South to the extremists but won the North, or an articulate segment of it, to its way of thinking."[51]

National politics inevitably reflected the moderation of sectional conflict in the early years of the century. In spite of the sectional basis of the national party system following the realignment of the 1890s, the nation's politics became less competitive and less intense in terms of party and sectional divisions. Given the dominance of the Republican party, meaningful divisions along regional lines were largely confined to intraparty differences, particularly among the Democrats. As a Virginian noted in 1897, "Even where Northerners and Southerners joined together for a common purpose, the reasons for the union were apt to be contradictory."[52] But when it came to politics, there were also divisions and contradictions among southerners.

Although the great majority of white southerners identified themselves as Democrats, the one-party system in the South was characteristically racked by vigorous factionalism. In national politics these factions developed as supporters and opponents of William Jennings Bryan. The South, as Vann Woodward once said, became the most thoroughly "Bryanized" part of the country.[53] The

50. See F. Garvin Davenport, Jr., *The Myth of Southern History: Historical Consciousness in Twentieth-Century Southern Literature* (Nashville, 1970), pp. 23–43. See also Williamson, *The Crucible of Race*, pp. 140–76.

51. Fredrickson, *The Black Image in the White Mind*, pp. 296, 299, 304, 310–11, 325. For a somewhat different interpretation, see Williamson, *The Crucible of Race*, pp. 109–284.

52. Lyon Gardiner Tyler to Woodrow Wilson, 23 July 1897, in *The Papers of Woodrow Wilson*, vol. 10, ed. Arthur S. Link et al. (Princeton, N.J., 1971), p. 279.

53. Woodward, *Origins of the New South*, p. 469.

Nebraskan was the most compelling national figure in the region from 1896 until the emergence of Woodrow Wilson in 1911 and 1912. He more than any other national leader of this period embodied the protest politics in the struggle of the South and West against the economic and political power of the Northeast. White southerners were drawn to the charismatic Bryan, savored his swelling oratory, and liked his Protestant Christianity, his emphasis on morality in politics, his enunciation of Jeffersonian principles, and his identification with rural progressivism. They also appreciated his endorsement of state rights and his acceptance of the white South's racial settlement at the turn of the century. Bryan's reform politics were perhaps even more important in his successful appeal to southerners: his opposition to monopoly, the "money trust," and the protective tariff; his proposals for currency and banking reform; his support of primary elections and the direct election of U.S. senators; his criticism of American imperialism; and his advocacy of prohibition and other social legislation.[54]

Bryan, whose supporters controlled the party machinery in most southern states, won the Democratic presidential nomination again in 1900. But his campaign, based on anti-imperialism and free silver, was easily overcome by President McKinley. Bryan carried only the South and five western states. The Republican ticket made a good showing in the upper South. The Democrats turned away from Bryan and the alliance of South and West in 1904, reorganizing the party along conservative lines, and nominating as its standard-bearer Judge Alton B. Parker of New York. Anti-Bryan factions in the South joined in the reorientation of the party. According to President Woodrow Wilson of Princeton University, the South had "a unique opportunity to perform a great national service. As the only remaining part of the Democratic party that can command a majority of the votes in its constituencies, let the South demand a rehabilitation of the Democratic party on the only lines that can restore it to dignity and power."[55] Many southerners were repelled by the aggressive partisanship of President Theodore Roosevelt, even though Roosevelt carefully avoided interjecting the race issue into the campaign. Southern politicians and journalists repeatedly attacked Roosevelt's appointment policies, asserted that he would abandon William McKinley's conciliatory approach, and denounced a Republican platform plank criticizing disfranchisement in the southern states as unconstitutional. "The real object of the Republican party," declared Representative John Sharp Williams of Mississippi, ". . . is to reduce Southern representation" and "to retain as 'a Republican asset,' the solid negro vote in Indiana, Illinois, [and] New Jersey." Such impassioned oratory did nothing to help the Democratic ticket in other sections. In the election Roosevelt led Parker by 2.5 million votes (out of a total of 13.5 million), losing only the twelve southern states and Maryland.[56]

54. For Bryan's political and social ideas, see Paul W. Glad, *The Trumpet Soundeth: William Jennings Bryan and His Democracy, 1896–1912* (Lincoln, Neb., 1960).

55. *New York Sun*, 30 November 1904, reprinted in *The Papers of Woodrow Wilson*, ed. Arthur S. Link et al., vol. 15 (Princeton, N.J., 1973), p. 547.

56. William H. Harbaugh, "Election of 1904," in *History of American Presidential Elections, 1789–*

Four years later the Democrats nominated William Jennings Bryan for a third time, and he challenged the Republican nominee, William Howard Taft. "A Conservative platform would ruin all of our chances for success," a Mississippi Democrat warned. "We must carry out the policies of Roosevelt that he borrowed from the Democratic party and add to the platform such planks as will give us a progressive campaign. Conservatism, as it is spelled by the politicians now, is cowardly and means a surrender to the interest of Wall Street and the trusts and corporations generally."[57] Bryan's energetic campaign and progressive platform brought him a million and a half more popular votes than Parker received in 1904. The Democrats were defeated again, however, carrying only the thirteen southern states (including the new commonwealth of Oklahoma) and three western states. Yet even in defeat there were signs of a Democratic revival outside the South. The party attracted more northern and western voters than it had in the past several years, elected more of its congressional nominees, and established itself more firmly as a progressive force in national politics.[58]

In the South the Republican ticket did better than usual in 1908, a consequence of conservative distaste for Bryanism and a desire for a larger southern role in national politics. The defectors contrasted the economic advances and bright industrial prospects of the South with its political intolerance, impotence in national affairs, and loss of "the old time southern force and character." Their spokesmen called for an end to the Solid South, for the expulsion of the region's "narrow and sectional spirit," for greater independence of thought, and for a discussion of national issues.[59] Little came of this new independence, however, and the South remained the mainstay of the Democratic party in national politics. In the presidential elections from 1896 through 1908, all won by the Republican party, the southern states accounted for more than 82 percent of the Democrats' electoral votes.

Some southern independents hoped that their section's political emancipation would be effected through presidential leadership. They spoke kindly of McKinley, were alternately encouraged and disappointed by Roosevelt, and for a brief time placed their confidence in Taft. But their hopes were never realized. In fact, the South during this period remained largely irrelevant to the nation's chief executives, both in their capacity as party leaders and as head of the federal government. This was true because of the overwhelming dominance of the Republican party in Washington and the fact that a sort of modus vivendi had emerged in the relationship between the South and the rest of the nation.

1968, ed. Arthur M. Schlesinger, Jr., and Fred L. Israel, vol. 3 (New York, 1971), pp. 1965–94 (quotation on p. 1981).

57. W. S. Chapman to E. F. Noel, 26 June 1908, Edmund F. Noel Papers, Mississippi Department of Archives and History, Jackson.

58. Paolo E. Coletta, "Election of 1908," in *History of American Presidential Elections*, ed. Schlesinger and Israel, vol. 3, pp. 2049–90; David Sarasohn, *The Party of Reform: Democrats in the Progressive Era* (Jackson, Miss., 1989), pp. 35–58.

59. Dewey W. Grantham, *Southern Progressivism: The Reconciliation of Progress and Tradition* (Knoxville, Tenn., 1983), pp. 352–54.

Nonetheless, the South was recurrently perceived as a national problem, though not one with high priority among most Americans. As President Roosevelt wrote a friend in 1904, "The southern question is not of immediate menace, but it is one of perpetual discomfort," given the "wrongheadedness and folly" of southern leaders.[60] Although the political expectations of black southerners had been severely dampened in the late-nineteenth century, they still looked to the Republican party and to the presidential administrations in Washington for help and recognition. As for white southerners, they viewed the national administrations of the early-twentieth century with a mixture of apprehension and cautious optimism. While critical of McKinley's black appointments, they responded warmly to his patriotic appeals and pleas for sectional accord. Yet McKinley was able to gain southern confidence "only by keeping silent on sensitive issues and thus by implicitly accepting the Negro's subservience." He made no public comment, for instance, following the terrible massacre of blacks in Wilmington, North Carolina, in 1898.[61]

When McKinley's assassination brought Theodore Roosevelt to the presidency in September 1901, southerners anticipated a new approach and even a new role for the South in national affairs. Roosevelt's exploits in the recent war and his generous praise of Robert E. Lee and the boys in gray made him popular in the South. His mother was a member of the prominent Bulloch family of Georgia, and two of his uncles had been conspicuously identified with the Confederate cause during the Civil War. While denying that he had "a sectional bone" in his body, Roosevelt declared that his "earliest training and principles were Southern."[62] The new president quickly committed himself to the elevation of federal appointments in the South and indicated his intention of appointing only qualified men, and if necessary, Democrats. But as one historian has written, "Quixotic reformism mingled strangely with an old brand of practical politics from the start."[63] Soon after assuming office, Roosevelt invited Booker T. Washington, a key adviser on southern appointments, to have dinner at the White House. This incident, coinciding with a rising tide of southern racism, provoked a violent reaction from white southerners. The New Orleans *States* described the president's act as "a studied insult" to the South, while another newspaper contended that by one foolish decision he had "destroyed the kindly, warm regard and personal affection for him which were growing up fast in the South." The Memphis *Scimitar* declared that Roosevelt had rudely shattered "any expectations that may have arisen from his announced intention to make the Republican party in the South respectable. He has closed the door to

60. Theodore Roosevelt to James Ford Rhodes, November 29, 1904, in *The Letters of Theodore Roosevelt*, ed. Elting E. Morison et al., vol. 4 (Cambridge, Mass., 1951), p. 1050.

61. Sherman, *The Republican Party and Black America*, pp. 12–13.

62. Willard B. Gatewood, Jr., *Theodore Roosevelt and the Art of Controversy: Episodes of the White House Years* (Baton Rouge, La., 1970), p. 5; Dewey W. Grantham, *The Regional Imagination: The South and Recent American History* (Nashville, 1979), p. 34.

63. Woodward, *Origins of the New South*, p. 463. Also see Williamson, *The Crucible of Race*, pp. 341–63.

any accessions of Southern white men to the Republican ranks."[64]

White southerners were also outraged when the president later closed the Indianola, Mississippi, post office because of the intimidation of the black post-mistress and appointed Dr. William D. Crum, a black physician, as customs collector for Charleston, South Carolina.[65] For all his talk of courageous action and higher standards of public service, Roosevelt himself made use of the southern "rotten-borough" system in searching for delegates to support him at the Republican convention of 1904. Although the South supplied no electoral votes to the GOP ticket in presidential elections, Republican leaders retained skeletal organizations that seemed to exist primarily for the purpose of obtaining federal offices in return for delegate votes at the national conventions. Nor did Roosevelt make an issue of southern disfranchisement. "The minute you mention the 'Fourteenth Amendment,' " Booker T. Washington cautioned him, "the whole Southern question looms up in the eyes of many timid people in the North and West."[66] Southerners could not entirely resist the ebullient Roosevelt, even though few of them were willing to vote for him. They gave him a hospitable welcome when he toured the South in 1905 and 1906. The president's action in ordering the discharge without honor of three companies of black soldiers, for their alleged complicity in a midnight raid on Brownsville, Texas, in 1906, brought widespread approval from white southerners and a wave of criticism from northerners.[67]

William Howard Taft wanted to be liked and respected by southerners. One scholar has suggested that Taft showed "more concern about the South than the Negro."[68] The twenty-seventh president's views on education were similar to those of Booker Washington, who served as one of his advisers. Many white southerners applauded Taft's announcement that he would not appoint blacks to office in communities where this would cause race friction and thus reduce the efficiency of the office. He forced the resignation of Dr. Crum, removed most of the remaining black officeholders in the South, and made only a few token appointments of African Americans to federal positions in the North.[69] Questioning the constitutional authority of Congress to take action against the widespread southern practice of lynching, Taft tried to avoid making any public reference to the problem. But his administration, like that of Roosevelt's, did initiate successful cases against peonage in the South.[70]

64. Grantham, *The Regional Imagination*, pp. 33–52 (quotations on pp. 38 and 42). See also Gatewood, *Theodore Roosevelt and the Art of Controversy*, pp. 32–61. It should be noted that Roosevelt's action was generally approved by other Americans.

65. Gatewood, *Theodore Roosevelt and the Art of Controversy*, pp. 62–134; Louis R. Harlan, *Booker T. Washington: The Wizard of Tuskegee, 1901–1915* (New York, 1983), pp. 3–31.

66. Booker T. Washington to Theodore Roosevelt, August 24, 1904, in *The Booker T. Washington Papers*, ed. Louis R. Harlan and Raymond W. Smock, vol. 8 (Urbana, Ill., 1979), p. 57.

67. George E. Mowry, *The Era of Theodore Roosevelt, 1900–1912* (New York, 1958), pp. 212–14; Woodward, *Origins of the New South*, pp. 463–65.

68. Sherman, *The Republican Party and Black America*, p. 80.

69. Harlan, *Booker T. Washington: The Wizard of Tuskegee*, pp. 338–58.

70. Pete Daniel, *The Shadow of Slavery: Peonage in the South, 1901–1969* (Urbana, Ill., 1972), pp. 43–109.

In one respect the South's participation in national politics was substantial during the first decade of the twentieth century: it dominated the Democratic party in Congress. The realignment of national parties in the 1890s severely weakened the Democratic party outside the South, thereby enhancing the role of its southern members, particularly in Congress. The Fifty-seventh Congress (1901–1903), for example, contained ninety-five Democratic representatives and twenty-two Democratic senators from southern states, as compared with fifty-six Democratic representatives and nine Democratic senators from other sections.[71] The southerners' habitual reelection usually made them the ranking members of the standing committees.[72] They mastered the organizational and procedural structure of the Senate and House of Representatives. They made adroit use of the committee system, usually dominated their party's congressional caucuses, and gradually assumed a position of power in the national government.[73]

Sectional divisions on congressional issues early in the twentieth century tended to fall along party lines, with the Republican Northeast and Midwest in opposition to the Democratic South and mountain West. Among the more salient issues that divided the economically developed core regions from the underdeveloped periphery to the south and west were a series of debates on American expansion at the turn of the century: recognition of the Cuban republic, annexation of Hawaii, the Platt Amendment limiting the independence of Cuba, and Philippine independence. A related sectional conflict grew out of the admission to the Union of new states such as New Mexico and Oklahoma. Most Americans seemed to accept the necessity for commercial expansion, to believe in the utility of foreign bases and coaling stations (for maritime trade and for the projection abroad of U.S. naval power), and to assume the superiority of their own institutions and of the "Anglo-Saxon race." But they differed over the means to achieve these ends.[74]

The southern periphery had reservations about the imperialism of the northern core, in part because of the regions' different positions in the world economy, in part because of racial fears growing out of the acquisition of "backward" elements in distant lands.[75] The South and the mountain West were producers of raw materials (cotton and metals) that sought industrial markets at home and abroad. Though undeveloped colonies might provide markets for

71. *Official Congressional Directory*, 57th Cong., 1st sess. (Washington, D.C., 1901). Also see Numan V. Bartley, "The South and Sectionalism in American Politics," *Journal of Politics* 38 (August 1976): 239–57.

72. Incumbency was a decided advantage in most primary elections for congressional seats in the South. The lack of Republican opposition in general elections was if anything even more significant in the long tenure of the average congressman from the South.

73. See David M. Potter, *The South and the Concurrent Majority*, ed. Don E. Fehrenbacher and Carl N. Degler (Baton Rouge, La., 1972).

74. Bensel, *Sectionalism and American Political Development*, pp. 88–103.

75. Edward W. Chester, *Sectionalism, Politics, and American Diplomacy* (Metuchen, N.J., 1975), pp. 151, 157–59; Tennant S. McWilliams, *The New South Faces the World: Foreign Affairs and the Southern Sense of Self, 1877–1950* (Baton Rouge, La., 1988), pp. 44–47, 66–67; Foster, *Ghosts of the Confederacy*, pp. 149–51.

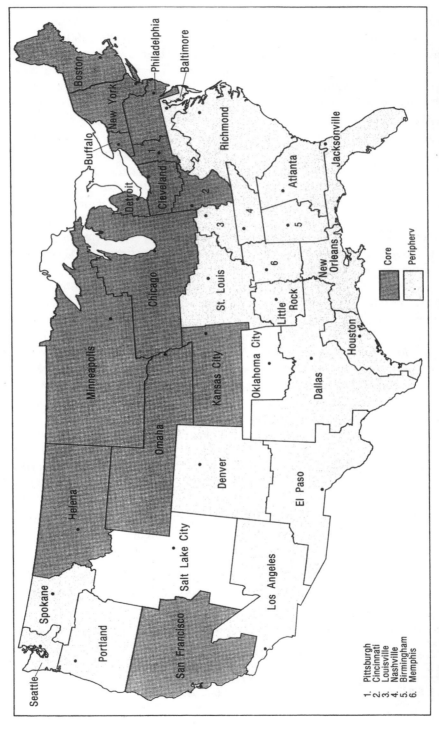

Opposing Sections in the 59th Congress (1905–1907). Source: Richard Franklin Bensel, *Sectionalism and American Political Development, 1880–1980* (Madison: University of Wisconsin Press, 1984), p. 41.

foodstuffs and manufactured goods produced in the Midwest and Northeast, such territories promised little help in the disposal of the South's "surplus" cotton. "Instead of neo-mercantile imperialism," Richard Bensel writes, "the periphery required the development of free trade in the world-system, which could only occur with the destruction of tariff barriers and elimination of exclusive exploitation of colonial markets by the major industrial powers."[76] Southerners feared that the most likely consequences of the new imperialism would be militarism and the political suppression of peripheral territory. They wanted to prevent "a subordinate economic role and political disadvantage from being translated into a permanent feature of the republic."[77] This concern also explains southern hostility to discriminatory preconditions on the admission of new states to the Union—preconditions placed by the northern core on territories in the periphery.

Southern congressmen were quick to react to any threat to the established system of race relations in their states and localities, whether in the form of black appointments in the South, the implementation of the Fourteenth Amendment, or other outside initiatives. Early in 1911, for example, when the Senate was considering a proposed constitutional amendment for the popular election of United States senators, the question of Negro suffrage touched off a heated debate. The progressive sponsors of the proposal, seeking to ensure its passage, agreed to an amendment offered by southern Democrats that would have denied congressional power, as provided in Article I, section 4, of the Constitution, to alter state regulations pertaining to the times, places, and manner of holding elections for senators. The southerners were intent upon preventing any possible basis for federal interference with the South's franchise laws. The southern proviso was eventually voted down, causing some southerners to vote against the amendment and delaying congressional approval of the Seventeenth Amendment by more than a year.[78]

Although many northerners viewed the southern congressmen as reactionary and anachronistic, their constructive leadership was greater than this image suggested. They were characterized, like many other Americans, by a rural, small-town orientation. Yet many of them were able legislators concerned with national as well as state and sectional problems. They supplied sturdy backing for railroad regulation, tariff and tax revision, and a variety of agrarian reforms during the Roosevelt and Taft administrations.[79] From 1905 to 1908, one scholar notes, "the nation grew accustomed to the spectacle of congressional Democrats providing the strongest support for a Republican president."[80] When the Democrats won control of the House of Representatives in the midterm elections of 1910, southern congressmen took the lead in organizing the

76. Bensel, *Sectionalism and American Political Development*, p. 92.

77. *Ibid.*, p. 93.

78. Sherman, *The Republican Party and Black America*, pp. 96–97.

79. See Anne Firor Scott, "A Progressive Wind from the South, 1906–1913," *Journal of Southern History* 29 (February 1963): 53–70, and "The Southern Progressives in National Politics, 1906–1916" (Ph.D. dissertation, Radcliffe College, 1957), pp. 1–16.

80. Sarasohn, *The Party of Reform*, p. 3.

House and supporting a series of progressive measures. They joined with northern and western liberals in reorienting and strengthening the Democratic party.

Sectionalism continued to intrude into almost every important aspect of American life, accompanied by the expression of mutual fears and recriminations. The interplay of conflict and accommodation between North and South was evident in the wave of reform movements known as progressivism. During the early years of the century, a series of reform campaigns was waged in the southern states and cities, as in other parts of the country. A number of tendencies—quickening social change, an emergent idea of southern progress, a broadening humanitarianism, and the transformation of politics—converged to provide a favorable setting for this reformism. Although rural southerners and agrarian influences played an important part in the reform movements, the most characteristic and significant progressives were middle-class men and women, inhabitants of the urban South and representatives of the new commercial and professional elements. They provided most of the leadership, created the new organizations, directed the reform campaigns, articulated the progressive rationale and mission, and gave the reform causes their distinctive tone and style. In general, southern progressives sought to impose a greater measure of social order, to foster economic development and opportunity, and, where possible, to protect the unfortunate.[81] The South's distinctive institutions and obsession with the race question no doubt gave a special cast to its social reform. But the region shared in the national reform ethos and interacted with other parts of the nation in developing its own brand of progressivism.

Political protest and reform in the South were frequently directed at outside interests and their assumed exploitation of southern people and resources. This sectional theme was notably manifest in the campaigns to regulate railroads, insurance companies, and other big corporations. In some cases reform in the South was influenced by the example of progressivism in other sections. That was evident in the case of the highly publicized regulatory campaigns led by progressive governors such as Robert M. La Follette of Wisconsin, Albert B. Cummins of Iowa, Charles Evans Hughes of New York, and Hiram W. Johnson of California. Northerners also influenced the movement to reform the prison system in the southern states, one of the most notorious of the institutions identified with the "backward South" at the turn of the century. Although the penal reform movement bore the distinctive imprint of the South's social and cultural priorities, it was encouraged by the innovations and advice of experts from outside the region. Southern reformers were prodded and stimulated by the financial contributions and uplift programs of northern philanthropists, and they sought to take advantage of the opportunities offered by federal legislation and appropriations. Occasionally, as in the structural changes associated with urban reform and the introduction of innovative farm demonstration tech-

81. A fuller treatment of the various reform movements in the South can be found in William A. Link, *The Paradox of Southern Progressivism, 1880–1930* (Chapel Hill, N.C., 1992); Ayers, *The Promise of the New South*, pp. 409–37; and Grantham, *Southern Progressivism*.

niques, the South was in the vanguard of national progressivism, and in the case of prohibition it was clearly the nation's leader.

Southern attitudes toward monopoly reflected the section's subordinate economic position in the nation and its hopes for more rapid growth. Thus large timber and oil companies were denounced for exploiting southern resources to enrich "foreign" entrepreneurs, insurance companies were attacked for draining away local capital, and railroads were criticized for establishing rate structures that placed the South at a distinct disadvantage in competition with other sections.[82] Southerners, including many businessmen, tended to be enthusiastic about President Roosevelt's trust-busting cases. Southern farmers and their representatives intensified their demand for the federal regulation of commodity markets, including trading in cotton futures. Southern bankers and other businessmen also became advocates of federal regulation. They were inclined to be suspicious of a political economy in which powerful eastern and midwestern business interests seemed to dominate both the national economy and government policies. Daniel A. Tompkins, a North Carolina business leader, opposed Senator Nelson W. Aldrich's plan for currency reform as a scheme of "Mr. Aldrich, the Standard Oil Company, and the Steel Trust."[83]

The major focus of antitrust activity in the southern states was on the section's railroads, which were firmly controlled by "northern men, money and management."[84] A series of statewide campaigns was waged against the railroads between 1905 and 1909. The result was that a majority of the southern states reorganized and strengthened their railroad commissions during this period, and almost every state in the region moved to secure lower passenger and freight rates and to prescribe a uniform system of intrastate rate classification. The surge of state regulation subsided after 1909, in part because of the interstate character of the corporations the states were trying to regulate. Regulatory campaigns in Alabama, North Carolina, and other states were crippled by the railroads' appeal to the federal courts. The state commissions found themselves increasingly dependent upon rulings of the Interstate Commerce Commission and edicts of the federal courts. With the enhanced role of the ICC and the expansion of federal controls came a corresponding restriction of the authority of state commissions and state laws.[85] Southern commercial interests, chambers

82. David M. Potter, "The Historical Development of Eastern-Southern Freight Rate Relationships," in *Law and Contemporary Problems* 12 (Summer 1947): 416–48; William B. Joubert, *Southern Freight Rates in Transition* (Gainesville, Fla., 1949), pp. 8, 19–21, 105.

83. Robert H. Wiebe, *Businessmen and Reform: A Study of the Progressive Movement* (Cambridge, Mass., 1962), pp. 43–45, 77–78 (quotation); Grantham, *Southern Progressivism*, pp. 144–45. For evidence of southern farmer reaction to the depredations of big business, see Louis Galambos, with the assistance of Barbara Barrow Spence, *The Public Image of Big Business in America, 1880–1940: A Quantitative Study in Social Change* (Baltimore, 1975), pp. 58–61, 90–91, 132–36.

84. John F. Stover, *The Railroads of the South, 1865–1900: A Study in Finance and Control* (Chapel Hill, N.C., 1955), p. 284.

85. Maxwell Ferguson, *State Regulation of Railroads in the South* (New York, 1916); James F. Doster, *Railroads in Alabama Politics, 1875–1914* (University, Ala., 1957); Grantham, *Southern Progressivism*, pp. 146–52.

of commerce, and reformers were convinced that the economic and political might of the Northeast and Midwest made it impossible to equalize railroad rates that penalized the South.

Another center of southern antagonism toward corporate wealth was the insurance company, which was scarcely less "foreign" or less exploitative in its operations than the great rail lines. Jeff Davis, for instance, a fiery leader of the white masses in Arkansas, successfully combined inflammatory attacks on "foreign" corporations with racist demagoguery. On one occasion in 1899, during his tenure as state attorney general, the irrepressible Jeff filed sixty-three antitrust suits against out-of-state fire insurance companies, which turned to the courts for protection.[86] All of the southern states created insurance departments in the late 1890s and early 1900s. They passed laws subjecting outside life and fire insurance companies to taxation, licensing, agents' residence, and deposit and liability requirements. The revelations of the Armstrong Committee concerning practices of the great New York insurance companies and the passage of a strong regulatory law by New York in 1906 stimulated state insurance regulation in the South and other parts of the country. The most notable of the state regulatory statutes was the Robertson Act of 1907, a Texas law designed to compel out-of-state companies to invest a portion of their Texas earnings in local securities or real estate. James H. Robertson, the sponsor of the legislation, said his purpose was "to stop the long continued practice of taking from Texas money belonging to the Texas people, and hoarding it in New York to be there used by the officials of the great insurance companies. . . ."[87]

By 1901 a number of sporadic and uncoordinated efforts were being made to persuade southern legislatures to deal with the problem of child labor in the South's new industries. These efforts developed into one of the first major social justice movements in the region. The employment of children in southern industries had increased during the hard times of the 1890s, and in the early years of the twentieth century children could be found in textile mills, tobacco factories, and fish canneries. They were an important source of labor in the section's burgeoning textile industry, symbol of the New South in action. An estimated 25 percent of the employees in southern cotton mills in 1900 were between the ages of ten and sixteen, and some workers were as young as seven or eight. They worked very long hours for extremely low wages. The rate of illiteracy among these children was high, three or four times that of other children in the same states according to the reformers. Yet the South, unlike the industrial states to the north, had enacted almost no legislation to prevent such abuses.[88]

The movement for regulation began in Alabama, where several labor

86. Raymond Arsenault, *The Wild Ass of the Ozarks: Jeff Davis and the Social Bases of Southern Politics* (Knoxville, Tenn., 1988), pp. 63–77, 89–91, 113–14, 125–28, 137–42, 207–209, 229–34.

87. James A. Tinsley, "Texas Progressives and Insurance Regulation," *Southwestern Social Science Quarterly* 36 (December 1955): 237–47 (quotation on p. 239).

88. Elizabeth H. Davidson, *Child Labor Legislation in the Southern Textile States* (Chapel Hill, N.C., 1939), pp. 11–16; Hugh C. Bailey, *Edgar Gardner Murphy: Gentle Progressive* (Coral Gables, Fla., 1968), pp. 66–77; Link, *The Paradox of Southern Progressivism*, pp. 161–82; Robert Hamlett Bremner, *From the Depths: The Discovery of Poverty in the United States* (New York, 1956), pp. 212–20.

CHILD–WOMAN RATIOS, NORTH AND SOUTH, 1880–1930 (CHILDREN AGED 0–4
PER 1,000 WOMEN AGED 15–44)

	South			Non-South		
Year	Total	White	Rural	Total	White	Rural
1880	741.5	711.4	—	545.9	547.5	—
1890	645.5	620.7	—	497.0	486.8	—
1900	636.0	638.1	—	467.7	460.6	—
1910	606.6	622.7	676.9	436.9	440.3	518.0
1920	537.2	546.9	615.9	445.6	446.1	533.4
1930	461.5	470.5	550.1	364.8	357.5	460.1

SOURCE: Dudley L. Poston, Jr., and Robert H. Weller, eds., *The Population of the South* (Austin: University of Texas Press, 1981), p. 7.

unions, women's organizations, and ministers began to advocate passage of a child labor law in the late 1890s. One of the moving spirits in the Alabama campaign was Edgar Gardner Murphy, the thirty-one-year-old rector of St. John's Episcopal Parish in Montgomery. Murphy took a leading part in the reformers' unsuccessful efforts to secure enactment of a state law in 1901, and he was the decisive figure in the formation of the Alabama Child Labor Committee. He became convinced that northern owners of Alabama cotton mills were primarily responsible for the failure of the reform bill of 1901. In a pamphlet entitled "An Appeal to the People and Press of New England," Murphy asserted that twice as many children under the age of twelve were working in the northern-owned mills of the state as in those operated by local capital. Murphy's "Appeal" brought a defense from representatives of New England companies with plants in Alabama and resulted in an exchange of open letters between businessmen and the Alabama clergyman. While conceding the undesirable character of child labor, the textile spokesmen attributed the reform movement in Alabama to a "skilled, female labor agitator," warned that it was the entering wedge of unionization, described Murphy as an "ill-advised humanitarian," and expressed the opinion that child labor legislation should be preceded by the enactment of a compulsory education law and that regulatory measures must be contingent upon action by other states.[89]

Perhaps the most insistent argument advanced by southern mill owners was the claim that child labor legislation would be ruinous to the section's textiles and would make it impossible for the South to compete with New England. The industrialists and their allies also tried to discredit the reformers, accusing them of exaggerating the evils of child labor and being overly sentimental in their

89. Davidson, *Child Labor Legislation in the Southern Textile States*, pp. 18–51; Hugh C. Bailey, "Edgar Gardner Murphy and the Child Labor Movement," *Alabama Review* 18 (January 1965): 47–59; Bailey, *Edgar Gardner Murphy*, pp. 65–108; "Child Labor in Alabama," *Outlook* 69 (December 14, 1901): 957–58. The "skilled, female labor agitator" was Irene M. Ashby, who carried out a thorough investigation of child labor for the American Federation of Labor in the winter of 1900–1901.

concern for the well-being of youthful workers. Richard H. Edmonds, editor of the *Manufacturers' Record,* characterized Edgar Gardner Murphy's arguments as impractical, inflammatory, and "Bryanesque." In Edmonds's opinion, "This whole child-labor agitation originated in the purpose to cripple the textile industry of the South, [so] that a small factor of that industry in New England might profit temporarily."[90] Opponents of regulatory laws also blamed the reform movement on organized labor, which was portrayed as a manifestation of northern intervention.

One reason for the increasing publicity given to child labor was that cotton textiles in the South were beginning to threaten New England's domination of the industry. Northern manufacturers pointed to the contrast in labor conditions in the two sections and charged that the South's competitive advantage resulted in large part from the exploitation of children and the subsequent depressed scale of adult wages. A second and more important factor in directing national attention to the problem of child labor in the South was the reform campaigns being conducted by Murphy and other humanitarians.

As the sentiment for child labor reform spread over the country, it was reflected in and no doubt stimulated by articles in such magazines as *Gunton's, Charities, Outlook,* and the *American Federationist.* These and other journals denounced the long hours, low wages, and exploitation of women and children in southern textile plants. In some cases there were sensational pieces depicting children in the southern mills as virtual slaves. This muckraking literature, focusing on the South and sometimes distorting actual conditions, helped create a national movement to stamp out child labor. But it also fanned the flames of southern sectionalism and stiffened the resistance to stronger legislation in the region.[91]

After 1903, when the first significant legislation was enacted, the efforts of child labor reformers in the southern states were slowly transformed into an organized movement that assumed a regional character. The principal instrument in this transformation was the National Child Labor Committee (NCLC), which was created in the spring of 1904 through the initiative of Felix Adler of New York and other social justice leaders, including Edgar Gardner Murphy. The committee hoped to assist local bodies in achieving child labor reform, to undertake investigations of its own, and to act as a clearinghouse for information and activities involving the child labor problem. Murphy served briefly as secretary of the committee and was instrumental in shaping its early policies.

90. Quoted in Yoshimitsu Ide, "The Significance of Richard Hathaway Edmonds and His *Manufacturers' Record* in the New South" (Ph.D. dissertation, University of Florida, 1959), p. 165. See also Bailey, *Edgar Gardner Murphy,* p. 79.

91. See Alexander J. McKelway, "Child Labor and Child Labor Legislation in the South," undated manuscript in Alexander J. McKelway Papers, Manuscript Division, Library of Congress; McKelway, "The Mill or the Farm?" supplement to *Annals of the American Academy of Political and Social Science* 35 (March 1910): 52–57; Harriet L. Herring, "Cycles of Cotton Mill Criticism," *South Atlantic Quarterly* 28 (April 1929): 120–21; Davidson, *Child Labor Legislation in the Southern Textile States,* pp. 54–62; and Stephen B. Wood, *Constitutional Politics in the Progressive Era: Child Labor and the Law* (Chicago, 1968), pp. 6–10.

He was responsible for the selection of Alexander J. McKelway of North Carolina as director of the NCLC's work in the South.[92]

In 1906 a significant change occurred in the slowly developing child labor movement in the South. It was the NCLC's decision to endorse Senator Albert J. Beveridge's congressional bill to outlaw child labor. A critical factor in the committee's decision was the failure of its efforts to promote state action in the southern states. In spite of McKelway's energetic campaigns, almost no further legislative progress seemed to have been made. Few southerners were affiliated with the NCLC, and the chances of going beyond the ineffective statutes already enacted appeared slight. Murphy, whose political conservatism led him to oppose the idea of federal legislation from the first, immediately resigned from the national committee. But McKelway was a champion of federal action, and he was soon dispatched to lobby for the Beveridge bill in Washington. Meanwhile, the NCLC continued to support the movement for effective state laws, and with the failure of the Beveridge measure in 1907, it turned with renewed energy to the state and local campaigns. For a decade after Senator Beveridge began to push for a national law, northern magazines were filled with "human interest" stories and pictures about the terrible conditions and wretched child workers in the South's mills. Southern spokesmen responded with countercharges of exaggeration and reports of improving conditions.[93]

By 1910 all of the southern states had established a minimum age for employment, at least in manufacturing. Yet only four southern states had a minimum age as high as fourteen, several state laws were weakened by broad exemption clauses, and only three of them required documentary proof of a working child's age. During the next few years, southern legislatures gradually raised their minimum age standards and extended the coverage of their child labor laws. The National Child Labor Committee also broadened the field of its work in the South, moving beyond its early preoccupation with the cotton textile industry to include night messenger service and street trades by 1911, and oyster and shrimp canneries on the Gulf Coast by 1913. In 1914 the committee turned once again to federal legislation as the best solution to the child labor problem.[94] The ensuing struggle represented a new phase in the evolution of the movement against child labor in the South.

In the meantime, social reformers had embraced other causes. The South's baffling social problems had become what has been called "the main laboratory for sociological experiments of organized Northern philanthropy and its Southern agents."[95] An "intersectional partnership of moderate progressives" set out to modernize the South through agencies like the Southern Education Board

92. Bailey, *Edgar Gardner Murphy*, pp. 86–90.

93. Herring, "Cycles of Cotton Mill Criticism," p. 121; Davidson, *Child Labor Legislation in the Southern Textile States*, pp. 129–41; Bailey, *Edgar Gardner Murphy*, pp. 94–102; John Braeman, *Albert J. Beveridge: American Nationalist* (Chicago, 1971), pp. 112–21.

94. Davidson, *Child Labor Legislation in the Southern Textile States*, pp. 249–52; John R. Commons et al., *History of Labour in the United States*, 4 vols. (New York, 1918–1935), vol. 3, pp. 414–15, 421, 429, 438–39.

95. Woodward, *Origins of the New South*, p. 396.

and the Rockefeller Sanitary Commission for the Eradication of Hookworm Disease. These organizations were coalitions of middle-class activists, reform-minded professionals, university presidents, and northern philanthropists.[96] Beginning in 1901, the Southern Education Board helped sustain a regionwide campaign for the establishment of a genuine public school system in the South. This educational crusade reminded contemporaries of a religious revival; it was carried on by state and local campaigns, surveys and reports, lobbying efforts in behalf of new school laws and taxes for education, and so on. The movement benefited from the vast resources of John D. Rockefeller's General Education Board, a foundation established in 1903. The GEB formed an interlocking directorate with several other philanthropies interested in southern problems, and with the boards of the Hampton and Tuskegee institutes. "Through education and health," William A. Link remarks, "reformers sought to attain a new standard of social efficiency and to transmit new values that, modernizing officials believed, would foster self-actuating development among southerners."[97]

In 1905 Edwin A. Alderman, a southern educator and leader in the public school movement, identified the major reasons for the South's educational problems. He singled out the section's "years of isolation and submersion," the fact that it had remained rural and thinly populated for so long, the duplication of educational effort resulting from its biracial society, the effects of war and defeat, its painful transition from "an agricultural order, depressed by poverty and misrule, to an industrial democracy wherein it must regain its national feeling," and its burden of a "backward race."[98]

Southern leaders argued that the beginning place in the crusade for public education was the white child. Northern representatives like Robert C. Ogden, who headed the Southern Education Board, were inclined to agree with their southern counterparts. Ogden and other northern philanthropists also used their money and influence to make vocational training the raison d'être of black schools in the South. Reflecting on the educational awakening in the South, *Outlook* magazine observed that "The Southerner has a keen sense of justice; what he needs most of all is not agreement with his view, but sympathy and the attempt to understand his conditions; to look at his problems, with a purely critical and certainly not in an antagonistic spirit, but from the standpoint of brotherly comprehension."[99] *The Nation* declared that the southern education reformers were "on the firing line in a battle for civilization, the echoes of which are to be heard far beyond the shores of our own country."[100]

Some southerners were suspicious of educational improvement schemes.

96. Louis R. Harlan, "The Southern Education Board and the Race Issue in Public Education," *Journal of Southern History* 23 (May 1957): 189–202; William A. Link, "Privies, Progressivism, and Public Schools: Health Reform and Education in the Rural South, 1909–1920," *Journal of Southern History* 54 (November 1988): 623–42.

97. Link, *The Paradox of Southern Progressivism*, p. 203. For the public school and public health crusades, see pp. 124–59.

98. Edwin A. Alderman, "The Achievement of a Generation," *South Atlantic Quarterly* 5 (July 1906): 237–38.

99. "Southern Education Again," *Outlook* 71 (May 17, 1902): 160.

100. "A Year's Progress in Southern Education," *Nation* 76 (January 15, 1903): 47.

Opponents warned of increased taxes, the danger of black schools, interference by northerners, and the political implications of the educational campaigns. Nor was local cooperation always forthcoming. Several prominent southern newspapers mounted a barrage of criticism against the Conference for Education and the northern philanthropists who contributed to its work. The *Manufacturers' Record,* which spoke for many of the section's industrialists, was especially aggressive in its attacks on the SEB, charging that its northern members were trying to bring back the era of Reconstruction and that its southern members were traitors to the traditions of the South. The race question was inevitably introduced. As late as 1906 the Charleston *News and Courier* was asserting that "the so-called Ogden movement . . . is for the negro primarily, and for the white man only to the extent that it can make the white man of assistance to the work of elevating the negro."[101]

Even so, most southerners showed an eager willingness to share in the benefits of outside generosity. Writing in 1915 of the General Education Board's

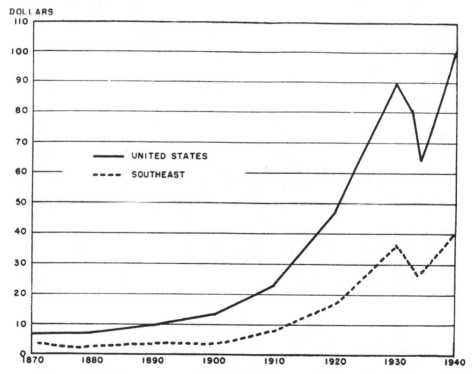

DOLLARS

Total Annual Expenditures per Pupil Enrolled in Public Schools, United States and Southeast, 1871–1940. SOURCE: Rupert B. Vance, in collaboration with Nadia Danilevsky, *All These People: The Nation's Human Resources in the South* (Chapel Hill: University of North Carolina Press, 1945), p. 418.

101. James W. Patton, "The Southern Reaction to the Ogden Movement," in *Education in the South: Institute of Southern Culture Lectures at Longwood College, 1959,* ed. R. C. Simonini, Jr. (Farmville, Va., 1959), pp. 63–82 (quotation on p. 75).

contributions, an appreciative southern woman concluded that "the Board's great work has been to invigorate and enrich the life and thought of the common people of the South, to increase their resources, and to help them to open for themselves the door of opportunity."[102] For their part, the northerners were extraordinarily sympathetic and tactful in approaching the southern states. The GEB, recalled one of its presidents, saw the South as "an educationally blighted region. The glaring inequity it chose to wage war against was not that which existed between the two races, but that which distinguished the South from the other regions of the United States."[103] On the other hand, a modern critic suggests that the spokesmen for "the philanthropic capitalist did not so much change Northern opinion as indicate its final capitulation to racism."[104]

The school campaigns early in the twentieth century did bring notable improvements in southern schools. During the decade and a half after 1900, the per capita expenditure for education in the South doubled, the average school term was substantially lengthened, teachers' salaries went up, thousands of schoolhouses were built, and the illiteracy rate among white children was cut in half. Yet the South lagged far behind other parts of the country, handicapped by its poverty, excessive number of children, rural environment, and dual school system. Meanwhile, southern blacks were pushed to the periphery of the regional crusade for schools and excluded from an equitable share of the educational benefits the movement brought. Discrimination against blacks in the section's state and local school systems was both flagrant and pervasive. Some black educators and editors criticized the Southern Education Board for ignoring their race's interests, but the temptation to use the African American's share for the white child proved irresistible. During the period 1900–1920, every southern state increased its public expenditures for the building of schoolhouses, but little of this money went to black schools. Between 1890 and 1910 the black-to-white ratio of per pupil expenditures in southern schools declined, and the relative quality of black public schools dropped in those years, with little change until the late 1920s.[105] Northern philanthropists did not entirely abandon the support of black education in the South during the progressive era. Black institutions were assisted by the General Education Board, the John F. Slater Fund, the Anna T. Jeanes Fund, and other foundations.[106] But the philanthropists' basic assumptions—and those of most white Americans in this pe-

102. Mrs. John D. Hammond, "The Work of the General Education Board in the South," *South Atlantic Quarterly* 14 (October 1915): 348–57 (quotation on p. 349).

103. Raymond B. Fosdick, *Adventure in Giving: The Story of the General Education Board, A Foundation Established by John D. Rockefeller* (New York, 1962), p. 324.

104. Louis R. Harlan, *Separate and Unequal: Public School Campaigns and Racism in the Southern Seaboard States, 1901–1915* (Chapel Hill, N.C., 1958), p. 81.

105. James D. Anderson, *The Education of Blacks in the South, 1860–1935* (Chapel Hill, N.C., 1988), pp. 79–156; Robert A. Margo, *Disenfranchisement, School Finance, and the Economics of Segregated Schools in the United States South, 1890–1910* (New York, 1985), pp. 7, 56–57; Margo, *Race and Schooling in the South, 1880–1950: An Economic History* (Chicago, 1990), p. 51; Wright, *Old South, New South*, pp. 80, 123.

106. James D. Anderson, "Northern Foundations and the Shaping of Southern Black Rural Education, 1902–1935," in *The Social History of American Education*, ed. B. Edward McClellan and William J. Reese (Urbana, Ill., 1988), pp. 287–312.

riod—were powerfully affected by the interregional agreement embodied in the Conference for Education in the South.

Public schools for African Americans in the southern states were supported in considerable part by the private contributions of black people themselves. Black efforts to establish good schools were part of a larger commitment to social reform. Although most black reformers were moderates who recognized the inviolability of white supremacy, they sought to encourage economic opportunities, build educational facilities, curb racial violence, promote justice in the courts, and foster racial pride and personal autonomy among men and women of color. They worked through religious and fraternal organizations, civic groups, and self-help agencies like the Neighborhood Union in Atlanta. Black women played a major role in these relief and improvement projects. The black reform spirit was sometimes manifested in protest and resistance: a series of boycotts organized against Jim Crow streetcars early in the century, demands for political and social change expressed by newspapers like the Nashville *Globe* and the Richmond *Planet*, and pioneer social investigations such as the *Publications* directed by W. E. B. Du Bois at Atlanta University. Thus, despite their racial subordination, black southerners participated in social reform activities and helped shape the contours of their region's progressivism.[107]

If northern philanthropy played an important role in the public school crusade in the South, it also gave impetus to the public health movement below the Potomac. A spectacular example was the campaign against hookworm disease. The campaign, which began in 1909 and lasted until 1914, combined many of the elements of social uplift in the region: a pervasive southern problem, northern philanthropy, the application of a scientific solution, and the involvement of southerners in organized efforts to deal with the problem. The hookworm, an intestinal parasite, infected and chronically debilitated a great many southerners, perhaps as many as two million persons. Walter Hines Page and other advocates of southern rehabilitation persuaded John D. Rockefeller to commit up to a million dollars for a regional campaign to wipe out the infection. The Rockefeller Sanitary Commission for the Eradication of Hookworm Disease made allocations to the various state boards of health, which supervised the actual work. The money was used for sanitary surveys, demonstrations, and organizational efforts, and the campaign elicited the cooperation of many local health officers and boards. Between 1909 and 1914 the clinics supported by the Sanitary Commission examined more than a million people and treated more than 440,000 infected persons. "Perhaps the Commission's most important legacy in the South," its historian concludes, "was the network of state and local public health agencies it left in its wake."[108] The progressives were not always

107. Grantham, *Southern Progressivism*, pp. 239–45. The range of reform endeavors undertaken by black southerners is illustrated in John Dittmer, *Black Georgia in the Progressive Era, 1900–1920* (Urbana, Ill., 1977), and Lester C. Lamon, *Black Tennesseans, 1900–1930* (Knoxville, Tenn., 1977).

108. John Ettling, *The Germ of Laziness: Rockefeller Philanthropy and Public Health in the New South* (Cambridge, Mass., 1981), p. 220. See also Allen Tullos, "The Great Hookworm Crusade," *Southern Exposure* 6 (Summer 1978): 40–49.

able to implement their reforms. Their pursuit of efficiency and modernization often resulted in popular antagonism and community resistance to coercive state intervention and centralized control. A leading student of southern progressivism suggests that two fundamental values were in conflict: "the paternalism of reformers and the localism and community power of traditionalists."[109]

In another area of progressive endeavor, agricultural improvement, the South provided a laboratory for the nation as a whole. Agricultural reform in the South during the progressive period took a variety of forms, most of which involved some type of farm organization and cooperation. One important emphasis in progressive efforts to rehabilitate the southern farmer was the widespread support of practical education and efficient methods in agriculture. This reform sentiment could be found in the section's farm journals, agricultural colleges and experiment stations, farm institutes, and in the work of Theodore Roosevelt's Country Life Commission. A striking illustration of the movement to improve agricultural techniques, increase production, and raise farm income was the demonstration system worked out by Seaman A. Knapp, a farm expert from Iowa selected in 1902 by the United States Department of Agriculture as a special agent for the promotion of agriculture in the South. Beginning in Texas, where the alarming spread of the boll weevil threatened to wipe out the state's cotton farmers, Knapp's demonstration program attracted widespread attention as a result of its dramatic success. It was soon introduced in other southern states. The new techniques were supported by congressional appropriations and Rockefeller's General Education Board as well as by local businessmen. It spread throughout the South and laid the basis for the nation's agricultural extension system involving federal funds, the USDA, agricultural colleges and experiment stations, and a network of county agents and home demonstration agents to advance the cause of scientific farming and domestic science. By 1920 GEB programs had expanded from demonstrating effective agricultural methods to providing extension services, sponsoring youth clubs, paying the salaries of supervisors for rural public schools, and supporting vocational agriculture in community programs, agricultural high schools, and state agricultural colleges.[110]

Efforts to promote social justice in the early-twentieth-century South were heavily dependent upon the activities of southern women. As a southern newspaper observed in 1912, in commenting on the activities of the North Carolina Federation of Women's Clubs, "The improvement of health, the betterment of morals, the modernizing of education and the humanizing of penology are perhaps the most vital matters of government in which North Carolina women

109. Link, *The Paradox of Southern Progressivism*, p. xii. See also *ibid.*, pp. 203–38, 268–95, and William A. Link, "The Social Context of Southern Progressivism, 1880–1930," in *The Wilson Era: Essays in Honor of Arthur S. Link*, ed. John Milton Cooper, Jr., and Charles E. Neu (Arlington Heights, Ill., 1991), pp. 55–82.

110. Theodore R. Mitchell and Robert Lowe, "To Sow Contentment: Philanthropy, Scientific Agriculture and the Making of the New South, 1906–1920," *Journal of Social History* 24 (Winter 1990): 317–40; Grantham, *Southern Progressivism*, pp. 320–48.

have interested themselves."[111] Through travel and the widening circle of their various organizations—Protestant missionary societies, temperance groups, women's clubs, the Young Women's Christian Association, the General Federation of Women's Clubs—a significant number of women in the South were brought into contact with magnetic leaders such as Frances Willard and Anna Howard Shaw and with the ideas and methods of advanced social reformers in the Northeast and Midwest. Southern women were active along a broad front in the struggle against social problems: the eradication of child labor, better schools, penal reform, legal rights for women, the public health movement, prohibition, development of organized charity and public welfare, establishment of missions, schools, and settlement houses in Southern Appalachia, and a complex of moral reforms to counter the breakdown of the family and to promote social efficiency. As the intensity of what was called "the woman's movement" increased, it found greater focus in the drive for the suffrage. The struggle to enfranchise women grew naturally out of their involvement in social reform. William A. Link argues that "there would have been no movement for woman suffrage without a prior large-scale entry of women into the public arena via the side door of social reform." The ballot symbolized early-twentieth-century feminism and the desire of many women "to break out of their narrow sphere and establish themselves as independent beings."[112] Enfranchisement was not only the supreme objective in the crusade for the emancipation of women; it also represented a pragmatic decision on the part of socially conscious women whose reform efforts in other fields had been consistently nullified or diminished because of their political impotence in the South.[113]

Though tiny woman suffrage groups existed in most southern states in the 1890s, they were feeble and most of them disappeared soon after the turn of the century. But in the years that followed a stronger and more concerted movement for women's rights gradually emerged in the South, aided by the General Federation of Women's Clubs and the National American Woman Suffrage Association (NAWSA). There were unmistakable overtones of class and caste in the ideas expressed by southern suffragists, and their campaign, like the movement in other parts of the country, was essentially "a struggle of white, native-born, middle-class women for the right to participate more fully in the public affairs of a society the basic structure of which they accepted."[114] Southern appeals, some of which were directed to northern women, elicited a sympathetic response from other sections. By the early 1900s, the national woman suffrage movement had broken with the abolitionist tradition and had become less egalitarian than in

111. Quoted in Anne Firor Scott, *The Southern Lady: From Pedestal to Politics, 1830–1930* (Chicago, 1970), p. 159.

112. Link, *The Paradox of Southern Progressivism*, p. 183 (first quotation); Scott, *The Southern Lady*, p. 165 (second quotation).

113. Link, *The Paradox of Southern Progressivism*, pp. 182–99; Ayers, *The Promise of the New South*, pp. 28, 316–17; Grantham, *Southern Progressivism*, pp. 200–208.

114. Aileen S. Kraditor, *The Ideas of the Woman Suffrage Movement, 1890–1920* (New York, 1965), p. x.

earlier years. One reason for the development of a national movement, in fact, was "the common cause made by Northern women who feared the foreign-born vote with Southern women who feared the Negro vote."[115]

Nevertheless, suffrage leaders outside the South eventually found it desirable to broaden their campaigns in order to attract the support of immigrant and working women. They also began to concentrate their efforts on a suffrage amendment to the U.S. Constitution. These developments alienated many southern suffragists. Kate M. Gordon of New Orleans, for example, was concerned about the influence black women might exert in the NAWSA, and she contended that a federal amendment would allow the national government and probably the Republican party to control federal elections. In 1913 Gordon was instrumental in organizing the Southern States Woman Suffrage Conference, which pledged itself to support "states' rights" and to work for woman suffrage through state action.[116] Even so, support for a federal amendment existed throughout the South, and it grew during the next few years.

In 1908 the historian William Garrott Brown called attention to the culmination of two processes of "sweeping legislation" in the southern states—the drastic regulation of railroads and the sudden prohibition of the traffic in intoxicating beverages. Brown thought the South had "recently come into that phase of democracy in which government stretches its authority to the uttermost in the endeavor to enforce moralities" and that government had become "wellnigh puritanized."[117] The movement to prohibit the manufacture and sale of alcoholic beverages may well have been the most dynamic and passionately supported "reform" in the South during the progressive era. In the late nineteenth century, widespread temperance sentiment and the perception of a growing moral crisis roused many southerners to action. While temperance advocates initially emphasized the responsibility of the individual for change and redemption, as time passed they increasingly embraced the idea of community responsibility, public solutions, and social reform.[118] Much of the South's regulatory energy in the decade after 1907 found an outlet in the anti-liquor movement, first in the drive for statewide prohibition and thereafter in the struggle for a national law. So powerful was its influence between the Potomac and the Rio Grande that prohibition leaders could describe the South, with considerable justification, as the "main-spring" of the movement in the United States, "the propagandic base" of the national agitation.[119]

115. *Ibid.*, p. 137. For a fuller discussion of the parallel between northern and southern arguments, see *ibid.*, pp. xi, 125–32, 163–68, 198–220.

116. Kate M. Gordon, "The Southern Woman Suffrage Conference," in *The History of Woman Suffrage, 1900–1920*, ed. Ida Husted Harper, vol. 5 (New York, 1922), pp. 671–73; Kenneth R. Johnson, "Kate Gordon and the Woman-Suffrage Movement in the South," *Journal of Southern History* 38 (August 1972): 365–81; Kraditor, *The Ideas of the Woman Suffrage Movement*, pp. 173–218; Marjorie Spruill Wheeler, *New Women of the New South: The Leaders of the Woman Suffrage Movement in the Southern States* (New York, 1993), pp. 133–71.

117. William Garrott Brown, "The South and the Saloon," *Century Magazine* 76 (July 1908): 462–63.

118. Link, *The Paradox of Southern Progressivism*, pp. 32–51.

119. John E. White, "Prohibition: The New Task and Opportunity of the South," *South Atlantic*

In 1907 and 1908 six of the thirteen southern states adopted prohibition. It had become a major issue in most of the other states, and the dry advance was continuing through local option elections. Then the movement slowed in the face of strong opposition and the difficulty of enforcing the prohibition statutes. But in 1914 the anti-liquor campaign regained momentum, and by the time the United States went to war in April 1917, the South was in the vanguard of the effort to secure national prohibition. The southern campaign both benefited from and contributed to the activities of national prohibition organizations such as the Anti-Saloon League of America and the Women's Christian Temperance Union. Prohibitionists in the South were encouraged by the passage in 1913 of the Webb-Kenyon Act, a congressional measure that outlawed the shipment of alcoholic beverages from a wet to a dry state.[120]

The easing of sectional tensions and the upsurge of national loyalties throughout the country at the turn of the century did not mark the demise of sectionalism in the United States. Southerners remained, as they had at the end of the Civil War, "a people who had had a history of separate aspiration and who still possessed the memory of a cause that was lost."[121] Northerners were inclined to think of their section as being more characteristically American than other parts of the country. Southerners, on the other hand, tended to think of their section as a unit within a larger unit. When a group of southern scholars and writers published a collaborative, multivolume history of the region early in the new century, they entitled it *The South in the Building of the Nation*. The editors were careful to explain that, "Owing to peculiar conditions the South was, and to some extent still is, a sort of political and economic unit—a definite section— with an interrelated and separate history, special problems and distinct life."[122] Although the harsh sectional clashes of the nineteenth century seemed to be a thing of the past, sectional consciousness and sectional conflicts, no less than political differences, economic disparities, and cultural distinctions of a regional nature, were still much in evidence. They would continue to have a strong effect on the American experience through most of the twentieth century.

Quarterly 7 (April 1908): 130–42. See also White, "Temperance Reform in the South," in *The South in the Building of the Nation* . . . , ed. Julian A. C. Chandler et al., 13 vols. (Richmond, 1909–1913), vol. 10, pp. 567–81, and Grantham, *Southern Progressivism*, pp. 160–77.

120. For the national prohibition movement, see James H. Timberlake, *Prohibition and the Progressive Movement, 1900–1920* (Cambridge, Mass., 1963), and Joseph R. Gusfield, *Symbolic Crusade: Status Politics and the American Temperance Movement* (Urbana, Ill., 1963).

121. Buck, *The Road to Reunion*, p. 42.

122. Chandler et al., eds., *The South in the Building of the Nation*, vol. 1, p. xvii.

CHAPTER 3

The Era of Woodrow Wilson

T HE second decade of the twentieth century brought a notable shift in the control of national politics in the United States. The resurgence of the Democratic party, the emergence of Woodrow Wilson as the party's leader, and Wilson's election as the nation's twenty-eighth president in 1912 set the stage for an extraordinary period of domestic reform, wartime mobilization, and international involvement for the American people. The South assumed an important role in these developments, and as a consequence its sectional character was altered. By the end of the Wilson administration, American sectionalism was manifesting itself in subtly different ways.

Democratic prospects appeared dim following the Republican presidential and congressional victories of 1908. But the new Taft administration was soon embroiled in a divisive intraparty struggle over tariff revision, and the progressive insurgency among the Republicans contributed to a surprising Democratic triumph in the midterm elections of 1910. Democrats captured control of the House of Representatives for the first time since 1892, with a solid majority of 228 to 161; Republicans retained control of the Senate by a margin of 51 to 41. Most of the Democratic newcomers in the House came from nonsouthern states, but southerners assumed a commanding position in organizing the Sixty-second Congress (1911–1913). Although the nominal leader of the House Democrats was Speaker Champ Clark of Missouri, the real leader was Oscar W. Underwood of Alabama, who became chairman of the Ways and Means Committee and floor leader. Most of the major House committees were headed by southerners.[1] This leadership soon gave the House a "southern" identity.

1. Anne Firor Scott, "A Progressive Wind from the South, 1906–1913," *Journal of Southern History* 29 (February 1963): 53–70; Evans C. Johnson, *Oscar W. Underwood: A Political Biography* (Baton Rouge, La., 1980), pp. 118–69; George E. Mowry, *The Era of Theodore Roosevelt, 1900–1912* (New York, 1958), pp. 238–73.

Meanwhile, another development was also enhancing the position of the South in national politics. This was the sudden emergence of Woodrow Wilson as a serious candidate for the Democratic presidential nomination in 1912 and his identification as a southerner. There was no doubt in Wilson's own mind about his southernism, even though he had left the South twenty-five years earlier and had entered politics by being elected governor of New Jersey in 1910. Born in Virginia on the eve of the Civil War, he had grown up in the South during the trying times of war and reconstruction. This helps explain why he thought of himself as a southerner. Yet Wilson became an ardent nationalist, and as a young man he was sometimes critical of the South's sectionalism. By the 1890s, however, he had rediscovered the South, whose traditions he came to idealize. He declared in 1896, for example, that there was "nothing to apologize for in the past of the South—absolutely nothing to apologize for." On a visit to North Carolina in 1911, Wilson began an address by saying, "It is very delightful to return to the Old North State and to feel that having been one of you I do not need any formal presentation or introduction to you. You know that it is only true of the region in which a man is born, that nothing there needs to be explained to him."[2]

Southerners were quick to claim Wilson as a native son. His nomination and subsequent election as governor of New Jersey brought a large number of enthusiastic letters from southerners as well as many favorable newspaper references in the South, some of which spoke of him as the Democratic party's best presidential hope in 1912. The speaker of the Virginia house of delegates wrote the governor-elect: "I regard you as the best & most available candidate for the Presidency on the democratic ticket of 1912."[3] Wilson-for-President clubs sprang up throughout the country, appearing first in Virginia in November 1910. And early in 1911 southern friends of Wilson in New York helped launch a movement to promote his nomination for president.[4] As his campaign began to take shape, Wilson looked to the South for indispensable support in the struggle for the nomination.

By the time the New Jersey governor began his campaign in earnest, he had begun to achieve a national reputation as a reformer, in large part because of the progressive ideas he enunciated and the progressive legislation he pushed through the New Jersey general assembly in 1911. Wilson's progressivism was the result of a metamorphosis in his thinking during the last year or two, and it was ironic that earlier, as president of Princeton University, he had been touted by Colonel George B. Harvey, editor of *Harper's Weekly*, as a conservative worthy of receiving the Democratic nomination for president. Southern conserva-

2. Arthur S. Link, *Wilson: The Road to the White House* (Princeton, N.J., 1947), p. 2 (first quotation); Link et al., eds., *The Papers of Woodrow Wilson*, vol. 23 (Princeton, 1977), p. 110 (second quotation); Link, "Woodrow Wilson: The American as Southerner," *Journal of Southern History* 36 (February 1970): 3–17.
3. Richard Evelyn Byrd to Woodrow Wilson, 10 November 1910, in *The Papers of Woodrow Wilson*, ed. Arthur S. Link et al., vol. 22 (Princeton, 1976), p. 20.
4. Link, *Wilson: The Road to the White House*, pp. 172, 312–13.

tives such as the journalists Henry Watterson and James C. Hemphill had joined in this promotion of Wilson.[5]

Wilson's emergence as a progressive reformer was primarily responsible for the movement to make him the Democratic party's presidential nominee in 1912. His backers tended to be progressive Democrats. That was also true in the South, where the more liberal party factions in states like Georgia, North Carolina, and Texas were the prime movers in organizing the governor's campaign. The more conservative—or "regular"—factions were usually opposed to Wilson. Most of these elements, particularly in the Deep South, threw their support to Representative Oscar W. Underwood, who first entered the race as a favorite son candidate. The Alabama congressman's hopes clearly rested on his appeal in his own section, and in contrast to Wilson he was publicized as a "Southerner living in the South." Underwood was respectable, generally conservative, and a bit dull. But he was an able legislator, and his success as majority leader in the Sixty-second Congress brought him favorable attention and made him something of a southern hero.[6]

Thus the South in the months before the Democratic national convention was a hotly contested region, not only by the supporters of Underwood and Wilson but by those of Speaker Champ Clark as well. The popular Clark portrayed himself as the heir to the great commoner, William Jennings Bryan. Wilson visited the South several times in 1911 and 1912, eliciting an enthusiastic response wherever he appeared. Yet his widespread popularity was not enough to bring him a sweeping victory there; he was forced to divide the southern delegations with his competitors. Wilson controlled the Texas and South Carolina delegations, three-fourths of North Carolina's, half of Louisiana's, and a portion of Virginia's and Tennessee's. But Underwood won Alabama, Florida, Georgia, and Mississippi, while Clark dominated the delegations of Kentucky, Arkansas, and Oklahoma. Slightly more than one-third of Wilson's votes on the first ballot at the national convention were cast by southern delegates. Nonetheless, the New Jersey governor was the second choice of many other southern delegates, and his nomination on the forty-sixth ballot was at least in part the result of the Underwood forces' refusal to shift their support to Clark even after the speaker obtained a majority (but not the required two-thirds majority) on the tenth ballot.[7]

In the meantime, the Republican party had split apart over the leadership

5. Willard B. Gatewood, Jr., "James Calvin Hemphill: Southern Critic of Woodrow Wilson, 1911–1912," *Georgia Review* 13 (Winter 1959): 378–92. In earlier years Wilson had asserted that the Populists should be read out of the Democratic party "as an alien faction." He had expressed the hope that the South's "latent conservatism" would contribute to "the reclamation of the Democratic Party." John M. Mulder, *Woodrow Wilson: The Years of Preparation* (Princeton, 1978), p. 233.

6. Johnson, *Oscar W. Underwood*, pp. 170–92; Arthur S. Link, "The Underwood Presidential Movement of 1912," *Journal of Southern History* 11 (May 1945): 230–45; George N. Green, "The Florida Press and the Democratic Presidential Primary of 1912," *Florida Historical Quarterly* 44 (January 1966): 169–80.

7. See Arthur S. Link, "The South and the Democratic Campaign of 1912" (Ph.D. dissertation, University of North Carolina, 1945), and Link, "The Baltimore Convention of 1912," *American Historical Review* 50 (July 1945): 691–713.

and policies of President Taft, and by early 1912 former president Theodore Roosevelt had entered the race for the Republican nomination. The result was a fierce conflict between Roosevelt and Taft for delegates to the GOP convention. Since the Taft forces controlled the convention, the president was awarded most of the numerous contested seats, and he was then renominated. Roosevelt and his supporters were furious, and they soon decided to organize the Progressive party under the former president's leadership. They adopted a liberal platform and began an energetic campaign, even in the South. John M. Parker, a Progressive leader from Louisiana, warned Roosevelt that the new party should be "a white man's party." That proved to be the case, and in every southern state except Oklahoma a "lily-white" Progressive party was organized. Roosevelt reached out to the southern white man. Speaking in Chattanooga, he declared: "I wish to see the South come back into its position of national importance which it formerly had, and which by right it should have."[8]

The general election campaign aroused exceptional interest in the South, not only because a southerner was the Democratic standard-bearer but because of Roosevelt's forays into the region. The contest was also marked by the campaigning of many southern Democrats in the North and West. The national outcome was scarcely in doubt, since Roosevelt's defection greatly diminished the Republicans' normal majority and enabled Wilson to win a large electoral majority with less than 43 percent of the popular vote. He won all thirteen southern states handily, but outside the South he carried a majority of the popular votes only in Arizona. Nevertheless, Wilson won forty states and demonstrated a genuinely national appeal. The Democrats also captured both houses of Congress, with an infusion of new strength from the mountain states, the wheat belt, and the large northern cities.[9]

Whether the Democrats could transform themselves into a real majority party remained to be seen. But for the South the meaning of the election was much clearer. As one historian has observed, the outcome "represented a revolution in the geographical distribution of power."[10] The reaction of most southerners was unmistakable—a feeling of exhilaration and of realizing long-deferred hopes. "Long ago," wrote a North Carolinian, "I had despaired of ever seeing a man of Southern birth President." Wilson's election, he declared, "marks an era in our national life. With it we have the ascendency of men of Southern birth and residence to the seats of power and responsibility such as has never been seen in our day."[11] Wilson's national role, the president of the

8. Arthur S. Link, "Theodore Roosevelt and the South in 1912," *North Carolina Historical Review* 23 (July 1946): 313–24 (quotation on p. 323). See also George E. Mowry, "The South and the Progressive Lily White Party of 1912," *Journal of Southern History* 6 (May 1940): 237–47.

9. George E. Mowry, "Election of 1912," in *History of American Presidential Elections, 1789–1968*, vol. 3, ed. Arthur M. Schlesinger, Jr., and Fred L. Israel (New York, 1971), pp. 2135–66, 2242; David Sarasohn, *The Party of Reform: Democrats in the Progressive Era* (Jackson, Miss., 1989), pp. 119–54.

10. C. Vann Woodward, *Origins of the New South, 1877–1913* (Baton Rouge, La., 1951), p. 481.

11. Benjamin F. Long to Walter Hines Page, 15 March 1913, Walter Hines Page Papers, Harvard University Library.

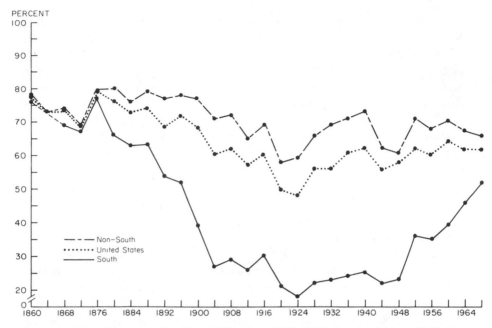

Estimated Voter Turnout in Presidential Elections, 1860–1968. Source: Numan V. Bartley and Hugh D. Graham, *Southern Politics and the Second Reconstruction* (Baltimore: Johns Hopkins University Press, 1975), p. 9.

University of Virginia declared, was "a sort of fulfillment of an unspoken prophecy lying close to the heart of nearly every faithful son of the South that out of this life of dignity and suffering, and out of this discipline of fortitude and endurance there would spring a brave, modern national minded man to whom the whole nation, in some hour of peril and difficulty would turn for succor and for helpfulness."[12] The southerners were at last "back in the house of their fathers."

Many political observers from other sections seemed prepared to give the southern congressmen an opportunity to demonstrate that they were capable of thinking in national terms. The journal *Current Opinion* reported in the spring of 1913 that the northern press was not disturbed over the political resurgence of the South; some newspapers actually expressed satisfaction in the fact. "We welcome the new emergence of the South into national affairs," the Chicago *Evening Post* declared, "however strong or weak it may prove to be."[13] President Taft thought that Wilson's election would give the South "a feeling of partnership" in the conduct of national affairs and do much to eliminate sectionalism.[14] Wilson himself expressed the hope that his election would mean "the final obliteration of everything that may have divided the great sections of this

12. Edwin A. Alderman, quoted in Gaines M. Foster, *Ghosts of the Confederacy: Defeat, the Lost Cause, and the Emergence of the New South, 1865 to 1913* (New York, 1987), p. 193.

13. "What Has Become of the Bloody Shirt?" *Current Opinion* 54 (April 1913): 271.

14. *Washington Post*, 13 November 1912.

country." The president-elect told a Chicago audience that "the happiest circumstances" of his election were the opportunities to put an end to the old feeling "that the Southerner was not of the same political breed and purpose as the rest of American citizens." His election would help Americans realize that the South "is a part of the Union, and that southern men—men born in the South—are not in the least inclined to draw sectional differences in guiding the policy of the nation."[15]

Still, there were disparaging comments about the southern atmosphere that characterized Washington early in 1913. The South, in the phrase of the day, was "in the saddle again." Some commentators suggested that southern leaders were too prejudiced, too provincial, too conservative to contribute much to the success of Wilson's progressive agenda. A writer in McClure's Magazine pointed out that one of the obstacles facing the new president was the fact that most of the important congressional committees were headed by "old Southern States'-rights Democrats."[16] Progressive Democrats in various parts of the South also let Wilson know of their fear that powerful "reactionary elements" in the southern congressional delegations would create problems for the president and use his administration as a means of defeating the section's progressives.[17] Wilson privately warned of "jealousies" in other parts of the country. "While I myself am deeply glad to be a Southern man and to have the South feel a sense of possession in me," he wrote Oscar W. Underwood, "we shall have to be careful not to make the impression that the South is seeking to keep the front of the stage and take possession of the administration."[18] These comments suggest that northern goodwill toward the South had become more restrained with the transfer of greater national power to southerners.

"In the Wilson era," one historian observes, "the South was not merely solid for the Democratic Party, not merely the party's bankable minimum at the ballot box, but its heart and soul."[19] The influential role of the South in the new administration was apparent from the outset. The nation had a southern-born president, five of Wilson's cabinet members were from the South or had been born in that region, and his closest adviser, Colonel Edward M. House, was a Texan. Southerners were in a position to receive more federal patronage than at any time since the Civil War.[20] And most important of all, southern senators

15. Arthur S. Link et al., eds., The Papers of Woodrow Wilson, vol. 25 (Princeton, 1978), p. 627; vol. 27 (Princeton, 1978), p. 34.

16. George Kibbe Turner, "What Wilson Is Up Against," McClure's Magazine 40 (February 1913): 176. See also A. Maurice Low, "The South in the Saddle," Harper's Weekly 57 (February 8, 1913): 20.

17. See, for example, Cone Johnson to Woodrow Wilson, 17 December 1912, and Thomas Bell Love to Wilson, 27 December 1912, in Link et al., eds., The Papers of Woodrow Wilson, vol. 25, pp. 603–605, 624–26.

18. Woodrow Wilson to Oscar Wilder Underwood, January 21, 1913, in Link et al., eds., The Papers of Woodrow Wilson, vol. 27, p. 66. Also see Wilson to William Jennings Bryan, 26 May 1913, p. 474.

19. David M. Kennedy, Over Here: The First World War and American Society (New York, 1980), p. 241.

20. John M. Blum, Joe Tumulty and the Wilson Era (Boston, 1951), p. 241. See also John W.

and representatives dominated Congress. Though comprising only about half of the Democratic senators and slightly over two-fifths of the Democratic representatives, the southerners made up a large majority of the party's senior members in the two houses. They exerted great weight in the two Democratic caucuses and headed almost all of the important congressional committees. Representative Underwood served as majority leader in the House, and when the Alabamian moved up to the Senate in 1915, he was replaced by Claude Kitchin of North Carolina. The majority leader in the Senate, John W. Kern of Indiana, was succeeded in 1917 by Thomas S. Martin of Virginia. The southerners made effective use of these formal positions, but their legislative power as a group was also the product of their parliamentary skill and mastery of the substantive details of congressional issues and proposals.[21]

As it turned out, most southern congressmen were in agreement with President Wilson's legislative proposals in 1913 and 1914, and they provided strong support for the basic features of his New Freedom. A few southerners in Congress did object to particular provisions of Wilson's tariff reform bill—to items affecting Texas wool, Louisiana sugar, and southeastern textiles—but on the final vote virtually all of them voted in favor of the measure. The legislation was skillfully guided through the two houses by Representative Underwood, chairman of the Ways and Means Committee, and Senator Furnifold M. Simmons of North Carolina, chairman of the Finance Committee. One of the novel provisions of the Underwood-Simmons Act was a federal income tax, which was drafted and shepherded through the House of Representatives by Cordell Hull of Tennessee. Representative John Nance Garner of Texas and Senator James K. Vardaman of Mississippi took the lead in amending the bill so that it included a graduated surtax on large incomes. Opponents of the income tax described it as class legislation and a sectional raid on eastern wealth. Hull responded by arguing that eastern wealth was derived from all sections of the country.[22]

Southern representatives and senators gave equally strong backing to two other central features of the New Freedom—banking and currency reform and antitrust legislation. The first of these resulted in the Federal Reserve Act, which was steered through Congress in 1913 by Representative Carter Glass of Virginia and Senator Robert L. Owen of Oklahoma. Glass, like most other southern congressmen, was a proponent of regional reserve banks, which were in-

---

Davidson, "The Response of the South to Woodrow Wilson's New Freedom, 1912–1914" (Ph.D. dissertation, Yale University, 1953).

21. For a penetrating analysis of southern influence in the modern Congress, see David M. Potter, *The South and the Concurrent Majority*, ed. Don E. Fehrenbacher and Carl N. Degler (Baton Rouge, La., 1972).

22. Arthur S. Link, *Wilson: The New Freedom* (Princeton, 1956), pp. 177–97; Johnson, *Oscar W. Underwood*, pp. 198–209; George Brown Tindall, *The Emergence of the New South, 1913–1945* (Baton Rouge, La., 1967), p. 11. See also Arthur S. Link, "The South and the 'New Freedom': An Interpretation," *American Scholar* 20 (Summer 1951): 314–24; Sarasohn, *The Party of Reform*, pp. 164–70; Philip A. Grant, Jr., "Tennesseans in the 63rd Congress, 1913–1915," *Tennessee Historical Quarterly* 29 (Fall 1970): 278–86; and Jack E. Kendrick, "Alabama Congressmen in the Wilson Administration," *Alabama Review* 24 (October 1971): 243–60.

cluded in the new system. Owen and other progressives, many of them southerners, successfully fought to exclude banker representatives from membership on the Federal Reserve Board, to make Federal Reserve notes obligations of the federal government, and to provide short-term ninety-day farm as well as commercial credit facilities. Southerners were less prominent in the passage of the Federal Trade Commission bill and the Clayton antitrust bill, although the latter was under the supervision in the House of Henry D. Clayton of Alabama. There was solid southern support for a provision in the Clayton Act designed to exempt farm and labor organizations from prosecution under the antitrust laws.[23]

In spite of their state rights tradition, southern congressmen during the Wilson period were forceful advocates of national aid, especially in the area of agriculture. They provided large majorities for long-term rural credits, a federal warehouse statute, an agricultural extension program, vocational education, and more effective regulation of commodity exchanges.[24] Among the southern lawmakers, particularly in the House, a group of agrarian reformers expressed a kind of neopopulism that looked to Washington both for antitrust action and federal aid to farmers and small businessmen. These southern agrarians—men such as Claude Kitchin, Robert Lee Henry and Rufus Hardy of Texas, Otis T. Wingo of Arkansas, and J. Willard Ragsdale of South Carolina—helped secure progressive changes in the Glass banking and currency bill, urged more rigorous antitrust legislation, worked for more democratic tax schedules, and championed a system of rural credits and other agricultural assistance.[25] A larger group of southern congressmen, supporters of the national administration, included leaders like Oscar Underwood, Duncan U. Fletcher of Florida, Lee S. Overman of North Carolina, William C. Adamson of Georgia, and Finis J. Garrett of Tennessee. The members of this group were generally conservative but reliable supporters of the party and the president.

Southerners tended to believe that their section had long been denied its fair share of federal benefits. Thus Senator John Sharp Williams of Mississippi wrote the director of the U.S. Geological Survey in June 1914 to complain that the agency "never can do anything in the South unless you can get an increased appropriation." According to Williams, "The South generally, and Mississippi in particular, has been neglected."[26] The desire for federal assistance, including administration patronage, was clearly one reason for southern support of the New Freedom. Wilson's appeal as a native son and the strong bond of party loyalty among southerners were also compelling factors. But there was still an-

23. Link, *Wilson: The New Freedom*, pp. 417–44.

24. Theodore Saloutos, *Farmer Movements in the South, 1865–1933* (Berkeley, Calif., 1960), pp. 213–35.

25. Link, "The South and the 'New Freedom,' " pp. 314–24; Tindall, *The Emergence of the New South*, p. 10. Different views are presented in Richard M. Abrams, "Woodrow Wilson and the Southern Congressmen, 1913–1916," *Journal of Southern History* 22 (November 1956): 417–37, and Howard W. Allen, "Geography and Politics: Voting on Reform Issues in the United States Senate, 1911–1916," *Journal of Southern History* 27 (May 1961): 216–28.

26. John Sharp Williams to George Otis Smith, 29 June 1914, John Sharp Williams Papers, Manuscript Division, Library of Congress.

other consideration of great importance: Wilson's major legislative reforms did not threaten local control or established institutions in the South. The southern power structure—planters, businessmen, professionals, and the local governing class—had no difficulty in assimilating the New Freedom. "They welcomed change," one historian writes, "that did not intrude upon the prerogatives of race and class and property, especially economic growth." In some measure, of course, that was true of the dominant political and social elements throughout the nation. A northern journalist who was following the racial situation closely concluded in the fall of 1913 that "there is not the slightest room for doubt that the Southerners in Congress have the tacit support of a large proportion of men from the North and West."[27]

In at least one respect southern leaders sought to promote change in the nation's capital. Many of them viewed the ascendancy of the Democratic party and the Wilson administration as a means of extending the southern formula for handling race relations to Washington and beyond. They introduced legislation in Congress to prevent racial intermarriage and to require racial segregation of public transportation facilities in the District of Columbia; they opposed any new black appointments and tried to remove or downgrade African Americans already in federal positions; and they brought pressure on the administration to introduce more thoroughgoing segregation in the various departments of the executive branch. The federal government, one scholar has remarked, was now controlled by "a party dominated by men determined to impose the caste system in the nation's capital."[28]

The southern offensive on the racial front posed a problem for Woodrow Wilson, who had openly appealed for northern black support in the campaign of 1912, assuring African Americans that he favored "justice executed with liberality and cordial good feeling." Wilson was the beneficiary of some black votes, perhaps as many as 100,000, and following his election Negro leaders and white civil rights advocates looked expectantly to the new administration for federal appointments and cooperation. Oswald Garrison Villard, a New York publisher and grandson of the abolitionist William Lloyd Garrison, urged Wilson on behalf of the National Association for the Advancement of Colored People to appoint a privately financed national race commission to conduct "a non-partisan, scientific study of the status of the Negro in the life of the nation." At first the president was receptive to this idea, but in the end he refused to act on it. The situation was "extremely delicate," he wrote Villard in August 1913, and "I find myself absolutely blocked by the sentiment of Senators; not alone Senators from the South, by any means, but Senators from various parts of the country." Wilson expressed a desire "to handle the matter with the greatest

27. I. A. Newby, *The South: A History* (New York, 1978), p. 379 (first quotation); John Palmer Gavit to Oswald Garrison Villard, 1 October 1913, in Oswald Garrison Villard Papers, Harvard University Library (second quotation). For evidence of how the conservative Democratic factions in several southern states actually used the Wilson administration to strengthen themselves against their progressive opponents, see Arthur S. Link, "Woodrow Wilson and the Democratic Party," *Review of Politics* 18 (April 1956): 146–56.

28. Link, *Wilson: The New Freedom*, p. 246.

possible patience and tact," but his attitude, while benevolent and well meaning, was that of the typical white southerner—and a great many nonsoutherners—of his class.[29]

By that time, it was apparent that black Americans, including black Democrats, could expect little help from the Wilson administration. The determined opposition of the more outspoken southern congressmen prevented the appointment of virtually any black to federal office, even though Wilson wanted to appoint a few prominent black Democrats to positions traditionally held by African Americans. Negro political appointees, in Washington and throughout the South, were quickly dismissed or downgraded in rank. In the spring of 1913, Wilson approved a plan for the segregation of black workers, most of whom were employed in the Post Office Department, the Treasury Department, and the Bureau of Printing and Engraving. The reaction to these decisions from black leaders and northern liberals seemed to surprise and upset the president, who asserted that many influential blacks approved the segregation of federal employees, that it was "as much in the interest of the negroes as for any other reason," and that he sincerely believed the policy to be "in their interest."[30] Wilson revealed his sympathy for the southern position in another episode when he agreed to a private showing of *Birth of a Nation* in the White House in 1915. The film, directed by David Wark Griffith, was based on Thomas Dixon's novel *The Clansman* (1905), a violently racist treatment of the South during Reconstruction. Nevertheless, Wilson did not capitulate to the Radical extremists. Segregation of the executive departments was piecemeal and incomplete, and apparently no explicit, written orders to implement such a policy were issued by the White House. In a few cases, such as the reappointment of Robert H. Terrell as a municipal court judge in the District of Columbia, the president stood by black appointees in the face of vigorous opposition. Indeed, Wilson contributed to the triumph of the conservative racialist mentality, which insisted upon the inferiority of African Americans but sought to define the nature and extent of that inferiority and to accommodate society to it.[31]

Blacks were understandably disappointed and disillusioned by the Wilson administration's racial policies. A black editor wrote that his race had been given "a stone instead of a loaf of bread."[32] Black Democrats who had worked for Wilson's election were distraught. One of them wrote that "We are publicly and frequently charged with having sold the Race into slavery and told that we

29. Woodrow Wilson to Oswald Garrison Villard, August 21, 1913, in Villard Papers. See also Arthur S. Link, "The Negro as a Factor in the Campaign of 1912," *Journal of Negro History* 32 (January 1947): 81–99, and Link, *Wilson: The New Freedom*, pp. 243–45.

30. Woodrow Wilson to Oswald Garrison Villard, 31 July 1913, Wilson Papers. See also Kathleen Long Wolgemuth, "Woodrow Wilson's Appointment Policy and the Negro," *Journal of Southern History* 24 (November 1958): 457–71; Nancy J. Weiss, "The Negro and the New Freedom: Fighting Wilsonian Segregation," *Political Science Quarterly* 84 (March 1969): 61–79; and Joel Williamson, *The Crucible of Race: Black-White Relations in the American South Since Emancipation* (New York, 1984), pp. 364–95.

31. Link, *Wilson: The New Freedom*, pp. 246–54; Williamson, *The Crucible of Race*, pp. 6, 387–95.

32. New York *Amsterdam News*, 3 October 1913, quoted in Link, *Wilson: The New Freedom*, p. 248.

ought to be beaten to death with clubs and forever despised by colored people."[33] After spending several days in Washington in the summer of 1913, Booker T. Washington said that he had "never seen the colored people so discouraged and bitter as they are at the present time." Yet, as Joel Williamson reminds us, "To the Wilsonians, as to the rest of the white nation at large, race relations was a minor matter."[34]

White southerners generally approved the Wilson administration's approach to race relations, though some moderates had reservations about the racist demagoguery of more assertive congressmen from their section. While the matter did not provoke a strong grass-roots reaction from outside the South, it did bring criticism from the NAACP, northern liberals, and many journals. According to Arthur S. Link, humanitarians, social workers, clergymen, liberal editors, and progressive political leaders outside the South denounced the administration's segregation policy as "vicious and offensive," "small, mean, petty discrimination," and "cruel, unjust and contrary to the spirit and the institutions of this country."[35] Between 1913 and 1917, the historian Morton Sosna has observed, "the direct impact of race consciousness upon national politics stemmed largely from the reinvigorated influence of Southern Democrats in Washington."[36] This was revealed not only in the adoption of legislation that discriminated directly against blacks but in federal proposals that were indirectly discriminatory or that were influenced by racial considerations. These measures inevitably possessed sectional implications. Three significant examples during the Wilson years were federal-state cooperative extension work, immigration restriction, and woman suffrage.

The Smith-Lever Act of 1914, sponsored by Senator Hoke Smith of Georgia and Representative Asbury F. Lever of South Carolina, appropriated federal funds for agricultural extension work through the land grant colleges. The money was to be allocated on the basis of each state's proportion of the country's total rural population, a condition that greatly favored the South. Significantly, state legislatures were given the sole discretion in distributing the funds within their jurisdictions, a stipulation that did not augur well for black colleges in the South. Southern congressmen were enthusiastic in their support of the Smith-Lever bill. Smith and other southern leaders defeated a Republican effort to guarantee Negro colleges a fair share of the federal money, and they beat back an attempt to change the basis for the allocation of federal funds from rural population to agricultural production, a criterion that would have benefited northern and western areas. The southerners argued that any sectional disparity in farm production could be attributed to race.[37]

33. Peter J. Smith to Joseph P. Tumulty, 1 June 1913, Wilson Papers.

34. Booker T. Washington to Oswald Garrison Villard, 10 August 1913, in *The Booker T. Washington Papers*, vol. 12, ed. Louis R. Harlan and Raymond W. Smock (Urbana, Ill., 1982), p. 248 (first quotation); Williamson, *The Crucible of Race*, p. 392 (second quotation).

35. Quoted in Link, *Wilson: The New Freedom*, pp. 250–51.

36. Morton Sosna, "The South in the Saddle: Racial Policies During the Wilson Years," *Wisconsin Magazine of History* 54 (Autumn 1970): 30.

37. Sosna, "The South in the Saddle," pp. 41–45; Dewey W. Grantham, *Hoke Smith and the*

Racial considerations also entered into congressional action on immigration-restriction legislation. In February 1914 the House of Representatives approved a restriction bill providing for a literacy test, a measure introduced by John L. Burnett of Alabama. The Senate passed a similar measure in January 1915, but the bill was vetoed by President Wilson. Southern representatives and senators were staunch backers of the Burnett bill, making common cause with restriction advocates such as Henry Cabot Lodge of Massachusetts and rabidly anti-Oriental lawmakers from the West Coast. A number of southern senators voted for an amendment that would explicitly have excluded black immigrants. The amendment was adopted by the Senate but rejected by the House.[38] Earlier John Sharp Williams had expressed the views of many of his southern colleagues when he warned the secretary of state against the possibility of extending the right of naturalization to Japanese immigrants. "The moment the Japanese are naturalized they can become voters and the moment they become voters you have a political race issue upon the Pacific Slope equal in its intensity, or much greater rather in its intensity than the race issue of the South."[39]

A third legislative issue in which race played a significant part during the early Wilson years was woman suffrage. Having failed during the first decade of the twentieth century to make much progress through campaigns for state enfranchisement of women, the National American Woman Suffrage Association (NAWSA) decided to push for an amendment to the Constitution that would grant women the right to vote. Sensitive to southern traditions, NAWSA leaders argued that federal action would neither infringe upon state rights nor undermine white supremacy in the southern states. But the section's representatives in Washington were afraid that the amendment would enable black women to vote. Most of them were even more concerned over the specter of federal interference with state and local control of the election process. Although opposition to woman suffrage in the South reflected a broader social and cultural conservatism on the place of women in society, racial fears infused the southern rhetoric directed at the suffrage resolution. "If you submit to this amendment," Representative Robert L. Henry of Texas asserted, "the next request will be for a law to prohibit the States from passing 'Jim Crow' laws, separate-coach laws, separate schools, [and] separate churches. . . . The next demand will be to place a Federal ban on the States where the intermarriage of the white and black races is prohibited."[40]

These fears brought a sympathetic response from some nonsouthern congressmen. Westerners spoke of the "yellow peril" and wondered if the suffrage

Politics of the New South (Baton Rouge, La., 1958), pp. 259–64. Ironically, at times during the debate on the Smith-Lever bill northerners argued for state rights, while southerners defended federal action.

38. Sosna, "The South in the Saddle," pp. 39–41. See also Rowland T. Berthoff, "Southern Attitudes Toward Immigration, 1865–1914," *Journal of Southern History* 17 (August 1951): 328–60, and John Higham, *Strangers in the Land: Patterns of American Nativism, 1860–1925* (New Brunswick, N.J., 1955), pp. 191–93.

39. John Sharp Williams to William J. Bryan, 16 June 1914, Williams Papers.

40. Quoted in Sosna, "The South in the Saddle," p. 48.

amendment might become a precedent for federal intervention to permit the Japanese ownership of property in their states. Senator William E. Borah, an Idaho Republican, openly associated the woman suffrage amendment with race; he called the Fifteenth Amendment a mistake, since its intent had been nullified, and opposed the insertion of another "hypocritical clause" in the Constitution. When the vote came, in 1914 and 1915, the amendment received a majority but not the required two-thirds majority in both houses of Congress. Ninety of the 104 representatives from the ex-Confederate states voted against the resolution in the House, while only 3 senators from those states voted for it in the Senate. The president's refusal to endorse federal action was no doubt a factor of considerable importance in the way southerners voted.[41]

The shift from state to federal legislation on two other social ills—child labor and alcoholic beverages—was less affected by racial considerations. But both issues possessed sectional connotations. When industrial child labor began to attract national attention around the turn of the century, the resulting publicity tended to focus on the South. This was true because of the revelations of extensive child labor that came with the campaigns to secure state legislation, and also because of the competitive threat that some southern industries posed to northern manufacturers. New England textile owners and other northern manufacturers charged that the South's competitive advantage was in large part a result of its exploitation of child labor and the consequent depressed wages of adult workers. In any case, the southern states became the major target of the work undertaken by the National Child Labor Committee. The committee's investigations of conditions in southern industrial plants caused widespread resentment in the region and a feeling that the child labor reform movement was an "alien" force. Alexander J. McKelway, one of the reformers, later referred to the "sectional prejudice" that the NCLC's activities were "directed against the South or one of its industries."[42]

After its repeated failure to obtain more effective state legislation in the South, the National Child Labor Committee turned once more to Washington. Its decision to seek federal legislation several years after the demise of the ill-fated Beveridge bill was also prompted by the revelations in a nineteen-volume report released by the Bureau of Labor (1910–1913) and the Supreme Court's ruling in 1913 upholding the constitutionality of the Mann Act, which struck at the interstate inducement of women into prostitution. The NCLC vigorously supported a bill introduced in both houses of Congress early in 1914 by Representative A. Mitchell Palmer of Pennsylvania and Senator Robert L. Owen. The debate on the Palmer-Owen bill reflected a certain sectional division, with the southeastern states leading the opposition. In congressional hearings and other forums, southern textile manufacturers strongly criticized the proposed law. David Clark, editor of the *Southern Textile Bulletin*, took the lead in organiz-

41. *Ibid.*, pp. 45–49; Link, *Wilson: The New Freedom*, pp. 257–59; Aileen S. Kraditor, *The Ideas of the Woman Suffrage Movement, 1890–1920* (New York, 1965), pp. 163–218.

42. Quoted in Stephen B. Wood, *Constitutional Politics in the Progressive Era: Child Labor and the Law* (Chicago, 1968), p. 59. See also pp. 1–13.

ing the Executive Committee of Southern Cotton Manufacturers. Opponents of the measure denounced it as unconstitutional, as unnecessary in light of existing conditions in the South, and as a matter that could best be dealt with by state action. They reiterated the old contention that textile mill work by children over the age of twelve or thirteen was not harmful. They were especially critical of the eight-hour-day provision for children under sixteen, asserting that it would be disastrous for their operations. There were overtones of the southerners' longtime complaint that New England textile interests were trying to destroy their southern competitors through legislative enactments. Clark referred derisively to the NCLC as "the New England organization."[43]

A powerful bipartisan coalition worked for the child labor bill, and it was passed by the House of Representatives in February 1915. Thirty-five of the forty-five negative votes came from six southern states; only one opposing vote came from outside the South. Since the Senate failed to act on the bill in 1915, it was reintroduced early in 1916 by Senator Owen and Representative Edward Keating of Colorado. It passed both houses easily, with most of the opposing votes coming from the southeastern textile states. Thus, while there was a sectional configuration in the struggle over federal child labor legislation, it was not, strictly speaking, a North-South division but rather a conflict between the southeastern textile region and the rest of the country. A majority of the southern representatives and senators voted for the child labor bill, and it was endorsed by many newspapers and organizations in the South.

Southern support constituted the bedrock of the prohibition movement during the Progressive Era. In 1913 five of the nine dry states in the United States were located in the South, and a new prohibition surge in the section during the next two years brought four more states into the dry column. Though many southerners hesitated to abandon state rights in exchange for federal intervention in controlling the liquor traffic, the ineffectiveness of state action, in the South as elsewhere, persuaded more and more of them to join the movement for reform at the national level.

In 1913 the Anti-Saloon League of America and other prohibition groups decided to concentrate their energies on federal legislation. A beginning was made with the passage of the Webb-Kenyon Act, which made it illegal to transport alcoholic beverages from a wet state to a dry one. Congressmen from the South were, by and large, firm supporters of the Webb-Kenyon bill and of the ASL prohibition amendment to the U.S. Constitution, which was introduced in the two houses by Representative Richmond Pearson Hobson of Alabama and Senator Morris Sheppard of Texas. The Hobson resolution came to a vote in the House in December 1914, receiving a narrow majority but falling short of the two-thirds needed for adoption. About a fourth of the southern representatives voted against the measure, which was not voted on in the Senate during

43. For the discussion in this paragraph and the one that follows, see *ibid.*, pp. 25–78; Elizabeth H. Davidson, *Child Labor Legislation in the Southern Textile States* (Chapel Hill, N.C., 1939), pp. 250–62; William A. Link, *The Paradox of Southern Progressivism, 1880–1930* (Chapel Hill, N.C., 1992), pp. 304–11; Dewey W. Grantham, *Southern Progressivism: The Reconciliation of Progress and Tradition* (Knoxville, Tenn., 1983), p. 369; and Sarasohn, *The Party of Reform*, pp. 184–86.

the Sixty-third Congress. Hobson became a full-time campaigner for national prohibition in 1915. James Cannon of Virginia headed the Anti-Saloon League's legislative committee, and Secretary of the Navy Josephus Daniels and other southern members of the Wilson administration became zealous champions of the movement. The prohibitionists won scores of endorsements in the congressional races of 1916, and the impetus provided by the war enabled them to win congressional approval of the prohibition amendment in 1917. Southern congressmen voted overwhelmingly in favor of the amendment. In Congress as a whole the votes on the prohibition resolution in 1914 and 1917 demonstrated a bipartisan character. They also revealed a sectional aspect, in which northern Democrats, whose support was based on wet cities, were opposed by the ASL, the Republican party, and a large number of southern Democrats.[44]

There were two periods of strain in the South's relationship with the Wilson administration between 1913 and 1917: the crisis that enveloped the cotton market in the autumn of 1914 and the next several months and the struggle over neutrality and preparedness in 1915 and early 1916. The two episodes were not unrelated and both were filled with overtones of southern sectionalism. The beginning of the war in Europe disrupted the normal pattern of cotton exports, brought a sharp drop in the price of the staple, and created a panic throughout the cotton belt. Organizations like the Farmers' Union, chambers of commerce, and banking groups quickly moved into action, formulating such schemes as the "buy a bale of cotton" movement and demanding relief action by Congress and the Wilson administration. Southerners flooded their congressmen with demands for federal relief. An Alabamian wrote Senator John H. Bankhead: "The Southern people claim that the United States Government is now run by Southern men, the Republicans saying the South is in the saddle again, and the South is looking to you for relief."[45] Dixie congressmen, led by Senator Hoke Smith of Georgia, responded by pressing for large-scale government purchases of cotton and other federal aid.

President Wilson resisted what he regarded as "class" legislation and, much to the disappointment of southern lawmakers, managed to head off the more extreme relief proposals. "The town is beginning to fill up with men of the restless, meddling sort," Wilson wrote a friend in mid-August 1915. "Some of them are southern congressmen with wild schemes, preposterous and impossible

44. See Andrew Sinclair, *Era of Excess: A Social History of the Prohibition Movement* (New York, 1964), pp. 154–64; Link, *Wilson: The New Freedom*, pp. 259–60; and Richard L. Watson, Jr., "A Testing Time for Southern Congressional Leadership: The War Crisis of 1917–1918," *Journal of Southern History* 44 (February 1978): 7–8, 24–29. For developments in one southern state, see Lewis L. Gould, *Progressives and Prohibitionists: Texas Democrats in the Wilson Era* (Austin, Tex., 1973), pp. 58–184.

45. W. J. Renfroe to John H. Bankhead, 7 September 1914, in John H. Bankhead Papers, Alabama Department of Archives and History, Montgomery. See also Arthur S. Link, "The Cotton Crisis, the South, and Anglo-American Diplomacy, 1914–1915," in *Studies in Southern History*, ed. J. Carlyle Sitterson (Chapel Hill, N.C., 1957), pp. 122–38; Saloutos, *Farmer Movements in the South*, pp. 237–47; and Grantham, *Hoke Smith*, pp. 277–91.

schemes to valorize cotton and help the cotton planter out of the Reserve Banks or out of the national Treasury—out of anything, if only they can make themselves solid with their constituents and seem to be 'on the job.' "[46]

The administration did undertake some initiatives to ease the crisis, and the gloom in the cotton areas gradually disappeared as British purchases and an economic upturn at home caused the price of the staple to go up. But some southern congressmen continued to attack the British blockade and to criticize the administration's neutrality policies. The audacious demands of the region's cotton spokesmen led the Wilson administration and much of the country, including Republican congressmen, to regard the South as obsessed with cotton and dominated by wild-eyed radicals bent on the application of impractical Populist schemes. This perception may also say something about the vitality of sectional stereotypes early in the twentieth century.

The Wilson administration's neutrality policies between the beginning of the war in August 1914 and U.S. involvement in April 1917 were imperiled by divisions among the American people—divisions among ethnic groups, economic interests, and geographic sections as to the course the nation should take. In sectional terms, one scholar suggests, the struggle over American involvement divided the country into three regions: the industrial and commercial core of the Northeast and Great Lakes, whose Republican congressmen and a smaller majority of their Democratic counterparts supported an aggresssive foreign policy and military expansion that went well beyond Wilson's preparedness proposals; the Great Plains and mountain West, whose predominantly Republican delegations usually opposed preparedness legislation but were often divided by questions of party loyalty and their party's commitment to military expansion; and the southern periphery, whose opposition to preparedness measures was more intense and generally more consistent.[47]

Economic considerations played a part in shaping southern attitudes. According to Arthur S. Link, the cotton crisis of 1914–1915 "left deep scars upon the South and a residue of intense anti-British sentiment." The section's prevailing rural pacifism and resentment at British trade violations "made the South one of the chief centers of resistance to military and naval expansion and to strong diplomacy vis-à-vis Germany between 1915 and 1917."[48] As a Texas congressman declared in February 1917, for more than two years Great Britain "forbade us to trade with her enemies, dragged our commerce from the seas, and with pusillanimous perfidy kept us from trading with Germany and Austria, and, through her minister of munitions and international financial agent in this country, Pierpont Morgan, she killed the cotton market of the

46. Woodrow Wilson to Edith Bolling Galt, 13 August 1915, in *The Papers of Woodrow Wilson*, vol. 34, ed. Arthur S. Link et al., (Princeton, 1980), p. 180.

47. Richard Franklin Bensel, *Sectionalism and American Political Development, 1880–1980* (Madison, Wis., 1984), p. 115.

48. Link, "The Cotton Crisis, the South, and Anglo-American Diplomacy," p. 138. See also Edward W. Chester, *Sectionalism, Politics, and American Diplomacy* (Metuchen, N.J., 1975), pp. 169–70.

South, robbed the Southland of nearly $400,000,000, [and] bought our cotton on a dead market at 5 and 6 cents a pound."[49]

Wilson's decision late in 1915 to seek congressional passage of a comprehensive preparedness program set off a heated debate. The administration's proposals went against the grain of "a widely prevalent rural-progressive opposition to war and militarism" in the South and a suspicion, particularly in rural areas, that preparedness was "a scheme for the profit of munitions makers and financial interests."[50] "One of the ridiculous phases of this preparedness agitation," a Texas representative declared in May 1916, "is the attitude of the New Yorkers, Bostonians, and Philadelphians. They are all for preparedness; and what they mean by preparedness is what the Army and Navy bluntly ask, 'all they can get.' The money is poured out along the Atlantic seaboard."[51] Claude Kitchin, the Democratic majority leader in the House of Representatives, openly opposed the president's program: "I feel that it is big ammunition and war equipment interests that are trying to manufacture public sentiment into favoring a big naval and military propaganda and with [an] attempt to intimidate Congress in entering upon it." Kitchin wanted to prevent these interests from piling "millions of additional burdens upon the people."[52] This Bryanesque attitude was not uncommon in the South; it reflected an agrarian antipathy toward the industrial and financial dominance of the North, as well as a suspicion of centralized military power.[53]

The sectional pattern of the debate over preparedness in 1916 was revealed in several roll call votes in the House in which amendments calling for large increases in the army and in the naval construction program were defeated. The strongest opposition to these military expansion proposals came from the South and the Midwest.[54] That was not the case in the vote to table a resolution introduced by Jeff McLemore of Texas calling on the president to warn Americans against traveling on armed belligerent vessels. Thomas P. Gore of Oklahoma introduced a similar measure in the Senate. A substantial majority of southern representatives, influenced by party loyalty and Wilson's leadership, as well as by nationalist sentiment, helped table the resolution. In this vote the core delegations of the Northeast and the periphery congressmen of the South were aligned against the agrarian plains and the West.[55]

Despite the mini-rebellion during the cotton crisis precipitated by the outbreak of war in 1914 and strong misgivings among some southerners about the

49. Representative James H. Davis, quoted in Bensel, *Sectionalism and American Political Development*, p. 121.

50. Tindall, *The Emergence of the New South*, pp. 40–41. See Arthur S. Link, *Woodrow Wilson and the Progressive Era, 1910–1917* (New York, 1954), pp. 175–96, for an authoritative treatment of the preparedness debate.

51. Oscar Callaway, quoted in Bensel, *Sectionalism and American Political Development*, p. 106.

52. Claude Kitchin to Clyde H. Tavener, 3 August 1915, and to Warren Worth Bailey, 3 August 1915, in Claude Kitchin Papers, Southern Historical Collection, University of North Carolina.

53. Bensel, *Sectionalism and American Political Development*, pp. 106, 112.

54. *Ibid.*, pp. 123–28.

55. *Ibid.*, pp. 122–24; Link, *Woodrow Wilson and the Progressive Era*, pp. 211–14.

administration's preparedness program, a majority of the southern representatives and senators supported Woodrow Wilson's foreign and defense initiatives. They did so in part because of the powerful hold Wilson had on them and their constituents, and also out of party loyalty, but there were other factors as well. Most southerners were disposed from the beginning of the war to take the side of the Allies, evidence no doubt of the strong British heritage and the absence of other ethnic attachments in the region. Many southerners resented the German atrocities and use of submarine warfare. There was, moreover, a military tradition in the South, notwithstanding the fear of militarism and corporate war profiteering. A survey of southern businessmen in May 1916 showed an overwhelming majority of them believing that the public approved of preparedness.[56]

Secretary of the Navy Josephus Daniels, a North Carolina progressive and longtime follower of William Jennings Bryan, supported the administration's preparedness program, but some aspects of the military buildup gave him pause. His progressive background led him to oppose the way in which large industrial corporations, particularly armor plate firms and oil companies, were profiting from navy contracts. He did his best to prevent war preparations from bringing private enrichment, and with the approval of Congress and the president, he converted the various navy yards from repair facilities to genuine shipyards for new construction when private bids exceeded authorized costs. With congressional support from men like Claude A. Swanson and Benjamin R. Tillman, both southern members of the Senate Committee on Naval Affairs, Daniels helped create a new complex. "In a kind of regional alliance," one historian has written, "they led the way to building up federally owned industry based in Norfolk and Charleston."[57]

If the congressional opponents of national preparedness were defeated on the essential features of the Wilson administration's program, they were more successful in determining how the military expansion would be paid for. Representative Kitchin, chairman of the House Ways and Means Committee, wrote Bryan early in 1916 to express his belief that "when the New York people are thoroughly convinced that the income tax will have to pay for the increases in the army and navy . . . preparedness will not be so popular with them as it now is."[58] The administration wanted to finance the program with excise taxes and other regressive levies. But a group of Democratic insurgents, aided by Kitchin's control of the Ways and Means Committee and a wave of popular support, was victorious. While the Revenue Act of 1916 retained the sugar duty

56. Tindall, *The Emergence of the New South*, p. 40; Chester, *Sectionalism, Politics, and American Diplomacy*, pp. 171–74.

57. Richard L. Watson, Jr., *The Development of National Power: The United States, 1900–1919* (Washington, D.C., 1982), p. 189 (quotation); Henry C. Ferrell, Jr., "Regional Rivalries, Congress, and MIC: The Norfolk and Charleston Navy Yards, 1912–1920," in *War, Business, and American Society: Historical Perspectives on the Military–Industrial Complex*, ed. Benjamin Franklin Cooling (Port Washington, N.Y., 1977), pp. 59–72; Melvin I. Urofsky, "Josephus Daniels and the Armor Trust," *North Carolina Historical Review* 45 (July 1968): 237–63.

58. Claude Kitchin to William Jennings Bryan, 31 January 1916, Kitchin Papers.

and raised the basic income tax from 1 to 2 percent, as Secretary of the Treasury William G. McAdoo recommended, it increased the surtax to a maximum of 13 percent on incomes above $2 million and imposed a graduated estate tax, a special tax on munitions profits, and new levies on corporation capital and on surplus and individual profits. "The new income and inheritance taxes," George B. Tindall concludes, "constituted the most clearcut victory of the agrarian radicals in the entire Wilson era, a victory further consolidated and advanced after war came."[59] Another scholar describes the new tax plan as "a great victory for Southern and Western progressive reformers, and a great defeat for conservative forces, heavily based in the Northeast."[60] There were charges in the Northeast that the South and West had combined in a gigantic raid on northern wealth.

Wilson and his advisers were acutely aware of the uphill battle the president would face in his reelection campaign of 1916. That was one reason for Wilson's move to the left in 1916 and for his renewed effort on behalf of additional and in many cases more advanced progressive legislation. He wanted to magnify his appeal to independents and progressives. Southern congressmen backed the administration's new agenda, though with some dissent in the passage of the Keating-Owen Child Labor bill and the confirmation of the well-known liberal Louis D. Brandeis's appointment to the Supreme Court. They were enthusiastic in their support of a rural credits bill and a measure promising independence to the Philippine Islands. They voted, with relatively little opposition, in favor of workmen's compensation for federal employees, for the Adamson eight-hour day legislation for railroad workers, and for the creation of a tariff commission.[61] A northern visitor reported early in 1916 that "The South is every year finding out more clearly how great a help the Federal Government is to her life and progress. For the eradication of the hookworm, for support in her plans for developing hydro-electric power in the Appalachian system of mountains, for aid against the boll weevil and the citrus canker and the cattle tick, for the deepening of her river channels, for the farm demonstration of new methods and processes of cultivation, for aid to the home economics courses for farmers' wives, the South has come to look to the National Government."[62] The Flood Control Act of 1917 provided a concrete illustration of this point. The law placed the major responsibility for controlling the frequent floods on the lower Mississippi River in the hands of the federal government.[63]

Becoming more conscious of their nationalism during the Wilson years, southern spokesmen seemed to be more inclined to express concern about national problems and to deny that the South was "backward and sectional." As

59. Tindall, *The Emergence of the New South*, pp. 43–44 (quotation on p. 44).

60. Kennedy, *Over Here*, p. 16. See also Link, *Woodrow Wilson and the Progressive Era*, p. 195.

61. Tindall, *The Emergence of the New South*, pp. 14–17; Link, *Woodrow Wilson and the Progressive Era*, pp. 223–30; Abrams, "Woodrow Wilson and the Southern Congressmen," pp. 430–37.

62. Frederick M. Davenport, "The Pre-Nomination Campaign: The National South," *Outlook* 112 (February 16, 1916): 387.

63. Donald C. Swain, *Federal Conservation Policy, 1921–1933* (Berkeley, Calif., 1963), pp. 103–106.

the North Carolina editor Clarence Poe wrote in the fall of 1916, "If the test of a section is 'not where it stands, but how it is moving,' the South is unmistakably progressive, and no section of America is more broadly National or patriotic." Poe appealed "to the men and women of the North for a clearer and fairer understanding of the heart and the spirit of their brothers and sisters 'south of the line.' "[64] Earlier that year Frederick M. Davenport, a New York professor of law and politics, provided evidence to support Poe's claim in articles he wrote for *Outlook* on the basis of a tour of the South. Davenport found many indications in the various southern states that the Wilson administration had "very perceptibly increased and established a new sense of loyalty to the National Government." The South, he reported, "does not follow Bryan in this crisis, although many of the leaders of the South still regard him highly." The section "feels that during the last two or three years it has come back in leadership and influence towards its own." The writer discovered "much evidence of earnest, serious, and concrete thoughtfulness about the condition of the country and its lack of preparedness both for peace and for war."[65] Woodrow Wilson deserved much of the credit for this change in southern outlook. "In personality and principle," a Charlestonian wrote of the president in November 1916, "he does not reach me, but his performance is truly thrilling in artistry, and it is much to a poor despised Democrat to have the master politician of his time at sword's play. . . . Another thing is the satisfaction I get at the ingrowing rage of the Tories and Bourbons hereabouts, most of whom hate Woodrow and don't dare to say so beyond the tiled recesses of the Charleston Club."[66]

To be sure, echoes of the nation's old sectional animosity could still be heard. During the neutrality period, outbursts of northern antipathy were directed at Representative Kitchin and other agrarian radicals in Congress. Such views were to some extent a reflection of the struggle for power in Congress. Thus Kitchin wrote a southern colleague in November 1915, "I have had many letters from Northern Members saying that some complaints are made in their section that the South is getting all the Chairmanships, and some insisting that several of the vacancies should be given to Northern Democrats. . . ."[67] A sectional division within the Democratic party was evident as early as the election of 1916, when western Democrats played a key role in Wilson's narrow reelection. Of that election one historian writes: "To the old Democratic alliance of the South and the urban machines, years of party policy and planning had added western progressives, renegade Bull Moosers, organized labor, Jewish voters, and liberal intellectuals in a proto–New Deal coalition."[68] Yet western-

64. Clarence Poe, "The South: Backward and Sectional or Progressive and National?" *Outlook* 114 (October 11, 1916): 328–31.

65. Davenport, "The Pre-Nomination Campaign: The National South," pp. 386–88. See also Davenport, "The Pre-Nomination Campaign: The Southern Renaissance," *Outlook* 112 (February 23, 1916): 427–30.

66. Thomas R. Waring to W. W. Ball, 11 November 1916, William Watts Ball Papers, Duke University Library.

67. Claude Kitchin to E. S. Candler, Jr., 1 November 1915, Kitchin Papers.

68. Sarasohn, *The Party of Reform*, p. 238. A somewhat different emphasis is provided in Link, *Woodrow Wilson and the Progressive Era*, p. 250: "It was, indeed, the South and West united again in

ers resented the proprietary attitude of party leaders in the East and South toward the president, and many of them felt that their hard work and personal sacrifices during the campaign had been taken for granted. These feelings were revived early in 1917 when Thomas S. Martin of Virginia was chosen over Thomas J. Walsh of Montana as the new Democratic majority leader in the Senate. Meanwhile, certain legislative proposals tended to divide Democrats along sectional lines. National prohibition, for example, was an issue that came to be identified with southern congressmen. Opposition to woman suffrage—a somewhat less divisive party issue—was also associated with southern lawmakers. To northern Democrats from large cities, prohibition symbolized the domination of the congressional hierarchy by southerners. One Boston Democrat was quoted as saying in 1917, "I am unalterably opposed to the Southern Democrats remaining in the saddle throughout the coming Congress."[69]

Southern support of the Wilson administration was intensified after the United States entered the war in 1917. Only one southern senator—James K. Vardaman—and a handful of the section's representatives voted against the war resolution. There was some resistance to the draft in the region—violent opposition on occasion in the Appalachian South, Oklahoma, Texas, and the upland areas of Alabama, Mississippi, and Arkansas—and "slackers" were rounded up in various southern cities. A few influential spokesmen such as Tom Watson of Georgia and Coleman L. Blease of South Carolina continued their earlier criticism of administration policies. But the dominant theme throughout the South was patriotic backing of the war effort. Pleasant A. Stovall, U.S. minister to Switzerland, made "patriotic appeals" in several Georgia and Florida cities during a visit home in the fall of 1917. "Any mention of your war policies," he wrote the president, "were applauded with enthusiasm, and I have yet to find a single town or city where the people were not ready and willing for any call or any sacrifice."[70]

When President Wilson addressed the Confederate Veterans' reunion in 1917, he reminded the old soldiers that the South was now "part of a nation united, powerful, great in spirit and in purpose," a nation that could be "an instrument in the hands of God to see that liberty is made secure for mankind."[71] Southern churches committed themselves to Wilson's definition of the war as a holy crusade. Sectionalism seemed to recede before the cry for unity, and the symbol of nationalism was taken up easily by southern leaders. "I thank

---

an emphatic mandate for progressivism and peace." See also Watson, *The Development of National Power*, pp. 205–209.

69. Quoted in Watson, "A Testing Time for Southern Congressional Leadership," p. 8.

70. Pleasant Alexander Stovall to Woodrow Wilson, 7 December 1917, in *The Papers of Woodrow Wilson*, vol. 45, ed. Arthur S. Link et al. (Princeton, 1984), p. 236. See also John Whiteclay Chambers II, *To Raise an Army: The Draft Comes to Modern America* (New York, 1987), pp. 205–37; Robert W. Dubay, "The Opposition to Selective Service, 1916–1918," *Southern Quarterly* 7 (April 1969): 301–22; and Judith Sealander, "Violent Group Draft Resistance in the Appalachian South During World War I," *Appalachian Notes* 7 (1979): 1–12.

71. Quoted in Charles Reagan Wilson, *Baptized in Blood: The Religion of the Lost Cause, 1865–1920* (Athens, Ga., 1980), pp. 179–80. For Wilson's remarks on this occasion, see Link et al., eds., *The Papers of Woodrow Wilson*, vol. 42 (Princeton, 1983), pp. 451–53.

God that one flag now floats over an indissoluble Union of indestructable [*sic*] States," Representative Robert L. Doughton of North Carolina declared to a northern audience on July 4, 1918, and that "the grandsons of the men who wore the blue and the grandsons of the men who wore the gray, are now marching with locked shields and martial step to the mingled strains of Dixie and the Star Spangled Banner."[72] The war spirit, Tindall suggests, nourished "the idea of a peculiarly pure Americanism in the South, with overtones of Anglo-Saxon racism and anti-radicalism, [and it] became an established article of the regional faith."[73]

Despite some quibbling and uneasiness over federal controls and the determined opposition of a handful of southern congressmen such as Senators Vardaman and Gore, most of the section's senators and representatives stood with Wilson on all of the major war measures. One of the recalcitrant congressmen from the South, Senator Thomas W. Hardwick of Georgia, explained his apprehensions early in 1918: "Frankly I am deeply alarmed at the tendency to centralize this government, to enthrone an autocrat, to abandon, one by one, the great fundamentals that underlie and protect our liberties—The form and substance of our government is being subverted, daily, *hourly*—and so many of the people seem not to realize it, or, worse, not to care."[74] But an overwhelming majority of southerners supported the president, even though the war legislation increased the functions and powers of the federal government and thus tended to undermine state rights principles. In the case of revenue policy, Claude Kitchin and like-minded agrarian progressives succeeded in forcing the acceptance of additional taxes on great wealth and war profits. These changes were embodied in the revenue acts of 1917 and 1918, which reduced personal exemptions and raised surtaxes to extremely high levels. For the most part, however, those who persisted in opposing the administration's war policies found themselves denounced in the southern press and confronted with grassroots petitions demanding that they either work with the administration or resign. Most southern congressional leaders, entrenched in powerful committee positions, provided indispensable legislative assistance to the enactment of the Wilsonian wartime program.[75]

The wartime patriotism of southerners and their willingness to adjust to the changes that came with American involvement were encouraged by the expansion of the region's economy. Agricultural prices rose sharply during the war, business flourished, and wages increased substantially. Army training camps, naval installations, shipyards, and new industries for the production of war ma-

---

72. Unpublished address, delivered at Trenton, N.J., 4 July 1918, Robert L. Doughton Papers, Southern Historical Collection, University of North Carolina.

73. Tindall, *The Emergence of the New South*, p. 64.

74. Thomas W. Hardwick to Mrs. W. H. Felton, 12 January 1918, Rebecca Latimer Felton Papers, University of Georgia Library.

75. Tindall, *The Emergence of the New South*, pp. 48–52; Grantham, *Southern Progressivism*, pp. 386–90; I. A. Newby, "States' Rights and Southern Congressmen during World War I," *Phylon* 24 (Spring 1963): 34–50; Watson, "A Testing Time for Southern Congressional Leadership," pp. 3–40; Richard L. Watson, Jr., "Principle, Party, and Constituency: The North Carolina Congressional Delegation, 1917–1919," *North Carolina Historical Review* 56 (July 1979): 298–323.

terials gave impetus to the South's economic development, as did the revival of old industries like cotton textiles, lumbering, and coal mining. Southerners had never known such exhilarating prosperity. Writing early in 1918, an Atlanta banker noted that, thanks to cotton bringing thirty cents a pound, "the South is coming into her own. The great borrowing section is a borrower no longer, but is beginning to lend. At the very time when the East is being drained of its liquid capital in order to provide the sinews of the war. . . ."[76]

Preoccupation with the war effort was evident in virtually every aspect of southern life. State and local leaders, in and out of government, set about implementing the mobilization measures. Numerous war-related agencies, emanating from federal bodies in Washington, devoted themselves to the endless tasks of organizing and coordinating the war effort on the home front. Thus the state and local councils of defense carried out an energetic campaign of patriotic education, food conservation, health protection, persecution of "slackers" and "radicals," and public support of labor recruitment, bond drives, and so on. The councils of defense, middle class in outlook and under business leadership, manifested a keen interest in creating greater order and stability in society. They expressed in large measure the prewar progressive faith in the value of efficiency and social control. Even the social agencies tried to do their part in mobilizing people and materials for the cause. The war's demands threw a revealing light on many of the social evils and inadequacies of the South. The national emergency brought more social workers—especially women—into southern communities, contributed to the professionalization of social workers in the section, and made them more acceptable to other southerners. It promoted the coordination and federated financing of social services and made the standards and procedures of social work in other parts of the country increasingly relevant to the amelioration of southern ills.[77]

Yet there were limits to the southerners' wartime fervor. It was soon clear that national mobilization threatened the South's low-cost wage structure, which had long been viewed as a regional advantage. According to a careful study of the mobilization process, southerners, in their efforts to control the migration of black labor and in their attempts to use the Department of Labor to achieve this objective, "consistently placed regional interests before national interests."[78] Sectional complaints could still be heard in the North and the South.

76. William Hurd Hillyer, "The South on Easy Street," *Independent* 93 (February 23, 1918): 320. See also Tindall, *The Emergence of the New South*, pp. 53–61, and Watson, *The Development of National Power*, pp. 219–316.

77. For this paragraph and the one that follows, see Grantham, *Southern Progressivism*, pp. 390–98, and Tindall, *The Emergence of the New South*, pp. 48–51, 61, 64. Additional information on wartime mobilization in region and nation can be found in Sarah McCulloh Lemmon, *North Carolina's Role in the First World War* (Raleigh, 1966); Kennedy, *Over Here*, pp. 93–190; Robert H. Ferrell, *Woodrow Wilson and World War I, 1917–1921* (New York, 1985), pp. 84–117; H. C. Peterson and Gilbert C. Fite, *Opponents of War, 1917–1918* (Madison, Wis., 1957); William J. Breen, "Black Women and the Great War: Mobilization and Reform in the South," *Journal of Southern History* 44 (August 1978): 421–40; and Breen, "Southern Women in the War: The North Carolina Woman's Committee, 1917–1919," *North Carolina Historical Review* 55 (July 1978): 251–83.

78. William J. Breen, "Sectional Influences on National Policy: The South, the Labor Department, and the Wartime Labor Mobilization, 1917–1918," in *The South Is Another Land: Essays on the*

Perhaps the primary focus of such criticism was Congress and the character of its southern leadership. After a close study of the wartime Congress, Richard L. Watson, Jr., concluded that sectionalism was "chronically not far from the surface" of debate in the House and Senate, sometimes in the form of good-natured gibes and sometimes in language that was blatantly accusatory. For instance, the decision to locate the sixteen camp sites of the National Army in the South and to train the drafted men there brought a hue and cry from northern politicians, who viewed it as a matter of pork-barrel and sectional discrimination.[79] In 1918 the *New York World*, a Democratic newspaper, predicted that, with southernism and particularly "Kitchinism" as an issue, there would never again be a Democratic Congress until "the Northern States have some reasonable assurance that such bodies will not be controlled by vengeful and parochial politicians from the South. . . ."[80]

Sectional ill will was a significant factor in the midterm elections of 1918, when many farmers in the western grain states deserted the Democrats. Reflecting on his party's congressional losses, a Democratic worker familiar with the western farm belt identified one of the problems: "The failure either to tax cotton or fix a price on it while limiting the price of the farmer's wheat and making him pay war prices on everything he had to buy, permitted the enemy to successfully raise the sectional issue, reviving many of the old Civil War prejudices, thereby losing practically all the members in the granger states and other country districts." This observer noted two other sources of resentment against southerners in Congress: an impression "that the north was being unduly taxed for the benefit of the south" and "the great body of southern members insisting on choking down the throats of unwilling communities national prohibition."[81]

Democratic reverses in the congressional elections of 1918 and after were the result of broader and more fundamental considerations than dissatisfaction with southern influence in Washington. Yet criticism of the South mounted during the postwar years, and in a sense the region seemed to symbolize the sad state of the Wilson administration following the president's devastating stroke in October 1919. Wilson himself had earlier expressed doubt that the Democratic party could be used as "an instrument" in postwar reformism, largely because of "the reactionary element in the South."[82] Conservative leaders pointed to "Southern reactionaries" as one reason for the administration's failure to establish a strong conservationist policy.[83] Other contemporaries cited the increase

Twentieth-Century South, ed. Bruce Clayton and John A. Salmond (New York, 1987), pp. 69–83 (quotation on p. 80).

79. Watson, "A Testing Time for Southern Congressional Leadership," pp. 36–38; Seward W. Livermore, *Politics Is Adjourned: Woodrow Wilson and the War Congress, 1916–1918* (Middletown, Conn., 1966), pp. 46–47.

80. Quoted in Watson, "A Testing Time for Southern Congressional Leadership," p. 37.

81. J. K. McGuire to Charles R. Crisp, 12 November 1918, Kitchin Papers. For the elections of 1918, see Livermore, *Politics Is Adjourned*, pp. 169–205.

82. Edward M. House diary, 24 February 1918, in *The Papers of Woodrow Wilson*, vol. 46, ed. Link et al. (Princeton, 1984), p. 436.

83. J. Leonard Bates, *The Origins of Teapot Dome: Progressives, Parties, and Petroleum, 1909–1921* (Urbana, Ill., 1963), p. 211.

in racial violence in the southern states as evidence of the section's backwardness.

Southern distinctiveness was apparent in several reform movements that came to fruition during the war period. One of these was the campaign for woman suffrage. A majority of the southern congressmen opposed the so-called Susan B. Anthony Amendment to the Constitution, despite President Wilson's endorsement of it and mounting support for the amendment as a result of women's war work. Though the House of Representatives approved the amendment in January 1918, 90 of the 101 Democratic votes against the measure came from the South. When the Senate narrowly rejected the amendment in October, only seven senators from the former Confederate states voted in the affirmative. Both houses approved the amendment by the necessary two-thirds majority in 1919, with stubborn resistance from most of the southern delegations. Only five southern states ratified the Nineteenth Amendment—Arkansas, Kentucky, Oklahoma, Tennessee, and Texas. Southern legislators, like the section's congressmen, tended to regard the proposal as a radical scheme that would subvert traditional cultural patterns, jeopardize state rights, and open the gates to federal intervention in race relations. Local opposition in the South was formidable. Nevertheless, suffrage for women had become a significant issue in southern politics. And when the general assembly of Tennessee in August 1920 became the thirty-sixth state to ratify the Nineteenth Amendment, most southern suffragists probably looked with satisfaction on the culmination of a process of nationalization in which they had been willing participants.[84]

Another reform movement, national prohibition, owed a great deal to southern congressmen, legislators, organizations, and public opinion. Although prohibition had become an accepted Democratic principle in most southern states well before the United States entered the war, some of the section's prohibitionists considered federal intervention a mistake, a violation of state rights and an infringement upon personal liberties and property rights. But most of these antisaloon people were advocates of rigorous state regulation, and for the most part the local optionists of earlier years shifted to the support of statewide prohibition as the strength of the national movement increased. The identification of prohibition with patriotism and the war effort proved to be a powerful weapon in the continuing crusade against alcohol in the South. Southern congressmen voted overwhelmingly in favor of the Eighteenth Amendment. Mississippi was the first state to ratify it, and all thirteen of the southern states approved it in 1918 and early 1919.[85]

One of the areas of war-spawned change that seemed most portentous to southerners was that of race relations. The mass movement of blacks out of the section during this period disturbed white southerners, while the upsurge of lynchings in 1918 and 1919, the widespread rumors of black uprisings after the

84. Grantham, *Southern Progressivism*, pp. 402–406; Link, *The Paradox of Southern Progressivism*, pp. 195–99, 296–304; Marjorie Spruill Wheeler, New Women of the *New South: The Leaders of the Woman Suffrage Movement in the Southern States* (New York, 1993), pp. 161–84.

85. Grantham, *Southern Progressivism*, pp. 401–402.

armistice, reports of African-American participation in organized labor activities, and the wave of race riots in 1919, several of them in northern cities, heightened the uneasiness in the white mind. A subtle alteration was discernible in the bearing and outlook of many black southerners, who had begun to demonstrate a new assertiveness and independence. In the postwar period evidence of the "New Negro" could be found even in Mississippi, with the appearance of the state's first NAACP branch, the revival of the state Federation of Women's Clubs, and the efforts of race uplift groups such as the Committee of One Hundred. The riots of 1919, the new militancy among blacks, and the hostile reaction of many whites galvanized southern progressives into action. In Nashville and several other cities, law and order leagues were formed in 1918 and 1919. But the most notable step was the organization in Atlanta in April 1919 of the Commission on Interracial Cooperation. Its distinguishing feature was its interracial contact among community leaders throughout the South.[86]

None of the changes associated with the war was more significant in the evolution of North-South relations than the exodus of almost half a million blacks out of the southern states. In the first place, as Carole Marks observes, "lines of communication between North and South had to be established to heighten awareness of the opportunities available in the North."[87] For the migrants themselves the experience was momentous and memorable, representing for many of them a kind of second emancipation. A third important consequence of the Great Migration was the effect it had in helping to break down the isola-

THE GREAT SOUTHERN EXODUS: NET MIGRATION, 1910–1960 (IN THOUSANDS)

	Whites	Blacks	Totals
1910s	−559.9	−482.3	−1,042.2
1920s	−764.4	−824.7	−1,589.1
1930s	−689.5	−458.0	−1,147.5
1940s	−1,126.9	−1,345.4	−2,472.3
1950s	−1,453.0	−1,362.9	−2,815.9
Totals	−4,593.7	−4,473.3	−9,067.0

NOTE: The South includes the ex-Confederate states except for Florida, plus Kentucky, Oklahoma, and West Virginia. Florida is excluded because its heavy white in-migration in the twentieth century would skew the statistical portrait of the region.
SOURCE: Adapted from Jack Temple Kirby, *Rural Worlds Lost: The American South, 1920–1960* (Baton Rouge: Louisiana State University Press, 1987), p. 320.

86. Edward Flud Burrows, "The Commission on Interracial Cooperation, 1919–1944: A Case Study in the History of the Interracial Movement in the South" (Ph.D. dissertation, University of Wisconsin, 1954), pp. 45–240; Jacquelyn Dowd Hall, *Revolt Against Chivalry: Jessie Daniel Ames and the Women's Campaign Against Lynching* (New York, 1979), pp. 59–106; Neil R. McMillen, *Dark Journey: Black Mississippians in the Age of Jim Crow* (Urbana, Ill., 1989), pp. 302–309; Arthur I. Waskow, *From Race Riot to Sit-In, 1919 and the 1960's: A Study in the Connections Between Conflict and Violence* (Garden City, N.Y., 1966), pp. 1–218.

87. Carole Marks, *Farewell—We're Good and Gone: The Great Black Migration* (Bloomington, Ind., 1989), p. 16.

tion of the southern labor market and eventually in contributing to the restructuring of the region's agricultural economy. Finally, this first great black exodus from the South brought a different kind of regional interaction and laid the basis for the phenomenon sometimes called "the South within the North," encapsulating the problems of the modern urban ghetto and creating new sources of North-South conflict.[88]

Perhaps it was fitting that the South should have become so strongly identified with Woodrow Wilson. The section's attitudes toward its famous native son reflected a mixture of pride, idealism, and self-interest. This sentiment was also an expression of southern sectionalism. In Wilson's ill-fated fight for ratification of the League of Nations, most of the southern senators vigorously defended his handiwork. Many of the state legislatures in the South adopted resolutions favoring the League, and a poll of editors in April 1919 revealed overwhelming southern support for Wilson's position. Commenting on North Carolina opinion, one historian writes: "From the speeches and statements of high Democratic officials down to ordinary citizens letters to newspapers, praise of Wilson as virtually a world savior was a recurring theme."[89] In the final vote on the treaty, in March 1920, twenty of the twenty-three senators who remained loyal to Wilson were from the South; only four of the twenty-one "disloyal" Democrats on that vote came from the ex-Confederate states.[90] One of the southern legacies of this "lost cause" was the idealization of Woodrow Wilson and a latent internationalism that reasserted itself a generation later.

The South experienced significant change during the era of Woodrow Wilson. Wilson's leadership of the Democratic party and of a national reform program went a considerable distance in nationalizing southern politics. It broadened the outlook of southern congressmen and gave them an opportunity to assume national responsibilities. Wilson lifted the horizons of the southern people and left them a heritage of reform politics and idealism in national and international affairs. At the same time, the configuration of sectional and national reform endeavors stimulated rather than diminished progressivism at the state and local levels, both in politics and government and in the work of private organizations and voluntary agencies. The war, in its turn, gave southern politi-

88. For the black migration of this period, see Jacqueline Jones, *The Dispossessed: America's Underclasses from the Civil War to the Present* (New York, 1992), pp. 146–47, 206–208; Marks, *Farewell—We're Good and Gone,* pp. 80–99, 110–51; Nancy J. Weiss, *The National Urban League, 1910–1940* (New York, 1974), pp. 93–128; Florette Henri, *Black Migration: Movement North, 1900–1920* (Garden City, N.Y., 1975), pp. 49–131; and James R. Grossman, *Land of Hope: Chicago, Black Southerners, and the Great Migration* (Chicago, 1989), pp. 13–119.

89. Ralph B. Levering, "Political Culture and Public Opinion: The League of Nations Controversy in New Jersey and North Carolina," in *The Wilson Era: Essays in Honor of Arthur S. Link,* ed. John Milton Cooper, Jr., and Charles E. Neu (Arlington Heights, Ill., 1991), pp. 159–97 (quotation on p. 166).

90. Tindall, *The Emergence of the New South,* p. 68; Chester, *Sectionalism, Politics, and American Diplomacy,* pp. 179–80, 183; Thomas A. Bailey, *Woodrow Wilson and the Great Betrayal* (New York, 1945), p. 272; Dewey W. Grantham, "The Southern Senators and the League of Nations, 1918–1920," *North Carolina Historical Review* 26 (April 1949): 187–205.

cians new opportunities for national leadership, brought a welcome season of economic prosperity to millions of southerners, and involved them in a great American cause. Yet neither Wilson's leadership nor the war seriously challenged the South's traditional sectional interests or seriously weakened intersectional suspicions and conflicts.

CHAPTER 4

Politics and Cultural Conflict

In the 1920s the Democrats were returned to their accustomed position as the nation's minority party. Although southern authority in Washington was diminished somewhat, southerners continued to dominate the Democratic party in Congress and to comprise a significant legislative element in dealing with national issues. The South was still the mainstay of the Democratic party in national elections, although as time passed the party gained strength in other regions, particularly the Northeast. This was reflected in a deepening conflict within the party along sectional lines, a conflict that involved cultural differences as well as economic and political objectives. While in political terms the South was hardly more than a passing problem or a long-range prospect for electoral gain, the region became the focus in the postwar decade of mounting northern criticism. In some ways this period was marked by notable change and declining provincialism below the Potomac; it witnessed the triumph of the "Atlanta spirit" and the emergence of an era of commercial and industrial expansion, urban boosterism, and growth psychology. But the opposition to social and cultural change remained strong.

The sweeping Republican victory in the election of 1920 weakened the ranks of northern Democrats in Congress, both in terms of their interparty significance and their role among Democratic congressmen. In the Sixty-seventh Congress (1921–1923), Republicans outnumbered Democrats 303 to 131 in the House of Representatives and 59 to 37 in the Senate. Southerners dominated the Democratic membership, with margins of 110 to 21 nonsouthern Democrats in the House and 24 to 13 in the Senate.[1] Democrats outside the South made significant gains in the congressional elections of 1922, although the Republicans retained control of both houses of Congress. In the Sixty-eighth Congress (1923–1925), southern Democrats had a numerical advantage of 116

---

1. The Sixty-seventh Congress contained thirteen Republican House members and two Republican senators from the thirteen southern states.

to 89 and 24 to 19 over their Democratic colleagues from other regions in the two houses. Southern congressional leaders held the major party posts and the ranking minority positions on most of the important committees. In the House of Representatives as the 1920s began, Finis J. Garrett of Tennessee was minority leader, John Nance Garner of Texas was the ranking member of the Ways and Means Committee, and William Oldfield of Arkansas was serving as party whip. In the upper house such veteran legislators as Furnifold M. Simmons, Duncan U. Fletcher, Joseph T. Robinson, Carter Glass, and Oscar W. Underwood were established in powerful positions.

In general, southern leadership in Congress during the 1920s was cautious and conservative. The agrarian radicalism associated with William Jennings Bryan was muted in the region's congressional ranks, and the outlook of the southern leaders in Washington seemed more responsive to the rising industrial and urban spirit of the postwar South. The good times of the new era encouraged this outlook, despite a series of agricultural crises and the straitened condition of the cotton textile industry. The Southern Tariff Association, an energetic new pressure group, met with some success in its effort to win converts to the doctrine of tariff protection. While a majority of southern congressmen opposed the high rates in the Fordney-McCumber Tariff Act of 1922, there was a discernible increase in the region's backing of protectionism.[2] Conservative northern Democrats looked to southerners for support, particularly in dealing with troublesome economic issues.

Even so, southern sectionalism had lost little of its vitality. This was evident in the determined opposition of the South's congressmen to an anti-lynching bill introduced by Representative Leonidas C. Dyer, a Republican from Missouri. Dyer was influenced by a new wave of lynchings, during the years 1917–1919, and by the race riots of 1919 in various parts of the country. His bill was backed by the National Association for the Advancement of Colored People and other groups. The measure passed the House of Representatives in 1922 but was defeated by a southern filibuster in the Senate. Before the proposal was voted on in the upper house, one southern observer asserted that "If the Republican Senators should force the bill through and the President sign it, they could not elect a Republican even to the office of 'dog-pelter' in the South for ten years to come."[3] White southerners viewed the measure as a cynical GOP maneuver to win black votes, and they accused Republican leaders of moral and political hypocrisy. They did not overlook the opportunity to identify northern failures in race relations such as the Chicago race riot of 1919. In the House passage of the bill, the division followed party lines; only eight northern and border state Democrats voted for the proposed law. Republican leaders abandoned the struggle at the end of 1922.[4] James Weldon Johnson of the NAACP

2. Charles M. Dollar, "The South and the Fordney-McCumber Tariff of 1922: A Study in Regional Politics," *Journal of Southern History* 39 (February 1973): 45–66; George Brown Tindall, *The Emergence of the New South, 1913–1945* (Baton Rouge, La., 1967), pp. 135–37.

3. J. E. McCulloch to Charles H. Brough, 4 February 1922, in Charles H. Brough Papers, University of Arkansas Library.

4. George C. Rable, "The South and the Politics of Antilynching Legislation, 1920–1940,"

later expressed the opinion that the controversy over the bill had served "to awaken the people of the Southern states to the necessity of taking steps themselves to wipe out the crime. . . ."[5]

A more complex manifestation of sectionalism in the 1920s grew out of the differences between the nation's economically developed northeastern core and the agrarian periphery. In much of the hinterland, the conflict over American neutrality and preparedness left a heritage of resentment against the industrial and commercial interests of the Northeast. After the war a sectional division was revealed in the struggle to liquidate such wartime agencies as the U.S. Shipping Board, a policy generally endorsed by the "free enterprise" Northeast. The agricultural recession of 1920–1921 exacerbated these sectional feelings, as did agriculture's worsening position in the national economy and the adverse effects of the changing economic order abroad.[6] Southern congressmen furnished substantial support to the relief program sponsored by the farm bloc early in the 1920s. Led by midwestern and western Republicans, this group of reform-minded congressmen pushed a series of remedial measures through the two houses: regulation of stockyards, meat-packing firms, and trading in grain futures; encouragement of cooperative marketing; a new type of federally guaranteed farm credit; a federal highway bill; and a three-year extension of the War Finance Corporation. Although congressmen from the southern states provided essential support to the farm bloc, they did not constitute a solid contingent in favor of its reform agenda, in part, perhaps, because some of the relief measures such as the tariff and business regulation seemed to offer only limited assistance to southern farmers. One historian concluded that only eight southern senators were involved in an "effective southern wing" of the farm bloc in the upper house.[7]

While the depressed agricultural prices improved in 1922, the fundamental problems of mounting costs and overproduction persisted. The search for a solution eventually led to the McNary-Haugen bill, a measure calling for federal action and the establishment of a two-price system for farm commodities as a means of raising domestic farm prices without sacrificing export markets for American crops. Southern leaders were inclined to oppose the bill, and most of them joined with eastern Republicans to defeat the proposal when it first reached the floor of the House in the summer of 1924. Many southerners disliked the tariff features of the bill, were suspicious of the "equalization fee" to be

Journal of Southern History 51 (May 1985): 203–208; Robert L. Zangrando, *The NAACP Crusade Against Lynching, 1909–1950* (Philadelphia, 1980), pp. 51–71.

5. Tindall, *The Emergence of the New South*, pp. 172–74 (quotation on p. 174); Dean Pope, "The Senator From Tennessee," *West Tennessee Historical Society Papers* 22 (1968): 120.

6. Richard Franklin Bensel, *Sectionalism and American Political Development, 1880–1980* (Madison, Wis., 1984), pp. 128–30.

7. Charles Dollar, "Southern Senators and the Senate Farm Bloc, 1921–1925" (M.A. thesis, University of Kentucky, 1963). See also Philip A. Grant, Jr., "Southern Congressmen and Agriculture, 1921–1932," *Agricultural History* 53 (January 1979): 338–51; Gilbert C. Fite, *Cotton Fields No More: Southern Agriculture, 1865–1980* (Lexington, Ky., 1984), pp. 91–119; and James H. Shideler, *Farm Crisis, 1919–1923* (Berkeley, Calif., 1957), pp. 95–117, 152–88.

assessed all producers, doubted that the scheme would prove beneficial to cotton growers because of their great dependence on exports, and were more interested in federal subsidies for the development of cooperative marketing. Congressmen from the South were also influenced by the fact that cotton prices were relatively good at that time.[8]

Record cotton crops in 1925 and 1926, with a resulting drop in prices, made the McNary-Haugen bill more attractive in the South. After suffering a second defeat in the House of Representatives in 1926, the sponsors of the legislation revised it, making cotton one of the basic commodities to be affected and changing certain other features in a way that appealed to cotton growers. Congress passed the measure in 1927 and again in 1928, with strong southern backing both times. On the other hand, northeastern congressmen, predominantly Republican and conservative, and fearful of inflation, voted in large numbers against the bill. In the end, McNary-Haugen never became law, falling to the vetoes of President Calvin Coolidge. After considering the sectional dimensions of congressional debate on the farm legislation of this period, one scholar concludes that "the growing cooperation between the plains, mountains, and southern periphery regions during the 1920s provided the foundation for passage of the Agricultural Adjustment Act and the creation of the Tennessee Valley Authority."[9]

In contrast to the troubled farm economy, the southern urban scene in the 1920s was dynamic and prosperous. The region made notable gains in urbanization and industrialization. The percentage of its urban population increased from 25.4 in 1920 to 32.1 in 1930, and most of its major cities grew rapidly during the decade—Nashville by 30 percent, Atlanta by 34.8 percent, Birmingham by 45.2 percent, and Memphis by 55.9 percent. While urban residence tended to standardize life throughout the nation, southern cities were smaller than their northern counterparts, more spread out, less ethnically diverse, and less dependent on manufacturing. Economic opportunities were accompanied by overcrowding, housing shortages, inadequate public services, immorality, and new threats to traditional values. "Southern cities," Blaine A. Brownell observes, "were often characterized in this period by violence, extreme conservatism on social and racial issues, religious frenzy, and moral absolutism." Yet urban consciousness spread through the region, and the cities and larger towns harbored an expanding middle class of businessmen, professionals, and white-collar employees. Urban business and civic leaders—the "commercial-civic elite"—emerged as a powerful and innovative element in making economic decisions and influencing public policy. Regional "progress" was increasingly identified with this urban South. "Progress," a noted historian has written, now appeared in "a subtly different context. It was more closely associated with the urban middle class, with chambers of commerce and Rotary Clubs. It carried the meaning of efficiency and development rather than of reform."[10]

8. Bensel, *Sectionalism and American Political Development*, pp. 141–46; Tindall, *The Emergence of the New South*, pp. 137–42.

9. Bensel, *Sectionalism and American Political Development*, p. 105.

10. Blaine A. Brownell, "The Urban South Comes of Age, 1900–1940," in *The City in Southern*

A new age of industrial enterprise swept through the South. Industry expanded, whether in the form of older products such as cotton textiles and tobacco or newer lines of production like electric power and chemicals. During the decade of "normalcy," the Southeast finally caught up with and surpassed the Northeast in almost every phase of cotton textile manufacturing. Although the industry as a whole faced fundamental problems, the southern branch continued to expand while northern mills lost their competitive advantage and began to collapse. By 1930 southern output was double that of the North. Industrial promotion was responsible for the building of an entire town—Kingsport, Tennessee—a planned community that boasted of its social harmony and business efficiency.[11]

But if the South seemed to be imitating the North in accordance with the New South formula, it continued to lag far behind the Northeast and Midwest on most measures of economic performance and well-being. At the end of the decade, the South received less than a fourth of its income from manufacturing. Half of the region's workers were employed in agriculture, and it was still overwhelmingly rural. Wages were 30 percent or more below the national average, and per capita income was only 53 percent of that enjoyed by nonsoutherners. Manufacturing continued to be concentrated in industries that could make effective use of the South's relatively cheap labor. On the eve of the Great Depression small, inefficient, nonproductive farms were all too typical of agriculture in the southern states. The southern labor market was still largely isolated from other regions. Despite the continuing outmigration, particularly of black workers, there was a labor surplus below the Potomac and the Ohio. Labor unions were weak, racial discrimination permeated the work force, and a wage differential based on race had developed, in which "black jobs" and "white jobs" were associated with low- and high-wage employment.[12]

Southern boosters explained their region's commercial and industrial expansion in terms of abundant natural resources, plentiful low-cost labor, and entrepreneurial resourcefulness. Among the developmental obstacles they identified was the South's colonial status in the national economy and its dependence on the North for capital and technology. Iron and steel, a regional disappointment, provides an example. Southerners attributed the failure of the Birmingham district to become a national center of heavy industry to discriminatory freight rates and monopolistic pricing dictated by northern steel corporations. Northern industrialists also had some sectional complaints. Northeastern textile lead-

History: The Growth of Urban Civilization in the South, ed. Blaine A. Brownell and David R. Goldfield (Port Washington, N.Y., 1977), pp. 123–58 (first quotation on p. 145); Blaine A. Brownell, The Urban Ethos in the South, 1920–1930 (Baton Rouge, La., 1975), pp. 1–38; George B. Tindall, "Business Progressivism: Southern Politics in the Twenties," South Atlantic Quarterly 62 (Winter 1963): 92–106 (second quotation on p. 95); Tindall, The Emergence of the New South, pp. 70–104.

11. Gavin Wright, Old South, New South: Revolutions in the Southern Economy Since the Civil War (New York, 1986), pp. 147–216; Nancy Frances Kane, Textiles in Transition: Technology, Wages, and Industry Relocation in the U.S. Textile Industry, 1880–1930 (New York, 1988), pp. 29–32, 44–45, 52; Margaret Ripley Wolfe, Kingsport, Tennessee: A Planned American City (Lexington, Ky., 1987).

12. Wright, Old South, New South, pp. 162–64, 177–207; Fite, Cotton Fields No More, p. 119.

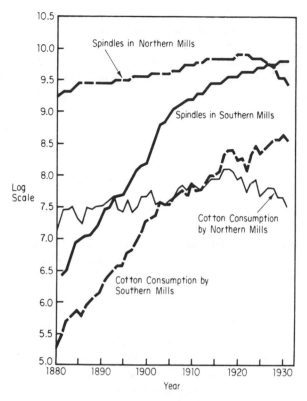

Northern and Southern Cotton Consumption and Spindles, 1880–1930. SOURCE: Gavin Wright, *Old South, New South: Revolutions in the Southern Economy Since the Civil War* (New York: Basic Books, 1986), p. 130.

ers, for instance, blamed their troubles on aggressive labor and "unfair competition" from the South.[13]

The South's yearning for economic development and its hope that the national government would contribute to this process were revealed in the long-continued controversy surrounding Muscle Shoals. The dispute grew out of the government's efforts during the war to construct two nitrate plants in northern Alabama and a dam on the nearby Tennessee River to provide the needed electric power. The disposition of these costly government facilities became a thorny issue in Congress in the immediate aftermath of the war, but the question was not settled until the authorization of the Tennessee Valley Authority in 1933. Throughout this long controversy, Richard F. Bensel writes, southern congressmen "consistently pursued a policy of expediency intended to bring economic aid to their region." And at every turn, this writer observes, southern tactics met solid opposition from representatives of the industrial East.[14]

13. Wright, *Old South, New South*, pp. 147–49, 165–72.
14. Bensel, *Sectionalism and American Political Development*, p. 137.

Muscle Shoals was infused with partisan and sectional politics from the beginning. Proposals for the public operation of the facilities, as well as charges of waste and mismanagement in their construction, were linked to the Wilson administration, under whose auspices they were launched. The South was obviously the section most interested in the development of the Muscle Shoals properties. A Minnesota Republican, speaking on a wartime measure to authorize additional support for the project, asserted: "Under the guise of doing something to help our military efficiency we are, in effect, erecting a gigantic enterprise in a certain part of the South for the manufacture and production of fertilizer. . . . The purpose is to have the Government provide cheap fertilizer for the South."[15] In the postwar period Republican leaders rejected the claim of southern lawmakers that the Muscle Shoals properties could be operated economically, charging that the real reason for southern enthusiasm was a desire to divert federal funds into the region.[16]

The prospect of cheap fertilizer, more than any other potential benefit, appealed to southerners and their representatives in Washington. When the automobile magnate Henry Ford formally offered to lease the Muscle Shoals facilities in 1921, his action aroused great excitement in the Tennessee Valley. The Ford offer promised not only to bring plenty of cheap fertilizer to southern farmers but to give a mighty boost to the development of the southern economy as well. Ford, it was said, planned to build a seventy-five-mile-long city in the Tennessee Valley. Boosters in the Muscle Shoals area dreamed of a great industrial center, and a huge real estate boom was set in motion by the excitement. For many residents, Henry Ford had become "the economic savior of the South."[17] In spite of enthusiastic southern support, the Ford offer was never approved by both houses of Congress, and it was withdrawn by the automobile manufacturer in 1924. Thereafter, the southern congressional bloc was less united on the Muscle Shoals issue. But the southerners, following "a policy of expediency designed to bring economic aid to the South,"[18] never lost sight of the opportunity presented by the federal project. They assumed, as George B. Tindall has noted, a succession of shifting positions: "first, support for governmental operation to produce cheap fertilizer, then for Henry Ford's offer to transform it into a vast industrial complex, then opposition to acquisition by Alabama Power or the American Cyanamid Company (despite substantial farm support for the latter), and finally support for the Norris idea of governmental development which seemed to promise the most widespread diffusion of cheap power."[19]

Southern congressmen were divided over the question of public versus pri-

15. Quoted in *ibid.*, pp. 131, 133.

16. Preston J. Hubbard, *Origins of the TVA: The Muscle Shoals Controversy, 1920–1932* (Nashville, 1961), pp. 21–22, 25. This study provides a comprehensive treatment of the controversy.

17. Hubbard, *Origins of the TVA*, pp. 39–40; Paul K. Conkin, "Intellectual and Political Roots," in *TVA: Fifty Years of Grass-Roots Bureaucracy*, ed. Erwin C. Hargrove and Paul K. Conkin (Urbana, Ill., 1983), pp. 14–16.

18. Hubbard, *Origins of the TVA*, p. 144.

19. Tindall, *The Emergence of the New South*, p. 241.

vate operation of the Muscle Shoals facilities. Many of them were not especially concerned over this question, as long as Muscle Shoals did not end up in the hands of the Alabama Power Company. By 1927, and with no solution in sight, the southerners in growing numbers began to endorse the public power proposal of Senator George W. Norris of Nebraska. A coalition of midwestern Republicans and southern Democrats was instrumental in passing the Norris bill in 1928 and again in 1931, although on both occasions the measure was killed by a presidential veto.[20] Nevertheless, Congress had approved a policy of public operation of Muscle Shoals. The policy emerged in late 1927, writes Preston J. Hubbard, when "Southerners in Congress as a whole began to veer toward the Norris idea, and it took definite form when the Republican members of the farm bloc in the House joined hands with the Southerners."[21]

The South's position in Congress mirrored the region's distinctive political institutions at the state and local levels. The one-party system, based on disfranchisement, the white primary, and low voter turnout, had been in place for two decades and had moved well into the secure confines of what would later be called the classic period of southern politics. The Democratic party was dominant in every southern state. Planters, industrialists, and the far-flung county-seat governing class exercised a controlling influence in political affairs even as they slowly made room for new business and professional groups. Poll taxes, literacy tests, and a restricted electorate characterized southern politics. In the 1920s, even after the enfranchisement of women, scarcely more than a fifth of adult southerners voted in either Democratic primaries or general elections. The only meaningful elections were the primaries, which were closed to most blacks until the 1940s. Political campaigns usually revolved around the personalities and qualifications of the candidates instead of more substantive issues.[22]

Some observers had anticipated that woman suffrage would have a profound effect upon politics in the South. But they were disappointed in their expectations, even though women became more active in the region's political affairs and made a vital contribution to social reform in the 1920s. Veterans of the long struggle for the ballot soon turned their suffrage organizations into leagues of women voters, continued to participate in legislative councils, and worked for desirable legislation such as stronger labor laws, the regulation of utility rates, and repeal of the poll tax as a voting prerequisite. They assumed a role in the organizational machinery of the two national parties and slowly became involved in the apparatus of their state parties. Those who ran for public office were not very successful, although by the end of the decade women had been elected to the legislatures of every southern state except Louisiana. In 1923 the governor of Georgia appointed the venerable Rebecca Latimer Felton to succeed Senator Thomas E. Watson, who had died. Felton was the first woman to serve in the United States Senate, but her appointment was purely honorary

20. Hubbard, *Origins of the TVA*, pp. 150–51, 223, 227, 232, 290–91, 308; Bensel, *Sectionalism and American Political Development*, pp. 131, 135–36.
21. Hubbard, *Origins of the TVA*, p. 297.
22. See Dewey W. Grantham, *The Life & Death of the Solid South: A Political History* (Lexington, Ky., 1988), pp. 78–101, for a discussion of state politics in the South during the 1920s and 1930s.

and she remained in office only one day. In 1931 Hattie Caraway of Arkansas was appointed to succeed her deceased husband in the Senate, and she was elected in her own right the next year, thus becoming the first woman to be *elected* to the U.S. Senate. Meanwhile, in 1924, Miriam A. Ferguson was elected governor of Texas (in the same year Nellie Tayloe Ross won the governorship of Wyoming) as a stand-in for her ineligible husband, and she was reelected in 1932. This random recognition of women's political arrival was less compelling, however, than the deep-seated suspicion of "the southern lady" in politics, especially among men, many of whom associated the suffrage movement itself with radical leaders in the North. Southern women also discovered that "inexperience and prolonged socialization impeded the acquisition of real power." Not surprisingly, outsiders looked on Dixie as the bastion of opposition to the rights of women.[23]

Spectacular political figures and colorful campaigners were encouraged by the individualistic and disorganized politics that existed in the one-party South. Factional division of the electorate on the basis of powerful personalities had become typical of the section's politics, sometimes providing an element of stability and structure in an essentially amorphous system. On occasion striking leaders of this type advanced the cause of reform, but more often than not they themselves became the central political issue. The emphasis on personality in politics was no doubt related to the longtime dominance of a rural, folk society, to the social paternalism carried over from the Old to the New South, and to the mythology that enveloped the Lost Cause and Reconstruction in the minds of white southerners. In the 1920s new political leaders rose to power in the region's state politics: Harry Flood Byrd in Virginia, O. Max Gardner in North Carolina, Edward H. Crump in Tennessee, Huey Pierce Long in Louisiana, and others. Long burst upon the political stage of Louisiana near the end of the decade. Challenging the planter-business-New Orleans machine alliance, he promised to increase state services if elected governor, and won after conducting a colorful, folksy campaign. Once in office, he pushed through an ambitious legislative program, created a powerful and ruthless state machine, and divided the electorate into Long and anti-Long supporters. The Kingfish, as he liked to be called, moved on to the U.S. Senate in 1932, and before his assassination in September 1935, he had become a national figure and a threat to President Franklin D. Roosevelt's reelection. About his manners, values, and idiom, Arthur M. Schlesinger, Jr., has written, "Huey Long remained a back-country hillbilly. But he was a hillbilly raised to the highest level, preternaturally swift and sharp in intelligence, ruthless in action, and grandiose in vision."[24]

23. Anne Firor Scott, "After Suffrage: Southern Women in the Twenties," *Journal of Southern History* 30 (August 1964): 298–318; Marjorie Spruill Wheeler, *New Women of the New South: The Leaders of the Woman Suffrage Movement in the Southern States* (New York, 1993), pp. 172–97; J. Stanley Lemons, *The Woman Citizen: Social Feminism in the 1920s* (Urbana, Ill., 1973), pp. 87, 106–109; Betty Brandon, "Women in Politics," in *Encyclopedia of Southern Culture*, ed. Charles Reagan Wilson and William Ferris (Chapel Hill, N.C., 1989), p. 1561 (quotation).

24. Arthur M. Schlesinger, Jr., *The Age of Roosevelt: The Politics of Upheaval* (Boston, 1960), p. 48. For Long's political career, see T. Harry Williams, *Huey Long* (New York, 1969), and William Ivy Hair, *The Kingfish and His Realm: The Life and Times of Huey P. Long* (Baton Rouge, La., 1991).

Two aspects of the regional political scene were especially significant in terms of the South's involvement in national politics during this period. Both of these themes were, in some respects, legacies of southern progressivism. One was the continuing commitment on the part of southern leaders to the goal of economic progress and the emphasis on efficiency, modernization, and public services. The other theme might be called the politics of morality, since it reflected a determination to preserve the South's traditional cultural values. As Numan V. Bartley says in his interpretation of Georgia politics, "The 1920s brought the first serious crisis for the old order and intensified the defense of traditional values."[25] Humanitarian and social justice concerns, while less salient than in earlier years, were still an important influence in voluntary endeavors and public welfare programs.

Although many professional groups were making the transition from "the missionary era to one of institutionalization and professionalism," social justice as well as social control remained a motivating factor in the reformism of the 1920s. One of the altered strains of southern progressivism took shape as a reform movement in race relations. The creation of the Commission on Interracial Cooperation reflected the white South's continuing interest in order, stability, and harmony in race relations. Other influences were also evident. Religious conviction, for example, was a powerful force in the leadership of Will W. Alexander, who became executive director of the commission. The interracial commission appealed not only to liberal sentiment in the South but also to progressives in other regions and to northern philanthropists, who provided much of the financial support for CIC activities. Unlike earlier white reform efforts in race relations, the commission could claim a concrete and realistic mode of action. It sought to avert racial violence and to secure specific improvements in community life. The concept of interracial organization, although anticipated in some of the wartime community programs, represented a departure from the past. The interracial movement had some effect in reversing the trend toward increasing separation between white and black southerners. The commission's approach was also different from previous reform movements in its interest in the scientific study of race relations, which was manifested in its emphasis on education, research, and publication. While its approach was cautious and its reforms largely superficial, the Commission on Interracial Cooperation was nonetheless a bolder and more liberal social experiment than the racial uplift of prewar progressives.[26]

One of the notable features of the interracial movement in the 1920s and 1930s was the important part played by southern women, black as well as white. The drive to improve the world in which they lived was a strong underlying motivation in the political and social-action endeavors of newly enfranchised southern women. The Woman's Committee of the Interracial Commis-

25. Numan V. Bartley, *The Creation of Modern Georgia* (Athens, 1983), p. 169.

26. Tindall, *The Emergence of the New South*, pp. 177–83, 219, 254; William A. Link, *The Paradox of Southern Progressivism, 1880–1930* (Chapel Hill, N.C., 1992), pp. 248–62; Wilma Dykeman and James Stokely, *Seeds of Southern Change: The Life of Will Alexander* (Chicago, 1962), pp. 52–164; Morton Sosna, *In Search of the Silent South: Southern Liberals and the Race Issue* (New York, 1977), pp. 20–59.

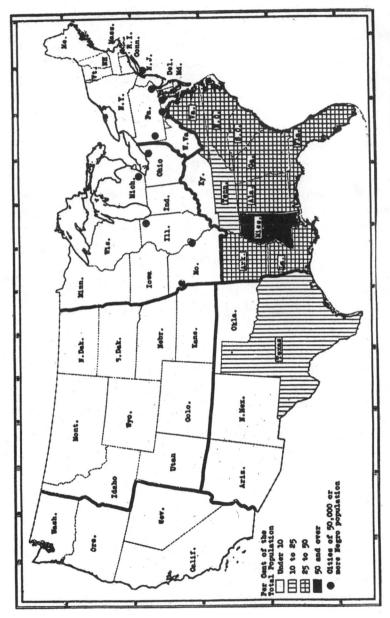

Negro Population, 1930. SOURCE: Howard W. Odum, *Southern Regions of the United States* (Chapel Hill: University of North Carolina Press, 1936), p. 14.

sion was, as one of its interpreters has noted, the earliest attempt in the South to build a woman's organization "explicitly devoted to overcoming the barriers of race."[27] The director of the committee was Jessie Daniel Ames of Texas, who took the lead in transforming the Interracial Commission's amorphous women's program into a well-organized, single-issue crusade against lynching. The Association of Southern Women for the Prevention of Lynching, founded in 1930, disavowed the "false chivalry" of lynching and set out to use the moral and social leverage of organized women to bring such acts of violence to an end.[28] Other social issues also attracted the attention of female reformers in the 1920s. "Having created a vast associational network," two scholars have observed, "southern women used it to promote prohibition, initiate the social welfare wing of southern progressivism, open higher education to women, establish kindergartens and settlement houses, and create a variety of welfare institutions."[29] Women below the Potomac supported congressional passage of the Sheppard-Towner Act for maternal and infant health in 1921 and worked effectively to secure the required matching funds from state legislatures. They campaigned against child labor, supported the expansion of public health facilities, helped bring about a dramatic increase in expenditures for public welfare, and strove to improve the public schools. Responding to the Young Women's Christian Association's stress on the problems of industrial labor, they lent their backing to such ventures as the Southern Summer School for Women Workers, an innovative education project. In 1929 many women textile workers took part in a wave of strikes that erupted in the southern Piedmont region.[30]

Southern preoccupation with economic growth gave impetus to the drive, in and out of government, for greater efficiency, professional standards, and public services. Good government and more adequate public services, southern leaders increasingly assumed, were as vital to economic development as natural resources, abundant labor, and able entrepreneurs. These emphases were apparent in the politics and policies of several southern states and municipalities during the 1920s, and "business progressives" like Byrd of Virginia, Bibb Graves of Alabama, and Austin Peay of Tennessee, stressing economy and efficiency, reorganized and modernized the structure of their state governments, developed new administrative and tax systems, and expanded state services.[31] Supported by businessmen, professional groups, and the urban middle class generally, political leaders in most of the southern states and municipalities made notable advances in the construction of highways, the improvement of public schools, the development of public health facilities, and the introduction

27. Jacquelyn Dowd Hall, *Revolt Against Chivalry: Jessie Daniel Ames and the Women's Campaign Against Lynching* (New York, 1979), p. 106

28. Hall, *Revolt Against Chivalry*, pp. x, 44–119, 123–28, 159.

29. Jacquelyn Dowd Hall and Anne Firor Scott, "Women in the South," in *Interpreting Southern History: Historiographical Essays in Honor of Sanford W. Higginbotham*, ed. John B. Boles and Evelyn Thomas Nolen (Baton Rouge, La., 1987), pp. 489–90.

30. *Ibid.*, pp. 484–504; Scott, "After Suffrage," pp. 299–312.

31. Tindall, "Business Progressivism," pp. 92–106; Tindall, *The Emergence of the New South*, pp. 224–38; Joseph T. Macpherson, "Democratic Progressivism in Tennessee: The Administrations of Governor Austin Peay, 1923–1927" (Ph.D. dissertation, Vanderbilt University, 1969).

of social welfare programs.[32] Medical care had joined education as a social panacea, at least in the minds of the reformers. The progressive spirit embodied in this reformism had a significant bearing on the relationship between region and nation. It put pressure on southern leaders to seek assistance from Washington in such fields as highway construction, flood control, and public health, and it encouraged private philanthropists in other regions to send money south to support change and modernization in education, health, and race relations.

Southern reformers concentrated much of their energy on the public schools, since they assumed that education could solve most problems. The schools were now supported by compulsory attendance laws, a standardized curriculum, and state certification of teachers. During the decade of the 1920s, school terms were lengthened, teacher salaries were increased, new school buildings were constructed, rural schools were consolidated, and eight of the southern states exceeded the national rate of increase in current expenditures for education. Yet there were marked disparities between public school facilities in poorer and wealthier districts. Despite the impressive contributions of black southerners and the assistance of the General Education Board and the Rosenwald Fund, the schools for African Americans struggled to hold their own against the pervasive discrimination by white authorities in the allocation of public school expenditures. The southern states provided little support for the training of black teachers. Louisiana, with a large black population, had 280 high schools for whites and only 3 for Negroes in 1923. In 1930 a mere $12.97 was spent for each black pupil in the South as compared with $44.31 for his white counterpart. The average salaries for African-American teachers were slightly more than one-third those of white teachers. For all the South's efforts, its expenditures per capita for public schools were scarcely half the national

PER PUPIL EXPENDITURES AS PERCENT OF U.S. AVERAGE, 1890–1940

	1890	1900	1910	1920	1930	1940
Alabama	28	17	33	39	43	37
Arkansas	40	35	38	34	39	34
Florida	46	51	51	63	58	71
Georgia	24	33	38	33	37	42
Louisiana	50	38	70	65	56	63
Mississippi	32	32	31	32	43	31
North Carolina	20	21	28	38	49	49
South Carolina	20	22	24	30	46	42
Tennessee	27	26	36	35	49	46
Texas	63	56	65	67	63	73
Virginia	47	48	51	54	51	54

SOURCE: Gavin Wright, *Old South, New South: Revolutions in the Southern Economy Since the Civil War* (New York: Basic Books, 1986), p. 80.

32. Tindall, *The Emergence of the New South*, pp. 254–84; Brownell, *The Urban Ethos in the South*, pp. 157–89.

average.[33] Southern educational reformers faced difficult problems, in addition to maintaining a dual school system. As William A. Link writes of the progressives' efforts in education and health, "Their challenge in creating a policy was more formidable than that of the other reformers. They had to create and then maintain administrative systems capable of reaching millions of long-isolated people accustomed to little outside intervention. Perhaps inevitably, these new administrative systems quickly became coercive and centralized, and they removed decision making from the community. Not surprisingly, the community response was often hostile, and by the late 1920s there was a kind of stand-off between centralizing officials and traditional localists."[34]

Another manifestation of the reform spirit in the 1920s was a series of campaigns to protect moral standards and traditional cultural values. This morality was closely identified with evangelical Protestantism, rural and small-town life, agrarian reformism, and the politics of William Jennings Bryan. Wartime dislocations and rapid social change in the postwar years heightened the social concerns of southern moralists and strengthened their resolve to defend the traditional culture. The region's defensive temper was intensified by what its moral custodians interpreted as challenges to southern orthodoxies. The result was a kind of "political fundamentalism," in which defenders of the old morality sought to deny divisions in southern society by appealing to regional loyalties and coercing a sense of unity. This fundamentalism contained an element of popular democracy, since it reflected the belief of many southerners that their society was being reshaped by a diverse but powerful economic group that seemed to disregard tradition and the idea of popular consent.[35] Southerners themselves were divided over their cultural preferences, and a growing number of urban-oriented men and women were no longer under the sway of religious fundamentalism and Victorian precepts. The mainstream southern churches were rent by a broad conservative-liberal factionalism and conflict over such issues as educational standards for ministers and the movement toward reunification of northern and southern Methodists.[36]

One example of the drive for cultural conformity was the zealous campaign to enforce prohibition, which remained a divisive issue in state politics during the 1920s. Throughout much of the South it was necessary to be "dry" in order to gain or retain public office. The prohibition movement and other anti-vice efforts were expressions of a widespread southern concern over immoral behavior, as well as an aspect of some reformers' commitment to the solution of social

33. Tindall, *The Emergence of the New South*, pp. 260–76; Link, *The Paradox of Southern Progressivism*, pp. 174–75, 196, 215, 217–38, 241, 243–47, 252, 268–95; James D. Anderson, *The Education of Blacks in the South, 1860–1935* (Chapel Hill, N.C., 1988), pp. 136, 145, 172, 203; Hair, *The Kingfish and His Realm*, p. 123.

34. Link, *The Paradox of Southern Progressivism*, pp. 268–69.

35. Robert A. Garson, "Political Fundamentalism and Popular Democracy in the 1920's," *South Atlantic Quarterly* 76 (Spring 1977): 219–33. See William E. Leuchtenburg, *The Perils of Prosperity, 1914–32* (Chicago, 1958), pp. 204–24, for a discussion of political fundamentalism in the context of national politics.

36. Kenneth K. Bailey, *Southern White Protestantism in the Twentieth Century* (New York, 1964), pp. 44–71.

problems. These moralistic campaigns were reminiscent of the earlier southern attacks on trusts and political "machines." Alarmed by the growing secularization of their society, southern fundamentalists became more involved in the support of prohibition, the anti-evolution movement, and the conservative Protestant opposition to Roman Catholicism.[37]

The conflict over evolution became a hot political question. William Jennings Bryan, now a resident of Florida, traveled over the South condemning the doctrine of evolution, while fiery evangelists like J. Frank Norris of Fort Worth, Texas, lashed out at religious modernism and defended the traditional faith. By 1921 a movement for the passage of laws to prevent the teaching of evolution in the public schools was under way, and the South became the stronghold of this movement. Between 1921 and 1929, five southern states enacted laws prohibiting the teaching of evolution. This fundamentalist crusade against religious modernism contributed to the image of a benighted South held by many Americans in other regions—a South that was viewed as socially backward, intolerant, and prejudiced. The melodramatic trial of John T. Scopes in the summer of 1925 for violating the Tennessee anti-evolution law was conducted in a circuslike atmosphere and attended by scores of reporters from outside the South, including H. L. Mencken. The Scopes trial, in the words of one scholar, solidified the mistaken notion that fundamentalism was simply "the baroque theology of southern hillbillies." Another writer suggests that, in the Scopes trial, "the provincialism of the city was arrayed against the provincialism of the country, the shallowness of Mencken against the shallowness of Bryan, the arrogance of the scientists against the arrogance of the fundamentalists."[38]

Another reason for the northern stereotype of the South as a land of cultural stagnation and reactionary politics was the Ku Klux Klan. Organized in Georgia in 1915, the secret order spread rapidly through the southern states during the early 1920s. Although the Klan became a national phenomenon, it first gained strength in the South, where about 40 percent of its members lived, and its southern "style" and essential Negrophobia gave it a southern cast even in later years.[39] Its membership and power were especially great in Georgia,

37. On Bryan and prohibition, see Lawrence W. Levine, *Defender of the Faith, William Jennings Bryan: The Last Decade, 1915–1925* (New York, 1965), pp. 93–131.

38. David Harrell, "Fundamentalism," in *Encyclopedia of Southern Culture*, ed. Wilson and Ferris, p. 1288 (first quotation); Leuchtenburg, *The Perils of Prosperity*, p. 221 (second quotation). See also Bailey, *Southern White Protestantism in the Twentieth Century*, pp. 72–91; Tindall, *The Emergence of the New South*, pp. 198–208; Levine, *Defender of the Faith*, pp. 243–92, 324–57; Willard B. Gatewood, Jr., ed., *Controversy in the Twenties: Fundamentalism, Modernism, and Evolution* (Nashville, 1969), pp. 285–329, 331–67; Gatewood, *Preachers, Pedagogues & Politicians: The Evolution Controversy in North Carolina, 1920–1927* (Chapel Hill, N.C., 1966); George M. Marsden, *Fundamentalism and American Culture: The Shaping of Twentieth Century Evangelicalism, 1870–1925* (New York, 1980); and Norman F. Furniss, *The Fundamentalist Controversy, 1918–1931* (New Haven, 1954).

39. See Robert Moats Miller, "The Ku Klux Klan," in *Change and Continuity in Twentieth-Century America: The 1920's*, ed. John Braeman, Robert H. Bremner, and David Brody (Columbus, Ohio, 1968), pp. 215–55. See also Charles C. Alexander, *The Ku Klux Klan in the Southwest* (Lexington, Ky., 1965); Kenneth T. Jackson, *The Ku Klux Klan in the City, 1915–1930* (New York, 1967), pp. 24–87; Shawn Lay, *War, Revolution, and the Ku Klux Klan: A Study of Intolerance in a Border City* (El Paso, Tex., 1985); Tindall, *The Emergence of the New South*, pp. 186–96; and J. Mills Thornton III, "Alabama

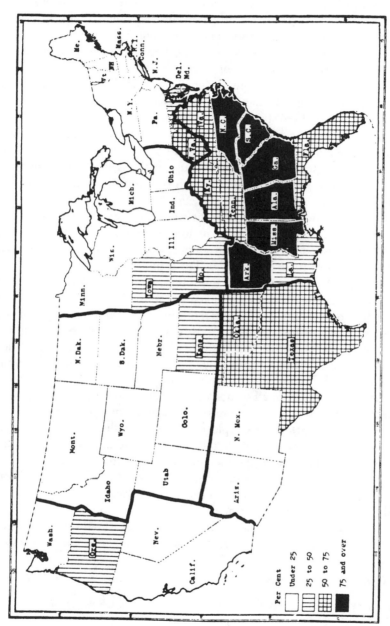

Percentage of Methodists and Baptists in Total Church Membership, 1926. SOURCE: Howard W. Odum, *Southern Regions of the United States* (Chapel Hill: University of North Carolina Press, 1936), p. 140.

Alabama, Arkansas, and Texas, as well as in cities such as Atlanta, Birmingham, Dallas, Houston, Little Rock, and Tulsa. In the South KKK members seemed to be motivated by religious and ethnic prejudices but also by fears of social change. Community morals were an overriding concern of the organization's members, whose activities represented, among other things, a general quest for moral and social conformity. The Klan's entry into politics was inevitable, and it enjoyed some success in state and local campaigns. It elected or had a hand in electing several governors and U.S. senators in Texas, Georgia, Oklahoma, and Alabama. The secret order declined in the late 1920s but for several years was a strong influence as well as an incendiary issue in the Democratic politics of the southern states. In Oklahoma it was an issue in every major political contest during the 1920s. Senator Oscar W. Underwood, a forthright opponent of the Klan, fought the organization not only because he disagreed with its fundamental principles but also because he thought "its continued operation in politics was going to make a breach between the democracy of the South and the North. . . ."[40]

By the 1920s, the South had become the most nativist part of the country. Aliens were defined in vague terms to include immigrants, Catholics, Jews, Negroes, Communists, and Socialists. In supporting the effort to restrict foreign immigration, Senator Morris Sheppard of Texas spoke of still another concern, warning of a "large element" among the foreign-born that "forms the main source and breeding ground of revolutionary and anarchistic propaganda in this country, such as Bolshevism, I.W.W.-ism, communism, and similar movements countenancing violence and disorder."[41] Although the modern South had attracted few immigrants, the nativist rhetoric of the Ku Klux Klan and other groups was nourished by racial forebodings and by anxieties over rapid cultural and social changes. While the success of immigration restriction in the 1920s was based on broad support from all sections of the nation, southern congressmen played a key role in the enactment of restrictive legislation. Pseudoscientific racial arguments in the North, for example, combined with the southern assertion of white rule over "colored people" to create a nationalism of race and to encourage the more complete incorporation of the South into the nation.[42]

Prohibition, Protestant fundamentalism, and the Ku Klux Klan became divisive issues in the struggle for control of the national Democratic party in the 1920s. This conflict was related to the changing composition of the party outside the South. The congressional elections of 1922, in which the Democrats gained seventy-eight House seats, proved to be a harbinger of things to come.

Politics, J. Thomas Heflin, and the Expulsion Movement of 1929," *Alabama Review* 21 (April 1968): 83–112.

40. Oscar W. Underwood to Mrs. W. H. Felton, 10 December 1924, Rebecca Latimer Felton Papers, University of Georgia Library.

41. Quoted in Edward W. Chester, *Sectionalism, Politics, and American Diplomacy* (Metuchen, N.J., 1975), p. 199.

42. *Ibid.*, pp. 190, 194–95, 199; William J. Cooper, Jr., and Thomas E. Terrill, *The American South: A History* (New York, 1991), vol. 2, pp. 621–23; Randall M. Miller, "Nativism," in *Encyclopedia of Southern Culture*, ed. Wilson and Ferris, pp. 415–17.

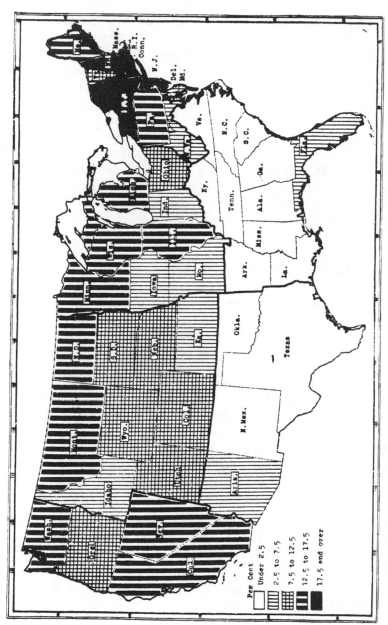

Percentage of Foreign-Born Whites in Total Population, 1930. SOURCE: Howard W. Odum, *Southern Regions of the United States* (Chapel Hill: University of North Carolina Press, 1936), p. 14.

The election results revealed a resurgence of Democratic strength in states like Missouri and Indiana, an increase in reform-minded congressmen from the West, and most important, a surprising shift toward the Democratic party in the metropolitan areas of the Northeast and Midwest.[43]

A fierce battle for the party's nomination in 1924 developed between William Gibbs McAdoo and Alfred E. Smith. McAdoo, a native southerner who had recently moved from New York to California, had served as secretary of the treasury in Woodrow Wilson's cabinet and had married Wilson's daughter. A progressive of sorts, he was a strong prohibitionist, had the support of a large number of Ku Klux Klan members, and was popular in the South and West. Like Wilson, McAdoo wanted to use federal power in the fields of business regulation and social reform. Governor Smith of New York, the grandson of immigrants and a product of Tammany Hall, was a critic of prohibition, an opponent of the Klan, and a champion of the urban masses. He was also a member of the Catholic Church. Another candidate was Senator Underwood of Alabama who challenged McAdoo in the South by opposing prohibition and condemning the KKK. But the Alabamian proved to be no match for McAdoo, who won a large majority of the southern delegates to the Democratic national convention in New York City.[44]

The contest between McAdoo and Smith presented the Democrats with a painful dilemma. "To reject McAdoo and nominate Smith," one historian has written, "would solidify anti-Catholic feeling and rob the party of millions of otherwise certain votes in the South and elsewhere. But to reject Smith and nominate McAdoo would antagonize American Catholics, who constituted some 16 per cent of the population and most of whom could normally be counted upon by the Democrats."[45] The convention, which lasted for sixteen days, was described by a newspaperman as a "snarling, cursing, tedious, tenuous, suicidal, homicidal rough-house."[46] A proposal to censure the Ku Klux Klan by name, opposed by most southern delegates, came within a few votes of passing. The sectional division within the party was vividly illustrated in the lengthy balloting for a presidential nominee, in which McAdoo and Smith were the leading contestants.[47] Neither could get the necessary two-thirds majority, however, and on the 103rd ballot the exhausted delegates finally selected John W. Davis of West Virginia as a compromise candidate. The southerners had

43. David Burner, *The Politics of Provincialism: The Democratic Party in Transition, 1918–1932* (New York, 1967), pp. 103–106; Burner, "Election of 1924," in *History of American Presidential Elections, 1789–1968*, vol 3, ed. Arthur M. Schlesinger, Jr., and Fred L. Israel (New York, 1971), p. 2460.

44. Burner, "Election of 1924," pp. 2467–69; Lee N. Allen, "The McAdoo Campaign for the Presidential Nomination in 1924," *Journal of Southern History* 29 (May 1963): 211–28; Allen, "The Underwood Presidential Movement of 1924," *Alabama Review* 15 (April 1962): 83–99; Douglas B. Craig, *After Wilson: The Struggle for the Democratic Party, 1920–1934* (Chapel Hill, N.C., 1992), pp. 30–50.

45. Burner, "Election of 1924," p. 2470.

46. Quoted in Burner, *The Politics of Provincialism*, p. 115.

47. Robert K. Murray, *The 103rd Ballot: Democrats and the Disaster in Madison Square Garden* (New York, 1976), provides a comprehensive account of the convention.

given Smith virtually no votes in the long balloting process. Davis's nomination was in some respects a tactical victory for Smith, since the West Virginian was a Wall Street lawyer who proved acceptable to the urban politicians of the North.[48] Yet Davis identified himself with the New South and with the leadership of Woodrow Wilson. In November all of the southern states except Kentucky dutifully cast their votes for the Democratic presidential ticket.

By the mid-1920s, the historian Robert K. Murray has observed, the Democratic party "was actually three parties: eastern and northern (urban and ethnic-dominated and opposed to prohibition); western (militantly farm-oriented and pro-prohibition); and southern (bone-dry, Klan-ridden, and fundamentalist-inclined)."[49] But it was the South that offered the greatest resistance to northern control of the party in the 1920s. Shortly before the election of 1924, the Harvard law professor Felix Frankfurter called attention to the fact that the South was "the single greatest cohesive factor of the Democratic party." The Solid South, Frankfurter lamented, was also "the greatest immoral factor of American politics, and to the extent that Northerners help to perpetuate it they are accomplices in all the evils that flow from it."[50] In the struggle for control of the Democratic party, Democrats confronted differences over economic and social policies as well as cultural schisms. The South, a valuable pawn in the struggle, wavered between a resumption of its old progressive alliance with the West and the blandishments of the more conservative Northeast.[51]

Sectionalism in the Democratic party reached a climax in the presidential election of 1928. It would be "a fatal mistake for the Democratic Party to nominate a man with the wet record of Governor Smith," warned former Secretary of the Navy Josephus Daniels, "it would tear us all to pieces in North Carolina."[52] Yet, as 1928 approached, Smith's nomination seemed increasingly certain. William G. McAdoo withdrew in September 1927 as a candidate for the party nomination, leaving the New York governor as a strong favorite for the honor. Smith, who was reelected to a fourth term as governor in 1926, had emerged as a formidable Democratic leader in a Republican era. Although there was widespread opposition to him throughout the South, as there had been in 1924, he was nominated on the first ballot at the Democratic national convention. Smith remained critical of national prohibition, but he sought in some ways to mollify the South. The national convention was held in Houston, Texas, and Joseph T. Robinson of Arkansas, the Senate minority leader, was chosen as Smith's running mate. Nevertheless, concerted opposition to the Democratic nominee developed swiftly in various parts of the South. "In the most profound sense," one student of the election observes, "the intensity of the fight to prevent the nomination of Smith measured the strength of an older and rural-minded America for continued dominance over the newer forces which

48. Burner, "Election of 1924," pp. 2471–78.
49. Murray, *The 103rd Ballot*, p. 24.
50. Quoted in Schlesinger and Israel, eds., *History of American Presidential Elections*, vol. 3, p. 2571.
51. Craig, *After Wilson*, pp. 2–3, 297.
52. Quoted in Tindall, *The Emergence of the New South*, pp. 245–46.

were concentrated in the large cities."[53] Smith's religion, while infrequently invoked directly, and his stand against prohibition made him particularly vulnerable in the southern states. As David Burner remarks, "Al Smith's stand against prohibition ended an alliance between the drys and the Democrats that had prevailed in the region for decades."[54]

Protestant leaders such as Bishop James Cannon, Jr., of the Methodist Episcopal Church, South, organized to defeat Smith. "By rumor, speech, and broadside," one historian notes, "the Roman menace was flaunted across the South."[55] Smith's choice of John J. Raskob, a devout Catholic and an ardent anti-prohibitionist, as chairman of the Democratic national committee and Smith's reliance on partisan advisers from New York struck many adherents of the Bryan-McAdoo wing of the party as an arrogant display of eastern control. While most Democratic politicians supported their party's ticket, though in many cases reluctantly, a number of prominent Democrats refused to vote for Al Smith. Among these leaders were Furnifold M. Simmons of North Carolina, J. Thomas Heflin of Alabama, Robert L. Owen of Oklahoma, Thomas B. Love of Texas, and Sidney J. Catts of Florida. Other Democrats simply ignored the Smith campaign. In most southern states the so-called Hoover-Democrat organizations mounted a spirited drive against Smith, encouraged by the Republican party.[56] The result was a rare division among southerners in a presidential campaign. Nicholas Murray Butler, the president of Columbia University, offered a flippant comment: "It is certainly a relief to find the South divided on almost everything, even if it be bigotry."[57]

The outcome of the presidential election in the South was startling. Herbert Hoover, the Republican nominee, carried seven of the southern states, and he came close to carrying another. His winning percentages in the South ranged from 51.8 in Texas to 63.8 in Oklahoma. Analyzing the election in 1949, V. O. Key, Jr., demonstrated that the most steadfast Democrats in the South were the white residents of the black belts, while the areas that showed the greatest shift to the Republicans were the counties with fewest Negroes.[58] Thus Democratic

53. Edmund A. Moore, *A Catholic Runs for President: The Campaign of 1928* (New York, 1956), p. 40. "This anti-Smith element," Robert K. Murray has written, "watched the New York governor's nomination in anguish and accepted him only by default." Murray, *The 103rd Ballot*, p. 273. See also Craig, *After Wilson*, pp. 80–86, 94–123.

54. Burner, *The Politics of Provincialism*, p. 224. For an authoritative study of the election, see Allan J. Lichtman, *Prejudice and the Old Politics: The Presidential Election of 1928* (Chapel Hill, N.C., 1979).

55. Tindall, *The Emergence of the New South*, p. 247. For Cannon's role in the campaign, see Virginius Dabney, *Dry Messiah: The Life of Bishop Cannon* (New York, 1949), pp. 173–89. See also Bailey, *Southern White Protestantism in the Twentieth Century*, pp. 92–110.

56. See, for example, Richard L. Watson, Jr., "A Political Leader Bolts—F. M. Simmons in the Presidential Election of 1928," *North Carolina Historical Review* 37 (October 1960): 516–43; Thornton, "Alabama Politics, J. Thomas Heflin, and the Expulsion Movement of 1929," pp. 83–112; and Craig, *After Wilson*, pp. 131–74.

57. Quoted in Norman D. Brown, *Hood, Bonnet, and Little Brown Jug: Texas Politics, 1921–1928* (College Station, Tex., 1984), p. 416.

58. This was not true in the case of Louisiana, where religion seems to have been the primary issue. Although Smith carried the state handily, his strongest support came from the Catholic and anti-prohibition parishes; he was weakest in the Protestant parishes, some of which had black

defections were least in Mississippi and South Carolina, the two states with the highest proportions of blacks. Key also identified other significant factors in the election results, including party loyalty, which aided the Democrats, and organization, which generally worked to the advantage of the Republicans. Hoover made his best showing in the peripheral South, and he won such growth-minded cities as Dallas, Houston, Birmingham, Atlanta, and Richmond.[59] Both parties tried to exploit racial fears in the South, but the major sources of Hoover's appeal to white southerners were a combination of Smith's religion, his opposition to national prohibition, and his New Yorkism, which to southerners symbolized a disquietingly different Democratic party. Hoover, hoping to make the Republican party more attractive to white southerners, employed a "southern strategy" during the campaign. He talked about reforming the GOP in the South and sought to exploit southern racism by purging blacks from positions of leadership in the party. In the end the reorganizing efforts were frustrated by intraparty feuds and black-white factionalism among southern Republicans.[60]

Some historians have argued that Al Smith was a sectional urban leader rather than a genuine national leader. In the election of 1928, one scholar suggests, "a provincial Protestant ruralism and a provincial Catholic urbanism stared at each other in uncomprehending hostility."[61] George Fort Milton, a southern journalist who strongly opposed Smith, touched on an important aspect of Democratic party sectionalism when he asserted that the New York governor's appeal was

> . . . to the aliens who feel that the older America, the America of the Anglo-Saxon stock is a hateful thing which must be overturned and humiliated; to the northern Negroes, who lust for social equality and racial dominance; to the Catholics, who have been made to believe that they are entitled to the White House; and to the Jews who likewise are to be instilled with the feeling that this is the time for God's chosen people to chastise America.[62]

Another interpreter contends that the Democratic party in the long period since Appomattox "had been held in virtual receivership by two social groupings often seen as fundamentally threatening to American unity: the plantocracy of the South and the Irish-Catholics of the North."[63] Religion, especially, and other cultural issues were important in the election of 1928, and they

majorities. See Steven D. Zink, "Cultural Conflict and the 1928 Presidential Campaign in Louisiana," *Southern Studies* 17 (Summer 1978): 175–97.

59. V. O. Key, Jr., with the assistance of Alexander Heard, *Southern Politics in State and Nation* (New York, 1949), pp. 318–29.

60. See Lichtman, *Prejudice and the Old Politics*, pp. 151–59, and David J. Ginzl, "Lily-Whites Versus Black-and-Tans: Mississippi Republicans During the Hoover Administration," *Journal of Mississippi History* 42 (August 1980): 194–211.

61. Burner, *The Politics of Provincialism*, p. 209. See also Murray, *The 103rd Ballot*, p. 282.

62. Quoted in Lawrence H. Fuchs, "Election of 1928," in *History of American Presidential Elections*, ed. Schlesinger and Israel, vol. 3, p. 2599.

63. Fuchs, "Election of 1928," p. 2586.

clearly contributed to the North-South division in the Democratic party and to the southern support for a northern Republican. But these factors should not be exaggerated in explaining the outcome. In his careful study of the election, Allan J. Lichtman concludes that "neither residence in city or country nor regional location skewed voting patterns in ways predicted by historians."[64] Still another scholar believes that a loose coalition of northeastern economic conservatives, who "clung to the doctrine of states' rights as a protection against federal regulation of business," controlled the Democratic party's nominating process and organization during the 1920s. Instead of following "the old West-South electoral strategy," this coalition based its presidential campaigns on "a North-South alliance."[65]

If the election of 1928 illustrated the North-South cleavage in the Democratic party, it also provided dramatic evidence of a divided South. For the first time since the Populist upheaval, the Solid South was disrupted. The dissenters in 1928, unlike those in the 1890s, made no attempt at third-party politics; instead, they tried to seize control of the Democratic party machinery at the state and local levels and to swing their states to the Republicans in the presidential contest. The differences among southerners were so great, at least momentarily, that this course seemed to offer real promise. But the resilience and strength of the Democratic party in the southern states soon enabled the traditional party to reassert its dominance over the insurgents and their would-be Republican collaborators.[66] In several southern states the personalities and issues of 1928 did offer an opportunity and a pretext for one group of politicians to challenge the control of the party by another faction. This seems to have occurred in Texas, where a group of young, self-styled Democrats challenged the control exercised by Thomas B. Love and the "old guard," who struck the insurgents as being fanatics in their support of prohibition.[67] In addition, the Smith campaign did foster on a small scale a new brand of southern liberalism, one that was suspicious of sectional shibboleths, more concerned with individual liberties, and even willing to accept an Irish-Catholic from New York as the Democratic presidential nominee.

It was not immediately apparent whether the events of 1928 would end the era of southern politics that began at the turn of the century. The intervening years constituted a period in which, except for the border states, any break in the South's Democratic solidarity was almost unthinkable. It was a period, moreover, in which southern handling of the race question encountered little interference from Congress or the president, met few challenges in the federal

---

64. Lichtman, *Prejudice and the Old Politics*, p. 241.

65. Craig, *After Wilson*, pp. 3, 42, 297.

66. The regular Democrats soon exacted a measure of revenge against the defectors. Senators Heflin and Simmons were denied reelection in 1930, the anti-Smith Democratic and Republican alliance failed in its bid for the Virginia governorship in 1929, Thomas B. Love was defeated in the Texas Democratic primary for governor in 1930, and the Republicans lost most of their southern congressional seats in the midterm elections of that year. Tindall, *The Emergence of the New South*, p. 253.

67. Brown, *Hood, Bonnet, and Little Brown Jug*, p. 409; Seth Shepard McKay, *Texas Politics, 1906–1944: With Special Reference to the German Counties* (Lubbock, Tex., 1952), pp. 178–79.

courts, and was generally approved in the country at large. Nor was that all. The South was the bulwark of the Democratic party, and the influence of its congressional delegations safeguarded its peculiar interests and obtained their share of federal benefits. But conditions were changing, and by the 1920s a more vigorous Democratic party had begun to emerge in other parts of the country. In 1928 the South was unable to prevent the nomination of a presidential candidate it strongly opposed. At that point many perceptive southerners could see that continued Democratic growth outside the South would eventually reduce their region's influence in the party.

The intemperate rhetoric that emanated from below the Potomac in the campaign of 1928 reinforced the widely held view in other regions that the South was the major repository of the nation's intolerance and bigotry. In the national press the South had long been identified with racial extremism, violence, political demagoguery, and cultural backwardness. This depiction of the benighted South had receded in the early years of the twentieth century, and the section was often viewed by outsiders as a stable, pastoral contrast to the increasingly industrialized and ethnically mixed North. In the 1920s the image changed, in part because of actual events—lynchings, night riding, Ku Klux Klan vigilantism, textile strike violence, religious intolerance, and so on. The image was also shaped by the accounts and reports of northern journalists and social commentators, and to some extent by southern critics and literary figures. It is also possible that, as northerners became more urbane, aggressively tolerant, and experimental, southerners stood out as opponents of modernism and leaders of reaction. Social fears and uncertainties among nonsoutherners may have encouraged them to focus on the South as the source of aberrant behavior. In any case, the Scopes trial precipitated a wave of outside criticism and ridicule directed at southerners. In the 1920s, Tindall has written, "a kind of neo-abolitionist image of the benighted South was compounded out of elements both old and new into a mind-set that has influenced strongly the outlook of the twentieth century." This sectional imagery, the historian suggested, might have served a function of national catharsis, creating for many Americans a convenient scapegoat on which to lay their own failures and shortcomings.[68]

"It is difficult now," wrote a southern journalist in 1924, "to find on the news stands a serious magazine without an article on some phase of life below the Potomac, or a discussion of one idea or another that has come out of the South. Critical pilgrims are perpetually exploring the section and sending back to their publications reports varying in quality from the highly valuable to the worthless and mischievous."[69] Books such as William H. Skaggs's *Southern Oligarchy* and Frank Tannebaum's *Darker Phases of the South*, both published in 1924, along

68. George B. Tindall, "The Benighted South: Origins of a Modern Image," *Virginia Quarterly Review* 40 (Spring 1964): 281–94 (quotation on p. 281). See also William J. Evitts, "The Savage South: H. L. Mencken and the Roots of a Persistent Image," *Virginia Quarterly Review* 49 (Autumn 1973): 596–611, and Fred Hobson, "The Savage South: An Inquiry into the Origins, Endurance, and Presumed Demise of an Image," *Virginia Quarterly Review* 61 (Summer 1985): 377–95.

69. Gerald W. Johnson, "Critical Attitudes North and South," *Journal of Social Forces* 2 (May 1924): 575.

with the National Association for the Advancement of Colored People's campaign against lynching, brought widespread public attention to the "backward" South in the 1920s. As Tindall puts it, "One Southern abomination after another was ground through the journalistic mills: Ku Kluxry, the Scopes trial, child labor, lynching, hookworm, pellagra." A number of sharecropper novels attracted attention beyond the South. One student of these developments observes that "the surreal potential of Dixie poverty, social customs, and history gained dominance in the media."[70] Writing in the 1930s, a sensitive southerner described the southern image in the mind of the metropolitan East: "The South—so the tale runs—is a region full of little else but lynchings, shootings, chain-gangs, poor whites, Ku Kluxers, hookworm, pellagra, and a few decayed patricians whose chief intent is to deprive the uncontaminated, spiritual-singing Negro of his life and liberty."[71]

The Baltimore editor and satirist Henry L. Mencken, in the words of one historian, "developed the game of South-baiting into a national pastime at which he had no peer."[72] Mencken derided southerners by referring to "morons," "hillbillies," "peasants," and the "degraded nonsense which country preachers are ramming and hammering into yokel skulls." He ridiculed the barrenness of southern culture and spoke contemptuously of the clerical tyranny of "Baptist and Methodist barbarism" in the region. He was disdainful of southern politics. Take the case of Virginia, the best of the lot: "The old aristocracy went down the red gullet of war; the poor white trash are now in the saddle. Politics in Virginia are cheap, ignorant, parochial, idiotic; there is scarcely a man in office above the rank of a professional job-seeker; the political doctrine that prevails is made up of hand-me-downs from the bumpkinry of the Middle West—Bryanism, Prohibition, vice crusading, all that sort of filthy claptrap; the administration of the law is turned over to professors of Puritanism and espionage; a Washington or a Jefferson, dumped there by some act of God, would be denounced as a scoundrel and jailed overnight."[73]

Mencken's mockery and ridicule were directed at unenlightened and bourgeois Americans in all parts of the country, although his most notorious assaults seem to have been made on the South and on southerners. At times his criticism may have been a calculated effort to stimulate cultural and literary advances in the South.[74] But southern spokesmen, always hypersensitive to northern disparagement, were quick to respond to such outside attacks. "The more defensive Southerners," observes one historian, "developed their own peculiar image of the benighted North, disfigured by slums, overrun by mongrel hordes, and fatally corrupted by gangsters and their henchmen."[75] In Arkansas, to cite one

70. Tindall, *The Emergence of the New South*, p. 212 (first quotation); Jack Temple Kirby, *Media-Made Dixie: The South in the American Imagination* (Baton Rouge, La., 1978), p. 49 (second quotation).
71. Quoted in Tindall, *The Emergence of the New South*, p. 215.
72. Tindall, *The Emergence of the New South*, p. 209.
73. H. L. Mencken, *Prejudices*, 2d series (New York, 1920), pp. 139–40. See also Mencken, *Prejudices*, 6th series (New York, 1927), pp. 136–45, and Tindall, *The Emergence of the New South*, pp. 208–209.
74. Oscar Cargill, "Mencken and the South," *Georgia Review* 6 (Winter 1952): 369–76.
75. Tindall, *The Emergence of the New South*, p. 216.

state, the reaction to Mencken's merciless pillorying was swift and certain. Arkansas newspapers competed with each other in denouncing Mencken, a state civic organization called for his deportation, and the Arkansas Knights of the Ku Klux Klan labeled him a "moral pervert."[76]

Other southerners, generally those committed to regional development based on industry, economic diversification, and education, defended the South in terms of progress. Thus the Richmond newspaper editor Virginius Dabney was at work on a book he called *Liberalism in the South* (1932), an effort to reveal the existence of a liberal tradition in the South. In 1926 Edwin Mims, a Vanderbilt University professor of English, published *The Advancing South: Stories of Progress and Reaction*. Mims's optimistic portrait of a progressive South was, at least in part, a response to the Scopes trial—to both the forces of obscurantism within the region that led to the trial and to the scathing criticism of the "monkey trial" from other sections. Mims conceded that "A section that is still solid in politics, however issues or candidates may change, that is a fertile ground for all sorts of intolerant ideas, that still gives little evidence that institutions of higher learning, fostered by state and private benevolence, have any appreciable influence on public opinion—surely such a section must seem a disappointment to the country as a whole."[77]

Yet not all northerners and westerners were disappointed in the South of Mims's day. There were many signs of modernization and progress. Also, an increasing number of northerners headed south to see the region for themselves, often by traveling to Florida, which held out "a promise of fulfilling one's dream of restored health or hedonistic pleasure." Even as the Great Migration continued out of the South, a swelling stream of tourists moved southward, almost two million by automobile in 1925 alone. "Up until the end of . . . World War I," one authority notes, "the region's reputation for unimproved, even dangerous, roads kept many American motorists away; but by the early 1920s, fear of traveling by car below the Mason-Dixon line disappeared, and tourists came south like never before."[78]

Criticism of the region by Mencken and other South-watchers provoked one group of southern intellectuals to a new awareness of their southernism and to a concerted attempt to define the essential elements of a distinctive southern tradition around which to rally. This band of writers and academics, many of whom were associated with Vanderbilt University in Nashville, Tennessee, also objected to the New South obsession with the Atlanta spirit of commercialism and industrialism and what they considered slavish imitation of the North.[79] As Donald Davidson, one of these southern agrarians, wrote a friend in 1927, "I

76. E. J. Friedlander, " 'The Miasmatic Jungles': Reactions to H. L. Mencken's 1921 Attack on Arkansas," *Arkansas Historical Quarterly* 38 (Spring 1979): 63–71.

77. Edwin Mims, *The Advancing South: Stories of Progress and Reaction* (Garden City, N.Y., 1926), p. 9.

78. Anne E. Rowe, *The Idea of Florida in the American Literary Imagination* (Baton Rouge, La., 1986), p. 91 (first quotation); Howard Lawrence Preston, *Dirt Roads to Dixie: Accessibility and Modernization in the South, 1885–1935* (Knoxville, Tenn., 1991), p. 109 (second quotation).

79. Tindall, *The Emergence of the New South*, pp. 216, 576–80.

can hardly read many of the observations about southern affairs now appearing here and there in New York magazines without getting sick at heart . . . we are in these days fallen prey to the mercies of a new sort of 'scalawags' and 'carpet-baggers.' "[80]

In 1930, just as the nation's celebrated industrial capitalism was threatened with collapse, Davidson and eleven other like-minded southerners published a manifesto entitled *I'll Take My Stand: The South and the Agrarian Tradition*. A series of provocative essays, the book eloquently described a South of rural virtues as distinguished from a nation increasingly dominated by the idea of progress and the pretensions of modern science. The essays presented a critique of the centralized state and of an expanding industrial system that seemed to dehumanize men and women. The fundamental choice facing southerners—and by implication all Americans—lay between industrialism and agrarianism. Emphasizing sectional differences in the United States, these articulate southerners yearned for an alternative South, a pastoral, conservative, and religious South. The publication of *I'll Take My Stand* precipitated widespread comment and on occasion heated debate, in and out of the South. It was destined to become, in the words of a recent interpreter, "one of the most influential documents of cultural dissent in American history."[81]

In retrospect it is clear that, for all its traditionalism, the South was experiencing important changes in the 1920s. One illustration of this transition was the appearance of a group of regional critics within the South who, as Tindall remarks, inadvertently made their own contribution to the imagery of an intolerant, prejudiced, and provincial South.[82] These endemic muckrakers, typified by journalists like Gerald W. Johnson of the Greensboro (N.C.) *Daily News* and Julian Harris of the Columbus (Ga.) *Enquirer-Sun* and by the novelist T. S. Stribling, reflected a diversity in the thinking of southern intellectuals. They also elicited a sympathetic response from northern observers. "It is difficult for the native born [southerner] to keep track of the transformations being wrought between the Potomac and the Gulf, so rapidly do they occur," Gerald Johnson wrote in 1924, adding, "how then shall the visitor note them and understand their significance?" Johnson called attention to "a new realization that Southern problems are necessarily American problems, that Southern progress is American progress, and that complete understanding of the South is essential to complete understanding of America."[83] On the other hand, Julian Harris, who won a Pulitzer Prize for his attacks on the Ku Klux Klan, wrote a northern friend in 1926, "All along I have been regarded among the less intelligent, and

80. Quoted in Fred C. Hobson, Jr., *Serpent in Eden: H. L. Mencken and the South* (Chapel Hill, N.C., 1974), p. 157.

81. Paul K. Conkin, *The Southern Agrarians* (Knoxville, Tenn., 1988), p. 88. See also Tindall, *The Emergence of the New South*, p. 579.

82. Tindall, *The Emergence of the New South*, pp. 214–15.

83. Johnson, "Critical Attitudes North and South," pp. 577–78. See also Darden Asbury Pyron, "The Cultural Awakening in the Inter-war South: A Review Essay," in *Perspectives on the American South: An Annual Review of Society, Politics and Culture*, vol. 2, ed. Merle Black and John Shelton Reed (New York, 1984), pp. 49–60, and Wayne D. Brazil, "*Social Forces* and Sectional Self-Scrutiny," in *ibid.*, pp. 73–104.

some of the intelligent, as a besmircher of Georgia, a negrophile, a Yankee lover, and a papist."[84]

In some respects the South seemed to have become less provincial and more like the nation as a whole in the 1920s—in its urbanization and industrialization, cultural and intellectual patterns, political developments, and national sentiment. But the decade's changes were ambiguous in their regional implications. The South in 1930 was still set apart from the rest of the country, still stigmatized by other Americans in terms of its economic and social deficiencies, cultural backwardness, and special problems. Its per capita wealth, income, public school outlays, and state revenue collections and expenditures were only about half the national average, and its high birth rate and infant mortality rate exacerbated efforts to narrow the regional gap. The North-South dialogue reflected sharp differences between the countryside and the city and between the highly developed and diversified North and the underdeveloped and homogeneous South. The interregional dialogue grew more rancorous, and the old image of a benighted South became more prevalent in other sections. For all its importance in national politics and the concessions made to it by other regions, the South found itself involved in bitter sectional conflict.

As the decade unfolded thoughtful observers like Gerald Johnson and Julian Harris must have become more aware of the extent to which sectional differences and suspicions still affected the relations between northerners and southerners. But it was this period—with its turbulent scenes of conflict between rapid change and adherence to traditional values—that gave rise to a new southern literature. Evidence of this Southern Renaissance was already available in the works of Ellen Glasgow, James Branch Cabell, T. S. Stribling, and a medley of talented local novelists and poets in Charleston, Richmond, Nashville, New Orleans, and other places. This early flowering of southern literature seemed to be confirmed with the publication in 1929 of Thomas Wolfe's *Look Homeward, Angel* and William Faulkner's *Sartoris* and *The Sound and the Fury*.[85] In the long run the literary creativity that welled up in the South following the World War would capture the American imagination and help change the cultural balance of trade between North and South.

84. Julian Harris to Oswald Garrison Villard, 23 October 1926, Oswald Garrison Villard Papers, Harvard University Library.

85. See Tindall, *The Emergence of the New South*, pp. 285–317, for a discussion of the southern literary scene in the 1920s.

CHAPTER 5

The Great Depression
and the New Deal

I N the 1930s southerners, like other Americans, experienced a great social crisis. The South, even more than other regions, was devastated by the collapse
of its economic life. Well before the election of a Democratic president in 1932,
southerners had begun to turn, with a mixture of desperation and hope, to the
federal government for emergency relief and economic assistance. With the
launching of the New Deal in the spring of 1933, they enthusiastically embraced the policies and programs of the new government in Washington. The
Great Depression and the New Deal brought fundamental changes to the
South, and those changes—painful and often traumatic—added to the crisis of
the decade. "Coupled with the reinforcing influences of World War II," two
scholars have observed, "the New Deal seems to have been the most powerful
force for change in the South since the Civil War."[1]

Although the South registered noteworthy economic expansion and urban
growth in the 1920s, its economy had manifested serious problems well before
the onset of the depression. Agriculture, the mainstay of the southern economy,
was plagued by chronic overproduction of staple crops in the late 1920s and by
millions of landless sharecroppers and tenants. The region's "farm problem"
was exacerbated by the collapse of export markets for cotton and tobacco. Fore-
casts of banner cotton crops, which had the effect of depressing the staple's
price, provoked a movement in 1931 led by Governor Huey P. Long of Louisiana to adopt a moratorium on the growth of cotton for a year. The movement
failed, but it did result in widespread discussion of the problem and how to deal
with it.[2] Meanwhile, natural disasters such as the ravages of the boll weevil, the
terrible Mississippi River flood of 1927, and a withering drought in the Southwest in 1930 and 1931 took their toll. The South's leading industry, cotton tex-

1. James C. Cobb and Michael V. Namorato, eds., *The New Deal and the South* (Jackson, Miss.,
1984), p. 5.
2. See Robert E. Snyder, *Cotton Crisis* (Chapel Hill, N.C., 1984).

tiles, also faced discouraging prospects in the late 1920s growing out of increasing competition, overproduction, and declining income.

The depression of the 1930s worsened an already bad situation. "Across the South it stretched," one historian has written of the South's single-crop system, "an endless belt of dirt, drudgery, and despair, where worn-out people, whom disease made feeble and lack of hope made shiftless, scratched at life against the background of overcrowded shacks, rusting Model T Fords, children with hookworm, clothes falling into rags, tumble-down privies, the cotton patch and the corn cob."[3] After traveling two hundred miles through the desolate countryside of South Carolina in 1930, a schoolteacher described having seen "deserted negro cabins by scores, ruined mansions, denuded fields, poor whites in huts, hound dogs, dust, cotton mills, paved roads and God knows the feelings that came to me as I rode along over a part of the state that I had never traversed before."[4] In Harlan County, Kentucky, 231 children died of malnutrition-induced disease between 1929 and 1931. Before committing suicide in 1930, a Houston mechanic wrote: "This depression has got me licked. There is no work to be had. I can't accept charity and I am too proud to appeal to my kin or friends, and I am too honest to steal." On one day in April 1932, a fourth of the farmland in Mississippi was sold at sheriff's sales, and between 1930 and 1932, 127 of that state's 307 banks failed. By early 1932, almost one-fourth of the Birmingham labor force was unemployed. In Arkansas 725 schools had been forced to close by February 1933, while 1,200 others had found it necessary to shorten the school year.[5]

As the depression worsened and state and local governments were unable to cope with the relief needs of their citizens, southern leaders increasingly turned to Washington for help. Those suffering from the agricultural crisis of the 1920s had already moved in that direction. As early as 1926, one southern cotton producer wrote President Calvin Coolidge, "I fear, Mr. President, if quick action is not taken by the government, we will have the most destructive panic the Nation ever had."[6] The historian Frank Freidel has noted that southerners, even in the 1920s, "were sufficiently in need of economic aid not to be frightened by the prospect of government intervention."[7] The mass meetings and special legislative sessions that spread over the South in the late summer of 1931 reflected the mounting support among southerners for drastic action in dealing with the depressed cotton market. But when the cotton growers and other

3. Arthur M. Schlesinger, Jr., *The Age of Roosevelt: The Coming of the New Deal* (Boston, 1958), p. 375.

4. Leonardo Andres to Oswald Garrison Villard, 3 July 1930, Oswald Garrison Villard Papers, Harvard University Libary.

5. Anthony J. Badger, *The New Deal: The Depression Years, 1933–40* (New York, 1989), pp. 11–28 (quotation on p. 11); Daniel C. Vogt, "Hoover's RFC in Action: Mississippi, Bank Loans, and Work Relief, 1932–1933," *Journal of Mississippi History* 47 (February 1985): 35–53; David Rison, "Federal Aid to Arkansas Education, 1933–1936," *Arkansas Historical Quarterly* 36 (Summer 1977): 192–93; Garry Boulard, " 'State of Emergency': Key West in the Great Depression," *Florida Historical Quarterly* 67 (October 1988): 166–83.

6. W. N. Malone to Calvin Coolidge, 13 October 1926, quoted in Snyder, *Cotton Crisis*, p. xvi.

7. Frank Freidel, *F.D.R. and the South* (Baton Rouge, La., 1965), p. 23.

southern groups sought help from the administration of President Herbert Hoover, they were disappointed. The president emphasized voluntarism, local initiative, and self-help in responding to the devastation of the depression. He urged farmers to reduce their output voluntarily and to make greater use of cooperatives. He was adamantly opposed to the appropriation of federal funds to relieve individual suffering. Although he eventually accepted the need for greater agricultural relief, financial loans, and public works, his policies were too limited to have much effect on the awful plight of millions of southerners and other Americans. Weary and disillusioned, some southern leaders taunted the beleaguered Hoover for being insensitive to the suffering of the masses and favoring the corporate interests of the North.[8]

The exigencies of the depression drastically changed the outlook in national politics, nowhere more so than in the South. While the bitter divisions of 1928 did not disappear, the collapse of the southern economy proved to be a powerful antidote to the region's internecine political strife in the last presidential election. Governor Franklin D. Roosevelt of New York was the chief beneficiary of Alfred E. Smith's overwhelming defeat in 1928. Most southerners viewed Governor Roosevelt as an attractive alternative to Smith. Roosevelt, who began to visit Warm Springs, Georgia, in the mid-1920s for the strengthening of his withered legs, had established himself as something of "a Georgia farmer-politician." Having cultivated southern political leaders in earlier years, he impressed many of them in the aftermath of the 1928 debacle as a man who might overcome the sectional division among Democrats and lead them to victory in 1932. Roosevelt, for his part, counted on southern politicians such as Senators Cordell Hull of Tennessee and Byron "Pat" Harrison of Mississippi to help him win the party nomination for president. He sought to mend the regional divisions within the Democratic party, to create an alliance between rural and urban Democrats, and to focus on economic rather than social and cultural issues. Emphasizing his party's Jeffersonian tradition, he was sensitive to "the rural Democrats, the dry Democrats, the antimonopoly Democrats, the progressive Democrats, the heirs of Bryan and Populism, [who] were growing increasingly restive."[9] The South had a disproportionate share of such Democrats.

Roosevelt's presidential candidacy attracted strong support from southern politicians, support that became even more impressive when Representative John Nance Garner of Texas decided to abandon his own campaign for the presidency and to accept the vice-presidential nomination. The New Yorker was then nominated on the fourth ballot at the national convention in Chicago. In November the Solid South reappeared: Roosevelt carried all thirteen south-

8. See, for example, Nan E. Woodruff, "The Failure of Relief During the Arkansas Drought of 1930–1931," *Arkansas Historical Quarterly* 39 (Winter 1980): 301–13, and Roger Biles, "The Persistence of the Past: Memphis in the Great Depression," *Journal of Southern History* 52 (May 1986): 189–212.

9. Arthur M. Schlesinger, Jr., *The Age of Roosevelt: The Crisis of the Old Order, 1919–1933* (Boston, 1957), p. 276. See also James MacGregor Burns, *Roosevelt: The Lion and the Fox* (New York, 1956), pp. 88, 100.

ern states. "For the South, in truth," a southern journalist later wrote, "it was almost as though the bones of Pickett and his brigade had suddenly sprung alive to go galloping up that slope to Gettysburg again and snatch victory from the Yankee's hand after all."[10] In the case of Georgia, one historian has written, the advent of Franklin D. Roosevelt seemed to be a godsend. "It appeared that their reaction to the new President stemmed from the prevailing Zeitgeist, the willingness to grasp at anything that was new and offered the promise of relief."[11]

Southerners were encouraged by the furious pace of the Roosevelt administration's activities in the spring of 1933. Between early March and mid-June, Congress followed the administration's recommendations in passing a long list of major bills. The Federal Emergency Relief Act made three-quarters of a billion dollars available to the states for direct relief (helping more than four million unemployed southerners in 1933), and when that proved inadequate, a new federal agency, the Civil Works Administration, dispensed $400 million for work relief in the winter of 1933–34. Other legislation established the Civilian Conservation Corps to make conservation and forestry work available for young unemployed men. More than a hundred CCC camps were eventually located in the southern states. In addition, Congress approved measures to save small home mortgages from foreclosure and to ease the burden of indebtedness in other areas.[12]

The New Deal also acted swiftly to relieve the farm crisis. The Agricultural Adjustment Act, passed in May 1933, and other measures introduced a combination of production controls, government payments, and price support loans, as well as authorizing marketing agreements to raise farm commodity prices. Unlike the Hoover agricultural policies, the new administration emphasized direct control of production and price support loans to farmers. It established the concept of parity as a means of maintaining a balance between commodity prices and farm costs. The Agricultural Adjustment Administration (AAA) was intended to increase the prices of staple crops, including southern-grown cotton, tobacco, and rice (sugar, peanuts, and cattle were later covered). The New Deal farm program helped the South more than any other region. The first New Deal Congress also resolved the long-standing Muscle Shoals controversy by passing the Tennessee Valley Authority Act, which promised to rehabilitate the Tennessee River drainage basin through a coordinated regional program of flood control, navigation, agricultural regeneration, and cheap hydroelectric power.[13]

10. W. J. Cash, *The Mind of the South* (New York, 1941), p. 365.

11. Michael S. Holmes, "From Euphoria to Cataclysm: Georgia Confronts the Great Depression," *Georgia Historical Quarterly* 58 (Fall 1974): 327.

12. George Brown Tindall, *The Emergence of the New South, 1913–1945* (Baton Rouge, La., 1967), pp. 473–81; Floyd W. Hicks and C. Roger Lambert, "Food for the Hungry: Federal Food Programs in Arkansas, 1933–1942," *Arkansas Historical Quarterly* 37 (Spring 1978): 23–43.

13. Tindall, *The Emergence of the New South*, pp. 391–403; Gilbert C. Fite, *Cotton Fields No More: Southern Agriculture, 1865–1980* (Lexington, Ky., 1984), pp. 120–62; Theodore Saloutos, *The American Farmers and the New Deal* (Ames, Iowa, 1982).

EFFECTS OF THE NRA ON REGIONAL WAGE DIFFERENTIALS

Industry	Pre-NRA Average Hourly Earnings (in cents)			NRA Average Hourly Earnings (in cents)		
	South	North	South ÷ North	South	North	South ÷ North
Furniture	28.4	44.9	.633	38.7	44.8	.864
Iron and Steel	28.3	45.9	.617	42.5	59.4	.715
Cotton Goods	23.9	32.4	.738	34.3	42.0	.817
Paints and Varnish	37.1	47.2	.786	45.1	54.3	.830
Lumber	17.0	38.9	.437	29.0	53.0	.547
Tobacco	27.9	38.0	.734	41.4	47.1	.879

SOURCE: Gavin Wright, *Old South, New South: Revolutions in the Southern Economy Since the Civil War* (New York: Basic Books, 1986), p. 217.

In responding to the depression in business and industry, Congress approved the National Industrial Recovery Act. This measure established the National Recovery Administration (NRA) and gave businessmen and the government extensive controls over production, wages, and prices, while exempting big business from antitrust prosecution. In addition, the legislation specified the right of labor to organize and engage in collective bargaining. It also authorized a huge public works program to help stimulate economic recovery. Meanwhile, President Roosevelt moved quickly to end the banking crisis and to obtain the enactment of legislation to restore order and confidence in the banking system. The Glass-Steagall Act of 1933 was meant to eliminate the most conspicuous deficiencies in the system. In 1933 and 1934, the Roosevelt administration extended federal regulation over Wall Street and the marketing of securities.[14]

Southerners approved of the New Deal for several reasons. For one thing, Roosevelt's program represented what one historian has called "a giant, nationwide cornucopia from which federal aid poured into the desperately Depression-ridden South."[15] Federal expenditures for relief, farm benefit payments, public works, and government employment had a profound effect upon life in the southern states. By October 1933, more than four million southerners (more than one in every eight) were receiving public relief dispensed by the federal government. From January 1933 through April 1939, the FERA (Federal Emergency Relief Administration), CWA, and WPA (Works Progress Administration) poured almost $2 billion into the South, providing relief and in the process bringing spectacular physical improvements. In 1936 Senator Josiah W. Bailey of North Carolina, a critic of the New Deal, boasted that he had

14. Tindall, *The Emergence of the New South*, pp. 433–42; Badger, *The New Deal*, pp. 67–80, 98–100.
15. Freidel, *F.D.R. and the South*, p. 48.

helped 4,000 North Carolinians find jobs with government agencies.[16] The sudden infusion of money through the farm price-support system, federal credit agencies, and public works programs regenerated the old dream of a New South. Although the benefits southerners received far surpassed their contributions to federal revenue collections, per capita federal expenditures in the South during the New Deal years were lower than those of any other region. This was true because the southern states found it difficult to raise matching funds and, doubtless in part, because guardians of the low-wage system did not really want the money spent in the region. In addition, regional differentials in work relief payments adversely affected the South. The concept of "security wages" introduced by the WPA reflected local wage standards and thus brought northern and western workers higher relief incomes than their southern counterparts. But the increasing use of direct grants meant that federal money accounted for a much larger percentage of relief spending in the southern states than in the nation as a whole.[17]

Another reason for the South's warm embrace of the New Deal was its traditional attachment to the Democratic party, its satisfaction over the party's national victories, and its pride in the influential position of southern congressmen in Washington. Southerners also anticipated a rich harvest of political patronage. One source of regional gratification was the number of southerners appointed to important administrative positions in federal departments and agencies. For example, three of the five Federal Emergency Relief Administration divisions were headed by southerners: Aubrey W. Williams of Alabama, Lawrence Westbrook of Texas, and Ellen S. Woodward of Mississippi. Woodward directed women's work under the FERA and the WPA. The new president looked to southern senators and representatives for cooperation and leadership in the enactment of his program. The response of these Dixie congressmen in 1933 and 1934 was all that Roosevelt could have hoped for. Like their Democratic colleagues from other regions, they gave the administration's proposals consistent and often enthusiastic support. They were moved by party loyalty, by Roosevelt's skill as a legislative leader, by their desire to ensure the success of the first Democratic presidency in twelve years, and by the desperate needs of their constituents. They were predisposed by experience and tradition to vote for such legislation as agricultural benefits and tariff reductions. Most of them liked the president, and they liked the power and prestige that came with responsible positions in a majority party.[18] For a time, moreover, many of them

16. Tindall, *The Emergence of the New South*, pp. 474, 476; James T. Patterson, "The Failure of Party Realignment in the South, 1937–1939," *Journal of Politics* 27 (August 1965): 611.

17. Per capita federal expenditures by region during the years 1933–1939 were: West $306, Midwest $224, Northeast $196, and South $189. See Gavin Wright, *Old South, New South: Revolutions in the Southern Economy Since the Civil War* (New York, 1986), p. 260. See also Badger, *The New Deal*, p. 193.

18. Freidel, *F.D.R. and the South*, pp. 34–70; Thomas H. Coode, "Tennessee Congressmen and the New Deal, 1933–1938," *West Tennessee Historical Society Papers* 31 (October 1977): 132–58; Lio-

assumed that the New Deal was no more than a revival of Woodrow Wilson's New Freedom—and would offer no greater threat to southern independence than had Wilson's administration. Southern leaders had implicit faith in the old assumption that Democratic control in Washington and defense of their region's peculiar institutions were synonymous.

The atmosphere on Capitol Hill in 1933 and the years that followed was reminiscent of the Wilson era. Southerners once again dominated the committee structure and the parliamentary proceedings of the two chambers. The Texas delegation alone included nine chairmen of permanent committees. In the Senate the majority leader was Joseph T. Robinson of Arkansas, a veteran of twenty years in the upper house and a dependable advocate of administration interests. When Robinson died suddenly in the summer of 1937, he was succeeded as majority leader by a strong New Dealer, Alben W. Barkley of Kentucky. Two other key Senate leaders from the South were Pat Harrison of Mississippi and James F. Byrnes of South Carolina. In his capacity as chairman of the Senate Finance Committee, Harrison steered the passage of such important administration measures as the National Industrial Recovery bill and the Social Security bill. Byrnes, an astute and influential senator, was the president's liaison with the upper house. A majority of the southern senators were veterans—men like Duncan U. Fletcher of Florida, Kenneth D. McKellar of Tennessee, and Morris Sheppard of Texas. But there were able younger men such as Hugo L. Black of Alabama, Claude Pepper of Florida, and Richard B. Russell of Georgia. Vice President John Nance Gardner was also a significant figure in the Roosevelt administration's legislative plans, particularly during the early years.

Southern influence was equally conspicuous in the House of Representatives. Three southerners served in succession as majority leader and then speaker during the Roosevelt years: Joseph W. Byrns of Tennessee, William B. Bankhead of Alabama, and Sam Rayburn of Texas. Before becoming majority leader in 1937, Rayburn had been chairman of the Committee on Interstate and Foreign Commerce, a position he used effectively to help pass the Securities Exchange Act of 1934, the Public Utilities Holding Company Act of 1935, the Rural Electrification Act of 1936, and other New Deal legislation. Rayburn, George B. Tindall has observed, "epitomized certain characteristics common among the Southern leaders: 'small-townish, agrarian, nationalistic, individualistic, anti-Wall Street,' men of rural background and humble origin who had struggled hard for an education, who felt an instinctive sympathy for the 'little fellow,' who 'savored the honors and prestige associated with Congressional leadership,' and who observed party regularity as an article of faith."[19] Another House stalwart was Robert Lee "Muley" Doughton of North Carolina who, as chairman of the Ways and Means Committee, guided such key measures as the

nel V. Patenaude, *Texans, Politics, and the New Deal* (New York, 1983); Martha H. Swain, "Ellen Woodward: Southern Gentlewoman and New Deal Official" (unpublished manuscript in possession of author), pp. 94–95.

19. Tindall, *The Emergence of the New South*, p. 609.

National Industrial Recovery and Social Security bills to passage in the lower house. Among other southern representatives who performed yeomanly service in support of New Deal legislation were Marvin Jones of Texas, chairman of the House Committee on Agriculture, and Henry B. Steagall of Alabama, who headed the Committee on Banking and Currency in the lower house.[20]

Southern congressmen gave the New Deal impressive backing during Roosevelt's first term. An analysis of the Arkansas congressional delegation during the years 1933–1936, for example, revealed that not a single negative vote was cast by the state's senators and representatives during that four-year period against measures that were central to the developing New Deal program. Like most other members of Congress, the Arkansas delegation generally exhibited more interest in legislation having a direct effect on their constituents—matters such as agriculture, mortgages, relief, and social security—than on broad questions of political and economic philosophy.[21] Yet the concerted influence of these southerners was sometimes remarkable. In the field of agriculture, for instance, one study concludes that the southern lawmakers in this period shaped the substantive content of farm legislation "to an extent far greater than their numbers warranted." The authors attribute this to the southerners' "unmatched cohesiveness, continuity, parliamentary skill, and positions of power."[22] The journalist Turner Catledge, who covered the congressional scene for the *New York Times* in the 1930s, thought the southerners were "more closely knit" than legislators from other regions. "They knew they were a minority and could have strength only by unity. They differed on details, but on the great issues—race, and a generally conservative approach to social and economic issues—they usually spoke with one voice."[23]

Franklin Roosevelt developed a special relationship with the South, which he considered his second home. He visited Warm Springs as often as possible, acquired a farm in the area, enjoyed the role of friendly neighbor, and went out of his way to be deferential to the region's political leaders. He struck a responsive chord among southerners, and his popularity in the South may have been greater than in any other part of the country. Southerners saw him not only as an agent of change but also as a man who, in the words of one of his biographers, "knew the area uncommonly well, loved it, and aspired to bring it a richer, more noble future."[24] In 1934 a contemporary observed that "if Roosevelt had announced himself the spiritual godchild of Lenin, the southern editor

20. Jack B. Key, "Henry B. Steagall: The Conservative as a Reformer," *Alabama Review* 17 (July 1964): 198–209; Irvin M. May, Jr., *Marvin Jones: The Public Life of an Agrarian Advocate* (College Station, Tex., 1980).

21. Travis M. Adams, "The Arkansas Congressional Delegation during the New Deal, 1933–1936" (M.A. thesis, Vanderbilt University, 1962).

22. Edward L. Schapsmeier and Frederick H. Schapsmeier, "Farm Policy from FDR to Eisenhower: Southern Democrats and the Politics of Agriculture," *Agricultural History* 53 (January 1979): 354.

23. Turner Catledge, *My Life and the Times* (New York, 1971), p. 67.

24. Freidel, *F.D.R. and the South*, p. 1. See also Paul K. Conkin, "It All Happened in Pine Mountain Valley," *Georgia Historical Quarterly* 47 (March 1963): 1–42, and Monroe Billington, "The Alabama Clergy and the New Deal," *Alabama Review* 32 (July 1979): 214–25.

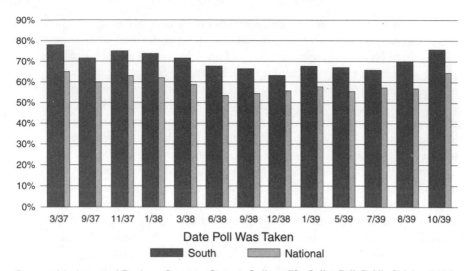

Roosevelt's Approval Ratings. SOURCE: George Gallup, *The Gallup Poll: Public Opinion, 1935–1971*, vol. 1 (New York: Random House, 1972), pp. 51, 68, 76, 83, 94–95, 98, 105–106, 118–19, 127–28, 134–35, 153, 166–67, 176, 187.

would have swallowed his embarrassment and let out an earnest whoop."[25] Whatever their ideological inclinations, most southerners were disposed to regard the president and the New Deal as allies in the struggle to curb the economic imperialism of the Northeast: to regulate Wall Street, equalize freight rates that discriminated against the South, liberalize credit, and supply badly needed capital for economic development, not to mention save the region's agricultural system and business enterprise. A recent study has pointed out still another consideration: "By not supporting civil rights issues or programs that would provide substantial, obtrusive aid to blacks, the Roosevelt administration avoided entangling the national government in the one issue that would assuredly have infuriated white southerners."[26]

By the time the Seventy-fourth Congress convened in January 1935, Roosevelt had decided to push for still further legislation and to give greater emphasis to reform. He was influenced by several considerations: the sweeping Democratic gains in the congressional elections of 1934, pressure from the left for more thoroughgoing reform, mounting distrust of business interests, and the failure of earlier administration programs to bring about economic recovery. The result was a new surge of far-reaching legislation in the spring and summer of 1935: a vast program of work relief, the Social Security Act, the National Labor Relations Act, the Public Utilities Holding Company Act, the Banking Act of 1935, and the Wealth Tax Act, as well as the creation of the Resettlement Administration and the Rural Electrification Administration. Although

25. John D. Allen, "Journalism in the South," in *Culture in the South,* ed. W. T. Couch (Chapel Hill, N.C., 1934), p. 146.
26. Earl Black and Merle Black, *Politics and Society in the South* (Cambridge, Mass., 1987), p. 214.

these measures provoked criticism from certain conservative interests in the South, most southerners and their representatives in Washington continued to give the New Deal strong support. In the presidential election of 1936, every southern state voted overwhelmingly in favor of FDR.

Nevertheless, the South's response to Roosevelt and the New Deal was one of approval mixed with uneasiness. One disquieting development was the reconstruction of the Democratic party. While the South remained an essential part of the Democratic coalition, it was suddenly changed by the partisan realignment of the 1930s from a majority faction in a minority party to a minority faction in a majority party. The massive Democratic gains outside the South had drastically reduced the dependence of the national party on southern voters and now threatened the traditional power of southern leaders in Washington. One of the region's longtime defenses—the two-thirds rule for making presidential nominations in national Democratic conventions—was abolished in 1936. Roosevelt, it seemed, was preparing to move beyond the traditional party base. The new Democratic coalition, as Arthur M. Schlesinger, Jr., has written, meant that the South "would now be just one element in a broad national coalition; the city machines, just another. Most of the other elements— labor, the newer immigrants, Negroes, women, intellectuals—were particularly accessible in great cities of the North, increasingly unresponsive to old-school bosses and machines, and increasingly insistent on direct representation in the new politics."[27] Although the Democratic party in Congress had become more northern and urban, it was still powerfully influenced by its southern leaders. And the southerners' key positions and skillful use of obstructionist tactics enabled them to turn back efforts to pass an anti-lynching bill and outlaw the poll tax as a voting prerequisite.

Whatever its long-range implications, Roosevelt's New Deal did not transform southern politics. Conservative officeholders, institutions, and attitudes were too firmly entrenched at the state and local levels to be dislodged by the president's reform programs. The New Deal, being dependent on home state authorities for the administration of its policies, did little to interfere with the distribution of political power within the region. "In effect," one historian says of the situation in Memphis, "the New Deal was filtered through the [Edward H.] Crump machine."[28] This helps explain the Roosevelt administration's willingness to accept racial discrimination in the operation of its own relief agencies, to tolerate wage differentials between blacks and whites, and to shy away from involvement in union-organizing efforts in the South. The result was that the New Deal tended to strengthen, not to undermine, the dominant political factions in most southern states. Influential southern liberals, moreover, were small in number and relatively weak, and the historian Alan Brinkley has argued that they were further hampered by the fear they shared with conservatives of "federal interference in the South's right to manage its own affairs and chart its own course." On occasion southern liberals complained about the ef-

27. Arthur M. Schlesinger, Jr., *The Age of Roosevelt: The Politics of Upheaval* (Boston, 1960), p. 423.
28. Roger Biles, *Memphis in the Great Depression* (Knoxville, Tenn., 1986), p. 86.

forts of "outside liberals" to impose a rigid kind of national reform on a region with its own special needs.[29] Although the South shared in the resurgence of American nationalism in the 1930s, its sectional interests and traditions qualified its nationalism.

Efforts to improve the condition of the more deprived southerners, inspired by liberal currents from Washington, were repeatedly frustrated by conservative opposition in the southern states and by the limits of New Deal power. In the case of agriculture, for example, crop reductions and federal subsidies and rental payments made it possible for landlords to evict many of their tenants even as they protested that relief payments and public works wages were too high to enable them to secure the seasonal workers they needed. Landlords generally refused to share federal benefit payments with their tenants, and when a group of liberals in the Agricultural Adjustment Administration tried to protect tenant rights, the liberals were forced to resign. An interracial organization called the Southern Tenant Farmers' Union (STFU), formed in 1934, struggled throughout the decade to advance the cause of the rural dispossessed, but without much success. The New Deal stimulated the growth of organized labor, and some progress was made in the enactment of more progressive labor legislation in the southern states. But many of the gains in union membership proved ephemeral, and organized labor won few of its major objectives.[30]

Even so, the ferment of the 1930s was pervasive. Not since the Populist revolt had ideological divisions been of such central importance in southern politics. The labels "liberal" and "conservative" acquired a more substantive meaning, and the fiscal, regulatory, and welfare functions of government generated heated debate among southerners. Roosevelt's leadership inspired and directed southern liberals in Congress, as well as a more numerous aggregation of New Deal partisans in statehouses and agencies throughout the South. Most of these Democrats shared FDR's desire to liberalize the Democratic party in Congress and in their respective states. They tended to accept the reality of the colonial South and to believe that a reactionary ruling class at home, in combination with powerful outside interests, was responsible for the South's social and political problems. They advocated repeal of the poll tax, favorable labor legislation, and the equalization of intersectional freight rates. The New Deal also encouraged a scattering of more radical activists in the South: the Highlander Folk School, the Southern Policy Committee, the Fellowship of Southern Churchmen, and the Southern Conference for Human Welfare.

At the same time, the New Deal aroused the political consciousness of millions of ordinary southerners—of poor farmers, coal miners, blacks, and working people generally. Franklin Roosevelt seemed to be the catalyst for this new political awareness. Reporting on a trip to the Carolinas in 1934, the journalist Martha Gellhorn observed that "Every house I visited—mill worker or unem-

29. Alan Brinkley, "The New Deal and Southern Politics," in *The New Deal and the South*, ed. Cobb and Namorato, pp. 98–109.

30. Fite, *Cotton Fields No More*, pp. 141–48; Tindall, *The Emergence of the New South*, pp. 505–26; Donald H. Grubbs, *Cry from the Cotton: The Southern Tenant Farmers' Union and the New Deal* (Chapel Hill, N.C., 1971).

ployed—had a picture of the President. . . . He is at once God and their inti-
mate friend; he knows them all by name, knows their little town and mill, their
little lives and problems."[31] "Negroes shud vote for Mistuh Roosevelt if they
kin," a black day laborer and Works Projects Administration worker told an
interviewer in 1940. "I been here twenty years, but since WPA, the Negro sho'
has started talkin' 'bout politics."[32]

Several southern governors became known as New Dealers. James V. Allred,
who served as governor of Texas during the years 1935–1939, brought that
state into the national social welfare system and in other respects cooperated
with New Deal programs. Bibb Graves, a liberal factional leader in Alabama,
was closely identified with the New Deal during his tenure as governor (1935–
1939). In Georgia, Eurith D. "Ed" Rivers, a former supporter of Eugene Talmadge, was elected governor in 1936. He gave Georgia a "Little New Deal"
and sponsored a series of measures that enabled the state to share in the Roosevelt programs. Rivers encountered revenue shortages, however, and his resort
to martial law and liberal use of the pardoning power, along with an investigation of wrongdoing in the highway department, weakened his administration
and caused him to leave office under a cloud. The difficulties that confronted
state reformers in the 1930s were illustrated in Virginia, where James H. Price,
a supporter of the New Deal, won the governorship only to face the implacable
opposition of Senator Harry Flood Byrd's machine. The Price administration
accomplished some of its objectives, but New Deal Democrats were unable to
create a viable organization of their own in the Old Dominion, even with a
measure of support from President Roosevelt. The ranks of the liberal, anti-
organization faction soon dwindled in the face of the regulars' strength, the organization's control of patronage, and the growing reaction against the New
Deal. Roosevelt, increasingly concerned with developments abroad, made
peace with Virginia's conservatives after 1939.[33]

Few opponents of FDR's reforms, North or South, were more vehement in
their denunciation than Governor Eugene Talmadge of Georgia. Talmadge set
out to obstruct his state's participation in the president's programs. "The New
Deal," the governor declared on one occasion, "is a combination of wet-
nursin', frenzied finance, downright communism, and plain damn-foolish-
ness."[34] Having presidential ambitions of his own, Talmadge helped organize
an anti–New Deal "Grass Roots Convention," which was held in Macon,
Georgia, in January 1936. "Jeffersonian Democrats" from seventeen southern
and border states were invited to attend the convention, which was sponsored

31. Quoted in Robert S. McElvaine, *The Great Depression: America, 1929–1941* (New York,
1984), pp. 115–16.

32. Quoted in Ralph J. Bunche, *The Political Status of the Negro in the Age of FDR*, ed. Dewey W.
Grantham (Chicago, 1973), p. 429.

33. Tindall, *The Emergence of the New South*, pp. 642–49; Merlin G. Cox, "David Sholtz: New
Deal Governor of Florida," *Florida Historical Quarterly* 43 (October 1964): 142–52; A. Cash
Koeniger, "The New Deal and the States: Roosevelt versus the Byrd Organization in Virginia,"
Journal of American History 68 (March 1982): 876–96; Jane Walker Herndon, "Ed Rivers and
Georgia's 'Little New Deal,' " *Atlanta Historical Journal* 30 (Spring 1986): 97–105.

34. Quoted in Allan A. Michie and Frank Ryhlick, *Dixie Demagogues* (New York, 1939), p. 184.

by the Southern Committee to Uphold the Constitution. The affair turned out to be a fiasco. "Our Gene" failed to control the Georgia delegation to the Democratic national convention in 1936, and he was trounced in his campaign for the Senate by Richard B. Russell, who defended the New Deal and his support of it in the Senate.[35]

The more conservative members of Congress from the South were torn between a desire to meet the pressing needs of their constituents and their dedication to a balanced budget, strong local government, and administrative efficiency. They were not unappreciative of their party's extraordinary success and of its leader's great popularity, but they were apprehensive and restless. Senator Carter Glass, perhaps the most impassioned of the New Deal's southern critics, soon concluded that Roosevelt's reforms represented an assault on southern traditions such as state rights, individualism, constitutional government, and white supremacy.[36] Another southern senator, Huey P. Long, gave the Roosevelt administration even more trouble than the conservatives. Until his assassination in 1935, the Louisiana senator condemned much of the New Deal as of little benefit to the poor and disadvantaged while serving the interests of the established and well-to-do. Early in 1934, Long launched his Share Our Wealth program and prepared to challenge Roosevelt's reelection in 1936. He was the subject of extensive media coverage and quickly became a national figure, perhaps the most compelling political leader from the South since Woodrow Wilson. No other southern politician could match his appeal outside the South. Long, one of his interpreters suggests, expressed the "dominant insurgent force in the depression South," a force that "drew from the region's own populist traditions, one that could produce both radical and reactionary demands, one that could find expression simultaneously in a Huey Long and a Eugene Talmadge."[37]

Roosevelt knew that men like Joe Robinson and Pat Harrison were troubled "about the whole New Deal." They wondered, FDR told a friend in the summer of 1935, "where that fellow in the White House is taking the good old Democratic party." Roosevelt went on to say, "I will have trouble with my own Democratic party from this time on in trying to carry out further programs of reform and recovery."[38] Yet he had not lost sight of the importance of main-

35. William Anderson, *The Wild Man from Sugar Creek: The Political Career of Eugene Talmadge* (Baton Rouge, La., 1975), pp. 105–67; Sarah McCulloh Lemmon, "The Ideology of Eugene Talmadge," *Georgia Historical Quarterly* 38 (September 1954): 226–48; Lemmon, "Governor Eugene Talmadge and the New Deal," in J. Carlyle Sitterson, ed., *Studies in Southern History* (Chapel Hill, N.C., 1957), pp. 152–68; Howard N. Mead, "Russell vs. Talmadge: Southern Politics and the New Deal," *Georgia Historical Quarterly* 65 (Spring 1981): 28–45.

36. A. Cash Koeniger, "Carter Glass and the National Recovery Administration," *South Atlantic Quarterly* 74 (Summer 1975): 349–64.

37. Brinkley, "The New Deal and Southern Politics," p. 111. See also Alan Brinkley, *Voices of Protest: Huey Long, Father Coughlin, and the Great Depression* (New York, 1982), pp. 194–215; Brinkley, "Huey Long, the Share Our Wealth Movement, and the Limits of Depression Dissidence," *Louisiana History* 22 (Spring 1981): 117–34; and Robert E. Snyder, "Huey Long and the Presidential Election of 1936," *Louisiana History* 16 (Spring 1975): 117–43.

38. Max Freedman, ed., *Roosevelt and Frankfurter: Their Correspondence, 1928–1945* (Boston, 1967), pp. 282–83.

taining the support of southern congressional leaders. "I did not choose the tools with which I must work," Roosevelt reminded Walter White of the National Association for the Advancement of Colored People. "Had I been permitted to choose them I would have selected quite different ones. But I've got to get legislation passed by Congress to save America. The Southerners by reason of the seniority rule in Congress are chairmen or occupy strategic places on most of the Senate and House committees. If I come out for the anti-lynching bill now, they will block every bill I ask Congress to pass to keep America from collapsing. I just can't take that risk."[39] Still, the president's patience was not unlimited and, following his triumphant reelection in 1936, he was in no mood to make large concessions to southern Democrats.

Frustrated by the Supreme Court's invalidation of much of his legislative program and emboldened by his electoral landslide in 1936, Roosevelt suddenly unveiled a plan to reform the court. His proposal to "pack" the Supreme Court created a great political crisis, gave his critics an effective issue, and brought conservatives from both parties together in opposition.[40] It also resulted in a major setback for the administration. Many southern congressmen backed the president in the court fight, and a Gallup poll revealed that a majority of the respondents approved the plan in every southern state except Kentucky and Oklahoma, while 53 percent of the national sample opposed it. But a good number of southern congressmen deserted Roosevelt for the first time. Conservatives throughout the South became more outspoken in their criticism of FDR and his administration. Some, like Frederick Sullens, editor of the Jackson (Miss.) *Daily News*, had progressed from "fervent support in 1933–34, through suspicion and disenchantment in 1935–36 to open hostility in the latter years of the decade."[41]

In the fall of 1937, an informal coalition of anti–New Deal Democrats and Republicans took shape. Southerners assumed a leading role in the coalescence of these congressional conservatives. The concern that united them was their opposition to much of the New Deal—to the growth of federal power and bureaucracy, to deficit spending, to industrial labor unions, and to most welfare programs. The timing of their action was obviously related to the defeat of Roosevelt's court reform proposal. In a statement of principles, drafted in December 1937 by Josiah W. Bailey of North Carolina and other conservative leaders, the dissidents presented a ten-point list of demands, including a balanced budget, tax reduction in order "to free investment funds," a new labor policy, maintenance of state rights and local self-government, and reliance upon the "American form of government and the American system of free en-

39. Walter White, *A Man Called White: The Autobiography of Walter White* (New York, 1948), pp. 169–70.

40. For an example of southern opposition, see Lionel V. Patenaude, "Garner, Sumners, and Connally: The Defeat of the Roosevelt Court Bill in 1937," *Southwestern Historical Quarterly* 74 (July 1970): 36–51.

41. John R. Skates, "From Enchantment to Disillusionment: A Southern Editor Views the New Deal," *Southern Quarterly* 5 (July 1967): 363–64.

terprise."[42] The coalition was a major factor in the failure of several New Deal measures in the late 1930s. Nevertheless, Southern congressional opposition to the legislative recommendations of the Roosevelt administration should not be exaggerated. On most issues the southerners continued to follow the party line. There was considerable diversity among the southern members, and their voting patterns revealed them to be only slightly more cohesive than the Republicans and nonsouthern Democrats. Genuine southern solidarity could be found only on the race question.[43]

Still, several other Roosevelt initiatives provoked resentment and criticism from southerners in and out of Congress. One of these was Roosevelt's behind-the-scenes intervention in the contest to elect a Senate majority leader following Joe Robinson's death in the midst of the court fight. Alben Barkley, a staunch administration man, defeated Pat Harrison, a more conservative and less reliable New Dealer, by one vote. The Louisville Courier-Journal, a pro-Roosevelt newspaper, argued that the election of Harrison would have "encouraged the tentative coalition between anti-Administrationists and Republicans to scuttle the New Deal."[44] The administration was also identified with an outbreak of sit-down strikes in 1937 and 1938, and its wages and hours bill threatened to wipe out regional wage differentials, against the wishes of many southern businessmen and politicians. Nor did the president's reference to the South as "the Nation's No. 1 economic problem," with the implication that the region's plight required liberal legislation and the election of liberal southerners to support the New Deal, improve his standing in the South.

Roosevelt, smarting over his defeat in the court struggle and his failure to get congressional approval of other reforms in 1937, moved to bolster his position by working to elect pro–New Deal Democrats in the midterm elections of 1938. Among the president's targets were a number of southerners, including Senators Walter F. George of Georgia and Ellison D. "Cotton Ed" Smith of South Carolina. Speaking on several occasions in the South, Roosevelt appealed for the election of congressmen who would cooperate with him in undertaking fundamental changes in southern economic and political practices. This attempt to "purge" Democratic conservatives focused national attention on the New Deal as an election issue, particularly in the South. Although Senators George, Smith, and Millard E. Tydings of Maryland were all reelected, Roosevelt was successful in several southern primaries, and a Gallup poll at about the same time showed that two-thirds of the southerners interviewed approved the president's performance in office. But many people resented his intervention.[45]

42. John Robert Moore, "Senator Josiah W. Bailey and the 'Conservative Manifesto' of 1937," *Journal of Southern History* 31 (February 1965): 21–39; James T. Patterson, "A Conservative Coalition Forms in Congress, 1933–1939," *Journal of American History* 52 (March 1966): 757–72; Patterson, *Congressional Conservatism and the New Deal: The Growth of the Conservative Coalition in Congress, 1933–1939* (Lexington, Ky., 1967).

43. V. O. Key, Jr., with the assistance of Alexander Heard, *Southern Politics in State and Nation* (New York, 1949), pp. 345–82.

44. Quoted in Philip A. Grant, Jr., "Editorial Reaction to the Harrison-Barkley Senate Leadership Contest, 1937," *Journal of Mississippi History* 36 (May 1974): 133.

45. Tindall, *The Emergence of the New South*, pp. 625–29; Patterson, "The Failure of Party Re-

Carter Glass warned that the South had better "begin thinking whether it will continue to cast its 152 electoral votes according to the memories of the Reconstruction era of 1865 and thereafter, or will have spirit and courage enough to face the new Reconstruction era that northern so-called Democrats are menacing us with."[46]

The events of the late 1930s heightened the concern of the "county-seat elites" and governing class in the South over the possible consequences of the national administration's welfare and labor programs, over the enlarged role of the federal government, and over Roosevelt's efforts to reform the courts and remove his conservative critics from office. A recent study of North Carolina in this period concludes that the state was most influenced by a "conservative, business-oriented ideology that survived the changes wrought by the New Deal."[47] Congressional leaders like Glass, Harrison, and Garner, reflecting the propertied interests of their region, were determined "to secure and maintain the existing socioeconomic society at home in the South."[48] Writing in 1935, a South Carolinian informed Senator James F. Byrnes of his dedication to the Democratic party and his faith in President Roosevelt. "At the same time," he observed, "I have always felt that he was surrounded by an aggregation of parlor communists and socialists and that too many of this unpractical type was even placed in his cabinet."[49] Southern liberals as well as conservatives were wary of the relationship between the New Deal, northern liberals, and Communists. The Birmingham journalist John Temple Graves, for instance, denounced northern Democrats for their failure, "in their approaches to the South, to separate themselves clearly from a communism which ruling Southerners hate and fear above all else."[50]

In some respects divisions among Americans—class, ethnic, regional— during the Great Depression were softened as a consequence of the universal hard times, deprivation, and suffering. Experiencing such an ordeal seemed to foster, at least at times, a heightened sense of unity, understanding, and compassion among the nation's citizens. But this mood did not obliterate longtime divisions among the American people, including sectional attitudes and issues. Many Americans outside the South, for example, resented the power wielded by

---

alignment in the South," pp. 602–17; J. B. Shannon, "Presidential Politics in the South: 1938," *Journal of Politics* 1 (May 1939): 146–70, (August 1939): 278–300; Luther Harmon Zeigler, Jr., "Senator Walter George's 1938 Campaign," *Georgia Historical Quarterly* 43 (December 1959): 333–52.

46. Quoted in Patterson, "The Failure of Party Realignment in the South," pp. 602–603.

47. Anthony J. Badger, *North Carolina and the New Deal* (Raleigh, 1981), p. 96. See also James T. Patterson, "The New Deal and the States," *American Historical Review* 73 (October 1967): 70–84; Don C. Reading, "New Deal Activity and the States, 1933 to 1939," *Journal of Economic History* 33 (December 1973): 792–810; and Anthony J. Badger, "The New Deal and the Localities," in *The Growth of Federal Power in American History*, ed. Rhodri Jeffreys-Jones and Bruce Collins (Edinburgh, 1983), pp. 102–15.

48. George E. Mowry, *Another Look at the Twentieth-Century South* (Baton Rouge, La., 1973), p. 60.

49. David S. Allen to James F. Byrnes, 6 March 1935, James F. Byrnes Papers, Clemson University Library.

50. Quoted in Brinkley, "The New Deal and Southern Politics," p. 106.

southern congressmen and the way in which the South's peculiar institutions imposed limits on the achievement of *national* reform. To be sure, every region sought to protect its own interests in Washington and thus applied constraints on the passage and implementation of new national legislation. It was southern interests and purposes, however, that were most conspicuously at odds with the rest of the nation in the depression decade, at least in domestic affairs.

Although the regional implications of New Deal policies were less salient than one might expect, they were manifest in the consideration of public works, industrial subsidies, immigration, agriculture, organized labor, the tariff, race relations, government regulation, and state rights. Inflation, relief programs, and demands for federal subsidies were major objectives of the peripheral South and West in the depression, while the northeastern and midwestern core increasingly turned to governmental regulation and subsidies. Both periphery and core favored the expansion of federal regulation and fiscal authority. Southern congressmen generally opposed the adoption of a national minimum wage but argued for a national standard in the allocation of relief funds. Northern lawmakers supported a national wage standard for private enterprise but insisted that regional differences in living standards should be reflected in public works payments. These regional differences were evident in the Democratic party. The northern wing of the party, despite periodic and largely symbolic efforts to pass anti-lynching and anti-poll tax legislation, was willing to tolerate racial discrimination in the South as a necessary political compromise.[51]

Southerners had long been sensitive to criticisms of their region's working conditions and wage levels, especially those involving intersectional competition in the textile industry. In 1929, for example, in response to a congressional call for a federal investigation of the southern textile industry, Senator Furnifold M. Simmons charged that the South had been slandered and had suffered from misleading propaganda concerning labor conditions in the region's cotton textile mills.[52] Though southern leaders succeeded in securing the adoption of regional wage differentials in the National Recovery Administration codes that most directly affected them, they were suspicious of New Deal labor legislation. John E. Edgerton of Tennessee, a former president of the National Association of Manufacturers, contended that the NRA "was devised, to a very large extent, to reform the South." Edgerton was instrumental in organizing the Southern States Industrial Council "to protect the South against discrimination"—that is, against higher wages.[53] In presenting the South's case against federal labor standards, southern senators maintained that the region could not afford to pay its workers as much as New England did, and that the South needed the kind of

51. Richard Franklin Bensel, *Sectionalism and American Political Development, 1880–1980* (Madison, Wis., 1984), pp. 147–74. See also Julius Turner, *Party and Constituency: Pressures on Congress* (Baltimore, Md., 1951).

52. Elmer L. Puryear, *Democratic Party Dissension in North Carolina, 1928–1936* (Chapel Hill, N.C., 1962), p. 22.

53. Tindall, *The Emergence of the New South*, pp. 443–44; Douglas Carl Abrams, *Conservative Constraints: North Carolina and the New Deal* (Jackson, Miss., 1992), ch. 2.

PER CAPITA FEDERAL EXPENDITURES, 1933–1939

	Expenditures Per Capita	Percentage of U.S. Average
United States	$224	
West	306	137
Midwest	224	100
Northeast	196	88
South	189	84
Alabama	175	78
Arkansas	256	114
Georgia	171	76
Louisiana	221	99
Mississippi	228	102
North Carolina	143	64
South Carolina	198	88
Tennessee	183	82
Texas	205	92
Virginia	175	78

SOURCE: Leonard Arrington, "The New Deal in the West: A Preliminary Statistical Inquiry," *Pacific Historical Review* 38 (August 1969): 312–14.

wage differentials built into the NRA and the public works agencies. They extolled their region's natural advantages, which Turner Catledge said featured "a plentiful supply of cheap, docile, dependable, and unorganized labor."[54] Many southerners believed that the Roosevelt administration's proposed wages and hours law was basically an attempt by northern business to remove the South's advantage in the labor market, that it was a "northern industrialist-inspired attempt to reduce the cost advantages of growing southern competitors."[55] Senator Byrnes asserted that "the hope, if not the purpose, of the principal advocates of this measure is to stop the movement of industries to the South, and to cause some to return to New England."[56]

Speaking on the wages and hours bill in December 1937, Representative Wade Hampton Kitchens of Arkansas referred to "lurking and concealed objectives" in the measure that struck him as being "selfish, sectional, discriminatory, and destructive to small industrial plants and their labor to the great advantage of the large monopolistic plants." Kitchens could not forget, he declared, "that the large industries and their labor in certain sections have been fostered and protected by tariffs and cheaper freight rates at the expense of all

54. Quoted in Chester M. Morgan, *Redneck Liberal: Theodore G. Bilbo and the New Deal* (Baton Rouge, La., 1985), pp. 172–73.
55. See, for example, Skates, "A Southern Editor Views the New Deal," p. 377, and Bensel, *Sectionalism and American Political Development*, p. 160 (quotation).
56. James F. Byrnes to "Dear Sir," 3 August 1937, in Byrnes Papers.

other labor, farmers, and other consumers, and thereby have been given special privileges and financial favors not enjoyed by others."[57] Southern spokesmen claimed that comparatively low wage scales in the South were justified by lower living costs in the region. They also argued that discriminatory freight rates, maintained through federal regulation, had retarded southern industrialization, and that a lower wage scale was the best way the South's industries had of overcoming that disadvantage.[58]

North-South differences were given more sensational exposure in the popular press. Outside newspapers and journals gave extensive coverage to the exploitation of industrial workers in the South, to the wretched condition of the region's tenant farmers, to the demagoguery and provincialism of southern politicians, and to the harsh treatment of blacks below the Mason-Dixon line. Anti-union violence also attracted the attention of outside commentators, who seized on evidence of anti-labor intimidation and force such as that provided by Senator Robert M. La Follette's committee on civil liberties in 1937.[59] When the young reporter Harry S. Ashmore proposed an investigation of northern industrial slums, his editors at the Greenville (S.C.) *Piedmont* jumped at the chance to respond to the sustained northern attacks on the low-wage, stretchout (increased workload) practices in the South's anti-union cotton mills. Ashmore found plenty of evidence to sustain his "prefabricated conclusions"— sweatshop labor in New York City, industrial ghost towns in New England, slums in Philadelphia, and "the universal fear" that industry would move away. Ashmore's articles appeared in twenty-two southern newspapers, and the enterprise even attracted the attention of *Time* magazine.[60]

A new kind of literature that combined "social reportage with photographic illustration often focused on the South."[61] Documentaries like Erskine Caldwell's and Margaret Bourke-White's *You Have Seen Their Faces* (1937) attracted many northern readers. It was not a pretty picture. A reviewer for the *Nation* described the South as "so sick from its old infections of prejudice and poverty that it is a menace to the nation."[62] The Southern Tenant Farmers' Union gained national attention in the mid-1930s, and an outpouring of photography and reportage, stimulated by New Deal agencies, graphically depicted rural poverty in the South. One historian has noted that the popularity of Erskine Caldwell's *Tobacco Road* (1932) inspired "a sharecropper fashion in the literature of the decade."[63] At the same time, some of the films of the 1930s intensified the

57. Quoted in Bensel, *Sectionalism and American Political Development*, p. 161. See also Coode, "Tennessee Congressmen and the New Deal," pp. 155–56, and H. M. Douty, "Recovery and the Southern Wage Differential," *Southern Economic Journal* 4 (January 1938): 314–21.

58. Bensel, *Sectionalism and American Political Development*, p. 160.

59. Jerold S. Auerbach, *Labor and Liberty: The La Follette Committee and the New Deal* (Indianapolis, 1966), pp. 116–20; Tindall, *The Emergence of the New South*, pp. 525–30.

60. Harry S. Ashmore, *Hearts and Minds: A Personal Chronicle of Race in America* (Washington, D.C., 1988), pp. 35–39.

61. Tindall, *The Emergence of the New South*, p. 589.

62. Quoted in Jack Temple Kirby, *Media-Made Dixie: The South in the American Imagination* (Baton Rouge, La., 1978), pp. 59–60 (quotation on p. 60).

63. Tindall, *The Emergence of the New South*, pp. 409–15 (quotation on p. 415).

northern imagery of a benighted South. Such motion pictures as *I Am a Fugitive from a Chain Gang* and *Hell's Highway*, both released in 1932, emphasized the backwardness and brutality of the southern prison system.[64]

Although racial discrimination and brutality at the hands of white southerners were only one aspect of northern criticism of the South, they were among the most important sources of intersectional condemnation and recrimination in the 1930s. A series of bizarre lynchings, an increase in peonage, and the flagrant unfairness of the southern criminal system all contributed to the South's unsavory reputation in other regions. The most conspicuous advocate of racial justice among northern liberals was the president's wife. "Eleanor Roosevelt," one scholar writes, "was made the symbol of everything wrong with the 'damnyankee,' race-meddling New Deal."[65] White southerners developed a litany of complaints: "She goes around telling the Negroes they are as good as anyone else." "Wherever she has spoken the Negroes always act like they are white folks." "She preaches and practices social equality."[66]

A federal anti-lynching law became the focus of legislative reform efforts undertaken by racial liberals during the 1930s. Despite the work of the Commission on Interracial Cooperation and the Association of Southern Women for the Prevention of Lynching, the decade brought an increase in mob violence directed at black southerners. The number of black lynching victims rose from seven in 1929 to twenty in 1930, twenty-four in 1933, and eighteen in 1935. The proposed statute, drafted late in 1933 under the leadership of the National Association for the Advancement of Colored People, would have made lynching a federal offense. It was finally passed by the House of Representatives in the spring of 1937, before being killed in the Senate by a southern filibuster early in 1938. President Roosevelt and other party leaders were keenly aware of the emerging role of black voters in northern and western elections—and as a component of the national Democratic coalition. During the Senate filibuster against the anti-lynching bill, southern spokesmen kept talking about the changing composition of the Democratic party—the new party of blacks, city bosses, and labor barons. Indeed, talk of a "nigger-loving New Deal" and condemnation of "the vile liberal appeal" for Negro votes punctuated congressional debate on relief, housing, and labor legislation in the late 1930s.[67]

One of the most spectacular episodes in the intersectional dialogue of the 1930s was the Scottsboro case. The case began in March 1931, when nine

---

64. Kirby, *Media-Made Dixie*, p. 57.

65. Harvard Sitkoff, *A New Deal for Blacks: The Emergence of Civil Rights as a National Issue*, vol. 1: *The Depression Decade* (New York, 1978), p. 106. See also John T. Kneebone, *Southern Liberal Journalists and the Issue of Race, 1920–1944* (Chapel Hill, N.C., 1985), pp. 80–82, and Walter T. Howard, "Vigilante Justice and National Reaction: The 1937 Tallahassee Double Lynching," *Florida Historical Quarterly* 67 (July 1988): 32–51.

66. Quoted in Nancy J. Weiss, *Farewell to the Party of Lincoln: Black Politics in the Age of FDR* (Princeton, N.J., 1983), p. 129.

67. Robert L. Zangrando, *The NAACP Crusade Against Lynching, 1909–1950* (Philadelphia, 1980), pp. 110–65; Sitkoff, *A New Deal for Blacks*, pp. 268–97; Weiss, *Farewell to the Party of Lincoln*, pp. 241–49; Freidel, *F.D.R. and the South*, pp. 71–102; Tindall, *The Emergence of the New South*, pp. 551–56.

young black men were arrested and charged with raping two white women while traveling on a freight train across northern Alabama. They were tried in the small town of Scottsboro, convicted, and all except the youngest sentenced to the electric chair. Several of them were retried and again convicted, even though one of the women reversed her previous testimony and denied that a rape had ever occurred. The Supreme Court twice overturned the convictions, and "the boys" were eventually released, a number of them after serving long prison terms. For most white southerners the case raised the specter of Communist subversion and racial insubordination. Many of them contended that "the South could have handled the case with justice if it had been left alone by the crusading Yankees."[68] Reaction outside the region was divided between the NAACP and the International Labor Defense (ILD), the legal affiliate of the Communist party, but as Dan T. Carter has said, for American liberals Scottsboro "became a tragic symbol of the sickness which pervaded the South's regional culture."[69] The ILD, which handled the defense until 1935, mounted an aggressive campaign of legal appeal and national propaganda that portrayed the youths as victims of a racist, capitalist society. Supporters of the Scottsboro boys organized rallies, marches, fund-raising drives, and letter-writing appeals in many parts of the North and West. Similar efforts were made in the case of Angelo Herndon, a young black Communist arrested in Atlanta for organizing a demonstration of the unemployed. Herndon was convicted of insurrection under an archaic Georgia law and sentenced to eighteen to twenty years in prison. After years of litigation and a Supreme Court ruling that invalidated the Georgia statute, Herndon finally won his freedom.[70]

Some southerners, including the historian Frank L. Owsley, accused the contemporary North of undertaking a "third crusade" against the South.[71] Owsley, one of the Southern Agrarians who wrote *I'll Take My Stand*, claimed that the South had long been the victim of the "industrial" power-hungry North, which was masquerading in the "robes of morality." In reality, he asserted, it was practicing a "sectionalism of exploitation." Then, wrote Owsley, the South and West combined in 1932 to overthrow the party of the "capitalists-industrialists." The latter now sought the assistance of the "proletarian-industrialists" or Communist element, which worked for the release of the Scottsboro boys and condemned the southern administration of justice as a means of creating friction between the races and providing still more "outrage-propaganda." In defending the South, Owsley referred to crooked lawyers and gangsters in the North who transformed justice there into "a cruel farce."[72]

68. Carroll Van West, "Perpetuating the Myth of America: Scottsboro and Its Interpreters," *South Atlantic Quarterly* 80 (Winter 1981): 36–48. For an illuminating account of the case, see Dan T. Carter, *Scottsboro: A Tragedy of the American South* (Baton Rouge, La., 1969).

69. Carter, *Scottsboro*, p. vii.

70. Charles H. Martin, "Communists and Blacks: The ILD and the Angelo Herndon Case," *Journal of Negro History* 64 (Spring 1979): 131–41.

71. Frank L. Owsley, "Scottsboro, the Third Crusade: The Sequel to Abolition and Reconstruction," *American Review* 1 (June 1933): 257–84.

72. *Ibid.*, pp. 275–77.

After the Great Depression and the New Deal, the South would never be the same again. Nor would the old relationship between the region and the larger nation ever be restored. Numan V. Bartley, among other recent scholars, has called the years 1935–1945 a "crucial decade" in the modern experience of the American South, for developments in that period eventually produced "massive changes in southern life."[73] Some of these changes were structural, such as those in agriculture, industrial labor, urban life, and government. Others involved new relationships, such as those between the cities and states and the national government. This was an aspect of the nationalization of American life in the 1930s, and while this nationalism encompassed a new appreciation of local and regional lore, it was also related to technological innovation and modernization, to political centralization and bureaucratization, and to the decline of geographical isolation and provincialism.

Franklin D. Roosevelt's leadership and the New Deal precipitated a great popular discussion of economic questions in the South, forced national issues into state and local political contests, and introduced codes and standards that did much to undermine local autonomy and state rights. The new programs brought a welcome stream of federal money into the southern states for relief and economic development. The New Deal also provided southern congressmen with an opportunity to contribute to the enactment of a momentous program of national reform and fostered the liberalism of many southerners. Without southern support, Frank Freidel notes, Roosevelt would never have been nominated in 1932. Furthermore, "It was Southern leadership in Congress that enacted the New Deal program and subsequently supplied to the President the requisite margin of votes to pass defense measures in the late thirties and early forties."[74] Nevertheless, much remained unchanged in the South on the eve of the Second World War. Roosevelt had not seriously challenged the region's conservative power structure or its one-party politics. The South's traditional system of race relations was still intact. Not much had been done to relieve the South's pervasive rural poverty or to improve the region's relative economic position in the nation. The South's status as a colonial appendage of the powerful Northeast and Midwest had not changed for the better.

Yet in other respects the southern role in the nation had changed, or was undergoing a significant alteration. Regional conflict, while frequently manifesting itself during the 1930s, was in some ways less intense than during the 1920s. Issues involving class differences and group interests had become more important. At the same time, the South's special interests and regional self-consciousness inevitably led to intersectional friction, debate, and compromise, altering the old regional equilibrium in the process. This was illustrated in the emergence of a new Democratic majority coalition, in the South's declining influence in the national party, and in the increasing strength of nonsouthern elements in the party. The emergence of this new and more powerful Demo-

73. Numan V. Bartley, "The Era of the New Deal as a Turning Point in Southern History," in *The New Deal and the South*, ed. Cobb and Namorato, p. 138.
74. Freidel, *F.D.R. and the South*, p. 2.

cratic coalition suggests that the changes the New Deal "wrought in American society at large [had] brought mounting external pressure for changes in the South."[75] Some northern liberals, including Franklin Roosevelt, had decided by the late 1930s to deal directly with the South as a national problem, in effect to sponsor the liberalization, economic development, and modernization of the region. Other northern liberals, particularly those interested in racial change in the South, were impatient with southern resistance to more thoroughgoing reform. These Democrats would soon be willing to confront the southerners in Congress and to use coercive measures against the South. Meanwhile, an influential group of southern conservatives had entered into an active collaboration with northern Republicans. This conservative coalition was a portent of things to come. These developments reveal that southern regionalism in the 1930s had become more complex, dynamic, and nationally important than at any time since the turn of the century.

75. Cobb and Namorato, "Introduction," in *The New Deal and the South*, p. 14.

Prophet of the New South: Henry W. Grady of the *Atlanta Constitution*. (*Robert W. Woodruff Library, Emory University*)

"Thomas E. Watson, of Georgia. Nominated by the Populists' National Convention for Vice-President at 1:40 A.M. This Morning" (*New York Times*). (*The Library of Congress*)

William Jennings Bryan of Nebraska, Democratic leader from 1896 to 1912 and a powerful figure in southern politics. (*The Library of Congress*)

Political hostility between a New York president and a South Carolina senator: Teddy Roosevelt and Pitchfork Ben Tillman. (*U.S. Senate Historical Office*)

Alabama chain gang, 1909. (*The Birmingham Public Library*)

Child labor in Georgia, 1913. (*Hargrett Rare Book and Manuscript Library, University of Georgia Libraries*)

Hookworm rally, Lutcher, Louisiana. (*Southern Historical Collection, University of North Carolina at Chapel Hill Library*)

Prohibition election in Lowndes County, Georgia, 1907. (*Georgia Department of Archives and History*)

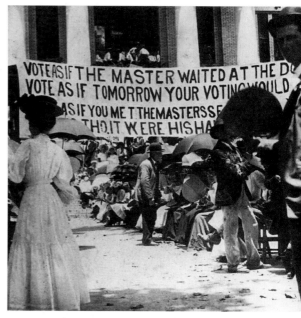

National Negro Business League Executive Committee. Booker T. Washington is seated, second from left. (*The Library of Congress*)

Southern congressional leaders: Representative Oscar W. Underwood of Alabama. (*The Birmingham Public Library*)

Southern congressional leaders: Senator Furnifold M. Simmons of North Carolina. (*U.S. Senate Historical Office*)

Preparedness parade, Mobile, Alabama, July 4, 1916. (*Erik Overbey Collection, University of South Alabama Archives*)

Women register to vote for the first time, Mobile, Alabama, 1920. (*Erik Overbey Collection, University of South Alabama Archives*)

Rebecca Latimer Felton of Georgia, champion of women's rights, advocate of black proscription, and the first woman to serve in the United States Senate. (*U.S. Senate Historical Office*)

A meeting of the Ku Klux Klan. In the 1920s the Invisible Empire spread from the South to many parts of the North and West. (*The Birmingham Public Library*)

Henry L. Mencken of Baltimore, critic and satirist of the "benighted South." (*The Library of Congress*)

Al Smith waving his famous derby in the campaign of 1928. (*The Library of Congress*)

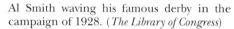

King Oliver's Creole Jazz Band. The trumpet player is Louis Armstrong, born in New Orleans in 1900. "Satchmo" became a jazz emissary to the world. (*William Ransom Hogan Jazz Library, Tulane University Library*)

Jimmie Rodgers (1897–1933), "The Father of Country Music." (*Courtesy Jimmie Rodgers Museum, Meridian, Mississippi*)

Thomas Wolfe . . . and a new generation of southern writers. (*The Library of Congress*)

CHAPTER 6

Regionalism and Reform

IF the Great Depression and the New Deal changed the South in many ways, the extraordinary developments of the troubled 1930s also brought unprecedented social and intellectual ferment to the region. One manifestation of this ferment was a vigorous outburst of criticism by southerners directed at their own region's mistakes and inadequacies. The extensive intervention of the federal government in the southern states contributed to a discussion of new ideas and to a sense of new possibilities, as did the reaction of outsiders to conditions in the South. These currents of change stimulated renewed interest in the southern identity and a regional approach to the solution of southern problems. *Regionalism* became the catchword of southern reformers and a new kind of liberalism took root. American liberals, including Franklin D. Roosevelt, identified the South as one of the nation's leading problems. Meanwhile, the late 1930s witnessed the reassertion of a more traditional kind of sectionalism based on antipathy toward the New Deal and a determination to protect the South's special interests, above all the institution of white supremacy.

Among the South's social critics of this period were the twelve southerners who published *I'll Take My Stand* in 1930. Most of these agrarians were identified with Vanderbilt University. Their celebration of rural virtues and their vision of an agrarian South provided a backdrop for their critique of the evils of American industrialism, materialism, and "progress." They were critical of the boosterism associated with the Atlanta Spirit and the New South's capitulation to the North's obsession with industrial capitalism and material profit. They expressed their dissatisfaction with southern politics—with the region's demagogues, machine politics, and the exaggerated influence of commercial interests. The specter of a malign northern invasion disturbed their cherished goal of preserving a strong southern tradition. After the appearance of their book, one scholar has noted, "Their generalized suspicion that somehow the North was to blame for the South's problems was elaborated into a full-fledged analysis of the South's 'colonial economy.'" At the same time, the Southern Agrarians hoped their manifesto would serve as a corrective to the nation's misplaced values. As Donald Davidson recalled, "Suddenly we realized to the full what we had long been dimly feeling, that the Lost Cause might not be wholly lost after all. In its very backwardness the South had clung to some secret which embodied, it seemed, the elements out of which its own reconstruction—and possibly even the reconstruction of America—might be achieved."[1]

The reaction to *I'll Take My Stand* outside the South tended to be negative. The writer Dixon Wecter described its authors as traditionalists who only wanted to wave the Bonnie Blue Flag. Other critics dismissed the Southern Agrarians as "Young Confederates" and "a socially reactionary band."[2] Yet their preference for an agrarian economy led several of these southerners to work for agricultural reform in the 1930s. Herman Clarence Nixon became a strong supporter of Roosevelt and the New Deal, and Frank L. Owsley and Donald Davidson endorsed many of the president's programs during his first administration. They championed tenant farmers and sharecroppers, advocated the redistribution of land, if necessary with government aid, and defended the Tennessee Valley Authority and the concept of public power. Their antimonopoly outlook reflected the region's Populist heritage, as did their belief in the desirability of renewing the political alliance between the South and the West. They turned hopefully to the farm tenancy bill introduced in 1935 by Senator John H. Bankhead of Alabama.[3]

While Nixon continued to be an ardent New Dealer, the other agrarians who advocated specific reforms turned away from Roosevelt and the New Deal after 1936. Their writings now revealed their disillusionment with Roosevelt's leadership and programs, their distaste for social planning, their fear of the centralization of political power, and their apprehension about federal intervention in southern race relations. In 1938 Davidson voiced his reservations in a book entitled *The Attack on Leviathan.* "The greatest present threat to the Federal Union," Davidson declared, "comes, not from any rising sectional movement, but from the advocacy and the more than incipient growth of a Leviathan State which, like the young of the cowbird, hatching where it did not build, shoulders the native brood from the nest."[4] By the late 1930s, the agrarians had become

1. John Shelton Reed, "For Dixieland: The Sectionalism of *I'll Take My Stand*," in *A Band of Prophets: The Vanderbilt Agrarians After Fifty Years*, ed. William C. Havard and Walter Sullivan (Baton Rouge, La., 1982), p. 49 (first quotation); Louis D. Rubin, Jr., "Introduction to the Torchbook Edition," in Twelve Southerners, *I'll Take My Stand: The South and the Agrarian Tradition* (New York, 1962), pp. viii–ix (second quotation). See also Paul K. Conkin, *The Southern Agrarians* (Knoxville, 1988); George Brown Tindall, *The Emergence of the New South, 1913–1945* (Baton Rouge, La., 1967), pp. 576–82; and Thomas Lawrence Connelly, "The Vanderbilt Agrarians: Time and Place in Southern Tradition," *Tennessee Historical Quarterly* 22 (March 1963): 22–37.

2. Connelly, "The Vanderbilt Agrarians," p. 22; Tindall, *The Emergence of the New South*, p. 578.

3. Connelly, "The Vanderbilt Agrarians," pp. 25–26; Mary Ann Wimsatt, "Political and Economic Recommendations of *I'll Take My Stand*," *Mississippi Quarterly* 33 (Fall 1980): 437–38; Andrew W. Foshee, "The Political Economy of the Southern Agrarian Tradition," *Modern Age* 27 (Spring 1983): 161–70.

4. Donald Davidson, *The Attack on Leviathan: Regionalism and Nationalism in the United States* (Chapel Hill, N.C., 1938), p. 106. See also Herbert Agar and Allen Tate, eds., *Who Owns America? A New*

an intellectual fringe of the growing conservative opposition to the New Deal in the South. As one scholar has remarked, "having said their piece," the Southern Agrarians "retired to their studies and left the darkling plain of struggle to the Farm Bureau, the tenant farmers' unions, the foundations, the sociologists, and the New Deal agencies."[5] One reason for their departure was a considerable amount of inconsistency in their assumptions. "In the South," one historian has written, "there is a pride in the old, individualistic self-subsistence, but also a worship of bigness and a sharp eye for the tobacco allotment paycheck."[6] The agrarians were not the first to misread the southern character. Their significance, in the 1930s and afterward, was not the validity of their social analysis but their contribution to the idea of the South and their critical perspective on the nature of industrial progress in the United States.

A very different perspective grew out of the "regionalist" school at the University of North Carolina. Like agrarianism, southern regionalism emerged with "the novel feature of academic trappings and affiliations."[7] The exponents of "regionalism" distinguished their approach from the "sectionalism" of the agararians. Sectionalism, according to the regionalists, would encourage interregional conflict, controversy, and separation, while regionalism, in the words of a later scholar, would "promote integration of the region into the nation, permitting diversity, but only in a larger framework of the national welfare."[8] Another writer distinguished between "the conservative aestheticism of Nashville" and "the liberal sociology of Chapel Hill."[9]

A research entrepreneur named Howard W. Odum took the lead in developing a comprehensive program of regional scholarship in the North Carolina village of Chapel Hill. More than any other single person he was "the father of the systematic scientific study of Southern society."[10] A native of Georgia (born in 1884), he was a graduate of Clark University and of Columbia University, where he encountered the new social sciences. He was also influenced by the southern education crusade and the nascent social welfare movement early in the twentieth century, as well as his work with the Southern Division of the American Red Cross during World War I. In 1920 he came to the University of North Carolina as head of the Department of Sociology and director of the new School of Public Welfare. Odum immediately became the central figure in the development of the social sciences at North Carolina, launching numerous in-

---

Declaration of Independence (Boston, 1936), and Edward S. Shapiro, "Frank L. Owsley and the Defense of Southern Identity," *Tennessee Historical Quarterly* 36 (Spring 1977): 75–94.

5. Tindall, *The Emergence of the New South*, p. 581.

6. Connelly, "The Vanderbilt Agrarians," p. 35.

7. Tindall, *The Emergence of the New South*, p. 576.

8. *Ibid.*, p. 585.

9. Michael O'Brien, *The Idea of the American South, 1920–1941* (Baltimore, 1979), p. xv. See also Marian D. Irish, "Proposed Roads to the New South, 1941: Chapel Hill Planners vs. Nashville Agrarians," *Sewanee Review* 49 (January–March 1941): 1–27.

10. George B. Tindall, "The Significance of Howard W. Odum to Southern History: A Preliminary Estimate," *Journal of Southern History* 24 (August 1958): 303–304.

stitutes and special programs in public welfare and social work, establishing the *Journal of Social Forces*, taking the lead in organizing the Institute for Research in Social Science, and assembling a strong cadre of assistants.[11]

From the beginning of his work in Chapel Hill, Odum was deeply interested in state and regional studies. The *Journal of Social Forces*, while concerned with many aspects of sociology, emphasized southern issues. Under Odum's leadership the Institute for Research in Social Science symbolized the new trend toward planned and cooperative research. The South became a great regional laboratory for the Institute, and its elaborately organized workshop reminded one of "the sort of room . . . in which a general's staff might plan its war."[12] In the late 1920s, Odum planned a comprehensive group of southern studies, and during the following decade an outpouring of monographs on black life, regional portraiture, and practical social problems issued from Chapel Hill. Although Odum was a modernist bent upon cultivating a new critical spirit in the South, he pursued a kind of poetic sociology. He had earlier begun to use a technique he identified as "descriptive studies" or "regional portraiture." Daniel J. Singal suggests that, once "he began to fathom the complexity of the South, no other method could have enabled him to express his conception of southern society with such exactitude."[13] Regionalism became Odum's intellectual preoccupation. In the early 1930s, the North Carolina scholar served as a member of the President's Research Committee on Social Trends, and his experience in that committee's task of inventorying the nation's social resources and trends undoubtedly contributed to the crystallization of his regional thought. In 1931 the General Education Board made a grant to the Social Science Research Council for a southern regional study. Odum was the obvious person to conduct the study, and in 1932 the SSRC put the project under his direction, with a southern regional committee in an advisory role. The result was Odum's epochal *Southern Regions of the United States* (1936), a huge inventory incorporating over seven hundred indices.[14]

Regionalism to Odum was a tool of analysis, an instrument for the effective synthesizing of the social sciences and to some extent other disciplines. In addition, it was a way to study the whole of society, for Odum emphasized what he described as the "folk-regional society," a gestalt "in which all factors are sought out and interpreted in their proper perspective."[15] Regionalism would

11. Louis R. Wilson, *The University of North Carolina, 1900–1930: The Making of a Modern University* (Chapel Hill, N.C., 1957), pp. 447–50, 462–68.

12. Jonathan Daniels, *Tar Heels: A Portrait of North Carolina* (New York, 1941), p. 274.

13. "Institute for Research in Social Science: Publications and Manuscripts," *Social Forces* 23 (March 1945): 309–28; Daniel Joseph Singal, *The War Within: From Victorian to Modernist Thought in the South, 1919–1945* (Chapel Hill, N.C., 1982), pp. 131–35 (quotation on p. 133).

14. Howard W. Odum, *Southern Regions of the United States* (Chapel Hill, N.C., 1936), pp. 621–28; Tindall, "The Significance of Howard W. Odum to Southern History," pp. 285–307; Rupert B. Vance and Katharine Jocher, "Howard W. Odum," *Social Forces* 33 (March 1955): 203–17; "From Community Studies to Regionalism," *Social Forces* 23 (March 1945): 245–58.

15. "From Community Studies to Regionalism," p. 253; George L. Simpson, Jr., "Howard W. Odum and American Regionalism," *Social Forces* 34 (December 1955): 101–106; O'Brien, *The Idea of the American South*, pp. 31–93; Singal, *The War Within*, pp. 115–52, 302–38.

also provide a framework for social planning and social action. The Chapel Hill sociologist saw a profound difference between a "national-regional" approach, which looked toward integration of the region into the nation, and a "sectional-local" perspective, which he associated with conflict and an exaggerated parochialism.[16] Other social scientists in the South contributed to the theory of regionalism, but none with the clarity and force of Odum's young colleague and protégé, Rupert B. Vance. In *Human Geography of the South: A Study in Regional Resources and Human Adequacy* (1932), Vance provided a valuable classification of the South's cultural areas and stated some of the requirements of the new regionalism. His later volume, *All These People: The Nation's Human Resources in the South* (1945), made skillful use of regional and population theory and extended the analysis presented in *Southern Regions*. The regionalism of the 1930s marked a milestone in the development of the social sciences in the South, and it produced a body of writing that did a great deal to illuminate southern life, to heighten regional awareness, and to help the nation view the South in a more positive light.

Odum hoped to implement his ideas through a Council on Southern Regional Development, an independent agency to be financed by foundations and individual contributions. He and his associates proposed an integrated program of social research and action to be carried on in four divisions: race relations, land tenure and farm relations, economic development and labor relations, and public relations and administration. The sociologist projected a twelve-year program with a budget of at least $2 million. The council was endorsed by a number of educators, businessmen, and labor leaders, and in 1938 an agreement was reached for it to merge with the Commission on Interracial Cooperation. These ambitious plans seemed to be part of a broader regional interest in social investigation and planning. "Discussion groups are springing up in many communities," wrote two members of the Odum group, "while civic clubs, religious and educational gatherings, college and high school debates, and public forums find topics on the Southern situation popular." The two regionalists cited, as an example, the recently organized Citizens' Fact Finding Movement in Georgia, sponsored by seventeen statewide groups and dedicated to the dissemination of authoritative information and analysis on topics such as agriculture, education, prison conditions, and politics.[17]

Howard Odum's plans for a program of constructive reform were never realized. Nevertheless, his ideas—and those of regionalism more generally—were influential in and out of the South: on the embryonic state and local planning boards, on some of the planning aspects of the Tennessee Valley Author-

---

16. In *American Regionalism: A Cultural-Historical Approach to National Integration* (New York, 1938), Odum and Harry Estill Moore applied the regional concept to the whole nation, with a sixfold delineation of regions in the United States. See also Katharine Jocher *et al.*, eds., *Folk, Region, and Society: Selected Papers of Howard W. Odum* (Chapel Hill, N.C., 1964), and "The Status and Future of Regionalism—A Symposium," *Journal of Southern History* 26 (February 1960): 22–56.

17. Arthur Raper and Ira DeA. Reid, "Old Conflicts in the New South," *Virginia Quarterly Review* 16 (Spring 1940): 218–29 (quotation on p. 226). See also Tindall, *The Emergence of the New South*, p. 586.

ity, and on the New Deal farm tenant programs. In 1939 the Southern Governors' Conference approved a ten-year program that borrowed generously from Odum's model. The North Carolinian also encouraged the research and development approach of the Southern Association for Science and Industry, founded in 1941.[18] Odum's greatest contribution, however, was the impetus he gave to the concept of the region and to the identity of the contemporary South. As George B. Tindall has suggested, "Regionalism quickened a generation of social scientists with its vision of the 'problem South,' a region with obvious deficiencies but with potentialities that demanded constructive study and planning."[19] But in its practical application the concept of regionalism proved almost as unrealistic as the proposals of the agrarians.

The Tennessee Valley Authority, established in 1933, also contributed to the popularization of the regional concept and to its identification with the South. The agency promoted the study of regional problems, became a center for the assembly and analysis of information on the southern states, and worked out arrangements with the land-grant colleges and state departments of education for a series of social and economic studies.[20] Discovering that it needed to know a great deal about state and local governments in the valley, the TVA developed a cooperative research program that involved academic people in various states and produced numerous studies. Similar arrangements resulted in archaeological investigations and social surveys. The authority subsidized and in other ways encouraged the establishment of bureaus of public administration in the southern universities; it also played a major part in the emergence of state and municipal planning commissions in the region.[21]

One of the agencies with which the Tennessee Valley Authority worked closely was the Bureau of Public Administration at the University of Alabama. The Alabama bureau played a key role in the early organization of southern research in politics and administrative affairs, and it quickly became a regional leader in the relatively new field of public administration.[22] The person who contributed most to the emergence of the bureau as a regional center was its first director, Roscoe C. Martin; he brought a new vitality to political science in the South, gave a regional scope to the study of political behavior there, and tried to bridge the gap between his discipline and the other social sciences.

In its early years the Alabama bureau emphasized research and service re-

18. Tindall, *The Emergence of the New South*, pp. 587–88.

19. *Ibid.*, pp. 583–88 (quotation on p. 588).

20. Joseph M. Ray, "The Influence of the Tennessee Valley Authority on Government in the South," *American Political Science Review* 43 (October 1949): 922–32; C. Herman Pritchett, *The Tennessee Valley Authority: A Study in Public Administration* (Chapel Hill, N.C., 1943), pp. 126–36; Gordon R. Clapp, *The TVA: An Approach to the Development of a Region* (Chicago, 1955), pp. 79–81.

21. Lawrence L. Durisch, "TVA and State and Local Government," in *TVA: The First Twenty Years, A Staff Report*, ed. Roscoe C. Martin (University, Ala., 1956), pp. 232–43; William E. Cole, "Personality and Cultural Research in the Tennessee Valley," *Social Forces* 13 (May 1935): 521–27; Clarence Lewis Hodge, *The Tennessee Valley Authority: A National Experiment in Regionalism* (Washington, D.C., 1938), pp. 98, 156–57; Albert Lepawsky, *State Planning and Economic Development in the South* (Washington, D.C., 1949).

22. See Rowland Egger and Weldon Cooper, *Research, Education, and Regionalism: The Bureau of Public Administration of the University of Alabama, 1938–1948* (University, Ala., 1949).

lated to governmental units and organizations in Alabama. A number of valuable monographs resulted, dealing with county and municipal government, state administration, and the legislative process.[23] Beginning in 1943, the bureau gave increasing attention to regional research and training, becoming a vehicle for the organization and management of a series of research and educational undertakings involving interstate and interinstitutional cooperation. This regional focus stemmed in part from the General Education Board's willingness to support comprehensive research programs in the South. But there were additional factors as well, including the TVA and other regional organizations, the southern campaign against the existing freight rate structure, and the example of the Chapel Hill regionalists.[24] In any case, the bureau carried through several important regional research projects during the 1930s and 1940s: studies of subsistence homesteads and federal rural housing; a cooperative survey of the administration of natural resources in the Southeast; a cooperative appraisal of technical services available to state and local officials in the region; a study of the electoral process in the South; and a regional training program in public administration.[25] These projects encouraged collaborative research in governmental affairs, led directly to the establishment of bureaus of public administration in several other states, and generally fostered the development of political science in the South.

The growing interest in basic research exhibited by the large foundations during the 1920s was even more evident in the 1930s. Almost every important project in social science research in southern colleges and universities was directly supported by such grants. Howard Odum recalled in 1954 that he himself had received $1.25 million from foundations. The General Education Board diverted more of its large resources to the needs of higher education in the South and in the late 1930s initiated a program to encourage the economic and social development of the region. The GEB and the Rosenwald Fund focused greater attention on black colleges and awarded hundreds of fellowships for advanced study to southerners of both races.[26] The Social Science Research Council, with Rosenwald money, awarded sixty-three Southern Fellowships in the Social Sciences during the years 1930–1933. The council also made a series of special grants-in-aid of research to southern faculty members in the social sciences during the 1930s and 1940s. In 1929 the SSRC created a South-

23. For examples, see Weldon Cooper, *Municipal Government and Administration in Alabama* (University, Ala., 1940), and Malcolm C. Moos, *State Penal Administration in Alabama* (University, Ala., 1942). By 1967 the bureau had published more than seventy books and monographs. Robert B. Highsaw to the author, 20 July 1967.

24. Egger and Cooper, *Research, Education, and Regionalism*, pp. 41–42.

25. Paul W. Wager, *One Foot on the Soil: A Study of Subsistence Homesteads in Alabama* (University, Ala., 1945); Rupert B. Vance and Gordon W. Blackwell, *New Farm Homes for Old: A Study of Rural Public Housing in the South* (University, Ala., 1946); Lawrence L. Durisch and Hershal L. Macon, *Upon Its Own Resources: Conservation and State Administration* (University, Ala., 1951).

26. O'Brien, *The Idea of the American South*, pp. 44–45; Raymond B. Fosdick, *Adventure in Giving: The Story of the General Education Board, a Foundation Established by John D. Rockefeller* (New York, 1962), pp. 266–97; Edwin R. Embree, *Julius Rosenwald Fund: Review of Two Decades, 1917–1936* (Chicago, 1936), pp. 24–35, 47; Tindall, *The Emergence of the New South*, pp. 499–504.

ern Regional Committee, which continued in existence for eighteen years. This committee investigated the status of the social sciences in the region and tried to stimulate academic research by sponsoring annual conferences and special studies of southern topics.[27]

An informal but influential directorate emerged during this period to establish lines of communication and understanding between the academic community in the South and the organizations interested in regional reform. The key figures were the triumvirate of Will W. Alexander, whose Commission on Interracial Cooperation became a clearinghouse for southern information and cooperation in race relations; Edwin R. Embree, president of the Rosenwald Fund; and Charles S. Johnson of Fisk University. These three were deeply involved in efforts to create black university centers in the South, in several of the fellowship programs, and in many of the special studies and reports sponsored by the Rosenwald Fund and other foundations. They organized, with support from the Rockefeller Foundation, a large-scale investigation of the South's rural economy in the mid-1930s that became the basis for a famous report entitled *The Collapse of Cotton Tenancy: Summary of Field Studies & Statistical Surveys, 1933–35* (1935).[28]

Charles Spurgeon Johnson was the leader in making Fisk University the major African-American center for social research in the South and one of the outstanding research institutions in the entire field of race relations. A sociologist who had served as director of research for the National Urban League, Johnson came to Fisk in 1928 to head the division of social sciences, which had just been reorganized with foundation help. An able organizer and promoter, Johnson secured outside financial support, brought in scholarly talent, and made his department a research center of real importance during the 1930s. The department published twenty-three books between 1928 and 1940 and carried out a variety of useful surveys. In 1944 Johnson expanded the program at Fisk by inaugurating the annual Institute of Race Relations.[29] The Fisk sociologist was also a productive scholar. His studies of Negro life in the black belt and of rural education, both based on extensive field work, were notable contributions.[30] One of his books, *Growing up in the Black Belt: Negro Youth in the Rural*

27. See the annual reports of the SSRC, 1929–1947, and *Problems of the Cotton Economy: Proceedings of the Southern Social Science Research Conference, New Orleans, March 8 and 9, 1935* (Dallas, Tex., 1936).

28. Edwin R. Embree and Julia Waxman, *Investment in People: The Story of the Julius Rosenwald Fund* (New York, 1949), pp. 73–74, 202–203; Wilma Dykeman and James Stokely, *Seeds of Southern Change: The Life of Will Alexander* (Chicago, 1962), pp. 164, 170–74, 185, 224; interview with Rupert B. Vance, 11 July 1967.

29. Edwin R. Embree, *13 Against the Odds* (New York, 1944), pp. 47–70; Patrick J. Gilpin, "Charles S. Johnson: An Intellectual Biography" (Ph.D. dissertation, Vanderbilt University, 1973); Joe M. Richardson, *A History of Fisk University, 1865–1946* (University, Ala., 1980); Edgar T. Thompson, "Sociology and Sociological Research in the South," *Social Forces* 23 (March 1945): 364–65; interview with Lewis W. Jones, 3 July 1967.

30. See, for example, Charles S. Johnson, *The Shadow of the Plantation* (Chicago, 1934), and Johnson et al., *Statistical Atlas of Southern Counties: Listing and Analysis of Socio-Economic Indices of 1104 Southern Counties* (Chapel Hill, N.C., 1941).

South (1941), was part of a large-scale investigation of black youth in the late 1930s.[31]

Scholarly investigations of black life and race relations were also being undertaken by other southerners. Among southern white scholars, for example, Thomas J. Woofter wrote several books that helped develop greater sophistication in the study of race in the South.[32] When Gunnar Myrdal launched his monumental study of black Americans a few years later, he turned to the southern sociologists for help.[33] Meanwhile, northern social scientists such as John Dollard and Hortense Powdermaker were undertaking community studies of blacks and whites in small southern towns.[34] This prompted one southern professor to remark on "the transition from the use of the South as an object of muckraking by northern journalists to its [current] use for anthropological field work by northern investigators."[35]

How can one explain this compulsion to investigate and analyze the South in the 1930s? In sociology, one writer suggests, "the primary motivation lay in the lure of the South itself as a territory ripe for research." Armed with the scientific method of their disciplines and supported by research organizations and foundations, social scientists were drawn to a region beset by a host of intractable problems: "Sharecropping, mill villages, chain gangs, lynchings, paternalism, legalized racial segregation, backwoods folk culture," and more.[36] The growth and professionalization of academic disciplines and the development of graduate studies in the South also contributed to the new social research. A spate of academic associations and periodicals, organized on a regional basis, appeared in the 1930s, adding their voices to the new regional analysis and discussion: the Southern Economic Association, the Southern Political Science Association, the Southern Sociological Society, the *Journal of Southern History*, the *Southern Economic Journal*, and the *Journal of Politics*. The *Southern Review* began publication at Louisiana State University in 1935, under the direction of Robert Penn Warren and Cleanth Brooks. The *Review* stimulated a new intellectual excitement and criticism as well as an innovative approach to the study of literature.[37]

31. These studies, sponsored by the American Youth Commission, were financed by the General Education Board. Fosdick, *Adventure in Giving*, pp. 244–46.

32. Few social scientists were associated with a wider array of organizations and research projects concerned with the South than Woofter. They included the Phelps-Stokes Fund, the Commission on Interracial Cooperation, the University of North Carolina, several New Deal agencies, and Gunnar Myrdal's *An American Dilemma*. See Woofter, *Southern Race Progress: The Wavering Color Line* (Washington, D.C., 1957).

33. Gunnar Myrdal, *An American Dilemma: The Negro Problem and Modern Democracy*, 2 vols. (New York and London, 1944).

34. See John Dollard, *Caste and Class in a Southern Town* (New Haven, Conn., 1937); Hortense Powdermaker, *After Freedom: A Cultural Study in the Deep South* (New York, 1939); and Allison Davis, Burleigh B. Gardner, and Mary R. Gardner, *Deep South: A Social Anthropological Study of Caste and Class* (Chicago, 1941).

35. Thompson, "Sociology and Sociological Research in the South," p. 361.

36. Singal, *The War Within*, p. 302.

37. Tindall, *The Emergence of the New South*, pp. 588–89; Dewey W. Grantham, "The Regional Imagination: Social Scientists and the American South," *Journal of Southern History* 34 (February 1968): 10–20; Robert B. Heilman, "Baton Rouge and LSU Forty Years After," *Sewanee Review* 88 (Winter 1980): 126–43.

The hard times of the Great Depression had a crippling effect on higher education in the southern states, as was true elsewhere. Scores of the region's "colleges" were too poor and inadequate to provide genuine higher education even in more normal times. Nevertheless, some of the state universities, such as those in Virginia, North Carolina, Louisiana, and Texas, made progress in the 1930s, as did private institutions like Duke, Tulane, Vanderbilt, and Rice Institute. According to a contemporary appraisal, the University of North Carolina had become "the Wisconsin of the South in wide community leadership and influence." While some observers lamented the "drag out of the South" of native scholars and intellectual talent, the region had begun to develop a handful of good graduate schools and to stress the need for modern research facilities. Outside foundations and New Deal agencies such as the National Youth Administration contributed to these efforts.[38] Public education struggled to survive "a desperate famine" early in the depression, and southern schools continued to lag far behind the national average in length of school terms, teacher salaries, libraries, and other facilities. Black schools faced even greater obstacles. However one explained "the backwardness of the South in education," a southern educator wrote in the mid-1930s, "the affliction itself stifles industry, represses effort, discourages enterprise, weakens the desire for excellence, and makes us satisfied with second-rate achievements."[39] Even so, state and local support of the public schools began to increase once more as the decade unfolded, and the region slowly began to improve its relative position in the national educational picture.

Looking for America in the 1930s, Burl L. Noggle has written, was in part "looking for regions and subcultures, and in that decade the South more than any region found itself photographed, stereotyped, and scrutinized."[40] The WPA Writers' Project and the Farm Security Administration's photographers reflected this fascination with the American South. In the South, as in all parts of the nation, a heightened social consciousness, an intense interest in the lives of ordinary people, and a renewed appreciation of provincial lore were revealed in the written and photographic documentaries of the decade—in such works as *You Have Seen Their Faces* (1937), by Erskine Caldwell and Margaret Bourke-White, and *These Are Our Lives* (1939), a publication of the Federal Writers' Project.[41] Writing of this regional documentation in 1942, Alfred Kazin spoke of "the cars on the unending white ribbon of road; the workers in the mills; the faces of

38. H. Clarence Nixon, "Colleges and Universities," in *Culture in the South*, ed. W. T. Couch (Chapel Hill, N.C., 1934), pp. 229–47 (quotation on p. 244).

39. Edgar W. Knight, "Recent Progress and Problems of Education," in *ibid.*, pp. 211–28 (quotation on p. 225); Tindall, *The Emergence of the New South*, pp. 493–504.

40. Burl L. Noggle, "With Pen and Camera: In Quest of the American South in the 1930s," in *The South Is Another Land: Essays on the Twentieth-Century South*, ed. Bruce Clayton and John A. Salmond (New York, 1987), p. 189.

41. Monty Noam Penkower, *The Federal Writers' Project: A Study in Government Patronage of the Arts* (Urbana, Ill., 1977), pp. 242–43; David H. Culbert, "The Infinite Variety of Mass Experience: The Great Depression, W.P.A. Interviews, and Student Family History Projects," *Louisiana History* 19 (Winter 1978): 43–63; Carol Schloss, "The Privilege of Perception," *Virginia Quarterly Review* 56 (Autumn 1980): 596–611.

farmers' wives and their children in the roadside camp, a thousand miles from nowhere; the tenant farmer's wife with her child sitting on the steps of the old plantation mansion . . . the Okies crossing the desert in their jalopy . . . the Baptist service in the old Negro church."[42] Reflecting on this outburst of regional expression, one scholar has suggested that "a combination of literary, artistic, political, and academic trends found common cause in regionalism."[43]

Much of the scholarship devoted to the "problem" South was published by the region's handful of university presses. The most important of these was the University of North Carolina Press, which itself became a powerful force in the emergence of a regional social science literature.[44] "As you probably know," the director of the press wrote a northern publisher in 1935, "we are attempting here at Chapel Hill to build a publishing organization that will do, in addition to the work usually done by university presses, a new and very important type of publishing for this region . . . to make the people in the South fully aware of the more important features of the region in which they live, including the natural life and resources and economic and social conditions."[45]

Another source of critical thinking in the 1930s was a group of liberal journalists who tended to support the New Deal and to accept the ideas of the Chapel Hill regionalists. They were represented by newspaper editors like Gerald W. Johnson of the Baltimore *Evening Sun*, Virginius Dabney of the Richmond *Times-Dispatch*, George Fort Milton of the Chattanooga *News*, Jonathan Daniels of the Raleigh *News and Observer*, Ralph McGill of the Atlanta *Constitution*, and Hodding Carter of the Greenville *Delta Democrat-Times*. Some of the liberal journalists had long been critical of what they considered malignant aspects of southern life—political demagoguery, the Ku Klux Klan, and the obsession with such issues as prohibition and the teaching of Darwinian evolution in the schools. Many of them rebelled against the sentimental tradition in the South, a tradition "designed to bolster up the ego of the south against the assaults of Yankeedom."[46] They were inclined to blame retrograde tendencies on lower-class susceptibility to racist politics, intolerance, and provincialism. Their own emphasis was on individual liberties.

By the early 1930s, the assumptions and commitments of these journalists

42. Quoted in Tindall, *The Emergence of the New South*, p. 590.

43. Marshall W. Fishwick, "What Ever Happened to Regionalism?" (unpublished paper, n.d., made available to the author in July 1967 by Edgar T. Thompson of Duke University).

44. By the end of 1945, the press had published about 500 titles, over 175 of which dealt with southern topics. See W. T. Couch, "The University Press," in *The Graduate School: Research and Publications*, ed. Edgar W. Knight and Agatha Boyd Adams (Chapel Hill, N.C., 1946), pp. 175–76, 183; Couch, "Twenty Years of Southern Publishing," *Virginia Quarterly Review* 26 (Spring 1950): 171–85; Lambert Davis, "North Carolina and Its University Press," *North Carolina Historical Review* 43 (Spring 1966): 149–56; and Singal, *The War Within*, pp. 265–301.

45. W. T. Couch to Oswald Garrison Villard, 21 May 1935, Oswald Garrison Villard Papers, Harvard University Library.

46. Wilbur J. Cash, quoted in Bruce Clayton, *W. J. Cash: A Life* (Baton Rouge, La., 1991), p. 122. For other liberal journalists, see John T. Kneebone, *Southern Liberal Journalists and the Issue of Race, 1920–1944* (Chapel Hill, N.C., 1985), and Charles W. Eagles, *Jonathan Daniels and Race Relations: The Evolution of a Southern Liberal* (Knoxville, Tenn., 1982), pp. 3–82.

had begun to change, encouraged by the effects of the depression and the early activism of the New Deal. They now turned their attention to the South's economic problems—to the plight of the farmer, the condition of industrial workers, and the need for regional development. Unlike the Southern Agrarians' desire to stop the advance of industrialism and to preserve the agrarian values of the past, these newpapermen looked with satisfaction on the beneficial changes that might come with an industrial and urban South. The region could not afford to isolate itself from the larger nation. The journalists also became more hopeful about the potential role of the southern masses in the wake of the latter's response to Franklin Roosevelt and his programs, and more interested in the example of Huey P. Long. Ordinary southerners, it seemed, were eager for reform and were seeking leaders to represent their real interests. Finally, the liberal newspapermen adopted more flexible ideas on the race question, joined in the effort to reverse a sudden increase in lynching, and supported the movement for a federal law to outlaw the poll tax. The Charlotte *News*, for instance, relentlessly documented and criticized the worst features of southern white racism.[47] Yet none of these southern liberals challenged racial segregation, and most of them accepted the prevailing white rationale for black disfranchisement. At the same time, the severe depression of the 1930s led them to deemphasize the matter of race relations, in part because they assumed that industrialization, urbanization, and economic development would go a long way toward settling the new controversies over racial questions.

Although the liberal journalists minimized state rights, were enthusiastic about FDR's leadership, and lent their backing to the New Deal, they eventually became critical of the president's move to the left. Their thinking had always betrayed an element of elitism and a strain of paternalism, and in the late 1930s they sometimes argued that, whatever the merits of New Deal proposals, they must not overthrow southern folkways. Fearful of increasing divisions within the South and of more extreme federal intervention, they insisted that regional "realities" must be taken into consideration. They differed with Roosevelt over his approach to the solution of rural poverty, criticized the sit-down strikes of 1937, and resented the president's attempt to "purge" the South's anti–New Deal congressmen in the elections of 1938. Still, they continued to share many of Roosevelt's goals, and their critical outlook and moderate reformism strongly conditioned what became known as "southern liberalism."

A number of southern journalists attempted broad interpretations of the South. Virginius Dabney wrote, for the University of North Carolina Press, a book with the significant title, *Liberalism in the South* (1932). It was, in the words of one historian, "the genealogy of a Southern liberalism stemming from Thomas Jefferson."[48] Another journalistic profile was Clarence Cason's *90° in the Shade* (1935), in which the author asserted that the South "would profit from a nice, quiet revolution . . . a revision of the region's implanted ideas, [and] a realistic

47. Clayton, *W. J. Cash*, p. 134.
48. Tindall, *The Emergence of the New South*, p. 217.

and direct recognition of existing social problems."[49] In 1938 Jonathan Daniels, editor of the Raleigh *News and Observer*, published *A Southerner Discovers the South*, based on a six-week tour of the region. Daniels described a South "self-consciously caught up in actual and potential social change, partly the product of the Depression's dislocations and partly the vigorous response to opportunities that New Deal programs had created."[50] But the most striking portrayal by a southern journalist was that of Wilbur J. Cash, an editorial writer for the Charlotte *News*. *The Mind of the South* (1941), a probing interpretation of the southern character, stressed the continuity of the southern experience and the unity of its culture. By "mind," the author meant the temperament, feelings, beliefs, sentiment, myths, and fantasies of southerners, primarily of white southerners. While crediting the South with significant virtues, Cash repeatedly cited its characteristic vices: "Violence, intolerance, aversion and suspicion toward new ideas, an incapacity for analysis . . . an exaggerated individualism and a too narrow concept of social responsibility, attachment to fictions and false values, above all too great attachment to racial values and a tendency to justify cruelty and injustice in the name of those values."[51]

In 1938 Donald Davidson expressed disappointment over the directions that were evident in contemporary southern letters. One group of southern writers, according to Davidson, wrote "charmingly" of mountaineers or Negroes; a second group "took refuge" in romantic irony; and a third employed a realism that would seem realistic on "the northern side of the Potomac." Davidson went on to say, "Most Southern writers seemed to think that they could not acknowledge their obligations to art without at the same time repudiating the Southern past and accepting the progressive view of the Southern present."[52]

The Vanderbilt professor may have exaggerated, but many of the South's creative writers in this period were critical of their native region and quite aware of their growing readership in other parts of the country. Commenting on the work of young writers like T. S. Stribling, Thomas Wolfe, William Faulkner, and Erskine Caldwell, Gerald W. Johnson praised them for dealing "courageously and vigorously with the problems of the modern South." Faulkner's *Sanctuary*, for example, suggested that "there are rotting spots in our civilization that are capable of producing things so revolting that the mind recoils from their contemplation." In Caldwell, Johnson observed, "One sees . . . the direct and appalling

49. Quoted in *ibid.*, p. 590. See also John M. Matthews, "Clarence Cason Among the Southern Liberals," *Alabama Review* 38 (January 1985): 3–18.

50. Jonathan Daniels, *A Southerner Discovers the South* (New York, 1938); Kneebone, *Southern Liberal Journalists*, p. 97.

51. W. J. Cash, *The Mind of the South* (New York, 1941), pp. 428–29. See also Charles W. Eagles, ed., *The Mind of the South: Fifty Years Later* (Jackson, Miss., 1992); Paul D. Escott, ed., *W. J. Cash and the Minds of the South* (Baton Rouge, La., 1992); Joseph L. Morrison, *W. J. Cash, Southern Prophet: A Biography and Reader* (New York, 1967); C. Vann Woodward, *American Counterpoint: Slavery and Racism in the North-South Dialogue* (New York, 1971), pp. 261–83; Richard H. King, *A Southern Renaissance: The Cultural Awakening of the American South, 1930–1955* (New York, 1980), pp. 146–72; and Clayton, *W. J. Cash*.

52. Davidson, *The Attack on Leviathan*, p. 92.

results of a slipshod social and economic system, the final effect of that rugged individualism which some of us have been foolish enough to praise."[53] Caldwell himself asserted, in responding to a Georgia congressman's harsh criticism of his novel and Broadway play, *Tobacco Road*, that "Stretching from South Carolina to Arkansas its [the South's] stench is a complacent nation's shame."[54]

Southern creative writers attracted even more attention from Americans in other regions than did scholars and journalists who focused on southern themes. One reason was the violence and sensationalism of authors like Faulkner and Caldwell. "For an audience long conditioned by attacks on the Benighted South and by the liberation from gentility," writes Tindall, "Southern literature seemed in the 1930's to be operating still in the context of those themes." Ellen Glasgow wondered if what she called the new school of "Southern Gothic" fiction had "become one vast, disordered sensibility."[55] Other Americans responded to the emphasis on the peculiarities and uniqueness of specific locales in the stories and novels of southern writers. The most famous example is Faulkner's mythical Yoknapatawpha County, located in the hill country of northern Mississippi. According to Cleanth Brooks, the novelist's use of local materials enabled him to present "the characteristic problems of modern man living in a world of drastic change; yet at the same time it gave him an opportunity to insist upon what he regarded as the eternal truths about the age-old and essentially unchanging human predicament."[56]

Gone With the Wind (1936) was the single most popular southern novel of the decade. Written by Margaret Mitchell of Georgia, this saga of the Old South, Civil War, and Reconstruction became an overnight success, won a Pulitzer Prize, and was made into a sensational film in 1939—the capstone of Hollywood's treatment of the South in the 1930s. While some critics found the book lacking in artistic skill and "coherent aesthetic vision," it proved to have universal appeal; no other work of the period did more to form the attitude of the general public toward the South. Indeed, it represented an important addition to the national culture. The heroine Scarlett O'Hara and her world, one scholar remarks, "entered the mainstream of American life, thereby incorporating the Old South, its beauties and its travails, firmly into the prevailing myth of the American past. In this respect, *Gone With the Wind* celebrated, even as it contributed to, the restoration of the South to the nation and the nation to the South."[57]

What became known as the Southern Literary Renaissance was under way

53. Gerald W. Johnson, "The Horrible South," *Virginia Quarterly Review* 11 (April 1935): 215, 217. See also Tindall, *The Emergence of the New South*, pp. 650, 662–65.

54. Quoted in Pete Daniel, *The Shadow of Slavery: Peonage in the South, 1901–1969* (Urbana, Ill., 1972), p. 170.

55. Tindall, *The Emergence of the New South*, p. 665.

56. Cleanth Brooks, "William Faulkner," in *The History of Southern Literature*, ed. Louis D. Rubin, Jr., et al. (Baton Rouge, La., 1985), pp. 341–42. See also Herschel Gower, "Regions and Rebels," in *ibid.*, pp. 399–406.

57. Elizabeth Fox-Genovese, "Scarlett O'Hara: The Southern Lady as New Woman," *American Quarterly* 33 (Fall 1981): 391–92. See also Darden Asbury Pyron, "*Gone with the Wind* and the Southern Cultural Awakening," *Virginia Quarterly Review* 62 (Autumn 1986): 565–87.

at least as early as 1929. That year brought the publication of William Faulkner's *Sartoris* and *The Sound and the Fury*, as well as Thomas Wolfe's *Look Homeward, Angel*. New books were published by Ellen Glasgow, James Branch Cabell, DuBose Heyward, T. S. Stribling, Allen Tate, and Stark Young. There were first books by Erskine Caldwell, Hamilton Basso, and Robert Penn Warren. In 1930 Katherine Anne Porter's *Flowering Judas* appeared, along with other first books by Caroline Gordon, Lillian Hellman, and Andrew Nelson Lytle.[58] The renaissance emerged more clearly and impressively during the 1930s. Faulkner was the major contributor; he "constructed a fictional world populated by southern figures of tragedy and comedy who acted out his major theme of the human heart in conflict with itself."[59] But there were others of great talent: Wolfe, Tate, Porter, Caldwell, Basso, Gordon, Jesse Stuart. There were gifted black writers as well, such as Richard Wright and Zora Neale Hurston. By the time war came in 1941, still other creative writers were about to be acclaimed, including Eudora Welty, Carson McCullers, and James Agee.

In an essay written many years later, C. Vann Woodward discussed some of the "necessary conditions" for the Southern Literary Renaissance. He identified six attributes of southern life as especially important: the concreteness of human relationships, including the concreteness of moral problems; the prevalence of conflict and tension, which made for drama; the pervading sense of community; the widespread sense of religious wholeness; the belief that human nature is mysterious and relatively intractable; and "a sense of the tragic dimension of life."[60] Although these conditions were not peculiar to the South in the 1930s, they were more characteristic of southerners than of other Americans, and they were important cultural determinants of southern distinctiveness in the nation. Yet, paradoxically, the South's rise to a position of respectability, perhaps even dominance, in the realm of American letters resulted in increasing recognition of the southern achievement from outside the region.

For advocates of the new regionalism and for southern reformers generally a series of developments set in motion by depression and federal policy raised their hopes and tested their liberalism. One of these was the Tennessee Valley Authority. A regional, multipurpose undertaking, the TVA was established as a government corporation with the mission of developing a 40,000-square-mile drainage area in seven states. The agency was given responsibility for navigation, flood control, the manufacture of fertilizer, and the production of electrical power; it was authorized to make "surveys of and general plans for said

58. C. Vann Woodward, "Why the Southern Renaissance?" *Virginia Quarterly Review* 51 (Spring 1975): 222–39; Louis D. Rubin, Jr., "Thomas Wolfe," in *The History of Southern Literature*, ed. Rubin et al., pp. 343–50.

59. M. Thomas Inge, "Literature," in *Encyclopedia of Southern Culture*, ed. Charles Reagan Wilson and William Ferris (Chapel Hill, N.C., 1989), p. 842. For the renaissance as a whole, see Louis D. Rubin, Jr., and Robert D. Jacobs, eds., *Southern Renascence: The Literature of the Modern South* (Baltimore, 1953); John M. Bradbury, *Renaissance in the South: A Critical History of the Literature, 1920–1960* (Chapel Hill, N.C., 1963); King, *A Southern Renaissance*; and Tindall, *The Emergence of the New South*, pp. 227–39.

60. Woodward, "Why the Southern Renaissance?" pp. 227–39.

Tennessee basin and adjoining territory . . . for the general purpose of fostering an orderly and proper physical, economic, and social development of said areas."[61] There was an aura of reform surrounding the project during its early years, growing out of its valleywide jurisdiction and multipurpose function, its commitment to planning and economic development, and the ideas of Arthur E. Morgan, its first chairman, about social engineering.

With a sympathetic president and powerful friends in Congress, the new agency was largely free to create its own identity and to translate a set of broad objectives into a structure of programs, relationships, and operations. This period was dominated by the unfolding of TVA's great construction projects and by a series of challenges to the authority's effectiveness, indeed, to its very existence.[62] But after surviving the most serious threats to its autonomy, as well as the adverse effects of its own internal disarray and a thoroughgoing congressional investigation, the enterprise was able to move forward with greater unity and concentration. The experiences of the 1930s clarified the agency's priorities and laid lasting foundations for most of its programs. The centrality of the hydroelectric program in the TVA's congeries of undertakings became apparent with the ascendancy of David E. Lilienthal among the directors. At the same time, Harcourt A. Morgan's dominant position in directing the course of the authority's various agricultural operations helped develop an infrastructure based on local interest groups. In spite of the growing importance of its power program, TVA was immersed in a multiplicity of other tasks.

The popular response to the Tennessee Valley Authority during these formative years was extraordinary. "There seems to be something about the boldness and vigor of the whole enterprise," the writer Stuart Chase noted in 1936, "which fires the imagination and enlists enthusiastic support."[63] The authority's projects received extensive coverage in American newspapers and magazines, and a steady stream of visitors, from the United States and abroad, moved through the valley to witness the wonders of the new experiment in the South. "As the great Leviathan rushed its physical works to completion and developed its numerous co-ordinated applications of physical and social science," one chronicler later wrote somewhat sardonically, "it became evident that here in the Tennessee Valley, of all places, was emerging one of the marvels of the modern world."[64] As enthusiasm for the TVA mounted, it was almost as if the region's inhabitants had discovered a new utopia. From its earliest settlement, one author remarked, "the Tennessee country had attracted utopians from afar

61. Tindall, *The Emergence of the New South*, p. 447.

62. For these and other aspects of the TVA's formative years, see Thomas K. McCraw, *TVA and the Power Fight, 1933–1939* (Philadelphia, 1971), and Richard Lowitt, "The TVA, 1933–45," in *TVA: Fifty Years of Grass-Roots Bureaucracy*, ed. Erwin C. Hargrove and Paul K. Conkin (Urbana, Ill., 1983), pp. 35–65.

63. Stuart Chase, *Rich Land, Poor Land: A Study of Waste in the Natural Resources of America* (New York, 1936), p. 277. See also Walter L. Creese, *TVA's Public Planning: The Vision, the Reality* (Knoxville, Tenn., 1990).

64. Donald Davidson, *The Tennessee*, vol. 2: *The New River, Civil War to TVA* (New York, 1948), p. 251.

and quickened utopian dreams among valley dwellers themselves."[65] There was evidence, too, of a remarkable esprit de corps among TVA staff members and a conviction among its employees that the agency's work was important and unprecedented.[66]

Nevertheless, the authority faced strong criticism, particularly outside the South. The big private utility companies, some of which had operating affiliates in the Tennessee Valley, vigorously opposed the TVA and the idea of public power, citing the agency's "unfair" advantages and "unfair" determination of "fair" rates. Opponents charged that TVA was using federal money to destroy legitimate business, that it was socialistic and un-American, and that its proponents planned to use it as a model for similar projects in other regions. It was said that the TVA ran through seven states and drained the nation. Some southerners, notably those outside the Tennessee Valley, were less than enthusiastic about the authority, and Senator Kenneth D. McKellar of Tennessee and Representative Andrew J. May of Kentucky repeatedly attacked the agency for their own reasons. Other southerners resented the self-righteous attitude and uplift goals of TVA officials. "These outlanders," George Fort Milton of Chattanooga recalled, "seemed to have come down here to reform an illiterate, godless lot who would not wear shoes."[67] Donald Davidson complained that the authority was primarily the creation of Senator George W. Norris and other "outsiders," and he considered it an attempt by the industrial North to remake the South in its own image. Davidson feared that TVA's transformation of the Tennessee Valley would bring with it the displacement of traditional society, and that the conquests of technology would take too great a toll in their effects on man, nature, and society.[68]

The TVA's evolution as a reform endeavor was closely related to the broader liberalism of the Roosevelt administration. As one of the president's favorite projects, the agency received invigorating assistance from Washington in the form of appropriations, public works loans, political support, and friendly counsel. At the same time, the Tennessee Valley experiment was an inspiration to Roosevelt and other New Dealers. Its antimonopoly objectives and decentralized features appealed strongly to the disciples of Justice Louis D. Brandeis, and it mirrored other important aspects of New Deal liberalism. The TVA's failure to launch a frontal attack on poverty, its racial discrimination, and its traditional social arrangements typified, rather than differed from, most New Deal undertakings. Whatever its hopes for more thoroughgoing social reform, the Roosevelt administration found it necessary to come to terms with existing

65. *Ibid.*, p. 145.

66. John Gunther, who spent some time investigating the authority in the 1940s, wrote that "never in the United States or abroad have I encountered anything more striking than the faith its men have in their work." Quoted in Marguerite Owen, *The Tennessee Valley Authority* (New York, 1973), p. 77.

67. Quoted in Tindall, *The Emergence of the New South*, p. 448. See also Daniels, *A Southerner Discovers the South*, pp. 48–49, 57–59, 72.

68. Donald Davidson, "Political Regionalism and Administrative Regionalism," *Annals of the American Academy of Political and Social Science* 207 (January 1940): 138–43; William C. Havard, Jr., "Images of TVA: The Clash over Values," in *TVA*, ed. Hargrove and Conkin, pp. 297–315.

centers of political and economic power. Still, TVA contributed to the sharp ideological split between the major political parties. Furthermore, the authority was one of the most successful of all New Deal ventures, and in later years it was perhaps the most visible legacy of Roosevelt's domestic reforms. It even won support from some of FDR's opponents. One such advocate was the Socialist Norman Thomas, whose deepening criticism of Roosevelt's presidency had gone so far by 1935 that he could approve only the TVA, which he called "a beautiful flower in a garden of weeds."[69]

In many respects the TVA was the centerpiece of the New Deal's response to the economic and social plight of the South. The region's depressed agriculture and colonial economy certainly provided a great challenge to the New Deal's recovery programs and reform efforts. Against this background, the agency became "a massive monument of economic growth and development."[70] The engineering achievements alone were remarkable: within a decade the agency transformed an unruly river into an impressive waterway providing navigation, flood control, and vast amounts of hydroelectric power. These benefits undoubtedly contributed to the industrial expansion and economic diversification of the Tennessee Valley, though it is impossible to be precise in measuring the authority's stimulative effects. New energy poured into the valley as a result of TVA's multipurpose activities: the electricity produced by the dams, the clearing of the rivers, the rebuilding of the forests, the replenishing of the soil, the improvement of agricultural methods, the development of recreation. But beyond this, as Arthur M. Schlesinger, Jr., has written, "there was something less tangible yet even more penetrating: the release of moral and human energy as the people of the Valley saw new vistas open up for themselves and for their children."[71]

In the Tennessee Valley, TVA gave rise to a new vision of progress. Southern liberals like George Fort Milton considered the authority the pinnacle of the New Deal and the best hope of the New South. Milton championed the undertaking as a means of developing the region, although he opposed any interference with the cultural heritage of the valley. He viewed the undertaking as a power development and coordinating agency that might bring about desirable economic and social changes in the South.[72] The TVA's popularity in the region was clearly related to the conviction that the project was promoting the

69. Arthur M. Schlesinger, Jr., *The Age of Roosevelt: The Politics of Upheaval* (Boston, 1960), p. 180. See also Schlesinger, *The Age of Roosevelt: The Coming of the New Deal* (Boston, 1958), p. 319, and William E. Leuchtenburg, *Franklin D. Roosevelt and the New Deal, 1932–1940* (New York, 1963), p. 149.

70. Tindall, *The Emergence of the New South*, p. 446.

71. Schlesinger, *The Coming of the New Deal*, pp. 333–34.

72. James A. Hodges, "George Fort Milton and the New Deal," *Tennessee Historical Quarterly* 36 (Fall 1977): 383–409, esp. pp. 405–408. See also Kneebone, *Southern Liberal Journalists*, pp. 125–27. Donald Davidson entitled one of the chapters in his history of the Tennessee River "At Last: The Kingdom Really Comes!" Davidson wrote that the establishment of the TVA was viewed, in and out of the region, as a means of overcoming the South's image as a backward and barbarous section—as a way "to wipe all sins away." Davidson, *The Tennessee*, vol. 2, pp. 211–18.

South's industrialization and economic growth.[73] Southerners were also stirred by the drama of the authority's political controversies and engineering feats. They applauded its accomplishments and savored its national recognition. Here was a southern enterprise whose achievements were admired in other parts of the country and whose style and joie de vivre nourished the image of a successful American institution.

Another focus of reform in the South during the 1930s was the region's extensive rural poverty and the terrible conditions that threatened to overwhelm its millions of landless farmers. The gaunt figures and dispirited faces of southern tenant farmers became a central feature of the new documentaries, familiarizing Americans with the most wretched of the South's dispossessed.[74] The problem eventually became the center of an array of reform efforts that included southern and northern liberals, large foundations, field surveys and scholarly analyses, federal agencies, and the farmers themselves. What began as a southern problem became, for a time, a matter of national concern.

Ironically, the New Deal's approach to the troubled agricultural situation, which emphasized recovery rather than reform, actually worsened the condition of many of the South's poorest farmers. Since the Roosevelt administration encouraged farmers to cut production, many large farmers dispensed with their tenants, with whom they were supposed to share benefit payments from the Agricultural Adjustment Administration. Landlords, who controlled the distribution of the benefit payments, frequently failed to share them with their sharecroppers and tenants, many of whom were evicted. Land was increasingly concentrated, large farmers shifted from mules to tractors, and thousands of sharecroppers were driven from the land. More than 111,000 tractors were introduced into the cotton-growing states in the 1930s, each tractor displacing several families.[75] As Rupert B. Vance observed in 1934, "With one hand the cotton landlord takes agricultural subsidies and rental benefits from his government, with the other he pushes his tenant on relief." After a visit to the Arkansas Delta, Norman Thomas declared that "under the operation of the AAA hundreds of thousands . . . are either being driven out on the roads without hope of absorption into industry or exist without land to cultivate by grace of the landlord in shacks scarcely fit for pigs."[76] A study published in 1935 concluded that "the landowner is more and more protected from risk by government activity,

73. See, for instance, Ted Leitzell, "Uncle Sam, Peddler of Electric Gadgets," *New Outlook* 164 (August 1934): 50–53, 63.

74. See, for example, Arthur F. Raper, *Preface to Peasantry: A Tale of Two Black Belt Counties* (Chapel Hill, N.C., 1936); Arthur F. Raper and Ira DeA. Reid, *Sharecroppers All* (Chapel Hill, N.C., 1941); James Agee and Walker Evans, *Let Us Now Praise Famous Men* (Boston, 1941); and Howard B. Myers, "Relief in the Rural South," *Southern Economic Journal* 3 (January 1937): 281–91.

75. Pete Daniel, *Breaking the Land: The Transformation of Cotton, Tobacco, and Rice Cultures since 1880* (Urbana, Ill., 1985), pp. 155–83; Gavin Wright, *Old South, New South: Revolutions in the Southern Economy Since the Civil War* (New York, 1986), pp. 226–38.

76. Quoted in Tindall, *The Emergence of the New South*, p. 409 (first quotation), p. 414 (second quotation).

while the tenant is left open to risks on every side."[77] There were widespread reports of violations of the tenancy provisions of the AAA contracts.

Receiving little help from their penurious local and state governments, the agricultural poor turned to the federal government for relief. Washington had provided some disaster relief for victims of the Mississippi River flood of 1927 and the drought of 1930–1931. The Federal Emergency Relief Administration and the New Deal work-relief programs tried to assist the rural unemployed, but these efforts were far from adequate and tended to neglect those residing in the countryside. In the meantime, the Division of Subsistence Homesteads in the Department of Interior and the FERA constructed a number of planned communities, largely agricultural, as a means of helping the dispossessed. Eventually more than a hundred such communities were built, a majority of them in the South.[78] Yet these projects could offer help to only a handful of the destitute. Widespread misery in the rural South, the enclosure of southern farmland, and the lack of industrial employment induced tens of thousands of southerners to leave the region. This stream of migrants included a great many victims of drought and depression in Oklahoma, Texas, Arkansas, and Missouri. These "Okies" and "Arkies," not all of whom were farmers, headed for California and other western states, a trek described with dramatic effect in John Steinbeck's *The Grapes of Wrath* (1939). Although the depressed condition of northern industry slowed the flow of migrants out of the South, 458,000 more blacks and 689,500 more whites left the region than moved in during the 1930s.[79]

Some tenant farmers attempted to defend themselves against their powerful

TENANTS, INCLUDING SHARECROPPERS, AS PERCENTAGE OF FARM
OPERATORS, 1880–1930

Year	South Atlantic	East South Central	West South Central	North
1880	36.1	36.8	35.2	19.2
1890	38.5	38.3	38.6	22.1
1900	44.2	48.1	49.1	26.2
1910	45.9	50.7	52.8	26.5
1920	46.8	49.7	52.9	28.2
1930	48.1	55.9	62.3	30.0

SOURCE: U.S. Special Committee on Farm Tenancy, *Farm Tenancy* (Washington, D.C.: Government Printing Office, 1937), p. 39.

77. Charles S. Johnson, Edwin R. Embree, and W. W. Alexander, *The Collapse of Cotton Tenancy: Summary of Field Studies & Statistical Surveys, 1933–35* (Chapel Hill, N.C., 1935), p. 51.

78. Daniel, *Breaking the Land*, pp. 65–151; Paul K. Conkin, *Tomorrow a New World: The New Deal Community Program* (Ithaca, N.Y., 1959); Conkin, "It All Happened in Pine Mountain Valley," *Georgia Historical Quarterly* 47 (March 1963): 1–42; Donald Holley, *Uncle Sam's Farmers: The New Deal Communities in the Lower Mississippi Valley* (Urbana, Ill., 1975).

79. Jack Temple Kirby, *Rural Worlds Lost: The American South, 1920–1960* (Baton Rouge, La., 1987), pp. 309–33; James N. Gregory, *American Exodus: The Dust Bowl Migration and Okie Culture in California* (New York, 1989), pp. 3–77.

landlords. The most notable of these resistance movements was the Southern Tenant Farmers' Union, which was organized in July 1934 in northeastern Arkansas.[80] Influenced by a few Socialists and organized on an interracial basis, the union was immediately concerned with establishing power to bargain with landlords and assuring tenants equitable treatment under AAA regulations. The movement spread to several surrounding states and may have included as many as 25,000 members. Among its supporters were the Fellowship of Southern Churchmen and prominent northerners such as Eleanor Roosevelt and Norman Thomas. The latter launched a campaign to arouse the conscience of Americans and to get the Roosevelt administration to do something about the distress of southern sharecroppers. But the STFU encountered determined and violent opposition from landlords, and its efforts to stop tenant evictions and to carry out cotton pickers' strikes enjoyed little success. Before the end of the decade, it had largely disappeared.[81] Even so, the union's brief existence revealed the desperation of its members and dramatized the plight of the rural poor in the South.

By 1935 the Roosevelt administration had become more conscious of the need to provide federal assistance to the mass of landless farmers in the southern states. In that year the president established by executive order the Resettlement Administation, which took over and completed the scattering of subsistence homesteads and farming communities and was authorized to make rehabilitation loans and grants to small farmers. Meanwhile, *The Collapse of Cotton Tenancy* (1935), a volume written by Charles S. Johnson, Edwin Embree, and Will Alexander, provided a vivid analysis of conditions in the southern cotton belt. Supported by the Rockefeller Foundation and based on scholarly investigations at the University of North Carolina and Fisk University, this work recommended a federal program for small farm ownership. The Southern Policy Committee, an organization created in 1935 to discuss various regional problems, also endorsed the idea of federal legislation to alleviate the tenant problem in the South. There was additional support within the administration for agricultural reform of this kind.

The first major effort along this line was a bill introduced in 1935 by Senator John H. Bankhead of Alabama. This measure called for the creation of a federal corporation authorized to make loans to deserving tenant farmers for the purchase of their own land. The bill passed the Senate but was not considered on the floor of the House. In 1936 President Roosevelt appointed a Special

80. An earlier Share Croppers' Union, organized in Alabama in the first part of the 1930s under the auspices of the Communist party, attracted about 5,000 members, mostly African Americans. But it accomplished little and had disappeared by 1935. Tindall, *The Emergence of the New South*, pp. 379–80; Kirby, *Rural Worlds Lost*, p. 151.

81. Donald H. Grubbs, *Cry from the Cotton: The Southern Tenant Farmers' Union and the New Deal* (Chapel Hill, N.C., 1971); M. S. Venkataramani, "Norman Thomas, Arkansas Sharecroppers, and the Roosevelt Agricultural Policies, 1933–1937," *Mississippi Valley Historical Review* 47 (September 1960): 225–46; Jerold S. Auerbach, "Southern Tenant Farmers: Socialist Critics of the New Deal," *Labor History* 7 (Winter 1966): 3–18; Thomas M. Jacklin, "Mission to the Sharecroppers: Neo-Orthodox Radicalism and the Delta Farm Venture, 1936–40," *South Atlantic Quarterly* 78 (Summer 1979): 302–16.

Committee on Farm Tenancy. Its report early in 1937 emphasized the extent of rural poverty, recommended the establishment of a Farm Security Administration, and pointed up the desirability of the privately owned family farm. A new bill, embodying a number of compromises, passed both houses of Congress in July 1937. The Bankhead-Jones Farm Tenancy Act authorized purchase loans repayable over forty years at 3 percent ($10 million the first year, rising to $50 million by the third year) and the creation of a new agency, the Farm Security Administration, which would supersede the Resettlement Administration.[82]

Although the Farm Security Administration's tenant purchase program and its other resettlement projects received widespread publicity, the agency's most vital function was its standard rural rehabilitation loan—for equipment, livestock, farm implements, and the like. A large part of the FSA's work focused on the South, where rural poverty was most acute. Between July 1935 and September 1943, the Resettlement Administration and FSA advanced rehabilitation loans to 399,000 southern families, about three-fifths of the loans in the country. Besides making loans for farm buying and rehabilitation, the FSA retired submarginal land, administered the resettlement of communities inherited from the RA, and operated camps for migratory farm workers.[83] The conservative resurgence of the 1940s resulted in the liquidation of this modest assault on the South's rural poverty, and FSA efforts made hardly a dent in relieving the problem of the depressed landless farmer in the region. A far more revolutionary change was brought about by New Deal acreage reduction and increasing mechanization during the 1930s, which forced hundreds of thousands of rural poor off the land.[84]

Southern liberals faced another challenge in the organized labor movement of the 1930s. For one thing, the South stood out as the least organized part of the country—as a bastion of anti-union sentiment. The region's major industry, cotton textiles, had repeatedly frustrated efforts to organize textile workers. Lacking a tradition of independent unionism, southern industrial labor confronted a number of formidable barriers: the worker's intense individualism, the region's pervasive poverty and abundant supply of cheap labor, the image of industrialists as community benefactors and leaders in the economic development of the South, and the anti-labor policies of state and local governments.[85] Management was also strengthened by the intersectional competition in indus-

82. Paul E. Mertz, *New Deal Policy and Southern Rural Poverty* (Baton Rouge, La., 1978), provides an authoritative treatment of congressional consideration of farm tenancy legislation in the mid-1930s.

83. Mertz, *New Deal Policy and Southern Rural Poverty*, pp. 190–93; Sidney Baldwin, *Poverty and Politics: The Rise and Decline of the Farm Security Administration* (Chapel Hill, N.C., 1968).

84. Pete Daniel, "The New Deal, Southern Agriculture, and Economic Change," in *The New Deal and the South*, ed. James C. Cobb and Michael V. Namorato (Jackson, Miss., 1984), pp. 41, 55.

85. Billy H. Wyche, "Southern Newspapers View Organized Labor in the New Deal Years," *South Atlantic Quarterly* 74 (Spring 1975): 178–96; Robert P. Ingalls, "Anti-Labor Vigilantes: The South during the 1930s," *Southern Exposure* 12 (November/December 1984): 72–78; Roger Biles, "Ed Crump versus the Unions: The Labor Movement in Memphis during the 1930s," *Labor History* 25 (Fall 1984): 533–52; Jim DuPlessis, "Massacre in Honea Path," *Southern Exposure* 17 (Fall 1989): 60–63.

tries like cotton textiles and the tendency of southern industrialists to seek a competitive advantage through the relative low wages of their workers. When the environment became more favorable to the labor movement in the 1930s, southern workers responded enthusiastically to the leadership of national unions based in the North. Moreover, they turned increasingly to the federal government for legislative encouragment and other assistance.

An outburst of strikes by workers in Elizabethton, Tennessee, Gastonia, North Carolina, and other textile mills in 1929 expressed the mounting alienation and resentment of industrial workers in the South, but these spontaneous demonstrations accomplished little except to publicize the deplorable condition of southern workers. In the spring of 1933 the feeble labor movement in the South was given new life by the promise of labor organization and collective bargaining contained in Section 7(a) of the National Industrial Recovery Act and the organizating campaigns of the United Mine Workers and other national and international unions. Affiliates of the American Federation of Labor, the railroad brotherhoods, and state federations and city labor centrals demonstrated unprecedented vitality in various parts of the region. Even the United Textile Workers responded to the prospect of labor reform, and in the late summer of 1934 militant textile workers in the South led the way in a national textile strike.[86]

In the mid- and late 1930s, the South was involved in the divisive struggle of organized labor, in the movement that led to the creation of the Congress of Industrial Organizations, and in the drive to unionize mass production industries. While John L. Lewis's United Mine Workers was especially active in these stirring events, workers, in and out of the South, were embattled in such industries as steel, rubber, oil, and tobacco. The struggle to organize the South was supported by national unions and labor leaders, in part because of the threat posed by the southern labor system to the standards being established in other regions. Despite some misgivings, most southerners supported the National Labor Relations Act of 1935, and a majority of the region's inhabitants approved the Fair Labor Standards Act of 1938. Yet many southern industrialists and business elements strongly opposed the act of 1938, fearing that its minimum wage features would destroy regional wage differentials and slow down the South's economic development. In some industries, however, northern entrepreneurs were much more favorably disposed toward the legislation. One such enterprise was cotton textiles, an industry in which the South had acquired three-fourths of the national plant capacity by 1940. According to one southern businessman, "A great many industrialists in the North, and especially politicians, believe that the South has an undue advantage and that labor is being sweated to the extent of destroying entire Northern industrial communities,

---

86. For these developments and other aspects of the southern labor scene in the 1930s, see F. Ray Marshall, *Labor in the South* (Cambridge, Mass., 1967), pp. 101–222; James A. Hodges, *New Deal Labor Policy and the Southern Cotton Textile Industry, 1933–1941* (Knoxville, Tenn., 1986); and Tindall, *The Emergence of the New South*, p. 505–39.

which are already moving South because of wage differentials and agitation from foreign labor elements in the North."[87]

Progress was made in the effort to organize southern industrial labor in the 1930s. But there were many setbacks, the most important being the failure to make significant inroads among textile workers. By the end of the decade, the percentage of organized workers in the southern states was only about half that of other regions, and they were concentrated in the older AFL unions and railroad brotherhoods. The South remained, in the words of one scholar, "predominantly nonunion and largely antiunion."[88] Strong obstacles to labor organization persisted, including the pervasiveness of an impoverished agriculture. Some of labor's gains during the New Deal years were made at the expense of blacks, who were frequently discriminated against by the white-controlled unions. Still, a genuine labor movement had finally come to the South, and World War II would strengthen it. Indeed, J. Wayne Flynt argues that the New Deal left a permanent impression on southern labor. Most important, perhaps, was the fact that southern workers had begun to turn to the federal government to redress their grievances. Industrial unionism, spearheaded by the CIO and supported by New Deal legislation, posed a serious threat to unorganized industries, challenged the southern system of segregation in the workplace, tried to protect the civil liberties of workers, and broadened the political involvement of working men and women. Federal labor reforms also reduced the wage differentials between workers based on skill, race, and region.[89] The New Deal took a giant step toward the establishment of national labor standards and ending the isolation of the southern labor market. The NRA, the work-relief programs, and especially the minimum wage provisions of the Fair Labor Standards Act raised the wage levels of hundreds of thousands of southern workers. The wages of southerners, far more than workers in other regions, were improved by these measures.[90]

Although the Roosevelt administration never sponsored a broad reform program for African Americans, the racial situation in the South during the Great Depression and the New Deal became a major concern of outside groups—black organizations, northern liberals, national foundations, labor unions, and even the federal government. This development captured the attention of many southerners, particularly black southerners, whose rising expectations and growing assertiveness made them more sensitive to the possibilities of racial change.[91] A few white southerners, described by one writer as "radicals and

87. Quoted in Wright, *Old South, New South*, p. 222.

88. Tindall, *The Emergence of the New South*, p. 522.

89. J. Wayne Flynt, "The New Deal and Southern Labor," in *The New Deal and the South*, ed. Cobb and Namorato, pp. 63–95; Frank Traver DeVyver, "The Present Status of Labor Unions in the South," *Southern Economic Journal* 5 (April 1939): 485–98; Marian D. Irish, "The Proletarian South," *Journal of Politics* 2 (August 1940): 231–58; Douglas L. Smith, *The New Deal in the Urban South* (Baton Rouge, La., 1988), pp. 186–208.

90. Wright, *Old South, New South*, pp. 214–19.

91. See, for example, Harvard Sitkoff, *A New Deal for Blacks: The Emergence of Civil Rights as a National Issue* (New York, 1978); John B. Kirby, *Black Americans in the Roosevelt Era: Liberalism and Race* (Knoxville, Tenn., 1980), pp. 153–86; and Edwin D. Hoffman, "The Genesis of the Modern

WPA MINIMUM MONTHLY WAGE RATES, 1935–1939

	May 1935	June 1938	August 1939
North			
Massachusetts	$40	$40	$39.00
Pennsylvania	40	40	39.00
Michigan	40	40	39.00
Illinois	40	40	39.00
Nebraska	32	40	39.00
South			
Virginia	21	26	31.20
North Carolina	19	26	31.20
South Carolina	19	26	31.20
Georgia	19	26	31.20
Alabama	19	26	31.20
Mississippi	19	26	31.20
Arkansas	21	26	31.20
Louisiana	21	26	31.20

SOURCE: Donald S. Howard, *The WPA and Federal Relief Policy* (New York: Da Capo Press, 1973, reprint of 1943 ed.), p. 160.

prophets," challenged the Jim Crow system and supported equal rights for blacks. People like Howard Kester, Myles Horton, James A. Dombrowski, and Lillian Smith fell into this category, along with organizations like the Highlander Folk School, the Fellowship of Southern Churchmen, and the Southern Tenant Farmers' Union.[92] But most southern liberals, though favoring the scientific investigation of race relations and open discussion of the subject, were reluctant to criticize the South's racial imperative. In the case of Howard W. Odum, for instance, the degree to which white southerners "could accept Negroes as fellow citizens represented . . . the limits of white racial liberalism in the South."[93] Leading southern interracialists such as Will W. Alexander, Clark Foreman, and Aubrey W. Williams were unwilling to go far beyond the moderate reformism of the Commission on Interracial Cooperation. At the same time, they helped shape the New Deal's approach to the treatment of black Americans. Except for a few people such as Harold L. Ickes and Eleanor Roosevelt, John B. Kirby writes, "it was the liberal southerner who most consciously brought black concerns to the attention of the Roosevelt administration and endeavored to see that those concerns were acted upon. In this regard, the New Deal's stress on economic reform and the ideas of individuals like Ickes fit

Movement for Equal Rights in South Carolina, 1930–1939," *Journal of Negro History* 44 (October 1959): 346–69.

92. Anthony P. Dunbar, *Against the Grain: Southern Radicals and Prophets, 1929–1959* (Charlottesville, Va., 1981), pp. 1–198.

93. Morton Sosna, *In Search of the Silent South: Southern Liberals and the Race Issue* (New York, 1977), pp. 42–87 (quotation on p. 59).

in with their own special need to reduce the South's isolation from the rest of the nation and the liberal's isolation from his fellow white southerner."[94]

The most conspicuous attempt on the part of southern white liberals to come to terms with the race issue was the Southern Conference for Human Welfare (SCHW). Organized in 1938, the conference attracted the support of many southern New Dealers, including political luminaries like Justice Hugo L. Black and prominent outside liberals such as Eleanor Roosevelt. It was a loose coalition of middle-class liberals, a sprinkling of progressive politicians, liberal journalists, CIO representatives, a few Communists, and an assortment of other reformers. Some southern liberals were too cautious to risk involvement in the group. The founding convention in Birmingham was attended by 1,200 enthusiastic people, black and white. The organization's first chairman was President Frank P. Graham of the University of North Carolina. The conference set out to modernize the South and to liberalize the region's Democratic party. It endorsed liberal economic policies, backed labor's right to organize, worked for the repeal of state poll taxes, sponsored several educational campaigns dealing with social problems, and spoke out against certain manifestations of racial discrimination. Its leaders eventually endorsed an anti-lynching law, federal aid to education, and a Fair Employment Practices Committee.[95]

Conservative southerners reacted strongly against the SCHW's racial liberalism, and the organization's members were condemned from the beginning as racial equality reformers. Indeed, many southern liberals were disquieted by the conference's position on the race question. "Until the South is prepared of its own volition to level racial barriers," declared the Chattanooga News, "no Conference resolutions are going to do anything but irritate and alienate the average Southerner."[96] Although the conference had only a handful of Communist members, it was widely criticized for its radical connections, and in the early postwar years the group's advanced racial stance and criticism of U.S. Cold War policies led to its frustration and disbandment in 1948. The conference marked what a sympathetic contemporary described as "a new stage in the development of southern progressive activities."[97] For a moment isolated southern reformers were brought together with the common purpose of modernizing their region. The moment was bright with promise. But the conference's contributions—to the labor movement and to the poll tax repeal campaign, for example—were modest. And its troubled experience revealed its inability to inspire a new political movement, as well as the limits of southern

---

94. Kirby, *Black Americans in the Roosevelt Era*, pp. 73–74. See also Dan T. Carter, "From Segregation to Integration," in *Interpreting Southern History: Historiographical Essays in Honor of Sanford W. Higginbotham*, ed. John B. Boles and Evelyn Thomas Nolen (Baton Rouge, La., 1987), pp. 414–20, and Alice G. Knotts, "Methodist Women and Interracial Fairness in the 1930s," *Methodist History* 27 (July 1989): 230–40.

95. Thomas A. Krueger, *And Promises to Keep: The Southern Conference for Human Welfare, 1938–1948* (Nashville, 1967); Sosna, *In Search of the Silent South*, pp. 88–104; Tindall, *The Emergence of the New South*, pp. 636–41.

96. Quoted in Kneebone, *Southern Liberal Journalists*, pp. 171–72.

97. Katherine DuPre Lumpkin, quoted in *ibid.*, p. 169.

liberalism, despite the popularity of Franklin Roosevelt and the New Deal among southerners.

"The Atlanta spirit," George Tindall has noted, "lay dormant only for a brief winter of depression; before the end of the 1930's it was in as full bloom as ever in the flourishing 1920's."[98] Despite the economic devastation wrought by the Great Depression, in no part of the country was the "growth psychology" more buoyant than in the South on the eve of World War II. In their quest for industrial plants and new capital, southern entrepreneurs looked to the North, as in the past. Qualms about outside control or exploitation seldom stopped southern boosters.[99] Southerners also welcomed another source of economic assistance from the outside—the federal government. Few southerners talked about federal intrusion or the threat to state rights when it came to expenditures for relief programs, public works, the TVA, or the Reconstruction Finance Corporation. The RFC made direct loans to banks, insurance companies, railroads, industrial concerns, and other business enterprises. The head of the agency, Jesse H. Jones of Texas, was sympathetic to southern credit needs, and he located thirteen of thirty-one RFC offices in the South. Almost all southerners were eager to accept this New Deal largess.

Nevertheless, the region's inhabitants remained sensitive to any aspersions or unfavorable comparisons directed at the South's economy. Thus when Secretary of Labor Frances Perkins, ineptly appealing for more purchasing power in May 1933, suggested that the South was "an untapped market for shoes," adverse reaction from "the barefoot South" continued for months.[100] Dixie sensibilities were also evident in the southern response to the publication of the National Emergency Council's *Report on Economic Conditions of the South* in 1938. The *Report* was largely written by southerners and incorporated the essential ideas of the Chapel Hill regionalists and other reformers in the South. Frank Freidel suggests that in effect it was "the southern reformers' manifesto for change." Published with the approval of President Roosevelt, it seemed to represent a concerted effort to reconstruct the southern economy. Roosevelt promised that his administration would develop the "despoiled" southern economy, "address the challenges of the new industrial era," and raise the living standards of all southerners.[101] The sixty-four-page pamphlet summarized the South's economic assets and shortcomings, emphasizing the region's abundant raw materials as well as the chronic poverty of the southern masses, the South's "colonial economy," and its dependence on northern credit. It pointed up the harm to the regional economy resulting from protective tariffs, discriminatory freight rates, monopoly, and absentee ownership. It endorsed the minimum wage and maximum hour provisions of the Fair Labor Standards Act, one objective of

98. Tindall, *The Emergence of the New South*, p. 457.

99. *Ibid.*, p. 463.

100. Tindall, *The Emergence of the New South*, p. 575; Gilbert C. Fite, *Richard B. Russell, Jr., Senator from Georgia* (Chapel Hill, N.C., 1991), pp. 130–31.

101. Frank Freidel, "The South and the New Deal," in *The New Deal and the South*, ed. Cobb and Namorato, p. 33; Bruce J. Schulman, *From Cotton Belt to Sunbelt: Federal Policy, Economic Development, and the Transformation of the South, 1938–1980* (New York, 1991), pp. 3–8, 39–62.

which was to impose national standards on the South. The *Report* aroused great interest, particularly in the South, and more than a million copies were distributed.[102]

In a preface to the *Report*, FDR declared that "The South presents right now the Nation's No. 1 economic problem—the Nation's problem, not merely the South's. For we have an economic imbalance in the Nation as a whole, due to the very condition of the South."[103] While southern liberals generally applauded the *Report*—the Southern Conference for Human Welfare used it as a program guide—the region's industrialists and conservatives tended to see it as a gratuitous indictment of the South. The president's attempt to use the document in his purge campaign during the summer of 1938 even bothered some southern liberals. "This section has been unwisely characterized as the economic problem No. 1 of the nation," the *Manufacturers' Record* protested. "Quite the opposite is true. The South represents the nation's greatest opportunity for industrial development."[104] The president of the Southern States Industrial Council thought the *Report* held the South up to "ridicule and shame" and was calculated to hinder his organization's efforts to attract capital and industry.[105] The Atlanta *Constitution*, while questioning the accuracy of some of Roosevelt's comments and attributing the study to New Deal political motives, declared that the number one economic problem statement was "not so much a criticism of the South [as of] . . . short-sighted interests in other sections which have been chiefly responsible for the condition, to the extent that it exists."[106]

One of the sectional themes discussed in the *Report on Economic Conditions of the South* had long been accepted by most southerners. This was the belief that the southern region was an economic "colony" of the North and that the South's subordinate status was the result, at least in part, of discriminatory policies of the federal government. As a southern historian asserted in 1942, "If it is true that the South is 'the Nation's No. 1 economic problem,' the fundamental historical explanation of that condition is to be found in the fact that for more than three centuries this region, in greater or less degree, has occupied the status of a colony."[107] Contemplating the South's undiversified economy, poverty, and feeling of inferiority, Representative Maury Maverick of Texas argued that the region had to get out from under "the hateful landlordism of the anonymous—the banks, the insurance companies, the distant investors, the credit lines, the bankruptcy receiverships, all the dreary apparatus of financial exploitation by remote control."[108] In *Divided We Stand: The Crisis of a Frontierless Democracy*

102. Steve Davis, "The South as 'the Nation's No. 1 Economic Problem': The NEC Report of 1938," *Georgia Historical Quarterly* 62 (Summer 1978): 119–32; Mertz, *New Deal Policy and Southern Rural Poverty*, pp. 221–47.

103. National Emergency Council, *Report on Economic Conditions of the South* (Washington, D.C., 1938), p. 1.

104. Quoted in Tindall, *The Emergence of the New South*, p. 599.

105. Mertz, *New Deal Policy and Southern Rural Poverty*, p. 236.

106. Quoted in *ibid*.

107. B. B. Kendrick, "The Colonial Status of the South," *Journal of Southern History* 8 (February 1942): 3.

108. Maury Maverick, "The South Is Rising," *Nation* 142 (June 17, 1936): 771.

(1937), Walter Prescott Webb of the University of Texas contended that about two hundred large corporations, mostly located in the North, owned or controlled most of the resources of the South and West, and were intent on subjugating their economies.[109]

For all the talk about regional disparities and discriminatory policies, the one question on which southern leaders gained some redress was that of freight rates. Various investigations of the nation's complex structure of railroad rates revealed that the South—and West—suffered from highly discriminatory rates, both within the region and on an intersectional basis. The rate structure favored the existing pattern of shipping out raw materials for refinement in the North and Midwest, while discouraging the introduction of manufacturing enterprises in the South. "This freight rate business is the heart of the whole Southern problem," Governor Bibb Graves of Alabama declared. "It explains nearly everything. Poverty. Low wages. Bad housing. We can't move till we get free."[110] Southern interests were divided on the question, generally between those dependent on the status quo and those eager for change and future gain. But the major voices of business and political leaders were forced to take "positive stands." Prodded by complaints from southern shippers in the mid-1930s, the Southeastern (later Southern) Governors' Conference took up the issue, conducting a regional "crusade" during the next several years. This campaign for uniform freight rates enjoyed great popular appeal in the South. Members of Congress from the South demanded an investigation of the problem by the Interstate Commerce Commission. In January 1939 they introduced bills designed to achieve rate uniformity, helped organize a southern-western bloc of supporters, and arranged committee hearings on the issue in both houses. Several reports by the Tennessee Valley Authority pointed up the need for rate reform. President Roosevelt endorsed the movement, and he began to appoint more southerners and westerners to the ICC. These developments encouraged the Interstate Commerce Commission to take remedial action. In 1939 the commission, in the Southern Governors' Case, introduced significant changes in commodity rates, and it soon launched a comprehensive investigation of the nation's freight rate structure. This inquiry culminated in 1945 when the ICC ordered the inauguration of a uniform classification system.[111] Southern leaders and their allies had apparently dismantled one of the supports of the region's colonial economy.

Depression and the New Deal did not usher in a new day for southerners. In spite of the disruption and ferment of the period, much remained unchanged. But the events of the 1930s did bring changes that eventually helped transform

109. Walter Prescott Webb, *Divided We Stand: The Crisis of a Frontierless Democracy* (New York, 1937).

110. Quoted in Tindall, *The Emergence of the New South*, p. 599.

111. John H. Goff, "The Interterritorial Freight-Rate Problem and the South," *Southern Economic Journal* 6 (April 1940): 449–60; William H. Joubert, *Southern Freight Rates in Transition* (Gainesville, Fla., 1949); Robert A. Lively, *The South in Action: A Sectional Crusade Against Freight Rate Discrimination* (Chapel Hill, N.C., 1949), especially pp. vii, 26, 33, 49, 67; Tindall, *The Emergence of the New South*, pp. 599–604.

the region. Federal policies and technological innovations, along with the Second World War, revolutionized the South's agricultural economy. By the end of the 1930s, the old debate over the character of the southern economy had been settled in favor of the New South formula. With the New Deal southerners discovered a new source of outside capital, as well as the potential benefits—and sometimes restraints—of federal action in areas like agriculture, credit, labor, and financial and monopoly regulation. For a time, southern workers who desired a genuine labor movement were encouraged by the federal government's commitment to the right of industrial laborers to organize and engage in collective bargaining. These changes gradually altered interregional relationships and the position of the South in the nation.

In the 1930s the reform spirit blossomed in the South, as it did throughout the nation. It reflected the new interest in regional problems and in the documentation, analysis, and reporting of southern conditions. It was stimulated by the wide-ranging initiatives of the New Deal, by the excitement and controversy over regionalism, and by the efforts of southern reformers to ease the plight of tenant farmers, to strengthen the embryonic labor movement, to abolish discriminatory freight rates, and so on. Southern reformers were also aided by liberal leaders, organizations, and philanthropic foundations from other regions, and by government agencies. In 1938 the southern liberals formed a regionwide organization and put forward a broad agenda for the economic development and reform of their region. As it turned out, however, the southern liberals—a relatively small and weak element—were unable to mount an effective challenge to the established political system in the South. Yet southerners shared in the resurgence of American nationalism in the 1930s and generally applauded the growing modernization of their region.[112] The national government furthered this process by assuming a more powerful role in American life and by developing new relationships with the states and municipalities. It was the federal government that established national standards in wages and hours, thereby breaking down the isolation of the southern labor market.

Meanwhile, however, economic and political differences between North and South continued to produce interregional conflict, although there was less frequent resort to harsh criticism and recrimination. The South welcomed federal programs and economic assistance as long as such intervention did not interfere with its traditional system of race relations and the existing structure of political and economic power in the region. Though unhappy over the changing shape of the national Democratic party, southern leaders could even tolerate the North's dominant role in the new majority coalition—as long as outside intrusion did not threaten their autonomy in matters of race and in the operation of one-party politics in their states and localities. Mounting apprehension eventually led them to collaborate with anti–New Deal Republicans from other regions in organizing a conservative coalition in Congress. In the 1930s northern-

112. See Charles C. Alexander, *Nationalism in American Thought, 1930–1945* (Chicago, 1969), and Paul H. Buck, "The Genesis of the Nation's Problem in the South," *Journal of Southern History* 6 (November 1940): 458–69.

ers seemed less concerned over social and cultural issues that had earlier embittered their relations with southerners and more concerned about economic and political differences of a sectional nature. Northern leaders were generally willing to make concessions to southern demands as long as such demands did not jeopardize their own regional advantages, did not cost too much, and did not undermine national business and labor standards. This was the situation that confronted the South when another momentous event from beyond its borders posed new challenges and opportunities for its inhabitants.

CHAPTER 7

The Stimulus of War

THE Second World War was a transforming experience for the South and a catalyst in altering its role in the nation. Once again, as in 1898 and 1917–1918, war brought a dramatic demonstration of the region's patriotism and nationalist feeling, and after the United States entered the struggle no other section was more zealous in its support of the war effort. The war encouraged the national economic integration of the South and significantly reduced the economic and social disparities between southerners and other Americans. It led to an infusion of new capital and industry into the South, quickened the pace of its urbanization, accelerated the restructuring of its agriculture, and brought a flood of soldiers to southern training camps from other regions. Some of these developments brightened the hopes of the region's liberals, but for the most part the circumstances of an all-out war strengthened the position of southern conservatives in their opposition to New Deal reforms, organized labor, and the influence of the national Democratic party. At the same time, the war years provoked sectional conflict—over the allocation of federal money and resources, over the process of mobilization, over national policy involving race relations, and over the meaning of American democracy. Many outsiders found new evidence during the early 1940s to support the old notion of the South as a national problem, a problem manifested in the region's pervasive poverty, backwardness, and undemocratic politics.

Southerners more than other Americans generally adopted a bellicose attitude during the national debate over foreign policy in 1940 and 1941. They were strong advocates of a British victory over the Axis powers, and no other region gave President Roosevelt such unified support in his efforts to aid the British against Germany and Italy. In the years before Pearl Harbor, one historian has noted, southerners "repeatedly displayed in the opinion polls a greater conviction that the United States would be drawn into war again, that overseas events were vital to American interests, that the nation should help France, Britain, China, and ultimately Russia, that the army and navy should be enlarged, that young men should be drafted, that neutrality legislation should be revised or repealed."[1] Southern congressmen provided overwhelming and at times indispensable support for the Roosevelt administration's key policies: for the first peacetime draft in 1940 and its extension a year later, for passage of the Lend-Lease Act in March 1941, for revision of the neutrality laws in 1939 and 1941, and for authorization to seize foreign merchant ships and to arm American vessels in 1941. Meanwhile, the isolationist America First Committee failed to develop substantial strength in the southern states, and before the draft went into effect southerners enlisted in the armed forces in greater numbers than men from other sections.[2]

Southern enthusiasm for a vigorous foreign policy was to some extent a reflection of Democratic party loyalty and the Wilsonian tradition of internationalism. As one noninterventionist complained in 1941, "If a Democratic President wants war, the south wants war. If a Republican President wanted war, the south would want peace."[3] Their historic attachment to the Democratic party predisposed the region's congressmen to support Franklin D. Roosevelt in a time of national crisis, although many of them were suspicious of the president's urban liberalism and not altogether mollified by his emphasis on rearmament and international leadership. But they were nationalists as well as provincialists. Economic considerations were also involved, particularly southern concern over the threat the Axis conquests posed to foreign markets for cotton and tobacco. In addition, psychological factors helped shape the regional outlook, including the South's long military tradition and the fact that its historical experience had "bred a psychology of danger and defense."[4] Historically, southerners had maintained sentimental ties with the British, and their ethnic homogeneity enabled them to escape much of the ethnic conflict found in other regions. Southerners, emphasizing the preponderance of the "native-born" among them, took pride in asserting that their section was the "most American" part of the nation.[5]

Thus, as his emphasis shifted from domestic reform to the international scene, Franklin Roosevelt was able to rely on the powerful leadership of southern congressmen. They provided a bulwark of support for the administration's foreign and defense policies throughout the war, and in the process helped the president maintain a high degree of party unity. The South also became conspicuously identified—through Secretary of State Cordell Hull, southern congressional leaders, and the force of public opinion—with Roosevelt's internationalism and his plans for a postwar system of collective security. Although

1. George Brown Tindall, *The Emergence of the New South, 1913–1945* (Baton Rouge, La., 1967), p. 688.

2. *Ibid.*, pp. 690–92; V. O. Key, Jr., with the assistance of Alexander Heard, *Southern Politics in State and Nation* (New York, 1949), pp. 352–54; Wayne S. Cole, "America First and the South, 1940–1941," *Journal of Southern History* 22 (February 1956): 36–47; Alexander DeConde, "The South and Isolationism," *Journal of Southern History* 24 (August 1958): 341–42; David L. Cohn, "Mr. Speaker," *Atlantic Monthly* 170 (October 1942): 73–78.

3. Quoted in Cole, "America First and the South," p. 45.

4. Tindall, *The Emergence of the New South*, p. 687.

5. DeConde, "The South and Isolationism," p. 344.

most southerners joined with a large majority of other Americans in backing the neutrality legislation of the mid-1930s, the region's congressmen, press, and public opinion had consistently expressed greater support for the League of Nations, the World Court, and the concept of international organization than any other sectional group. An American Institute of Public Opinion poll in 1937 revealed that 44 percent of southerners thought the United States should join the League, compared with 33 percent of northeasterners, 31 percent of midwesterners, and 27 percent of westerners.[6] Southern advocates of a Wilsonian organization, one scholar has written, "seemed to rejoice in the possibility that their benighted region had, after all, produced an idea that would rescue the world from itself and establish a new order under a progressive American leadership."[7] Southerners, in and out of Congress, used their influence to help make the United Nations a reality during the last years of the war.[8]

The South responded like other regions to the national appeals for voluntary involvement in the myriad demands of homefront mobilization—running the local draft boards, implementing the rationing of scarce goods, serving in civilian defense activities, and so on.[9] But in some respects the southern contribution was distinctive. For one thing, the region became the location of a disproportionate number of the nation's military bases and training centers, in part because of its moderate climate, abundance of open space, and congressional influence. More than 60 of the army's 100 new camps were located in the South, and two-fifths of the wartime expenditures for new military and naval installations went to the southern states. An older base, Fort Benning in Georgia, became the army's largest basic training center. Army bases, naval stations, military airfields, and specialized educational operations like the navy's V-5 and V-12 programs were scattered over the region. Many of these installations dramatically transformed the South's quiet countryside. The War Department bought huge amounts of land for military use. One survey of military purchases in Alabama, Georgia, and South Carolina revealed acquisitions of 710,000 acres and the displacement of 25,000 people. Starke, Florida, a drowsy town of 1,500 people in 1940, emerged overnight as the home of Camp Blanding and the state's fourth-largest city. "By March, 1941," one writer observed,

6. Tennant S. McWilliams, *The New South Faces the World: Foreign Affairs and the Southern Sense of Self, 1877–1950* (Baton Rouge, La., 1988), p. 143; Alfred O. Hero, Jr., *The Southerner and World Affairs* (Baton Rouge, La., 1965), p. 223; Tindall, *The Emergence of the New South*, pp. 688–92.

7. McWilliams, *The New South Faces the World*, p. 138.

8. See, for example, Caroline K. Pruden, "Tennessee and the Formative Years of the United Nations: A Case Study of Southern Opinion" (unpublished paper [1989], in possession of author); Ralph B. Levering, *American Opinion and the Russian Alliance, 1939–1945* (Chapel Hill, N.C., 1976), p. 201; and George H. Gallup, *The Gallup Poll: Public Opinion, 1935–1971*, 3 vols. (New York, 1972), vol. 1 p. 382.

9. For the experience of two southern states, see Sarah McCulloh Lemmon, *North Carolina's Role in World War II* (Raleigh, N.C., 1964), and C. Calvin Smith, *War and Wartime Changes: The Transformation of Arkansas, 1940–1945* (Fayetteville, Ark., 1986). See also Robert J. Norrell, with the assistance of Guy C. Vanderpool, *Dixie's War: The South and World War II* (Tuscaloosa, Ala., 1992); Virginia Historical Society, *V for Virginia: The Commonwealth at War, 1941–1945* (Richmond, 1991); Lonnie E. Maness, "A West Tennessee Town and World War II," *West Tennessee Historical Society Papers* 32 (October 1978): 110–19.

"more than 20,000 men were busily sawing, hammering, bricklaying and mixing to construct a permanent camp for 60,000 soldiers."[10] Farther south in the same state, Miami Beach suddenly became a major military center; scores of hotels were taken over to house thousands of new recruits.[11] Many other communities in the South experienced similar changes.

New defense industries stimulated the southern economy even more than the military installations. Over $4 billion went into military facilities and about $5 billion into defense plants (about a fifth of which represented private investment). Although the most industrialized parts of the country received a large percentage of the defense contracts, especially in the early years of the struggle, war production increasingly moved south and west. The South received 17.6 percent of the national investment in war plants, much less than its percentage of the national population (28 percent) but still a powerful stimulus to the expansion of the region's manufacturing capacity. Its most important defense industries included shipyards in Newport News, Norfolk, Charleston, and along the Gulf Coast; aircraft plants in Dallas-Fort Worth and Marietta, Georgia; ordnance plants, alumimum production, petroleum refineries and pipelines, metal fabrication plants, and synthetic rubber production in various parts of the South. In May 1941, four shipyards on the Gulf Coast were working around the clock on warships and merchantmen, and four new shipyards were under construction. The Oak Ridge, Tennessee, facility for the production of uranium required 110,000 workers during its construction and 82,000 workers at the height of its production in 1945.[12]

Military installations, defense plants, and related industrial enterprises were eagerly sought by southern business and political leaders. The pressure they exerted had some effect. The Tennessee Valley Authority, with a mandate to expand its production of electrical power and to assume the role of a defense agency, became a strong promoter of industrial growth in the valley. Perhaps even more important were the decisions made by the Roosevelt administration and key mobilization agencies to take advantage of the war emergency to develop and modernize the South—to move forward in the spirit of the *Report on Economic Conditions of the South* and the establishment of minimum wages in 1938. This was evident in the military buildup of 1940 and 1941. In 1940, for example, Congress amended the Maritime-Naval Expansion Act of 1938 to make it possible for southern and West Coast shipbuilders to secure contracts without

10. Geoffrey Perrett, *Days of Sadness, Years of Triumph: The American People, 1939–1945* (New York, 1973), p. 85. See also Morton Sosna, "War and Region: The South and World War II" (unpublished manuscript), pp. 46–50.

11. Perrett, *Days of Sadness, Years of Triumph*, p. 238; William T. Schmidt, "The Impact of Camp Shelby in World War II on Hattiesburg, Mississippi," *Journal of Mississippi History* 39 (February 1977): 41–50.

12. William J. Cooper, Jr., and Thomas E. Terrill, *The American South: A History*, 2 vols. (New York, 1991), vol. 2, pp. 689–90; Charles W. Johnson and Charles O. Jackson, *City Behind a Fence: Oak Ridge, Tennessee, 1942–1946* (Knoxville, Tenn., 1981); Tindall, *The Emergence of the New South*, pp. 695–700; Perrett, *Days of Sadness, Years of Triumph*, p. 84; Lewis N. Wynne and Carolyn J. Barnes, "Still They Sail: Shipbuilding in Tampa During World War II," *Gulf Coast Historical Review* 5 (Spring 1990): 179–91.

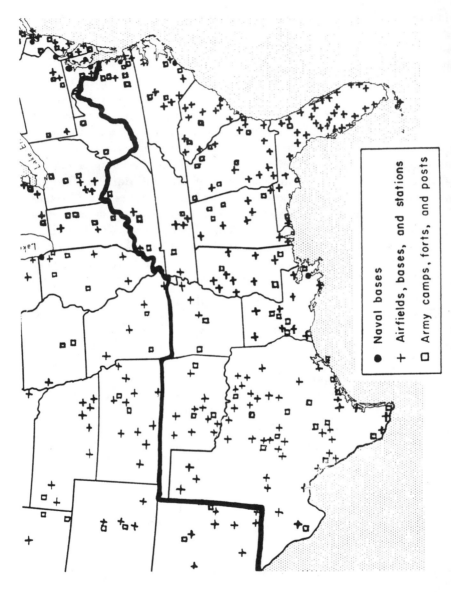

The South in World War II: Army Camps, Naval Bases, and Airfields. SOURCE: Adapted from Clifford L. Lord and Elizabeth H. Lord, *Historical Atlas of the United States*, rev. ed. (New York: Henry Holt and Co., 1953), p. 193.

necessarily presenting the lowest bids. During the war, the War Production Board, the National War Labor Board, and other agencies adopted policies that facilitated the decentralization of war plants, improving wages for southern and western workers and encouraging the economic growth of the periphery. As Bruce J. Schulman observes, "it was the effort to modernize the southern economy that brought officials such as Donald Nelson of the WPB and George Taylor of the NWLB into the national government in the first place. FDR's affection for his 'other home' and his horror at southern underdevelopment led him to look kindly on efforts to build the South during the war. So did the conviction of war agency administrators that industrialization of the South would stave off future economic depression and secure national prosperity."[13]

By 1945 the southern economy had undergone a series of remarkable changes. The productive capacity of the economy, stimulated by Washington's investments in new plants and equipment, had increased by about 50 percent. The number of production workers doubled during the war. The production of ships and planes, as well as petrochemicals, oil pipelines, and light metals, gave a decided boost to the region's industrialization, diversified the industrial economy, encouraged the emergence of new industrial centers along the Gulf Coast and in the Southwest, and led to the accumulation of new industrialized knowhow, a pool of skilled workers, and a cadre of experienced managers. This industrial expansion also sparked the acquisition of sizable amounts of investment capital, the growth of financial institutions, and the emergence of an unprecedented consumer market in the South. Although a considerable part of this industrial expansion proved to be ephemeral, it fundamentally reshaped the southern economy and, with changes in the agricultural sector, constituted the "take-off" phase of the region's subsequent industrial and commercial growth.[14] Intangible aspects of the war experience were also important, including what George B. Tindall has described as "the demonstration of industrial potential, new habits of mind, [and] a recognition that industrialization demanded community services."[15]

The South's economic expansion was accompanied by accelerated urban growth. Thirty-nine of the region's metropolitan areas increased in population during the war. Whereas the South's farm population declined by about 20 percent between 1940 and 1945, its cities gained nearly 30 percent, surpassing the rate of urbanization in other parts of the country. "The urban South," one scholar notes, "was changing its basic function from serving as a market for the surrounding countryside to serving as a magnet for economic opportunity."

13. Bruce J. Schulman, *From Cotton Belt to Sunbelt: Federal Policy, Economic Development, and the Transformation of the South, 1938–1980* (New York, 1991), pp. 63–134 (quotation on p. 100). Also see Sosna, "War and Region," ch. 1.

14. Cooper and Terrill, *The American South*, vol. 2, pp. 690–92; Jack Blicksilver, "World War II," in *The Encyclopedia of Southern History*, ed. David C. Roller and Robert W. Twyman (Baton Rouge, La., 1979), p. 1361; Sosna, "War and Region," ch. 1; Tindall, *The Emergence of the New South*, pp. 697–701. For the national picture, see Harold G. Vatter, *The U.S. Economy in World War II* (New York, 1985).

15. Tindall, *The Emergence of the New South*, p. 701.

Southern cities such as Norfolk, Charleston, and Mobile became overnight boomtowns, while others such as Memphis and Tampa acquired new regional importance as a result of their wartime dynamism. The nation's capital was transformed. David Brinkley recalled long afterward how the "languid Southern town with a pace so slow that much of it simply closed down for the summer grew almost overnight into a crowded, harried, almost frantic metropolis struggling desperately to assume the mantle of global power, moving haltingly and haphazardly and only partially successfully to change itself into the capital of the free world."[16] The mushrooming growth of cities like Norfolk produced overcrowding, an acute housing shortage, inadequate schools, the collapse of community services, and widespread vice and juvenile delinquency.

More than three million persons made at least one move within the South during the war. The region's rural population dropped by 3.5 million. Of the 677,000 persons who comprised the agricultural work force in Arkansas in 1940, only 292,000 were left by the spring of 1944. Some two million civilians, two-thirds of them black, left the South during the war years, usually for cities in the Northeast and Midwest. The pace of Appalachian migration quickened, and during the 1940s between two and three of every ten of that subregion's residents moved away. Meanwhile, millions of soldiers and their families came into the southern states from other parts of the country.[17]

Changes in the South's agricultural economy were momentous. Prosperity came to the southern countryside with a rush. Farm prices rose sharply—cotton prices more than doubled during the war—and the cash income of the region's farmers from commodity sales and government payments increased more than 100 percent between 1940 and 1944. In some areas farm wages more than tripled. The war years brought increased yields of traditional crops and of newer products like peanuts and livestock, despite some shrinkage in acreage.[18] Nevertheless, not all of the ills of southern farmers were remedied. As Gilbert C. Fite

16. David R. Goldfield, "Southern Cities Unbound and Unwound: The Urban South in World War II" (1993; unpublished paper in possession of author), p. 5 (first quotation); David Brinkley, *Washington Goes to War* (New York, 1988), p. xiv (second quotation).

17. David R. Goldfield, *Cotton Fields and Skyscrapers: Southern City and Region, 1607–1980* (Baton Rouge, La., 1982), p. 142; Edward F. Haas, "The Southern Metropolis, 1940–1976," in *The City in Southern History: The Growth of Urban Civilization in the South*, ed. Blaine A. Brownell and David R. Goldfield (Port Washington, N.Y., 1977), pp. 159–62, 173; Jacqueline Jones, *The Dispossessed: America's Underclasses from the Civil War to the Present* (New York, 1992), p. 227; Tindall, *The Emergence of the New South*, pp. 701–703; Smith, *War and Wartime Changes*, p. 122; Blicksilver, "World War II," p. 1361; Blaine A. Brownell, "Urbanization," in *Encyclopedia of Southern Culture*, ed. Charles Reagan Wilson and William Ferris (Chapel Hill, N.C., 1989), p. 1438; John Hammond Moore, "No Room, No Rice, No Grits: Charleston's 'Time of Trouble,' 1942–1944," *South Atlantic Quarterly* 85 (Winter 1986): 23–31.

18. Tindall, *The Emergence of the New South*, pp. 703–707; Cooper and Terrill, *The American South*, vol. 2, pp. 693–94; Edward L. Schapsmeier and Frederick H. Schapsmeier, "Farm Policy from FDR to Eisenhower: Southern Democrats and the Politics of Agriculture," *Agricultural History* 53 (January 1979): 352–71; Gilbert C. Fite, *Cotton Fields No More: Southern Agriculture, 1865–1980* (Lexington, Ky., 1984), pp. 168, 171–72.

writes, "If one had traveled from Raleigh, North Carolina, through neighboring South Carolina, on through Georgia, Alabama, Mississippi, Louisiana, and as far west as Dallas, Texas, in 1945, he would have observed many more similarities than differences in the rural landscape from any prewar trip." A traveler "would have passed poorly fed and poorly clothed people living in unpainted, weather-beaten shacks made worse with age, eroded fields, much idle land grown up in brush and weeds, and other signs of low productivity and poverty."[19]

There were also other continuities. One was the continued reliance of southern farmers on cotton as their major cash crop. Despite a substantial reduction in the acreage devoted to cotton during the war years, the annual carryovers of the staple remained very large, never less than the prewar surpluses; it was clear that the postwar years would be difficult for cotton producers. Even so, the war hastened the emergence of important structural changes in the rural South and "speeded the uneasy transition from labor-intensive to capital-intensive production."[20] The use of tractors, grain combines, and other labor-saving equip-

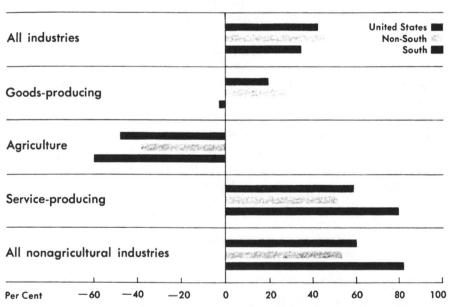

Percentage Changes in Employment, by Major Industry Group, United States, Non-South, and South, 1940–1960. SOURCE: James G. Maddox, with E. E. Liebhafsky, Vivian W. Henderson, and Herbert M. Hamlin, *The Advancing South: Manpower Prospects and Problems* (New York: Twentieth Century Fund, 1967), p. 25.

19. Fite, *Cotton Fields No More*, p. 173.
20. Pete Daniel, "Going among Strangers: Southern Reactions to World War II," *Journal of American History* 77 (December 1990): 886–911 (quotation on p. 889).

ment increased sharply, while the number of sharecroppers and tenants dropped dramatically. New Deal programs had begun to change southern agriculture in the 1930s, but they had been unable to open up opportunities for the South's surplus farm population. The war created such opportunities.[21] One way in which large farm operators tried to meet their labor shortages was by employing German prisoners of war, almost 250,000 of whom were located in the southern states by 1945. These prisoners proved to be satisfactory workers.[22]

Whatever its limitations, the new prosperity of the war period narrowed the gap in the standard of living and general well-being of southerners and other Americans. Income payments in the South increased two and a half times between 1940 and 1945, and per capita income rose 140 percent, as compared with an increase of about 100 percent in other regions. Southern per capita income rose from 59 percent to 65 percent of the national average during the war years. The levels of purchasing power and savings reached new heights. Employment was now available to all who wanted to work, including the region's poorest and most depressed elements. "These jobs," observed one student of the war period, "not only gave them their first taste of prosperity but began to tear apart the paternalistic pattern to which many southern whites as well as the great majority of blacks had been subjected."[23] Indeed, the Second World War set the South on a new course. It brought an abrupt departure from the South's economic backwardness, poverty, and distinctive rural life, as the region moved "perceptibly closer to the mainstream of national economic and social life." Meanwhile, dramatic social and demographic changes swept over the region.[24]

Southern support of the war and of President Roosevelt's wartime leadership was apparent in Congress as well as in the press and public opinion polls. At the same time, southern lawmakers were not always reliable supporters of the administration's domestic proposals. Southern Democrats constituted the largest and most cohesive regional group in Congress. The elections of 1942, which

21. Fite, *Cotton Fields No More*, pp. 168, 171, 174, 176; Jack Temple Kirby, *Rural Worlds Lost: The American South, 1920–1960* (Baton Rouge, La., 1987), pp. 275, 304–305, 325–27.

22. Most German POWs in the United States were located in the South—in some 70 major and 270 branch camps. See Sosna, "War and Region," pp. 270–315. Two of the ten Japanese-American relocation centers were situated in southeastern Arkansas. But the 10,000 inmates in those centers were not an important source of farm labor for the surrounding area. Smith, *War and Wartime Changes*, pp. 63–75.

23. Morton Sosna, "World War II," in *Encyclopedia of Southern Culture*, ed. Wilson and Ferris, p. 674. See also Tindall, *The Emergence of the New South*, p. 701, and Cooper and Terrill, *The American South*, vol. 2, p. 689.

24. See Bruce J. Schulman, " 'This Truly American Section': Federal Policy and the Nationalization of the South, 1938–1960" (paper presented at the annual meeting of the American Historical Association, December 1986); Blicksilver, "World War II," p. 1362 (quotation); Ralph C. Hon, "The South in a War Economy," *Southern Economic Journal* 8 (January 1942): 291–308; and Dillard B. Lasseter, "The Impact of the War on the South and Implications for Postwar Developments," *Social Forces* 23 (October 1944): 20–26.

enlarged the Republican membership and brought the defeat of many northern and western Democrats, strengthened the southern position. The elections also increased the power of the conservative coalition. In the Seventy-eighth Congress (1943–1944), southern Democrats outnumbered nonsouthern Democrats in the House and held just under 44 percent of the party's seats in the Senate. Continuity and the rule of seniority enabled the southerners to assume the chairmanships and ranking positions of a majority of the most important committees in the two houses. The southerners' mastery of the committee structure and parliamentary proceedings of the House and Senate enhanced their influence during the war, as it had in the past. Thus Congress was sometimes described as a "southern institution."[25]

The South's congressional leaders were for the most part quite satisfied to have, in Roosevelt's words, "Dr. Win the War" replace "Dr. New Deal." The region's congressmen enjoyed the influence they exerted in the operation of the committee system and in parliamentary proceedings, for they were important players in the unfolding drama of the nation at war. While they were ardent backers of the Roosevelt administration's defense programs and international initiatives, the southerners were jealous of their political independence, which was strengthened by the growth of conservatism during the war years. In most cases, the southern wing of the Democratic party went along with administration policy; one reason was the continuation of New Deal programs that favored the South—TVA, agricultural supports, and administration efforts to use the war to dismantle protectionist barriers to free trade. Southerners also tended to approve federal controls on business and heavy war taxes, which promised to prevent a recurrence of the spectacular profits enjoyed by northern industries during World War I. Southern leaders applauded the War Production Board's attempt to disperse new industrial capacity to "uncongested areas" of the South and Far West. "It is essential for small Texas manufacturing plants to have a share in defense production," Representative Lyndon B. Johnson told the newspaper editors of that state on one occasion, for ". . . Texas not only wants to do everything it can for defense, but it foresees the need for preserving and expanding its manufacturing plants for normal demands of the future."[26]

In his study of congressional politics during World War II, Roland Young classified all members of the two houses, on the basis of party votes, into three groups of roughly equal size. Group I contained strong party supporters, Group II moderate party supporters, and Group III mild or weak party supporters. The largest number of southern Democrats in both the House and Senate was located in Group III, and the combined percentage of southerners in Groups II

25. *Official Congressional Directory*, 78 Cong., 1 Sess., 2d ed. (Washington, D.C., 1943), pp. 133–42, 177–83, 197–209; Thomas L. Stokes, "The Congress," in *While You Were Gone: A Report on Wartime Life in the United States*, ed. Jack Goodman (New York, 1946), pp. 133–64.

26. Quoted in Robert Dallek, *Lone Star Rising: Lyndon Johnson and His Times, 1908–1960* (New York, 1991), p. 228. See also Richard Franklin Bensel, *Sectionalism and American Political Development, 1880–1980* (Madison, Wis., 1984), pp. 181–82.

and III was 80 percent in the Senate and 83 percent in the House. The southerners found common ground with conservative Republicans on such principles as state rights, fiscal conservatism, limited government, and the abolition of
agencies that might "disrupt social relations in their states."[27] In the Seventy-
eighth Congress conservative southerners and their Republican allies carried
out a concerted attack on a number of New Deal agencies, reduced the progres-
sively oriented National Resources Planning Board to a skeleton, defeated a
federal aid to education bill, and helped turn back a proposal by northern Democrats for a massive public housing program. The voting alliance between
southern Democrats and Republicans reached its peak in 1944, when the conservative coalition manifested itself on about 40 percent of close votes in the
Senate. The index of likeness between Republicans and southern Democrats in
the upper chamber that year, according to one study, reached 63.4 percent, as
compared with a likeness score for nonsouthern Democrats and southern Democrats of only 57 percent.[28] James MacGregor Burns once described the southerners and other old barons who dominated Capitol Hill as "masters of proce-
dure, evokers of memories, voices of ideology—and contrivers of deadlock."
Roosevelt was quoted by an administration official as saying that "for all practical purposes we have a Republican Congress now."[29]

Among their regional interests, the protection of agriculture received top priority in the thinking of southern congressmen, and in contrast to labor policy
the wartime handling of agricultural issues was strongly influenced by the legislative branch. Increased demand for farm commodities eventually brought a
dramatic rise in the price of agricultural products, but farm leaders and their
political representatives in Washington did not wait for market forces to bring
this about. Pressured by the American Farm Bureau Federation and led by determined congressmen such as Senator John H. Bankhead and Representative
Henry B. Steagall, the farm bloc worked unrelentingly to raise government support prices on basic commodities, to revise the parity formula, and to defer farm
laborers from the draft. By 1944 Congress had increased the government loan
rate to 90 percent of parity, and the Stabilization Act of that year directed the
president to take all lawful action to assure that producers of basic farm crops
received at least 100 percent of parity. In addition, the southerners and their
allies in other regions secured legislation requiring that the price supports of

27. Roland Young, *Congressional Politics in the Second World War* (New York, 1956), pp. 15, 239–
65; James T. Patterson, *Mr. Republican: A Biography of Robert A. Taft* (Boston, 1972), p. 260.

28. John Morton Blum, *V Was for Victory: Politics and American Culture During World War II* (New
York, 1976), pp. 222, 231, 234–36; Richard Polenberg, *War and Society: The United States, 1941–
1945* (Philadelphia, 1972), pp. 73–98; Allan M. Winkler, *Home Front U.S.A.: America during World
War II* (Arlington Heights, Ill., 1986), pp. 84–85; Key, *Southern Politics*, pp. 346, 349, 357–58, 361–
62, 366, 374–75; John Robert Moore, "The Conservative Coalition in the United States Senate,
1942–1945," *Journal of Southern History* 33 (August 1967): 368–76; J. Donald Kingsley, "Congress
and the New Deal," *Current History* 4 (March 1943): 25–31; Floyd M. Riddick, "Congress Versus
the President in 1944," *South Atlantic Quarterly* 44 (July 1945): 308–15; Cooper and Terrill, *The
American South*, vol. 2, p. 698.

29. James MacGregor Burns, *Roosevelt: The Soldier of Freedom* (New York, 1970), p. 426 (first
quotation); Polenberg, *War and Society*, p. 199 (second quotation).

major agricultural commodities be maintained for two years after the war at 90 percent of parity. The farm defenders were less successful in the long battle they waged against the Office of Price Administration's regulations and the related issue of food subsidies, which farm leaders feared would place a ceiling on agricultural prices and provide an undeserved bonus for consumers. The farm alliance tried again and again to weaken the price control structure, winning some concessions but never managing to overturn the system. Congress voted twice to terminate the food subsidy program, only to be blocked by presidential vetoes.[30]

In three other areas, southern Democrats in Congress reacted defensively in wartime developments—the growing influence of organized labor, changing currents in race relations, and the nomination of the Democratic presidential ticket in 1944. The expansion of organized labor in the South, particularly the growth of the Congress of Industrial Organizations (CIO), provoked strong resistance in the region and the enactment of several state laws designed to hamstring labor unions. In Congress many southerners were outspoken in their criticism of strikes in war industries and vehemently opposed to the liberal demands and political activities of organized labor. Although virtually all important labor controls emerged from within the executive branch, Congress made full use of its investigatory power in an effort to shape the development of labor policy. Representative Howard W. Smith of Virginia and an anti-labor bloc in the House of Representatives sponsored an anti-strike bill and contributed to the passage of the War Labor Disputes Act, a measure introduced by Smith and Senator Thomas T. Connally of Texas and passed over Roosevelt's veto in 1943. Strongly supported by southern members, its purpose was to curb the freedom of labor unions and to prevent the use of union funds in political campaigns. Southern congressional leaders were motivated by concern over the threat organized labor posed to the South's existing labor system and the part a reinvigorated labor movement might play in the national Democratic coalition.[31]

Congress provided an important forum for wartime decisions affecting African Americans, and southern members spent a great deal of time on such issues. Southern support of the move to abolish the National Youth Administration (NYA), for example, resulted in part from disapproval of the agency's efforts to recruit and train black workers for war industries. The southerners fiercely resisted an anti-poll tax bill, which twice passed the House during the war only to die in the Senate as a result of filibusters. The 1944 filibuster, in David Brinkley's pungent words, was "a charade, a political carnival: a con-

30. Young, *Congressional Politics in the Second World War*, pp. 103, 107–10; Polenberg, *War and Society*, pp. 31–32; Stokes, "The Congress," pp. 154–55; Bruce J. Dierenfield, *Keeper of the Rules: Congressman Howard W. Smith of Virginia* (Charlottesville, Va., 1987), pp. 103–104; Patterson, *Mr. Republican*, pp. 261, 264–65.

31. F. Ray Marshall, *Labor in the South* (Cambridge, Mass., 1967), pp. 225–45; Bensel, *Sectionalism and American Political Development*, pp. 179–80, 186, 188–90; Dierenfield, *Keeper of the Rules*, pp. 95–100; Randall L. Patton, "The CIO and the Search for a 'Silent South,' " *Maryland Historian* 19 (Fall/Winter 1988): 1–14.

UNION MEMBERSHIP IN THE SOUTH, 1939–1964

Union Members (in thousands)	1939	1953	1964
South	627	1,788	1,961
Non-South	5,891	14,616	15,227
Percent of nonagric. workers org. in South	10.7	17.2	14.4
Percent of nonagric. workers org. in Non-South	21.5	34.1	29.5

SOURCE: Adapted from F. Ray Marshall, *Labor in the South* (Cambridge: Harvard University Press, 1967), p. 299.

trived, tedious, often odious discussion of a bill that every member realized would ultimately be defeated." Southerners vigorously protested the Supreme Court's invalidation of the Democratic white primary in *Smith* v. *Allwright* (1944). They took the lead in emasculating the Roosevelt administration's proposal for a federal ballot to be used by out-of-state soldiers in the election of 1944, charging that it represented an assault on state rights, including the power of southern states to limit the enfranchisement of black servicemen. Representative Hatton W. Sumners of Texas warned that the administration's recommendation would "strengthen the stranglehold of this great Federal bureaucracy upon the throats of the States."[32] The southern lawmakers' most impassioned denunciation was reserved for the Fair Employment Practices Committee (FEPC), the target of a sectional crusade throughout the war.

President Roosevelt created the agency by executive order in 1941 and reorganized it in 1943 in an effort to end discrimination against blacks in war-related industries. Many white southerners denounced the committee. Governor Ellis G. Arnall of Georgia, a liberal on many issues, complained that the FEPC was an irritant to most southerners, who regarded it as "a successor to the Lodge Force Bills."[33] The agency had only limited success, particularly in the Deep South, where it encountered determined resistance from management, labor unions, and white workers. Most skilled jobs in this subregion were reserved for white workers, and the newly created training programs were grossly discriminatory against African Americans. Industrial expansion heightened racial tensions, and in some cases, such as the Birmingham steel mills, white fears prompted union leaders to commit themselves to the maintenance of white supremacy. Southern congressmen like Howard W. Smith, chairman of the House Committee on Executive Agencies, sniped at the FEPC throughout the war, attacking it as coercive, bureaucratic, and a threat to the stability of race relations in the South. Early in 1944 Smith turned an investigation of the agency into "a public forum for segregationists." Roosevelt's own support of

32. Brinkley, *Washington Goes to War*, p. 203 (first quotation); Young, *Congressional Politics in the Second World War*, pp. 84–86 (second quotation on p. 84). See also Robert A. Garson, *The Democratic Party and the Politics of Sectionalism, 1941–1948* (Baton Rouge, La., 1974), pp. 24–25, 42–47, 52, 86–87, 89–90, 92; Polenberg, *War and Society*, pp. 110–11, 119, 195–97.

33. Ellis Gibbs Arnall, *The Shore Dimly Seen* (Philadelphia, 1946), p. 101.

FEPC was halfhearted and vacillating. He seemed intent above all else on winning the war and, if possible, on holding the Democratic coalition together through the election of 1944. He apparently encouraged Attorney General Francis Biddle to abandon a possible move to prosecute Alabama officials for denying blacks the right to vote in the Democratic primary of 1944, and he failed to act promptly in supporting the FEPC's ongoing effort to force southern railroads to stop discriminating against Negroes. In 1945 the committee's enemies in Congress, led by southern delegations, succeeded in cutting its budget by half and providing for its dissolution within a year.[34]

The wartime controversy over the committee revealed once again the division between northern and southern Democrats. Southern leaders wanted to promote economic progress in their states but not at the cost of disrupting social order. As Gilbert C. Fite has said, Senator Richard B. Russell found himself "in the grasp of a great contradiction from which he was unable to escape." His very success in helping to expand old federal facilities and to bring new ones into Georgia during the war "worked against the status quo in race relations."[35] Finally, the southern outcry against wartime racial change contributed to the northern image of a reactionary and undemocratic region fundamentally at odds with the national struggle against totalitarianism and intolerance abroad.

As the presidential election of 1944 approached, sectionalism assumed a more prominent place in Democratic party affairs than at any time since 1928. The Democrats were divided along sectional lines, divided into what some commentators referred to as a northern liberal wing and a southern conservative wing. Political leaders in the South talked ominously about leaving the Democratic party. They made much of the changing character of the national party—of the activities of the CIO's Political Action Committee, urban bosses, and black organizations—and of the South's declining role in the party. They noted that, by the summer of 1944, Roosevelt had indicated his intention of reviving the New Deal following the war and that he had advocated new social welfare legislation, a federal ballot for soldiers, and noninterference with the rights of organized labor. The president's southern critics linked his administration with the challenge to the South's established racial order, with labor racketeering, and with Communist sympathies. They charged Roosevelt with the construction of a gigantic federal bureaucracy and with a relentless assault on constitutional government, state rights, and local self-government.

Late in 1942 and early in 1943, Governors Frank M. Dixon of Alabama and Sam Houston Jones of Louisiana suggested that southerners might be forced to

34. Merl E. Reed, "The FEPC, the Black Worker, and the Southern Shipyards," *South Atlantic Quarterly* 74 (Autumn 1975): 446–67; Reed, "FEPC and the Federal Agencies in the South," *Journal of Negro History* 65 (Winter 1980): 43–56; Reed, *Seedtime for the Modern Civil Rights Movement: The President's Committee on Fair Employment Practice, 1941–1946* (Baton Rouge, La., 1991); Charles W. Eagles, *Jonathan Daniels and Race Relations: The Evolution of a Southern Liberal* (Knoxville, Tenn., 1982), p. 117; James A. Nuechterlein, "The Politics of Civil Rights: The FEPC, 1941–46," *Prologue* 10 (Fall 1978): 171–91; Robert J. Norrell, "Caste in Steel: Jim Crow Careers in Birmingham, Alabama," *Journal of American History* 73 (December 1986): 669–94; Blum, *V Was for Victory*, p. 215.

35. Gilbert C. Fite, *Richard B. Russell, Jr., Senator from Georgia* (Chapel Hill, N.C., 1991), p. 185.

break the bonds of party loyalty. New Deal policies, Jones asserted, "have continued to kick an already prostrate South in the face."[36] A few months later Senator Josiah W. Bailey warned, "We can form a southern Democratic party and vote as we please in the electoral college, and we will hold the balance of power in this country."[37] Leon C. Phillips, a former governor of Oklahoma, denounced the New Deal for undermining the Constitution, for attempting "to destroy individual initiative . . . through regimentation," and for permitting "labor racketeers" to become "the bosses of our people."[38] Phillips announced that he was joining the Republican party. Gessner T. McCorvey, chairman of the Alabama Democratic executive committee, spoke out against the activities of the FEPC, the Roosevelt administration's handling of "the racial issue," and outside meddling in "our racial problems in the South."[39]

Although these complaints reflected extensive and growing alienation among anti–New Deal southerners, they were not typical of the region's rank and file. A Gallup poll taken in the summer of 1943 revealed that 80 percent of the southerners questioned favored FDR's renomination for a fourth term. Roosevelt, the journalist John Temple Graves remarked, was "the Democratic party, the rebel yell, Woodrow Wilson and Robert E. Lee rolled into one."[40] To defy him would be equivalent to repudiating the South's political heritage. This was enough to give pause even to the region's conservatives, especially the politicians. As Gessner McCorvey reminded fellow Alabamians, "We can certainly expect nothing from the Republican Party in return for our having voted against them for three-quarters of a century, whereas the Democratic Party owes us an everlasting debt of gratitude as we have been the back-bone of that party for several generations and have really prevented it, on several occasions, from passing into oblivion."[41]

The Roosevelt administration was encouraged by the appearance of several new Democratic leaders at the state level. Robert S. Kerr, who was elected governor of Oklahoma in 1942, worked to unify the Democratic party in his state. A popular and successful wartime governor, Kerr rallied Oklahomans around such themes as the need for economic growth, governmental assistance, and administrative efficiency. Though hardly a New Deal liberal, he was loyal to the national Democratic party and became the chief spokesman in Oklahoma for Democratic administrations in Washington.[42] In Georgia Ellis G. Arnall, the

36. Quoted in Fletcher M. Green, "Resurgent Southern Sectionalism, 1933–1955," *North Carolina Historical Review* 33 (April 1956): 225. See also Thomas Sancton, "Trouble in Dixie II. The Bloody Shirt Once More," *New Republic* 108 (January 11, 1943): 50–51, and Carroll Kilpatrick, "Will the South Secede?" *Harper's Magazine* 186 (March 1943): 415–21.

37. Quoted in Garson, *The Democratic Party and the Politics of Sectionalism*, p. 48.

38. Leon C. Phillips, "A Southern Democrat Renounces the New Deal Party," *Manufacturers' Record* 112 (August 1943): 33, 60.

39. Gessner T. McCorvey, "Democratic Party Regulations Explained," *Alabama Historical Quarterly* 6 (Spring 1944): 64–70.

40. John Temple Graves, *The Fighting South* (New York, 1943), p. 114.

41. McCorvey, "Democratic Party Regulations Explained," p. 70.

42. Anne Hodges Morgan, *Robert S. Kerr: The Senate Years* (Norman, Okla., 1977), pp. 13–32; James R. Scales and Danney Goble, *Oklahoma Politics: A History* (Norman, Okla., 1982), pp. 221–41.

state's young attorney general, emerged as leader of the anti-Talmadge faction. Taking advantage of Governor Talmadge's controversial interference in the state system of higher education, Arnall defeated Talmadge in the gubernatorial primary of 1942. Arnall proved to be an able governor and a successful reformer. He restored the independence of the university system, strengthened the state's commitment to higher education, reformed the penal and parole systems, spearheaded the adoption of a new state constitution, reduced the voting age to eighteen, took the lead in abolishing the poll tax, and accepted Negro suffrage following the invalidation of the white primary. His leadership attracted strong support from "the expanding and increasingly aggressive suburban-uptown bourgeoisie."[43] In addition, Arnall won the plaudits of South-watchers in other regions. In 1945, for instance, a writer in *Life* magazine declared that the governor "has succeeded within three short years in lifting his state from the benightedness of Tobacco Road to the position of runner-up to North Carolina for the title of 'most progressive Southern state.' "[44]

It was not easy to be a liberal in the South, Arnall later wrote. One handicap was "the attitude of a group of [outside] critics, who form a coterie of professional liberals, and who can find nothing in America to view with alarm except the atmosphere of the Southern States." Assailed on the one hand by northern critics and on the other by "native reactionaries, scalawags and demagogues with vocabularies of invective of which 'Communist,' 'traitor to Southern ideals,' 'fellow-traveller,' and 'nigger lover' are the least opprobrious and only the beginning, most Southern liberals search for another tag to wear."[45] Yet they shied away from political conservatism, whose effect, another liberal noted, was "to conserve the domination over the South of the big non-southern interests of this country."[46] Governor Arnall condemned "centralization of industry within an imperial and favored region," called for an attack on monopolies, and urged the removal of other impediments to economic decentralization and industrial growth in the "distressed colonial appendages."[47] As governor, Arnall joined and became one of the most forceful spokesmen for the regional campaign to equalize discriminatory freight rates. The Interstate Commerce Commission upheld the southern position in 1945, although uniform rates were not fully established until 1952.[48]

43. Numan V. Bartley, *The Creation of Modern Georgia* (Athens, Ga., 1983), pp. 184–86. See also Harold Paulk Henderson, *The Politics of Change in Georgia: A Political Biography of Ellis Arnall* (Athens, Ga., 1991), pp. 33–115, 137–58, and Henderson, "Ellis Arnall and the Politics of Progress," in *Georgia Governors in an Age of Change: From Ellis Arnall to George Busbee*, ed. Henderson and Gary L. Roberts (Athens, Ga., 1988), pp. 25–39.

44. John Chamberlain, "Arnall of Georgia," *Life* 19 (August 6, 1945): 69–76 (quotation on p. 69).

45. Arnall, *The Shore Dimly Seen*, p. 87.

46. See the unpublished article by Senator Claude Pepper, September 1944, in Ralph McGill Papers, Emory University Library.

47. Arnall, *The Shore Dimly Seen*, pp. 138–46; Bartley, *The Creation of Modern Georgia*, p. 186.

48. Henderson, *The Politics of Change*, pp. 116–36; Milton S. Heath, "The Uniform Class Rate Decision and Its Implications for Southern Economic Development," *Southern Economic Journal* 12 (January 1946): 213–37; Sam Hall Flint, "The Great Freight Rate Fight," *Atlanta Historical Journal* 28 (Summer 1984): 5–22.

By 1944 it was clear that, if he decided to run for a fourth term, Roosevelt would be renominated. Even so, most of the South's political leaders were determined to prevent the renomination of Vice President Henry A. Wallace, whom they identified as a champion of sharecropper rights, equal rights for blacks, and advanced liberalism.[49] In the meantime, southern conservatives had found their own hero in Senator Harry Flood Byrd of Virginia. A Byrd-for-President Committee was established, and conservative revolts were attempted in three southern states. In South Carolina the insurgents were turned back by Governor Olin D. Johnston's faction, which controlled the state convention. The Mississippi Democratic convention placed a slate of uninstructed electors on the ballot, but they were replaced by a loyal slate after the party's national convention. A struggle between pro- and anti-Roosevelt Democrats also occurred in Texas, which sent two delegations to the national convention. Later, after the pro-Roosevelt faction gained control of the state party, a group of conservative rebels known as Texas Regulars managed to get an independent slate of electors on the ballot. It was pledged to vote for any Democrat other than Roosevelt. The Texas Regulars received only 11.7 percent of the vote, however, and Roosevelt won easily in the Lone Star State.

"One who listened to the noise from the South," remarked the journalist Mark Ethridge in September, "got the feeling that everybody in the seaboard and Gulf states hated Roosevelt with a passion matched only by a Union Leaguer; but, as it turned out, the revolters haven't won a[n] election in the South this year. . . ."[50] Southern political leaders could claim some credit for helping prevent the renomination of Vice President Wallace and replacing him with Senator Harry S. Truman of Missouri.[51] But Roosevelt was too popular and too strong a wartime leader to lose in the South in 1944. The president was the commander in chief, he was the leader of most southerners' party, and he was the central figure in the Allies' march toward victory. Southern congressmen were conscious of the fact that, with their backing, the South had fared exceedingly well in the allocation of agricultural benefits, military bases, defense contracts, and federal support generally. They realized as well that FDR remained popular with their constituents.

Roosevelt's reelection in 1944 did little to blunt the edge of the conservative coalition in Congress. Early in 1945 the president forced Secretary of Commerce Jesse H. Jones to resign and replaced him with Henry Wallace. The conservatives, led by Senators Bailey and Walter F. George, began an attack on this nomination. They succeeded in stripping the Commerce Department of its

49. Garson, *The Democratic Party and the Politics of Sectionalism*, pp. 94–130; Blum, *V Was for Victory*, pp. 281, 288–89; Oswald Garrison Villard, "The Democratic Revolt in the South," *Christian Century* 61 (June 28, 1944): 771–72; "The South's Bitterness Centers on Wallace," *Christian Century* 61 (July 19, 1944): 844.

50. Mark Ethridge to Ralph McGill, 7 September 1944, McGill Papers. For the Texas Regulars, see Seth Shepard McKay, *Texas Politics, 1906–1944: With Special Reference to the German Counties* (Lubbock, Tex., 1952), pp. 431–65.

51. John W. Partin, "Roosevelt, Byrnes, and the 1944 Vice-Presidential Nomination," *Historian* 42 (November 1979): 85–100; Brenda L. Heaster, "Who's on Second: The 1944 Democratic Vice Presidential Nomination," *Missouri Historical Review* 80 (January 1986): 156–75.

lending agencies (including the Reconstruction Finance Corporation) and then almost prevented the Iowan's confirmation. At about the same time, Senate conservatives refused to confirm Aubrey W. Williams of Alabama as head of the Rural Electrification Administration. They regarded Williams, who had directed the NYA, as a left-winger in the same class with Henry Wallace. The outspoken Williams had denounced the "Republican-Southern Tory coalition."[52]

Sectional suspicion and ill will spawned by the war encouraged many Americans to believe that the South constituted a worsening national problem, not the economic problem that Roosevelt had identified in 1938, but one rooted in the region's social backwardness and racial prejudice. "Of all the United States," one northerner living in the South wrote near the end of the war, "the South is most trapped by poverty and disease, illiteracy, political corruption, and a deep want of ambition. She holds no prevailing social convictions newer than those of the Reconstruction years. She is unable to participate in modern American democracy. In conflict with our times, she is a demoralizing influence."[53] Critics of the great power the South wielded in Congress resented what they perceived as the southern lawmakers' arrogant and contemptuous insistence on protecting their section's special interests. Northern liberals condemned the southerners' assault on the New Deal agencies, their opposition to organized labor, and their challenge to Roosevelt's domestic policies and to the Democratic party as a reform vehicle. They could cite many examples, such as the efforts by state leaders in the South to continue the ban on black voters in Democratic primaries despite the Supreme Court's decision in *Smith* v. *Allwright*.[54] Oswald Garrison Villard spoke despairingly of southern "reactionaries," of antisocial forces at work in the South, and of "oligarchies of the rich and powerful" controlling southern politics.[55]

A great many northerners were appalled at the crudeness and intolerance of some southern politicians. Few Dixie congressmen could outdo Senator Theodore G. Bilbo of Mississippi in this respect. Bilbo, an outspoken opponent of the FEPC, asserted on the Senate floor that "If you go through the government departments there are so many niggers it's like a black cloud all around you. . . . The niggers and the Jews of New York are working hand in hand on this damnable, Communist, poisonous piece of legislation."[56] Bilbo's fellow Mississippian in the House of Representatives, John E. Rankin, was no less restrained. Although Rankin was a champion of the TVA, rural electrification, and soldiers' benefits, his extreme prejudices led a contemporary reporter to describe him as "a ranting demagogue," "a wild-eyed Jewbaiter," and "a

52. Leonard Dinnerstein, "The Senate's Rejection of Aubrey Williams as Rural Electrification Administrator," *Alabama Review* 21 (April 1968): 133–43; Blum, *V Was for Victory*, p. 300.
53. Ruth Landes, "A Northerner Views the South," *Social Forces* 23 (March 1945): 379.
54. Darlene Clark Hine, *Black Victory: The Rise and Fall of the White Primary in Texas* (Millwood, N.Y., 1979), pp. 212–32; C. Calvin Smith, "The Politics of Evasion: Arkansas' Reaction to Smith v. Allwright, 1944," *Journal of Negro History* 67 (Spring 1982): 40–51.
55. Villard, "The Democratic Revolt in the South," pp. 771–72.
56. Quoted in Perrett, *Days of Sadness, Years of Triumph*, p. 322.

travesty of a true democrat."[57] It mattered little to most outside viewers that a majority of southern political leaders were not demagogues. The extravagant rhetoric of men like Bilbo and Rankin attracted national attention, and the vigorous and vehement efforts of the region's representatives in Washington to ward off even the slightest outside threat to southern racial practices contributed to the idea of an intransigent and oppressive section out of step with the democratic nation.

Equally telling in arousing northern condemnation were the attitudes and practices of white southerners in dealing with black soldiers and workers. The systematic segregation of black soldiers—on and off military bases—and the discriminatory treatment of black workers in the new defense plants led to complaints and criticisms. Interracial conflict, vigilante violence, and other racial disturbances spread through the southern states—in places like Fayetteville in North Carolina, Mobile, and El Paso. One contemporary estimate identified at least twenty race-related riots or mutinies in southern military installations or base towns.[58] Off military reservations, racial tension grew out of segregated transportation and discrimination in employment. In a wartime volume on race relations, the sociologist Howard W. Odum noted "an almost universal assumption on the part of the rest of the Nation that 'something must be done about' the South's treatment of the Negro."[59] Meanwhile, rumors were rife in the South. It was said that blacks, now in a more independent and militant mood, were intent upon widespread and concerted rebellion. One of the rumors had it that black domestic servants were organizing "Eleanor Clubs" to make sure that there was "a white woman in every kitchen."[60] Rural whites resented increases in black income and complained that Negroes were becoming too "independent." Representative spokesmen like the journalists Virginius Dabney, Jonathan Daniels, and John Temple Graves expressed alarm over what they viewed as African-American agitation and a heightening of black consciousness. According to Dabney, "A small group of Negro agitators and another small group of white rabble-rousers are pushing this country closer and closer to an interracial explosion."[61]

Interracial friction was not restricted to the South, and clashes between blacks and whites became a national problem. A series of racial confrontations and riots developed in northern cities. The worst of these erupted in Detroit in June 1943, leaving twenty-five blacks and nine whites dead. White southerners were quick to instruct the North on its failures in race relations. In the wake of

57. Russell Whelan, "Rankin of Mississippi," *American Mercury* 59 (July 1944): 31–37. For a more general picture of southern naysayers, see Tindall, *The Emergence of the New South*, pp. 724–26.

58. Sosna, "War and Region," pp. 133–34; James A. Burran, "Urban Racial Violence in the South During World War II: A Comparative Overview," in *From the Old South to the New: Essays on the Transitional South*, ed. Walter J. Fraser, Jr., and Winfred B. Moore, Jr. (Westport, Conn., 1981), pp. 167–77.

59. Howard W. Odum, *Race and Rumors of Race: Challenge to American Crisis* (Chapel Hill, N.C., 1943), p. 6.

60. Tindall, *The Emergence of the New South*, pp. 716–18; Perrett, *Days of Sadness, Years of Triumph*, pp. 146–53, 313–14; Cooper and Terrill, *The American South*, vol. 2, pp. 695–97.

61. Quoted in Tindall, *The Emergence of the New South*, p. 718.

the violent disorder in Detroit, Representative Rankin spoke of it as "one of the most disastrous race riots in history." The trouble, he declared, had been "hastened by the crazy policies of the so-called Fair Employment Practices Committee in attempting to mix the races in all kinds of employment." The Jackson (Miss.) *Daily News* found Eleanor Roosevelt "morally responsible" for the riot. "It is blood on your hands, Mrs. Roosevelt. You have been personally proclaiming and preaching social equality at the White House and wherever you go. . . ." And in Detroit, "a city noted for the growing impudence and insolence of its Negro population, an attempt was made to put your preachments into practice. . . ."[62] Some northerners attributed the racial disturbances in their midst to large-scale black and white migration from the South. In Detroit, they noted, the Ku Klux Klan had flourished in recent years and the openly racist Southern Society had claimed a membership of sixteen thousand.[63]

During the war, almost five million men and women from other parts of the country spent some time in army camps, naval bases, or airfields in the South. Few of them had ever been in the region before. Their letters, diaries, and memoirs reveal their wary approach to the southern landscape and its inhabitants—and to their exotic, unpleasant, and threatening qualities. The effect of this exposure tended to be lasting and negative. One historian states, perhaps with some exaggeration, that "mobilizing a military force of over twelve million men and women had the unintended effect of mobilizing an army of critics against the South."[64] Nothing was more important in stimulating these critics than the daily injustice borne by black southerners. "However much these northern GIs may have been impervious to racial injustices in their own areas," Morton Sosna writes, "or were themselves prejudiced against blacks, given the time and place, not to mention the circumstances of war, most did not find the white South's highly visible efforts to enforce segregation compatible with the democratic ideals they were ostensibly defending."[65]

One response of black southerners to the restraints and opportunities of wartime was migration to other regions, an option taken by perhaps a million African Americans. Blacks who remained in the South showed a greater willingness than in earlier years to demand the right to vote, to insist upon equitable employment in defense industries, to compare their own treatment at the hands of white southerners with that accorded German prisoners of war, and to join in the black "Double V" campaign—victory over the nation's enemies abroad and over enemies of black Americans at home. The mood of many Negroes was captured in a book published in 1944 under the title *What the Negro Wants*. In this

62. Quoted in Robert Shogan and Tom Craig, *The Detroit Race Riot: A Study in Violence* (Philadelphia, 1964), p. 98. Also see Blum, *V Was for Victory*, pp. 200–204, and Harvard Sitkoff, "The Detroit Race Riot of 1943," *Michigan History* 53 (Fall 1969): 183–206.

63. Perrett, *Days of Sadness, Years of Triumph*, pp. 311–12.

64. Morton Sosna, "The GIs' South and the North-South Dialogue During World War II," in *Developing Dixie: Modernization in a Traditional Society*, ed. Winfred B. Moore, Jr., Joseph F. Tripp, and Lyon G. Tyler, Jr. (Westport, Conn., 1988), pp. 311–26 (quotation on p. 312). See also Sosna, "War and Region," pp. 84–116.

65. Sosna, "World War II," p. 675.

volume, fifteen African-American contributors demanded political and civil rights, equal educational and job opportunities, and equal access to public facilities—at once.[66] This volume's condemnation of segregation embarrassed William T. Couch, the director of the University of North Carolina Press, which published the book. Couch took the unusual step of including a "Publisher's Introduction" in the work, arguing that a sudden end to segregation "would be disastrous for everyone and more so for the Negro than the white man."[67] This action by Couch, an authentic white liberal, was revealing; it made clear the fact that few white southerners were prepared to go very far in meeting the demands for racial change in the South.

This may also say something about the growing precariousness of the liberals' position in the South. Nevertheless, southern liberals were encouraged by several developments during the last year of the war: by Roosevelt's reelection in 1944, by the growth of organized labor in the region, particularly the gains of the Congress of Industrial Organizations, and by the establishment of the Southern Regional Council.[68] The Southern Regional Council, organized in Atlanta early in 1944, superseded the Commission on Interracial Cooperation. The SRC set out to coordinate the programs of various reform agencies, to undertake studies of specific problems, and to publish educational materials. Its fundamental objective was the "improvement of social, civic, economic, and racial conditions in the South."[69] Meanwhile, Clark Foreman and other leaders of the Southern Conference for Human Welfare launched a campaign to strengthen the conference: to expand its activities, organize state conferences, and put the movement on a more solid financial footing. The *Smith* v. *Allwright* decision, striking down the white primaries, was encouraging. While the newly energized SCHW attracted new members and enjoyed some success, it faced an increasingly hostile environment in the postwar period.[70] That was generally true of southern liberals, most of whom were unwilling to accept the racial reforms advocated by the SRC and the SCHW.

The response of many white southerners to black protest, mounting interra-

66. Rayford W. Logan, ed., *What the Negro Wants* (Chapel Hill, N.C., 1944). See also Kenneth Robert Janken, *Rayford W. Logan and the Dilemma of the African-American Intellectual* (Amherst, Mass., 1993), pp. 145–66; Richard M. Dalfiume, "The 'Forgotten Years' of the Negro Revolution," *Journal of American History* 55 (June 1968): 90–106; Harvard Sitkoff, "Racial Militancy and Interracial Violence in the Second World War," *Journal of American History* 58 (December 1971): 661–81; and Lee Finkle, "The Conservative Aims of Militant Rhetoric: Black Protest During World War II," *Journal of American History* 60 (December 1973): 692–713.

67. Quoted in Tindall, *The Emergence of the New South*, p. 718.

68. For the growth of organized labor in the South during the war, see Marshall, *Labor in the South*, pp. 225–45; Leo Troy, "The Growth of Union Membership in the South, 1939–1953," *Southern Economic Journal* 24 (April 1958): 407–20; and Rudolf Heberle, "War-Time Changes in the Labor Force in Louisiana," *Social Forces* 24 (March 1946): 290–99.

69. "The Southern Regional Council, 1944–1964," *New South* 19 (January 1964): 1–32; William Clifton Allred, Jr., "The Southern Regional Council, 1943–1961" (M.A. thesis, Emory University, 1966).

70. Thomas A. Krueger, *And Promises to Keep: The Southern Conference for Human Welfare, 1938–1948* (Nashville, 1967), pp. 119–38; Numan V. Bartley, "The Southern Conference and the Shaping of Post–World War II Southern Politics," in *Developing Dixie*, ed. Moore, Tripp, and Tyler, pp. 179–97.

cial tension, and increasing criticism of the South's racial practices from outside the region was to rally to the defense of their biracial system. Once again they assumed a siege mentality and a position of white solidarity. At the same time, powerful new currents were beginning to alter American thinking on the place of African Americans in the nation's life. One manifestation of these new currents was the appearance in 1944 of a monumental two-volume study by the Swedish scholar Gunnar Myrdal entitled *An American Dilemma: The Negro Problem and Modern Democracy*, in which the author argued that Americans could not long postpone coming to grips with the nation's racism and correcting this blatant contradiction of its democratic creed. Myrdal drew a negative image of the South, although he was generous in his appraisal of southern liberals.[71] Many northern readers concluded, as often in the past, that the race problem in America was peculiarly southern.

In the late 1930s and early 1940s, the threat of totalitarianism and alternative ideologies gave rise to a renewed interest among Americans in the meaning of democracy. The result was an extensive literature on the subject and a wide-ranging discourse on the nature of Americanism and the nation's common ideals. This democratic revival brought, among other things, an assumption that racial discrimination constituted not merely a sectional problem but a national and even worldwide problem. Yet the question was frequently asked, "What shall we do about the South?" Was not its racial caste system an egregious violation of American ideals? "Not since the Civil War era," a recent study observes, "had the South's distinctiveness seemed so threatening." In her wartime study of the American character, *And Keep Your Powder Dry* (1942), the anthropologist Margaret Mead wrote: "The generalizations in this book should be based primarily on the North, Middle West, and West, and should not be called in question because certain elements of Southern culture differ from them, as this is inevitable." As Morton Sosna has said, American nationalism during the Second World War contained "a strong antisouthern undercurrent."[72] It was ironic that a region that had rallied so ardently to the survival of American democracy in a great national crisis should be singled out by inhabitants of other parts of the country as a mortal threat to the nation's democratic institutions. There was a deeper irony in the fact that people in every region seemed to accept the American democratic creed without giving much thought to the pervasiveness of racial discrimination and prejudice throughout the nation, as well as the removal of Japanese Americans to relocation camps, the concentration of American Indians on reservations, and the continued use of "gentlemen's agreements" to limit the educational and social opportunities of American Jews.

71. David W. Southern, *Gunnar Myrdal and Black-White Relations: The Use and Abuse of an American Dilemma, 1944–1969* (Baton Rouge, La., 1987), pp. 1–69; Walter A. Jackson, *Gunnar Myrdal and America's Conscience: Social Engineering and Racial Liberalism, 1938–1987* (Chapel Hill, N.C., 1990). For the first reactions to *An American Dilemma*, see Southern, *Gunnar Myrdal and Black-White Relations*, pp. 71–99.

72. Sosna, "War and Region," pp. 176–218 (first quotation on p. 186, second quotation on pp. 188–89).

The vast intermingling of people from different regions—in and out of the South, in the armed forces, in defense plants and civilian life—brought unprecedented contacts, associations, and experiences across regional lines. Whatever their impressions, whether hostile or sympathetic, many visitors retained mental pictures of the South that possessed an unforgettable vividness and verisimilitude. For all the outside criticism of racial discrimination and injustice in the South during the war years, northerners had some positive views of southerners. One was that of "the fighting South," of the region's patriotism, heroism in battle, and strong support of the war effort.[73] People in other regions also appreciated the continuing vitality of the Southern Renaissance in letters.[74] Established writers such as Faulkner, Warren, Caldwell, and others added to their national reputations during the war. Two notable wartime books dealt with the nation's racial malaise: Lillian Smith's best-seller, *Strange Fruit* (1944), a novel that probed the interrelationship of race, class, and gender in southern society, and Richard Wright's *Black Boy* (1945), a vivid and moving account of growing up black in the South. Meanwhile, new southern writers were emerging, including Eudora Welty, Tennessee Williams, and Randall Jarrell. This evidence of the South's literary imagination appeared to lessen the region's isolation, even though outsiders frequently regarded the stories and novels of southern authors as bizarre, in the manner of "hillbilly music" or fundamentalist religion.

Students of the southern experience agree that the era of the New Deal and World War II set in motion extraordinary changes in the lives of southerners, changes that transformed the South during the next half-century. The events of the war prepared the way for the region's impressive economic progress and a great reordering of its socioeconomic ranks after 1945. A dynamic new middle class began to emerge. The war also affected the status and outlook of disadvantaged elements in southern society such as black people, tenant farmers, and women. Southern women joined the industrial work force in significant numbers in the early 1940s—in aircraft plants, ordnance depots, shipyards, and textile mills. Many rural women moved to town and began to work outside their homes, sometimes in defense plants. Many black women moved out of low-paying domestic and laundry service into industrial jobs and other work. According to a recent study of one southern state, the war did not "bring about long-term changes in women's status in Alabama but did open the door to the possibility of expanding and enlarging their role in the society and the economy."[75]

The war years were a time of continuity as well as change. This is apparent in two notable—and rather paradoxical—aspects of southern regionalism in

73. See Graves, *The Fighting South*, and Sosna, "War and Region," pp. 229–62.

74. Morton Sosna, "More Important than the Civil War? The Impact of World War II on the South," in *Perspectives on the American South: An Annual Review of Society, Politics and Culture*, vol. 4, ed. James C. Cobb and Charles R. Wilson (New York, 1987), pp. 155–58.

75. Mary Martha Thomas, "Rosie the Alabama Riveter," *Alabama Review* 39 (July 1986): 196–212 (quotation on p. 212). See also Daniel, "Going among Strangers," p. 895, and Goldfield, "Southern Cities Unbound and Unwound," pp. 19–20.

this period. The first was the economic and social convergence of North and South during the war; interregional disparities declined sharply in the face of quickening southern urbanization, industrialization and economic diversification, the restructuring of the agricultural economy, unparalleled prosperity and a rising standard of living. With all of this came an awareness that not within living memory had the South assumed such a vital role in the life of the nation. A second significant aspect of the South's wartime regionalism was the disjunction between regional social change and regional ideology. One historian of the South in World War II has identified the growing contrast "between the South as a social and economic category whose conformity to national patterns was greatly accelerated by the war, and the South as an intellectual and cultural entity whose alterity challenged fundamental tenets of American life more than at any time since the Civil War. . . ."[76]

Some southerners were troubled by the contrast between rapid social change and the strength of traditional values in the South. Allen Drury, a young southerner who covered the Senate for the United Press during the war, captured the depth of congressional uneasiness in a diary entry in the spring of 1944: "We seem to be perched on a cliff, in Washington, above a vast and tumbled plain that stretches far below us: the South, unhappy, restless, confused, embittered, torn by pressures steadily mounting. As far as the eye can see there is discontent and bitterness, faint intimations of a coming storm like a rising wind moving through tall grass. . . ."[77] The "rising wind" Drury spoke of portended a heightening of interregional friction and a resurgence of sectionalism in the years ahead.

76. Sosna, "War and Region," pp. 17–18.
77. Allen Drury, *A Senate Journal, 1943–1945* (New York, 1963), p. 141.

CHAPTER 8

Resurgent Southern Sectionalism

Following the war, the South participated in the nation's remarkable prosperity. Virtually every index of economic activity revealed that the region was rapidly improving its position in the national economy. In some cases, moreover, the southern landscape was undergoing a profound metamorphosis: one after another of "the old monuments of regional distinctiveness" was disappearing in the path of what was aptly called a Bulldozer Revolution.[1] Southerners, perennially relegated to the category of abnormal, were beginning to "nibble at the apple of [national] conformity."[2] In a study of population change published in 1956, two scholars concluded that "the South is becoming an urban and even metropolitan region at a rapid rate, that the ethnic complexion of its population is changing with great speed, that its type of work and worker shows significant changes, and that the composition and characteristics of the people as a whole reflect these fundamental trends."[3] Two years later the journalist Harry S. Ashmore wrote an epitaph for the South he had known in the 1930s and 1940s. Notwithstanding bitter opposition and rearguard fighting, he asserted, nothing could "turn back the forces that are reshaping the Southern region in the nation's image."[4]

The southern industrial expansion of the war years achieved added momentum in the postwar period, fueled by the region's energetic search for manufacturing enterprises, the continued flow of federal funds into the southern states, and the emergence of an impressive new consumer market. Nonagricultural employment grew swiftly as the regional economy became more diversified and

1. C. Vann Woodward, "The Search for Southern Identity," *Virginia Quarterly Review* 34 (Summer 1958): 321–27.
2. Robert Bechtold Heilman, *The Southern Connection: Essays by Robert Bechtold Heilman* (Baton Rouge, La., 1991), pp. 241–46.
3. John M. Maclachlan and Joe S. Floyd, Jr., *This Changing South* (Gainesville, Fla., 1956), p. 146.
4. Harry S. Ashmore, *An Epitaph for Dixie* (New York, 1958), p. 22.

a revolution in the countryside brought larger, more mechanized, and more productive farms accompanied by a vast movement of farm tenants and workers from the land. By 1960 only 10 percent of the southern population was still engaged in farm labor. New Deal labor policies and the developments of the war period ended the isolation of the southern labor market and quickened the process of integrating southern labor into the national work force. Between 1940 and 1960, the South's population shifted from 65 percent rural to 58 percent urban, and cities like Atlanta, Dallas, Memphis, and Norfolk increasingly came to resemble the great metropolitan centers outside the South. Southern per capita income tripled during the 1940s and by 1960 had risen to about three-fourths of the national average.[5]

Ironically, a surge of sectional distrust and disagreement, sparked by the rise of civil rights as a national issue, appeared at this time. Thus, one historian notes, southern white resistance to changes in race relations occurred "at a time when economic and demographic changes made the South statistically more similar to the rest of the nation and thereby made regional behavior appear particularly distinctive."[6] The democratic revival of the war years had increased the notoriety of the South's racial practices and intensified anti-southern sentiment in other regions. For their part, many white southerners attributed the new assertiveness of blacks to the National Association for the Advancement of Colored People and the intervention of the Fair Employment Practices Committee. A series of racial controversies in the early postwar years added to sectional suspicions and animosities. Although North and South were internally divided over questions of race, the two regions gradually adopted a more rigid confrontational posture in the emerging national debate. As so often in the past, the North became identified with what proved to be a national concern, and the South with sectional opposition to it. As time passed, the northern and southern wings of the Democratic party were increasingly estranged over racial issues. The Supreme Court's school desegregation decision in *Brown* v. *Board of Education* in 1954 brought widespread defiance and resistance from white southerners, and the accelerating civil rights movement resulted in a national effort to reconstruct the South. Sectional antagonism had not reached such heights since Reconstruction.

An example of the growing divisiveness of race was the southern assault on the FEPC. Although opposition to this wartime agency came from all parts of the country, it was the South that provided the most concentrated and determined resistance to efforts to continue it after the war. The most outspoken opponent of the committee in Congress was Senator Theodore G. Bilbo, who warned his fellow southerners that it was "nothing but a plot to put niggers to work next to your daughters." Employing extreme racial rhetoric, Bilbo re-

5. E. William Noland, "Industry Comes of Age in the South," *Social Forces* 32 (October 1953): 28–35; Stefan H. Robock, "Industrialization and Economic Progress in the Southeast," *Southern Economic Journal* 20 (April 1954): 307–27; James C. Cobb, "Industry and Commerce," in *Encyclopedia of Southern Culture,* ed. Charles Reagan Wilson and William Ferris (Chapel Hill, N.C., 1989), pp. 718–20.

6. Numan V. Bartley, ed., *The Evolution of Southern Culture* (Athens, Ga., 1988), p. x.

sorted to filibusters on two occasions in an attempt to end the agency's existence. He and other southern leaders were instrumental in drastically curtailing
the committee's operation in 1945 and in defeating a measure to establish a
permanent FEPC in 1946.[7]

Meanwhile, a politics of race and reaction had begun to develop in the
southern states, particularly in the Deep South. Many state and local politicians
in the region were angered by the Supreme Court's decisions striking at racial
discrimination in interstate transportation and in labor unions, and they were
alarmed by the invalidation of the white primary and the prospect of a great
increase of black voters. Several of the southern states set about tightening their
voting requirements as a means of deterrence. The white primary decision
dominated the gubernatorial contest of 1946 in Georgia, an election in which
former governor Eugene Talmadge launched a white supremacy drive and encouraged a widespread resort to voter purges, intimidation, and violence directed at black Georgians. These tactics ensured Talmadge's election.[8]

Senator Bilbo adopted Talmadge's approach in his campaign for reelection
in Mississippi. Bilbo made race and particularly the FEPC the centerpiece of his
campaign. He declared that "the way to keep the nigger from the polls is to see
him the night before." The senator was challenged by four other Democrats,
but his real opponent was Hodding Carter, the nationally known editor of the
Delta Democrat-Times and longtime detractor and critic of Bilbo. Carter's national reputation, enhanced by the Pulitzer Prize he won in 1946, aroused
unusual interest in the national media and brought a number of outside reporters to Mississippi during the campaign. Many of these writers ridiculed Bilbo as
the laughingstock of the nation, while portraying Carter as a brave, reform-
oriented editor resisting backwoods tyranny. As the intensity of this outside criticism mounted and the *New York Times*, Philadelphia *Inquirer*, *New Republic*, and
other journals exposed Bilbo's demagoguery, racism, and social insensitivity,
the senator was able to depict himself as a victim of the "Yankee, mongrelizing
press" and of massive anti-Mississippi bias in the North. Bilbo lashed out at "the
Drew Pearsons, the Walter Winchells . . . old Lady Roosevelt, Harold Ickes and
Hank Wallace, together with all the negroes, communists, negro lovers and advocates of social equality who poured out their slime and money in Mississippi."[9] Assuming the role of martyr enabled the senator to rally white voters to

7. David R. Goldfield, *Promised Land: The South Since 1945* (Arlington Heights, Ill., 1987), p. 54
(quotation); Robert J. Bailey, "Theodore G. Bilbo and the Fair Employment Practices Controversy: A Southern Senator's Reaction to a Changing World," *Journal of Mississippi History* 42 (February 1980): 27–42; Robert A. Garson, *The Democratic Party and the Politics of Sectionalism, 1941–1948*
(Baton Rouge, La., 1974), pp. 135–44.

8. Joseph L. Bernd, "White Supremacy and the Disfranchisement of Blacks in Georgia, 1946,"
Georgia Historical Quarterly 66 (Winter 1982): 492–513; Ralph McGill, "How It Happened Down in
Georgia," *New Republic* 116 (January 27, 1947): 12–15.

9. Quoted in Chester M. Morgan, *Redneck Liberal: Theodore G. Bilbo and the New Deal* (Baton
Rouge, La., 1985), pp. 250–51. See also Garry Boulard, " 'The Man' versus 'The Quisling': Theodore Bilbo, Hodding Carter, and the 1946 Democratic Primary," *Journal of Mississippi History* 51
(August 1989): 201–17, and "Senator Bilbo Meets the Press," *American Mercury* 63 (November
1946): 525–34.

his cause and win a close victory in the Democratic primary. A great many outside observers no doubt agreed with Senator Robert A. Taft of Ohio, who associated men like Bilbo with "the sudden outbreak of hate and intolerance" directed at minority groups and who denounced the Mississippian as "a disgrace to the Senate."[10]

Several racial incidents in the early postwar years revealed the explosive violence inherent in confrontations between the new black militancy and the southern white determination to preserve traditional racial practices. A number of these incidents received nationwide publicity, galvanized civil rights groups into becoming more active in protecting African-American rights, and pushed the administration of President Harry S. Truman to make civil rights a part of its national agenda. One manifestation of racial violence occurred in Columbia, Tennessee, early in 1946. An altercation in a local department store resulted in the arrest of two Negroes, the arming of the black community, including several black veterans, the gathering of a white mob, rumors of lynchings, and a race riot that led the governor to dispatch the Highway Patrol and the state militia to the scene. Two blacks were killed during the riot, a number of people were wounded, and many black businesses were destroyed or damaged.[11] Later that year two black couples were shot in cold blood in Monroe, Georgia. When William F. Knowland, a Republican from California, rose in the Senate to deplore these murders, Richard B. Russell of Georgia was quick to defend the South. Although Russell denounced the crime and emphasized his opposition to mob violence, he reminded his colleagues that murders also took place in other regions. The Georgian reiterated a point he had often made. "There seems to be an effort to make political capital out of the crimes in which Negroes are the victims if they are committed in the South," he declared, "and we hear a clamor for Federal intervention which is never raised in the case of similar crimes committed in other sections of the country." The senator was convinced that the agitation of northern blacks and white liberals was disrupting a broad North-South consensus on the race issue. He developed a scheme to equalize the races throughout the nation by subsidizing the voluntary migration of southern blacks to the North and northern whites to the South. The plan was intended to force northerners to experience the reality of a biracial society, to show the necessity for and the fairness of segregation, and to expose northern hypocrisy. Introduced in the Senate in 1949, Russell's bill attracted some favorable notice in and out of the South but was never reported out of committee.[12]

Mob violence against blacks in the South was accompanied by new evidence of the pervasive failure of black southerners to obtain justice in the region's legal system. This evidence also illustrated the impotence of the federal government

10. "Senator Bilbo Meets the Press," p. 527.

11. Dorothy Beeler, "Race Riot in Columbia, Tennessee: February 25–27, 1946," *Tennessee Historical Quarterly* 39 (Spring 1980): 49–61; Garson, *The Democratic Party and the Politics of Sectionalism,* pp. 193–202.

12. Gilbert C. Fite, *Richard B. Russell, Jr., Senator from Georgia* (Chapel Hill, N.C., 1991), p. 230 (quotation); David Potenziani, "Striking Back: Richard B. Russell and Racial Relocation," *Georgia Historical Quarterly* 65 (Fall 1981): 263–77.

in protecting the civil rights of blacks in the South. As late as 1945, the Justice Department characterized its own policy as one of "strict self-limitation." Some of the postwar cases reminded observers of the Scottsboro trials of the 1930s in the interest they created outside the South, the efforts they inspired to raise money in the North, the energetic role of the NAACP on behalf of black defendants, and even attempts by the left-wing, Communist-influenced Civil Rights Congress to appeal more broadly to African Americans by involving itself in such legal controversies.[13]

The enormous migration of people—blacks and whites—out of the South during the 1940s and 1950s made the "southern problem" a more immediate concern for many Americans. These swelling streams of humanity tended to settle in urban slums and "hillbilly ghettos," and, as one historian suggests, they "changed the nature of life . . . in every industrial area that offered relief from the grinding poverty of southern rural existence."[14] The interaction of southern newcomers and their northern hosts constitutes an important theme in the modern American experience. This interaction was filled with sectional implications, not all of them happy. Northerners frequently regarded the southern influx with a jaundiced eye, being reminded of the "backward South" from which the migrants came and perceiving in their urban concentration, lack of formal education, and attachment to southern ways the genesis of serious social problems. Despite the economic and political benefits they found in the North, the transplanted southerners were often misunderstood, stereotyped, and discriminated against. The presence of large numbers of southern blacks in the heart of the North not only enhanced the political strength of African Americans in northern elections and gave rise to humanitarian efforts to ameliorate their condition, but also fostered the desire of many northerners to make the South more hospitable for blacks, in part as a means of deterring their continued migration.

One repository of sectional stereotypes and of the low opinion that outsiders tended to have of the South in the mid-1940s was John Gunther's *Inside U.S.A.* (1947). A widely read best-seller, Gunther's book is a huge travel guide and an impressionistic portrait of the nation. The depiction of the South is harsh, unflattering, and consistent with many northern stereotypes of the region. "Once or twice, traveling from town to town," the author remarks, "I felt that I wasn't

---

13. See, for example, Charles H. Martin, "Race, Gender, and Southern Justice: The Rosa Lee Ingram Case," *American Journal of Legal History* 29 (July 1985): 251–68; Steven F. Lawson, David R. Colburn, and Darryl Paulson, "Groveland: Florida's Little Scottsboro," *Florida Historical Quarterly* 65 (July 1986): 1–26; and Michal R. Belknap, *Federal Law and Southern Order: Racial Violence and Constitutional Conflict in the Post-Brown South* (Athens, Ga., 1987), pp. 18–26.

14. Jon C. Teaford, "The Twentieth Century's Great Migration," *Reviews in American History* 18 (June 1990): 222. See also Lewis M. Killian, "The Adjustment of Southern White Migrants to Northern Urban Norms," *Social Forces* 32 (October 1953): 66–69; Thompson Peter Omari, "Factors Associated with Urban Adjustment of Rural Southern Migrants," *Social Forces* 35 (October 1956): 47–53; Homer L. Hitt, "Migration Between the South and Other Regions, 1949 to 1950," *Social Forces* 36 (October 1957): 9–16; C. Vann Woodward, "The North and the South of It," *American Scholar* 35 (Autumn 1966): 647–58; and Jacqueline Jones, *The Dispossessed: America's Underclasses from the Civil War to the Present* (New York, 1992), pp. 209–46.

in the United States at all, but in some utterly foreign land. . . . The South highlights almost every American problem. . . . It is a kind of laboratory, an exotic testing ground. . . . That it is *the* problem child of the nation is of course indisputable. But how it resents being told so!"[15] Gunther describes the rural slums of the South as "almost beyond doubt the most revolting in the nation"; finds the region's public health "at the bottom of the heap"; and characterizes the southern artistic scene as a "cultural wasteland." In religion the South is pictured as a land "replete with Bible marathons, revivalists, Gaelic fundamentalism, and a fierce retentive hostility to other creeds." Nor is that the end of it: "The South contains a great number of pronouncedly schizoid people; the whole region is a land of paranoia, full of the mentally sick; most Southerners feel a deep necessity to hate something, if necessary even themselves." In sexual matters southerners combined "a heavy puritanical facade with almost epochal lubricity." In both crime and civil liberties "the South is probably the darkest place in the nation." Finally, according to Gunther, "the southern bloc of Tory Democrats is the chief single factor in the United States militating against the progress of the nation as a whole." Even so, the author concedes, the region "leads the nation" in "the quality of charm."[16]

Racial violence in the South, the growing importance of black voters in the North, and the increasing pressure of African-American leaders and organizations were telling considerations in President Truman's decision to embrace a program of civil rights for blacks. In December 1946, Truman created the President's Committee on Civil Rights, a panel made up of fifteen distinguished leaders. The committee's report, *To Secure These Rights*, was published in October 1947. It was a comprehensive set of recommendations for congressional and administrative action to overcome racial discrimination in the United States. Though these recommendations may have gone further than he expected, Truman sent a special message to Congress in February 1948 urging passage of broad civil rights legislation. He proposed enactment of an antilynching law, abolition of the poll tax as a voting prerequisite, establishment of a permanent FEPC, the outlawing of segregation in interstate transportation, the strengthening of the Department of Justice, and several other steps.[17] In July 1948, the president issued an executive order ending racial segregation in all federal agencies, including the armed services.

Truman's recommendations dismayed most white southerners, aroused strong southern opposition in Congress, and as time passed provoked a chorus of denunciation from the region's newspapers. As the South's political resistance intensified, white public opinion below the Potomac hardened and became inflamed. Public opinion polls in 1948 revealed that only 23 percent of white southerners (as contrasted with 51 percent of nonsoutherners) thought the

15. John Gunther, *Inside U.S.A.* (New York, 1947), pp. 653–78 (quotation on pp. 657–58).

16. *Ibid.*, pp. 663, 666–67, 669–71, 675–77.

17. William C. Berman, *The Politics of Civil Rights in the Truman Administration* (Columbus, Ohio, 1970), pp. 53–78; William E. Juhnke, "President Truman's Committee on Civil Rights: The Interaction of Politics, Protest, and Presidential Advisory Commission," *Presidential Studies Quarterly* 19 (Summer 1989): 593–610.

federal government should intervene to prevent lynchings; white southerners by a margin of five to one (compared with fewer than two out of five nonsoutherners) asserted that Negroes should be required to occupy a separate part of buses and trains in traveling from one state to another; and only 22 percent of white respondents in the South (compared with 50 percent outside the region) thought Congress should enact legislation guaranteeing the right of blacks to vote.[18]

The southerners won this first major skirmish in the modern struggle for black equality, bottling up Truman's legislative proposals in Congress. Southern congressmen had a good deal of support, some of it covert, from their non-southern colleagues. But civil rights had become a national issue, and the events of 1948 gave great impetus to the resurgence of southern sectionalism. The Truman administration's proposals convinced many southern leaders that Truman no longer had any real concern for the South and that he had become the spokesman for an urban coalition made up of labor unions, ethnic groups, intellectuals, and blacks. The national Democratic party could no longer be counted on to represent the South. As a Democratic leader in South Carolina wrote in 1948, southerners "know that they have kept the democratic party alive for the past seventy-five years; that but for them there would have been no Cleveland or Wilson administrations and, perhaps, no Franklin Delano Roosevelt administration." Hence, southern Democrats had assumed "that they had the right to expect fair treatment at the hands of the democratic party. They didn't expect to be maligned and misrepresented by its leaders; nor did they expect that the democratic doctrine of state sovereignty, fundamental principle of our constitutional scheme of government, would be repudiated, or that the party would move to destroy [the] social standards of the South, under which the relations between the white and Negro races of the South have steadily improved."[19]

As the election of 1948 approached, a movement spread through the southern states to deny the party's nomination to President Truman or any other liberal Democrat. Most southern Democrats preferred Senator Richard B. Russell, and most of the southern delegates to the national Democratic convention cast their votes for him in a symbolic protest against Harry Truman and the leadership of the national party. The convention adopted a liberal civil rights plank following an intense debate that reflected sectional divisions. Truman won the nomination on the first ballot. Northern liberals had discovered in the civil rights issue a means of ensuring the support of the large black vote in northern cities, of striking at the powerful position of southern conservatives in the party, and of strengthening their own role in party affairs. A bone of conten-

18. Robert A. Garson, "The Alienation of the South: A Crisis for Harry S. Truman and the Democratic Party, 1945–1948," *Missouri Historical Review* 64 (July 1970): 448–71; *Public Opinion Quarterly* 12 (Winter 1948–49): 757–58; George H. Gallup, *The Gallup Poll: Public Opinion, 1935–1971*, 3 vols. (New York, 1972), vol. 1, pp. 747–48; Monroe Billington, "Civil Rights, President Truman and the South," *Journal of Negro History* 58 (April 1973): 127–39.

19. Edgar A. Brown to Joe Blythe, 11 October 1948, Edgar A. Brown Papers, Clemson University Library. See also Garson, *The Democratic Party and the Politics of Sectionalism*, pp. 220–31, and Fite, *Richard B. Russell*, pp. 231–36.

tion between the northern and southern wings of the party, the conflict over civil rights was fundamentally a struggle over the nature and control of the Democratic party. There were many party leaders from all parts of the country, including Truman, who hoped to assuage southern apprehensions and to retain the region's support. But liberals like Mayor Hubert H. Humphrey of Minneapolis, many members of the Americans for Democratic Action (ADA), and others were outspoken in their criticism of the southern position on civil rights.[20]

When the liberal position carried the day in the struggle over civil rights in the Democratic convention, the Mississippi delegation and half of the delegates from Alabama walked out. A few days later a group of the more rebellious southern Democrats convened in Birmingham, where they held their own convention. Calling themselves States' Rights Democrats, they proceeded to nominate Governor J. Strom Thurmond of South Carolina for president and Governor Fielding L. Wright of Mississippi for vice president. The insurgents, who were dubbed Dixiecrats, were determined to retain the Democratic party label, since it had been an instrument of white unity for generations and was too much a part of the South's political culture to be discarded by southern voters. Emphasizing state rights and stirring appeals to the South's racial and sectional traditions, Governor Thurmond and his associates set out to capture all of the South's electoral votes. A close observer of the southern political scene described the response the Dixiecrat orators received: "the serious upturned faces of the 'wool-hat boys,' the 'get tough' attitude of the free-enterprise claque, the clusters of old-timers talking of the days when Wade Hampton's Red Shirts rode, the rebel yells, the strains of 'Dixie,' the Confederate uniforms and the Confederate flags, the inscrutability of the Negroes on the fringes of the audience, the frolicking of young Negro boys up close to the speaker's platform and their joining in the applause and the fun."[21]

The Dixiecrat leaders hoped to carry all or most of the southern states and thereby prevent either of the major parties from gaining a majority in the electoral college. The election would then devolve to the House of Representatives, where southern influence might well determine the outcome. The Dixie rebels wanted, at the very least, to prevent the election of Harry Truman. They assumed, along with most southerners, that Truman would be defeated and that as a consequence the leadership of the national Democratic party would be more sensitive to southern demands in the future. But to the surprise of most Americans, Truman won the election. As for the States' Rights Democratic insurgents, they carried only four Deep South states and less than one-fifth of the

20. Garson, *The Democratic Party and the Politics of Sectionalism*, pp. 232–80; Berman, *The Politics of Civil Rights in the Truman Administration*, pp. 79–114; Samuel Lubell, *The Future of American Politics*, 3d rev. ed. (New York, 1965), pp. 89–105; Fite, *Richard B. Russell*, pp. 238–41; Richard S. Kirkendall, "Election of 1948," in *History of American Presidential Elections*, 4 vols., ed. Arthur M. Schlesinger, Jr., and Fred L. Israel (New York, 1971), vol. 4, pp. 3099–3211; Clifton Brock, *Americans for Democratic Action: Its Role in National Politics* (Washington, D.C., 1962), pp. 95–104; Peter J. Kellogg, "The Americans for Democratic Action and Civil Rights in 1948: Conscience in Politics or Politics in Conscience?" *Midwest Quarterly* 20 (Autumn 1978): 49–63.

21. William G. Carleton, "The Fate of Our Fourth Party," *Yale Review* 38 (Spring 1949): 454.

southern votes. Truman won all of the other southern states.[22]

Truman's relatively good showing in the South suggested that loyalty to the national Democratic party, particularly in the peripheral South, was still strong among the region's white inhabitants, that civil rights had not yet become an overriding issue in the South, and that the interests of many southerners were too diversified and too dependent on national politics and policies for them to join a sectional assault on Washington and the Democratic party.[23] But Dixie congressmen and their allies were able to frustrate the administration's civil rights proposals in 1949, and with the beginning of the Korean War in June 1950, Truman placed less emphasis on domestic reform and reached out to southern leaders for backing in the implementation of his defense and foreign policy initiatives. Adlai E. Stevenson, the Democratic nominee for president in 1952, sought to reinvigorate the party in the South and adopted a moderate position on civil rights.

Nevertheless, the Dixiecrat revolt of 1948 disrupted the Solid South. "Whatever courses southerners subsequently took," Robert A. Garson writes, "the Democratic party was never again upheld as the embodiment of race, country, God, and southern womanhood."[24] By the end of the 1940s, another scholar observes, the South was no longer a part of the New Deal coalition. The New Deal party—"the party of the urban masses, union labor, Negroes, civil rights, and social reform"—had become "an affront to the conservative, rural-minded, and rural-dominated, if no longer rural, South."[25] Racial protest was a factor in the reelection of Governor Herman Talmadge of Georgia and in the gubernatorial victory of James F. Byrnes of South Carolina in 1950. In the same year Senators Claude Pepper of Florida and Frank P. Graham of North Carolina, two of the South's best-known liberals, were defeated in hotly contested primary campaigns. Racist charges and innuendos were used with telling effect against both men, and they were identified with outside forces attacking the South.[26]

22. Emile B. Ader, "Why the Dixiecrats Failed," *Journal of Politics* 15 (August 1953): 356–69; Numan V. Bartley, *The Rise of Massive Resistance: Race and Politics in the South During the 1950's* (Baton Rouge, La., 1969), pp. 28–46; Garson, *The Democratic Party and the Politics of Sectionalism*, pp. 281–314; V. O. Key, Jr., with the assistance of Alexander Heard, *Southern Politics in State and Nation* (New York, 1949), pp. 329–44; Alexander Heard, *A Two-Party South?* (Chapel Hill, N.C., 1952), pp. 251–79; Robert Sherrill, *Gothic Politics in the Deep South: Stars of the New Confederacy* (New York, 1968), pp. 235–54; William D. Barnard, *Dixiecrats and Democrats: Alabama Politics, 1942–1950* (University, Ala., 1974), pp. 95–124; Carleton, "The Fate of Our Fourth Party," pp. 449–59.

23. See, for example, James R. Sweeney, "The Golden Silence: The Virginia Democratic Party and the Presidential Election of 1948," *Virginia Magazine of History and Biography* 82 (July 1974): 351–71; A. G. Grayson, "North Carolina and Harry Truman, 1944–1948," *Journal of American Studies* 9 (December 1975): 283–300; and John E. Borsos, "Support for the National Democratic Party in South Carolina during the Dixiecrat Revolt of 1948," *Southern Historian* 9 (Spring 1988): 7–21.

24. Garson, *The Democratic Party and the Politics of Sectionalism*, p. xi.

25. Robert J. Steamer, "Southern Disaffection with the National Democratic Party," in *Change in the Contemporary South*, ed. Allan P. Sindler (Durham, N.C., 1963), p. 170.

26. David R. Goldfield, *Black, White, and Southern: Race Relations and Southern Culture, 1940 to the Present* (Baton Rouge, La., 1990), pp. 65–70; Lubell, *The Future of American Politics*, pp. 106–14;

Picking cotton in the Mississippi Delta in the late 1930s. (*The Library of Congress*)

Street musicians in the Great Depression, Maynardsville, Tennessee, October 1935. (*Photograph by Ben Shahn. The Library of Congress*)

Norris Dam in East Tennessee, the first dam completed by the TVA. (*Courtesy Tennessee Valley Authority*)

The Southern Agrarians: Cartoon of Donald Davidson, Allen Tate, and John Crowe Ransom on the cover of the Vanderbilt University humor magazine, 1933. (*Photographic Archives, Vanderbilt University*)

The Southern Regionalists: Howard W. Odum of the University of North Carolina, academic entrepreneur and promoter of regionalism. (*Southern Historical Collection, University of North Carolina at Chapel Hill Library*)

Three southern congressional leaders in the early 1930s: Senators Carter Glass of Virginia (left), Joseph T. Robinson of Arkansas (center), and Cordell Hull of Tennessee. (*U.S. Senate Historical Office*)

James F. Byrnes of South Carolina, an astute liaison between the Roosevelt administration and southern senators. (*U.S. Senate Historical Office*)

Southern leaders on Capitol Hill: Alben W. Barkley of Kentucky, Senate majority leader (on left), and Vice President John Nance Garner of Texas. (*U.S. Senate Historical Office*)

Senator Josiah W. Bailey of North Carolina, a critic of the New Deal and an organizer of the conservative coalition in Congress. (*U.S. Senate Historical Office*)

Senator Huey P. Long of Louisiana challenged the New Deal from the left. (*U.S. Senate Historical Office*)

FDR and the Court fight. (*U.S. Senate Historical Office*)

ALL I SAID WAS 'GIMME SIX MORE JUSTICES!"

President Roosevelt visits Georgia to oppose Senator Walter F. George's reelection in 1938: Senator George (left), Senator Richard B. Russell (center), and the president. (*U.S. Senate Historical Office*)

President Truman signs the National School Lunch Act, June 1946. Southern congressional sponsors shown with the president are Senators Russell of Georgia and Allen J. Ellender of Louisiana (third and fourth from left), Representative Malcolm C. Tarver of Georgia (second from left), and Representative John W. Flannagan of Virginia (extreme right). (*U.S. Department of Agriculture photograph, courtesy Harry S. Truman Library*)

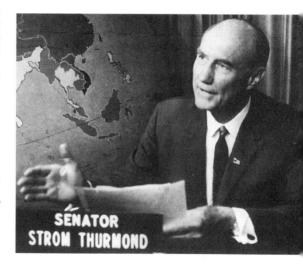

J. Strom Thurmond of South Carolina, States' Rights Democratic nominee for president in 1948. (*U.S. Senate Historical Office*)

SENATOR STROM THURMOND

Senate majority leader Lyndon B. Johnson of Texas (right) and Senator Russell B. Long of Louisiana. (*U.S. Senate Historical Office*)

President Eisenhower shares a light moment with several members of Congress, including Speaker of the House Sam Rayburn of Texas (second from left). *(U.S. Senate Historical Office)*

President Eisenhower and Attorney General William P. Rogers (third from right) meet with prominent black leaders at the White House. Among those attending the meeting were Martin Luther King, Jr. (second from left), A. Philip Randolph (fourth from right), and Roy Wilkins (extreme right). *(National Park Service photograph, courtesy Dwight D. Eisenhower Library)*

Conflict during the Little Rock school crisis, September 1957. *(The Library of Congress)*

President Eisenhower confers with Governor Orval Faubus of Arkansas on September 14 in Newport, Rhode Island, where the president was vacationing. Representative Brooks Hays of Arkansas (at right) helped arrange the meeting, which failed to resolve the crisis. *(National Park Service photograph, courtesy Dwight D. Eisenhower Library)*

Jonathan Daniels, liberal journalist and editor of the Raleigh *News and Observer*. (*Southern Historical Collection, University of North Carolina at Chapel Hill Library*)

Ralph McGill, liberal journalist and editor of the Atlanta *Constitution*. (*Robert W. Woodruff Library, Emory University*)

William Faulkner, preeminent southern writer, recipient of the Nobel Prize for Literature in 1950. (*The Library of Congress*)

The spread of southern evangelicalism: Billy Graham addressing a large crowd in Trafalgar Square, London, April 1954. (*The Library of Congress*)

Johnny Cash and Elvis Presley at the Grand Ole Opry in Nashville, December 1957. (*Photograph by Elmer Williams, courtesy Center for Popular Music, Middle Tennessee State University*)

Hank Williams (center) and the Drifting Cowboys. (*Center for Popular Music, Middle Tennessee State University*)

Writing early in 1950, Ralph McGill, editor of the Atlanta *Constitution* and a prominent southern liberal, presented a rosy, optimistic view of the contemporary South, citing "a ferment of change, enthusiasm, hope, and determination" in the region. Most southerners, McGill wrote, were "normal" Americans.

> But what often seems to the South almost a national policy of hostile criticism and suspicion, in which misrepresentation and error are not uncommon, makes for a stubborn defense of leaders and policies for which the South actually has only contempt. This is one of the great frustrations of the South—it must so often defend its wrongs. Something of Lincoln's spirit and of Roosevelt's policy of aid to the South would be helpful now, because, as nearly always, fears outweigh realities.[27]

The fears that McGill spoke of were evident in southern politics at the state level. Although the South's politics in the late 1940s and early 1950s continued to reflect the economic and class alignments stimulated by the New Deal, the racial apprehensions that gave rise to the Dixiecrat movement did not dissipate. The national Democratic party was committed to a policy of civil rights and an extension of New Deal reforms.

In the 1950s efforts to bring about fundamental change in American race relations assumed new directions and gathered greater momentum. They also brought a heightening of North-South conflict. Four aspects of this sectional conflict were especially important. One of these was the catalytic role of the federal government, both in the policies of the Truman administration and in the decisions of the courts. A second was the increasing strength of black protest, within as well as outside the South. A third development of central importance was the emergence of an organized movement of white resistance against racial change in the southern states. Still another aspect of this resurgent sectionalism was the intensifying emotional involvement of white Americans in other regions, whose reactions to momentous racial events of the decade included rising antipathy toward white southerners, mounting sympathy and support for black southerners, and an increasing identification of the South as the source and embodiment of the race problem in the United States. In the eyes of northern liberals, the "southern problem" was no longer a matter of economic underdevelopment and the absense of industrial democracy; it had reemerged as a moral problem.

By the late 1940s, Thurgood Marshall and his associates in the NAACP's Legal Defense and Education Fund were making plans to launch a direct attack on the "separate but equal" doctrine in the field of public education. The return of prosperity in the early 1940s, the infusion of federal funds in the form of

---

Whittington B. Johnson, "The Vinson Court and Racial Segregation, 1946–1953," *Journal of Negro History* 63 (July 1978): 221–22.

27. Ralph McGill, "The Real Reconstruction Begins," *Reporter* 2 (March 28, 1950): 5–7 (quotation on p. 7).

military contracts and defense programs, and the heightened expectations with which southerners entered the postwar period had rekindled the region's New South hopes and renewed its commitment to educational progress and interregional parity. During the 1950s and 1960s most of the southern states customarily spent a larger percentage of their income on education than the nation as a whole. As one authority has observed, "The effects of increased financial support showed in the enlarged libraries, expanded curricula, special enrichment programs, and instructional developments in the southern schools."[28] The region's support of its universities and colleges was equally impressive. But the educational plans of southern white leaders were complicated by the demands of black southerners for the improvement of their own schools and for more equitable treatment in the allocation of public funds for education. In the 1930s and 1940s the NAACP had sought relief in the federal courts, concentrating on school facilities and teachers' salaries. These efforts brought some results. Belatedly recognizing a threat to the principle of segregated schools, state authorities moved precipitately in the years after World War II to strengthen the black school system. Thus in 1951 South Carolina adopted a $75 million bond program designed to improve black schools. By 1948 Negro teachers were being paid 79 percent as much as their white counterparts, and by 1952 the southern states were spending 70 percent as much to educate a black child as a white child (in 1940 the amount had been only 43 percent).[29] Meanwhile, two Supreme Court cases decided in 1950 demonstrated that the "separate but equal" doctrine enunciated in *Plessy* v. *Ferguson* (1896) was being undermined in graduate and professional education. Speaking in 1955, the black educator Benjamin E. Mays remarked that "the millions poured into Negro education in the last 20 years were appropriated not so much because it was right but in an endeavor to maintain segregation."[30]

Carefully selecting its cases, the NAACP began a far-flung campaign in the federal courts during the early 1950s. The Supreme Court eventually accepted jurisdiction, and after consolidating five related cases under the title *Brown* v. *Board of Education of Topeka, Kansas*, handed down a decision on May 17, 1954. Chief Justice Earl Warren, speaking for a unanimous court, declared that "separate educational facilities are inherently unequal." Warren went on to assert that to separate certain schoolchildren "from others of similar age and qualifications solely because of their race generates a feeling of inferiority as to their status in the community that may affect their hearts and minds in a way unlikely

28. Charles P. Roland, *The Improbable Era: The South since World War II* (Lexington, Ky., 1975), pp. 98–118 (quotation on p. 101).

29. George Brown Tindall, *The Emergence of the New South, 1913–1945* (Baton Rouge, La., 1967), pp. 563–64; C. Vann Woodward, *The Strange Career of Jim Crow*, 3d rev. ed. (New York, 1974), pp. 145–46; Harvard Sitkoff, *The Struggle for Black Equality, 1954–1980* (New York, 1981), pp. 19–20; Robert A. Margo, *Race and Schooling in the South, 1880–1950: An Economic History* (Chicago, 1990).

30. See *McLaurin* v. *Oklahoma State Regents for Higher Education* (1950) and *Sweatt* v. *Painter* (1950). It should be noted that in the 1930s blacks in several southern states began to apply, usually with the support of the NAACP, for admission to white graduate and professional schools in the region. For the statement by Mays, see Benjamin E. Mays, "The Moral Aspects of Segregation," paper delivered at the Southern Historical Association meeting in Memphis, 10 November 1955.

PER PUPIL EXPENDITURES IN THE SOUTH

State	1940	1950	1960	1968
Virginia	$43.80	$145.56	$274	$554
North Carolina	39.56	140.82	237	461
South Carolina	34.08	122.39	220	427
Georgia	34.12	123.37	253	508
Florida	58.12	181.27	318	554
Kentucky	39.93	120.82	233	475
Tennessee	37.77	132.17	238	461
Alabama	30.55	117.09	241	403
Mississippi	24.89	79.69	206	346
Arkansas	27.43	111.71	225	441
Louisiana	51.06	214.08	372	618
Oklahoma	53.85	207.05	311	547
Texas	59.50	208.88	332	493
Southern average	41.13	146.53	266.15	483.69
National average	81.50	208.83	375	623
Southern average as a percentage of national average	50%	70%	71%	78%

SOURCE: James C. Cobb, *The Selling of the South: The Southern Crusade for Industrial Development, 1936–1980* (Baton Rouge: Louisiana State University Press, 1982), p. 163.

ever to be undone." The *Brown* decision, perhaps the most famous ever issued by the Supreme Court, became a symbol of racial equality and laid the basis for a series of rulings striking down segregation laws in virtually all areas of southern life.[31]

Reactions to *Brown* v. *Board of Education* followed sectional—and racial—lines. Most blacks, in and out of the South, were elated and cautiously optimistic. Some southern politicians were bitterly defiant. Senator Russell condemned the decision as "a flagrant abuse of judicial power," and Senator James O. Eastland of Mississippi proclaimed the refusal of the southern states to "abide by or obey this legislative decision by a political court." Writing in the period of frenzied opposition to school desegregation, one southern historian remarked that in his region "It is safe to attack the Supreme Court, the National Association for the Advancement of Colored People (NAACP), 'nigger lovers,' both local and outsiders, sociologists, and meddlesome Yankees."[32] Many southerners were more moderate in their initial reaction to *Brown*. The Louisville *Courier-Journal* editorialized that "the end of the world has not come for the South or for

31. Richard Kluger, *Simple Justice: The History of Brown v. Board of Education and Black America's Struggle for Equality* (New York, 1976), pp. 700–10; J. Harvie Wilkinson III, *From Brown to Bakke: The Supreme Court and School Integration, 1954–1978* (New York, 1979), pp. 26–39; Melvin I. Urofsky, *The Continuity of Change: The Supreme Court and Individual Liberties, 1953–1986* (Belmont, Calif., 1991), pp. 199–203. For the text of the *Brown* decision, see Kluger, *Simple Justice*, pp. 779–85.

32. Thomas D. Clark, *The Emerging South*, 2d ed. (New York, 1968), p. 200.

the nation. The Supreme Court's ruling is not itself a revolution." In general the southern response was surprisingly mild, in part, no doubt, because the court had decided not to order immediate desegregation of the schools. When the implementation decree came a year later, most white southerners were relieved because of its ambiguity. Although the second *Brown* decision ordered the integration of segregated schools "with all deliberate speed," it failed to establish a definite timetable and placed the responsibility for formulating desegregation plans with local school authorities. The burden of supervising the process was turned over to federal district court judges, who in most cases would be native southerners.[33] One journalist noted in 1956 that "the prevailing mood is escapist; actuality is not yet at hand, and most Southerners still hope that somehow it will go away."[34]

Some communities in the border states soon began to comply with the *Brown* decision, but in the South as a whole political leaders and school authorities adopted a wait-and-see attitude. Harry S. Ashmore, editor of the *Arkansas Gazette*, predicted that desegregating the South's public schools would be a major ordeal. "Interest in the schools is universal," he wrote, "and it is an interest that directly involves not only the tax-payer but his family, and therefore his emotions. Those who are indifferent to all other community affairs tend to take a proprietary interest in the schools their children attend, or will attend, or have attended."[35] No other public activity was so closely identified with local mores. Surveys of public opinion revealed that over 80 percent of white southerners opposed school desegregation. Segregationists dominated the South's congressional delegations and legislatures, its county and municipal school boards, and its legal structures. Southern leaders soon demonstrated their resourcefulness in resisting the implementation of the *Brown* decree. North Carolina, for example, adopted a scheme in 1955 that transferred authority over pupil enrollment to its 167 county and city school boards.[36] As the *Southern School News* observed, this would make "individual school units, and not the state as a whole, defendants in

33. Kluger, *Simple Justice*, pp. 710–11; Wilkinson, *From Brown to Bakke*, pp. 61–77; Urofsky, *The Continuity of Change*, pp. 203–206; Woodward, *The Strange Career of Jim Crow*, pp. 139–54; Benjamin Muse, *Ten Years of Prelude: The Story of Integration Since the Supreme Court's 1954 Decision* (New York, 1964), pp. 16–28.

34. Quoted in Goldfield, *Promised Land*, p. 65. For the reaction of southerners to the *Brown* decision, see Bartley, *The Rise of Massive Resistance*, pp. 67–81; David W. Southern, *Gunnar Myrdal and Black-White Relations: The Use and Abuse of An American Dilemma, 1944–1969* (Baton Rouge, La., 1987), pp. 155–85; Hugh Davis Graham, *Crisis in Print: Desegregation and the Press in Tennessee* (Nashville, 1967), pp. 29–61; Roy E. Carter, Jr., "Segregation and the News: A Regional Content Study," *Journalism Quarterly* 34 (Winter 1957): 3–18; R. Ray McCain, "Reactions to the United States Supreme Court Segregation Decision of 1954," *Georgia Historical Quarterly* 52 (December 1968): 371–87; and Joseph A. Tomberlin, "Florida Whites and the *Brown* Decision of 1954," *Florida Historical Quarterly* 51 (July 1972): 22–36.

35. Harry S. Ashmore, *The Negro and the Schools* (Chapel Hill, N.C., 1954), p. 82.

36. Muse, *Ten Years of Prelude*, pp. 62–71; Sitkoff, *The Struggle for Black Equality*, pp. 23–24; Jonathan T. Y. Houghton, "The Politics of Sly Resistance: North Carolina's Response to *Brown*," paper presented at the annual meeting of the Organization of American Historians, Louisville, Kentucky, April 1991; Wilma Peebles-Wilkins, "Reactions of Segments of the Black Community to the North Carolina Pearsall Plan, 1954–1966," *Phylon* 48 (June 1987): 112–21.

any school litigation so one lawsuit will not be binding upon all units."[37]

The civil rights movement of the postwar period owed a great deal to new leaders, organizations, and tactics that went beyond the NAACP approach of challenging racial discrimination in the courts. One of the dramatic starting points of black protest in the South was the simple, unpremeditated act of a forty-two-year-old Negro seamstress in Montgomery, Alabama, named Rosa Parks. Tired after a hard day's work, Mrs. Parks on December 1, 1955, suddenly decided that she would not surrender her bus seat to a white person. She was promptly arrested. The response of the black community could scarcely have been predicted. Under the leadership of the Montgomery Improvement Association, the city's blacks rallied overwhelmingly to support a crippling boycott of the local bus system. The boycott was maintained for almost a year and ended in an impressive victory for African Americans after the federal courts invalidated the Alabama segregation laws. J. Mills Thornton has concluded that segregation in Montgomery "could have been disestablished only in the way in which it was disestablished: by internal pressure sufficient to compel intervention from outside the South."[38] The Montgomery bus boycott was a portent of things to come. Its church meetings, singing of religious hymns, frequent reference to American ideals, nonviolent tactics, and black unity would be characteristic of the "movement" during the years ahead.

The leader of the Montgomery Improvement Association was an eloquent young Baptist minister named Martin Luther King, Jr. The son of a successful Atlanta minister and a doctoral graduate of Boston University in theology, King developed during the long months of the Montgomery struggle a program of nonviolent resistance. It was based on the evangelical Christianity in which he had been nurtured and on Mahatma Gandhi's satyagraha philosophy, to which King had been attracted for some time. King would use "nonviolent direct action" to provoke crisis and "creative tension," which would force the white community to confront its racism. "If we are arrested every day, if we are exploited every day, if we are trampled over every day," the minister declared at one of the Montgomery mass meetings, "don't ever let anyone pull you so low as to hate them. We must use the weapon of love. We must have compassion and understanding for those who hate us."[39] In 1957 King organized the Southern Christian Leadership Conference, with headquarters in Atlanta, and the influence of his leadership spread throughout the South. He soon became a national figure.

Black protest like that in Montgomery reflected not only the mounting impa-

37. Quoted in Houghton, "The Politics of Sly Resistance."

38. J. Mills Thornton III, "Challenge and Response in the Montgomery Bus Boycott of 1955–1956," *Alabama Review* 33 (July 1980): 163–235 (quotation on p. 234). See also Aldon D. Morris, *The Origins of the Civil Rights Movement: Black Communities Organizing for Change* (New York, 1984), pp. 17–76; David J. Garrow, ed., *The Walking City: The Montgomery Bus Boycott, 1955–1956* (Brooklyn, N.Y., 1989); Jo Ann Gibson Robinson, *The Montgomery Bus Boycott and the Women Who Started It: The Memoirs of Jo Ann Gibson Robinson* (Knoxville, Tenn., 1987); and Sitkoff, *The Struggle for Black Equality*, pp. 41–64.

39. Quoted in David J. Garrow, *Bearing the Cross: Martin Luther King, Jr., and the Southern Christian Leadership Conference* (New York, 1986), p. 66.

tience of African Americans with their second-class citizenship, but also a realization that civil rights had begun to attract national attention, that black votes
had become a critical factor in many closely contested elections in northern
cities and states, and that American race relations were vitally linked to the
United States' search for support in the Cold War from colored peoples in
Africa and Asia. Black protest in the South was related to the swelling urbanization of the region's African Americans, to the growing percentage of black
skilled and semiskilled workers, clerical employees, and professionals, to the
steadily increasing ranks of black voters in the South, and to the leadership of
people such as Martin Luther King, Jr.

In the mid-1950s, school desegregation became a compelling public issue in
the South. Most of the border states, including Missouri, Kansas, and the District of Columbia, soon began to comply with the *Brown* decision. Although the
states to the south were not prepared to desegregate their public schools "with
all deliberate speed," as the Supreme Court had decreed in May 1955, their
defiance was largely rhetorical for several months. The reason was that the
desegregation decision had no immediate effect on southern schools, which remained segregated. This state of affairs did not last long. Local school boards,
particularly outside the Deep South, were soon being petitioned by black parents to admit their children to previously all-white schools. The NAACP encouraged these petitions. In 1955 and 1956, the federal courts ordered the admission of black students to a number of public schools in Kentucky,
Tennessee, and Texas. These court orders resulted in a series of riots and acts of
violence. In February 1956 a mob of students and townspeople forced the expulsion of Autherine Lucy, a young black woman who had just been admitted
to the University of Alabama by court order. In the fall of 1956, Governor Allan
F. Shivers of Texas exercised the state's police power to prevent violence and
maintain order—and preserve segregation—in two communities under court
order to desegregate public schools. Governors Albert B. Chandler of Kentucky
and Frank G. Clement of Tennessee were forced to use state police and national guardsmen to restore order and enable desegregation to continue in their
states. Only 723 of the South's 10,000 school districts had been desegregated by
September 1956, and the eight South Atlantic and Gulf Coast states—from
Virginia through Louisiana—remained completely segregated at the primary
and secondary school levels.[40]

School desegregation quickly became a volatile political issue in the South.
The *Brown* decision was the object of harsh condemnation in several Democratic primaries in 1954, and it dominated the state campaigns in Georgia and
South Carolina. Those two states foreshadowed the development of racially obsessed politics in much of the South. Both states were led by determined, resourceful, and influential politicians: South Carolina by James F. Byrnes and J.
Strom Thurmond, Georgia by Herman Talmadge. All three were powerful
transitional figures in the shift to a politics of all-out resistance. In 1954 Gover-

40. This discussion of massive resistance is based on Dewey W. Grantham, *The Life & Death of
the Solid South: A Political History* (Lexington, Ky., 1988), pp. 134–48.

nor Talmadge succeeded in securing voter approval of a constitutional amendment permitting the substitution of a private school system for the public schools. Beginning in the lower South, state legislatures soon laid down a barrage of defensive enactments. The Louisiana lawmakers, who were in session when the *Brown* decision was handed down in May 1954, censured the Supreme Court, created a joint legislative committee to devise strategy for the maintenance of segregation, passed a measure requiring segregation in all primary and secondary schools, and enacted a pupil assignment law that authorized local superintendents to assign individual students to public schools.[41] Similar bills and constitutional amendments, including measures authorizing the abolition of entire public school systems and a variety of other segregation legislation, were adopted later in the year by a number of other states.[42]

By the early part of 1956, a movement of "massive resistance" to public school desegregation had taken shape in the South. Segregationist organizations, including a revived Ku Klux Klan, threw themselves into the campaign against school desegregation. They applied economic pressure—and sometimes violence—against integrationists, worked for the passage of legislation to frustrate their opponents, and endeavored to "purify" voting lists and prevent further black registration. "The atmosphere of violence, boycott, reprisal, and caste solidarity," Numan V. Bartley has written, "both set the stage for and announced the arrival of the Citizens' Council movement."[43] The Citizens' Council soon became the most vocal of all pressure groups opposing desegregation. First organized in July 1954 in the Delta town of Indianola, Mississippi, the council spread to surrounding counties and shortly afterward formed a state association. The movement quickly dominated political life in Mississippi. The council was also powerful in Alabama, and it became an influential organization in Louisiana and South Carolina. Virginia, the fifth state with a strong white supremacy organization, was represented by the Defenders of State Sovereignty and Individual Liberties. Other segregationist organizations, including the Patriots of North Carolina and the States' Rights Council of Georgia, appeared in the region. Citizens' Councils existed in most southern states, and at the movement's height in 1956 the organization had about 250,000 members. Encouraged by its growth in the southern states, the council contemplated the creation of a nationwide organization. While its efforts in a few states such as California and Maryland enjoyed some success, the movement encountered hostile forces and made only limited gains outside the South.[44]

Another manifestation of the South's growing political defiance came in March 1956, when 101 of the 128 congressmen from the ex-Confederate states issued a "Southern Manifesto." Originally proposed by Senator Strom Thur-

41. The pupil assignment laws provided for the individual assignment of students to schools and established prerequisites for the use of local administrators in making such placements. They also created a system of administrative remedies for parents dissatisfied with the results.

42. Bartley, *The Rise of Massive Resistance*, pp. 67–81.

43. *Ibid.*, p. 83.

44. See Neil R. McMillen, *The Citizens' Council: Organized Resistance to the Second Reconstruction, 1954–64* (Urbana, Ill., 1971).

mond and quickly endorsed by Senator Harry Flood Byrd of Virginia, the "Declaration of Constitutional Principles," as it was formally known, was devised by a committee headed by Senator Russell. Byrd explained that the manifesto was "a part of the plan of massive resistance we have been working on and I hope and believe it will be an effective action." The document denounced the *Brown* decision as "a clear abuse of judicial power" and commended the motives of those states that were determined "to resist forced integration by any lawful means." The manifesto's signers pledged themselves to use all lawful means to reverse the desegregation decision and to prevent its enforcement.[45]

The doctrine of "interposition" provided massive resistance with a theory and a rallying cry. Reviving concepts associated with Thomas Jefferson and John C. Calhoun, advocates of interposition invoked the state rights tradition, the compact theory of the Union, and a strict constructionist view of the Constitution. They argued that, by consolidating public school authority in the state government and interposing the "sovereignty" of the state between local school officials and federal courts, the *Brown* decision could be reversed. The proposition seemed to offer a strategem that would turn back federal intervention in the South's traditional pattern of race relations and offer a solution to the region's problems resulting from *Brown* v. *Board of Education*. Early in 1956 Virginia's general assembly adopted a joint resolution "interposing the sovereignty" of the state "against encroachment upon the reserved powers" of the Old Dominion. The five states of the Deep South soon followed Virginia's lead, and by mid-1957 eight southern states had approved interposition resolutions. Meanwhile, the peripheral South had become the scene of a pivotal struggle to solidify the region in support of massive resistance. Led by moderate business-oriented chief executives, most of these states stopped short of massive resistance, but they increased their opposition to complying with desegregation rulings. They enacted local option school closing laws, authorized tuition grants to students attending private schools, and passed various other segregationist measures.[46]

State legislatures in the eleven ex-Confederate states passed, by one count, no fewer than 450 pro-segregation measures during the decade following the issuance of the *Brown* decision. Since the burden of initiating litigation to force school desegregation fell on the NAACP, segregationists singled out that organization and its allies by special legislation and legal harassment. "Attacking the NAACP in the South," one scholar has observed, "was politically analogous to assaulting the Communist Party in the rest of the nation."[47] In fact, southern segregationists soon linked their cause with anti-communism, and they appealed to right-wing patriots in the North as well as the South by painting the

45. Bartley, *The Rise of Massive Resistance*, pp. 116–17.

46. *Ibid.*, pp. 126–49; McMillen, *The Citizens' Council*, pp. 159–88; Earl Black, "Southern Governors and Political Change: Campaign Stances on Racial Segregation and Economic Development, 1950–69," *Journal of Politics* 33 (August 1971): 703–34; Edward R. Crowther, "Alabama's Fight to Maintain Segregated Schools, 1953–1956," *Alabama Review* 43 (July 1990): 206–25.

47. Bartley, *The Rise of Massive Resistance*, p. 213.

NAACP and its friends in reddish hues.[48] Several states required the organization to register and provide membership lists and the names of contributors. Other statutes stipulated that no member of the NAACP should be employed by a state agency. Criminal sanctions were also directed at the association, including efforts in six states to curtail the organization's access to the courts. Governmental harassment of dissenters and coercion of the uncommitted were most extreme in the investigations and other activities of state sovereignty commissions and special legislative committees created throughout the region. These groups did their best to prevent any deviation from orthodox thinking and behavior among southern educators, launched harsh probes of black institutions such as South Carolina State College in Orangeburg, and severely restricted academic freedom and civil liberties in many parts of the South. In addition, they initiated a vigorous propaganda campaign, published a flood of segregationist tracts, and attempted to bolster their arguments with scientific evidence.[49] "When is the South going to stop beating itself over the head with this race prejudice business?" an Alabama liberal demanded at the end of 1956. "It is bad any way you look at it. It will destroy any man or people if indulged in long enough. It is keeping industry out of the South, and is causing our best young people to leave the South."[50]

It was not surprising that segregationists should turn to science as a means of discrediting the *Brown* decision. In challenging the court, I. A. Newby writes, "They sought not only to refute the social science incorporated in the decision, but more importantly, they endeavored to develop a systematic scientific defense of segregation, especially segregation in the public schools of the South."[51] Professor Henry E. Garrett of Columbia University, a leading authority on psychometrics and psychological testing, Dr. Wesley C. George, professor of anatomy at the University of North Carolina Medical School, and other "field marshals of scientific racism" devoted themselves assiduously to this campaign. They were joined by a number of northerners, among them a popularizer of scientific racism named Carleton Putnam, former airline executive and biographer of Theodore Roosevelt.[52] For a time these intellectual defenders of segregation attracted national attention and encouraged segregationists, particularly in the South. But their arguments seemed to exert little influence among mainstream American scientists and scholars.

Federal intervention and the prospect of radical changes in "the southern

48. McMillen, *The Citizens' Council*, pp. 189–204; Don E. Carleton, "McCarthyism in Houston: The George Ebey Affair," *Southwestern Historical Quarterly* 80 (October 1976): 163–76; George N. Green, "McCarthyism in Texas: The 1954 Campaign," *Southern Quarterly* 16 (April 1978): 255–76.

49. Bartley, *The Rise of Massive Resistance*, pp. 170–236; McMillen, *The Citizens' Council*, pp. 159–88, 235–46; I. A. Newby, *Challenge to the Court: Social Scientists and the Defense of Segregation, 1954–1966*, rev. ed. (Baton Rouge, La., 1969); James Graham Cook, *The Segregationists* (New York, 1962); Waldo W. Braden, "The Rhetoric of a Closed Society," *Southern Speech Communication Journal* 45 (Summer 1980): 333–51.

50. Aubrey W. Williams, "The Man With the Hammer," *Southern Farm & Home Almanac* (First Quarter, 1957), copy in Estes Kefauver Papers, University of Tennessee Library.

51. Newby, *Challenge to the Court*, p. 63.

52. *Ibid.*, pp. 62–212.

way of life" encouraged "a sense of beleaguered solidarity" among white southerners in the 1950s. According to one close observer, "a fever of rebellion and a
malaise of fear spread over the region," and "the lights of reason and tolerance
and moderation began to go out under the resistance demand for conformity."[53] "It was a frightening thing to go into a small city," Pat Watters of the
Southern Regional Council recalled, "and to realize that not merely the semi-
literate poor white gas station attendant, but also the bankers, the mayor, the
editor, even some of the preachers, all those who are personages in such a place
supported it [resistance] fervently."[54] One reason, as Anthony Lewis of the *New
York Times* wrote in 1964, was that segregationists "have invested their cause
with a searing emotional impact. It has been made to appeal to the most suscep-
tible tribal impulses: patriotism, racial purity, religious dogma, group solidarity,
status and personal pride."[55]

Public opinion polls suggested the extent of sectional polarization over
school desegregation in the United States. In February 1956, over 70 percent of
northern whites who were interviewed supported the Supreme Court's rulings
of 1954 and 1955, while 80 percent of southern whites were opposed. During
the late 1950s, southern whites disapproved of the *Brown* decision by a four-
to-one margin, while nonsoutherners approved of it almost three-to-one. When
asked, in August 1958, if they favored court-ordered school desegregation in
their communities, 14 percent of the southerners interviewed answered yes, as
opposed to 75 percent who answered no (11 percent had no opinion).[56] These
questions may have had an abstract quality for many northerners, since school
desegregation had little relevance in the North at that time. Yet it is significant
that by midcentury nineteen nonsouthern states had passed civil rights laws.

In national politics, as well, the South seemed to be increasingly alienated
from the rest of the nation. Approximately one out of every three recorded
votes in Congress during the mid-1950s found a majority of the southern Democrats voting against the Democratic majority from other regions. The "southern" position on racial issues was also different from that of congressional
Republicans, although the two groups tended to agree on questions having to
do with domestic welfare spending, organized labor, and state rights. Southern
congressional attitudes toward world affairs were also becoming more distinctive. Congressmen from the South, one scholar contended in 1960, were going
through "a sharp swing away from their former active support of a positive and
multilateralist approach to the international problems facing the United
States," and except for military defense and military alliances, were moving toward "a modernized version of old-fashioned isolationism." This writer sug-

53. Woodward, *The Strange Career of Jim Crow*, p. 165. See also Stan Opotowsky, "Silence in the
South," *Progressive* 21 (August 1957): 10–12.
54. Quoted in Goldfield, *Promised Land*, p. 79.
55. Anthony Lewis and the *New York Times*, *Portrait of a Decade: The Second American Revolution*
(New York, 1964), p. 57. See also Bartley, *The Rise of Massive Resistance*, pp. 293–319.
56. Gallup, *The Gallup Poll*, vol. 2, pp. 1401–1402, 1465–66, 1487, 1518, 1566–67; vol. 3, pp.
1616, 1723.

gested that, where "you find an isolationist, you usually also find a state righter of a particularly rigid and mechanistic sort, a budget-cutter, an opponent of 'socialism'—from which he usually excludes cotton supports and the depletion allowance—and increasingly only a racist who is free with his prophecies of bloodshed."[57]

One group of southerners found itself caught in the cross fire between the coercive pressures for regional conformity and outside demands for national conformity on how to deal with race relations in the South. This group contained the southern liberals, who soon became an endangered species. Liberalism in the South had achieved a new vitality and sense of purpose during the 1930s, stimulated by the ravages of the Great Depression, the collapse of the agricultural system, New Deal reforms, and the emergence of new voices within the region advocating change. The "southern liberal," acutely aware of his section's pressing problems, shared with many other southerners a dedication to the improvement of the South. Southern liberalism, as Gunnar Myrdal observed in 1944, *"gets its power from outside the South."* Its main strategic function over the years had been to serve as "a liaison agent with the North," to act as advisers and executors of northern philanthropists "who wanted to do something for the region," and, beginning in the 1930s, "to bring the New Deal into effect in the South." A relatively small band of intellectuals, editors, university professors, and politicians, with "little organized support among the broad masses of workers, farmers and lower middle class," southern liberals were both critics and defenders of the South, which they often spoke of as "hopelessly backward" but at the same time "flattered in the most extravagant terms of regional mythology." The southern populace "must not be enraged into resistance," and it was absolutely imperative "to tread most cautiously around the Negro problem." Thus, Myrdal concluded, the southern liberal was "inclined to stress the need for patience and to exalt the cautious approach, the slow change, the organic nature of social growth."[58]

This was true of their approach to the explosive racial issue in the post–World War II period. The historian Anthony L. Newberry has described their plight in the late 1950s. "Convinced of the need to retain credibility with the white community even while pushing for change, buffeted from the right and left by 'irresponsible extremists,' devoted to racial justice yet loyal to their native land, liberal gradualists often cast themselves in the part of an impartial arbiter among the contending forces converging upon southern racial ills."[59] These liberals were more circumspect and possibly more effective than a handful of more

57. Charles O. Lerche, Jr., "Southern Congressmen and the 'New Isolationism,' " *Political Science Quarterly* 75 (September 1960): 321–37 (quotations on pp. 321 and 335); Frank E. Smith, "Valor's Second Prize: Southern Racism and Internationalism," *South Atlantic Quarterly* 64 (Summer 1965): 296–303; Grantham, *The Life & Death of the Solid South*, p. 140.

58. Gunnar Myrdal, with the assistance of Richard Sterner and Arnold Rose, *An American Dilemma: The Negro Problem and Modern Democracy*, 20th anniversary ed. (New York, 1962), pp. 466–73.

59. Anthony Lake Newberry, "Without Urgency or Ardor: The South's Middle-of-the-Road Liberals and Civil Rights, 1945–1960" (Ph.D. dissertation, Ohio University, 1982), p. 208.

forthright reformers such as Lillian Smith, Aubrey W. Williams, and Myles Horton.[60]

Southern liberals had seen their mission as that of internal critics, and they set out, in C. Vann Woodward's words, "to sting the conscience of the South into an intensified awareness of the inconsistency between creed and custom."[61] At the same time, they were extraordinarily sensitive to the misrepresentations and stereotypes directed at the South by outside critics. In 1942 in *Below the Potomac: A Book About the New South*, for example, Virginius Dabney wrote contemptuously of those northerners who pictured the South as a "reactionary and backward land, incredibly sleazy and down at heel, inhabited by degenerates drooling tobacco juice, whose penchant for lying is exceeded only by [their] predilection for divers varieties of lechery."[62] Frank P. Graham and Dorothy M. Tilly, highly respected southern liberals who served on the President's Committee on Civil Rights, protested the depiction of conditions in the South in the 1947 draft report of *To Secure These Rights*. So much plain talk in a federal report, Tilly explained, would "undo the social progress the South has made in the last twenty years." The language of the report was then extensively revised and examples of northern racial discrimination were added.[63] The southern gradualists criticized northern reformers for allegedly viewing African Americans in abstract, ideological terms and caring little for them as human beings. The strong implication was that southern liberals, alone among white friends of "the Negro," really understood their "needs and wants" and cared about them as individuals. Thus Harry S. Ashmore accused northern critics of treating the black man as "a sort of abstraction, a social worker's case history representing Something That Should Be Done About."[64]

The Dixie liberals tried to function as interracial mediators, and they did discredit some of the worst racial rumors and stereotypes. But they were more important in the 1940s and 1950s in the role of interpreting southern ways to northern audiences. Liberal journalists like Hodding Carter, Virginius Dabney, and Gerald W. Johnson attracted a sizable readership outside the South. They produced a large amount of social commentary on their native region, much of which was published in mass circulation magazines, liberal journals, and widely read books. These interpreters were often admired in northern circles as "astute, dispassionate analysts," and Anthony Newberry suggests that they were influential "in shaping educated and nonsouthern perspectives on the region's racial problem."[65]

Yet, as the currents of racial reform gathered force in the 1950s, southern liberals found themselves in an increasingly untenable position. Most of them,

60. See, for example, Richard A. Reiman, "Aubrey Williams: A Southern New Dealer in the Civil Rights Movement," *Alabama Review* 43 (July 1990): 181–205, and Lillian Smith, "No Easy Way, Now," *New Republic* 137 (December 16, 1957): 12–16.

61. Woodward, *The Strange Career of Jim Crow*, p. 126.

62. Quoted in Newberry, "Without Urgency or Ardor," p. 214.

63. *Ibid.*, pp. 218–19.

64. *Ibid.*, pp. 88, 214 (quotation).

65. *Ibid.*, pp. 16, 27, 213.

after all, were moderates and gradualists. They wanted an orderly, locally controlled process of racial change that would take account of community conditions and regional economic growth. They preferred the principles of personal
responsibility and local and state initiative to the concept of "overweening federal power." They believed in the efficacy of educational progress, industrialization, a growing urban middle class, the expanding influence of black consumers, and the enlightened self-interest of businessmen in the South. As the
crisis over school desegregation deepened, southern moderates tended to abandon their role as critics of their region's racial practices and to stress their role as
friendly interpreters and tacit defenders of southern ways. This was not enough
to shield them from the suspicion and denunciation of southern conservatives.
Nor did it protecct them from the criticism of black activists and northern liberals. In the post-*Brown* years southern moderates found it more difficult to justify
their faith in the beneficial effects of educational advances and economic progress in the South, as well as their sensitivity to outside scrutiny, ambivalence
about segregation, qualms over the desirability of federal intervention to protect
civil rights, and lectures to NAACP activists on "What the Negro Wants."[66]

Most of the region's liberals, along with a majority of white southerners,
wanted the Supreme Court to move slowly in implementing the *Brown* decision.
They pointed to the importance of community attitudes, warned of strong opposition to desegregation in the Deep South, and expressed faith in "southerners of good will." Benjamin Muse, a former state senator in Virginia, argued
that the time had come for the NAACP to "relax . . . and reflect on the vast
significance of its present gains." This would not only allow the Deep South to
"cool off" but would enable the "fine flower of tolerance" to bloom once more
among enlightened whites who had been put off by the association's "indis-
criminate aggressiveness." The *New Republic*, which published Muse's article,
observed that, in the absence of "moderate Southern white leadership, the
Southern plea for 'moderation' amounts to a plea for moratorium." Some
northern liberals would no doubt have agreed with a comment made in 1946
by the writer Bernard DeVoto, who spoke disdainfully of "alleged southern liberals who tell us that there is no moral issue in anti-negro discrimination . . . and
that if we will only let the South handle the negro problem . . . everything will
work out all right."[67]

In March 1956, *Life* magazine published "A Letter to the North" from William Faulkner. The Mississippi novelist urged civil rights activists to "go slow
now" and to "stop now for a time, a moment," so that the southerner could
assimilate what had happened on the race issue, including the North's resolve
to address it. Faulkner described himself as occupying the moderate "middle
ground" between equally dogmatic integrationists and segregationists. Northerners, he asserted, did not understand that the race question was a deeply

66. *Ibid.*, pp. 2–3, 16, 122, 124, 155, 221, 429.
67. *Ibid.*, pp. 322, 394; Benjamin Muse, "Moderates and Militants," *New Republic* 134 (April 2,
1956): 8–10; Bernard DeVoto to Oswald Garrison Villard, 18 March 1946, Oswald Garrison
Villard Papers, Harvard University Library.

rooted cultural concern for southerners, and they did not see the moral ambiguity in southern race relations. He thought that the South, if given some time, would move on its own to remedy racial inequities. The Civil War, he remarked, should have proved to the North that the South "will go to any length, even that fatal and already doomed one, before it will accept alteration of its racial condition by mere force of law or economic threat."[68] Many other gradualists lamented the "plight of the southern moderate," appealed for understanding and sympathy from outsiders, and spoke of their "grueling emotional ordeal." In December 1958, for instance, a group of southern liberals from Alabama wrote the *Saturday Review* to say that "we have the feeling down here that there's no real interest in the North in our problem, the problem of the liberal Southerner, that is." The Alabamians reported that "external and internal pressures have just about put the Southern liberal out of business." They complained about the impractical advice and sharp criticism given by their northern counterparts. "Don't condemn us out of hand," the southerners concluded. ". . . And please don't think that the only thing that is keeping us from being effective is an insufficiency of moral judgments from the North."[69]

If southern moderates lost much of their raison d'être in the late 1950s, that was not true of liberals in other parts of the country. Encouraged by the reform proposals of the Truman administration and the ground-breaking decisions of the Supreme Court, as well as the determined efforts of black Americans, northern liberals found a worthy cause in the civil rights movement. There was, not surprisingly, a pronounced sectional theme in their support of civil rights. As Harry Ashmore pointed out, "The conviction that one could not be pro-Negro without being anti-South was as firmly held among neo-abolitionists as it was among Daughters of the Confederacy."[70] The commitment to civil rights had become apparent in the national Democratic coalition, among liberal politicians outside the South, urban machines, labor leaders, and intellectuals, in addition to black leaders and organizations. The Americans for Democratic Action, a group that tried to adapt New Deal liberalism to postwar realities, strongly endorsed the goal of racial equality. Northern foundations also lent their assistance. For example, the Fund for the Advancement of Education, an agency created by the Ford Foundation, provided the money for an appraisal of the South's segregated educational system. It resulted in the publication, the day before the 1954 *Brown* decision, of a valuable book on *The Negro and the Schools.*[71] The widening sectional division in the Democratic party clearly re-

68. William Faulkner, "A Letter to the North," *Life* 40 (March 5, 1956): 51–52. See also Robert Penn Warren, "Faulkner, the South and the Negro," *Southern Review* 1 (July 1965): 501–29; Louis Daniel Brodsky, "Faulkner and the Racial Crisis, 1956," *Southern Review* 24 (Autumn 1988): 791–801; and John T. Kneebone, "Liberal on the Levee: Hodding Carter, 1944–1954," *Journal of Mississippi History* 49 (May 1987): 153–62.

69. Norman Cousins, "The Plight of the Southern Liberal," *Saturday Review* 41 (December 20, 1958): 26; Newberry, "Without Urgency or Ardor," pp. 403–404.

70. Harry S. Ashmore, *Hearts and Minds: A Personal Chronicle of Race in America* (Cabin John, Md., and Washington, D.C., 1988), p. 38.

71. *Ibid.*, pp. 201–204.

flected differences between the South and the rest of the nation that were centered in the conflict over race.

Nothing was more important in attracting the attention of outsiders to the massive resistance of the South to school desegregation and other racial reforms than the mass media. The dramatic conflict that punctuated the desegregation process brought a growing number of reporters and photographers into the South, attracted by what the *New York Times* described as "actions of violence and the unleashing of malevolent moods." The *Times* reported that "Men, women and children with wrathful faces have shouted epithets and obscenities and even danced in the street to express their delight at thwarting the purpose of a neighbor. In some instances these scenes have been framed by the glistening bayonets and khaki uniforms of militiamen called to preserve law and order."[72] Several developments reinforced the image in the minds of Americans outside the South of a reactionary and repressive section: evidence of the fanatical determination of white southerners in resisting racial change, the recalcitrance of southern congressmen in opposing civil rights measures, and on occasion the resort to brutality and murder to keep blacks "in their place." A notorious example of the last was the lynching in 1955 of a black teenager named Emmett Till for allegedly whistling at a white woman in the Mississippi Delta. In the aftermath of that gruesome murder, the northern media conducted a kind of anti-Mississippi campaign.[73]

The Montgomery bus boycott, which began in December 1955 and lasted almost a year, introduced a new tactic in the struggle against Jim Crow. This was the televised mass demonstration, which would become a powerful catalyst for racial change in the early 1960s.[74] The Montgomery boycott was also the crucible that transformed Martin Luther King, Jr., into a national figure. King emerged from the boycott, one of his biographers has written, "as a national leader with a popular backing of a depth and intensity unknown in America since the days of Booker T. Washington." By the spring of 1957, he was known in "almost every corner" of the country. He had been the subject of long and generally approving articles in virtually all major American and many foreign newspapers and magazines. *Time*, the leading white-oriented news magazine, and *Jet*, the leading African-American news magazine, had carried cover stories on him. *Jet* captured the general tenor of the press's treatment of King, declaring that he had become "a symbol of divinely inspired hope," "a kind of modern Moses who has brought new self-respect to Southern Negroes."[75]

When the governors of Arkansas and Virginia closed public schools in their

72. Quoted in Albert P. Blaustein and Clarence Clyde Ferguson, Jr., *Desegregation and the Law: The Meaning and Effect of the School Segregation Cases*, 2d ed. (New York, 1962), p. 212.

73. Stephen J. Whitfield, *A Death in the Delta: The Story of Emmett Till* (New York, 1989); James C. Cobb, *The Most Southern Place on Earth: The Mississippi Delta and the Roots of Regional Identity* (New York, 1992), pp. 217–21; Warren Breed, "Comparative Newspaper Handling of the Emmett Till Case," *Journalism Quarterly* 35 (Summer 1958): 291–98.

74. William J. Cooper, Jr., and Thomas E. Terrill, *The American South: A History*, 2 vols. (New York, 1991), vol. 2, p. 710.

75. Quoted in Lerone Bennett, Jr., "When the Man and the Hour Are Met," in *Martin Luther King, Jr.: A Profile*, ed. C. Eric Lincoln (New York, 1970), p. 33.

states under court orders to desegregate, the national media gave their actions extensive coverage. *Time* magazine and the *New York Times* devoted articles to "the lost class of '59," and the Columbia Broadcasting Company and other television channels gave the issue prime-time coverage. A Georgian conveyed the feeling of many southerners when she complained that the South "is being insulted every day either singularly or collectively by the daily press, radio, television and movies, not to mention some of the Southern preachers and politicians. . . ."[76] Nevertheless, another intersectional consideration affected the thinking of southerners in the late 1950s, particularly in the peripheral South. That was the reluctance of outside business interests to locate plants or make investments in communities experiencing racial conflict and tension. Some southern business leaders began to moderate their resistance to racial change and to endorse compromise measures that promised peace and stability in the community.[77]

Sectional conflict in the 1950s was countered by powerful national forces, institutions, and leaders ready to compromise in order to minimize the South's isolation within the nation, and to strengthen political and economic bonds between North and South. This was evident in the continued influence of the conservative coalition of southern Democrats and northern Republicans in Congress. Southern Democrats and nonsouthern Republicans found common cause, for example, in an attack on the Supreme Court. The House of Representatives passed five measures in 1958 designed to curb the court's power, while the Senate came close to nullifying several Supreme Court decisions and within one vote of prohibiting the court from excluding states from any legislative area occupied by Congress unless that body specifically agreed. Not all of this assault was fueled by racial concerns, since much of the opposition outside the South was directed at the broader liberalism of the Warren Court.[78] Some northern and southern congressmen found common ground in equating opposition to racial equality with fervent anti-communism.

Certain basic issues that faced Congress elicited responses that were very different from the simple polarity of North versus South. The question of agricultural control and support legislation, for instance, tended to divide the core industrial area of the Northeast and Midwest from the agrarian periphery that made up much of the rest of the country. Widespread farm distress resulted from the extraordinary commodity productivity and chronic surpluses of the postwar period. Debate over agricultural policy in the 1950s revealed a regional pattern in which the high-support, interventionist philosophy of the periphery (which included the South) was pitted against the free-market orientation of the industrial core, whose position was backed by the Eisenhower administration. The representatives of the periphery were generally successful in preventing the

76. Nonie M. Wells to Estes Kefauver, 19 June 1957, Kefauver Papers.

77. Elizabeth Jacoway and David R. Colburn, eds., *Southern Businessmen and Desegregation* (Baton Rouge, La., 1982); Cooper and Terrill, *The American South*, vol. 2, p. 714.

78. Woodward, *The Strange Career of Jim Crow*, pp. 167–68; Grantham, *The Life & Death of the Solid South*, p. 144.

introduction of free-market competition in the farm economy.[79]

The longtime conflict between the industrial core and the agrarian periphery was itself ameliorated by several economic and political developments, including the economic interdependence of agricultural interests in the two areas and the increasing economic diversification of the periphery. There were also political considerations, most notably in negotiations between farm bloc and industrial labor representatives within the New Deal Democratic coalition. The committee system in the two houses of Congress—particularly the committees on Agriculture, Education and Labor, and Rules—facilitated logrolling between the two sectional wings of the Democratic party in the 1950s. A close student of modern sectionalism in Congress has written, "In hearings, committee reports, and floor debates, leaders of the party, allied bureaucrats, and private interest groups would forge a political justification which could bridge the sectional cleavage."[80] Thus, even in the midst of renewed sectional conflict, there were strong pressures promoting interregional accord.

Another illustration of these unifying influences was the leadership of the two major political parties, which were soon engaged in unaccustomed competition for southern support in national politics. In 1952 Democratic leaders, confronted with the candidacy of General Dwight D. Eisenhower and a rehabilitated Republican party, adopted a conciliatory approach toward the South. Party unifiers prevailed in the Democratic national convention, a strongly worded civil rights plank was defeated, and Governor Adlai E. Stevenson of Illinois and Senator John J. Sparkman of Alabama (whose selection reflected party leaders' concern about the South) were nominated for president and vice president, respectively. Although Stevenson was identified with northern liberalism, he made a special effort to attract southern support, and his position seemed to be more moderate than that of two southerners who had campaigned for the party's presidential nomination that year: Estes Kefauver on the left and Richard Russell on the right. While the Solid South was again disrupted, Stevenson and Sparkman carried eight of the southern states. Still, the Republicans made an important breakthrough in the South. Eisenhower won millions of southern votes and carried five of the region's states. His southern victories represented a significant triumph for presidential Republicanism in the South.

Despite the growing strength of massive resistance, the presidential election of 1956 did not precipitate a southern rebellion against the national leadership of the Democratic party, nor even a protest in the manner of Richard Russell's candidacy in 1952. The party's nominee, once again Adlai Stevenson, was conciliatory toward the South, and the national convention was unusually harmonious. The party platform omitted a direct endorsement of the *Brown* decision and specifically rejected the use of force in implementing the ruling. Although Stevenson divided the southern states with President Eisenhower, he carried all

79. Richard Franklin Bensel, *Sectionalism and American Political Development, 1880–1980* (Madison, Wis., 1984), pp. 191–206; Fite, *Richard B. Russell*, pp. 304–308, 310–12, 314–15.

80. Bensel, *Sectionalism and American Political Development*, pp. 206–22 (quotation on p. 219).

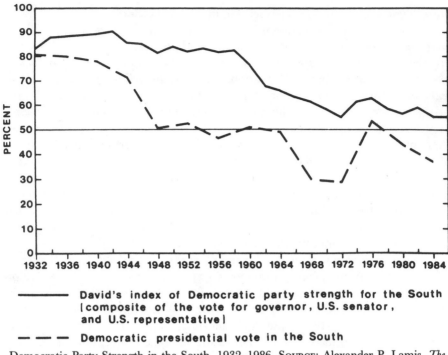

———— David's index of Democratic party strength for the South
(composite of the vote for governor, U.S. senator, and U.S. representative)

— — — Democratic presidential vote in the South

Democratic Party Strength in the South, 1932–1986. SOURCE: Alexander P. Lamis, *The Two-Party South*, 2d rev. ed. (New York: Oxford University Press, 1990), p. 42.

of the Deep South states except Louisiana. Indeed, the South provided the bulk of the party's electoral votes in 1952 and 1956. On the other hand, Eisenhower did even better in 1956 than he had done four years earlier; he carried seven southern states and won a larger percentage of the region's popular votes than his Democratic opponent. Republicans sought to take advantage of increasing southern alienation from the national Democratic party, and one consequence of their southern successes was to create a new position for the South in the orbit of national politics. Eisenhower's victories below the Potomac gave the minority party a new respectability among southerners, particularly middle-class and suburban dwellers.

Meanwhile, southerners continued to exert great influence in Congress, dominating the committee system and playing a major role in national decision making. The Democratic leaders in the two houses were Senator Lyndon B. Johnson and Representative Sam Rayburn, both moderate Texans. Although the sweeping Democratic victory in the midterm elections of 1958 brought an influx of new liberal congressmen to Washington, the imprint of the South's remarkable power in the shaping of national policy was still clearly defined. This does a good deal to explain the persistence of Democratic loyalties in the South. Equally important was the fact that the political power structure of the southern states and localities had a strong vested interest in Democratic control. That interest included not only its domination of local and state politics in the

South—massive resistance won one victory after another in Democratic primaries—but also the fact that southerners were reluctant to abandon their traditional identification with the Democratic party.

President Eisenhower's refusal to speak out in support of the *Brown* decision and the conservative approach he took to civil rights also gave aid and comfort to white southeners, at least during his first term. Eisenhower had considerable sympathy for southern conservatives like Governor James F. Byrnes of South Carolina who stressed the local nature of school systems, the limited authority of the Supreme Court, and danger to the federal system if the court extended federal control into the arena of public schools. He was especially concerned about the possibility that too rapid desegregation would cause some southern states to abolish public education altogether. The president favored a gradual approach to the implementation of *Brown* v. *Board of Education*, and he supported the decision only to the minimum extent he believed the law required. His administration did sponsor the civil rights acts of 1957 and 1960, both concerned with voting rights for blacks in the South, but southern opposition led by Senator Russell succeeded in weakening both measures. In the case of the 1957 bill, Eisenhower accepted some of the southern arguments and helped undermine the legislation that originated in his own Justice Department.[81] Thus the Eisenhower administration's extreme caution and hands-off approach encouraged southern resistance to racial change and contributed to the conservative nature of national policy in the field of civil rights during the 1950s.

Massive resistance encountered a major setback in 1957–1958. Early in the fall of 1957, the movement was tested in a dramatic confrontation over the desegregation of Central High School in Little Rock, Arkansas. The Arkansas capital city was an unlikely scene for such a confrontation in view of its moderation in race relations and its early formulation of plans to desegregate Central High. But the breakdown of community leadership and the pressure exerted by such groups as the Citizens' Council, as well as the popularity of massive resistance in many parts of the South, led Governor Orval Faubus to intervene with state militiamen in order to prevent desegregation. When a federal court enjoined this action and a frenzied mob surrounded the school, the president sent in federal troops to remove the obstruction.[82]

News of the Little Rock crisis sent shock waves through the South and placed Arkansas in the forefront of massive resistance. Governor Faubus was suddenly transformed, in the eyes of many white southerners, into a heroic defender of the embattled South. The immediate result of the crisis was to embarrass or

81. Robert Fredrick Burk, *The Eisenhower Administration and Black Civil Rights* (Knoxville, Tenn., 1984), pp. 142–73, 204–27, 243–48, 261–63; Steven F. Lawson, *Running for Freedom: Civil Rights and Black Politics in America Since 1941* (New York, 1991), pp. 40–58; Michael S. Mayer, "With Much Deliberation and Some Speed: Eisenhower and the *Brown* Decision," *Journal of Southern History* 52 (February 1986): 43–76; Fite, *Richard B. Russell*, pp. 329–49.

82. Burk, *The Eisenhower Administration and Black Civil Rights*, pp. 174–203; David Wallace, "Orval Faubus: The Central Figure at Little Rock Central High School," *Arkansas Historical Quarterly* 39 (Winter 1980): 314–29; Tony A. Freyer, "Politics and Law in the Little Rock Crisis, 1954–1957," *Arkansas Historical Quarterly* 40 (Autumn 1981): 195–219; Colbert S. Cartwright, "The Improbable Demagogue of Little Rock, Ark.," *Reporter* 17 (October 17, 1957): 23–25.

silence southern moderates and to strengthen extremist elements. It also brought the collapse of "Operation Dixie," an ambitious plan to develop the Republican party in the southern states. State governments throughout the region were galvanized into action, reinforcing barriers to desegregation and stepping up their attacks on the NAACP. Yet many thoughtful southerners were beginning to understand that the power of the national government could now be expected to enforce the decrees of the federal courts. After Little Rock it was scarcely possible to use violence to nullify decisions of the federal courts, and courtroom litigation over school desegregation during the next few years proved to be a vital means of undermining massive resistance. The federal courts eventually ruled that a state could not selectively close its public schools; they also refused to approve the concept of publicly subsidized private schools. Early in 1959, a federal court found that Virginia's action in closing nine public schools under orders to desegregate was unconstitutional. Still, the politics of massive resistance had not yet run its course. The conservative trend was unmistakable in the gubernatorial elections of 1958, and by the end of the year ten southern states had adopted school-closing laws.[83]

The first decisive defeat for the segregationist cause occurred in Virginia, where a shift away from interposition had become apparent by the fall of 1958. Some Virginia leaders had begun to weigh the relative importance of traditional white supremacy and public education. An open-schools movement was launched, and influential business interests raised questions about the wisdom of massive resistance. After the courts overturned the state's school-closure policy in January 1959, the Old Dominion was forced to reconsider its position. Governor J. Lindsay Almond, a strong advocate of massive resistance, gradually assumed a more moderate stance, and under his guidance the general assembly approved a series of measures compatible with token desegregation. An unfavorable court decision also contributed to the defeat of massive resistance in Arkansas in 1959. The balance of political pressure was narrow, but, as in Virginia, a coalition of educators, citizen supporters of the schools, and business leaders was successful. The compromise worked out in Virginia and Arkansas suggested the feasibility, from the segregationist point of view, of shifting from all-out defiance to a more moderate position and a willingness to accept token desegregation. That seemed preferable to most southern leaders when faced with a choice between segregation and traditional values, on the one hand, and social stability, business pursuits, and "progress," on the other. By the end of the decade, only the five states of the Deep South remained completely segregated, and they, too, succumbed in the early 1960s.[84]

Most southerners, even in the Deep South, were primarily concerned in the

83. Bartley, *The Rise of Massive Resistance*, pp. 251–92; Lewis, *Portrait of a Decade*, pp. 40–59, 92–94; J. W. Peltason, *Fifty-Eight Lonely Men: Southern Federal Judges and School Desegregation* (New York, 1961), pp. 48–55, 164–77; Sherrill, *Gothic Politics in the Deep South*, pp. 74–117.

84. Bartley, *The Rise of Massive Resistance*, pp. 320–39. See also Luther J. Carter, "Desegregation in Norfolk," *South Atlantic Quarterly* 58 (Autumn 1959): 507–20, and David Pace, "Lenoir Chambers Opposes Massive Resistance: An Editor Against Virginia's Democratic Organization, 1955–1959," *Virginia Magazine of History and Biography* 82 (October 1974): 415–29.

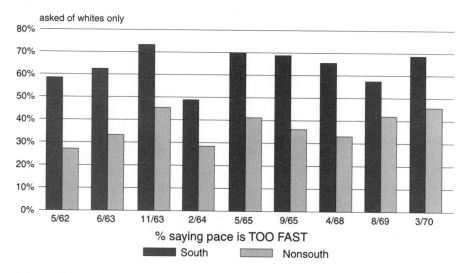

Is Racial Integration's Pace Too Fast, Not Fast Enough, or About Right? Source: George H. Gallup, *The Gallup Poll: Public Opinion, 1935–1971*, vol. 3 (New York: Random House, 1972), pp. 1769, 1823, 1852, 1867, 1939, 1961, 2122, 2210, 2240.

1950s with the pressures and necessities of their daily lives. The struggle over racial change did not completely dominate their existence. Yet the emotional conflict and turmoil that centered in the South in the 1950s was extraordinary. One result was increasing alienation in the relationship of black and white southerners—and of northerners and southerners. Although a variety of interregional agencies promoted compromise and accommodation between North and South, the emergence of civil rights as a national issue sparked a resurgence of southern sectionalism and a rising tide of anti-southern feeling in the North. By the time John F. Kennedy was inaugurated as president in 1961, the stage was set for the Second Reconstruction of the South.

CHAPTER 9

The Second Reconstruction

UNTIL 1960, C. Vann Woodward writes, southern resistance was "able to persuade itself that the civil rights movement was wholly the result of 'outside agitators,' that Southern Negroes were contented and happy with the 'Southern way of life,' that they preferred segregation, and that left to themselves they would never think of protesting."[1] White southerners had reason to be hopeful. The national political scene, reflecting the cautious moderation of Dwight D. Eisenhower, provided few opportunities for major breakthroughs in civil rights; the South continued to exert great influence in Congress; and the liberal coalition committed to racial reform had not yet achieved broad national support. Nevertheless, a number of developments in the 1950s prepared the way for the momentous civil rights struggle of the 1960s: *Brown* v. *Board of Education*, the emergence of Martin Luther King, Jr., as a dynamic champion of racial justice, the heightened expectations of black Americans and their determination to bring about a new day in race relations, and the widespread assumption among northerners that the South was responsible for the terrible racial problem in American life.

The presidential election of 1960 revealed the growing importance of the civil rights movement, and early in the 1960s the new Democratic administration was forced to respond to a series of demands for federal action to advance the cause of racial equality. Meanwhile, black students turned to new forms of protest and King, employing the tactics of Christian nonviolent protest, showed the effectiveness of mass demonstrations against the Jim Crow system in the southern states. These dramatic events brought reporters and photographers to the region in unprecedented numbers, captured the attention of the nation, and contributed, along with an emerging liberal coalition dedicated to racial re-

---

1. C. Vann Woodward, *The Strange Career of Jim Crow*, 3d rev. ed. (New York, 1974), pp. 168–69.

form, to the eventual creation of a national consensus in favor of civil rights for African Americans. In 1963 President John F. Kennedy decided to sponsor a comprehensive civil rights bill, and following his assassination the new president, Lyndon B. Johnson, led the way in the passage of the Civil Rights Act of 1964, the Voting Rights Act of 1965, and other measures of racial reform. The South was the object of a Second Reconstruction—more comprehensive and far-reaching than the first Reconstruction a century earlier. Then, at the very moment of its triumph, the civil rights movement lost momentum, racked by internal division, an outbreak of urban riots throughout the country, the appearance of a new and more doctrinaire black militancy, and the increasing preoccupation of the Johnson administration with the Vietnam War. By the end of the decade, the Second Reconstruction seemed to be over.

There were many vital elements in the rise and decline of the Second Reconstruction, including the changing context of national politics, the role of political leadership, and the part played by the federal government. But below the surface of political debate and public policy other essential forces were involved. Among these were powerful external pressures on the South emanating from black leaders and organizations, a civil rights coalition that included church groups, foundations, and labor unions, and broad, grass-roots support. Developments within the South were probably even more important, especially the protest and community-action programs of students and the demonstrations led by King and the Southern Christian Leadership Conference (SCLC). Two other internal elements contributed to the equal rights movement in the South. One of these was a growing minority of white liberals and moderates who began to use their influence to restore social order and tranquillity, even at the cost of racial change. The other was the most confirmed practitioners of massive resistance—the bitter-enders—whose repressive tactics, violence, and rhetorical extremism stirred the wrath of most Americans and helped pave the way for a national consensus.

Southerners approached the presidential election of 1960 in a mood of uncertainty, but many of them hoped that the outcome would enable the South to retain a large measure of political autonomy and to ease the threat of more drastic racial change. Both of the major parties looked to the southern states in 1960 for essential support in a national election that promised to be extremely close. The absence of Dwight Eisenhower from the ticket made the Republicans less formidable than in 1952 and 1956, but the GOP undertook an energetic campaign in the South, under the leadership of the party's nominee, Vice President Richard M. Nixon. Yet in some respects southern Republicans were inhibited in exploiting the troubled racial situation in the region, given the Eisenhower administration's use of federal troops at Little Rock and its part in the passage of the 1957 and 1960 civil rights laws. As an Alabama newspaper warned, in reflecting on the results of the southern defection to Eisenhower in 1952: "What did we gain by . . . dereliction? We got Earl Warren and the NAACP, we got Little Rock and Federal troops on Southern soil again; we got the rights of the individual states here in the South ground under foot, and if

Slick Dick Nixon has his way, we will have carpetbag rule all over again."[2] In addition, the Republican platform of 1960 contained a strong civil rights plank. Nixon, a moderate on racial issues, hoped to attract southern voters on the basis of his party's economic policies and state rights principles. He made a vigorous appeal for southern support, campaigning in every southern state. Speaking in Atlanta late in August, Nixon was given an enthusiastic reception by almost 200,000 people. The *Constitution's* Ralph McGill wrote that it was "the greatest thing in Atlanta since the premiere of *Gone With the Wind*."[3]

Southern interest in the election was quickened because of the role assumed by Senator Lyndon B. Johnson. The Texan sought his party's presidential nomination on the basis of his strong congressional support and his success as Senate majority leader. In an effort to go beyond his regional base, he stressed his western orientation and reached out for delegates in other parts of the country. One reason he helped enact civil rights legislation in 1957 and 1960 was his desire to "nationalize" his southern image. Johnson had worked hard as majority leader to keep the race question from becoming a disruptive issue between the two major geographical divisions of the Democratic party.[4] Nevertheless, he was widely viewed as the *southern* candidate, receiving backing in the national convention from virtually all of the southern states except Florida. His strength in other regions was limited, however, and he was unable to prevent the nomination of Senator Kennedy on the first ballot. Johnson's loss embittered many of his southern supporters. One Texas delegate asserted, "They crammed a civil rights plank down our throats, a liberal for president, then asked us to help sell the deal to the South with Johnson's aid."[5] This resentment was alleviated when Kennedy persuaded Johnson to become the party's vice-presidential nominee. During the campaign that followed, the Texan devoted much of his time to the South. Touring the region by rail on the "LBJ Special," Johnson traveled almost 3,000 miles, made about sixty speeches at southern stops, and worked with his accustomed political flair to gain the cooperation of Democratic leaders.

Kennedy himself campaigned in six southern states. Although the Democratic platform included a forthright endorsement of civil rights, the Massachusetts senator attempted to reach out to southern whites. He was concerned about the religious as well as the racial sensibilities of white southerners. Kennedy reassured many southern Protestants when he appeared in Septem-

2. Anniston (Ala.) *Star*, 28 February 1960, quoted in Gary W. Reichard, "Democrats, Civil Rights, and Electoral Strategies in the 1950s," *Congress & the Presidency* 13 (Spring 1986): 71.

3. Quoted in M. Lee Smith, "The Nixon Campaign in the South: A Chapter in the Rise of a Two-Party South" (Honors essay, Vanderbilt University, 1964), pp. 47–48. For the election of 1960 in the South, see Numan V. Bartley and Hugh D. Graham, *Southern Politics and the Second Reconstruction* (Baltimore, 1975), pp. 90–95; Stephen E. Ambrose, *Nixon: The Education of a Politician, 1913–1962* (New York, 1987), pp. 535–608; Earl Black and Merle Black, *The Vital South: How Presidents Are Elected* (Cambridge, Mass., 1992), pp. 189–99; and Guy Paul Land, "John F. Kennedy's Southern Strategy, 1956–1960," *North Carolina Historical Review* 56 (January 1979): 41–63.

4. Robert L. Riggs, "The South *Could* Rise Again: Lyndon Johnson and Others," in *Candidates 1960: Behind the Headlines in the Presidential Race*, ed. Eric Sevareid (New York, 1959), pp. 280–321.

5. Quoted in O. Douglas Weeks, *Texas in the 1960 Presidential Election* (Austin, 1961), p. 38.

ber before the Greater Houston Ministerial Association to assert his belief in the separation of church and state. During the campaign, he also promised to protect the southern textile industry against low-price foreign imports. He made a point of appealing to black voters, who had abandoned the Democratic party in significant numbers in the presidential election of 1956. In accepting his party's nomination, Kennedy declared that new reforms were needed in a time of rapid change, including support for the "peaceful revolution" that was demanding an end to racial discrimination in "all parts of our community life." Senator Johnson assured blacks that a Democratic administration would "do more in the field of civil rights than has been accomplished in the last century." When Martin Luther King, Jr., was arrested at a demonstration in Atlanta on October 19 and quickly sentenced to four months of hard labor in a state penitentiary, Kennedy called the black leader's wife to express his concern; his brother Robert F. Kennedy was able to arrange for King's release. These initiatives were not widely publicized among white southerners, much to the relief of the Kennedy campaign staff, but the news spread rapidly through black districts and clearly influenced many Negro voters. "When John Kennedy captured the presidency," Robert Weisbrot has written, "many in the civil rights movement believed that they had done so as well."[6]

Kennedy and Johnson carried a majority of the southern states in 1960, winning 50.47 percent of the vote in the former Confederate states, as compared with the Democrats' 47.76 percent in 1956. Yet the election in the South was almost as close as in the nation at large. The Republicans carried most of the outer South—Virginia, Kentucky, Tennessee, Florida, and Oklahoma—and came within a few thousand votes of winning Texas. Nixon led his Democratic opponent in the metropolitan counties of the South, and he did better than Eisenhower had done in the southern black belts. These gains resulted in part from the Republicans' vigorous campaign in the region; they also reflected the accumulating distrust of the national Democratic party felt by many white southerners, a distrust that was exacerbated by the civil rights movement and by Kennedy's Catholicism. The religious issue undoubtedly hurt the Democratic ticket in several states, and the Survey Research Center at the University of Michigan estimated that the defection of Protestant Democrats from Kennedy in the southern and border states represented 17.2 percent of the two-party vote in those states.[7] Still, Kennedy was popular among many southerners. His stand on civil rights appeared moderate, and he seemed to have a genuine interest in the South. He received impressive support from black southerners. Beyond that, the prospect of federal appropriations and patronage from a new Democratic administration was certainly an important consideration in the minds of southern politicians. Many observers believed, with Sena-

6. Robert Weisbrot, *Freedom Bound: A History of America's Civil Rights Movement* (New York, 1990), pp. 45–49 (quotation on p. 49).

7. Philip E. Converse, Angus Campbell, Warren E. Miller, and Donald E. Stokes, "Stability and Change in 1960: A Reinstating Election," *American Political Science Review* 55 (June 1961): 269–80; Bernard Cosman, "Presidential Republicanism in the South, 1960," *Journal of Politics* 24 (May 1962): 303–22.

tor John C. Stennis of Mississippi, that Lyndon Johnson "made the difference in the 1960 campaign."[8] Not only did Johnson's moderate record and southern background reassure the region's whites, but his strenuous electioneering and great influence among southern Democratic leaders made an indispensable contribution to his party's victory.

Notwithstanding John F. Kennedy's considerable success in reviving the national Democratic coalition of earlier years, the election returns provided evidence of strong sectional conflict in the voting behavior of Americans. The most obvious manifestation of this sectionalism was the continuing North-South cleavage in the Democratic party. In the North the Democrats were the party of liberals and intellectuals, of blacks and the newer ethnic groups, of urban dwellers and organized labor, of Catholics and Jews, as well as Protestants. Kennedy's strength lay in the Northeast and Midwest, and in key industrial states such as Pennsylvania and Michigan his appeal to blacks, ethnic groups, and organized labor ensured his election. In the South the Democrats were the party of whites and old-stock Americans, many of whom still opposed the enfranchisement of blacks; of rural and small-town people whose leaders continued to exercise great influence in southern politics even as the region was being transformed into an urban society; and of the most religious citizenry in the nation, most of whom were Protestant. Ninety-five percent of the southern electorate was Protestant, as compared with less than two-thirds of the voters in other regions. Kennedy's Catholicism brought him some gains among nonsoutherners, but anti-Catholic sentiment cost him heavily in the South. In one respect, though, the election of 1960 marked an advance in the nationalization of southern politics: like the elections of the 1950s, it resulted in intense two-party competition at the presidential level.[9]

During the campaign Kennedy had promised an "innovative and vigorous" approach to civil rights, and his election raised the hopes and expectations of blacks and other Americans working for a major victory in the struggle for equal rights. But the new president soon disappointed those who expected him to pursue a bold and far-reaching civil rights program. The reasons for his cautious approach were soon apparent. Realizing how narrow his margin of victory was in 1960 and that Richard Nixon had attracted more votes from white southerners than he had, Kennedy was unusually solicitous of those southerners, whose support he needed in Congress and in the election of 1964. Kennedy counted on the cooperation of southern congressmen in order to get his legislative program enacted. As he said to an aide, "If we drive [John] Sparkman, [Lister] Hill and other moderate Southerners to the wall with a lot of civil rights demands that can't pass anyway, then what happens to the Negro on minimum wages, housing and the rest?"[10] And while the president agreed with the general

8. Quoted in Reichard, "Democrats, Civil Rights, and Electoral Strategies," p. 73.

9. The voter turnout increase in the South, the largest in the nation, represented a 25 percent gain over the election of 1956. See Converse, Campbell, Miller, and Stokes, "Stability and Change in 1960," pp. 269–70.

10. Quoted in Carl M. Brauer, *John F. Kennedy and the Second Reconstruction* (New York, 1977), p. 62.

objectives of the civil rights movement, he was not yet convinced of the need for or the desirability of comprehensive federal involvement in the struggle.

Thus at the outset the Kennedy administration emphasized executive action in such areas as voting rights, employment, transportation, and education. The administration was able to get a two-year extension of the Civil Rights Commission in 1961, established the President's Committee on Equal Employment Opportunity, under the chairmanship of Vice President Johnson, and endorsed two voting rights proposals in 1962. Kennedy also appointed blacks to high-level positions in the federal government, and he supported the civil rights division in the Department of Justice, which was headed by Robert F. Kennedy. In the early 1960s, the number of voting rights suits initiated by the Justice Department was greatly increased. On the other hand, the chief executive refused to act on a recommendation that nondiscrimination be made a condition of federally aided programs in the states. Pressured by southern senators, he appointed a number of staunch segregationists to federal judgeships in the South. And despite his campaign promise to ban discrimination in federally subsidized housing, he delayed such action for almost two years, and even then his executive order was issued in a narrow and ineffective form. While the administration encouraged the voluntary acceptance of the civil rights of black people in the South, it avoided even the appearance of federal coercion.[11]

Black protest entered a new phase on February 1, 1960, when four students from North Carolina Agricultural and Technical College, an all-black institution in Greensboro, took seats at a Woolworth's lunch counter and refused to move when they were denied service. This new tactic, based on King's nonviolent ethic, provided a means of publicizing discrimination against blacks in many public places in the South. A wave of sit-ins at lunch counters and restaurants and other challenges to segregated facilities swept over the South. A new social movement took shape, encouraged by the Student Nonviolent Coordinating Committee (SNCC), which was organized in April 1960. By that time, thousands of students had conducted sit-in demonstrations in some 60 communities, and before the end of the year protests had been carried out in over 200 cities and towns. The sit-ins provoked white resistance and retaliation. "As student protest continued," one historian has noted, "the veneer of racial harmony in Southern cities cracked, then fell away to reveal a core of racial antagonism."[12] Meanwhile, in the North sympathy boycotts were conducted against Woolworth's and other chain stores whose southern branches refused to serve blacks at lunch counters. The pressure of the sit-ins had some effect, as southern merchants, community leaders, and moderate politicians decided to make concessions in the interest of social order and a resumption of business.[13]

11. Brauer, *John F. Kennedy and the Second Reconstruction*, pp. 61–88; Herbert S. Parmet, *JFK: The Presidency of John F. Kennedy* (New York, 1983), pp. 249–76; Allen J. Matusow, *The Unraveling of America: A History of Liberalism in the 1960s* (New York, 1984), pp. 60–96.

12. Weisbrot, *Freedom Bound*, pp. 19–44 (quotation on p. 25).

13. Harvard Sitkoff, *The Struggle for Black Equality, 1954–1980* (New York, 1981), pp. 69–96; Clayborne Carson, *In Struggle: SNCC and the Black Awakening of the 1960s* (Cambridge, Mass., 1981), pp. 1–30.

In the spring of 1961, the equal rights movement took another turn when the Congress of Racial Equality (CORE) sponsored a "freedom ride" through the South to test the Supreme Court's recent decision prohibiting segregation in bus- and train-terminal accommodations. Thirteen black and white volunteers left Washington, D.C., by bus early in May, bound for New Orleans. CORE leaders abandoned the undertaking after the riders were attacked by white mobs in Anniston and Birmingham, Alabama. The Kennedy administration was hesitant to get involved, in spite of the failure of local authorities to protect the demonstrators, since Governor John Patterson, a dedicated segregationist, had been the first southern political leader to endorse John Kennedy for president. But when a new group of student activists resumed the ride to Montgomery, Attorney General Kennedy managed to persuade Governor Patterson to guarantee the safety of the bus as far as the Montgomery city limits. At the downtown terminal, however, an angry mob viciously attacked the riders. When a second riot developed the next day outside a black church where Martin Luther King, Jr., was leading a rally in support of the freedom riders, the president sent 400 federal marshals to Montgomery; the governor finally acted as well, declaring martial law in the city and mobilizing the National Guard. A newly organized Freedom Ride Coordinating Committee then recruited thousands of "freedom riders" to continue the trip; 360 of the riders were arrested when they arrived in Jackson, Mississippi.[14]

The freedom rides led the Interstate Commerce Commission, under pressure from the Kennedy administration, to issue a ruling in September 1961 prohibiting segregated facilities in interstate travel. The rides also inspired other students in the South to protest against segregated transportation facilities and helped create a community of militant activists dedicated to social justice. Meanwhile, the sit-ins had accelerated the rate of social change in race relations, inaugurated a period of unprecedented rivalry among the racial reform groups, and "made nonviolent direct action the dominant strategy in the struggle for racial equality during the next half-decade."[15] The young rebels brought to the southern movement unconventional and increasingly militant tactics, an emphasis on local initiative and decentralized control, and a heightened sense of racial consciousness among civil rights participants. While black ministers were at the center of the struggle for racial equality, SNCC, one scholar observes, "stood alone in its unselfish determination to confront the segregationist power structure."[16] Entering local communities, the youthful activists began to mobilize poor and working-class blacks. In urban areas, especially in the upper South, they organized large-scale demonstrations to desegregate public facili-

14. The riders were tried for violating the segregation laws, fined, and given two-month suspended sentences. The demonstrators all went to jail rather than pay their fines. August Meier and Elliott Rudwick, *CORE: A Study in the Civil Rights Movement, 1942–1968* (New York, 1973), pp. 135–58; Carson, *In Struggle*, pp. 31–44; Weisbrot, *Freedom Bound*, pp. 55–63; Brauer, *John F. Kennedy and the Second Reconstruction*, pp. 98–112.

15. Meier and Rudwick, *CORE*, p. 101.

16. Manning Marable, *Race, Reform and Rebellion: The Second Reconstruction in Black America, 1945–1982* (Jackson, Miss., 1984), pp. 66–72 (quotation on p. 72).

ties, improve housing and job opportunities for African Americans, and eliminate discriminatory public policies. They organized marches and rallies to show
black resolve and to encourage federal intervention on behalf of blacks. And
they helped popularize "freedom songs," often based on traditional religious
music, that contributed to the creation of a distinctive *movement* culture.[17]

SNCC and its collaborators had a significant influence on Martin Luther
King, Jr., who sought to control them and was both stimulated and challenged
by their activities. Although King's oratory and presence often aroused black
enthusiasm and attracted publicity, his Southern Christian Leadership Conference had done little to organize and conduct demonstrations and protest campaigns since its founding in 1957. Sit-ins, freedom rides, and community programs provided vivid examples of new and potentially more fruitful approaches
in the movement for equal rights. King, a political realist as well as an idealist,
learned from these examples and supported some of them. His own commu-
nity-based demonstrations started in Albany, Georgia, a town in the southwestern part of the state. Beginning in November 1961 and lasting more than a
year, thousands of blacks led by King endeavored to win the franchise and to
secure the desegregation of public facilities in the Georgia town. Many of the
demonstrators were arrested, but Sheriff Laurie Pritchett and other city authorities were careful to maintain order and avoid the use of violence in dealing with
the protesters. In the end, the Albany campaign collapsed. Meanwhile, the
Kennedy administration refused to become involved, in part because it wanted
to enhance the chances of Carl Sanders, a moderate candidate in the Democratic gubernatorial primary of 1962.[18]

But in the fall of 1962 President Kennedy was drawn into a dramatic confrontation with intransigent white supremacists in Mississippi. The federal
courts had ordered the admission to the state university of a black Mississippian
named James H. Meredith; Governor Ross Barnett, who had been elected with
Citizens' Council backing, aroused the public with demagogic rhetoric and talk
of nullification. He defied the court orders and personally denied Meredith's
enrollment in the University of Mississippi. The Kennedy administration tried
persuasion with Barnett, and the president addressed the nation over television,
urging the students and people of Mississippi to comply with the court ruling.
Such pleas were unavailing. Meredith's appearance on campus was greeted by
an outbreak of violence, and an angry white mob fought the 320 federal marshals Kennedy had dispatched with stones, clubs, bottles, gasoline bombs, and
firearms. "This was not an attack on Negroes or demonstators," Vann Woodward later wrote. "It was an insurrectionary assault on officers and soldiers of
the United States Government and the most serious challenge to the Union

17. Clayborne Carson, "Black Freedom Movement," in *Encyclopedia of Southern Culture*, ed.
Charles Reagan Wilson and William Ferris (Chapel Hill, N.C., 1989), pp. 159–60; Carson, *In
Struggle*, pp. 45–82.

18. Adam Fairclough, *To Redeem the Soul of America: The Southern Christian Leadership Conference and
Martin Luther King, Jr.* (Athens, Ga., 1987), pp. 57–109; Brauer, *John F. Kennedy and the Second Reconstruction*, pp. 154–55, 168–79.

since the Civil War."[19] Only after a night of terror and a pitched battle involving thousands of students and outside segregationists, on the one hand, and 400 federal marshals and a small contingent of army troops, on the other, was the lone black man enrolled. Kennedy moved to quell the riot by sending in regular troops and federalizing the state's National Guard. Two people were killed and 375 injured in the melee.[20]

The "Battle of Oxford" added fuel to the flames of intersectional animosity. The Ole Miss crisis also pointed up the extent to which Mississippi had become a "closed society." The doctrine of white supremacy was passionately subscribed to by most of the state's Caucasian inhabitants, and white leaders, fortified by the Citizens' Council and other organizations, worked anew to legitimize segregation through appeals to religion and revered historical figures. While praising defenders of segregation, they vehemently attacked integrationists and found scapegoats in the NAACP, outside liberals, and the Communist party. Meanwhile, the guardians of the Magnolia State's "closed society" made effective use of powerful symbols like the Confederate flag and the song "Dixie" as a means of invoking southern myths.[21]

Many northerners were disgusted with Mississippi's recalcitrance, and liberal leaders, including some Republicans, urged the president to move more forcefully in dealing with racial violence and white defiance in the South. White southerners tended to blame the confrontation on King, SNCC, and other "Communist-inspired" groups as well as John F. Kennedy. Black activists, frequently encountering economic pressure, intimidation, and physical attack, turned increasingly to the federal government for protection and to newspaper and television reporters in an effort to influence public opinion. As the civil rights struggle in the South became more intense and as the movement became the focus of national attention, the Kennedy administration found itself pressed to do more than support the right of black southerners to vote and rely on the voluntary cooperation of political and business leaders to abandon segregation and racial discrimination. Between the fall of 1961 and the spring of 1963, 20,000 protesters were arrested. In 1963 alone another 15,000 were imprisoned, as 1,000 desegregation protests took place in more than 100 cities and towns. A small group of black demonstrators had become a large mass movement for racial reform and civil rights.[22] But the protesters had not yet achieved a dramatic breakthrough.

Then, in the spring of 1963, King led a number of large demonstrations in Birmingham, Alabama. Birmingham was perhaps the most notorious center of

19. Woodward, *The Strange Career of Jim Crow*, p. 175. See also Brauer, *John F. Kennedy and the Second Reconstruction*, pp. 180–204.

20. For two firsthand accounts of the Ole Miss crisis, see James W. Silver, *Mississippi: The Closed Society* (New York, 1964), and Russell H. Barrett, *Integration at Ole Miss* (Chicago, 1965).

21. See, for example, Harold Mixon, "The Rhetoric of States' Rights and White Supremacy," in *A New Diversity in Contemporary Southern Rhetoric*, ed. Calvin M. Logue and Howard Dorgan (Baton Rouge, La., 1987), pp. 166–87.

22. Steven F. Lawson, *Running for Freedom: Civil Rights and Black Politics in America Since 1941* (New York, 1991), p. 87; Marable, *Race, Reform and Rebellion*, pp. 75–76.

racial repression and violent resistance to civil rights in the South. A local black movement led by the Reverend Fred L. Shuttlesworth and a group of concerned business leaders had helped change the city government and elect a moderate mayor in March 1963, but these changes were challenged in the courts and powerful opposition to King's campaign was directed by the city's public safety commissioner, T. Eugene "Bull" Connor. King wanted both to win the support of southern whites through a "persuasive" policy and to provoke federal intervention through a "coercive" policy. SCLC leaders arranged their demonstrations to coincide with the Easter shopping season; they hoped to desegregate public facilities, to obtain employment opportunities for blacks in downtown businesses, and to improve services in black neighborhoods. A few days after the SCLC protests began, King was arrested for ignoring a state court injunction against further protests. While in prison over Easter weekend, the SCLC leader wrote his "Letter from Birmingham Jail," a response to an open letter from white ministers and rabbis criticizing the demonstrations and praising the police for upholding the law. In deeply moving language, King talked about the fundamentals of his nonviolent philosophy, distinguishing between just laws and unjust laws, and stressing the morality rooted in divine justice and opposed to the degrading statutes of segregation. The minister's letter was soon being circulated as a pamphlet printed by the American Friends Service Committee, and it was excerpted in journals like the *Christian Century* and in national newspapers.[23]

As the demonstrations dragged on without noticeable success, Martin Luther King, Jr., made the decision deliberately to provoke "Bull" Connor and his men by employing black children in the demonstrations. Connor responded by arresting 900 of these youthful protesters on May 2. On the following day, when a thousand young protesters were prepared to march, Connor's policemen turned on them and other demonstrators with billy clubs, police dogs, and high-pressure water hoses. On May 6, this scene was repeated. By then, King's army had lost its discipline, and many blacks, particularly young adult males, responded to the sustained police brutality with a hail of bricks and bottles. Vivid pictures of the brutal police repression in Birmingham were seen on television screens throughout the country, arousing indignation among many Americans who had never before been concerned about the mistreatment of blacks. One photograph that appeared on the front page of newspapers around the world showed a huge, snarling police dog lunging at a black woman.[24]

Finally, the pressure for a settlement had its effect. As King wrote later,

23. Weisbrot, *Freedom Bound*, pp. 68–70; Lawson, *Running for Freedom*, pp. 91–92; David R. Goldfield, *Black, White, and Southern: Race Relations and Southern Culture, 1940 to the Present* (Baton Rouge, La., 1990), pp. 124–38; Adam Fairclough, "Martin Luther King, Jr. and the Quest for Nonviolent Social Change," *Phylon* 47 (March 1986): 1–15.

24. Weisbrot, *Freedom Bound*, pp. 70–72; Fairclough, *To Redeem the Soul of America*, pp. 111–39; David J. Garrow, *Bearing the Cross: Martin Luther King, Jr., and the Southern Christian Leadership Conference* (New York, 1986), pp. 231–86; Taylor Branch, *Parting the Waters: America in the King Years, 1954–63* (New York, 1988), pp. 673–707, 734–802.

"There were Negroes on the sidewalks, in the streets, standing, sitting in the aisles of downtown stores. There were square blocks of Negroes, a veritable sea of black faces. . . . Downtown Birmingham echoed to the strains of the freedom songs."[25] Many Birmingham residents were alarmed over the threat of an all-out race war. Businessmen, worried over declining sales and profits, and in some cases pressured by southern industrialists and executives, began to show a more genuine willingness to negotiate. President Kennedy threatened to use federal troops to restore order in the city. After new discussions, encouraged by local civic leaders and federal officers, an agreement was reached. The demonstrators won their demands for the desegregation of lunch counters, rest rooms, and certain other facilities, as well as the hiring and promoting of blacks "on a nondiscriminatory basis throughout the industrial community of Birmingham." When prodded by black leaders, the new mayor, Albert Boutwell, eventually opened the library, municipal golf courses, and other facilities to both races. Even so, the end of the Birmingham protests was marked by two bombings and a Ku Klux Klan rally. A few months later, on September 15, 1963, the Sixteenth Street Baptist Church, a rallying point for the previous spring's demonstrations, was the object of a mysterious bombing that cost the lives of four young black girls worshiping inside.[26]

The Birmingham demonstrations and the growing momentum of the civil rights movement altered the attitude of the Kennedy administration. Robert Kennedy, increasingly frustrated by the tactics of southern opponents of racial change and sharply criticized by young black activists for failing to protect them, soon concluded that a more vigorous federal role would have to be undertaken. Other advisers were more cautious, warning the president that a thoroughgoing commitment to civil rights legislation might well bring the collapse of his presidency and prevent his reelection. In the meantime, King's Birmingham campaign had sparked one protest after another. By midsummer, almost 800 demonstrations, involving a broader range of blacks and a growing number of whites, had taken place in some 200 southern cities and towns. By the end of the year, over a hundred thousand people had participated in equal rights demonstrations, leading to nearly fifteen thousand arrests.[27] These protests left their imprint on the Kennedy administration.

President Kennedy was more directly affected in June 1963 by the challenge posed by Governor George Corley Wallace of Alabama. When Governor Wallace threatened to defy a court order admitting two black students to the University of Alabama, Kennedy acted quickly, federalizing the state's National Guard and forcing the governor to stand aside when he personally sought to prevent their registration. "To Americans trying to forget the horrors of Birmingham," one scholar writes, "the sight of a governor seeking physically to

25. Martin Luther King, Jr., *Why We Can't Wait* (New York, 1964), p. 111.

26. Robert Corley, "In Search of Racial Harmony: Birmingham Business Leaders and Desegregation, 1950–1963," in *Southern Businessmen and Desegregation*, ed. Elizabeth Jacoway and David R. Colburn (Baton Rouge, La., 1982), pp. 185–90; Lawson, *Running for Freedom*, pp. 93–94; Goldfield, *Black, White, and Southern*, pp. 140–41.

27. Weisbrot, *Freedom Bound*, pp. 72–74.

prevent students from entering a school was at once tragic and ludicrous." In an eloquent television address following his encounter with Wallace, on June 11, the president declared that America was faced "primarily with a moral issue." The nation would not be fully free, he warned, "until all its citizens are free." A week later, Kennedy sent Congress a comprehensive civil rights bill.[28]

Kennedy's address marked a turning point in the history of the civil rights movement. Although civil rights leaders and liberals generally commended the president, it was clear that the legislation he sought would be difficult to enact. Strong opposition persisted in the South, along with apathy and doubts in other regions. Only hours after the chief executive's national address, the NAACP's field secretary in Mississippi was murdered from ambush as he returned to his home in Jackson. Kennedy soon began to take a more active part in advancing the cause of equal rights. In addition to sponsoring a major civil rights law, he authorized Attorney General Kennedy to undertake suits against segregated schools and strengthened federal authority to deny funds for discriminatory programs. He made personal appeals to separate groups representing business leaders, governors, mayors, educators, blacks, southern whites, clergymen, labor spokesmen, and others. With Kennedy's approval, a Democratic party official organized a citizens' lobby to work for the civil rights bill.[29]

Like a great many other Americans, John F. Kennedy was unexpectedly caught up in the huge march on Washington on August 28, although he chose not to speak at the affair. The demonstration was a revival of A. Philip Randolph's threatened march in 1941; it brought together a wide range of black leaders, as well as politicians, teachers, musicians, movie stars, labor leaders, and others of both races. More than 200,000 people sprawled out along the Mall facing the Lincoln Memorial, making it the largest political assembly in American history. When Martin Luther King, Jr., delivered his powerful address on that occasion, he warned of the "whirlwind of revolt" that would sweep over the country if the rights of blacks were delayed any longer. President Kennedy praised the rally for its "deep fervor and quiet dignity."[30] By the fall of 1963, the Kennedy administration had become a full-fledged supporter of the civil rights movement. Kennedy and his lieutenants were working energetically to develop grass-roots backing for the administration's proposed legislation and to rally support for it in Congress. Despite the likelihood of losing several southern states in 1964 and signs of a "white backlash" in northern suburbs, Kennedy continued until his death to fight for the civil rights bill.

But it was clear that Congress would be in no hurry to pass Kennedy's civil rights legislation. The Senate Judiciary Committee, under the chairmanship of Mississippi's James O. Eastland, held hearings on the measure but took no further action during the session. Southern congressmen vowed that, if the bill did reach the floor, they would filibuster it to death. One poll showed that 4.5 mil-

28. *Ibid.*, p. 75; Brauer, *John F. Kennedy and the Second Reconstruction*, pp. 252–62.
29. Weisbrot, *Freedom Bound*, pp. 75–76; Lawson, *Running for Freedom*, p. 95.
30. Brauer, *John F. Kennedy and the Second Reconstruction*, pp. 290–93; Branch, *Parting the Waters*, pp. 846–87.

lion white southerners had become disillusioned with Kennedy since his election. A North Carolina housewife was quoted as saying, "He's stirred up all the colored people to get their vote. It's terrible; he encouraged them to break state laws."[31] Meanwhile, intensive negotiations between the Kennedy administration and congressional leaders of both parties began to lay the groundwork for ultimate success. On October 29 the Judiciary Committee in the House of Representatives reported the administration's civil rights bill with a recommendation that it be passed.[32] Three weeks later the young president was dead.

In his first address to Congress as president, late in November 1963, Lyndon B. Johnson called for "the earliest possible passage" of the Kennedy civil rights bill. The new chief executive soon made it clear that he was totally committed to the enactment of this broad civil rights measure. "We have talked long enough in this country about equal rights," Johnson declared on November 27, 1963. "We have talked for one hundred years or more. It is time now to write the next chapter, and to write it in the books of law."[33]

When the second session of the Eighty-eighth Congress began its work in January 1964, the Johnson administration mobilized all of its powers behind the effort to enact a comprehensive civil rights statute. The threat of a discharge petition that would force consideration persuaded the House Rules Committee to clear H.R. 7152 for floor action by late January, and the bill was passed with strong bipartisan support on February 10, by a vote of 290 to 130. One hundred and four southern Democrats voted against the measure, while only eleven of the region's Democratic representatives supported it. In steering the bill through the lower house, Emanuel Celler, the floor manager, was assisted not only by liberal party members identified with the Democratic Study Committee but also by such Republican leaders as William H. McCulloch, the ranking minority member of the House Judiciary Committee. In the meantime, thousands of people poured into Washington early in 1964 to press for congressional approval, and scores of civil rights, religious, and labor groups participated in the movement through the Leadership Conference on Civil Rights.[34]

Prospects were much less encouraging in the Senate, given the strategic positions of southern leaders in that body and the difficulty of overcoming filibusters. The senators from southern states, led by Richard B. Russell, condemned the bill, particularly the provisions banning discrimination in public places. They regarded the measure as unconstitutional because it restricted personal freedom and the right to control one's private property. The central issue, according to Russell, was the unrestrained power the bill gave to the executive

31. Weisbrot, *Freedom Bound*, pp. 77–84 (quotation on p. 84).

32. Charles Whalen and Barbara Whalen, *The Longest Debate: A Legislative History of the 1964 Civil Rights Act* (New York, 1985), pp. 1–71; Hugh Davis Graham, *Civil Rights and the Presidency: Race and Gender in American Politics, 1960–1972* (New York, 1992), pp. 46–48, 53–66.

33. *Public Papers of the Presidents of the United States: Lyndon B. Johnson, 1963–64*, 2 vols. (Washington, D.C., 1965), vol. 1, p. 9. See also Matusow, *The Unraveling of America*, pp. 180–216.

34. For congressional action on H.R. 7152, see Whalen and Whalen, *The Longest Debate*, pp. 72–233, 247–54, and Graham, *Civil Rights and the Presidency*, pp. 67–86.

branch of the federal government, which would permit political persecution of citizens by an ambitious and ruthless attorney general and other bureaucrats. The Georgia senator argued that the proposal originated in politics, was punitive in nature, and would be sectional in its application. It was aimed primarily at the South, like the Reconstruction laws of the 1860s. Indeed, Russell declared, "the white people of the Southern states" were "the most despised and mistreated minority in the country."[35] In this case the southern congressmen reflected the feeling of the preponderance of their white constituents. Although the racial thought of southerners differed—between the black belt and the hill country, the upper South and the lower South, and so on—segregation was too deeply rooted in their culture for most white southerners to accept such a drastic change as the abolition of Jim Crow in race relations. Only gradually, following the Second World War, did a sprinkling of the region's white liberals begin to reconcile themselves to the idea of comprehensive civil rights for blacks. For most white southerners alterations in attitude usually came after behavioral modifications that resulted from the Second Reconstruction.

Russell and his embattled compatriots hoped to bury the House-approved bill in Eastland's Judiciary Committee, but administration leaders skillfully avoided that trap and persuaded the Senate on February 26 to place the measure directly on the upper chamber's calendar. Hubert H. Humphrey, who managed the bill in the Senate, and other supporters succeeded in creating a sturdy coalition and in preventing its disruption as a result of partisan politics, a constant danger. The southerners' last hope was to attract enough conservative Republican backing to prevent the adoption of cloture, which would make it possible to end a filibuster. Since 1938, eleven votes had been taken in the Senate on cloture in connection with civil rights, and Richard Russell had led successful opposition to every one of them. Now the southern senators once again employed the tactic of delay. As Eric F. Goldman wrote a few years later:

> Senator Russell had a band of eighteen Southern senators whom he deployed in three platoons of six each, a fresh platoon each day. They talked on and on— about the "amalgamation and mongrelization of the races," the source of the grits that people in Minnesota eat, the living habits of Hungarian immigrants, sometimes about the bill itself, calling it, to use the phrase of Senator Russell Long, "a mixed breed of unconstitutionality and the NAACP."[36]

For eighty-two days after March 9, 1964, discussion of civil rights totaled some ten million words and filled more than six thousand pages of the *Congressional Record*.[37] Administration spokesmen carried on intensive negotiations with Senate leaders of both parties in an effort to work out an agreement that would halt debate and enable the bill to pass. The pivotal figure in these negotiations

35. Gilbert C. Fite, *Richard B. Russell, Jr., Senator from Georgia* (Chapel Hill, N.C., 1991), pp. 407–15 (quotation on p. 414).
36. Eric F. Goldman, *The Tragedy of Lyndon Johnson* (New York, 1969), p. 69.
37. Fite, *Richard B. Russell*, pp. 407, 414. See also Weisbrot, *Freedom Bound*, pp. 88–89.

was minority leader Everett M. Dirksen of Illinois, with whom the White House held painstaking conferences. Dirksen slowly moved toward a compromise, and in mid-May, during the seventh week of floor debate, a package of amendments was agreed to in the negotiations and incorporated into a "clean bill" to be offered as a substitute for H.R. 7152. On June 10 the Senate adopted a cloture resolution by a vote of 71 to 29, and for the first time in its history the upper house had voted to close debate on a civil rights bill. The power of the southern bloc had been broken. In demanding unconditional surrender, Russell and his confederates may have missed an opportunity to weaken the bill that was finally passed.

After adopting cloture, the Senate approved a few minor amendments, voted down a large number designed to undermine the measure, and passed it on June 19 by a roll call vote of 73 to 27. Twenty-one of the twenty-six senators from the South voted against cloture and final passage of the bill. The House accepted the Senate version, and President Johnson signed it on July 2. The Civil Rights Act of 1964 was the most sweeping affirmation of equal rights ever made by a U.S. Congress. The law assured access to public accommodations such as motels, restaurants, and places of amusement; authorized the federal government to bring suits to desegregate public facilities and schools; contained provisions to help guarantee black voting rights; extended the life of the Civil Rights Commission for four years and gave it new powers; provided that federal funds could be cut off when programs were administered discriminatorily; prohibited discrimination by firms with twenty-five or more employees on the basis of race, color, sex, or religion; created a five-member Equal Employment Opportunity Commission; and authorized the Justice Department to enter into pending civil rights cases. Compliance was by no means universal, but the law was generally obeyed throughout the South, in part because of careful preparation by federal and local officials.

The civil rights breakthrough of the mid-1960s represented in some measure a national commitment to act on the long-deferred promise to end legal discrimination against African Americans in the United States. Congress had joined the executive branch and the judiciary of the federal government in making this a reality. But politicians and public officials had responded to the pressure exerted by a variegated and wide-ranging civil rights movement. While the focus of that movement was the harsh system of racial practices that prevailed in the southern states, the struggle for black equality was not simply a conflict between North and South. Much of the energy and inspiration that infused the civil rights movement came out of the South itself, and ironically the waning of the movement owed a great deal to opposition in other parts of the country. The sectional interaction in the Second Reconstruction was complex and subtle; it was also one of the most important forces in postwar American politics.

In its origins the Second Reconstruction was clearly the result of outside forces impinging on the South, among them the older black organizations and an emergent political liberalism sensitive to racial injustice. The ultimate triumph of the civil rights movement—its successes in the federal courts, in the executive branch, and in Congress—reflected the swelling support of northern and western reform elements and, eventually, more conservative Americans who for various reasons came to see the question of race relations in the South as a national problem. But the dramatic upheaval of black protest in the South was equally important, for it brought with it dynamic new leaders, organizations, and tactics that were largely endemic in nature. The most significant manifestation of this southern black protest was the leadership of Martin Luther King, Jr., a young and compelling figure of great power whose leadership was indelibly associated with the black clergy, the immorality of racial segregation, and the tactic of nonviolence. King represented a new and impatient black leadership in the South, which was also symbolized by the roles of Rosa Parks, E. D. Nixon, Jo Ann Robinson, and Ralph D. Abernathy in the Montgomery bus boycott.

A second indigenous element in southern black protest was that of student activists, who first came to public attention in the sit-ins of 1960, the freedom rides of 1961, and the activities of the Student Nonviolent Coordinating Committee. Emphasizing community organization and voter registration drives, the young protesters tried to involve poor and working-class blacks who had seldom participated in earlier demonstrations. While initially cooperating with King and his associates, they soon began to challenge the SCLC leader as well as the Kennedy and Johnson administrations, pushing for more thoroughgoing change and providing a stimulus for federal intervention and reform.

A third—and less conspicuous—source of change in race relations from within the South came from the region's white liberals and moderates: writers, journalists, ministers, professors, and others who in varying degree endorsed the objectives of the civil rights movement. One illustration was the Southern Regional Council, an Atlanta-based and foundation-financed reform agency. The SRC supported the major goals of the black struggle, coordinated the various organizations involved in the Voter Education Project, and gained a national reputation for its analysis and interpretation of the racial situation in the southern states. Most white southerners were neither idealists nor crusaders, certainly not on the race question, but a growing number of them could be described as moderates or pragmatists. As a close observer noted, "at one stage of the struggle or another, enough local politicians, public officials, and businessmen made the decision for compliance and conciliation to render impossible a solid phalanx of Southern resistance and a hideous national crisis."[38] It was ironic that Lyndon Johnson, whose national ambitions as late as 1960 appeared thwarted by his provincial background and regional identity, should have become the great champion of the Second Reconstruction. Johnson's sponsorship of a broad program of social reform was inextricably connected with his support of civil rights, and one suspects that his determination to transcend his sectional heritage and lead the way in providing a national solution to the most intractable of America's social problems became the catalyst for his Great Society.

38. William G. Carleton, "The South's Many Moods," *Yale Review* 55 (Summer 1966): 638–39.

One other regional aspect of the Second Reconstruction needs to be considered. This was the way in which the media identified the race issue with the South and helped create support for a national solution to the problem. Both print and electronic journalism produced dramatic images of the South during the civil rights movement, a time that coincided with the rise of national network news reporting in the United States. Television news, in fact, developed into a national medium partly through its experience in the South, and many reporters and photographers first achieved recognition when they came South to cover the civil rights story. The three television networks devoted much of their news budgets to racial protest in the southern states. Television news enabled advocates of racial equality to overcome the indifferent or hostile coverage of local newspapers and area TV stations. Moreover, TV's record of the brutal treatment inflicted on demonstrators by southern police had a much greater impact than written accounts.

By the early 1960s, vivid reports from the civil rights front in the South had become a staple of national network news. Early in 1963, for example, SNCC's direct action and voter registration in Greenwood, Mississippi, provoked local whites into initiating a reign of violence against the equal rights activists. When SNCC responded with a series of protest marches, national television cameras for two weeks filmed peaceful demonstrators under siege by the police and their snarling dogs. Martin Luther King's demonstrations in Birmingham during the spring of 1963 resulted in television and newspaper accounts of "Bull" Connor's men attacking black children and other demonstrators with police dogs and fire hoses. In March 1965 the American Broadcasting Company interrupted its regularly scheduled program to broadcast the startling images of people being trampled by police horses at the Edmund Pettus Bridge in Selma, Alabama. These scenes of "Bloody Sunday" brought a stream of people to join King's march from Selma to Montgomery. Civil rights leaders soon learned to plan events that would attract the attention of the national press, especially television crews, and, as one writer observed, the national media "became the ally of civil rights leaders in presenting their case to an American public."[39] According to Robert MacNeil of the National Broadcasting Company, "The tone of network programming has been emphatically liberal, identifying the advancement of the American Negro—toward equality as unquestionably linked to the health of this nation."[40] Senator Russell spoke for many southern segregationists when he accused outside journalists of fostering "bitterness and hatred against southern whites" to such an extent that it had become "a national disease."[41]

Other elements of the news media also played a significant part in reporting

39. Marie Antoon, "Civil Rights and Media," in *Encyclopedia of Southern Culture*, ed. Wilson and Ferris, pp. 912–14.
40. Quoted in James L. Baughman, *The Republic of Mass Culture: Journalism, Filmmaking, and Broadcasting in America since 1941* (Baltimore, Md., 1992), p. 109. See also Robert J. Donovan and Ray Scherer, *Unsilent Revolution: Television News and American Public Life, 1948–1991* (New York, 1992), pp. 3–22.
41. Fite, *Richard B. Russell*, p. 411.

the struggle for equal rights in the southern states. In his analysis of congressional reaction to the violence suffered by voting rights demonstrators in Alabama, David J. Garrow stresses the importance of newspaper coverage, especially stories in the *New York Times* and the Washington *Post*. News magazines like *Time*, *Newsweek*, and *U.S. News & World Report* devoted extensive space to articles and photographs about the civil rights movement in the southern region.[42] In short, the news media became the primary instrument in shaping the image of the South in the nation and the world.

Several other events of 1964 and 1965, in addition to the Birmingham demonstrations and the passage of the Civil Rights Act of 1964, reveal the interplay of sectional and national currents at the height of the Second Reconstruction. One of these was the civil rights program conducted by SNCC and other equal rights groups in Mississippi during the summer of 1964. It was called Freedom Summer. Another was the presidential election of 1964. A third was the climactic Selma-to-Montgomery march of the next year, followed by the passage of the Voting Rights Act of 1965. Meanwhile, southern white opposition to the dismantling of Jim Crow continued even as an increasing number of southerners reconciled themselves to the desegregation of the schools and public accommodations and to the enfranchisement of black southerners.

The Mississippi Freedom Summer grew out of an earlier emphasis on black voter registration and the failure of civil rights workers to make much progress in the Magnolia State. Equal rights leaders assumed that the vote would gradually improve the condition of the black masses and provide a political means of attacking both racism and poverty. Southern blacks themselves showed a growing interest in the ballot. Shortly after the November election of 1963 in Mississippi, SNCC leaders devised a Freedom Election to prove that African Americans wanted to vote. On the same day that white Mississippians voted, nearly 80,000 disfranchised blacks cast "freedom ballots." Yet the success of the registration campaign in Mississippi was limited. The Southern Regional Council's Voter Education Project reported that 688,800 blacks had qualified to vote for the first time in the eleven states of the old Confederacy between April 1, 1962, and November 1, 1964. But most of that increase came in urban areas and the upper South. Less than 7 percent of the adult black population of Mississippi was registered in 1964. This led voter-registration leaders to concentrate on exposing the hazards of trying to enfranchise blacks in the state. "The whole of Mississippi became the stage," Neil R. McMillen has written, "its public officials and law-enforcement personnel unwitting, but perfectly cast, villains, its 400,000 disfranchised adult Negroes the principal players, and the nation at large the audience to which 'live' television presentations were offered each evening with the news."[43]

42. Baughman, *The Republic of Mass Culture*, pp. 109–11; David J. Garrow, *Protest at Selma: Martin Luther King, Jr., and the Voting Rights Act of 1965* (New Haven, Conn., 1978), pp. 78–84, 161–69; Richard Lentz, *Symbols, the News Magazines, and Martin Luther King* (Baton Rouge, La., 1990).

43. Neil R. McMillen, "Black Enfranchisement in Mississippi: Federal Enforcement and Black Protest in the 1960s," *Journal of Southern History* 43 (August 1977): 364. See also John Dittmer, "The

In 1964 the Council of Federated Organizations (COFO), a coalition of civil rights groups such as SNCC and CORE, launched the Mississippi Freedom Summer Project. A massive voter registration drive, the undertaking was designed to attract national attention to the repressive means used to prevent blacks from voting, in part by exposing northern students to the dangers blacks faced on a daily basis. Although many white Americans scarcely noticed the discrimination and brutality habitually experienced by black Mississippians, they could be expected to express alarm and hostility at such treatment of young northern volunteers. Almost a thousand such students participated in "Freedom Summer" of 1964, while another 650 persons included clergymen, volunteer lawyers, and medical specialists who provided support for the project participants. Most of the young volunteers were white, sons and daughters of middle- and upper-middle-class America, students in major colleges and universities, idealists committed to the cause of racial justice. To these volunteers, Mississippi stood as "the living embodiment of the [American] potential for inhumanity and injustice"—as "mute testimony to the changeless quality of the 'Southern Way of Life.' "[44]

The student volunteers were assigned to projects scattered over the state but they were most numerous in the heavily black population of the Mississippi Delta. Living in rural areas and hamlets, they busied themselves in working for voter registration, political organization, and the operation of "freedom schools." The climax of their voter enrollment campaign was a challenge to the state Democratic party delegation to the Democratic national convention in Atlantic City. Their activities brought fierce opposition from local whites and the death of at least four volunteers, the beating of eight workers, a thousand arrests, and the bombing or burning of more than sixty black churches, businesses, and homes. One student of Freedom Summer says that most of the volunteers left Mississippi "politically radicalized and intent on carrying on the fight in the North."[45]

Events in Mississippi also tended to involve and radicalize the parents of the student participants. They were horrified by the murder of three volunteers early in the project, not to mention the arrests or beatings of their own sons and daughters and the failure of the Justice Department to protect the civil rights workers. Often prodded by memos from SNCC, the parents besieged their congressmen and the Department of Justice with letters and telephone calls demanding protection for the volunteers, disseminated information about the Mississippi project to local newspapers and radio and television stations, and organized their own support groups. The unfolding drama in Mississippi became the nation's top news story that summer. As one of the students wrote in

Politics of the Mississippi Movement, 1954–1964," in *The Civil Rights Movement in America*, ed. Charles W. Eagles (Jackson, Miss., 1986), pp. 65–93.

44. Doug McAdam, *Freedom Summer* (New York, 1988), p. 24.

45. *Ibid.*, pp. 66–118 (quotation on p. 117). See also Mary Aickin Rothschild, *A Case of Black and White: Northern Volunteers and the Southern Freedom Summers, 1964–1965* (Westport, Conn., 1982); Carson, *In Struggle*, pp. 111–29; McMillen, "Black Enfranchisement in Mississippi," pp. 364–68; Sitkoff, *The Struggle for Black Equality*, pp. 169–75; and Weisbrot, *Freedom Bound*, pp. 92–100.

his journal on June 25, 1964, "We were all watching the CBS TV show—about 100 of us. . . . Walter Cronkite told how the whole country was watching Mississippi. And then the television was singing our freedom song, 'We shall overcome, we shall overcome. . . .' So we all joined hands and sang with the television. We sang with all our hearts—'justice shall be done . . . we shall vote together . . . we shall live in freedom. . . .' "[46] In a sense, sociologist Doug McAdam has written, "the entire country had visited Mississippi courtesy of the national news media. And given the editorial tone of most of the coverage, many of those who visited vicariously came away with a generally favorable view of the civil rights movement, college students, and activism in general."[47] In the meantime, millions of nonsoutherners were drawn into a position of sympathetic approval of, if not active participation in, the civil rights movement. They were influenced not only by the attitude and behavior of their sons and daughters, and by the examples of college students and other civil rights workers, including dedicated black southerners, but also by the role of their own churches, professional organizations, labor unions, and civic and political leaders. For a moment, at least, they became part of an overriding national commitment to racial justice in America.

By the summer of 1964, persistent attacks on voter registration workers and acts of racist terrorism, in Mississippi and elsewhere in the South, increasingly threatened constitutional rights, held out the possibility of widespread lawlessness, and challenged the emphasis of the Johnson administration on the importance of local responsibility for law enforcement and the futility of federal prosecutions in the South. The result was another crisis in the nation's federal system. Southern leaders had long insisted that the federal system ruled out any national interference in southern law enforcement, indeed, that the abdication of state and local authority in this realm would destroy American federalism. Yet the movement to expand rights for black southerners inevitably raised the pressing question of what the national government should do about racial violence in the South. The federal policy of refusing to assume responsibility in dealing with anti–civil rights violence was, as one scholar has noted, "a casualty of the bloody Freedom Summer of 1964."[48]

President Dwight Eisenhower had made no move to challenge the doctrine of federal nonintervention until forced to do so in the Little Rock school crisis of 1957. His administration did accept the relatively mild anti-bombing provisions included in the Civil Rights Act of 1960. Eisenhower's successor, John F. Kennedy, was also reluctant to make use of federal force, partly because he hoped to avoid alienating the Democratic South. But he found it necessary on several occasions to use federal force to protect the victims of violent resistance to racial change. His administration was more active in pushing for black voter registration and in voting rights litigation. As for the pleas of civil rights workers

46. Quoted in McAdam, *Freedom Summer*, p. 71.
47. *Ibid.*, pp. 116–18 (quotation on p. 118).
48. Michal R. Belknap, *Federal Law and Southern Order: Racial Violence and Constitutional Conflict in the Post-Brown South* (Athens, Ga., 1987), pp. ix–xi, 128–29 (quotation on p. xi).

for protection from white intimidation and violence in the South, the administration, in Michal R. Belknap's words, "spurned these calls for help, responding to them only with rhetorical hand-wringing and further obeisance to the supposed demands of federalism."[49] The violence and murder that accompanied the Mississippi Summer Project compelled Washington to search for new ways of maintaining law and order in the South.

President Johnson, having committed himself to the central goals of the civil rights movement and with the enactment of a comprehensive civil rights law in sight, was willing to act. Suddenly, the Federal Bureau of Investigation began to assume a more vigorous role, conducting an all-out search for the bodies of James Chaney, Andrew Goodman, and Michael Schwerner, arresting those suspected of murdering them, and launching an attack on the Ku Klux Klan. The Justice Department initiated federal cases against the alleged murderers of the three civil rights volunteers and against those accused of slaying a black army reserve officer in Georgia. The Supreme Court lent its assistance by reinterpreting old laws and the Constitution so that the prosecution could proceed. Federal prosecution brought convictions of some of those tried for murders in Georgia and Mississippi, and a federal jury returned guilty verdicts against klansmen in Alabama for a murder there in 1965. Congress, reacting to these developments and to the president's strong support, passed a sweeping statute in 1968 that expanded federal authority to punish anti–civil rights violence.[50]

Hoping to attract broad support for his Great Society reform program and to win a great triumph in the election of 1964, Lyndon Johnson pursued the

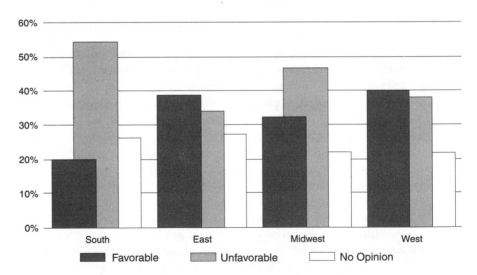

What Is Your Opinion of LBJ's Great Society Program? 4 December 1966. SOURCE: George Gallup, *The Gallup Poll: Public Opinion, 1935–1971*, vol. 3 (New York: Random House, 1972), pp. 2038–39.

49. *Ibid.*, pp. 27–127 (quotation on p. 106).
50. *Ibid.*, pp. 128–82, 205–28.

politics of consensus with extraordinary energy and skill. Although he stressed his role as the national leader of all the people, he faced a serious problem in his own region, where many white southerners opposed the new civil rights legislation and were disturbed by the president's liberal policies. The party images of southerners between 1961 and late 1964 changed dramatically. An analysis of interviews conducted in 1964 by the Survey Research Center of the University of Michigan revealed that the proportion of southern blacks with strongly pro–Democratic party images had more than doubled during this period, from 24 to 52 percent, while the proportion of southern whites with strongly pro–Republican party images had doubled, from 9 to 18 percent.[51] During the campaign of 1964, Johnson appealed for unity and party loyalty on the part of southern Democrats, and on one occasion, in New Orleans, he sought to call forth the South's "finest instincts" in defending his administration's support of civil rights. It was time, he declared, for southerners to hear "a Democratic speech" about helping the common people, instead of only "Negro, Negro, Negro!" at election time.[52]

While Johnson was consolidating his national leadership, the two political parties were making preparations for the presidential election of 1964. The Republicans, torn by internal conflict and upset by the resurgence of Democratic strength, turned abruptly from the moderate course followed by their presidential candidates since 1940 and began a militantly conservative campaign to regain the White House. The GOP right wing found a political figure to rally around in Senator Barry M. Goldwater of Arizona. The South and the "heartland" of the Midwest were of vital importance in the movement for Goldwater's nomination. Conservative sentiment in the South, exacerbated by the civil rights demonstrations and increasingly opposed to the liberal Democratic administrations in Washington, was attracted to Goldwater. An early indication of this conservative response came in the midterm elections of 1962, when Senator Lister Hill of Alabama was almost defeated by James D. Martin, a staunch Republican conservative, and Senator Olin D. Johnston of South Carolina was seriously challenged by another Republican conservative, William D. Workman, Jr.[53] Southern Republicans were leaders in winning control of their party's machinery for the senator from Arizona. The outspoken Goldwater, an advocate of state rights and an opponent of federal civil rights legislation, received enthusiastic backing from white southerners. "We're not going to get the Negro vote as a bloc in 1964 and 1968," Goldwater had asserted in 1961, "so we ought to go hunting where the ducks are."[54] The best prospects were among the growing number of politically alienated southerners. When the

51. Meanwhile, the proportion of southern whites with pro–Democratic party images declined from 62 to 52 percent. See Donald R. Matthews and James W. Prothro, *Negroes and the New Southern Politics* (New York, 1966), pp. 385–86.

52. Roman Heleniak, "Lyndon Johnson in New Orleans," *Louisiana History* 21 (Summer 1980): 274.

53. Walter Dean Burnham, "The Alabama Senatorial Election of 1962: Return of Inter-Party Competition," *Journal of Politics* 26 (November 1964): 798–829.

54. Quoted in Black and Black, *The Vital South*, p. 150.

GOP national convention met, Goldwater was nominated on the first ballot and was given a platform decidedly more conservative than that of the Democrats. He received the vote of virtually every southern delegate. During the campaign he pursued what came to be called "the southern strategy" in appealing to the region's disaffected whites.[55]

As the campaign began, it was clear that President Johnson would face strong opposition from southern white voters, particularly in the lower South. Senator Strom Thurmond of South Carolina left the Democrats and joined the "Goldwater Republican party." Governor Wallace of Alabama was so disillusioned with the Johnson administration that he opposed the president's nomination in several northern primaries, although he eventually gave up the venture, apparently in order to allow southern conservatives to rally behind Goldwater in the November election. The Alabama governor's impressive showing in these primaries suggested that his opposition to federal civil rights legislation and other features of the Great Society appealed to many voters outside the South. Johnson also encountered other regional problems. When the regular Mississippi delegation to the national convention was challenged by the insurgent, largely black Mississippi Freedom Democratic party (MFDP), Johnson's lieutenants worked out a compromise that permitted the regular delegates to take their seats if they would sign a party loyalty pledge and surrender two convention seats to the challenging group. Although the insurgents refused this token recognition, they were able to tell their story to millions of Americans during nationally televised credentials hearings.

The credentials committee's recommendation, that in the future a state must ensure that "all voters, regardless of race, color, creed or national origin, will have the opportunity to participate fully in party affairs," was one of the antecedents of the delegate-selection reforms adopted at the Democratic national convention in 1972. On the other hand, the civil rights workers in Mississippi, who had enrolled almost 60,000 disfranchised blacks in the MFDP, were offended and discouraged by the way they were patronized and manipulated by the president and other national party leaders. And, ironically, when the regular party delegates returned to Mississippi, a majority of them opposed Lyndon Johnson.[56]

Johnson won the election by a landslide, carrying forty-four states and 61 percent of the popular vote. He won eight southern states. The president was helped by the endorsement he received from the party organization in several southern states, and he was given overwhelming support by the region's black voters. Many southerners, black and white, were impressed by Johnson's accomplishments and were put off by Goldwater's impulsive pronouncements about the desirability of selling the Tennessee Valley Authority, abandoning

55. See Bernard Cosman, *Five States for Goldwater: Continuity and Change in Southern Presidential Voting Patterns* (University, Ala., 1966).

56. Jack Bass and Walter DeVries, *The Transformation of Southern Politics: Social Change and Political Consequence Since 1945* (New York, 1976), pp. 204–205; Sitkoff, *The Struggle for Black Equality*, pp. 179–86; McAdam, *Freedom Summer*, pp. 118–22; Weisbrot, *Freedom Bound*, pp. 114–23; Lawson, *Running for Freedom*, pp. 100–104.

farm subsidy and social security programs, and undertaking a more vigorous war in Vietnam. Nor did the Republican nominee benefit substantially from the anticipated backlash among northern whites, despite riots in several cities outside the South in the summer of 1964 and evidence that some nonsoutherners were opposed to the course of the civil rights movement. Goldwater was essentially a sectional candidate.[57]

Senator Goldwater made his best showing in the South. He carried five Deep South states (winning 87 percent of the votes in Mississippi) and only his home state of Arizona outside the southern region. The race question was an ever-present concern in the lower South. As one historian has said of Louisiana, the state "seemed engulfed by a wave of pro-segregationist and anti-Johnson feelings that fall."[58] According to the novelist Walker Percy's interpretation of the vote in Mississippi, "it would not have mattered if Goldwater had advocated the collectivization of the plantations and open saloons in Jackson; he voted against the Civil Rights bill and that was that."[59] The perception of Goldwater as the segregation candidate clearly influenced many white voters in the Deep South, although the continuing rebellion against the national Democratic party was a motivating factor as well. Polling data revealed that nearly nine of every ten white southerners thought that the civil rights movement was proceeding too fast and were opposed to the use of busing to achieve racial balance in the schools. "By coming south," the journalist Richard H. Rovere suggested, "Barry Goldwater had made it possible for great numbers of unapologetic white supremacists to hold great carnivals of white supremacy."[60] Surveys of white voters outside the South showed that Johnson received 91 percent of the vote cast by Democrats, 69 percent of that by independents, and 27 percent of that by Republicans—an overwhelming Democratic victory. Unlike the Republican pattern in the three previous elections, Goldwater's greatest southern strength lay in the old Dixiecrat belt and in the rural areas generally. But he carried an estimated 55 percent of southern white voters, and a startling 71 percent of such voters in the Deep South. For the first time in American history, the Republican party had won a larger percentage of the popular vote in the ex-Confederate states than in any other region.[61] Moreover, for the first time in U.S. history, the GOP had played the role of the "traditional" party of the South.[62]

Despite the efforts of SNCC and other civil rights organizations, the voter registration drives in the South had achieved only modest success by the fall of 1964. The Mississippi Summer Project and other enfranchisement campaigns demonstrated the continuing resistance to black voter registration and made it clear to civil rights leaders that, as long as they were denied the ballot, the harassment and mistreatment of black southerners would go on. The Civil

---

57. Matusow, *The Unraveling of America*, pp. 131–52.
58. Heleniak, "Lyndon Johnson in New Orleans," p. 269.
59. Quoted in Goldfield, *Black, White, and Southern*, p. 196.
60. Quoted in Black and Black, *The Vital South*, p. 151.
61. *Ibid.*, pp. 147–58, 199–210.
62. Cosman, *Five States for Goldwater*, p. 55.

Rights Act of 1964 seemed unlikely to remove such obstructions to the ballot box as literacy tests, discriminatory treatment by local registrars, economic pressure, and intimidation. Late in 1964, Martin Luther King, Jr., and other members of SCLC worked out plans to arouse the nation to the need for a national voting rights law. They planned a series of demonstrations centering in Selma, Alabama, in the heart of the black belt. They anticipated that these non-violent protests would meet violent resistance, that indignant Americans in other sections would demand "federal intervention and legislation," and that the Johnson administration, under mass pressure, would quickly intervene and sponsor a "remedial" law.[63]

Speaking in Selma early in January 1965, King announced a "determined, organized, mobilized campaign to get the right to vote everywhere in Alabama." If necessary, he continued, "we will seek to arouse the Federal Government by marching by the thousands to the places of registration. We must be willing to go to jail by the thousands. We are not asking, we are demanding the ballot."[64] Dallas County, in which Selma was located, had a black majority but only 325 Negroes were registered to vote, as compared with 9,800 whites. In some other black belt counties, not a single black man or woman was entitled to vote. King and his associates spent two months leading black people—eventually hundreds of them—to the courthouse to register and staging demonstrations in the area. Few were allowed to register, many were assaulted by Sheriff Jim Clark's men and white onlookers, and about two thousand of them were jailed. Frustrated by these developments, King called for a "march on the ballot boxes throughout Alabama," moving from Selma to Montgomery, the state capital, fifty-four miles away. Governor Wallace refused to permit such a march, and when the demonstrators tried to proceed without his approval on March 7, they were savagely attacked by men with clubs, whips, and tear gas.

Pictures on national television and in newspapers portrayed an appalling scene of white violence and black helplessness and fear. The White House was inundated with demands for federal intervention, and within two days of the assaults Selma was denounced in fifty congressional speeches. The president finally stepped in, federalizing the Alabama National Guard, and the march, involving thousands of black and white participants, was completed between March 21 and 25, culminating in a great civil rights gathering at the Alabama capitol. The dramatic events that unfolded in and around Selma represented a peak experience in the civil rights movement and set the stage for congressional action on voting rights legislation.[65]

Having become committed to the passage of an effective voting rights statute, Lyndon Johnson addressed a nationally televised joint session of Congress on March 15, 1965, to urge prompt passage of such legislation. He had become convinced that the ballot was indispensable for black integration into American

63. Fairclough, *To Redeem the Soul of America*, pp. 225–30.

64. *Ibid.*, p. 229.

65. *Ibid.*, pp. 230–51; Garrow, *Bearing the Cross*, pp. 357–430; Sitkoff, *The Struggle for Black Equality*, pp. 187–96; Weisbrot, *Freedom Bound*, pp. 128–49.

society. Two days later he submitted a carefully developed proposal to Congress. From March until August, the voting rights coalition maintained its impetus. It was a bipartisan effort, under the zealous eye of the president and with important assistance from the Leadership Conference on Civil Rights and other groups. The Senate adopted a cloture motion on May 25—the second one in two years—and the bill was passed on the following day. The House, after rejecting a weaker Republican substitute, passed a similar measure on July 9, and after a compromise was worked out by the conference committee of the two houses, the president signed the bill early in August. Most of the negative votes on final passage were cast by southerners, although thirty-six representatives and a few senators from the South voted for the bill.[66] One historian notes that the act "enjoyed broader, more sustained public support than any previous civil rights measure" and that the struggle for its passage "fit perfectly with the liberal call for expanded federal action to protect the rights of all citizens."[67]

The Voting Rights Act of 1965 called for direct federal action to enable blacks and other disfranchised citizens to register and vote. It empowered the attorney general to appoint federal examiners to supervise voter registration in states or voting districts where a literacy test or similar qualifying devices existed or where fewer than 50 percent of the voting-age residents had voted or were registered to vote in the presidential election of 1964. This brought the federal registration machinery to bear on seven southern states—Alabama, Georgia, Louisiana, Mississippi, South Carolina, Virginia, and twenty-six counties in North Carolina.[68] To register under the new law, an applicant merely had to fill out a simple form (with assistance from a registrar if necessary), giving name, age, length of residence, and whether he or she had ever been convicted of a felony. Stiff penalties were provided for interference with voter rights. Justice Department officials moved cautiously in implementing the new statute, hampered in the beginning by subterfuge and lack of cooperation on the part of many local officials in the Deep South. Nevertheless, the Voting Rights Act has been aptly described as "the grand turning point in modern times for the reentry of blacks into southern politics."[69] The number of black voters in the region increased by more than a million between 1964 and 1968. This dramatic growth was accompanied by an equally sharp increase in white registration. Federal intervention in the 1960s also resulted in the invalidation of the poll tax as a voting requirement and the reapportionment of legislative and congressional seats.

Within a year or two, the Second Reconstruction lost its momentum. Black

66. For the legislative history and significance of the statute, see Garrow, *Protest at Selma*, pp. 31–132; Graham, *Civil Rights and the Presidency*, pp. 87–98; Matusow, *The Unraveling of America*, pp. 180–216; Steven F. Lawson, "Civil Rights," in *The Johnson Years, Volume One: Foreign Policy, the Great Society, and the White House*, ed. Robert A. Divine (Lawrence, Kans., 1987), pp. 93–125; and Steven F. Lawson and Mark I. Gelfand, "Consensus and Civil Rights: Lyndon B. Johnson and the Black Franchise," *Prologue* 8 (Summer 1976): 65–76.

67. Weisbrot, *Freedom Bound*, pp. 152–53.

68. Alaska and one county each in Arizona, Idaho, and Maine were also affected.

69. Earl Black and Merle Black, *Politics and Society in the South* (Cambridge, Mass., 1987), p. 136.

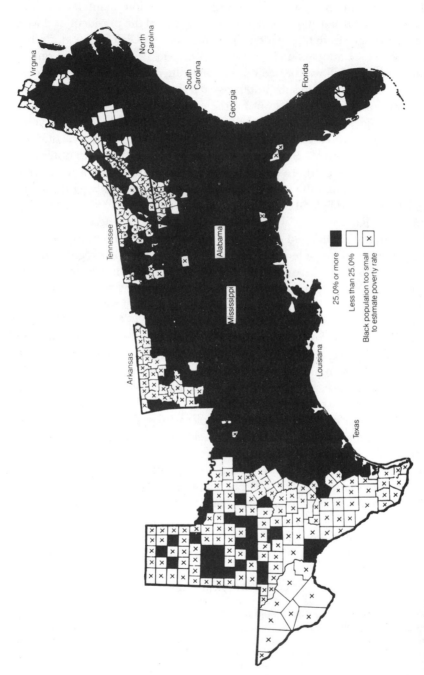

The Geography of Black Poverty. Southern counties in 1969 in which at least 25 percent of African-American families reported incomes below the poverty level. SOURCE: Earl Black and Merle Black, *Politics and Society in the South* (Cambridge, Mass.: Harvard University Press, 1987), p. 165.

impatience and white resistance grew even as the structure of legal segregation was being dismantled. Internal division and conflict destroyed the unity of the civil rights movement, as more militant groups parted company with moderate leaders and organizations. Stokely Carmichael, the new chairman of SNCC, transformed that group into an all-black organization. Frustration and rage found expression in "black power," which embodied racial pride and solidarity, as well as an angry reaction against nonviolence as a tactic and integration as a goal. "Shattering the fragile alliance of civil rights forces," Clayborne Carson notes, "the black power upsurge challenged the assumptions underlying previous interracial efforts to achieve national civil rights reforms."[70] In the meantime, President Johnson's increasing preoccupation with the war in Vietnam both weakened the Great Society and absorbed the energies of many reformers and their organizations. Racial tension mounted throughout the country, and by the summer of 1966 a "white backlash" was evident in many northern and midwestern areas; "law and order" emerged as a major political issue.[71] *The Report of the National Advisory Commission on Civil Disorders* in 1968, the work of a special commission appointed by President Johnson and headed by Otto Kerner, a former governor of Illinois, cited the growing concentration of blacks in cities; the chronic discrimination and segregation in employment, education, and housing; the oppressive effects of ghetto life upon the young and the increase in crime, drug addiction, and welfare dependency; and the fact that two million "hard-core disadvantaged" urban blacks were making no real economic gains.

By early 1967, the civil rights movement seemed to have lost its steam and much of its support. While urban riots raged out of control during the following summer, the House of Representatives voted down rent subsidy and rat control legislation. The assassination of Martin Luther King, Jr., on April 4, 1968, touched off the most widespread rioting that had yet occurred in African-American areas and contributed further to black disillusionment and alienation. The murder of Robert F. Kennedy a few weeks later also dealt the civil rights cause a heavy blow. King's assassination did help bring the passage of the Civil Rights Act of 1968, which featured a much-discussed fair housing provision. The challenge to Lyndon Johnson's renomination in 1968, first by Senator Eugene McCarthy of Minnesota and then by Senator Robert Kennedy of New York, the reassessment of the administration's policies in Vietnam, and the president's decision not to run for reelection cast a shadow on Johnson's leadership and the Democrats as the party of reform. Meanwhile, Democratic prospects in the South were dimmed by a number of unfavorable developments.

In the Deep South several governors were carrying on a war against the national party. In Congress southern Democratic dissidence manifested itself in hostility to urban social and welfare programs, opposition to increased federal spending and federal services, and concern for state control of various

70. Carson, *In Struggle*, p. 215. See also Fairclough, *To Redeem the Soul of America*, pp. 309–31, and Matusow, *The Unraveling of America*, pp. 347–75.
71. Lawson, *Running for Freedom*, pp. 117–34; Sitkoff, *The Struggle for Black Equality*, pp. 199–224.

programs. This southern defiance of national Democratic policies also found expression in the growing strength of the conservative coalition in the late 1960s. Controversies over the recognition and seating of Alabama, Georgia, and Mississippi delegations, leading to the unseating of some regular delegates, as well as the nomination of Hubert H. Humphrey and Senator Edmund S. Muskie as the party's standard-bearers, alienated many southern Democrats, as did the platform's strong endorsement of civil rights. Many other Americans were appalled by a series of acrimonious and bloody clashes that took place in downtown Chicago between youthful antiwar demonstrators and the city police. "I have about given up hopes of ever really reforming the Democratic Party," Richard Russell informed a constituent late in the campaign. "We have to live with it as it is. It has been an oil and water mixture and, if Humphrey wins . . . I am afraid that you will not see a housecleaning job but only the spreading on of several new layers."[72]

Even more ominous for the Democrats was George C. Wallace's decision to bolt the party and run for president as the head of the America Independent party. Wallace had become the most compelling politician in the region and a symbol of resistance to civil rights throughout the South. His appeal was especially great among white southerners deeply committed to rural and traditional values. The Alabama governor explained his appeal as resulting in part from his role in restoring confidence and pride to southerners, who had long resented the criticisms, sneers, and patronizing attitude of outsiders. Wallace developed surprising strength in 1968, not only among white southerners but also among blue-collar workers and the lower middle class in other regions, where rising tension between whites and blacks was apparent. The Wallace movement was basically a reaction against the racial changes associated with the Great Society. Displaying a quick wit and a folksy speaking style, the Alabamian campaigned throughout the country. He liked to assert that there was not "a dime's worth of difference" between the two major parties. His jibes at the "pointy-headed bureaucrats" and the "intellectuals who look down their noses at you" were calculated to take advantage of the "white backlash" as well as the growing sense of alienation, resentment against demonstrators, and feeling of powerlessness among blue-collar workers, rural dwellers, and hard-pressed members of the lower middle class. Early in the fall Wallace was receiving more than 20 percent of the preference votes in public opinion polls.[73]

Wallace's new third party also alarmed Republican leaders in the South, where the minority party had high hopes for electoral success in 1968. Former vice president Richard M. Nixon, who became the party's presidential nominee, employed a "southern strategy" in appealing to white southerners by expressing agreement with them on issues like the use of busing as a means of achieving school desegregation and a get-tough policy against crime and dis-

72. Richard B. Russell to John H. Dillard, 30 October 1968, Richard B. Russell Papers, University of Georgia Library.

73. Jody Carlson, *George C. Wallace and the Politics of Powerlessness: The Wallace Campaigns for the Presidency, 1964–1976* (New Brunswick, N.J., 1981), pp. 27–132; Marshall Frady, *Wallace*, enlarged and updated (New York, 1976); Black and Black, *The Vital South*, pp. 161–69.

order. Southern influence was an important factor in Nixon's nomination and also in the choice of Governor Spiro T. Agnew of Maryland for vice president. The Republican platform emphasized an "all-out" attack on crime, reform of the welfare laws, an end to inflation, and a stronger national defense.[74]

Although Humphrey and Muskie managed to bring a measure of unity to their party and to mount an effective appeal to labor unions and working-class people outside the South, often at the expense of Governor Wallace, they lost to Nixon and Agnew in a close election in November. The southern states played a vital role in the Republican victory. Nixon carried six states in the peripheral South, plus South Carolina, while Wallace won the other four Deep South states as well as Arkansas. Humphrey captured only one southern state— Texas, where Johnson's vigorous support probably made the difference. Nixon and Wallace both received a larger percentage of the southern vote than Humphrey, whose strongest support came from southern blacks. In addition to carrying five southern states, Wallace influenced GOP leaders throughout the region to move closer to his own position. The defections that began with the Dixiecrat revolt of 1948 had culminated in an almost solid non-Democratic South.[75]

Somewhat surprisingly, the waning of the Second Reconstruction owed more to rising resistance in the North and West than to the attitudes and behavior of southerners. By the mid-1960s, the struggle for black equality was moving northward. Black leaders challenged residential segregation, poor schooling, high unemployment among racial minorities, and alleged police brutality. Efforts to integrate public schools in these nonsouthern areas met mounting white resistance. "So long as school desegregation was considered a 'Southern problem,' " C. Vann Woodward remarked, "the heat was on. . . . Once it appeared that the courts were going to move against *de facto* school segregation in Northern cities, however, the commitment to integration quickly cooled." Yet it was clear that school desegregation was more than a "southern problem." Many of the old southern arguments began to reemerge "from Northern mouths."[76] A white backlash spread through the North and West, fueled by a wave of urban riots, demands for "black power," and the proposal of new remedies for racial discrimination that seemed to go beyond the national consensus in favor of equality. Enthusiasm for the Second Reconstruction declined sharply among white Americans.[77]

Many people outside the South sympathized with the southern resistance to school desegregation and the demands of the equal rights demonstrators. This was apparent in the surprising strength George Wallace showed in 1964, when

74. Stephen E. Ambrose, *Nixon: The Triumph of a Politician, 1962–1972* (New York, 1989), pp. 133–222.

75. Black and Black, *The Vital South*, pp. 298–303; Matusow, *The Unraveling of America*, pp. 395–439.

76. Woodward, *The Strange Career of Jim Crow*, pp. 216–17 (quotation on p. 216).

77. Carson, *In Struggle*, pp. 229–303; Weisbrot, *Freedom Bound*, pp. 262–87; James W. Button, *Black Violence: Political Impact of the 1960s Riots* (Princeton, N.J., 1978); Joseph Boskin and Robert A. Rosenstone, eds., *Seasons of Rebellion: Protest and Radicalism in Recent America* (Lanham, Md., 1980).

he challenged President Johnson's consensus politics in the Democratic presidential primaries of Wisconsin, Indiana, and Maryland, and four years later when he ran for president as an independent candidate. In earlier years southern congressional leaders had been able to count on support from conservative Republicans in other regions in preventing the passage of civil rights legislation. But more recently, according to some southern leaders, northern whites had been misled by agitators and the media. In the early 1960s, for example, Richard B. Russell received letters from other regions expressing agreement with and appreciation of his last-ditch efforts to prevent the enactment of a comprehensive civil rights bill. Russell interpreted this reaction as evidence that "thinking Americans" throughout the country saw the dangers in such legislation.[78]

On August 11, 1965, five days after the president signed the Voting Rights Act, a terrible race riot broke out in Watts, a black community in Los Angeles. It resulted in thirty-four deaths, four thousand arrests, and millions of dollars lost to property damage. It was Watts that first aroused Americans to the danger of large-scale ghetto violence. It revealed a growing mood of frustration, bitterness, and anger among northern blacks, highlighted interracial tensions, and contributed to the alienation of white sympathizers throughout the nation. The Watts uprising and more than a hundred others that exploded in U.S. cities over the next three years reflected the urban decay, high unemployment, inadequate housing, discrimination at the hands of employers and labor unions, and increasing segregation in urban America. Between 1940 and 1960 more than five million southerners left their native region, and the exodus continued through the 1960s. Over a million black migrants from the South moved into crowded northern ghettos during the 1960s, and neither expanded federal programs nor private efforts did much to improve conditions there. "For black migrants," Jacqueline Jones writes, "Northern workplaces often seemed to recapitulate historic Southern patterns of racial prejudice. . . . In the Midwest, countless Southern black migrants watched poorly educated whites from Kentucky or Tennessee take advantage of skin color and kin ties to secure jobs, confirmation of the fact that all blacks would be prevented 'from making our fullest contribution—not for lack of ability but for lack of whiteness.' "[79] It was ironic that, at the very time the civil rights movement was gaining momentum, the American suburban explosion was heightening the separation of the races. As Richard Polenberg has written, "The process of suburbanization, it turned out, was strengthening the de facto basis for racial segregation even as judicial rulings, militant protest, congressional action, and executive intervention were weakening its de jure basis."[80] The black influx led to conflict between the new arrivals and recent ethnic groups still struggling to attain their own economic

78. Fite, *Richard B. Russell*, pp. 411–12; David D. Potenziani, "Look to the Past: Richard B. Russell and the Defense of Southern White Supremacy" (Ph.D. dissertation, University of Georgia, 1981), pp. 126, 148, 272, 277.

79. Jacqueline Jones, *The Dispossessed: America's Underclasses from the Civil War to the Present* (New York, 1992), pp. 224, 234–35 (quotation).

80. Richard Polenberg, *One Nation Divisible: Class, Race, and Ethnicity in the United States Since 1938* (New York, 1980), p. 153.

and social security. Since a majority of the black migrants came from the South, northerners often associated ghetto problems with the South and the notion of "the South within the North."[81]

The outbreak of race riots in northern and western cities in the mid-1960s coincided with—and was no doubt related to—the shift in the focus of the civil rights movement from the South to the North. As this happened other changes were also discernible in the civil rights movement: the move from a religious to a secular emphasis, from nonviolence and integration to greater militancy and black separatism, from attacking the immorality of segregation to a harsh critique of the economic and social order. By the time of the climactic riots in Detroit and Newark in 1967, the extent of northern opposition to the demands of the civil rights advocates was unmistakably clear. When Martin Luther King, Jr., tried to transfer his nonviolent protest movement to Chicago in 1966, he suffered a frustrating setback. As one historian observes, "SCLC discovered in Chicago that discrimination was a far more insidious and tenacious enemy than segregation."[82] Reflecting on this example of northern racial prejudice, King confessed that "I've never seen anything like it. I've been in many demonstrations all across the south, but I can say that I have never seen—even in Mississippi and Alabama—mobs as hostile and as hate-filled as I've seen in Chicago."[83]

Many white northerners viewed the ghetto riots as evidence of black ingratitude, since they themselves in large numbers had supported the earlier objectives of the equal rights movement. But now the reformers were going beyond the overthrow of Jim Crow to demand things like jobs, open housing, and better schools. By 1968 the Equal Employment Opportunity Commission had shifted the focus of its hearings to white-collar discrimination in the North and West. White southerners soon saw the anomaly of the South's lagging behind the North in the matter of race riots. One gleeful reaction was, "Well, for once, we've got the niggers and the Yankees fighting each other. Now maybe they'll leave us alone."[84] Northern resistance to the demands for racial equality was apparent in the long struggle by the Johnson administration and its liberal backers, in and out of Congress, to enact a new federal law against racial terrorism and an end to housing discrimination. Southern congressmen led the opposition but with vigorous assistance from many of their northern colleagues, who seemed to be more interested in punishing urban rioters than in protecting civil rights workers in the South or guaranteeing open housing. Collaboration between North and South repeatedly stymied the bill's passage, and only King's

81. C. Vann Woodward, *American Counterpoint: Slavery and Racism in the North-South Dialogue* (Boston, 1971), pp. 7–8.

82. Fairclough, *To Redeem the Soul of America*, pp. 279–307 (quotation on p. 307); Garrow, *Bearing the Cross*, pp. 431–74, 489–525.

83. Quoted in Weisbrot, *Freedom Bound*, p. 183. For King's protest movement in Chicago, see James R. Ralph, Jr., *Northern Protest: Martin Luther King, Jr., Chicago, and the Civil Rights Movement* (Cambridge, Mass., 1993).

84. Quoted in Pat Watters, *The South and the Nation* (New York, 1969), p. 39. See also Graham, *Civil Rights and the Presidency*, pp. 124–27.

assassination in April 1968 and a new outbreak of rioting across the country made possible the approval of the Civil Rights Act of 1968.[85]

Northern opposition to school desegregation was also pronounced. Powerful northern and western political leaders such as Mayor Richard J. Daley of Chicago used their influence to weaken the desegregation guidelines set forth by the Department of Health, Education and Welfare. At the beginning of the 1960s, seventy-five of Detroit's public schools were all white and eight were all black; thirty-one had at least a 90 percent white student enrollment and seventy had at least a 90 percent black enrollment. Critics of the school administration's policies charged that, as blacks moved westward in the 1950s, school authorities redrew the boundaries of the school districts so as to maintain a pattern of segregation. By the mid-1970s, the Supreme Court had begun to limit the use of busing as a means of achieving racial balance in the schools; it had decided that the nation's suburbs were not obligated to share either their children or their wealth with nearby urban blacks in the quest for educational equality. De facto segregation was widespread. In the mid-1970s, for example, 90 percent of the schoolchildren in Wilmington, Delaware, were nonwhite, while 90 percent of those elsewhere in New Castle County were white. At that time, 259 of Chicago's 537 schools reported enrollments of 90 percent or more blacks, while 109 other schools had enrollments that were 90 percent or more white. So it went across the country.[86]

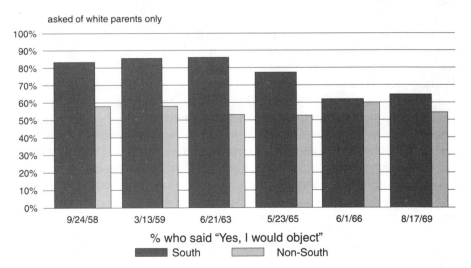

Would You Object to Your Child Attending Schools with A MAJORITY of Blacks? Source: George Gallup, *The Gallup Poll: Public Opinion, 1935–1971*, vol. 3 (New York: Random House, 1972), pp. 1569, 1598, 1824, 1941, 2010, 2211.

85. Belknap, *Federal Law and Southern Order*, pp. 207–28.
86. For this paragraph and the one that follows, see Sidney Fine, *Violence in the Model City: The Cavanagh Administration, Race Relations, and the Detroit Riot of 1967* (Ann Arbor, Mich., 1989), p. 8; Richard Kluger, *Simple Justice: The History of Brown v. Board of Education and Black America's Struggle for Equality* (New York, 1976), pp. 769–73, 777–78; Raymond Wolters, *The Burden of Brown: Thirty*

The de facto nature of segregation outside the South made it exceedingly difficult to bring about genuine integration of the public schools in those areas. Southern congressmen, eager to arouse northern opposition to school integration, tried unsuccessfully to secure the adoption of legislation calling for uniform federal action against racial segregation in all parts of the country, whatever its source. In addition, the concept of "affirmative action" provoked resistance from white Americans. Most whites, North and South, opposed any kind of preferential treatment—viewing it as reverse discrimination—and rejected any program that established a fixed number of positions, or quotas, for minorities as a violation of the historic American principle of equal opportunity. A survey carried out in 1972 showed that 82 percent of the nation's whites opposed affirmative action plans that favored blacks over equally qualified whites.

Richard M. Nixon's southern strategy of 1968 and later years was based upon the assumption that millions of Americans, north and south of the Mason-Dixon line, shared a broad agreement on the "excesses" of the civil rights movement. During the campaign of 1968, Nixon spoke out against court-ordered busing, took a tough stand on crime, and went to great lengths to satisfy the demands of conservative Republicans like Senator Strom Thurmond. As president, Nixon opposed busing, sought to delay the progress of school desegregation, encouraged private segregated schools, and attempted to place a "strict constructionist" southerner on the Supreme Court. Meanwhile, he tried to take advantage of the backlash against rising crime rates, campus disorders, black militancy, and moral permissiveness, appealing not only to white southerners but to "white ethnics," who were deeply disturbed by the social ferment of the late 1960s and early 1970s. In the election of 1972, Nixon swept the country, winning large percentages of southern whites, blue-collar workers, Catholics, and other ethnic groups. Surveys revealed that former Wallace voters went to Nixon by a margin of three to one in the South and six to five in the North. It appeared that the president had indeed found a formula to enhance intersectional unity in national politics. Another meaning of the election, as Vann Woodward has noted, seemed to be "an end to the crusade against Jim Crowism."[87]

Thus, by the end of the Second Reconstruction, regional differences over the meaning of race in America had been substantially narrowed. Attitudes and practices involving race were now similar throughout the nation, many non-southerners had experienced a "loss of innocence" in their racial assumptions, and the pejorative stereotypes associated with the racist South had begun to dissipate. But if the Second Reconstruction encouraged a process of convergence in the thinking and behavior of northerners and southerners on racial matters—a process that brought changes on both sides—it was the South that

Years of School Desegregation (Knoxville, Tenn., 1984), p. 175; Melvin I. Urofsky, *The Continuity of Change: The Supreme Court and Individual Liberties, 1953–1986* (Belmont, Calif., 1991), pp. 233–34; and Lawson, *Running for Freedom*, pp. 197–98.

87. Woodward, *The Strange Career of Jim Crow*, p. 214. Also see Black and Black, *The Vital South*, pp. 246–48, 303–306, and Ambrose, *Nixon: The Triumph of a Politician*, pp. 579–652.

experienced the most profound social change. Though racial prejudice remained pervasive in the South, as elsewhere in the United States, the elaborate structure of Jim Crow was torn down. Southern schools became the most desegregated in the country. Fearful of a breakdown of law and order in their communities, southerners themselves assumed much of the responsibility for controlling and punishing racial violence.[88] The enfranchisement and empowerment of black southerners, along with reapportionment of legislative seats and other reforms, transformed and democratized the region's politics. The white South had always wanted to show the North a thing or two but, as the journalist Pat Watters once remarked, "it was the persecuted black South that kept doing it."[89] One aspect of this dramatic political transformation was the reversal of the historic roles the major parties had played since Reconstruction. Increasingly the Republican party became the party of white southerners, at least in presidential elections, while the Democratic party became the party of blacks and liberal whites. The preemption of the race issue by their Republican adversaries forced Democratic leaders in the South to cultivate a politics of black and white coalitions and to accept blacks in the party's organization and leadership.

In the years that followed, racial polarization in politics, resegregation of the schools, and the worsening plight of a black underclass seemed to mock the idealistic hopes of the Second Reconstruction. Problems of black poverty, illiteracy, and hopelessness confronted northerners and southerners alike. Racial inequality and injustice still plagued all parts of the country. Some observers suggested that the South had begun to adopt the subtle ways of racial discrimination in the North.[90] Perhaps so, but the nationalization of the "race problem" did a great deal to nationalize the thinking of southerners. Nor was that all. The reversal of the flow of black migrants from the southern states seemed to indicate that life below the Potomac now offered opportunities and satisfactions scarcely imaginable in the era of Jim Crow. That was a significant measure of the enduring changes wrought by the Second Reconstruction. One feature of the new regional environment was the South's economic expansion and diversification.

88. See Belknap, *Federal Law and Southern Order*, pp. 229–51.
89. Watters, *The South and the Nation*, p. 328.
90. See, for example, Richard Current, *Northernizing the South* (Athens, Ga., 1983), p. 113.

CHAPTER 10

The Sunbelt South

In 1971 two sociologists with an interest in the American South published an article on the region's transformation since the 1930s and what they called its "national incorporation." Citing the South's industrialization, occupational redistribution, income, and education, they depicted a region that was rapidly abandoning its "geographic, mental, and social" isolation and being fully integrated into the larger American system. Writing several years later, an economic historian observed that "it is now virtually impossible to find an essentially regional southern identity in economic life."[1] The theme of regional convergence emphasized by these scholars, a theme that found expression in the commentaries of other students of the postwar South, reflected the region's astonishing economic expansion and social metamorphosis in the years after 1940. In the process the contrasts and disparities between North and South receded, although differences remained along with recurrent sectional conflicts and rivalries. But for many southerners good times and a booming economy seemed to be the realization of the old dream of a triumphant New South.

The vision of a New South based on the region's economic regeneration had inspired southern leaders since the days of Henry W. Grady, and for almost three-quarters of a century the doctrine of industrialization, economic diversification, and outside investment was viewed by southerners as the surest means of overcoming their inferior position in the nation. The southern economy did respond to this incentive, but in the period before the Second World War it remained an economy dominated by agriculture and low-wage extractive industries. It was basically a colonial appendage of the more highly developed Northeast and Midwest, with a depressed and isolated labor system. As late as

1. John C. McKinney and Linda Brookover Bourque, "The Changing South: National Incorporation of a Region," *American Sociological Review* 36 (June 1971): 399–412; Gavin Wright, *Old South, New South: Revolutions in the Southern Economy Since the Civil War* (New York, 1986), p. 241 (quotation).

1945, per capita income in the South was only about half that of the national average. Then economic progress came with a rush. The stimulus of World War II and the prosperity of the postwar era created a milieu in which the regional economy experienced unprecedented growth and diversification.

Revolutionary changes in agriculture made up a significant part of the South's postwar economic transformation. Within a generation the structure of the region's agriculture was profoundly reshaped. The number of farmers in the South plummeted, the number of farms declined sharply while the average size of those that remained steadily increased, the production of cotton and other traditional crops gave way to new farm commodities, and farming became more capital-intensive, more centralized in operation, more mechanized and scientific, and more efficient and productive. Sharecroppers and tenants almost disappeared. The Great Depression and the New Deal farm policies helped set some of these changes in motion, and the disruption of the war gave them added momentum. The increasing capitalization and mechanization of southern agriculture, along with employment opportunities in the cities, furthered the process. Federal policies and the organizational strength of the American Farm Bureau Federation enhanced the position of large-scale commercial agriculture in the South.[2] Reflecting on these changes, one historian writes, "The vigorous work cultures that thrived at the turn of the century have withered. Farm work, like factory work, has become specialized, mechanized, and sapped of the human relations that blessed and cursed the rural South."[3]

The number of farmers in the ex-Confederate states shrank from 2.1 million in 1950 to 720,000 in 1975, while the average size of the region's farms increased from 93 acres to 216 acres during this period. Over a million farm families were displaced altogether between 1945 and 1969, and between 1940 and 1980 almost 14 million people left the farms of the southern states. By 1960 only 10 percent of the southern population was still working in agriculture. Crop diversification was vividly illustrated in the shift from cotton and corn to soybeans, livestock, dairy and poultry products, and tree farming. By 1975 not a single southern state ranked cotton first in marketing receipts. "As the traveler of the 1970s rode north from New Orleans to Virginia," one scholar observes, "he saw about him vast stretches of green fields and grazing cattle, broken only by tracts of timber, where a few years before he would have seen cotton fields and pine barrens."[4] Increasingly the small farmer and the family-size farm, in the South as elsewhere in the United States, disappeared from the rural scene. Meanwhile, the highly capitalized and business-oriented planter profited, not

2. Charles P. Roland, *The Improbable Era: The South since World War II* (Lexington, Ky., 1975), pp. 20–26; Theodore Saloutos, "Agricultural Organizations and Farm Policy in the South After World War II," *Agricultural History* 53 (January 1979): 377–404; Gilbert C. Fite, "Mechanization of Cotton Production Since World War II," *Agricultural History* 54 (January 1980), 190–207; Charles Reagan Wilson, "Agribusiness," in *Encyclopedia of Southern Culture*, ed. Charles Reagan Wilson and William Ferris (Chapel Hill, N.C., 1989), pp. 13–15.

3. Pete Daniel, *Breaking the Land: The Transformation of Cotton, Tobacco, and Rice Cultures since 1880* (Urbana, Ill., 1985), p. 298.

4. Roland, *The Improbable Era*, p. 21.

only because of his scientific efficiency but also because of high price supports southern congressmen helped guarantee from the federal government. Many of these producers were involved in what came to be known as "agribusiness," the large-scale and vertically integrated control, frequently through corporations, of the production, processing, and marketing of agricultural commodities.[5] The dramatic restructuring of southern agriculture since the 1930s, for all its costs in human suffering, relieved the economy of its dependence on an inefficient farm system.

Industry boomed in the postwar South. Between 1939 and 1972, the number of factories in the region grew by more than 200 percent. The South's share of new capital investment in manufacturing increased from about 25 percent in 1939 to 38 percent in 1976, and the southern growth rates for manufacturing industries after 1960 surpassed those for the non-South by substantial margins. The southern states enjoyed an overall relative gain of approximately 1.7 million employees in the manufacturing sector between 1957 and 1979. Some of this growth took place in older industries such as textiles, coal, and steel, but the boom was also evident in defense industries, construction, food processing, and consumer durables. Newer industries such as petrochemicals and automobile components emerged. Commerce and trade flourished, including international trade in the seaboard cities.[6] "In the South," the journalist Marshall Frady later wrote, "the land of Canaan came to consist of a horizon of smokestacks. Industrialization—the devout acquisition of factories—became a kind of second religion there: the secular fundamentalism."[7]

Industrialization was not directly linked to the rapid urbanization of the postwar South, although the two proceeded in tandem. The military installations and defense industries of the Second World War quickened the pace of urban growth in the region, as did the increase in mobility and the depopulation of the countryside following the war. New transportation and communications technologies facilitated the rise of this urban South. Between 1940 and 1960 the South's population shifted from 65 percent rural to 58 percent urban, and by the 1980s three-fourths of all southerners were classified as urban dwellers, not very different from other Americans.[8] The landscape of southern cities,

5. Gilbert C. Fite, *Cotton Fields No More: Southern Agriculture, 1865–1980* (Lexington, Ky., 1984), pp. 180–231; Daniel, *Breaking the Land*, pp. 239–98; Wilson, "Agribusiness," pp. 13–15.

6. James C. Cobb, *Industrialization and Southern Society, 1877–1984* (Lexington, Ky., 1984), pp. 39–67; Robert J. Newman, *Growth in the American South: Changing Regional Employment and Wage Patterns in the 1960s and 1970s* (New York, 1984), pp. 5, 12, William J. Cooper, Jr., and Thomas E. Terrill, *The American South: A History*, 2 vols. (New York, 1991), vol. 2, pp. 758–61; E. William Noland, "Industry Comes of Age in the South," *Social Forces* 32 (October 1953): 28–35; Robert Estall, "The Changing Balance of the Northern and Southern Regions of the United States," *Journal of American Studies* 14 (December 1980): 365–86; John M. Maclachlan and Joe S. Floyd, Jr., *This Changing South* (Gainesville, Fla., 1956).

7. Quoted in Cobb, *Industrialization and Southern Society*, p. 2.

8. Cobb, *Industrialization and Southern Society*, p. 53; Blaine A. Brownell, "Urbanization," in *Encyclopedia of Southern Culture*, ed. Wilson and Ferris, pp. 1438–41; Joseph Persky, "The Dominance of the Rural-Industrial South, 1900–1930," *Journal of Regional Science* 13 (December 1973): 409–19; Leonard Reissman, "Urbanization in the South," in *The South in Continuity and Change*, ed. John C. McKinney and Edgar T. Thompson (Durham, N.C., 1965), pp. 79–100; Randall M. Miller, "The

increasingly like their northern and western counterparts, underwent dramatic changes with the appearance of shopping malls, apartment complexes, subdivisions, and traffic loops, as well as inner-city decay and noisome ghettos. The age of the metropolis had arrived in the South. By 1980 the population of Atlanta, Houston, and Dallas-Fort Worth had grown to more than two million each, and eleven metropolises in the ex-Confederate states were listed among the nation's fifty most populous cities. Although the South was still more rural than the rest of the country, it had experienced "a pervasive standardization of entertainment, information, architecture, and expectations."[9]

By the 1970s, Americans outside the South had begun to view the southern region in a new and more appreciative light. This changing perspective was related to the South's burgeoning economy, population growth, racial change, and political transformation. Commentators identified the South with the so-called Sunbelt, a dynamic area stretching from the South Atlantic states to southern California. Definitions of the Sunbelt varied, but most interpreters identified the concept with an expanding southern and southwestern region characterized by a casual and inviting lifestyle, a favorable climate, and a conservative politics increasingly inclined toward the Republican party. As Blaine A. Brownell puts it, "Here interstate highways, satellite relays, lower taxes, the relative absence of labor unions, a good climate, more land, and a 'better quality of life' underwrote a shift in population from the Northeast and Midwest to the South and Southwest."[10] Newspapers and journals in the North suddenly discovered the South's attractions and the "good life" it had to offer. In 1976, for example, in what seemed to be a banner year for selling the Sunbelt, *U.S. News & World Report* published numerous enthusiastic articles about the region, including one headlined "The New South: Pushing Forward on All Fronts."[11] "For the first time since the Civil War," an urban historian writes, "the idea of a Sunbelt allowed the newest New South to deny its dependence on and subordination to the North. . . . In a sense, the idea of a Sunbelt allowed the South to escape its own history and to transform [itself] instantly from a 'backward' to a 'forward' region."[12]

Southerners were inclined to attribute their region's economic expansion in

Development of the Modern Urban South: An Historical Overview," in *Shades of the Sunbelt: Essays on Ethnicity, Race, and the Urban South*, ed. Randall M. Miller and George E. Pozzetta (New York and Westport, Conn., 1988), pp. 1–20.

9. Blaine A. Brownell, "Introduction," in *Searching for the Sunbelt: Historical Perspectives on a Region*, ed. Raymond A. Mohl (Knoxville, Tenn., 1990), p. 6. See also Bradley R. Rice, "Searching for the Sunbelt," in *ibid.*, pp. 212–21, and Richard M. Bernard and Bradley R. Rice, eds., *Sunbelt Cities: Politics and Growth since World War II* (Austin, Texas, 1983).

10. Brownell, "Urbanization," p. 1438. See also Estall, "The Changing Balance of the Northern and Southern Regions," pp. 365–86, and James R. Adams, "The Sunbelt," in *Dixie Dateline: A Journalistic Portrait of the Contemporary South*, ed. John B. Boles (Houston, 1983), pp. 141–44.

11. Gene Burd, "The Selling of the Sunbelt: Civic Boosterism in the Media," in *The Rise of the Sunbelt Cities*, ed. David C. Perry and Alfred J. Watkins (Beverly Hills, Calif., 1977), pp. 129–49 (quotation on p. 140).

12. Carl Abbott, "New West, New South, New Region: The Discovery of the Sunbelt," in *Searching for the Sunbelt*, ed. Mohl, p. 16.

263

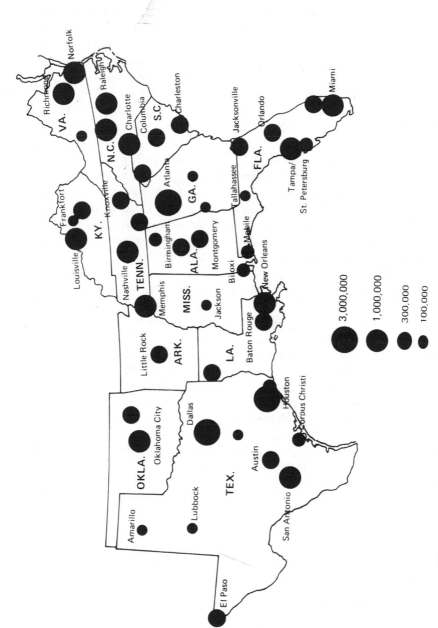

Population of Southern Urban Areas, 1980s. SOURCE: William J. Cooper, Jr., and Thomas E. Terrill, *The American South: A History*, vol. 2 (New York: McGraw-Hill, 1991), p. 658.

considerable part to its natural resources and energy reserves. As the *Report on Economic Conditions of the South* noted in 1938, "The paradox of the South is that while it is blessed by Nature with immense wealth, the people as a whole are the poorest in the country. Lacking industries of its own, the South has been forced to trade the richness of its soil, its minerals and forests, and the labor of its people for goods manufactured elsewhere."[13] The region's natural environment contained extensive forests, abundant water, and much open space. In an optimistic essay written in 1958, the historian Walter Prescott Webb emphasized the great potential of the South's renewable resources, farmland, rainfall, and long growing season.[14] In the 1970s the region provided more than a third of the nation's commercial timberland and almost the same percentage of its electric generating capacity; it produced 65 percent of U.S. crude petroleum.[15] The South also had a warm and inviting climate, a significant factor in its acquisition of military installations, new industry, tourism, and increasing population. Relatively inexpensive railroad transportation, the new interstate highway system, and the rapid shift to other shipping modes made these resources more accessible. The air-conditioning revolution had worked its magic throughout the southern states by the 1970s, drastically changing the environment, encouraging the growth of population, and accelerating the Americanization of Dixie.[16]

Population growth was a major factor in the emergence of the Sunbelt phenomenon. Since midcentury the South has been the second fastest-growing region behind the West, and in less than a generation the southern states moved from a heavy net migration loss to a very large gain. Between 1970 and 1975, nearly a million more people left the Northeast for the South than moved in the opposite direction. During the years 1975–1980, the South enjoyed a net gain of 800,000 migrants from the Northeast, 700,000 from the Midwest, and 160,000 from the West. Black in-migration lagged behind that of whites, but by the mid-1970s the South was gaining black migrants from each of the nation's other major regions. Foreign immigration was also becoming more important in a few southern states, most notably Mexicans in Texas and Cubans and other Caribbean newcomers in Florida.[17]

The character of this in-migration was also changing. Younger, better-

13. National Emergency Council, *Report on Economic Conditions of the South* (Washington, D.C., 1938), p. 8.

14. Walter Prescott Webb, "The South and the Golden Slippers," *Texas Quarterly* 1 (Spring 1958): 11–13.

15. Cobb, *Industrialization and Southern Society*, p. 57.

16. Mancur Olson, "The South Will Fall Again: The South as Leader and Laggard in Economic Growth," *Southern Economic Journal* 49 (April 1983): 929–32; Rembert W. Patrick, "The Mobile Frontier," *Journal of Southern History* 29 (February 1963): 3–18; Raymond Arsenault, "The End of the Long Hot Summer: The Air Conditioner and Southern Culture," *Journal of Southern History* 50 (November 1984): 597–628.

17. Bernard L. Weinstein and Robert E. Firestine, *Regional Growth and Decline in the United States: The Rise of the Sunbelt and the Decline of the Northeast* (New York, 1978), pp. 1–5, 10; Curtis C. Roseman, "Migration Patterns," in *Encyclopedia of Southern Culture*, ed. Wilson and Ferris, pp. 551–52; Rex R. Campbell, Daniel M. Johnson, and Gary Stangler, "Return Migration of Black People to the South," *Rural Sociology* 39 (Winter 1974): 514–28.

educated persons began to move south, and the migrants included a growing number of managers, technicians, and skilled workers. While economic opportunities drew these people southward, they were also attracted by the quality of life the region afforded—by the moderate climate, recreational opportunities, low crime rate, and lower cost of living. In 1976, for example, a family of four at a middle-income budget level required 36 percent more income in the Boston metropolitan area than in Austin, Texas.[18] In the meantime, the South became a haven for elderly Americans. In contrast to its earlier pattern of age distribution, the region by 1970 led the nation in the percentage of its residents over sixty-five. Florida, first in the nation in this respect, was the most spectacular magnet for this incoming stream. These older migrants often transformed both the nature of southern old age and the communities in which they resided.[19]

Abundant natural resources, an increasing population, and an inviting lifestyle were not alone responsible for the South's economic growth in the postwar period. Nor was this expansion altogether the result of manufacturing growth since the war. Several southern states had earlier developed a significant manufacturing sector, as well as an expanding commercial economy, a larger tax base, and more generous public services. Per capita income in most southern states was increasing faster than in the nation as a whole. In short, the South in the late-nineteenth and early-twentieth centuries had begun to acquire the infrastructure, institutions, skills, and habits necessary for rapid industrialization.[20]

The vision of a New South based on industrialization and a diversified economy continued to inspire southern leaders. Writing in 1961, the historian George B. Tindall remarked that the promotion of industry had become "almost the central theme of Southern history in the past two decades, despite spectacular headlines about more stirring events."[21] By midcentury the southern states had turned with renewed energy to the task of "selling the South" to outside industrialists and entrepreneurs. Governors, legislators, mayors, industrial development commissions, chambers of commerce, and newspapers joined in the effort. In earlier years the southern obsession with industrialization had resulted in what one scholar described as a "chaotic, hell-for-leather scramble for industrial payrolls."[22] But following the war a well-organized though highly competitive search for industrial plants took shape. Its organizational aspects were anticipated by an experiment Mississippi undertook in the 1930s

18. Weinstein and Firestine, *Regional Growth and Decline in the United States*, p. 26.

19. *Ibid.*, pp. 25–26; Carole Haber, "Elderly," in *Encyclopedia of Southern Culture*, ed. Wilson and Ferris, pp. 1539–40.

20. See in this connection Peter A. Coclanis and Lacy K. Ford, "The South Carolina Economy Reconstructed and Reconsidered: Structure, Output, and Performance, 1670–1985," in *Developing Dixie: Modernization in a Traditional Society*, ed. Winfred B. Moore, Jr., Joseph F. Tripp, and Lyon G. Tyler, Jr. (New York and Westport, Conn., 1988), pp. 93–110, and David L. Carlton, "The Revolution from Above: The National Market and the Beginnings of Industrialization in North Carolina," *Journal of American History* 77 (September 1990): 445–75.

21. George B. Tindall, "The South: Into the Mainstream," *Current History* 40 (May 1961): 270.

22. James C. Cobb, "The Sunbelt South: Industrialization in Regional, National, and International Perspective," in *Searching for the Sunbelt*, ed. Mohl, p. 29.

known as the Balance Agriculture with Industry (BAWI) program. Under this plan the state authorized and supervised the use of municipal industrial bonds to finance plant construction and start-up.[23]

State-approved industrial bonds as a means of recruiting industry from other regions and abroad were widely used in the postwar years. By the early 1960s, the southern states accounted for an estimated 87 percent of the industrial development bonds issued in the United States. There were other subsidies as well, including tax exemption, free plant sites, and special training programs. Industrial parks were established by local development corporations, for lease to new plants on attractive terms. Georgia had more than a hundred such parks by 1960. In the mid-1960s most southern communities could claim at least one industrial development organization. In small towns and rural areas, clusters of counties began to join together to form development districts, with each district having its own planning staff to survey needs, make recommendations, and negotiate with interested firms.[24]

In addition to these inducements, the South offered other attractions to cost-conscious industrialists. Low corporate taxes, which had once been the highest in the nation, appealed to outside companies, as did state and local governments that tended to be conservative and pro-business. It was not an environment that fostered the growth of labor unions. In fact, organized labor in the South lagged far behind that of other regions, even though the labor movement made modest gains in the postwar period. By the 1950s, virtually every southern state had enacted a right-to-work law, with an eye to the preferences of industrialists looking south. In the early 1970s, U.S. Department of Labor statistics showed that the average annual pay for workers in right-to-work states was 16 percent lower than for workers in all other states. Anti-labor policies were not the only barriers to unionization in the South, but such measures clearly discouraged the growth of labor organizations in the region. In the 1980s fewer than 10 percent of southern textile workers belonged to independent unions. One reason for the weakness of organized labor below the Potomac—and for the failure of a more vigorous labor tradition to take root in the South—was the persistent charge by industrial promoters that labor unions would handicap the economic development of the region. In many cases the workers themselves feared that joining a union would mean closing their plant.[25] By the end of the 1970s, one writer remarks, "antiunionism had sup-

23. James C. Cobb, *The Selling of the South: The Southern Crusade for Industrial Development, 1936–1980* (Baton Rouge, La., 1982), pp. 5–34.

24. Cobb, *The Selling of the South*, pp. 35–50; Cobb, *Industrialization and Southern Society*, pp. 27–50; Roland, *The Improbable Era*, pp. 12–14; David R. Goldfield, *Promised Land: The South Since 1945* (Arlington Heights, Ill., 1987), pp. 27–33; John Fischer, "Georgia: Mother of Social Invention," *Harper's Magazine* 244 (March 1972): 10–20.

25. Cobb, *The Selling of the South*, pp. 96–121; Cobb, *Industrialization and Southern Society*, pp. 88–98; F. Ray Marshall, *Labor in the South* (Cambridge, Mass., 1967), pp. 246–331; Marshall, "Organized Labor," in *Encyclopedia of Southern Culture*, ed. Wilson and Ferris, pp. 1395–98; "Workers' Compensation: Understanding the Problem," Southern Regional Council, *Legislative Bulletin* No. 13 (Summer 1993): 9. See also Barbara S. Griffith, *The Crisis of American Labor: Operation Dixie and the*

The Democratic ticket in 1960: Senators John F. Kennedy of Massachusetts and Lyndon B. Johnson of Texas. (*Lyndon Baines Johnson Library*)

President John Fitzgerald Kennedy and his closest adviser, Attorney General Robert Francis Kennedy. (*John F. Kennedy Library/Imagefinders, Inc.*)

A new president assumes office aboard Air Force One, Dallas, Texas, November 22, 1963. (*Lyndon Baines Johnson Library*)

President Johnson makes a point in meeting with black leaders Roy Wilkins (on left) and Martin Luther King, Jr. (*Photograph by Yoichi R. Okamato, courtesy Lyndon Baines Johnson Library*)

Senator Richard B. Russell presides over the southern caucus resisting passage of civil rights legislation. (*U.S. Senate Historical Office*)

President Johnson addresses a joint session of Congress on March 15, 1965, urging passage of a federal voting rights law. (*Photograph by Cecil Stoughton, courtesy Lyndon Baines Johnson Library*)

Lyndon works on Ev: The president applies the LBJ treatment to Everett M. Dirksen, the Senate minority leader. (*U.S. Senate Historical Office*)

Richard B. Russell, spearhead of the opposition in the Senate to civil rights laws. (*U.S. Senate Historical Office*)

J. William Fulbright of Arkansas, chairman of the Senate Committee on Foreign Relations and, after the escalation of the war in Vietnam in 1965, a strong critic of President Johnson's policies in Southeast Asia. (*U.S. Senate Historical Office*)

Inauguration of the thirty-seventh president, January 20, 1969. (*U.S. Senate Historical Office*)

Senator Sam J. Ervin of North Carolina presides over the Watergate hearings in 1973. Senator Howard H. Baker of Tennessee (on left) was the ranking Republican member of the Ervin committee. (*U.S. Senate Historical Office*)

Senator Ervin goes after President Nixon with the notorious White House tapes. (*Cartoon by Ranan R. Lurie. Copyright by Cartoonews International Syndicate, N.Y.C., USA. Courtesy U.S. Senate Historical Office*)

The president and his lady walk down Pennsylvania Avenue on January 20, 1977. (*Jimmy Carter Library*)

By Draper Hill in the *Detroit News.* © 1977, reprinted with permission.

Ronald Reagan and George H. W. Bush: Republicans in the White House, 1981–1993.
(*The Library of Congress*)

Bill Monroe (third from left) and the Bluegrass Boys, 1989. (*Photograph by Paul F. Wells, courtesy Center for Popular Music, Middle Tennessee State University*)

Country music stars: Johnny Cash and June Carter Cash. (*Center for Popular Music, Middle Tennessee State University*)

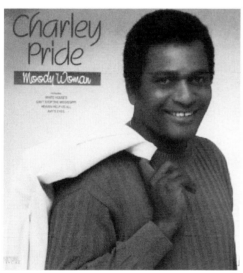

Charley Pride. (*Courtesy Opryland Music Group, Inc.*)

Black gospel music rendered by the Fairfield Four. (*Photograph by Paul F. Wells, courtesy Center for Popular Music, Middle Tennessee State University*)

Jerry Falwell, famous televangelist and founder of the Moral Majority. (*Courtesy Liberty University, Lynchburg, Virginia*)

Ted Turner, Atlanta-based media entrepreneur and influential figure in southern culture. (*Photograph by George Bennett, courtesy Turner Broadcasting System, Inc.*)

planted racism as the South's most respectable prejudice."[26]

Thus selling the South to northern industrialists and investors seemed to require a variety of subsidies, pro-business policies, enticing advertisements, and the wooing of outside entrepreneurs—all essential elements of a successful promotional campaign. The most prominent participants in these campaigns were southern governors, most of whom became tireless missionaries in the quest for new plants and firms. Some, like Luther H. Hodges and Terry Sanford of North Carolina, became supersalesmen of their individual states' special attractions and business opportunities. Governor Hodges traveled more than 67,000 miles in the search for new industries in 1959 alone. Dixie governors became frequent visitors to the offices of northern—and foreign—business firms. One author wrote facetiously of a particular governor's visit:

SECRETARY: There's a salesman here to see you.
MANAGER: Does he have an appointment?
SECRETARY: No.
MANAGER: What's he selling?
SECRETARY: A state.
MANAGER: A what? Who is he?
SECRETARY: He claims he's the governor.[27]

News that a governor had "bagged" an industry, observes James C. Cobb, "often seemed to be perceived as a sectional victory for the southern underdogs over the rich and powerful Yankees. Many southern editors and politicians delighted in baiting northern leaders who complained about such industrial 'piracy.' "[28]

Southern promotional campaigns apparently paid off. One example was the small industrial city of Spartanburg, South Carolina. Mobilized by an energetic chamber of commerce leader, the city by 1973 had brought in twenty-four foreign companies, employing 4,000 local workers. Its location in the center of the American textile industry was important. But a journalist noted that the city could also offer "cheap land, no inventory taxes on manufactured goods warehoused in the state, a five-year moratorium on some property taxes, little unionization and, best of all, a unique series of state-supported technical education centers that would train workers for specific jobs at no cost to the companies involved."[29] A leading student of this period concluded that "the South's growth was closely related to its ability to provide a highly desirable combina-

Defeat of the CIO (Philadelphia, 1988), and Gilbert J. Gall, *The Politics of Right to Work: The Labor Federations as Special Interests, 1943–1979* (New York and Westport, Conn., 1988).

26. Cobb, *The Selling of the South*, p. 259.

27. Quoted in *ibid.*, p. 74. See also Cobb, *Industrialization and Southern Society*, p. 50; Roland, *The Improbable Era*, pp. 12–13; and Goldfield, *Promised Land*, pp. 145–52.

28. Cobb, *Industrialization and Southern Society*, p. 46.

29. Roul Tunley, "In Spartanburg, The Accent Is on Business," *Reader's Digest,* January 1974, pp. 165–68 (quotation on p. 167).

tion of markets, cheap labor, low taxes, and cooperative state and local governments."[30] Despite many successes, the South's pursuit of new industry did not
always add to its economic vitality. Many of the new plants represented foot-
loose industries engaged in low-wage, labor-intensive manufacturing.

Seeking to attract more sophisticated industrial and commercial concerns,
southern leaders turned to the improvement of education and the provision of
advanced technological facilities as a more promising approach. As early as
1946, the National Planning Association created a Committee of the South,
which sponsored a series of research projects, one of which resulted in the 1951
publication of *Economic Resources and Policies of the South*, by Calvin B. Hoover and
B. U. Ratchford. The Southern Research Institute was established in Birmingham soon after the end of the war, and in 1948 the Southern Regional Education Board (SREB) made its appearance with headquarters in Atlanta. The
SREB, an experiment in regional cooperation, was inspired in part by the conviction that the region's rapid industrialization and urbanization required improvement in the quality of its higher education. Beginning in 1958, the Inter-
University Committee for Economic Research on the South commissioned
another group of publications on the region's economic development. Late in
the 1950s, North Carolina leaders launched a plan designed to take advantage
of the research potential of the Raleigh-Durham-Chapel Hill area, where three
major universities were concentrated. The resulting Research Triangle Park
offered facilities and support to enterprises dependent upon advanced research
and high technology. Firms such as General Electric, Union Carbide, and Atlantic Refining, as well as several government agencies, speedily moved into the
Research Triangle. Similar research centers soon appeared throughout the
country, including several other southern states.[31]

If southern promoters were prepared to enhance their region's educational
facilities as a means of encouraging economic growth, they were also willing,
though sometimes grudgingly, to adopt more controversial reforms for the
same purpose. Apprehensive about the image they projected to outside business
elements, local civic leaders and developers frequently sought to improve their
reputations by working to better the living conditions, public facilities, educational opportunities, and political practices in their communities. A desire for
new and better industry sometimes brought important reforms and innovations. As one student of southern industrialization has said, "Beautification, expansion and improvement of hospitals, parks, and other public facilities clearly
contributed to an improved quality of life for many Dixie residents."[32] A more
clear-cut reform challenge came with the civil rights movement and vehement

30. Cobb, *The Selling of the South*, p. 227.
31. Tindall, "The South: Into the Mainstream," pp. 270–72; Cobb, *The Selling of the South*, pp.
174–77; W. B. Hamilton, "The Research Triangle of North Carolina: A Study in Leadership for
the Common Weal," *South Atlantic Quarterly* 65 (Spring 1966): 254–78; L. V. Berkner, "Educating
Southern Manpower for Technological Change," *South Atlantic Quarterly* 64 (Autumn 1965): 434–
43; E. William Noland, "Technological Change and the Social Order," in *The South in Continuity
and Change*, ed. McKinney and Thompson, pp. 167–97.
32. Cobb, *Industrialization and Southern Society*, p. 117.

white resistance to school desegregation and black protest. The bitter division and social disorder manifested in the Little Rock school controversy of 1957 and in other southern cities in later years had an adverse effect on industrial growth and economic prosperity in those municipalities. This may explain the more moderate course followed by Atlanta, Charlotte, Dallas, and a few other cities. In any case, business leaders and promoters, concerned about the economic consequences of racial friction and social turmoil, were generally active in working to accept at least some racial change. In Jackson, Mississippi, for instance, "When businessmen became convinced that sustained racial upheaval would imperil economic development, they provided a climate for change in southern customs by taking a stand on upholding 'law and order.' "[33] An illuminating study of southern businessmen and school desegregation suggests that, while the region's business leaders did not become advocates of "meaningful desegregation," they did become active agents of change.[34]

One consequence of the rise of the Sunbelt South was the growing convergence of South and non-South—in income and material prosperity, in the character of their economies, in the configuration of their cities, and in the na-

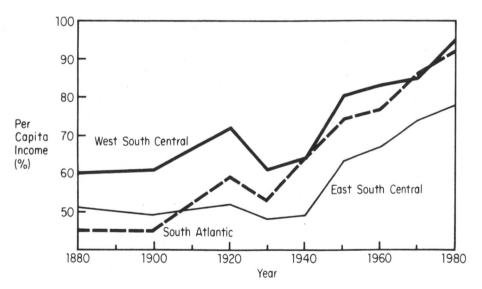

Per Capita Income as Percentage of U.S. Average, 1880–1980. SOURCE: Gavin Wright, *Old South, New South: Revolutions in the Southern Economy Since the Civil War* (New York: Basic Books, 1986), p. 240.

33. Charles Sallis and John Quincy Adams, "Desegregation in Jackson, Mississippi," in *Southern Businessmen and Desegregation,* ed. Elizabeth Jacoway and David R. Colburn (Baton Rouge, La., 1982), p. 247. See also the other essays in this volume, as well as Cobb, *The Selling of the South,* pp. 122–50; Cobb, *Industrialization and Southern Society,* pp. 99–120; M. Richard Cramer, "School Desegregation and New Industry: The Southern Community Leaders' Viewpoint," *Social Forces* 41 (May 1963): 384–89; and G. Donald Jud, "Public Schools and In-migration in North Carolina Counties, 1975–80," *American Journal of Economics and Sociology* 43 (July 1984): 313–22.

34. Elizabeth Jacoway, "An Introduction: Civil Rights and the Changing South," in *Southern Businessmen and Desegregation,* ed. Jacoway and Colburn, p. 5.

ture of the work done by their inhabitants. The North-South wage differential virtually disappeared and the South's "colonial" economy no longer seemed meaningful. The region's long period of economic dependency seemed to be ending. New Deal farm programs and the labor shortages of World War II contributed to the disintegration of southern tenancy and sharecropping, and sent a stream of migrants northward. Federal labor policies, beginning in the 1930s with the establishment of minimum wages, raised the level of base wage rates in the southern states. Following the war, the movement of northern capital to the South also helped end the isolation of the southern labor market. Meanwhile, trends in communications and technology reduced geographic differences generally. The economist Gavin Wright emphasizes the steady movement in recent years toward an integrated national labor market, in which wage and salary differentials reflect only cost of living and locational amenities. "The ironic conclusion to the story," Wright remarks, "is that the only major act of conscious economic suppression by northern forces, the imposition of national wage and labor standards beginning in the 1930s, was the decisive step in abolishing the separate Southern economy."[35]

This suggests that federal policy played a significant part in the emergence of the Sunbelt South, particularly in the creation of development capital and a more expansive consumer market. One illustration of such federal policy was, as Gavin Wright notes, the imposition of national standards in areas like labor conditions and race relations; these standards helped free the South of restraints that limited its economic development and made it more attractive to outsiders. Equally important was federal spending, which brought a sustained infusion of outside capital into the region. Southern congressional leaders, who dominated the committee structure of the two houses and exerted great influence on legislative and executive decisions, were strategically located to protect the interests of their constituents.

Although southern congressmen had discovered the benefits that could be derived from federal expenditures at least as early as the administration of Woodrow Wilson, they were slow in taking full advantage of that source, partly because they feared the consequences of federal intervention. The New Deal, with its multiplicity of federal relief and recovery programs, began to change the southerners' outlook. Increasingly conscious of the South's economic colonialism, some southern leaders began to envisage federal dollars as a means of overcoming the region's lack of development capital. But the fiscal conservatism of many southern congressmen and the region's inability or unwillingness to provide the required matching funds for some federal benefits limited such expenditures in the South. Despite being the poorest section of the nation, the South received the lowest level of federal spending per capita of any region, 84 percent of the national average in the 1930s.[36] The war brought a change.

35. Wright, *Old South, New South*, pp. 239–74 (quotation on p. 270). See also *Joseph J. Persky, The Burden of Dependency: Colonial Themes in Southern Economic Thought* (Baltimore, Md., 1992), pp.143–51.
36. Wright, *Old South, New South*, p. 260. The percentages for other regions during the years 1933–1939 were: Northeast, 88; Midwest, 100; and West, 137.

Southern leaders worked energetically to secure military installations and defense contracts for their states and localities, and federal funds poured into the South in unprecedented amounts. This federal largess continued in the postwar period.

One avenue for the transfer of federal funds to the South was agricultural programs, the tangible benefits of which southerners had realized as far back as Seaman A. Knapp's demonstration work and the development of the agricultural extension system. New Deal programs revealed the possibilities of federal support on a grand scale, support that might help overcome the region's chronic poverty and bring in much-needed capital. Southern congressmen became ardent champions of high price supports and other farm expenditures. During the war and after, they used their powerful positions in Congress to this end. One of the most proficient players in this game was Senator Richard B. Russell of Georgia, who served for many years as chairman of the Appropriations Committee's subcommittee on agriculture. Although Russell became increasingly disenchanted with the liberalism of the Democratic party in the 1950s and 1960s, he never lost his enthusiasm for the pursuit of federal dollars. While he might vote against a particular measure, if it became law, he said, "I take my tin cup and try to fight my way to the head of the line."[37] Results showed that the Georgian was never very far back in the line.

Russell had reason to boast, as he sometimes did, of the federal funds that poured into Georgia as a consequence of his efforts—high price supports for farmers, military installations, research facilities, dams, and other federal projects. He could point to some 60,000 Georgians employed at fifteen military bases in the state, to federal military and civilian payrolls in Georgia of over $1 billion in 1965, and to about $850 million spent by the federal government to harness four of his state's rivers.[38] Southern congressmen worked assiduously to enlarge their share of federal funds for highways, airport systems, education, and public health. As government entitlement programs proliferated, they stressed the principle of equality in the disbursement of federal funds. The South's deficient public services and economic infrastructure clearly benefited from such federal expenditures. The South—and also the West—fared well in terms of federal payments to state and local governments as a percentage of state and general revenues. Between midcentury and the 1970s, the region's share of federal government expenditures per capita grew steadily, virtually to parity by the end of the period.[39]

With the onset of the Cold War, the military became the major representative of the national state in the South—more so than in any other section. Southern influence in the House and Senate Armed Services committees and in Congress generally, the South's long military tradition, and the advantages its

---

37. Quoted in Gilbert C. Fite, *Richard B. Russell, Jr., Senator from Georgia* (Chapel Hill, N.C., 1991), p. 434.

38. *Ibid.*, pp. 301–23, 349–70.

39. It stood at 97 percent for the years 1974–1976. Wright, *Old South, New South*, p. 261. Also see Bruce J. Schulman, *From Cotton Belt to Sunbelt: Federal Policy, Economic Development, and the Transformation of the South, 1938–1980* (New York, 1991), pp. 112–26.

climate and terrain offered for military training all contributed to the region's success in acquiring defense dollars. Encouraged by the long years of the Cold War, the South became the most powerful base of support for the U.S. military buildup. No other part of the country could boast more military, naval, and air installations. In the late 1970s, twenty-four of the nation's forty-six major military posts were located in the South. In 1980, 48 percent of all men and women in the service were in the southern states and Washington, D.C., and at some point in their careers most military personnel were assigned to a southern camp or station. Almost 40 percent of all Department of Defense expenditures went to the South in 1980. In addition, National Aeronautics and Space Administration outlays were primarily directed toward the southern states and Washington, D.C., and the Veterans Administration spent large sums in the South. Although these various expenditures were not evenly distributed among southern states and cities, they represented close to 10 percent of the region's total income and about a third of all federal spending in the South. Southerners had taken a giant step toward the militarization of their economy.[40]

NASA Favors the South. SOURCE: Reprinted from the *Times-Picayune/The States Item,* August 25, 1963.

40. Schulman, *From Cotton Belt to Sunbelt,* p. 135; Thomas J. Anton, "The Regional Distribution of Federal Expenditures, 1971–1980," *National Tax Journal* 36 (December 1983): 429–42; James Clotfelter, "The South and the Military Dollar," *New South* 25 (Spring 1970): 52–56; John Hawkins Napier III, "Military Bases," in *Encyclopedia of Southern Culture,* ed. Wilson and Ferris, pp. 640–41; Alvin R. Sunseri, "Military and Economy," in *ibid.,* pp. 731–32.

Southern enthusiasm for military installations and contracts reflected both the region's traditional military spirit and its commitment to economic expansion. According to a recent study of defense contracting since the beginning of World War II, "Southern politicians, rather than working out a policy to redress low per capita incomes with government-sponsored and regionally targeted industrialization programs, turned instead to the Pentagon, for both the military bases that are disproportionately located in the South and the contracts for everything from uniforms to C-5A transport planes." Thus the South—and the West—"could recruit a highly educated work force at the nation's expense."[41] At the same time, military officers of southern birth and rearing made up a disproportionate percentage of the armed services, and a larger percentage of enlistees came from the South than any other region. Alabama had the largest National Guard in the nation, and in many small southern towns armories and American Legion posts habitually served as social clubs for local men. Though opposition to the Vietnam War damaged the Reserve Officer Training Corps in much of the country, ROTC programs continued to flourish in the South during that long war. Meanwhile, colonies of military retirees sprang up along the Florida coast and in cities like San Antonio and El Paso. Military bases produced their share of friction and antagonism between local residents and "Yankees," especially during World War II and the early postwar years, but in general the camps tended to diminish intersectional prejudices; more often than not the military bases fostered a sense of community among active and former service personnel.[42]

The quest for federal funds and outside investment was strengthened by the rise of what one historian calls new "Whigs" or "business progressives," politicians dedicated to the economic development of the South, skillful in promoting consensus, and moderate on volatile issues such as civil rights. These moderate Whigs bestirred themselves to find the matching funds needed to take advantage of federal programs for highways and other facilities. They understood that the Interstate Highway Act of 1956 could have a profound effect on southern geography and the region's economic growth. They appreciated the fact that military spending sometimes involved complex scientific and engineering work that helped to create new facilities and groups of scientists and engineers and to expand existing ones.[43]

Defense spending and federal expenditures generally should not be exaggerated as a force behind the South's remarkable postwar growth.[44] But the

41. Ann Markusen et al., *The Rise of the Gunbelt: The Military Remapping of Industrial America* (New York, 1991), p. 244.

42. Morris Janowitz, *The Professional Soldier: A Social and Political Portrait* (New York, 1960), pp. 79, 87–89; Napier, "Military Bases," pp. 640–41; Sunseri, "Military and Economy," pp. 731–32.

43. Schulman, *From Cotton Belt to Sunbelt*, pp. 112–34; Cooper and Terrill, *The American South*, vol. 2, p. 762.

44. Wright, *Old South, New South*, p. 262. Weinstein and Firestine, *Regional Growth and Decline in the United States*, p. 65, argue that "market and institutional forces" had a much greater impact on the redistribution of people and economic activity than did federal spending or public policy. For two other dissenting views, see E. Blaine Liner and Lawrence K. Lynch, eds., *The Economics of Southern Growth* (Durham, N.C., 1977), and Clyde E. Browning, "The Role of the South in the Sun

MILITARY PRIME CONTRACT AWARDS, SELECTED
YEARS, FISCAL YEARS 1951–1980—SOUTH AS A
PERCENTAGE OF THE UNITED STATES TOTAL (%)

Fiscal Year	South's Share (%)
1951	7.6
1953	12.5
1955	12.5
1958	16.1
1960	15.3
1963	15.8
1967	23.5
1970	25.4
1975	22.0
1980	24.2

SOURCE: Bruce J. Schulman, *From Cotton Belt to Sunbelt: Federal Policy, Economic Development, and the Transformation of the South, 1938–1980* (New York: Oxford University Press, 1991), p. 140.

historian Bruce J. Schulman argues persuasively that the federal government figured prominently in the South's economic transition during the last half-century, in what Schulman calls the region's odyssey from Cotton Belt to Sunbelt.[45]

It was no doubt inevitable, as southern economic prospects brightened and parts of the Northeast and Midwest began to experience industrial decline and a depressed economy, that regional conflict should develop over the economic effects of various federal policies. In Congress the most sectionally divisive policies in the post–civil rights years were those that channeled federal funds to the industrial core or retarded the shift of population and economic activity to the periphery. An early example in the postwar period was the struggle over industrial decentralization or dispersal as a safeguard against nuclear attack, a proposal endorsed by some military spokesmen. During the Korean War, southern congressmen introduced legislation to require the Department of Defense in awarding contracts to take into account the need for industrial dispersal. Debate on the issue divided lawmakers along sectional lines, with the South and much of the West arrayed against the Northeast and Midwest. The advocates of industrial dispersal, who eventually won, saw their proposal as a means of bettering their economic position at the expense of the more highly industrialized regions.[46]

Belt–Snow Belt Struggle for Federal Funds," in *Perspectives on the American South: An Annual Review of Society, Politics and Culture*, vol. 1, ed. Merle Black and John Shelton Reed (New York, 1981), pp. 253–61.

45. Schulman, *From Cotton Belt to Sunbelt*, pp. 219–21.

46. Roger W. Lotchin, "The Origins of the Sunbelt-Frostbelt Struggle: Defense Spending and City Building," in *Searching for the Sunbelt*, ed. Mohl, pp. 47–68; Richard Franklin Bensel, *Sectionalism and American Political Development, 1880–1980* (Madison, Wis., 1984), pp. 256–316.

Early in the 1950s, a number of depressed northern industries, including New England textiles, turned to Washington for federal assistance. They were encouraged by Defense Manpower Policy Number Four, which made it possible for surplus-labor areas to obtain defense contracts after being informed of low bids and matching such offers. Charges that DMP No. 4 showed economic favoritism to the Northeast led the Truman administration to remove certain industries from the policy, including textiles and shoes. During the congressional debate that ensued, spokesmen for New England cities and industries accused the South of unfair competition, violating the wage standards of the Walsh-Healy Public Contracts Act, and suppressing the development of organized labor. Southern spokesmen, in and out of Congress, defended their region, citing the increase in wages and contending that the South had developed its own industry rather than pirating that of the North. The sectional rhetoric was sometimes bitter. When DMP No. 4 was voted on in the Senate in July 1953, it was defeated. The proposal did not receive a single vote from a southern senator.[47]

Representative John F. Kennedy of Massachusetts and other congressional critics of the South's industrial promotion practices were particularly distressed by the use of public subsidies to lure industries to the South. In 1952 Representative George M. Rhodes of Pennsylvania introduced a bill that would have effectively destroyed the use of municipal bonds as industrial subsidies. Rhodes's bill failed, but it was followed by many other proposals to restrict the employment of industrial development bonds. By mid-1966, fourteen such measures had been introduced to abolish or curtail the issuance of municipal industrial securities. Southern congressional leaders led the opposition to these bills, which made little progress until early 1969. Encouraged by the Treasury Department's decision to remove the tax exemption on industrial development issues larger than $1 million, northern lawmakers moved to give congressional sanction to the Treasury ruling. In the debate that followed, sectional charges and countercharges were made—charges of southern "stealing" of northern industry and of the colonial exploitation of the South by the North. Representative Clement J. Zablocki of Wisconsin declared that northerners were tired "of having our pockets picked in extra taxes to pay the way for tax-exempt bonds for building factories in other states."[48] Others argued that the large industrial issues had forced interest rates up on more "legitimate" municipal securities and that their increasing use was denying the Treasury needed revenue. Congress finally placed the exemption limit at $5 million. But the restriction on bond financing did not end industrial subsidies by southern states and communities.[49]

The expansiveness of the southern economy in the 1970s, in vivid contrast to evidence of economic problems in the industrial North, brought a more spectacular manifestation of interregional rivalry and resentment. For a time, na-

47. Lotchin, "The Origins of the Sunbelt-Frostbelt Struggle," pp. 58–64.
48. Cobb, *The Selling of the South*, pp. 42–46 (quotation on p. 45).
49. *Ibid.*, pp. 45–46.

tional journals carried glowing reports on the South's economic progress. In 1977, for example, an article in *Fortune* magazine proclaimed that "Business Loves the Sunbelt (and Vice-Versa)." But other northern opinion-makers asserted that the South's rise had come at the expense of the North. Kirkpatrick Sale, in his 1975 *Power Shift: The Rise of the Southern Rim and Its Challenge to the Eastern Establishment*, identified the "six pillars" of the Sunbelt's economic power as agribusiness, defense, technology, oil, real estate, and leisure. But he pictured the South as a parasitic region draining away more than its share of federal money. *Business Week* warned in 1976 of "The Second War Between the States."[50]

In a series of articles in 1976 devoted to the South's economic success, the *New York Times* emphasized the role of federal spending in the region's expansion. The *Times* described the southern states as being "first in line at the pork barrel." Other well-publicized journal articles stressed the same theme. In June 1976, for instance, the *National Journal*, a Washington, D.C., weekly, stimulated widespread interest with an article entitled "Federal Spending: The North's Loss Is the Sunbelt's Gain." Considering defense contracts and salaries, federal expenditures for highways and sewers, and welfare and retirement payments, the *Journal* estimated that the South had received $918 in federal disbursements per resident in fiscal 1975, as compared with $863 for the Northeast and $706 for the Midwest (the figure for the West was $1,119). According to the *Journal*, the southern states took in $11.5 billion more in federal funds than they paid in federal taxes; by contrast ten northern states suffered an aggregate deficit of $30.8 billion. Many commentators made the point that out-migration from the Northeast and Midwest was depriving the cities of those regions of talent and human resources in a time of urban fiscal crisis and mounting inner-city problems. After absorbing millions of impoverished southern migrants, the North watched in dismay as the tax base necessary to accommodate that influx shifted steadily toward the South.[51]

Northern resentment of "unfair competition" from southern states eventually brought concerted action from the North. An early example of this cooperation was the formation in 1973 of the New England Congressional Caucus, a group interested in influencing federal spending policies. In 1976 the Northeast-Midwest Congressional Coalition was organized, and in the same year five northern governors established the Coalition of Northeastern Governors to combat what they regarded as sectional discrimination. "It was largely tax dollars from our urban states," explained Governor Milton Sharp of Pennsylvania, "that built the Tennessee Valley Authority. Now we find the lower cost of TVA

50. Kirkpatrick Sale, *Power Shift: The Rise of the Southern Rim and Its Challenge to the Eastern Establishment* (New York, 1975), pp. 17–53; Burd, "The Selling of the Sunbelt: Civic Boosterism in the Media," pp. 129–49; Richard M. Bernard, "Sunbelt South," in *Encyclopedia of Southern Culture*, ed. Wilson and Ferris, pp. 732–33; Cobb, *Industrialization and Southern Society*, p. 61; Cobb, *The Selling of the South*, p. 194.

51. Cobb, *The Selling of the South*, pp. 193–96; Estall, "The Changing Balance of the Northern and Southern Regions," pp. 365–86.

power used against us to attract our industry."[52] Northern political leaders gradually organized a coordinated campaign to equalize the regional distribution of federal funds. By early 1979, twelve coalitions were working to redirect federal money to the Northeast and Midwest. In addition to lobbying in the interest of their particular region or subregion, these groups endeavored to change the formulas for the allocation of federal grant funds. Their first success came in 1977, when Congress amended the Community Development Block Program to spend more in northern cities and created the Urban Development Action Grant Program to aid the most distressed urban areas. The amendment adopted in 1977 authorized an alternative formula for the allocation of federal grants to the nation's cities, one that worked to the advantage of northern cities. Two years earlier Congress had approved an emergency aid bill to relieve the desperate plight of New York City. Meanwhile, states outside the South had increased their own promotional efforts to stimulate economic growth, and by the early 1970s the southern states were only slightly ahead in the percentage of their total state budgets devoted to industrial promotion.[53]

Startled by the northern counterattack, southern political and business leaders began to consider defensive measures and intraregional cooperation. The section's governors began to show greater interest in the benefits that might be derived from pooled resources and orderly, desirable growth. The most notable outcome of this thinking was the creation, in December 1971, of the Southern Growth Policies Board (SGPB), which by 1978 represented every southern state except Texas. The board employed a full-time staff to administer programs and conduct research, and it soon began to prepare reports on such topics as the objectives of economic growth and how best to achieve social progress. The SGPB also assumed a role in the southern response to the northern counterattack of the 1970s, encouraging southerners to maintain the pace of the South's growth and development. One of the board's position papers, "The Snowbelt and the Seven Myths," systematically attacked the northern claim that the South was receiving a disproportionate share of federal funds or was stealing northern industry or that poverty was no longer a problem in the South.[54]

Southerners were understandably proud of the advances their region had made since the Second World War. The South was the site of new industries and jobs, of high-tech urban complexes, of a new landscape and lifestyle. By 1980 a majority of white southerners were engaged, for the first time, in middle-class occupations. Economic prospects were bright. On the other hand, one

52. Quoted in Cobb, *The Selling of the South*, p. 198.

53. Robert Jay Dilger, *The Sunbelt/Snowbelt Controversy: The War over Federal Funds* (New York, 1982), pp. 48–123; Bensel, *Sectionalism and American Political Development*, pp. 275–79; Cobb, *The Selling of the South*, pp. 196–99; Diana Yiannakis Evans, "Sunbelt Versus Frostbelt: The Evolution of Regional Conflict over Federal Aid to Cities in the House of Representatives," *Social Science Quarterly* 67 (March 1986): 108–17.

54. Cobb, *The Selling of the South*, pp. 200–202; Charles P. Roland, "Sun Belt Prosperity and Urban Growth," in *Interpreting Southern History: Historiographical Essays in Honor of Sanford W. Higginbotham*, ed. John B. Boles and Evelyn Thomas Nolen (Baton Rouge, La., 1987), pp. 439–41.

writer observes, "the previously dominant Northeast and Midwest—now known as the Frostbelt—languished in population declines, factory closings, and inclement winters."[55] Even though the Sunbelt boom lost some of its momentum in the 1980s, the southern economy continued to surpass the national average in employment growth. The South, at long last, seemed about to overtake the North, as disparities between South and non-South disappeared or diminished in categories like industrialization, occupations, income, urbanization, and education. The collective spirit of the region's inhabitants changed, becoming less defensive, more confident, more optimistic about the future. At the same time, the North as the South's "significant other" receded.[56] The South appeared to be "shedding its history." William H. Nicholls, a leading southern economist, argued forcefully in *Southern Tradition and Regional Progress* (1960) that historically the southern economy had failed to develop not because of northern domination but because of the South's own traditions—its rigid social structure, undemocratic politics, conformity of thought, penchant for violence, and lack of social responsibility. The region must choose between tradition and progress.[57]

If the South's self-esteem rose in the 1960s and 1970s, its reputation in other parts of the nation also improved. Its eventual accommodation to the civil rights revolution of the 1960s, the alteration of its political system, and the election of a president from the Deep South in 1976 impressed many outsiders. The disillusioning experience of Vietnam and Watergate, as well as the migration of racial conflict to northern and western cities, destroyed some of the illusions and innocence of Americans outside the South and subtly changed the perceptions of southerners. The Sunbelt phenomenon, the historian Carl Abbott suggests, enabled southerners to deny their dependence on the North: "Regional progress could suddenly be defined in terms of convergence or kinship with the dynamic West, as part of a new leading sector marked by fast growth and fast living."[58]

In a 1974 book entitled *The Americanization of Dixie: The Southernization of America*, the writer John Egerton examined the homogenizing processes that were steadily eroding the distinctiveness of the South and making North and South increasingly alike. "The South," Egerton declared, "is no longer simply a colony of the nation, an inferior region, a stepchild; it is now rushing to rejoin the Union, and in the process it is becoming indistinguishable from the North and East and West. The Union is meeting the South at the front door with overtures of welcome."[59] Commenting on the theme of regional convergence, the novelist

55. Brownell, "Introduction," p. 3. See also Earl Black and Merle Black, *Politics and Society in the South* (Cambridge, Mass., 1987), pp. 23–72.

56. George Brown Tindall used this phrase in *The Ethnic Southerners* (Baton Rouge, La., 1976), p. 9.

57. William H. Nicholls, *Southern Tradition and Regional Progress* (Chapel Hill, N.C., 1960); Persky, *The Burden of Dependency*, pp. 143–51.

58. Abbott, "New West, New South, New Region," p. 16. See also Cobb, *The Selling of the South*, pp. 182–86.

59. John Egerton, *The Americanization of Dixie: The Southernization of America* (New York, 1974), p. xix.

Walker Percy remarked, "I sometimes think that some parts of the South are more like the North than the North itself."[60] It was also true that the southern states had been forced to bend to the national will. They had found it necessary to respond, sometimes eagerly, sometimes defiantly, to federal policies that set national standards, brought military installations into the South, and subjected the region to a Second Reconstruction. But in the meantime the South changed the character of the rest of the country. For one thing, it exported millions of blacks—and whites—to northern and western cities, not to mention country music, soul food, and southern religion. The influence southerners exerted in national politics, the formulation of foreign policy, the growth of the U.S. economy, and even the civil rights movement also illustrates the point. The victorious North had provided the defeated South with the model industrial society for more than a hundred years. Now, southerners began to discover that imitation was attended with peril. As George B. Tindall has warned, "We will have to make the same mistakes [made by the North] all over again, and we will achieve the urban blight, the crowding, the traffic jams, the slums, the ghettos, the pollution, the frenzy, and all the other ills that modern man is heir to."[61]

One problem was that the Sunbelt image, while containing an element of truth, conveyed a distorted impression of reality. Indeed, despite its extraordinary economic advances and its social and political transformation, the South still lagged behind the rest of the nation in several important respects. The evolution from a rural-agrarian to an urban-industrial economy created new problems, the most intractable of which was a large, unskilled, poorly educated work force no longer needed to till the land and inadequately trained to meet the needs of an industrial and post-industrial economy. The South's great need was to increase the productivity of its economy.[62] David L. Carlton suggests that the South's modern problems are rooted in the very nature of its industrial order: "Southern industrial society, after all, has never really matched the prevailing image of an industrial society. Its manufacturing has never built great cities; its factories have relied heavily on low-wage labor; its workers have been the least unionized in the nation; and its state governments have been the most laggard in regulating industry, in providing social welfare services, and in developing the region's human capital."[63]

The South was still the nation's number one economic problem. While Florida, Virginia, Texas, and Oklahoma were near or above the national average in per capita income in 1982, most of the other southern states were well below it. While the South contained about 25 percent of the nation's population, it had over 40 percent of America's poor people, including a startlingly high percentage of poor blacks. The region had the highest percentage of poor children in the country—26 percent of those under the age of six. Appalachia and many rural areas with heavy black populations enjoyed little of the South's

60. Quoted in Richard N. Current, *Northernizing the South* (Athens, Ga., 1983), p. 113.
61. Tindall, *The Ethnic Southerners*, p. 241.
62. See James G. Maddox et al., *The Advancing South: Manpower Prospects and Problems* (New York, 1967), esp. pp. 79–121, 216.
63. Carlton, "The Revolution from Above," p. 446.

economic prosperity. Industrial decay also affected the South, as it had earlier affected the manufacturing belt of the North, and industries such as textiles, coal, iron and steel, and wood products suffered losses. Determined to promote economic growth, state governments were slow in establishing and implementing safeguards against industrial pollution and despoliation of the environment. Southern cities increasingly conformed to the national pattern of urban development: inner-city decay, suburban sprawl, growing racial tension, and ineffective government.[64]

Nevertheless, the emergence of the Sunbelt South represents an important chapter in the recent history of the region and the nation. By the end of the 1960s, a new southern economy had taken shape, "not an advanced version of the old economy, but a new economy."[65] This postwar South, one scholar writes, "seemed truly to become an integral piece of the national polity and economy, a part of the main."[66] The enormity of this transformation is suggested by the environmental historian Albert E. Cowdrey when he observes, "For men and women who are middle-aged in the 1980s, as for their great-grandparents in the 1880s, there will always be the feeling that they are separated from their youth by more than years." He goes on to say, "The changes in the metaphorical landscape of culture have been mirrored in the physical landscape, whose forms, more than ever before, are shaped by super-abounding human power. Cottonfields have changed to pastures or to woods; marshes to soybean fields or rolling Gulf; wild land to neon strips. A generation after World War II, healthier, more prosperous, and more numerous southerners confront common American dilemmas without altogether shifting the burden of a peculiar past."[67] The changes alluded to by Cowdrey and described in these pages are richly infused with themes of interregional conflict and convergence.

64. J. Wayne Flynt, *Dixie's Forgotten People: The South's Poor Whites* (Bloomington, Ind., 1980), pp. 107, 125–61; Jacqueline Jones, *The Dispossessed: America's Underclasses from the Civil War to the Present* (New York, 1992), pp. 269–70; Schulman, *From Cotton Belt to Sunbelt*, pp. 174–91; Cobb, *The Selling of the South*, pp. 229–68; Cobb, *Industrialization and Southern Society*, pp. 121–35; Peter Schrag, "A Hesitant New South: Fragile Promise on the Last Frontier," *Saturday Review* 55 (February 12, 1972): 51–58; Cooper and Terrill, *The American South*, vol. 2, pp. 758–61, 765; Jack Bass, "Hunger? Let Them Eat Magnolias," in *You Can't Eat Magnolias*, ed. H. Brandt Ayers and Thomas H. Naylor (New York, 1972), pp. 273–83.

65. Wright, *Old South, New South*, p. 241.

66. Schulman, *From Cotton Belt to Sunbelt*, p. 219.

67. Albert E. Cowdrey, *This Land, This South: An Environmental History* (Lexington, Ky., 1983), p. 169.

CHAPTER 11

The Nationalization of Southern Politics

ALTHOUGH the rise of the Sunbelt South undermined the economic and so-cial order that had supported the Solid South, external forces, including the edicts of the federal courts and the civil rights laws of the 1960s, spear-headed the overthrow of racial segregation and voter disfranchisement, which had long provided institutional props for the southern political system. Mean-while, the disruption of the South's one-party system, beginning with the Dixie-crat movement of 1948, proceeded apace as the alienation of white southerners from the liberal commitments of the national Democratic party increased in the 1960s. Moving to take advantage of these defections, the Republican party adopted a "southern strategy" that proved attractive to more and more white southerners, especially in presidential elections. Black southerners, by contrast, identified themselves with the national Democratic party and sought to find a place for themselves in that party in the South. A new party system began to emerge in the southern states, and politics in the South, though retaining a dis-tinctive southern cast, became more fully integrated into the national political system.

Confusion and uncertainty characterized the southern political scene in the aftermath of the presidential election of 1968. The long-dominant Democratic party of the South, with only one state victory in the national election, had been battered and left adrift. Millions of southern Democrats had voted for George Wallace's third party, which carried five of the region's states. The Republicans had not been so competitive in the South since Reconstruction; they won seven southern states and were particularly strong in the upper South and in Florida. The three-way cleavage of 1968 made it difficult to forecast the immediate di-rection southern politics would take.

President Richard M. Nixon, conscious of his narrow margin of victory in the recent election, and aware of the mounting opposition of white southerners to the national Democratic party, saw in the South an unmatched opportunity to strengthen his political base and that of his party. The immediate obstacle that stood in his way was Governor Wallace, whose conservative ideas and rhetoric overlapped his own. Intent upon congressional support and the best means of assuring his own reelection, Nixon pursued a calculated approach to the South from the beginning of his presidency. He set out to counter the Wallace movement and to enhance his chances of carrying the South against the Democratic nominee in 1972. Conceding the loss of black votes and those of white liberals, the new president reached out for the backing of white southerners, suburbanites, and ethnic workers troubled by the threat of racial equality and social disorder. He combined law and order appeals with economic conservatism.

Although Nixon identified himself with the goal of achieving racial justice, he launched a wide-ranging campaign to exploit the racial fears and prejudices of white Americans, particularly in the South. He attempted to slow the progress of school desegregation in the South, weakened civil rights offices in the Justice Department and in the Department of Health, Education and Welfare, fought unsuccessfully to obtain drastic changes in the Voting Rights Act of 1965, and urged Congress to impose a moratorium on court-ordered busing to bring about school integration. In 1969 HEW relaxed its policy against five school districts in South Carolina and flip-flopped in handling thirty-three Mississippi school districts (after having earlier approved desegregation plans for the fall term).[1] In other respects, the president followed a policy of willful neglect in dealing with civil rights questions.

In promising to "get tough on crime" and in condemning drugs and pornography, President Nixon tried to take advantage of the backlash against rising crime rates, antiwar protest, campus disorders, black militancy, and moral permissiveness. This appeal to the "silent majority" and "Middle America" elicited a sympathetic response from many white southerners. Nixon's eagerness to add "strict constructionists" to the Supreme Court and to overcome the liberal majority that had dominated the Warren Court also pleased southern conservatives. After Earl Warren retired as chief justice in June 1969, the president chose Warren Burger, a respected conservative, to replace him. In making a second appointment to the court later that year, Nixon turned to the South, selecting Clement F. Haynesworth, Jr., a federal circuit judge from South Carolina. Haynesworth was vigorously opposed by several civil rights groups and labor organizations, and after a stormy debate the Senate voted against his confirmation. Nixon then nominated another southerner, G. Harrold Carswell, a federal circuit court judge from Florida. Carswell, who was attacked for having been a racist earlier in his career and for having a mediocre record on the bench, was also rejected. Richard Nixon was furious, and he charged liberal

1. The Supreme Court eventually overruled the delaying action in the Mississippi case, and in *Alexander* v. *Holmes County Board of Education* (1969) Chief Justice Warren E. Burger, speaking for a unanimous court, declared that "the obligation of every school district is to terminate dual school districts at once and to operate now and hereafter only unitary schools." For the Nixon administration's civil rights policies, see Steven F. Lawson, *In Pursuit of Power: Southern Blacks and Electoral Politics, 1965–1982* (New York, 1985), pp. 121–90.

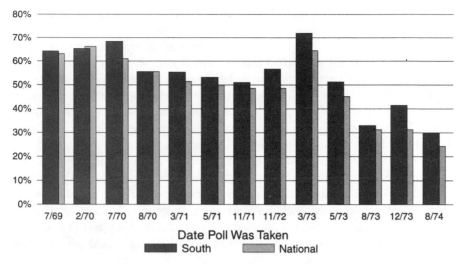

Nixon's Approval Ratings. SOURCE: George Gallup, *The Gallup Poll: Public Opinion, 1935–1971*, vol. 3 (New York: Random House, 1972), pp. 2204, 2237, 2257, 2259–60, 2291, 2305–06, 2231; George Gallup, *The Gallup Poll: Public Opinion, 1972–1977*, vol. 1 (Wilmington, Del.: Scholarly Resources, Inc., 1978), pp. 2–4, 101, 124, 154–55, 217, 325–26.

Democrats with denying qualified southerners an opportunity to serve on the nation's highest court.[2]

Nixon looked to the midterm elections of 1970 for popular endorsement and legislative support of his program. He had come to believe that a major party realignment was under way, and he accepted journalist Kevin P. Phillips's thesis that a new Republican majority was evolving, centered in the South and West and in the "Middle American" urban-suburban districts.[3] President Nixon and Vice President Spiro T. Agnew joined other Republican leaders in conducting a strenuous campaign in 1970. Nixon's southern strategy was designed to win support from Wallace sympathizers, while his attempts to exploit the more conservative aspects of cultural politics were aimed at middle-class Americans throughout the country. A central theme in the president's Dixie appeal was that southerners should elect Republicans to Congress so that they could back his determined stand against school busing. Two southern journalists who followed the administration's campaign described it as "a cynical strategy, this catering in subtle ways to the segregationist leanings of Southern vot-

2. Stephen E. Ambrose, *Nixon: The Triumph of a Politician, 1962–1972* (New York, 1989), pp. 315–17, 330–31, 337–38; Kirkpatrick Sale, *Power Shift: The Rise of the Southern Rim and Its Challenge to the Eastern Establishment* (New York, 1975), pp. 156, 235, 245–47. Following the defeat of Carswell, the president selected Harry A. Blackmun, a highly regarded federal judge from Minnesota. He was unanimously confirmed. In 1971 Nixon was able to make two other appointments to the Supreme Court, including Lewis F. Powell, a conservative lawyer from Virginia, who was confirmed by the Senate.

3. Kevin P. Phillips, *The Emerging Republican Majority* (New Rochelle, N.Y., 1969). For a somewhat similar analysis that emphasizes the political power of the Southern Rim, see Sale, *Power Shift*.

ers—yet pretending with high rhetoric that the real aim was simply to treat the South fairly, to let it become part of the nation again."[4]

The outcome of the congressional elections was disappointing to the Nixon administration. While the Democrats lost two Senate seats, they gained nine in the House. Nixon's southern strategy heightened the sectional sensibilities of many white southerners and drew forth their strong approval, but it brought few immediate Republican gains in the region. Except for Tennessee, where Winfield Dunn was elected governor and Representative William E. Brock defeated the liberal senator Albert Gore, the Republicans enjoyed little success in the southern states. They lost the governorship in Arkansas and in Florida and were unable to win any other statewide offices in the region. Most Democratic candidates opposed busing and identified themselves with the social conservatism of their white constituents. In some cases, moreover, Nixon was reluctant to oppose southern Democrats, since he counted on their support in Congress, where southern Democratic dissidence remained strong and southerners still dominated the committee system.

George Wallace continued to pose a problem for Richard Nixon. The administration's southern strategy failed to undermine Wallace's formidable hold on the South. Wallace appealed not only to the white backlash but also to what two students of southern politics have described as "the growing sense of alienation, resentment against war protesters, and frustrations of powerlessness expressed by blue-collar workers and others in public opinion polls."[5] Following his narrow victory in the Alabama gubernatorial election of 1970, Wallace consolidated his political base in his home state and became a candidate for the Democratic presidential nomination in 1972. Describing himself as a national candidate, he criticized both President Nixon and leading Democratic aspirants Edmund S. Muskie, Hubert H. Humphrey, and George S. McGovern. In March 1972 Wallace won a surprising victory in the Florida preferential primary, prompting Republican leaders to intensify their own efforts in the southern states. The Alabama governor moved on to win primary victories in Tennessee, North Carolina, Michigan, and Maryland, while making an impressive showing in the Wisconsin, Pennsylvania, and Indiana primaries. Indeed, the most noteworthy primary campaigns were those of Wallace and Senator McGovern, the candidates of the right and left, respectively. Then, as Wallace rattled "the eyeteeth of the Democratic party," fate intervened: the governor was shot by a would-be assassin on May 15 while campaigning in Maryland. Left paralyzed from the waist down, he was unable to continue his pursuit of the Democratic nomination.[6]

Senator McGovern, the beneficiary of new Democratic delegate-selection

4. Reg Murphy and Hal Gulliver, *The Southern Strategy* (New York, 1971), p. 3.

5. Jack Bass and Walter DeVries, *The Transformation of Southern Politics: Social Change and Political Consequence Since 1945* (New York, 1976), p. 67.

6. Numan V. Bartley and Hugh D. Graham, *Southern Politics and the Second Reconstruction* (Baltimore, 1975), pp. 164–74; Bass and DeVries, *The Transformation of Southern Politics*, pp. 64–67; Jody Carlson, *George C. Wallace and the Politics of Powerlessness: The Wallace Campaigns for the Presidency, 1964–1976* (New Brunswick, N.J., 1981), pp. 133–79.

procedures that favored minority and liberal elements, won his party's presidential nomination in 1972. The reform of the selection process, as well as McGovern's liberalism, endorsement of civil rights and school busing, and forthright opposition to the war in Vietnam, alienated many conservative Democrats, particularly in the South. Few Democratic leaders in the region campaigned for the South Dakota senator, and several prominent Democrats, including former governors John B. Connally of Texas and Mills E. Godwin, Jr., of Virginia, actively supported Nixon's reelection. Sam Nunn, a Democratic nominee for the U.S. Senate from Georgia, announced his intention to vote for the GOP ticket. President Nixon did his best to take advantage of white segregationist sentiment in the southern states. The controversy over "forced busing" enabled Republicans to exploit regional divisions within the Democratic party while drawing a distinction between busing and legal segregation.

Republican hopes were overwhelmingly realized in the South—and throughout the nation. Nixon and Agnew carried every southern state, winning more than 70 percent of the region's popular vote, as compared with slightly less than 60 percent in the rest of the country. McGovern received only 28.9 percent of the region's popular vote. Seldom had the color line been more visible in southern politics. Seventy-nine percent of the South's white voters cast their ballots for Nixon, while most of the black electorate—plus a majority of the Chicano voters in Texas and the Jewish voters in Florida—supported McGovern. The major difference between the elections of 1968 and 1972 in the South was the absence of the Wallace alternative in 1972. Three out of four of those southerners who voted for Wallace in 1968 cast their ballots for Nixon four years later. In capturing all of the South's electoral votes, the president profited from white resentment over civil rights and a preference for fiscal conservatism and state rights.[7] Democratic loyalties in presidential elections had worn perilously thin.

Although the Republican landslide in the South in 1972 did not extend below the presidential level, the party did make gains in other races. Republicans won six of twelve Senate elections in the South and increased their southern seats in the House of Representatives by seven, giving them about a third of the region's membership in the two houses of Congress. They were most successful in Virginia and North Carolina, in part because of their exploitation of the "social issue" and their efforts to identify Democratic candidates with McGovern's brand of liberalism. In the Old Dominion, the GOP captured a Senate seat in 1972, and a year later Mills Godwin, a former Democratic governor, won the governorship as a Republican, with the help of a great many conservative Democrats. North Carolina Republicans did even better in the elections of 1972, winning the governorship, a U.S. Senate seat, and four of the eleven seats in the House of Representatives. The new Republican senator was

7. Earl Black and Merle Black, *The Vital South: How Presidents Are Elected* (Cambridge, Mass., 1992), pp. 303–306; Bartley and Graham, *Southern Politics and the Second Reconstruction*, pp. 172–75; Alexander P. Lamis, *The Two-Party South*, 2d expanded ed. (New York, 1990), pp. 28–30; Thomas Byrne Edsall, with Mary D. Edsall, *Chain Reaction: The Impact of Race, Rights, and Taxes on American Politics, with a New Afterword* (New York, 1992), pp. 74–98.

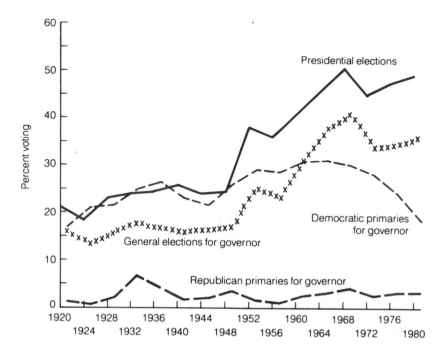

Changing Patterns of Participation in Southern Elections. SOURCE: Earl Black and Merle Black, *Politics and Society in the South* (Cambridge, Mass.: Harvard University Press, 1987), p. 177.

Jesse A. Helms, an extreme conservative who defeated the liberal Democrat Nick Galifianakis.[8]

If the Second Reconstruction alienated millions of white southerners and led them to support the Republican party in growing numbers, it also brought about a recomposition of the Democratic party in the region. Black southerners flocked to the polls in the years after 1965, creating a new biracial electorate in the South. Most of these new voters entered the Democratic party, giving it a stronger liberal flavor. Despite efforts by white authorities to make their registration difficult, especially in the Deep South, black voter enrollment mounted rapidly. In Mississippi, where only 6.7 percent of the state's adult African Americans were registered in 1964, the proportion enrolled climbed to 67 percent by 1970. One historian has written that, even before the Voting Rights Act breakthrough of 1965, the mock elections of 1963 and 1964, the Freedom Summer of the latter year, and the Mississippi Freedom Democratic party had contributed

8. Bartley and Graham, *Southern Politics and the Second Reconstruction*, pp. 175–83; Lamis, *The Two-Party South*, pp. 134–36, 153–54; Louis M. Seagull, *Southern Republicanism* (Cambridge, Mass., 1975); Merle Black and Earl Black, "The Growth of Contested Republican Primaries in the American South, 1960–1980," in *Contemporary Southern Political Attitudes and Behavior: Studies and Essays*, ed. Laurence W. Moreland, Tod A. Baker, and Robert P. Steed (New York, 1982), pp. 121–43.

Roy Justus

There's Something on That Line! Source: Reprinted by permission
from the *Star Tribune*, Newspaper of the Twin Cities.

to "a proud new black psyche, a new sense of militancy and racial solidarity."[9]
Registration drives in black communities and federal intervention—or the
threat of such intervention— encouraged the process, though often at a slower
pace in rural counties and small towns. The number of blacks registered in the
ex-Confederate states increased from 1.5 million in 1960 to 5.6 million (as compared with 28 million whites) in 1984. By the latter year, the registered percentage of the black voting-age population had almost reached that of the white—
66.2 to 75.3.[10]

9. Neil R. McMillen, "Black Enfranchisement in Mississippi: Federal Enforcement and Black
Protest in the 1960s," *Journal of Southern History* 43 (August 1977): 351–72 (quotation on p. 369). See
also Pat Watters and Reese Cleghorn, *Climbing Jacob's Ladder: The Arrival of Negroes in Southern Politics*
(New York, 1967).

10. Earl Black and Merle Black, *Politics and Society in the South* (Cambridge, Mass., 1987), pp.
112–25, 134–44; David Campbell and Joe R. Feagin, "Black Politics in the South: A Descriptive
Analysis," *Journal of Politics* 37 (February 1975): 129–62; Ronald J. Terchek, "Political Participa-
tion and Political Structures: The Voting Rights Act of 1965," *Phylon* 41 (March 1980): 25–35;
Jeffrey E. Cohen, Patrick R. Cotter, and Philip B. Coulter, "The Changing Structure of Southern
Political Participation: Matthews and Prothro 20 Years Later," *Social Science Quarterly* 64 (Septem-

It did not take long for the expanding black electorate to have an effect on southern politics. For one thing, Democratic candidates began to broaden their appeals to include blacks, even as the latter's presence led thousands of white Democrats to leave their traditional party. Attitudes and practices began to change all across the South. In Alabama, for instance, the state Democratic party in 1966 removed the party motto—"White Supremacy—For the Right"—from the ballot. Ernest F. Hollings of South Carolina, the first U.S. senator from the South to be elected after passage of the Voting Rights Act, illustrated the response of many politicians to the altered political environment by leading a successful Senate battle in 1969 to expand federal food stamps and other programs to combat hunger and malnutrition, an effort that would be especially helpful to blacks. A more fundamental change occurred in the politics of the southern black belts, the traditional bulwark of regional conservatism and solidarity. As African-American men and women began to register and vote in large numbers, the black belts began to shed their accustomed conservatism and to express a more moderate and even liberal position on political issues. In South Carolina Hubert H. Humphrey won thirteen of the fifteen counties with black majorities in 1968; only one of those counties had voted Democratic in 1964.

Meanwhile, many white southerners tried to limit or dilute the black vote. In the lower South blacks were sometimes subjected to voter reregistration, harassment at the polls, and economic pressure. Black office holding was minimized through the use of at-large elections for municipal and county offices, multimember districts, racial gerrymandering, and other forms of electoral discrimination. The intervention of the Justice Department and the federal courts, as well as the Voting Rights Act amendments of 1982, encouraged the shift from

THE POLITICAL MOBILIZATION OF SOUTHERN BLACKS, 1940–1984

Year	South	Peripheral South	Deep South	Difference between Peripheral South and Deep South
1940	3	5	1	+4
1947	12	17	8	+9
1956	25	29	21	+8
1964	43	52	30	+22
1966	52	58	46	+12
1968	62	67	57	+10
1976	63	62	64	−2
1984	59	58	59	−1

NOTE: Each entry is the percentage of eligible blacks who were estimated to be registered to vote. SOURCE: Earl Black and Merle Black, *Politics and Society in the South* (Cambridge, Mass.: Harvard University Press, 1987), p. 137.

ber 1983): 536–49; Lorn S. Foster, "The Voting Rights Act: Political Modernization and the New Southern Politics," *Southern Studies* 23 (Fall 1984): 266–89.

multimember to single-member districts for legislative, city council, and school district seats. Another obstacle to the election of African Americans was the reluctance of white southerners to vote for black candidates. When the Mississippi courts finally ordered a change to single-member legislative seats in 1979, black leaders had high expectations in thirty districts with large African-American populations. But black candidates were successful in only fifteen house and two senate races. In 1982 state representative Robert Clark became the first black candidate in Mississippi to win a Democratic nomination for Congress—with 57 percent of the primary vote. But he lost in the general election when many whites defected and voted for his Republican opponent.[11]

Nevertheless, the number of black elected officials in the South rose steadily, increasing from fewer than a hundred in 1965 to about 3,500 in 1984. Most of these officials were members of city councils, county commissions, school boards, and law enforcement agencies. In Mississippi the number rose from zero in 1965 to 521 in 1986, making that state the leader in black elected officeholders. By 1983, 236 black mayors had been elected, mostly in small towns but including Atlanta, Birmingham, New Orleans, Raleigh, and Richmond. Following the election of 1972, Greene County, Alabama, the poorest county in the state, became the first biracial political unit in the United States to be completely black-governed. The first modern black congressional representatives from the South—Barbara Jordan of Texas and Andrew Young of Georgia—were elected in 1972. In 1989 L. Douglas Wilder of Virginia became the first black candidate to win the office of governor in the South. The number of African Americans in southern legislatures also increased, rising from 3 in 1965 to 176 in 1985. Even so, in 1980 blacks held only 4 percent of the elective county offices and 3 percent of the elective municipal offices in the South.[12]

11. Lester M. Salamon and Stephen Van Evera, "Fear, Apathy, and Discrimination: A Test of Three Explanations of Political Participation," *American Political Science Review* 67 (December 1973): 1288–1306; Chandler Davidson and George Korbel, "At-Large Elections and Minority-Group Representation: A Re-Examination of Historical and Contemporary Evidence," *Journal of Politics* 43 (November 1981): 982–1005; Peyton McCrary, "Racially Polarized Voting in the South: Quantitative Evidence from the Courtroom," *Social Science History* 14 (Winter 1990): 507–31; Chandler Davidson, ed., *Minority Vote Dilution* (Washington, D.C., 1984); Beeman C. Patterson, "The Three Rs Revisited: Redistricting, Race and Representation in North Carolina," *Phylon* 44 (September 1983): 232–43. For a study that questions federal intervention in state and local electoral affairs, see Abigail M. Thernstrom, *Whose Votes Count? Affirmative Action and Minority Voting Rights* (Cambridge, Mass., 1987).

12. Charles S. Bullock III, "The Election of Blacks in the South: Preconditions and Consequences," *American Journal of Political Science* 19 (November 1975): 727–39; Margaret K. Latimer, "Black Political Representation in Southern Cities: Election Systems and Other Causal Variables," *Urban Affairs Quarterly* 15 (September 1979): 65–86; Huey L. Perry, "The Socioeconomic Impact of Black Political Empowerment in a Rural Southern Locality," *Rural Sociology* 45 (Summer 1980): 207–22; James W. Button and Richard K. Scher, "The Election and Impact of Black Officials in the South," in *Public Policy and Social Institutions*, ed. Harrell R. Rodgers, Jr. (Greenwich, Conn., 1984), pp. 183–215; David Campbell and Joe R. Feagin, "Black Electoral Victories: Progress and Problems," *Phylon* 45 (December 1984): 331–45; Bernard Grofman and Lisa Handley, "The Impact of the Voting Rights Act on Black Representation in Southern State Legislatures," *Legislative Studies Quarterly* 16 (February 1991): 111–28; Steven F. Lawson, *Running for Freedom: Civil Rights and Black Politics in America Since 1941* (New York, 1991), pp. 146–70.

Notwithstanding the dramatic upsurge in their enfranchisement, black southerners remained less active politically than their white counterparts. Their voting percentages were generally lower than those of whites. Once in office, black leaders found it difficult to translate their electoral success into policies that would improve the lives of their black constituents. As the political scientists Donald R. Matthews and James W. Prothro had forecast in the mid-1960s, "the concrete, measurable payoffs from Negro voting in the South will *not* be revolutionary."[13] "None of the new leaders," wrote Roy Reed, the *New York Times* southern correspondent, in 1974, "has made real headway in providing industrial jobs for the multitudes of poor people who still live in the black belts. None has found the answers to newer problems such as urban blight and the growing concentration of economic power in fewer hands."[14] Blacks were a minority in most parts of the region. In 1920 they made up 32 percent of the population in the ex-Confederate states, but by 1980 that proportion had declined to 20 percent (29 percent in the Deep South and 15 percent in the peripheral South). African Americans constituted less than one-fifth of the southern electorate. In addition, blacks were poorer, less educated, and subjected to far worse living conditions than were whites. These disparities helped account for sharp differences between blacks and whites on such political issues as the government's responsibility for jobs, expenditures for welfare programs, and the relative importance of dealing with unemployment and inflation.[15] It soon became apparent that the strong Democratic proclivity of black southerners was potentially both an advantage and a liability for the Democrats.

Southern Democrats benefited, at least in the short run, from the frustration and collapse of the second Nixon administration. Though white southerners tended to support Nixon's policies in Vietnam and were slow to condemn his behavior in the Watergate scandal, they shared in the national disillusionment over his conduct. The leading roles played by Democrat Sam J. Ervin and Republican Howard H. Baker in the Senate investigation of Watergate also encouraged southern disaffection with Nixonian Republicanism. Ervin emerged as a southern folk hero and achieved a national audience in the 1970s, as Senator J. William Fulbright of Arkansas had among critics of American foreign policy in the 1960s. Fulbright, a moderate on most social questions, had voted against the civil rights legislation of the mid-1960s, but his outspoken and eloquent opposition to the continuing escalation of the war in Vietnam made him an admired figure among "dovish" Americans, particularly outside his own region. The early 1970s brought what one journalist described, with some exaggeration, as a "new breed" of southern congressmen—"more independent and tolerant and more national in their outlook than their counterparts of previous decades."[16]

13. Donald R. Matthews and James W. Prothro, *Negroes and the New Southern Politics* (New York, 1966), p. 481.

14. Quoted in David R. Goldfield, *Promised Land: The South Since 1945* (Arlington Heights, Ill., 1987), p. 192.

15. Black and Black, *Politics and Society in the South*, pp. 203–207, 214–19.

16. Jack Nelson, "South from the Potomac," in *I'll Still Take My Stand*, ed. Frank E. Smith

Another manifestation of Democratic renewal in the South was the election of a group of moderate governors during the 1970s. These governors were able to construct majority coalitions that included working-class whites and blacks as well as middle-class and professional people. Having been largely emancipated from the burden of the racial issue, they emphasized economic development and opportunity. Programmatic and goal-oriented, they tried to modernize their state governments and to extend public services. Their ranks included Reubin O. Askew of Florida, Dale Bumpers of Arkansas, James Earl "Jimmy" Carter, Jr., of Georgia, Edwin W. Edwards of Louisiana, James B. Hunt, Jr., of North Carolina, and John C. West of South Carolina. William Winter, who won the Mississippi governorship in 1971, began to bring blacks into the state's politics and government, and Charles "Cliff" Finch, who was elected as his successor in 1975, went further in creating a black-white Democratic coalition. Even George Wallace, who was reelected to a third term as governor of Alabama in 1974, moved toward the center of the political spectrum.[17] A new spirit was evident in gubernatorial rhetoric. As one scholar remarks, "New faces appeared, and strategies were planned to accommodate an expanded electorate . . . [that would include] blacks, women, blue-collar workers."[18]

A resurgent Democratic party in the South, along with the weakening effects of Watergate on the Republican party, set the stage for the rise of Jimmy Carter and his accession to the presidency. Carter helped rejuvenate the Democratic party in Georgia from its threatened collapse in the late 1960s. Lester Maddox had won the governorship in 1966 with a racist and reactionary campaign, and in 1968 the Democratic presidential ticket had come in third behind George Wallace and Richard Nixon. Carter, a former naval officer and a successful agribusinessman from southwest Georgia, was elected to the state senate in 1962 over the opposition of local politicians. He was reelected two years later, and in 1966 lost a bid for his party's gubernatorial nomination. But in 1970 he defeated former governor Carl Sanders for the Democratic gubernatorial nomination and then won the general election. Carter opposed school busing and appealed to the social conservatism of rural and small-town Georgians; he attracted much of the Talmadge-Maddox-Wallace following in his campaign against the racially moderate Sanders. Yet, as governor, Carter expressed liberal racial views, set about reorganizing the state government, and began to put together a coalition that included blacks and rural and small-town workers. In his inaugural address, he declared that "the time for racial discrimination is over. Our people have already made this major and difficult decision. No poor,

---

(Vicksburg, Miss., 1980), p. 9. See also David Zarefsky, "Fulbright and Ervin: Southern Senators with National Appeal," in *A New Diversity in Contemporary Southern Rhetoric*, ed. Calvin M. Logue and Howard Dorgan (Baton Rouge, La., 1987), pp. 114–65.

17. Bass and DeVries, *The Transformation of Southern Politics*, pp. 12–13, 94–98, 124–31, 261–64; Dewey W. Grantham, *The Life & Death of the Solid South: A Political History* (Lexington, Ky., 1988), pp. 181–84.

18. Waldo W. Braden, "The Speaking of the Governors of the Deep South, 1970–1980," in *A New Diversity in Contemporary Southern Rhetoric*, ed. Logue and Dorgan, pp. 188–205 (quotation on p. 203).

rural, weak, or black person should ever have to bear the additional burden of being deprived of the opportunity for an education, a job, or simple justice."[19] Carter's term as governor, one interpreter suggests, seemed to confirm "the triumph of a metropolitan ideology that stressed economic expansion, businesslike administration, and free market individualism."[20]

In 1972, while in the middle of his term as governor, the Georgian decided to run for president. Beginning with his own state, Carter worked to commit the rest of the South to his candidacy as he entered a large number of presidential primaries in and out of the South. Meanwhile, the Georgia governor traveled extensively throughout the United States in preparation for the preconvention campaign of 1976. He stressed the innovative character of his governorship and his commitment to a new approach in race relations. After Senator Edward M. Kennedy, the early favorite, withdrew for personal reasons in September 1974, several other candidates entered the competition for the Democratic nomination. Among these Democratic aspirants, in addition to Carter, were Senator Henry M. Jackson of Washington, Representative Morris K. Udall of Arizona, and Governor George Wallace of Alabama. To the surprise of most observers, Carter led the nine candidates in the party's New Hampshire primary in February 1976. He had been campaigning for more than a year. He had a disarming smile, adopted an earnest and folksy approach, and employed a personal, face-to-face style. According to a journalist covering his campaign, "Carter is selling only two products—his personality and the image of the outsider who will clean up Washington."[21]

In his own region, Carter faced a formidable obstacle in the person of George Wallace, who once again sought the Democratic presidential nomination by conducting a grass-roots campaign. Opinion polls in the spring of 1975 showed Wallace to be the leading candidate among the Democratic leaders who were actively working for the nomination. But the political situation had changed since 1972, and in Carter, Wallace was confronted with a strong adversary. Carter presented himself as a moderate, New South alternative to Wallace, but he tried not to alienate his fellow governor. The Georgian won a decisive victory over Wallace in the Florida preferential primary on March 9, and he went on to defeat the Alabamian in North Carolina, Georgia, Arkansas, Kentucky, and Tennessee. Wallace eventually endorsed Carter, who had succeeded in unifying the South behind his own candidacy.[22] Carter's national strategy was also working, and he captured the delegates of eleven nonsouthern states in presidential primaries. Despite late challenges from Senator Frank Church of Idaho and Governor Jerry Brown of California, Carter was nomi-

19. Quoted in Numan V. Bartley, "1940 to the Present," in *A History of Georgia*, ed. Kenneth Coleman (Athens, Ga., 1977), p. 402. See also Gary M. Fink, *Prelude to the Presidency: The Political Character and Legislative Leadership Style of Governor Jimmy Carter* (Westport, Conn., 1980).

20. Numan V. Bartley, *The Creation of Modern Georgia* (Athens, Ga., 1983), p. 206.

21. Thomas W. Ottenad, "Jimmy Carter: A Smile and a Shoeshine," *Progressive* 40 (May 1976): 24.

22. Black and Black, *The Vital South*, pp. 248–54; Carlson, *George C. Wallace and the Politics of Powerlessness*, pp. 181–252.

nated on the first ballot when the Democratic national convention assembled in New York City in July. His choice of Senator Walter F. Mondale of Minnesota as his running mate gave the ticket ideological balance and helped unify the party.

In the meantime, President Gerald R. Ford and former governor Ronald Reagan of California engaged in a hard-fought struggle for the Republican nomination. The South played a part in this struggle, since Reagan's outspoken conservatism attracted many southerners. In March the Californian won an upset victory in North Carolina, and he moved on to defeat the president in several Sunbelt primaries.[23] But Ford clung to a narrow lead and was nominated by the GOP convention in August. Senator Robert Dole of Kansas was named the party's vice-presidential nominee.

Recognizing how Watergate had changed the public mood, Carter talked about restoring morality and integrity to the national government. He declared again and again that the nation deserved a government "as good as its people." Ford tried to take advantage of his position in the White House and to identify his presidency with moderation and constructive leadership. Starting from far behind, Ford's campaign began to gain momentum, and by election day he and his challenger were almost even in the polls. Although the Democrats retained a comfortable lead in congressional seats and governorships, they barely managed to win the presidential election. Carter and Mondale received 40.8 million votes (50.1 percent) to 39.1 million (48 percent) for Ford, who actually carried two more states than his opponent. The Democrats made their best showing in the South, winning eleven of the thirteen southern states and receiving 54 percent of the popular votes cast in the region. Carter also ran well in the Northeast, while Ford carried most of the western states. With strong support from Congressman Andrew Young and other African-American leaders, the Democrats captured over 90 percent of the southern black votes. But Ford and Dole had a lead of 53 to 47 percent among the South's white voters. The pollster Louis Harris concluded that the Democratic nominee won not because of his personal qualities but because of "the revival of the old coalition that first sent Franklin D. Roosevelt to the White House in 1932." "Even so," the historian Robert Kelley said of Carter's election, "his Southern accent, Southern Baptist style, and Southern populist aura almost defeated him, so widely do these diverge from the Northern WASP manner and outlook that seem to have become the basis for a national culture."[24]

Southerners were exhilarated by the election of a president from the heart of their region. Humbled, isolated, and largely bereft of a positive role in national

23. Black and Black, *The Vital South*, pp. 273–79.

24. William E. Leuchtenburg, *In the Shadow of FDR: From Harry Truman to Ronald Reagan*, rev. ed. (Ithaca, N.Y., 1989), p. 183 (first quotation); Robert Kelley, "Ideology and Political Culture from Jefferson to Nixon," *American Historical Review* 82 (June 1977): 560 (second quotation). See also Betty Glad, *Jimmy Carter: In Search of the Great White House* (New York, 1980), pp. 204–405; Black and Black, *The Vital South*, pp. 329–37; Lamis, *The Two-Party South*, pp. 37–39; Paul R. Abramson, "Class Voting in the 1976 Presidential Election," *Journal of Politics* 40 (November 1978): 1066–72; and Numan V. Bartley, *Jimmy Carter and the Politics of the New South* (St. Louis, 1979), pp. 11–12.

affairs for generations, they savored a moment of vindication. According to the poet and novelist James Dickey, the South had finally won out "after all these years" and had become the "political pivot" of the nation. Carter's election also seemed to symbolize the South's more complete integration into national life. This theme was widely sounded during and after the campaign of 1976. "Whatever else he may do," the liberal journalist Tom Wicker wrote, "Jimmy Carter has removed the last great cause of Southern isolation; and even in the remote little farm towns that dot the Southern countryside, it is already possible to sense that Southerners are coming to believe that they finally belong to something larger than the South."[25] Eugene Patterson, publisher of the St. Petersburg *Times*, observed that "the enormous leadership potentials that the South has always nurtured need never again be wasted in the political isolation the old South brought down on itself."[26] If Americans outside the southern states were more restrained in their reactions, most of them seemed disposed to give the president from Georgia a chance to demonstrate his capacity as a national leader.

Jimmy Carter was the first president from the Deep South since Zachary Taylor. He struck some observers as a more authentic southerner than his southern predecessor Lyndon Johnson. Carter came from an old family in Georgia that represented three major strands of the southern political tradition—bourbonism, populism, and progressivism. He himself typified, as Robert C. McMath, Jr., has pointed out, "the southern populist as outsider and prophet, and the middle-class southerner as engineer and progressive."[27] During the campaign of 1976, Carter reached out for liberal support, emphasizing his commitment to full employment, civil rights, and international human rights. Yet he probably benefited from widespread doubts among Americans about the consequences of Keynesian economics, liberal diplomacy (that led to war in Southeast Asia), "open" life-styles, and a bland liberal religion. The Georgian was somewhat ambiguous in his attitude toward modern American liberalism. In an earlier day he would have been considered a "business progressive," certainly not a Populist redistributionist. He believed in efficiency, preferred a prudent fiscal policy, denounced "special interests," and sought to elevate the nation's moral tone.

In his inaugural address Carter proclaimed "a new beginning, a new dedication within our government, a new spirit within us all." He worked hard at the task of finding solutions to the nation's troublesome economic and social problems. But he realized few successes. One reason was that he came to the presi-

25. *Nashville Tennessean*, 26 December 1976. See also David D. Lee, "The South and the American Mainstream: The Election of Jimmy Carter," *Georgia Historical Quarterly* 61 (Spring 1977): 7–12, and Dewey W. Grantham, *The Regional Imagination: The South and Recent American History* (Nashville, Tenn., 1979), p. 222.

26. Quoted in Reg Murphy, "Not Since Jefferson and Madison . . . ," *Saturday Review*, 4 September 1976, p. 10.

27. Robert C. McMath, Jr., "Jimmy Carter: A Southerner in the White House?" in *The Adaptable South: Essays in Honor of George Brown Tindall*, ed. Elizabeth Jacoway et al. (Baton Rouge, La., 1991), pp. 237–63 (quotation on p. 262).

dency after waging a highly personalized campaign, which left him without a clear policy mandate and without the loyalty of established Democratic leaders. Suspicious of insiders and special interests, he had trouble with Congress, including the members of his own party. Critics charged that his legislative strategy was "essentially anti-political," that he had neither a clearly defined program nor a coherent philosophy, and that he was an ineffective leader of a "passionless presidency."[28] Despite Carter's good intentions and some notable accomplishments, especially in foreign affairs, he was eventually frustrated by intractable problems, a resurgent Congress, and a divided Democratic party. New crises near the end of Carter's term heightened the mood of futility and impotence that surrounded his administration and contributed to his defeat in 1980. Nor did the Carter presidency clarify the ambiguity that characterized the role of the South in national politics. Ironically, the leadership of this southern Democrat opened the door wider to Republican advances in the South. In the midterm elections of 1978, efforts by the Carter administration to unseat several Republican senators were unsuccessful, and GOP candidates won the governorship of Texas and a Senate seat in Mississippi for the first time in the twentieth century.[29]

Carter's troubled administration was epitomized by Edward M. Kennedy's challenge to his renomination in 1980. The Massachusetts senator portrayed the president as a weak and ineffectual leader who had abandoned the Democratic party's tradition of domestic reformism and was unable to forge a successful foreign policy. In the end, Carter won a series of presidential primaries, including all of the eight held in the South, and turned back Kennedy's challenge. The Democratic national convention then renominated Carter and Mondale. The Republicans turned to ex-governor Ronald Reagan, who had come close to winning the GOP nomination in 1976 and had a great deal of support in the West and South. The conservative Reagan urged a reduction of federal spending and promised to "take government off the backs of the people." The festering resentment among many Americans over questions of race and taxes strengthened the hands of Republican leaders, who identified their Democratic opponents with the "rights revolution" (for the protection of criminal defendants, the poor, women, and so on) and the reform movement that focused on the right to guaranteed representation. Reagan also blamed the Carter administration for the nation's economic doldrums and accused it of allowing the Soviet Union to achieve an advantage in strategic striking power. While Carter fought back, he remained on the defensive throughout the campaign, battered by a faltering economy, deteriorating relations with the Soviet Union, and a humiliating crisis precipitated by the holding of American diplomats as hos-

28. Charles O. Jones, *The Trusteeship Presidency: Jimmy Carter and the United States Congress* (Baton Rouge, La., 1988), pp. 2–3, 81, 210–15; Emmet John Hughes, "The Presidency vs. Jimmy Carter," *Fortune*, 4 December 1978, pp. 50–64; James Fallows, "The Passionless Presidency: The Trouble with Jimmy Carter's Administration," *Atlantic* 243 (May 1979): 33–48, *Atlantic* 243 (June 1979): 75–81; Glad, *Jimmy Carter*, pp. 409–72.

29. M. Glenn Abernathy et al., eds., *The Carter Years: The President and Policy Making* (London, 1984); Erwin C. Hargrove, *Jimmy Carter as President: Leadership and the Politics of the Public Good* (Baton Rouge, La., 1988); *New York Times*, 9 November 1978.

tages in Iran, which seemed to symbolize the bankruptcy of the president's leadership. Galloping inflation and the sluggish economy undermined public confidence in the Carter administration. In addition, the Republicans conducted a spirited and well-organized campaign, in contrast to the Democrats' loosely organized and uninspired efforts. The South became a critical battleground in the contest, and part of the Republican strategy was to force Carter to campaign extensively in his native region.[30]

In an election that attracted the lowest turnout in the twentieth century, Reagan won with 43.9 million popular votes (51 percent) to 35.5 million (41 percent) for Carter. Representative John B. Anderson, an independent candidate from Illinois, received 5.7 million votes. The Republicans had an overwhelming electoral margin of 489 to 49. Carter and Mondale carried only six states, including Carter's home state of Georgia. The Republican ticket won the other twelve southern states, six of them narrowly. One of the significant reversals of the 1976 results was the fact that Carter, who described himself as a born-again Christian, failed to win substantial support from the growing Religious Right, a loosely organized, Christian political movement that actively opposed his reelection in 1980. Although Carter captured virtually all of the black ballots in the South, he received only about 36 percent of the region's white votes. Among southern whites, he did best with older, low-income, and less-educated voters. The Republicans also made gains below the presidential level in the South. They won new Senate seats in North Carolina, Georgia, Florida, and Alabama, gained nine southern seats in the House of Representatives, and captured the governorship of Arkansas. To their delight, the Republicans won control of the Senate for the first time in a quarter-century, while making sizable gains in the House of Representatives.[31]

The election of 1980 paved the way for Republican domination of presidential politics in the South. The Republican presence in the region was enhanced because the party's southern leaders included persons of influence and power. Howard H. Baker, the new majority leader in the Senate, became a serious candidate for the presidency in the 1980s. J. Strom Thurmond, John G. Tower, and Jesse A. Helms took over the chairmanships of important Senate committees in 1981. Southern Republicanism was also boosted by the Reagan administration, which showed its solicitude for the South in ways that were both tangible and symbolic. "Reagan's popularity," the columnist David Broder observed in 1986, "has created a real opportunity for political realignment of the region, down to the courthouse level." Reagan's policies at home and abroad were popular among white southerners and received considerable support from

30. Black and Black, *The Vital South*, pp. 254–56, 279–82; Edsall, *Chain Reaction*, pp. 3–4, 99–136; Grantham, *The Life & Death of the Solid South*, pp. 186–87.

31. Lamis, *The Two-Party South*, pp. 210–24; Black and Black, *The Vital South*, pp. 307–12; Larry Light, "Independent Reagan Groups Have Shaved Spending Plans," *Congressional Quarterly Weekly Report* 38 (October 18, 1980): 3152–53; Warden Moxley, "GOP Wins Senate Control for First Time in 28 Years," *ibid.* (November 8, 1980): 3300–03; Jeffrey L. Brudney and Gary W. Copeland, "Evangelicals as a Political Force: Reagan and the 1980 Religious Vote," *Social Science Quarterly* 65 (December 1984): 1072–79.

southern Democrats in Congress. This regional response involved more than racial considerations. White southerners generally liked Reagan's emphasis on lower taxes, economic growth, reduction of federal regulatory activities, resistance to redistributive welfare programs, opposition to a "predatory" Soviet Union, and insistence upon the importance of patriotism and traditional values and institutions.[32]

Results from the presidential election of 1984 in the South, as in other parts of the country, gave southern Republicans further cause to be optimistic about their party's progress in the region. The outlook for the GOP was favorable from the beginning of the contest. Economic recovery was in full swing following the recession of 1981–1982, foreign affairs had assumed a less hazardous complexion, and President Reagan's popularity remained gratifyingly high. Reagan dominated the Republican party, which was united in support of his reelection. Democratic prospects, on the other hand, were never very bright. The party went through a long and bruising preconvention struggle. Former vice president Walter Mondale, the early front-runner, received vital support from the South. Mondale was challenged by Jesse Jackson, a charismatic black minister. Jackson, a native of South Carolina and a civil rights leader based in Chicago, argued that blacks as a group had been taken for granted by the Democratic party. As the leader of the "Rainbow Coalition" of blacks, Hispanics, and low-income whites, he emerged as a serious candidate for the Democratic nomination. But he was forced to share black primary votes with the liberal Mondale, who seemed to have a better chance than Jackson to be elected president. Mondale won the nomination and chose Representative Geraldine A. Ferraro of New York as his running mate.[33] The Democrats waged a forceful

THE GREAT WHITE SWITCH IN PRESIDENTIAL ELECTIONS

	Percent Voting Republican			
	1976	1980	1984	1988
White voters only				
South	53	61	72	67
Rest of nation	52	55	63	57
Difference (S − N)	+1	+6	+9	+10
All voters				
South	46	53	64	59
Rest of nation	50	51	58	52
Difference (S − N)	−4	+2	+6	+7

SOURCE: Earl Black and Merle Black, *The Vital South: How Presidents Are Elected* (Cambridge, Mass.: Harvard University Press, 1992), p. 349.

32. Charlotte *Observer*, 8 August 1986 (quotation); Edsall, *Chain Reaction*, pp. 154–71.
33. Black and Black, *The Vital South*, pp. 256–60; E. Lee Bernick and Charles L. Paysby, "Reactions to the Jackson Candidacy among Southern Black Democratic Party Activists," in *Blacks in Southern Politics*, ed. Laurence W. Moreland, Robert P. Steed, and Tod A. Baker (New York, 1987), pp. 191–208.

and energetic campaign, but they were no match for the confident and unified Republicans. Both nominees gave special attention to the South.

Reagan and his running mate, George H. W. Bush of Texas, won by a landslide, receiving 54.5 million votes (59 percent) to 37.6 million (41 percent) for the Democratic ticket. The electoral vote was a staggering 527 to 13, with the Republicans carrying every state except Minnesota and the District of Columbia. Reagan and Bush did better in the South than in the rest of the nation. By capturing all of the South's electoral votes, the Republicans needed only one-third of the electoral votes in the rest of the country to be successful. Race clearly influenced the outcome of the election. Jesse Jackson's candidacy probably accelerated the movement of white southerners into the GOP column. The southern vote was sharply polarized along racial lines: over 70 percent of the region's white ballots went to Reagan, while almost 90 percent of its black votes supported Mondale. Yet white southerners were influenced by many factors, including Reagan's personal popularity and the approval of his policies. Mondale's liberal image, his willingness to increase taxes, and the nomination of Ferraro also put the Democrats at a disadvantage.[34]

Seeking to enhance the role of the South in the presidential nominating process, southern leaders were able to arrange a regional primary for the two parties in 1988. This Super Tuesday was scheduled for March 8, two weeks after the New Hampshire primary; it would be held in ten southern states (South Carolina decided on a caucus rather than a primary election). Unfortunately for the Democrats, they did not have a consensus candidate, and the outcome was a three-way division of votes. Jesse Jackson, once more an active candidate, carried four Deep South states plus Virginia, with 29 percent of the region's popular vote; Senator Albert Gore, Jr., of Tennessee won three upper South states and 29 percent of the southern votes; and Governor Michael Dukakis of Massachusetts captured Florida and Texas with 24 percent of the South's popular votes. The southern states turned out to be indispensable for the candidacy of Vice President George Bush, who it was said ran as a carbon copy of Ronald Reagan. After winning the South Carolina delegates, Bush swept over his opponents on Super Tuesday, carrying 57 percent of the Republican vote in the ten states. "The South's contribution to Super Tuesday," two students of southern politics observe, "was perhaps the most striking evidence in recent years of the influence of the united conservatives on behalf of the most electable conservative candidate."[35]

Both parties courted the South in 1988. The two national conventions as-

34. Linda F. Williams, "Blacks and the 1984 Elections in the South: Racial Polarization and Regional Congruence," in *Blacks in Southern Politics*, ed. Moreland, Steed, and Baker, pp. 77–98; David O. Sears, Jack Citrin, and Rick Kosterman, "Jesse Jackson and the Southern White Electorate in 1984," in *ibid.*, pp. 209–25; Lamis, *The Two-Party South*, pp. 233–64; Harold W. Stanley, "The 1984 Presidential Election in the South: Race and Realignment," in *The 1984 Presidential Election in the South: Patterns of Southern Party Politics*, ed. Robert P. Steed, Laurence W. Moreland, and Tod A. Baker (New York, 1986), pp. 303–35; Black and Black, *The Vital South*, pp. 312–15; Wayne Greenhaw, *Elephants in the Cottonfields: Ronald Reagan and the New Republican South* (New York, 1982).

35. Black and Black, *The Vital South*, pp. 260–68, 282–87 (quotation on p. 287); Lawson, *Running for Freedom*, pp. 247–57.

sembled in the region—the Democrats meeting in Atlanta and the Republicans in New Orleans. "It has been a long time," the historian C. Vann Woodward remarked, "since the South has enjoyed the feeling of being really wanted and needed in the national business of electing a president."[36] The Democrats proceeded to nominate Governor Dukakis for president and Senator Lloyd Bentsen of Texas as his running mate, while the Republicans chose Vice President Bush and Senator J. Danford Quayle of Indiana as their standard-bearers. All of the nominees campaigned in the South. Speaking in Montgomery, Dukakis declared, "I'm serious . . . about campaigning hard in the South, working hard in the South and winning the South."[37] But he showed little understanding of the nuances of the southern situation, and his chances of doing well in the region were never very good. Republican speakers stressed the nation's economic growth, prosperity, and low inflation rate, and they launched a telling assault on Dukakis's character, judgment, and values. They pictured him as a "Teddy Kennedy liberal" from Massachusetts who opposed gun ownership, the Pledge of Allegiance, prayer in the schools, and an anti-crime program. Once again the GOP won a decisive majority, with 53.4 percent of the popular vote to 45.6 percent for the Democrats. Dukakis and Bentsen carried only ten northern and northwestern states. In the South, where the Republicans ran well ahead of their performance in other regions, Bush and Quayle won every state. Returns from the South revealed a pronounced racial polarization: the Democratic ticket received about 90 percent of the region's black votes but only 32 percent of its white ballots. In a postmortem Tom Wicker pointed out that "peace, prosperity and patriotism" were all working to ensure Bush's election. But Wicker also remarked that "white flight into the Republican Party, in all regions of the country but most spectacularly in the South, will be a palpable, continuing, virtually fatal problem for the Democrats as far ahead as a poll-taker can see."[38]

Four years later the Democrats tried a different tack, moving toward the political center in an effort to identify their campaign with the broad middle class and the American mainstream. The South became a crucial battleground in that endeavor. The struggle for the Democratic presidential nomination, featuring a crowded field of aspirants and a drawn-out series of preferential primaries, was won by Governor Bill Clinton of Arkansas. To the surprise of many observers, Clinton selected Senator Albert Gore, Jr., of Tennessee as his running mate, making it clear that the Democrats intended to challenge the Republicans for the South's electoral votes and to reverse the GOP's stranglehold on the region in the last three elections. Meanwhile, the Republicans renominated President Bush and Vice President Quayle, and a hard-fought

36. C. Vann Woodward, "The Particular Politics of Being Southern," in *The Prevailing South: Life & Politics in a Changing Culture*, ed. Dudley Clendinen (Atlanta, Ga., 1988), p. 18.

37. Quoted in Lamis, *The Two-Party South*, p. 305.

38. Quoted in *ibid.*, p. 310. See also Black and Black, *The Vital South*, pp. 25–27, 315–25, 339–40; Alexander P. Lamis, "The Future of Southern Politics: New Directions for Dixie," in *The Future South: A Historical Perspective for the Twenty-first Century*, ed. Joe P. Dunn and Howard L. Preston (Urbana, Ill., 1991), pp. 57–64; and Monte Piliawski, "Racial Politics in the 1988 Presidential Election," *Black Scholar* 20 (January–February 1989): 30–37.

campaign ensued, enlivened by the third-party candidacy of Ross Perot, a wealthy Texas financier and advocate of drastic deficit reduction and other reforms. Clinton and Gore focused on the sluggish performance of the economy and worsening unemployment, while asserting that it was "time for a change" and committing themselves to an array of social reforms. Bush's approval rating had declined dramatically since the high level of his popularity during the Persian Gulf War of 1991, and he found himself on the defensive throughout the campaign.

Clinton won the election with only 43 percent of the popular vote but a substantial majority of 370 votes in the electoral college; Bush garnered 37.4 percent of the popular vote and 168 electoral votes, while Perot received a remarkable 18.9 percent of the popular vote without any electoral votes. Clinton and Gore made their best showing in the Northeast, but they won 41 percent of the southern popular vote and carried five of the region's states. Yet in defeat the Republican ticket did well in the South, receiving 43 percent of the ballots and carrying eight southern states. Bush and Quayle acquired 116 of their 168 electoral votes in the South. While the Democrats retained control of both houses of Congress, the Republicans made some congressional gains in the southern states.[39] In Bill Clinton, the nation had summoned another president from the South. But Clinton, who admired the leadership of John F. Kennedy, was unmistakably national in his thinking, and his administration developed an ambitious reform agenda. Even so, the role of the South in the election of 1992 and in the early years of Clinton's presidency was striking. All three of the major candidates in the election of 1992 identified themselves with the South, and no other part of the country was more fiercely contested than that region. The new administration in Washington was headed by a southern president and vice president, and the fate of its programs and policies would depend in no small measure on the powerful influence of southern congressional leaders from both political parties.

The number of Republican members of Congress from the South had steadily risen in recent years. Unlike the situation in earlier times when Democratic ascendancy was so overwhelming that the Republicans left many congressional seats uncontested, the minority party had begun to field candidates for most House and Senate seats. The 1970s brought "a core of right-wing Republican strength [from the South] in Congress."[40] After the 1980 election, Republicans held eleven of the region's twenty-six Senate seats[41] and one-third of the House seats. Despite some ups and downs, the party maintained this southern congressional strength during the 1980s. It gained nine new House positions in the election of 1984, for example, but lost four of its Senate seats in 1986. Following the election of 1992, Republicans held 11 of the 26 Senate seats from the South and 52 of the region's 147 House seats. Congress was no

39. "Democrats Reclaim Electoral College," *Congressional Quarterly Almanac*, vol. 48 (Washington, D.C., 1993), pp. 3A–24A.

40. Jack Bass, "V. O. Key Revisited," *South Atlantic Urban Studies* (1979): 267.

41. One of the other Senate seats was held by Harry F. Byrd, Jr., of Virginia, who classified himself as an independent but usually voted with the Republicans.

longer a "southern" institution, as it had been in some sense for more than half a century. Meanwhile, congressional Republicans from the southern states began to assume important positions of leadership. When the GOP won control of the Senate in 1980, Howard Baker became the new majority leader, while Strom Thurmond and other southerners headed key committees. In the House, Trent Lott of Mississippi and Newt Gingrich of Georgia later rose to positions of prominence and influence.[42]

By the 1970s the South's once-powerful Democratic delegations were becoming less formidable, partly because of the increasing numbers of Republican members from the southern states. Southerners were now less dominant in the committee structure and leadership positions of the two houses. The towering figures of an earlier day—Richard B. Russell, Harry Flood Byrd, John L. McClellan, James O. Eastland, Howard W. Smith, Wilbur Mills—had disappeared from the scene. Southerners now headed fewer committees and were less influential as a regional group, although some individual members such as Representative Jaime Whitten of Mississippi, longtime chairman of the House Appropriations subcommittee on agriculture, wielded enormous power. In 1981 southern Democrats presided over only six of twenty-two standing committees in the House and served as ranking minority members on only four of sixteen committees in the Republican-controlled Senate. Beyond that, the committee system itself was losing strength. New rules in the House of Representatives had diminished southern power, and in the mid-1970s a revolt of young liberals in that body was instrumental in the removal of two southern Democrats from important chairmanships.[43]

The conservative coalition—the informal voting alliance between southern Democrats and northern Republicans—did not disappear, although it became somewhat less prevalent in the 1970s. Roll call votes on which congressional Democrats split along sectional lines were likewise a continuing feature of proceedings in Congress. One study of House roll calls for selective years between 1951 and 1967 revealed that southern Democrats were more like Republicans than like northern Democrats on 37.6 percent of the votes.[44] The North-South split among Democrats showed up on 38 percent of the roll call votes in 1971, involving issues like defense appropriations, foreign aid, agricultural price sup-

42. Lamis, *The Two-Party South*, pp. 249–97, 314–21; William D. Snider, *Helms and Hunt: The North Carolina Senate Race, 1984* (Chapel Hill, N.C., 1985); Frederick A. Day and Gregory A. Weeks, "The 1984 Helms-Hunt Senate Race: A Spatial Postmortem of Emerging Republican Strength in the South," *Social Science Quarterly* 69 (December 1988): 942–60; "Democrats Reclaim Electoral College," pp. 9A–24A.

43. Richard Franklin Bensel, *Sectionalism and American Political Development, 1880–1980* (Madison, Wis., 1984), pp. 353–67, 381–85; Monroe Billington, *Southern Politics Since the Civil War* (Malabar, Fla., 1984), pp. 162–63; Grantham, *The Life & Death of the Solid South*, p. 188; Norman C. Miller, "The Farm Baron: Rep. Jaime Whitten Works behind Scenes to Shape Big Spending," *Wall Street Journal*, 7 June 1971, pp. 1, 25.

44. This was based on the 274 roll calls on which majorities of Democrats opposed majorities of Republicans. See W. Wayne Shannon, "Revolt in Washington: The South in Congress," in *The Changing Politics of the South*, ed. William C. Havard (Baton Rouge, La., 1972), pp. 649–50.

ports, efforts to broaden coverage of the minimum wage, equal employment opportunities, election reform, and school prayer. In 1973 a majority of the southern Democrats voted with a majority of the Republicans on 256 of the 318 roll calls involving a regional split among the Democrats. The conservative coalition won 61 percent of these votes. The coalition was evident in numerous aspects of Ronald Reagan's program in 1981, including the adoption of curbs against abortion and school busing. It appeared on only 14 percent of all roll call votes in 1985 but was successful on 89 percent of those. Coalition victories included spending for the MX missile system, for the "strategic defense initiative," and for Nicaraguan rebels.[45] A careful study of the phenomenon concludes that it "exists as an essentially permanent cross-party majority in Congress."[46]

Below the level of presidential voting, southern Republicans were most successful in the election of United States senators, U.S. representatives, and governors. A few GOP senators and governors were elected in the 1960s, but the number rose substantially in the 1970s. The election of 1980 represented a real breakthrough for the Republican party in the South. GOP candidates that year won 45.4 percent of the contests for the Senate and governorship in the former Confederate states. After the midterm elections of 1986, Republicans held about a third of the region's congressional seats and governorships, and by the end of the decade every southern state had elected a Republican governor since the mid-1970s. Progress at the municipal and county level was slower and quite uneven. The number of Republican state legislators began a slow increase early in the 1960s, reaching 416 of 1,782 seats (23.3 percent) by 1988.[47] Interparty competition, so long anticipated by political reformers in and out of the South, had become a reality in the region. It was no longer a rarity to find Republican officeholders in congressional and statewide positions. The GOP was organized in every southern state, and it had begun to contest all statewide and congressional offices and an increasing number of local elections.[48]

A dramatic change in the party loyalties of southerners was evident, espe-

45. *Ibid.*, pp. 637–87; "Democratic Split: Highest Percentage Since 1960," *Congressional Quarterly Almanac* 27 (1971): 107–10; "Regional Divisions Among Democrats Declined in 1973," *Congressional Quarterly Almanac* 29 (1973): 942–45; "Influence of Conservative Coalition Declined in 1973," *ibid.*, pp. 946–51; "Conservatives Hit New High in Showdown Vote Victories," *Congressional Quarterly Almanac* 37 (1981): 35c–40c; "Conservative Strength Falters in Wake of United Democrats," *Congressional Quarterly Almanac* 39 (1983): 37c–42c; "Conservative Strength Is High but Infrequent," *Congressional Quarterly Almanac* 41 (1985): 36c–41c; David W. Brady and Charles S. Bullock III, "Is There a Conservative Coalition in the House?" *Journal of Politics* 42 (May 1980): 549–59.

46. Mack C. Shelley II, *The Permanent Majority: The Conservative Coalition in the United States Congress* (University, Ala., 1983), p. 157.

47. Lamis, "The Future of Southern Politics," p. 67; Lamis, *The Two-Party South*, pp. 22, 32, 265, 314–16; Grantham, *The Life & Death of the Solid South*, p. 191.

48. Greenhaw, *Elephants in the Cottonfields, passim*; Earl Black and Merle Black, "The Partial Transformation of Southern Democracy: State Intraparty Politics, 1920–85," paper presented at the annual meeting of the American Political Science Association, August 1986; Harold W. Stanley, "Southern Partisan Changes: Dealignment, Realignment, or Both?" *Journal of Politics* 50 (February 1988): 64–88.

cially in national politics. A process of "dealignment" seemed to be dissolving the familiar Democratic hegemony in the South. The electorate had splintered into minorities of Democrats, Republicans, and independents. Whereas Democrats in the region had outnumbered Republicans almost eight to one in the early 1950s, their advantage in party identification in presidential elections had disappeared. As late as 1968, survey data showed that 60 percent of southerners called themselves Democrats and only 18 percent Republicans. Polls revealed that the percentage of southern whites favorably disposed toward the Republican party nearly doubled between 1976 and 1984. Political scientists estimate that the Democrats suffered a net loss of 25 percent between the 1950s and the 1980s, while the Republicans enjoyed a net gain of 20 percent during the same period. In the meantime, a sharp drop occurred in the percentage of white southerners who considered themselves *strong* Democrats. Only black southerners continued overwhelmingly to vote for Democratic candidates and to identify themselves positively as Democrats. Surveys conducted by the National Election Study in the fall of 1988 showed that among white southerners 35 percent described themselves as Democrats, 26 percent as Republicans, and a whopping 39 percent as independents. The realignment of southern whites had a profound effect on the national party system. White southerners, who had once made up a third of the Democratic party, now constituted barely a fifth of all Democrats. The Republican party had become the party of southern whites as well as northern white Protestants. The white South was, in fact, the major element of the national party realignment in presidential elections. It provided the base for what had become a normal Republican presidential majority.[49]

Why did southerners, particularly white southerners, abandon their traditional loyalty to the Democratic party? Why did more and more of them identify themselves with the Republican party? Broadly speaking, white southerners were increasingly disaffected by the liberalism of the national Democratic party, while growing numbers of them were attracted to the conservatism of the Republican party. The GOP attraction was especially notable among middle-class and upper-middle-class whites, the college educated, and the younger generation. A substantial majority of the South's white residents had come to identify themselves as conservatives, and in many respects the political outlook of the white working class was quite similar to that of the white middle class. Southern Republicanism was also nourished by the growing numbers of outsiders moving into the region; people from other sections eventually comprised about 20 percent of the electorate. The occupations, professions, education,

49. William Schneider, "The New Shape of American Politics," *Atlantic Monthly* 259 (January 1987): 39–54; John R. Petrocik, "Realignment: New Party Coalitions and Nationalization of the South," *Journal of Politics* 49 (May 1987): 347–75; Martin P. Wattenberg, "The Building of a Republican Regional Base in the South: The Elephant Crosses the Mason-Dixon Line," *Public Opinion Quarterly* 55 (Fall 1991): 424–31; Lamis, *The Two-Party South*, p. 321. See also James F. Lea, ed., *Contemporary Southern Politics* (Baton Rouge, La., 1988); Robert H. Swansbrough and David M. Brodsky, eds., *The South's New Politics: Realignment and Dealignment* (Columbia, S.C., 1988); and Tod A. Baker et al., eds., *Political Parties in the Southern States: Party Activists in Partisan Coalitions* (New York, 1990).

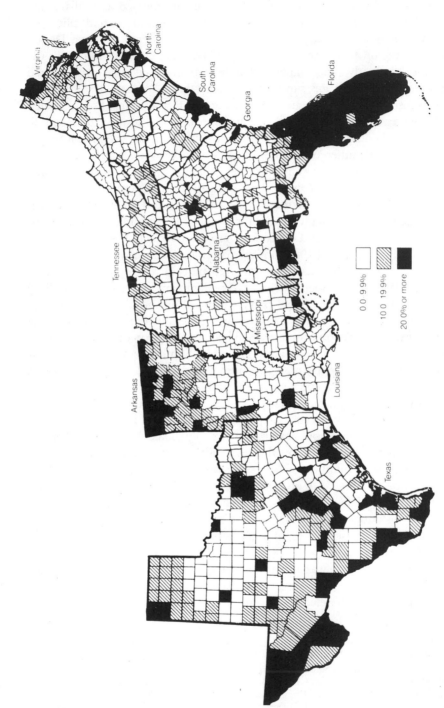

The Geography of Northernization. Percentage of native whites in 1980 who were born outside of the southern states. SOURCE: Earl Black and Merle Black, *Politics and Society in the South* (Cambridge, Mass.: Harvard University Press, 1987), p. 18.

and political preferences of these migrants predisposed a majority of them to conservatism and Republicanism. Middle-class conservatives had still another advantage: greater financial resources. Organized labor's lack of influence enhanced the political strength of conservatives. The failure of southern liberalism, Earl Black and Merle Black suggest, resulted from the fact that "too many white voters welcome conservative positions and candidates and reject the symbols, policies, and beneficiaries of contemporary liberalism."[50] The conservatism that exerted such a strong appeal among white southerners included a powerful racial component. A poll conducted by the Center for Political Studies at the University of Michigan in the spring of 1988 revealed that 69 percent of black southerners favored preferential hiring and promotion for their race, while 86 percent of white southerners opposed such preferential treatment of African Americans.[51]

By the 1980s, a majority of southern whites had entered the region's dynamic new middle class, and that class was persistently drawn to conservative political positions. As two close students of recent southern politics have written, "The reigning political philosophy of the new southern middle class is the entrepreneurial version of the individualistic political culture, a blend of conservative and progressive themes. In its emphasis on low rates of taxation, minimal regulation of business, and resolute opposition to unions and redistributive welfare programs for have-nots and have-littles, the current political ideology retains important continuities with the traditionalistic political culture."[52] Committed to the virtues of economic growth, the new class approved the use of government funds to build the facilities needed for such development. But it tended to condemn liberal policies that might restrain entrepreneurial ventures, redistribute income, or expand the welfare state. Meaningful symbols for this class included police, whites, southerners, the military, conservatives, and Republicans. Public opinion polls showed that white southerners, more than most other Americans, believed in the principle of individual responsibility, questioned the wisdom of enlarging the domestic powers of the federal government, and had steadily lost confidence in decisions made in Washington. These attitudes do much to explain George Wallace's regional popularity and, after the decline of his movement, the mounting support for Republican candidates. Working-class southerners also increasingly adhered to many of these conservative positions, as the pattern of their votes revealed.[53]

In addition, the conservative tendencies of white southerners were shown in their attitudes on "social issues" such as the use of busing to achieve racial bal-

50. Black and Black, *Politics and Society in the South*, p. 230.

51. Black and Black, *The Vital South*, pp. 6–7.

52. Black and Black, *Politics and Society in the South*, p. 297. See also Helmut Norpoth, "Under Way and Here to Stay: Party Realignment in the 1980s?" *Public Opinion Quarterly* 51 (Fall 1987): 376–91. In *American Federalism: A View from the States*, 3d ed. (New York, 1984), Daniel J. Elazar characterizes the South's dominant political culture as a combination of "traditionalist" and "individualistic" themes.

53. Black and Black, *Politics and Society in the South*, pp. 213–31, 246–48, 298, 313; Lamis, *The Two-Party South*, pp. 220–21.

ance, prayer in the public schools, and abortion. Although most whites gradually abandoned the doctrine of strict segregation, adopting a position in between segregation and desegregation, they remained racial conservatives. Most whites and most blacks had conflicting views on the form of race relations they preferred, and they differed profoundly on an array of specific racial issues— the responsibility of the federal government in providing citizens with a job and a good standard of living, the role of affirmative action policies, the need for individual responsibility, and so on. The economic priorities of the two racial groups diverged, since poverty and marginal economic status affected them very differently. These divergent social perspectives made it difficult for liberal and moderate politicians to create black and white coalitions. "In order to hold together their ideologically diverse biracial coalition," one scholar observes, "southern moderates need to be skilled practitioners of the art of the political straddle, and they certainly are."[54]

Attitudinal differences along racial lines also help account for the alienation of white southerners from the national Democratic party, as well as the continuing political impotence and frustration of black southerners. Thus, while Douglas Wilder of Virginia became the first African American to be elected governor of a U.S. state (in 1989), his "color," a student of Virginia politics writes, "probably cost him tens of thousands of votes on election day. . . . [since] many conservative Democrats and independents otherwise inclined to vote Democratic simply could not pull Wilder's lever."[55] Election returns and survey research data not only point up a sharp racial split in southern politics; they also suggest marked differences between North and South, with southerners taking a tougher stance on national security issues and a more conservative position on a cluster of social questions. Southerners as a group appear to be more socially conservative, nationalistic, and religious than nonsoutherners. They also seem to be better satisfied, regardless of class, race, or party, with their states and communities than is true of other Americans. This, too, fostered conservatism.[56]

Although Democratic power in the South had waned, the party remained the largest political organization in the region. The Democrats retained their superiority in party identification, with an estimated 50 percent of the voting-age population. They were still the dominant party in state and local elections. If a party realignment was under way in the southern states, it was not yet complete; thus far it was only a "split-level realignment" manifesting itself mainly in presidential elections. Democratic leaders could take some comfort in survey data showing that economic class continued to differentiate white southern voters, and evidence that white Democrats in the South were more numerous

54. Lamis, "The Future of Southern Politics," p. 56.
55. Quoted in Lamis, *The Two-Party South*, p. 317. See also *ibid.*, pp. 222–23; and Black and Black, *Politics and Society in the South*, pp. 195–231, 270–71, 295–96.
56. Alan I. Abramowitz, "Ideological Realignment and the Nationalization of Southern Politics: Party Activists and Candidates in Virginia," in *Perspectives on the American South: An Annual Review of Society, Politics and Culture*, vol. 1, ed. Merle Black and John Shelton Reed (New York, 1981), pp. 83–106; Black and Black, *The Vital South*, pp. 220–37, 383–86; Lamis, "The Future of Southern Politics," pp. 71–77.

among "those who have less."[57] Democrats could also anticipate support from southern women, who had become more active in politics as voters, party workers, candidates, and officeholders, particularly in local and municipal politics. In recent presidential elections, women in the South, as in other regions, had outpolled men, and in all but the oldest age cohort women seemed to be more Democratic than men in the white South. Southern women were still less active than men in traditional politics, although the two sexes appeared to show about equal interest in community matters. But there was evidence that southern women were becoming steadily more active in partisan politics. Within three years of the organization of the North Carolina Women's Political Caucus in 1972, for instance, the number of female legislators in that state increased from two to thirteen. Thirty-one of the party nominees for Congress in the South in 1992 were women. In describing a bicentennial program on Women and the Constitution, held in Atlanta in 1988, one writer spoke of the presence in full array of "the foot soldiers of the civil rights and recent women's movements, the lawyers and professors, political partisans, clubwomen, and even survivors of 'Ladies for Lyndon' and 'The Peanut Brigade.' "[58]

Democratic party leaders sought to adapt to a political constituency that included blacks and whites. By the mid-1980s, more than five million black voters had become supporters of the Democratic party in the southern states. This meant that Democratic candidates in the Deep South could usually win with no more than 40 percent of the white vote (45 percent in the peripheral South). Yet they had to be cautious: while "most politically active blacks are Democrats, most southern Democrats are whites."[59] Blatant racism no longer dominated southern politics, but racial considerations were still a powerful influence, particularly in the lower South. Thus, in their efforts to construct coalitions of black and white voters, Democratic politicians tended to adopt moderate, central positions. As a Democratic congressman from Mississippi explained in 1982, "no one could really stamp me as a liberal or a conservative. I never did anything to alienate the black support that I had. I never did anything to alienate the business support that I had."[60] Jack Bass and Walter DeVries mention "the conservative Dixie Democrat who gets black votes by being a Democrat and white votes by voting conservative."[61] It was like walking a tightrope. But Democrats depended on such biracial coalitions in every southern state.

In many respects the transformation of southern politics during the last three decades represents a remarkable nationalization of political life in the region. One manifestation of this change was the increasing similarity in the political

57. Black and Black, *Politics and Society in the South*, pp. 239–40, 259, 282; Lamis, *The Two-Party South*, pp. 215–16, 309.

58. Margaret Ripley Wolfe, "The View from Atlanta: Southern Women and the Future," in *The Future South*, ed. Dunn and Preston, pp. 123–57 (quotation on p. 126); Bass and DeVries, *The Transformation of Southern Politics*, pp. 243–44; Wattenberg, "The Building of a Republican Regional Base in the South," p. 430; Rhodes Cook, "Democratic Clout Is Growing As the Gender Gap Widens," *Congressional Quarterly Weekly Report* 50 (October 17, 1992): 3265–68.

59. Black and Black, *Politics and Society in the South*, p. 312.

60. Quoted in Lamis, *The Two-Party South*, p. 230.

61. Bass and DeVries, *The Transformation of Southern Politics*, p. 75.

practices and political culture of the South and non-South. Nothing was more important than the disruption of the Solid South, the decline of Democratic primaries as the only meaningful elections in the region, and the emergence of genuine bipartisan competition. With the growing appeal of Republican candidates, politics became more competitive in every southern state. This in turn stimulated Democrats to strengthen their position in state and local contests. These developments were related to the expansion of the southern electorate— to the enfranchisement of the black masses, to the dramatic increase in the registration of white southerners, and to the marked rise in voter turnout. "Today," Earl Black and Merle Black remark, "one looks at the South and sees America." For the modern South "is the largest, the most cohesive, and, arguably, the most important region in the United States in terms of establishing the partisan direction of presidential politics."[62]

Southern politics became more open and more democratic. This resulted in part from court decisions that forced the redistricting of congressional and legislative seats, from the invalidation of the poll tax and other disfranchising devices, and from the effects of the Voting Rights Act of 1965 and hundreds of registration drives. It also stemmed from increasing registration of southern whites, often in response to the enfranchisement of blacks. Reapportionment hastened the decline of rural influence and the transfer of political power to metropolitan and urban areas. In 1941 the political scientist Herman Clarence Nixon described the typical southern legislature as "chiefly a body of Democratic, small-town or rural, white men, a majority of whom represent a minority of the population of the state, not to mention the restricted suffrage by which the members were chosen in a party primary."[63] Thirty years later the composition of the region's legislatures had undergone a decided change. By the 1970s they were much more urban-oriented, and their members included increasing numbers of blacks, women, and Republicans. Competition for legislative seats had become keener. Politics had become significantly more accessible and more meaningful to southerners than at any time since the late-nineteenth century. Many of the disparities that once distinguished political affairs in the South from other parts of the country had disappeared.

The integration of the South into the national economy contributed to the nationalization of the region's politics. "In every southern state," a recent study notes, "industrialization has multiplied and diversified the number of institutions—banks, insurance companies, utilities, construction firms, real estate interests, transportation companies, communications businesses, leading law firms—that make up state power structures, while simultaneously augmenting the collective resources at the disposal of state 'establishments.' "[64] The political

62. Black and Black, *The Vital South*, pp. 344, 366. See also Paul Allen Beck and Paul Lopatto, "The End of Southern Distinctiveness," in *Contemporary Southern Political Attitudes and Behavior*, ed. Moreland, Baker, and Steed, pp. 160–82, and Carol A. Cassel, "Change in Electoral Participation in the South," *Journal of Politics* 41 (August 1979): 907–17.

63. H. C. Nixon, "The Southern Legislature and Legislation," in *The Southern Political Scene, 1938–1948*, ed. Taylor Cole and John H. Hallowell (Gainesville, Fla., 1948), p. 412.

64. Black and Black, *Politics and Society in the South*, p. 23.

leverage of the old county-seat governing class declined dramatically. The rural South, including the once-dominant black belts, was no longer a major source of political leadership and power, while the urban sector began to exert much greater weight in election campaigns and policy outcomes. The large metropolitan and medium-city electorates provided 70 percent of the southern vote in the presidential election of 1980. The new middle class, in which white women constituted a notable part, reflected these economic and social changes. As two authorities point out, "Middle-class southerners occupy most of the region's political offices, dominate its key decisionmaking institutions in the private sector, and control most of its communications and mass media."[65] In these and other respects North and South were increasingly alike.

In the South, as elsewhere, old-style personal politics and other traditional forms of campaigning began to give way to expensive and high-powered media appeals to the mass of voters and to a diminished role for the political party. The changing technology of mass communications hastened the adoption of new techniques of campaigning based on telephone polling and television advertising. Segregation-type politicians virtually passed from the scene. Governors became more important as party leaders. They tended to be moderates and centrists rather than neo-Populists, but most of them were willing to spend money for public services, especially education. Meanwhile, in the 1970s and 1980s, state governments throughout the South were modernized in an effort to make them more effective in carrying out their enlarged functions. National issues relating to education, health care, the environment, and the like had become as salient in the southern states as in other regions. In Washington the South's overrepresentation in Congress resulting from malapportionment and restricted electorates had ended. Sectional differences still hampered the operation of the Democratic party, but there seemed to be greater agreement and less friction, in and out of Congress, between the southern and nonsouthern wings of the party.[66]

Southern politics had changed enormously since midcentury, and the region's political affairs had, outwardly at least, become Americanized. Nevertheless, there was continuity as well as change in the new southern politics, and in some respects political life in the South remained distinctive within the nation as a whole. This was revealed in the continued existence of a certain folksiness in state and local politics, in the emphasis on personality in election campaigns, in the colorful speech and behavior of southern politicians, and in the traditional views in the region about the role of women in public affairs. Thus politics presented, in the words of one historian, a "dissonant picture, with socio-

65. Ibid., p. 58.

66. John S. Jackson III and Robert A. Hitlin, "The Nationalization of the Democratic Party," Western Political Quarterly 34 (June 1981): 270–86; William M. Lunch, The Nationalization of American Politics (Berkeley, Calif., 1987), pp. 109–12; Kenny J. Whitby and Franklin D. Gilliam, Jr., "A Longitudinal Analysis of Competing Explanations for the Transformation of Southern Congressional Politics," Journal of Politics 53 (May 1991): 504–18; Charles S. Bullock III, "Congressional Voting and the Mobilization of a Black Electorate in the South," Journal of Politics 43 (August 1981): 662–82; Black and Black, Politics and Society in the South, pp. 210, 251–55.

economic *dis*continuity accompanied by striking continuities of conservative political dominance."[67] In spite of the enfranchisement of millions of black and white southerners, the electorate of the typical southern state remained less active and less influential than its counterpart in other regions. Labor unions in the South continued to be weak. The political system was less responsive to the public needs of the disadvantaged than was true of other sections. Finally, southern politics, in contrast to politics in other regions, was still pervasively affected by racial considerations. While race was a significant factor throughout the nation in the ascendancy of the conservative presidential majority of the 1980s, it was an especially potent influence among white southerners. A close student of southern politics has noted that the central tendency of Republican efforts in the South since the early 1960s was an attempt to construct a new "white man's party."[68] These regional differences point to the persistence of distinctive cultural patterns in the contemporary South.

67. Hugh Davis Graham, "Beyond V. O. Key: The Normativ: Legacy of *Southern Politics*," *Georgia Historical Quarterly* 72 (Spring 1988): 87–101 (quotation on p. 91).

68. Earl Black, "Competing Responses to the 'New Southern Politics': Republican and Democratic Southern Strategies, 1964–1976," in *Perspectives on the American South*, vol. 1, ed. Black and Reed, pp. 151–64. See also Edsall, *Chain Reaction*, p. 256.

CHAPTER 12

The Persistence of Southern Distinctiveness

ANY nonsoutherners had long hoped that someday the South would be, "in character and culture," identical with the North.[1] Southerners themselves, particularly those who through the years had advocated a "New South," assumed that in some important respects the region would eventually remake itself along the lines of the powerful and triumphant North. The theme of convergence seemed to reach fruition in the extraordinary changes that swept over the South during the decades following World War II—its economic expansion, the revolution in its race relations, and the transformation of its politics. No one could doubt that the region had changed more rapidly than the rest of the nation in the postwar period. The image of a defeated, poverty-stricken, racially obsessed, and tragic region was replaced by one of prosperity, good fortune, and success.

In many respects the South had become almost indistinguishable from other parts of the country. As one southerner remarked, "On any given day in . . . Atlanta or Richmond or Raleigh or New Orleans or Birmingham or Houston, it would be easy to believe not only that the South [had] thoroughly lost the War, but that since then it has been effaced, ploughed under, and covered with asphalt. Has vanished forever in a total and final Yankee triumph."[2] Or the interregional convergence could be viewed as the triumph of the South. When Will Barrett, the protagonist in Walker Percy's *The Last Gentleman*, returns to the South after a long absence, he suffers a kind of culture shock. As Percy writes, "The South he came home to was different from the South he had left. It was happy, victorious, Christian, rich, patriotic and Republican."[3] The journalist Joseph B. Cumming, Jr., concluded as early as 1971 that the South had become

---

1. See, for example, Richard N. Current, *Northernizing the South* (Athens, Ga., 1983), p. 1.
2. George Garrett, "Southern Literature Here and Now," in Fifteen Southerners, *Why the South Will Survive* (Athens, Ga., 1981), p. 123.
3. Walker Percy, *The Last Gentleman* (New York, 1966), p. 185.

Americanized in virtually every way. Thus, southern racism "has grown close enough to the national style of racism, as described by the Kerner Report, to lose its value as a national news story."[4]

By the 1970s, moreover, sectional hostility between North and South had become less strident. The depiction of a savage and benighted South in the national media during the 1950s and 1960s—sustained by the dramatic civil rights struggles that erupted in Little Rock, Birmingham, Selma, and dozens of other southern cities and towns—was replaced by the image of the Sunbelt South. The region had emerged as what Fred Hobson describes as "a superior South, a region cleaner, less crowded, more open and honest, more genuinely religious and friendly, and suddenly more racially tolerant than any other American region."[5] The phenomenon of Jimmy Carter seemed to mark the South's political redemption and national approval of southern leadership. Indeed, one scholar notes, "the craze for things southern began to mushroom like skyscrapers in Atlanta or mellow accents in Washington."[6] Americans outside the South, having experienced military defeat in Vietnam, an unnerving constitutional crisis in Watergate, and racial conflict in their own communities, were no longer in a mood to refashion the South in the likeness of the North. Southerners, for their part, were no longer acutely conscious of living under a powerful external threat.

At the same time, the South demonstrated a capacity to absorb economic and demographic change with relatively little social and cultural disruption. Commenting in 1966 on the decline of "southernism," a close observer predicted that "a thousand and one cultural nuances—ranging from speech peculiarities and food preferences to the tempo of life, and from 'gasconade mixed with plaintiveness' to 'hedonism combined with puritanism' "—would survive "for some time the encroaching and flattening uniformity of our industrialized age."[7] Writing in the mid-1980s, an English student of the American South remarked that the region still inhabited two worlds, "two moral territories." While its material culture had changed substantially since the Second World War, its "non-material culture, although altered, still enables Southerners to think and talk of themselves in terms of their regional identity, the inherited codes, and, to some extent, still permits Northerners to do the same."[8] The South did remain a distinctive American region. Southernness continued to embody, on the one hand, "an undeniable core of shared meanings, understandings, and ways of doing things," and on the other, an insistence by outsiders that the southerner's "group membership was significant."[9]

4. Joseph B. Cumming, Jr., "Been Down Home So Long It Looks Like Up to Me," *Esquire*, August 1971, pp. 84–85, 90, 110, 114 (quotation on p. 85).

5. Fred Hobson, *Tell About the South: The Southern Rage to Explain* (Baton Rouge, La., 1983), p. 14.

6. George B. Tindall, "The Resurgence of Southern Identity," in *The American South: Portrait of a Culture*, ed. Louis D. Rubin, Jr. Baton Rouge, La., 1980), p. 161.

7. William G. Carleton, "The South's Many Moods," *Yale Review* 55 (Summer 1966): 640.

8. Richard Gray, *Writing the South: Ideas of an American Region* (Cambridge, England, 1986), pp. 230–31.

9. John Shelton Reed, "The Same Old Stand?" in Fifteen Southerners, *Why the South Will Survive*, p. 19.

In 1972 a young sociologist named John Shelton Reed provided persuasive evidence to support the argument that the South had not lost its cultural identity, that it had not been swallowed up in an increasingly homogenized and standarized America. Reed maintained, in *The Enduring South: Subcultural Persistence in Mass Society*, that "regional cultural differences have existed and still exist, and that they correspond at least roughly to Americans' perceptions of them."[10] Reed employed public opinion polls covering a period of three decades in an investigation of three broad cultural areas: attitudes toward religion, violence, and localism. The South, he concluded, comprises a regional subculture with a strong sense of group membership. He argued that southerners' differences from "the American mainstream" are similar to those of the immigrant ethnic groups. He contended that southerners "are more likely than non-Southerners to be conventionally religious, to accept the private use of force (or the potential for it), and to be anchored in their homeplace."[11] This regional differentiation did not seem to result from differences in urbanization, occupation, or education. As for the sources of the South's continuing distinctiveness, Reed emphasized the role of the family and the church, which he found to be more important in the southern states than in other regions. Historically, the sociologist noted, the image of the South was that of "a people defined in opposition to a powerful, external threat." Thus "localism, violence, and a conservative religion are all plausible responses for a minority group, surrounded by a culture which is viewed as powerful, hostile, and unresponsive; all can be seen as adaptive reactions to the situation in which Southerners have, time and again, found themselves."[12]

Survey data as well as less quantitative evidence reveal that southerners seem more likely than other Americans to identify closely with their own communities—to think of themselves as "distinct from and preferable to other regions, states, and localities." The theme of place and community apparently has special meaning for most southerners. Polls indicate that they are more inclined than other Americans to pay relatively greater attention to state politics than to national and international affairs; to choose their "normative reference individuals" from neighbors and family members; to have a high opinion of their home states and of their colleges; and to express regret over having left their states and region. In the South there was a "symbiotic relation" between regional culture and local institutions. As Reed observes, a localistic orientation— "an attachment to their place and their people"—is one of the cultural characteristics that continue to make southerners distinctive in the larger nation.[13]

10. John Shelton Reed, *The Enduring South: Subcultural Persistence in Mass Society* (Lexington, Mass., 1972), p. 83. See also Reed, "The South: What Is It? Where Is It?" in *The South for New Southerners*, ed. Paul D. Escott and David R. Goldfield (Chapel Hill, N.C., 1991), pp. 18–41.

11. Reed, *The Enduring South*, p. 83.

12. *Ibid.*, pp. 88–89. See also John Shelton Reed, *Southerners: The Social Psychology of Sectionalism* (Chapel Hill, N.C., 1983).

13. Reed, *The Enduring South*, pp. 33–43 (quotations on pp. 33 and 43). See also John Shelton Reed, *One South: An Ethnic Approach to Regional Culture* (Baton Rouge, La., 1982), pp. 11–32, 154–61; Stephen A. Smith, *Myth, Media, and the Southern Mind* (Fayetteville, Ark., 1985), pp. 116–32; Earl Black and Merle Black, *Politics and Society in the South* (Cambridge, Mass., 1987), pp. 219–29; and

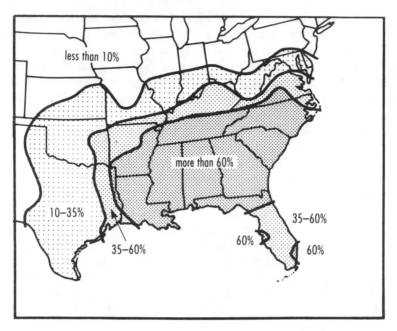

"Southern" Listings as Percentage of "American" Listings in Telephone Directories, ca. 1975. SOURCE: John Shelton Reed, "The Heart of Dixie: An Essay in Folk Geography," *Social Forces* 54 (June 1976): 929.

Perhaps the most distinguishable aspect of modern southern culture is the church and the "old-time religion." There was reason for outsiders to refer to the South as the "Bible Belt," for religion had long been a powerful influence in the lives of southerners. For much of its history, the South was almost as solid in religion as in politics. One scholar has aptly spoken of the "Anglo-Saxon Protestant hegemony" in the region.[14] The essence of this "southern religion" was what two authorities describe as "the distinctive, relatively stable, and culturally integrated Protestantism of the region's native-born whites." It was a religion characterized by "high visibility, conservatism, and emotionalism."[15] At an earlier time the religious beliefs and practices of southerners had not been very different from those of other Americans. In the first half of the nineteenth century, evangelical Protestantism distinguished the religious orientation of the North as well as the South. During the second half of the century, however, the North changed radically, moving toward a more pluralistic culture under the influence of immigration and secularization, while the South remained a land

Merle Black, "North Carolina: The 'Best' American State?" in *Politics and Policy in North Carolina,* ed. Thad L. Beyle and Merle Black (New York, 1975), pp. 13–34.

14. Samuel S. Hill, Jr., cited in David Edwin Harrell, Jr., "Religious Pluralism: Catholics, Jews, and Sectarians," in *Religion in the South,* ed. Charles Reagan Wilson (Jackson, Miss., 1985), p. 60.

15. Joseph H. Fichter and George L. Maddox, "Religion in the South, Old and New," in *The South in Continuity and Change,* ed. John C. McKinney and Edgar T. Thompson (Durham, N.C., 1965), p. 359.

of revivalism and religious fundamentalism. Although religious expression in the North and South has grown more alike in cc.temporary America, the pervasiveness and intensity of religion below the Potomac continue to set the region apart within the nation.[16]

Evangelicalism and fundamentalism are deeply rooted in southern life. "In its heart of hearts," one scholar observes, "southern religion puts its faith in the personal piety of converted individuals whose lives reflect biblical righteousness in daily behavior."[17] Evangelical Protestantism and Christian orthodoxy became dominant. Even the minority churches mirrored a discernible regional culture. African-American religious life in the South paralleled that of the white community, in spite of racial segregation and the fierce independence of the two groups. Even the minority Caltholics, Jews, and sectarians, with their own distinctive theological traditions and their alienation in "an unfriendly evangelical culture," were molded by the South's peculiar history, shared in a kind of southern civil religion, and generally felt at home with their religious neighbors in the region.[18] The powerful role of the Southern Baptist and Methodist churches in the South, like that of Mormons and Roman Catholics in some other parts of the country, permits one to describe those churches as "cultural religions." Such religions "so dominate a geographical region that the line between the church and the surrounding culture grows increasingly hard to draw and the force of this unofficial alliance tends to make the religious body ever stronger and more inclusive."[19]

"Southerners," Time magazine pointed out in 1976, "are the most churchgoing people in the nation, and from camp meeting through riverside baptisms to huge urban congregations, the tone and temper of Southern Protestantism is evangelical."[20] Church membership is a major element of personal identity among southerners, and they are more likely than people in other regions to attend church and to tune into worship services on radio and television. The South is more Protestant than the rest of the country—90 percent of white southerners identify themselves as Protestant—and the region's population is much more homogeneous in its Protestantism than is true of other sections. Nearly half of southern white Protestants are Baptists, and about eight out of ten are Baptist, Methodist, or Presbyterian. The percentage is even higher for southern black Protestants. Churches of Christ have also grown rapidly in the twentieth century, and Pentecostal and Holiness bodies have attracted many followers in the South. Although not all southerners are fundamentalists, a ma-

16. Carl N. Degler, "Thesis, Antithesis, Synthesis: The South, the North, and the Nation," *Journal of Southern History* 53 (February 1987): 12–14; Samuel S. Hill, Jr., *The South and the North in American Religion* (Athens, Ga., 1980), pp. 90–135, 141.

17. Samuel S. Hill, "Religion and Politics in the South," in *Religion in the South*, ed. Wilson, p. 148.

18. Harrell, "Religious Pluralism: Catholics, Jews, and Sectarians," pp. 59–82.

19. Edwin S. Gaustad, "Regionalism in American Religion," in *Religion in the South*, ed. Wilson, p. 171.

20. Quoted in Howard L. Preston, "Will Dixie Disappear? Cultural Contours of a Region in Transition," in *The Future South: A Historical Perspective for the Twenty-first Century*, ed. Joe P. Dunn and Howard L. Preston (Urbana, Ill., 1991), p. 200.

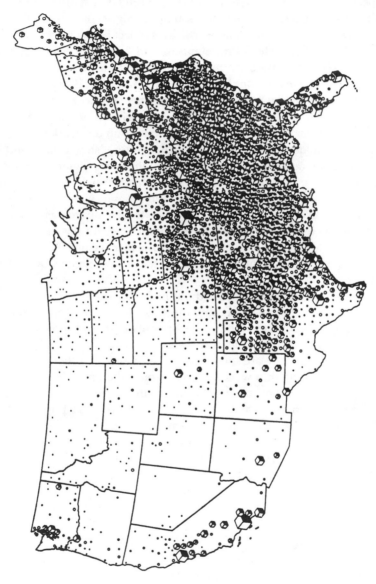

Members of Baptist Churches, 1952. SOURCE: Wilbur Zelinsky, "An Approach to the Religious Geography of the United States: Patterns of Church Membership in 1952," *Annals of the Association of American Geographers* 51 (June 1961): 172.

jority of them are evangelical Protestants. Most southerners, in fact, belong to low-church evangelical Protestant denominations, which does much to explain the democratic and anti-authoritarian traditions of those churches.[21] Even the radical churches of the dispossessed participate in and help shape the cultural life of the region.[22] This is notably true of the black church, whose importance is suggested by the role it played as a major source of and a sustaining force in the civil rights movement. It would be hard to imagine the rise of Martin Luther King, Jr., without the crucible of the black church.[23]

Samuel S. Hill has identified four common convictions as forming "a normative southern religious position": the Bible is the sole reference point of belief and practice; direct and dynamic access to the Lord is open to all; morality is defined in individualistic and personal terms; and worship is informal.[24] According to a number of national polls over the last several decades, southerners are more likely than northerners to speak specifically of heaven, hell, judgment, and bodily resurrection. One Gallup poll indicated that 86 percent of white southern Protestants believe in the Devil, as compared with 52 percent of their counterparts in other regions. Southerners are twice as likely as nonsoutherners to report that they have had a "moment of sudden religious insight or awakening," and in a poll taken in 1959, 81 percent answered yes to the question, "Do you think Jesus Christ will ever return to earth?" Analysts have found that using statistical measures to control for such factors as education, occupation, and rural residency does not substantially reduce regional religious differences. Southerners continue to place great weight on individual salvation. Their churches have persistently denied "the illusion of human perfectibility," and this "Calvinistic skepticism toward human possibilities carries over into the region's attitude toward all sorts of programs for the improvement of society."[25]

The post–World War II South produced the nation's leading Protestant evangelists. The most famous of these evangelists was Billy Graham of North Carolina. He employed organizational skills and sophisticated techniques to

21. John Shelton Reed, "Southerners," in *Harvard Encyclopedia of American Ethnic Groups*, ed. Stephan Thernstrom (Cambridge, Mass., 1980), p. 946; Reed, *The Enduring South*, pp. 57–81; David Edwin Harrell, Jr., *White Sects and Black Men in the Recent South* (Nashville, Tenn., 1971); Corwin Smidt, "Evangelicals Within Contemporary American Politics: Differentiating Between Fundamentalist and Non-Fundamentalist Evangelicals," *Western Political Quarterly* 41 (September 1988): 601–20; Samuel S. Hill, "Religion," in *Encyclopedia of Southern Culture*, ed. Charles Reagan Wilson and William Ferris (Chapel Hill, N.C., 1989), pp. 1269–1331.

22. See Harrell, *White Sects and Black Men in the Recent South*; David Edwin Harrell, Jr., ed., *Varieties of Southern Evangelicalism* (Macon, Ga., 1981); Samuel S. Hill, Jr., "The Strange Career of Religious Pluralism in the South," in *Perspectives on the American South: An Annual Review of Society, Politics and Culture*, vol. 2, ed. Merle Black and John Shelton Reed (New York, 1984), pp. 197–214; Christopher H. Walker, "Three Pentecostal Churches," in *ibid.*, pp. 215–25; and Steven M. Kane, "Appalachian Snake Handlers," in *Perspectives on the American South: An Annual Review of Society, Politics and Culture*, vol. 4, ed. James C. Cobb and Charles R. Wilson (New York, 1987), pp. 115–27.

23. Lewis V. Baldwin, " 'Let Us Break Bread Together': Martin Luther King, Jr. and the Black Church in the South, 1954–1968," in *Cultural Perspectives on the American South*, vol. 5: *Religion*, ed. Charles Reagan Wilson (New York, 1991), pp. 119–42.

24. Hill, "Religion," in *Encyclopedia of Southern Culture*, ed. Wilson and Ferris, p. 1269.

25. Charles P. Roland, "The Ever-Vanishing South," *Journal of Southern History* 48 (February 1982): 10. See also Reed, *The Enduring South*, pp. 57–81, and Reed, "Southerners," pp. 946–47.

carry southern revivalism's traditional message to millions of people around the world. Many other revivalists followed in Graham's wake, including Oral Roberts, Jimmy Swaggert, Jerry Falwell, and Pat Robertson. Using radio and television with spectacular results, these "televangelists" attracted huge audiences by presenting the old-time religion in contemporary terms. Their message was personal and intense, and it stressed traditional values of family, home, and community. Although these evangelists attracted millions of followers throughout the country, the "electronic church" was a uniquely southern phenomenon. Virtually all of the leading televangelists came from the South or moved into the region to establish their ministries. Their audiences were drawn disproportionately from the South—perhaps as much as half of them.[26]

This revitalized Christian evangelicalism embraced a broader agenda than saving souls. Long opposed to such evils as alcohol, tobacco, and gambling, southern ministers in the postwar years involved themselves in the fight against communism, in efforts to restore prayer to the public schools, in opposing abortion, and in defending other traditional values. They found additional targets as well: pornography, feminism, rock music. They sometimes favored the censorship of school and library books, the teaching of "creation science" as an alternative to evolution, and the support of Christian schools rather than public education. Large numbers of southerners approved the reform agendas of the Moral Majority, Christian Voice, Religious Roundtable, National Christian Political Action Committee, and other groups identified with the "New Christian Right." In 1982 the Louisiana state legislature passed the Balanced Treatment for Creation-Science and Evolution-Science Act, which required the teaching of creationism whenever evolution was taught. "The South," one historian remarks, "is probably the only area of the country in which a major political issue, such as the equal rights amendment to the Constitution, will prompt state legislators to ask the opinion of a prominent evangelist's family."[27]

Historically the emphasis on personal morality and individual responsibility in southern Protestantism contributed to the region's political conservatism. Indeed, the church's influence in this regard has been pervasive. Its subordination of women—by excluding them from boards of deacons and denying their ordination—carried over into politics, even though the Methodist Church in particular sometimes offered opportunities for feminine social action. White southerners' faith in individual responsibility and opposition to the welfare state

26. Jeffrey K. Hadden and Charles E. Swann, "Religious Broadcasting," in *Encyclopedia of Southern Culture*, ed. Wilson and Ferris, pp. 1277–79; William J. Cooper, Jr., and Thomas E. Terrill, *The American South: A History*, 2 vols. (New York, 1991), vol. 2, p. 774.

27. Donald G. Mathews, "Religion," in *The Encyclopedia of Southern History*, ed. David C. Roller and Robert W. Twyman (Baton Rouge, La., 1979), p. 1047. See also Willard B. Gatewood, Jr., "From Scopes to Creation Science: The Decline and Revival of the Evolution Controversy," *South Atlantic Quarterly* 83 (Autumn 1984): 363–83; Rodney A. Grunes, "Creationism, the Courts, and the First Amendment," *Journal of Church and State* 31 (Autumn 1989): 465–86; Cooper and Terrill, *The American South*, vol. 2, p. 774; Hill, "Religion and Politics in the South," pp. 139–53; Preston, "Will Dixie Disappear?" pp. 201–203; and Stacy F. Sauls and James L. Guth, "White Clergymen in Southern Politics: A Case Study," in *Perspectives on the American South: An Annual Review of Society, Politics and Culture*, vol. 1, ed. Merle Black and John Shelton Reed (New York, 1981), pp. 347–65.

strongly conditioned the political culture of the contemporary South.[28] Political-religious conservatism provided the foundatic.1 for the New Christian Right in the region. Jerry Falwell's Moral Majority lent vigorous support to Ronald Reagan's candidacy and presidency, while Pat Robertson actively sought the Republican nomination for president in 1988. The New Christian Right specifically and southern religion in general have strengthened political conservatism and the Republican party in the southern states. To be sure, Christian evangelism has experienced a nationwide resurgence since the 1960s, in part no doubt because of the swift changes and unsettling disruptions in American society. But the movement also owes a good deal to the southern-rooted evangelical revival. As two historians of the South have recently written, "Protestant evangelicalism has joined southern literature, jazz, blues, rock and roll, and country music as a major means by which the South has shaped the nation's life and culture."[29]

Another important cultural distinction between North and South was anchored in regional differences in the use of force and a propensity for violent behavior among southerners. Outsiders have long viewed the South as a savage and sadistic society. Southern violence ranged from dueling to family feuds, from lynching to Ku Klux Klan terrorism, from night-riding to assaulting civil rights workers. "Beneath the image of a gracious, hospitable, leisurely folk," John Shelton Reed writes, "has lurked that of a hot-tempered, violent, even sadistic people. . . ."[30] The southern reputation for violence reflected a regional pattern of behavior that stood in sharp contrast to the rest of the nation.

Close observers pointed out as early as the 1870s and 1880s that homicide rates among black and white southerners were well above the national averages. In the early-twentieth century, several southern cities became notorious for their spectacular murder rates; sociologist H. C. Brearley found that during the five years from 1920 to 1924 the homicide rate for the southern states was two and a half times greater than that of the remainder of the United States. Southerners murdered each other—in many cases a friend or family member—much more frequently than did nonsoutherners. Statistics for later decades confirmed this regional contrast. The southern states led the nation in the percentage of violent offenses against persons, in the percentage of people imprisoned for crimes of violence, and in the number of death sentences and executions. In 1880 ten of the eighteen states with the highest homicide rates were southern states. Although regional differences had declined by the 1980s, a significant North-South distinction remained.[31] Some of the violence, physical brutality, and verbal abuse that erupted in the South during the 1950s and 1960s grew

28. Black and Black, *Politics and Society in the South*, pp. 213–31, is suggestive on this point.

29. Cooper and Terrill, *The American South*, vol. 2, p. 775.

30. Reed, *The Enduring South*, p. 45.

31. Raymond D. Gastil, "Violence, Crime, and Punishment," in *Encyclopedia of Southern Culture*, ed. Wilson and Ferris, pp. 1473–76; Gastil, *Cultural Regions of the United States* (Seattle, Wash., 1975), p. 97; Sheldon Hackney, "Southern Violence," in *Violence in America: Historical and Comparative Perspectives*, rev. ed., ed. Hugh Davis Graham and Ted Robert Gurr (New York, 1970), pp. 505–506; Reed, *The Enduring South*, pp. 45–55; Cooper and Terrill, *The American South*, vol. 2, pp. 617, 776.

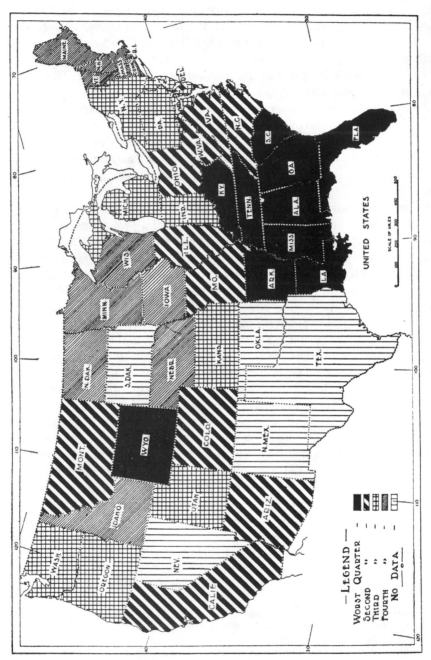

Distribution of Homicide in the United States, 1918–1927. Source: W. T. Couch, ed., *Culture in the South* (Chapel Hill: University of North Carolina Press, 1934), p. 682.

out of racial conflict over school desegregation and the civil rights movement. Televised scenes of demonstrators being attacked with fire hoses and police dogs, reports of the bombing of black churches, and the beating and murder of civil rights volunteers shocked millions of people in the United States and reinforced the outside perception of the South as the nation's most violent and savage section.[32]

John Shelton Reed has found, after carefully analyzing a variety of opinion polls, that there is an important difference between northern and southern attitudes toward violence. His investigations reveal that southerners are more in favor of gun ownership and of corporal punishment of children than are nonsoutherners, and he suggests that this can be viewed "as aspects of a more general acceptance of violence and the use of force."[33] Commenting on the southern habit of owning firearms, another scholar observes that "virtually every household in the rural and small-town South had a closetful of shotguns and rifles, and many had a pistol for good measure."[34] Southerners also seem to endorse the use of force as an agent of national policy. They exhibit a collective "military-patriotic" personality that lends strong support to the armed forces and an American presence abroad.[35]

While demographic and economic factors may explain some of the regional differences with respect to violence, a significant part of it must be attributed to

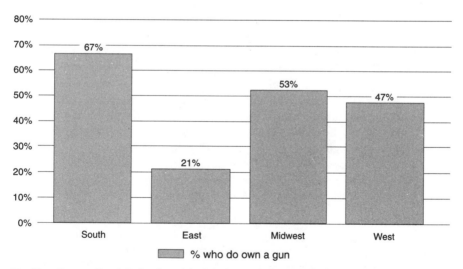

Do You Own a Gun? Poll taken 9/4/59. SOURCE: George Gallup, *The Gallup Poll: Public Opinion, 1935–1971*, vol. 3 (New York: Random House, 1972), p. 1626.

32. Richard Maxwell Brown, "Southern Violence vs. the Civil Rights Movement, 1954–1968," in *Perspectives on the American South*, vol. 1, ed. Black and Reed, pp. 49–69. It should be noted that not all of this violence was confined to white attacks on blacks.

33. Reed, *The Enduring South*, pp. 45–55.

34. Charles P. Roland, *The Improbable Era: The South Since World War II* (Lexington, Ky., 1975), p. 177.

35. *Ibid.*, pp. 177–78.

"southernness." Something about the culture of the South has been particularly conducive to violence. The historian Sheldon Hackney contends that the southern identity "has been linked from the first to a siege mentality," and that a valid explanation of the region's violent proclivities is likely to be found in the development of a southern worldview "that defines the social, political, and physical environment as hostile and casts the white Southerner in the role of the passive victim of malevolent forces."[36] In any case, the South's predisposition to resort to violence can be understood best in terms of its history and culture.[37] Some commentators have speculated, for instance, about the possible relationship between the southerner's passion for football and the region's penchant for violence. The relationship, if there is one, is not clear. "What is clear," writes one historian, "is that one of the most violent sports played in the United States enjoys its greatest success and has its greatest following in the one region that has historically embraced violence as an accepted means of self-expression."[38] This association, while suggestive, is not entirely convincing in light of the national enthusiasm for football, the popularity of boxing and hockey in other regions, and the great affection for golf, a pacific sport, in the South.

The South's culture of violence, according to a leading authority, has been a source of the nation's high homicide rate. It can be shown, for example, "that outside of the centers of Southern and Northern society, state homicide rates grade into one another in rough approximation to the extent to which Southerners have moved into mixed states."[39] In some categories of crime, the South makes a better showing. Relative to the North, the South has high rates of homicide and assault, moderate rates of crime against property, and low rates of suicide.[40] The theme of regional convergence is also evident in this cultural realm. If the South's overt use of violence has diminished somewhat in recent decades, that of other regions has increased. As Reed noted in 1972, the South appeared to have "the dubious distinction of being in the vanguard of a national trend—it was the most violent region in an increasingly violent nation."[41]

Both the South's cultural distinctiveness and its influence on other parts of the country were apparent in the development of modern southern music. In fact, music was one of the South's great natural resources and one of its most valuable exports. Originating in the folk music of the early South, it reflected

36. Hackney, "Southern Violence," p. 524. Frank E. Vandiver had earlier identified what he described as an "offensive-defense" mechanism in explaining the South's reaction to outside threats. This concept throws light on the strain of violence in the southern experience. See Vandiver, "The Southerner as Extremist," in *The Idea of the South: Pursuit of a Central Theme*, ed. Frank E. Vandiver (Chicago, 1964), pp. 43–55.

37. See Gastil, *Cultural Regions of the United States*, pp. 97–116; Hackney, "Southern Violence," pp. 505–27; John Shelton Reed, "To Live—and Die—In Dixie: A Contribution to the Study of Southern Violence," *Political Science Quarterly* 86 (September 1977): 429–43; and Jerry L. Butcher, "Violence," in *The Encyclopedia of Southern History*, ed. Roller and Twyman, pp. 1274–75.

38. Preston, "Will Dixie Disappear?" pp. 198–99. See also John Shelton Reed, "Below the Smith and Wesson Line: Reflections on Southern Violence," in *Perspectives on the American South*, vol. 1, ed. Black and Reed, pp. 18–19, and Cooper and Terrill, *The American South*, vol. 2, p. 776.

39. Gastil, *Cultural Regions of the United States*, p. 116.

40. Hackney, "Southern Violence," pp. 506–507.

41. Reed, *The Enduring South*, p. 55.

the cultural influences of the region's African and British heritage.[42] Like the southern historical experience, Charles P. Roland observes, southern music has been "exceptionally dramatic, poignant, and colorful."[43] It mirrored what one writer has described as "the harshness of life in a poverty-stricken, race-divided, rural, and often violent region." But it also echoed the southerner's "faith, family, and pride in the land." And it touched on the mythic theme of place and community, as in the rock and roll message of Alabama's "My Home's in Alabama." According to a North Carolinian, country music "has become the music of our region precisely because a few of our number can, through it, relate the events that have happened to us all."[44]

Black southerners greatly enriched musical expression in the South. "Closely related in rhythm, scale, and vocal mannerisms," one writer notes, "both secular and sacred black music grew out of twentieth-century African-American Southern culture and the segregation that characterized contemporary race relations." Music also nurtured the growth of the region's mythology, often with the help of outsiders, in which the South was seen as a land of romance and mystery as well as hardship and tragedy. These qualities attracted the interest of northerners in the nineteenth century and strongly influenced American music generally in the twentieth century. The South provided the nation with a source of images and symbols that fired the imagination of musicians and songwriters, and it contributed entertainers and styles that did much to shape popular music in the United States.[45]

American musical styles that had their beginning in the South included ragtime, blues, and jazz; country and bluegrass; and rock and roll. A series of developments beginning in the 1920s nationalized southern music: its growing commercialization and professionalization, the role of radio and other technological innovations, massive population movements during and after World War II, the emergence of national music centers in cities like Nashville and Atlanta, and changes in the stylistic structure of the region's music. Southern musicians and entertainers—from Jimmie Rodgers to Loretta Lynn, from Louis Armstrong to Elvis Presley, from Bessie Smith to Dolly Parton—became national stars. The music industry became one of the region's economic success stories; it also provided southern women as well as southern men with an inviting professional field for individual achievement and recognition. The defeat

42. Bill C. Malone, *Country Music, U.S.A.*, rev. ed. (Austin, Tex., 1985), pp. 1–29; Malone, *Singing Cowboys and Musical Mountaineers: Southern Culture and the Roots of Country Music* (Athens, Ga., 1993); Malone, "Southern Music—American Music," in *The American South Comes of Age*, ed. Jack Bass and Thomas E. Terrill (New York, 1986), p. 348.

43. Charles P. Roland, "Editor's Preface," in Bill C. Malone, *Southern Music, American Music* (Lexington, Ky., 1979), p. ix.

44. David R. Goldfield, *Promised Land: The South since 1945* (Arlington Heights, Ill., 1987), p. 129 (first quotation); David B. Santelle, "Listen and Remember," in Fifteen Southerners, *Why the South Will Survive*, p. 151 (second quotation); Smith, *Myth, Media, and the Southern Mind*, p. 118; Katie Letcher Lyle, "Southern Country Music: A Brief Eulogy," in *The American South*, ed. Rubin, pp. 140–60.

45. Nell Irvin Painter, " 'The South' and 'The Negro': The Rhetoric of Race Relations and Real Life," in *The South for New Southerners*, ed. Escott and Goldfield, pp. 49–58 (quotation on p. 57); Malone, *Southern Music, American Music*, pp. 1–2.

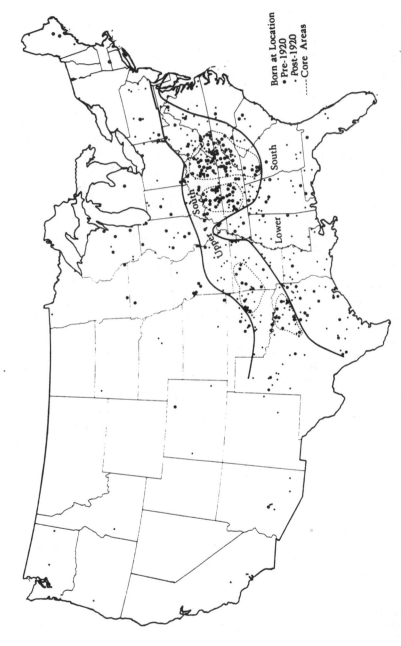

Birthplaces of Country Music Performers, 1870–1970. Map by George O. Carney. SOURCE: John F. Rooney, Jr., Wilbur Zelinsky, and Dean R. Louder, eds., *This Remarkable Continent: An Atlas of United States and Canadian Society and Cultures* (College Station: Texas A & M University Press, 1982).

and disillusionment of Vietnam and Watergate seemed to heighten the appeal of country music for many Americans in the 1970s, and the themes of loneliness, failure, and alienation, of "drinking, cheating, and heartbreak," struck a responsive chord far beyond the South, particularly among working-class and lower-middle-class Americans. Country music's newfound respectability was manifest, for example, in its identification with presidential politics, from Richard Nixon to George Bush. The growing popularity of southern musical styles and musicians clearly helped change outside perceptions of the South and encouraged its acceptance as a part of the national culture.[46]

Southern music seemed to have become American music. "Much of the music now bearing the 'country' label," Bill C. Malone has recently pointed out, "has little relationship to southern, rural, or working-class life, but instead is aimed at middle-class urban listeners who presumably have little regional or class identification."[47] This was also true of other varieties of southern music, with the exception of "southern gospel." Yet most musical styles that originated in the South maintained the imprint of southern culture. Elvis Presley, the "King of Rock and Roll," became a major figure in American popular culture, but he symbolized—in life and death—many of the tensions and contradictions in southern culture. Although country music produced a protest strain against the Vietnam War, that music generally "reflected both the South's support of its traditional values of duty, honor, courage, and country, and the region's inability to comprehend why so many in other sections of the nation perceived Vietnam as a national debacle."[48] At the same time, southern musicians continued to perpetuate their own versions of the southern myth. As Malone says, "The South of imagery endures even as its performers and musical forms gradually become absorbed in the national mainstream."[49]

"By 1945," George B. Tindall has observed, "the South, whatever deficiencies it might suffer in other fields, was far advanced toward, if indeed it had not already seized, triumphant 'possession of the American literary world.' "[50] Another commentator on the southern literary scene, writing in the mid-1960s,

46. Malone, *Country Music, U.S.A.*, pp. 177–415; Malone, *Southern Music, American Music*, pp. 58–105; Bill C. Malone and Judith McCulloh, eds., *Stars of Country Music: Uncle Dave Macon to Johnny Rodriquez* (Urbana, Ill., 1975); Wayne W. Daniel, *Pickin' on Peachtree: A History of Country Music in Atlanta, Georgia* (Urbana, Ill., 1990); Mary A. Bufwack and Robert K. Oermann, *Finding Her Voice: The Saga of Women in Country Music* (New York, 1993); Roland, *The Improbable Era*, pp. 163–66; James C. Cobb, "From Muskogee to Luckenbach: Country Music and the 'Southernization' of America," *Journal of Popular Culture* 16 (Winter 1982): 81–91; Kent Blaser, " 'Pictures from Life's Other Side': Hank Williams, Country Music, and Popular Culture in America," *South Atlantic Quarterly* 84 (Winter 1985): 12–26. See also the essays and articles under "Music" in *Encyclopedia of Southern Culture*, ed. Wilson and Ferris, pp. 985–1091.

47. Bill C. Malone, "Music," in *Encyclopedia of Southern Culture*, ed. Wilson and Ferris, p. 991.

48. Melton McLaurin, "Country Music and the Vietnam War," in *Perspectives on the American South: An Annual Review of Society, Politics and Culture*, vol. 3, ed. James C. Cobb and Charles R. Wilson (New York, 1985), p. 158 (quotation); Richard Welch, "Rock 'n' Roll and Social Change," *History Today* 40 (February 1990): 32–39.

49. Malone, *Southern Music, American Music*, p. 150.

50. George Brown Tindall, *The Emergence of the New South, 1913–1945* (Baton Rouge, La., 1967), p. 686.

pointed out that the region's current writers of distinction had a different focus from earlier giants like William Faulkner and Thomas Wolfe, for the members of the new generation "have moved from the rural South to a broader world, and have lost much that was distinctively southern in the movement."[51] Yet even as southern life was increasingly moving into the American mainstream, the literary South remained distinctive. The literary flowering among southern writers that occurred between the two world wars came to be known as the Southern Literary Renaissance. Some of these writers have been discussed previously. Ironically, this literary growth became apparent soon after the appearance in 1917 of H. L. Mencken's famous essay on the artistic sterility of the South, "The Sahara of the Bozart." There was no cause-and-effect relationship between the two, however. William Faulkner was the major figure to emerge from the renaissance, but he was only one of a score or more of talented contemporaries who made the South what Louis D. Rubin has described as "the creative center of American literary achievement."[52] These southern writers—most notably novelists, poets, and critics—shared a pervasive historical sense, a commitment to place and community, a fascination with morality and evil, and an eye for folk tradition and mythology. They were also gifted tale tellers.[53]

A second generation of renaissance writers emerged following World War II. Some of the prewar writers were still productive, including Faulkner, Robert Penn Warren, Katherine Anne Porter, Eudora Welty, and Richard Wright. But the new southern writers constituted an imposing group: James Agee, Truman Capote, James Dickey, Ralph Ellison, Ernest J. Gaines, Randall Jarrell, Flannery O'Connor, Walker Percy, Reynolds Price, Elizabeth Spencer, William Styron, Peter Taylor, Tennessee Williams, and others. In addition, a growing number of university teachers devoted themselves to southern literary studies, and a group of liberal journalists—ranging from Hodding Carter and Ralph McGill to Tom Wicker and Edwin M. Yoder, Jr.—made their own contribution to southern writing.[54]

Faulkner still cast a long shadow, and several of the young writers were strongly influenced by the Mississippian. Faulkner himself continued to write steadily until his death in 1962. Perhaps the most talented of all modern American writers, he turned out a succession of novels in the postwar period, among them *Intruder in the Dust* (1948), a Pulitzer Prize winner concerned with race relations. *The Town* (1957) and *The Mansion* (1959) completed his triology on the Snopes clan. Faulkner was also a master of the short story. The award of the Nobel Prize for Literature in 1950 added to his national and international sta-

51. C. Hugh Holman, "A Cycle of Change in Southern Literature," in *The South in Continuity and Change*, ed. McKinney and Thompson, p. 402.

52. Louis D. Rubin, Jr., "Literature," in *The Encyclopedia of Southern History*, ed. Roller and Twyman, p. 727.

53. *Ibid.*, pp. 724–28; Louis D. Rubin, Jr., et al., eds., *The History of Southern Literature* (Baton Rouge, La., 1985), pp. 261–459; Tindall, *The Emergence of the New South*, pp. 650–86; Cleanth Brooks, "Southern Literature: The Wellsprings of Its Vitality," *Georgia Review* 16 (Fall 1962): 238–53.

54. M. Thomas Inge, "Literature," in *Encyclopedia of Southern Culture*, ed. Wilson and Ferris, pp. 839–44.

tures. Another major literary figure who continued to write in the postwar years was Robert Penn Warren, who bridged the gap between the first and second generations of modern southern writers. Warren was possibly the most versatile of twentieth-century southern writers. He began his career as a poet, won academic recognition as an innovator in the teaching of literature, gained a public reputation as a novelist, and then emerged as one of the nation's greatest poets. His fiction constitutes what one scholar has called "a lifelong philosophical discourse on the meaning of history, the nature of man, and the compromises necessary in building a workable political and social system."[55] His best-known novel, *All the King's Men* (1946), revealed his interest in the South's propensity toward violence, his fascination with time and its meaning, and his ability to dramatize human experience through large dialectical patterns like good and evil.[56] Warren's profound interest in southern history and in race relations was evident in several works of nonfiction: *The Legacy of the Civil War* (1961), *Segregation: The Inner Conflict in the South* (1956), and *Who Speaks for the Negro?* (1957).

Like their prewar counterparts, the second generation of modern southern writers had much in common, particularly their self-consciousness as southern literary authors. Although these writers differed in many ways, they tended to emphasize family history, race, religion, a sense of place, "of concreteness, and of the imperfectibility of man."[57] While some of these novelists and poets left the South, their regionalism often manifested itself in an unfavorable view of the North, in images of a wasteland, of a freezing prison, even of horror.[58] Some of the postwar writers introduced new techniques, such as the grotesque, in books like Flannery O'Connor's *Wise Blood* (1952). A few literary critics, such as Walter Sullivan, concluded that the quality of southern writing had declined and that the Southern Literary Renaissance had ended by the mid-1950s. One reason, according to Sullivan, was the passing of the ambiguities of the southern social scene following the upheaval of the civil rights movement and a situation in which good and evil seemed readily apparent. This new theme was "vastly inferior" to the old one as a stimulus to the writing of great literature.[59]

Yet the best of the postwar literature mirrored the tensions of a rapidly changing society, a society shifting from an agrarian to an industrial and urban base, with a disintegrating tradition and older values under attack. Peter Taylor's stories of individuals and families whose roots are in small southern towns

55. *Ibid.*, p. 842.

56. James H. Justus, "Robert Penn Warren," in *The History of Southern Literature*, ed. Rubin et al., pp. 450–59; William C. Havard, "The Burden of the Literary Mind: Some Meditations on Robert Penn Warren as Historian," *South Atlantic Quarterly* 62 (Autumn 1963): 516–31; Mark Royden Winchell, "Robert Penn Warren's *Brother to Dragons*: Irony and the Image of Man," in *The Vanderbilt Tradition: Essays in Honor of Thomas Daniel Young*, ed. Mark Royden Winchell (Baton Rouge, La., 1991), pp. 105–16.

57. Roland, "The Ever-Vanishing South," p. 12.

58. Robert White, "North in Literature," in *Encyclopedia of Southern Culture*, ed. Wilson and Ferris, pp. 858–60.

59. Walter Sullivan, "Southern Literature: The Last Twenty Years," in *Two Decades of Change: The South Since the Supreme Court Desegregation Decision*, ed. Ernest M. Lander, Jr., and Richard J. Calhoun (Columbia, S.C., 1975), pp. 55–67; Sullivan, *Death by Melancholy: Essays on Modern Southern Fiction* (Baton Rouge, La., 1972).

have as a central theme the clash between traditional values and the demands of modern life. Taylor's fictional world witnessed the breaking down of old loyalties, faiths, and relationships. *Losing Battles* (1970), Eudora Welty's novel about a hill-country family in Mississippi, revolves around the conflict over the incompatibility between the traditional agrarian life and the forces of modernism. Tennessee Williams, whose dramas did much to make the world aware of the South, was concerned in many of his works with what he perceived to be a declension in regional standards and ideals and his own distrust and dislike of the modern world. The deterioration of family structure and the older domestic virtues is a major theme in numerous other works of fiction, such as Anne Tyler's *Dinner at the Homesick Restaurant* (1982).[60]

Although few if any of the postwar generation of southern writers were diehard defenders of the prewar South, their fiction revealed their ambivalence about their region's transformation and their misgivings about the social consequences of modernization and homogenization. For example, the theme of displacement and mobility infuses Flannery O'Connor's story "The Displaced Person" and Walker Percy's novel *The Last Gentleman* (1966). Will Barrett, the main character in *The Last Gentleman*, is a southern expatriate at the outset of the story, and he becomes a wanderer through the South and West. A seeker who sometimes suffers from amnesia, Barrett is torn between the old and the new, between manners and leveling, between memory and forgetting.[61] The Percy trademarks, according to one critic, were "a sardonic tone, a crisp, cool prose style, sly knowingness . . . and a preoccupation with the *detritus* of post-industrial culture."[62]

Though the shift from a closely knit, orderly community to a society without traditional values is a prominent concern in the work of postwar southern writers, organized religion seems to have little influence on the characters in this fiction. This was not true in the case of Flannery O'Connor, a devout Roman Catholic who boldly connected art and religion in her work. O'Connor found rich materials for religious allegory in her native region and brilliantly exemplified the "Southern Gothic" form in such books as *A Good Man Is Hard to Find* (1955) and *The Violent Bear It Away* (1960). Her stories have been described as tragicomic morality plays on man's fall, redemption, and faith in God; one

60. Thomas Daniel Young, "A Second Generation of Novelists," in *The History of Southern Literature*, ed. Rubin et al., pp. 466–69; David Marion Holman, "Peter Taylor," in *ibid.*, pp. 494–96; Peggy Whitman Prenshaw, "Eudora Welty," in *ibid.*, pp. 470–75; Suzanne Marrs, "Eudora Welty: The Southern Context," in *Perspectives on the American South*, vol. 4, ed. Cobb and Wilson, pp. 26–35; Gray, *Writing the South*, pp. 237–51; Jacob H. Adler, "Modern Southern Drama," in *The History of Southern Literature*, ed. Rubin et al., pp. 436–42; Nancy M. Tischler, "The South Stage Center: Hellman and Williams," in *The American South*, ed. Rubin, pp. 323–33.

61. J. O. Tate, "Civility, Civil Rights and Civil Wars: Walker Percy's Centennial Novel," in *Perspectives on the American South*, vol. 3, ed. Cobb and Wilson, pp. 29–43; James C. Cobb, "Southern Writers and the Challenge of Regional Convergence: A Comparative Perspective," *Georgia Historical Quarterly* 73 (Spring 1989): 15–17.

62. Gray, *Writing the South*, pp. 251–70 (quotation on p. 269). See also Bertram Wyatt-Brown, "Walker, Will, and Honor Dying: The Percys and Literary Creativity," in *Looking South: Chapters in the Story of an American Region*, ed. Winfred B. Moore, Jr., and Joseph F. Tripp (New York, 1989), pp. 229–58.

scholar says she used "religious fundamentalism of baroque intensity to satirize the hollowness of modern rationalism."[63]

Another theme expressed in much of the postwar southern fiction is that of "the complex and ambiguous relationships" between blacks and whites. These writings often illuminate "the unique characteristics of a biracial society" and the changing relationships between the races. Elizabeth Spencer's *The Voice at the Back Door* (1956), Jesse Hill Ford's *The Liberation of Lord Byron Jones* (1965), Madison Jones's *A Cry of Absence* (1971), and other widely read novels deal with the relationships in small southern towns arising from racial conflicts and divisions, and in some cases, the effects of racial tension within the context of the civil rights revolution. Harper Lee, who wrote only a single novel, *To Kill a Mockingbird* (1960), won a Pulitzer Prize for fiction. Set in a small Alabama town in the 1930s, the novel tells the story of the white lawyer Atticus Finch's courageous but unsuccessful defense of a black man wrongly accused of raping a white woman.[64]

A group of black writers from the South dealt with the dehumanizing effects that African Americans experienced during the era of Jim Crow. Alice Walker, in *The Third Life of Grange Copeland* (1970), and Ernest J. Gaines, in *The Autobiography of Miss Jane Pittman* (1971), provide memorable examples of the genre. Some of the younger black writers who participated in the civil rights campaigns of the 1960s made the movement a major focus of their work. In *Meridian* (1976), for example, Walker portrayed the involvement of her protagonist at the height of the movement and in later years. Meanwhile, a host of young black poets were writing passionately about racial injustice, antagonism, and discord.[65]

By the 1970s, there was talk of an outburst of new literary talent below the Mason-Dixon line, but just how regionally distinctive the new writers were and to what extent they were influenced by the South's earlier literary flowering was not clear. Fred Hobson has remarked that the problem for the neo-Gothic novelist in the contemporary South is that southern social reality no longer so dramatically supports the writer's fiction.[66] For this new generation of southern writers, the 1960s seem to have been a pivotal decade in southern life and letters, such as the 1920s had been. It was a time of southern defiance, of southern crimes against humanity, of outside condemnation, and of great intellectual ferment. This uncomfortable matrix made a deep impression on young southern writers, and in some respects a new southern fiction resulted. The South had

63. Roland, *The Improbable Era*, p. 141. See also Young, "A Second Generation of Novelists," p. 468, and Louise Y. Gossett, "Flannery O'Connor," in *The History of Southern Literature*, ed. Rubin et al., pp. 489–93.

64. Young, "A Second Generation of Novelists," p. 467; Mark Royden Winchell, "A Golden Ball of Thread: The Achievement of Elizabeth Spencer," *Sewanee Review* 97 (Fall 1989): 580–86; Peggy Whitman Prenshaw, "Elizabeth Spencer," in *The History of Southern Literature*, ed. Rubin et al., pp. 497–500; Martha E. Cook, "Old Ways and New Ways," in *ibid.*, pp. 527–34.

65. Trudier Harris, "Black Writers in a Changed Landscape, Since 1950," in *The History of Southern Literature*, ed. Rubin et al., pp. 566–77; J. Lee Greene, "The Pain and the Beauty: The South, the Black Writer, and Conventions of the Picaresque," in *The American South*, ed. Rubin, pp. 264–88; Roland, *The Improbable Era*, pp. 143–47.

66. Fred Hobson, *The Southern Writer in the Postmodern World* (Athens, Ga., 1991), p. 7.

survived its time of crisis, accommodating itself to the civil rights revolution, experiencing Sunbelt prosperity, and witnessing the election of a native son as president. While this was happening, other Americans were beginning to understand their own complicity in social evil and undergoing defeat abroad and a constitutional crisis at home. Regional assumptions and perspectives changed. "What was the writer of the seventies and eighties to do with a suddenly Superior South, optimistic, forward-looking, more virtuous and now threatening to become more prosperous than the rest of the country?"[67]

Contemporary southern writers seem to be less conscious of the past in the present, less influenced by Faulkner and his generation, less absorbed in place and family and community—in short, less "southern"—than their literary forebears. Writers such as Josephine Humphreys, Lee Smith, Barry Hannah, Clyde Edgerton, and Jill McCorkle create characters who are conditioned by television, movies, rock music, and other manifestations of popular culture. The fictional world of Bobbie Ann Mason is the superficial present-day South—a South of mobile homes, plastic restaurants, and Parthenon-like shopping malls.[68] Some of the new novelists and storytellers do not seem southern at all. As Hobson observes in the case of Richard Ford, here was a "southern expatriate for the eighties, with no interest in past, place, family, religion, community, guilt, and burdens of history, family, or otherwise."[69]

Nevertheless, most contemporary writers of fiction and poetry from the South, including Richard Ford, are conscious of their southern identity and of the fact that they belong, in some degree at least, to a southern literary tradition. Much of their work is set in the South, deals with southern themes, including family and community, features southern characters and the southern idiom, and is widely perceived as an expression of contemporary southern culture. This is notably true of several black writers from the South. One example is Alex Haley's prize-winning novel *Roots* (1976), which re-created the history of his family in America. Ernest Gaines, in *A Gathering of Old Men* (1983), vividly illustrates the power of a black community in southern Louisiana. Fred Hobson believes that African-American fiction, within contemporary southern literature, is analogous to the place of southern fiction in earlier decades within the national literature—"a powerful, folk based, past-conscious, often mythic expression of a storytelling culture within a larger literature."[70]

These cultural patterns—extending from attitudes toward religion and physical violence to musical expression and literary creativity—suggest that, in spite of drastic change, the South remains the most distinctive region in the nation. Southerners continue to be profoundly conscious of their regional identity. As two sociologists remarked in 1965, "The South has seemed to live inside its people like an instinct. In contrast, the Middle West and New England have

67. *Ibid.*, p. 8.

68. *Ibid.*, pp. 8–10; Doris Betts, "Many Souths and Broadening Scale: A Changing Southern Literature," in *The Future South*, ed. Dunn and Preston, p. 173; Cobb, "Southern Writers and the Challenge of Regional Convergence," pp. 21–25.

69. Hobson, *The Southern Writer in the Postmodern World*, p. 49.

70. *Ibid.*, pp. 93–100 (quotation on p. 93).

appeared to exist in the inhabitants of those areas more like a habit."[71] This may account for what one interpreter calls the southerner's habit of explaining, justifying, and affirming the South. Analyzing the mind and soul of the South "assumed epidemic proportions" in the decades following the Second World War. "Every journalist, politician, and scholar in the late Confederacy, it seemed, was probing his homeland, writing a book about it, assigning it a new label."[72] Change itself no doubt inspired much of this regional stock-taking. If southern distinctiveness persisted, differences between North and South had steadily diminished over the last half-century, whether in terms of economic activity, socioeconomic condition, or political practices. One aspect of this nationalization was "the Southernization of America," including the export of southern music and literature and the increasing importance of political and religious conservatism outside the South.[73] By the 1970s the national media was depicting a sympathetic South, even in such rustic television series as "The Andy Griffith Show," "The Beverly Hillbillies," and "The Waltons."[74] At the same time, Hollywood continued to ensure that the South "was a distinct section which drew unrelenting curiosity."[75]

In 1958 C. Vann Woodward, noting the swift disappearance of old monuments of regional distinctiveness and the way "the Bulldozer Revolution" was plowing under "cherished old values of individualism, localism, family, clan, and rural folk culture," pondered the question of "southern identity." The time was approaching, Woodward wrote, "when the Southerner will begin to ask himself whether there is really any longer very much point in calling himself a Southerner."[76] The Bulldozer Revolution has continued in the years since Woodward wrote, remaking the face of the landscape, transforming such regional institutions as race relations and politics, and changing the thinking and behavior of the southern people. Woodward had hoped that the South's history—its long and un-American experience with failure, poverty, and guilt— along with cultural contributions like "the magnificent body of literature" produced by its writers would nourish the more constructive side of the region's heritage. As it turned out, the South's cultural heritage in all its protean character proved to be among the most powerful manifestations of the southern identity in contemporary America.

71. McKinney and Thompson, *The South in Continuity and Change*, p. xi.

72. Hobson, *Tell About the South*, pp. 297–98.

73. See John Egerton, *The Americanization of Dixie: The Southernization of America* (New York, 1974), pp. 172–208.

74. Smith, *Myth, Media, and the Southern Mind*, p. 110; Jack Temple Kirby, *Media-Made Dixie: The South in the American Imagination*, rev. ed. (Athens, Ga., 1986), pp. 141–44.

75. Edward D. C. Campbell, Jr., *The Celluloid South: Hollywood and the Southern Myth* (Knoxville, Tenn., 1981), p. 191.

76. C. Vann Woodward, *The Burden of Southern History* (Baton Rouge, La., 1960), pp. 3–25 (quotation on p. 3).

CHAPTER 13

The South, the North, and the Nation

A LTHOUGH the end of Reconstruction lowered the level of intersectional animosity in the United States, it did little to reduce the disparities of condition that favored the North or to change the attitudes and behavior that had set southerners apart from other Americans. To be sure, southerners participated in national politics, shared a common culture with northerners, and responded to the cumulative effects of a national business system and powerful new channels of transportation and communication. But they were profoundly affected by sectional interests, and no other Americans were so clearly and self-consciously identified along sectional lines. Fifteen years after Appomattox, the New York journalist Whitelaw Reid noted that the South "still sits crushed, wretched, busy displaying and bemoaning her wounds."[1] The South had also become a rich repository of social myths—of "mental pictures that portray the pattern of what a people think they are (or ought to be) or what somebody else thinks they are."[2]

One source of southern self-consciousness in the late-nineteenth century was the section's laggard economy, at least in comparison with the dynamic economic development of the Northeast and Midwest. The South remained overwhelmingly agricultural and rural, its industries mostly devoted to the extraction and processing of raw materials, its commerce and trade decentralized and starved for credit. Northern entrepreneurs acquired an increasing share of the ownership and control of southern industries and resources. As C. Vann Woodward has observed, "The Morgans, Mellons, and Rockefellers sent their agents to take charge of the region's railroads, mines, furnaces, and financial corpora-

1. Quoted in C. Vann Woodward, *Origins of the New South, 1877–1913* (Baton Rouge, La., 1951), p. 107.
2. See George B. Tindall, "Mythology: A New Frontier in Southern History," in *The Idea of the South: Pursuit of a Central Theme,* ed. Frank E. Vandiver (Chicago, 1964), pp. 1–15 (quotation on p. 1).

tions, and eventually of many of its distribution institutions."[3] Southerners were poorer than other Americans. Those who farmed—a great majority of the region's inhabitants—were growing steadily more landless, and southern workers possessed few industrial and vocational skills. The South was "a low-wage region in a high-wage country."[4] In 1880 the per capita wealth in the South was $376, while that in the North was $1,086. In the 1880s southerners' per capita income was barely half that of the national average. These ratios had undergone little change by the end of the century.

Southerners differed from their fellow Americans in other ways as well. The region attracted few foreign immigrants and its ethnic homogeneity and overwhelming Protestantism contrasted sharply with other parts of the country. Southern rates of illiteracy, births, mortality, and homicides were far higher than the national average. At the turn of the nineteenth century, the ratio of children to adults in the southern states was nearly double that of the rest of the nation, while the section's expenditures per child for education averaged less than one-half that of other regions. Small wonder that northerners tended to assume an air of superiority and condescension toward the South, or that they were inclined to consider it a land of racial injustice, economic backwardness, and undemocratic politics. Although home rule had become a reality in the post-Reconstruction South and the North had largely lost interest in reforming the southern states, many white southerners continued to fear "Yankeefication."

Following Reconstruction, northern interest in the South seemed to shift from political control to taking advantage of economic opportunity, to embody the "transition from the missionary and political to the economic and exploitative phase" of northern policy.[5] The South, though divided in its response to the altered emphasis of the North's intervention, was receptive to the promise of northern investment and economic development. Southern leaders adopted a strategy of imitation and cooperation in dealing with northern representatives, helping to fashion an intersectional rapprochement. In the 1880s they elaborated "the New South creed," a doctrine of "progress, prosperity, sectional reconciliation, and racial harmony." Its advocates envisioned the regeneration of the region on the basis of industrialization, urbanization, and economic diversification.[6] The vision of a triumphant New South was based on a number of realistic premises, but it gave rise to an elaborate myth of southern potential and success. Even so, a new urban business class rose in the late-nineteenth and early-twentieth centuries that did much to direct the modern South. "It was," Don H. Doyle writes, "a business class fashioned on the northern model and devoted to reshaping the South in the image of the North."[7] Northern reaction

3. Woodward, *Origins of the New South*, p. 292.
4. Gavin Wright, *Old South, New South: Revolutions in the Southern Economy Since the Civil War* (New York, 1986), p. 76.
5. Woodward, *Origins of the New South*, p. 115.
6. See Paul M. Gaston, *The New South Creed: A Study in Southern Mythmaking* (New York, 1970).
7. Don H. Doyle, *New Men, New Cities, New South: Atlanta, Nashville, Charleston, Mobile, 1860–1910* (Chapel Hill, N.C., 1990), p. 158.

was decidedly favorable. As Charles Dudley Warner observed in 1889, "Southern society and Northern society are becoming every day more and more alike."[8]

A second manifestation of this North-South reconciliation was the political orientation of the Redeemers, the political leaders who dominated political affairs in the South from Reconstruction to 1890. Their regimes were generally aligned with the conservative leadership of Grover Cleveland and other northern Democrats. They embraced the New South movement and were prepared to use the example and support of the North in the service of southern "progress." Not all southerners endorsed the Redeemer–New South approach, and it was seriously challenged in the stormy politics of the 1890s. Indeed, on many congressional issues in the post-Reconstruction years a clear-cut sectional pattern revealed itself. More often than not, southern senators and representatives voted with the more radical West and against the conservative East on currency, revenue, protective tariff, and internal improvement proposals, as well as federal regulatory measures. The agrarian upheaval of the late 1880s and the Populist revolt of the 1890s undermined the hegemony of the Redeemers, led to a repudiation of the Cleveland administration, and reoriented the Democratic party in the South toward the West and the leadership of William Jennings Bryan. Thus there were important sectional considerations in the politics of the 1890s. Southern Populists challenged not only the conservative regimes of the Redeemers but also the informal alliances the latter had long maintained with northern Democrats. The fusion of southern Populists and Bryan Democrats resulted in a more thoroughgoing North versus South (and a good deal of the West) division in the presidential campaign of 1896. The outcome of that election, which changed the contours of national politics for a generation, followed sectional lines.

But the sectional hostility engendered by the political struggles of the 1890s did not last. For one thing, the nation's sudden resort to war in 1898 brought a patriotic response from the South and the spectacle of southerners and northerners united in support of the flag. Sectional animosities receded before the surging tide of nationalism. The political realignment of the 1890s also diminished the force of sectionalism. That realignment entrenched the Republicans as the nation's dominant party, ended the GOP's real interest in southern support, and enabled southern Democrats to disfranchise most blacks, overcome their insurgent challengers, and create the Solid South. Thus, paradoxically, the realignment reduced the threat of northern intervention in the South and at the same time made the national party system more sectional than before. Not only did the outcome of the political upheaval of the 1890s solidify the South politically and enhance the region's independence by weakening the Democratic party in other regions, it strengthened the role of the southern states in the national Democratic party. At the same time, the New South vision and the enthusiasm for economic development caused southerners to turn expectantly to the North—and to Washington—for helpful policies and assistance. Mean-

8. Quoted in Gaston, *The New South Creed*, p. 197.

while, new social problems and changing ideas among Americans generally about the need for a more active federal government, paved the way for new initiatives in the nation's capital.

Still other factors lessened the intensity of sectionalism in the new century. In the aftermath of the troubled 1890s, the spirits of southerners and northerners alike were lifted by the return of good times and the brightening economic outlook. The emergence of a new national consensus on the treatment of black Americans, one that followed the lead of southern "accommodationists" on the race question, also eased sectional tensions. In the meantime, southern congressional leaders assumed a larger role in Congress, since they now dominated the Democratic party in Washington.

Sectional interests had by no means disappeared from the American scene. In Congress differences between the dominant northeastern and midwestern "core" and the southern and western "periphery" continued to be evident on economic policies relating to the nation's empire overseas and the extent of federal regulation at home. Sectional themes were also evident in southern progressivism, particularly in legislative efforts to curtail monopolistic practices by outside railroad, insurance, and industrial corporations. The movement to restrict child labor, encouraged by northern reformers and organizations, was weakened by strong sectional currents resulting from the growing competition between New England and southern textile manufacturers. The use of child labor and the low-wage structure in the southern industry, some northern businessmen charged, gave the South an unfair advantage in the production of cotton textiles. Southern textile men countered by asserting that the campaign to banish child labor was a scheme devised by their northern competitors to drive the southern mills out of business. The southern "problem" assumed various other forms in northern thinking. Among these was the desperate need for financial help to reform and modernize public education and health facilities in the South. One response to this need was an intersectional accord involving northern philanthropists and businessmen, on the one hand, and southern educators and reformers, on the other, to provide solutions.

Although southern progressivism bore its own indigenous stamp, it reflected an unusual amount of regional interaction and cooperation. The South joined and sometimes led in the regulation of business, agricultural improvement, and structural changes in city government. It provided a laboratory for the development of farm demonstration techniques. In other cases southerners turned to the examples of outside regions, as in prison reform, the movement to organize good schools, and the struggle for woman suffrage. And in still other areas, such as the new dispensation in race relations and the prohibition of alcoholic beverages, the South led the nation. By the turn of the century, some southerners were contemplating a new role for the South in American life, a role made possible by the North's understanding of the burden of the southern past and its ultimate approval of the southern mission to preserve the nation's racial purity.

These tendencies were heightened during the presidential administration of Woodrow Wilson. The South reacted enthusiastically to Wilson's election and provided strong support for his New Freedom legislation and international leadership. Southerners responded to Wilson's leadership for many reasons, not least because he was a southerner and a Democrat. Furthermore, southern congressional leaders, who now dominated the two houses, welcomed the prestige and responsibility that came to them with Wilson's election in 1912. Nor were they averse to the unaccustomed federal patronage made possible by the Wilson administration and new federal appropriations for agricultural extension programs, vocational education, road construction, and similar improvements. Wilson's conduct of the presidency broadened and helped nationalize the outlook of southern congressmen, whose cooperation and skill made a major contribution to Wilson's success as a legislative leader. Southerners generally endorsed the twenty-eighth president's war leadership and his peace plans; they rallied to Wilson's defense in his ill-fated struggle to win approval of the League of Nations.

The South's prominent role in national affairs during the Wilson era was not without its sectional repercussions. Southern congressmen opposed the appointment of blacks to federal office, pressed Wilson to extend racial segregation in the executive departments, and, urged on by the more extreme among them, even agitated for the application of a Jim Crow system to public accommodations in the District of Columbia. Some congressional votes in this period, such as those on child labor, prohibition, and woman suffrage, revealed a sectional pattern, one dimension of which was a North-South division among Democrats. On occasion, northern and western Democrats expressed resentment at the powerful influence exerted by southerners in Congress and in Democratic party affairs. Some northerners bridled in 1916 and 1917 at what they regarded as agrarian radical schemes among southern congressmen to devise revenue laws that would force the more industrialized and prosperous North to pay most of the costs of defense preparedness and the war. Democratic losses in the grain-producing states of the Midwest in the elections of 1918 resulted, in some part, from resentment over the government's failure to control cotton prices while regulating the price of wheat and other grains. Sectionalism divided and weakened the Democrats, although more fundamental factors were also involved.

In the 1920s, a period of Republican ascendancy in national politics, the Democrats resumed their accustomed position as minority party. But the South remained influential in Congress, where it held a majority of the Democratic seats. While southern congressmen endorsed federal legislation to ease the plight of the distressed farmer and supported federal action to use the wartime facilities at Muscle Shoals, Alabama, to produce cheap fertilizer and hydroelectric power, their outlook also reflected the region's accelerating industrial and urban growth. During the 1920s, the southern economy became more diversified than ever before, and southern institutions experienced significant modernization. In this sense, the South became more like other parts of the nation. In some respects, however, sectional conflict flared up with renewed intensity. This conflict manifested itself in a series of cultural and political issues involving such questions as national prohibition, efforts to restrict the teaching of evolution in public schools, Catholicism, and the role of the Ku Klux Klan. These issues as well as ideological differences were sharply focused in the widening sectional cleavage within the Democratic party, which was soon caught up in a bitter struggle over questions of this kind and control of the party. The Democratic party's controlling faction, a loose coalition of northeastern economic conservatives, sought to develop a North-South alliance, while the more economically progressive elements identified with the leadership of Bryan and Wilson struggled to revitalize the old western and southern axis.

One of the obstacles to Democratic unity was the intense friction in the relationship between the rural-Protestant-Anglo-Saxon South and the urban-Catholic-immigrant North throughout the 1920s. In 1924 the two sectional wings deadlocked the Democratic national convention, and 103 ballots were required to select a presidential nominee. Four years later the South was unable to prevent the nomination of Governor Alfred E. Smith of New York, the son of Irish immigrants, a Roman Catholic, a critic of prohibition, and an opponent of the Klan. The result was the rupture of the Solid South and the defection of seven southern states from the Democratic ticket in 1928. These sectional differences also contributed to a new outburst of northern criticism of the "benighted South"—of its barbarous habits and backward institutions. Southern lynchings, inhumane prison conditions, political demagoguery, and religious intolerance were all fair game for northern chastisement and ridicule. Southerners, always sensitive to outside disparagement and challenges to their honor, were quick to reply in kind.

The terrible ordeal of the Great Depression seemed to reduce the urgency of sectional disagreements and to encourage a greater appreciation of local and regional diversity among Americans. Preoccupied with the problems of economic survival, most people showed greater tolerance for and understanding of human eccentricities and frailties, including those associated with the South. The advent of the presidential administration of Franklin D. Roosevelt moved southern congressional leaders back into positions of national responsibility and enabled them, as in the Wilson administration, to make a vital contribution to the enactment of a remarkable recovery and reform program. At the same time, the political realignment of the 1930s diminished the importance of the South in the Democratic party, making it only one of several components in a new majority coalition. Yet Roosevelt's New Deal made it possible for southerners to obtain much-needed federal appropriations and relief. The president and his administration elicited strong support from southern politicians and their constituents. But as Roosevelt embraced more thoroughgoing reform proposals, some southern leaders turned against him, and by the fall of 1937, in the aftermath of FDR's bold attempt to reform the Supreme Court, an informal coalition of southern Democrats and northern Republicans emerged. It was an interregional alliance destined to exert immense influence in national politics.

In the meantime, southern problems became the focus of extensive commentary and organized reform efforts, by southerners and other Americans. A group of regionalists approached the South as "a case for analysis and a cause for social action." The condition of southern sharecroppers, industrial workers, and blacks aroused the sympathy and ire of outside reformers. Late in the

1930s, the Roosevelt administration committed itself to the regeneration of the southern economy. While this was happening, the Southern Literary Renaissance burst into full flower, gradually attracting an audience outside the South. A much more popular work, Margaret Mitchell's *Gone with the Wind* (1936), enthralled millions of readers on both sides of the Mason-Dixon line.

The developments of the 1930s represented a major turning point in the relationship between the South and the nation. In the first place, the extent of federal intervention—in the South and throughout the country—was unprecedented. The national government became a palpable force in the lives of southerners, and new links were established between Washington and the states and municipalities. The New Deal initiated vast changes in southern agriculture, set national wage and hour standards, encouraged the unionization of the region's labor force, and turned to the task of removing economic disparities between the South and the rest of the nation. In the second place, most southerners responded favorably to these federal initiatives. Even southerners who looked on Franklin Roosevelt's policies with a jaundiced eye found succor and satisfaction in the federal largess. Southern congressional leadership was instrumental in the enactment of Roosevelt's programs. A third aspect of federal intervention was the effect the New Deal had in arousing the political consciousness of southerners, including poor farmers, coal miners, blacks, and working people generally. Although the president's politics and policies did little to change the distribution of political power in the South, it did a good deal to change the political outlook of southerners. It helped create a politics of class and economic interest in the South, as in other regions. It both reinforced southerners' regional self-consciousness and heightened their awareness of being an integral part of the nation.

In the long run, the New Deal engendered opposition from many southern conservatives and much of the region's traditional governing class. Apprehensive about the new labor policies, resentful over the South's declining influence in the national Democratic party, and fearful of federal interference in southern race relations, anti–New Deal southerners gradually coalesced into groups that openly opposed any extension of the New Deal, particularly in the South. They employed the rhetoric of state rights and constitutionalism in defending their position, and in Congress they rallied to the support of the conservative coalition. In time they would launch a full-blown sectional movement against liberal Democrats and against the northern wing of their party.

If the 1930s brought notable changes to the South and its place in the nation, the years of the Second World War were perhaps even more crucial in their long-term effects. The enormous expenditures in the southern states were a great stimulus to the region's industrial and urban growth, preparing the way for more substantial economic development in the postwar period. Wartime prosperity and a multitude of military camps and defense industries, as well as the movement of millions of outsiders to southern training sites and assignments narrowed regional differences. At the same time, southern congressmen took a leading part in steering Roosevelt's defense measures and international policies through the two houses. Nevertheless, sectional issues provoked controversy, especially those involving African Americans. Southerners helped terminate several New Deal agencies and joined the conservative coalition in opposing domestic reform and federal encroachment on state rights.

Following World War II, the South's economic expansion, unprecedented prosperity, and rapid urbanization created conditions increasingly similar to those in other regions. The South, it seemed, was finally entering the American mainstream. But appearances were illusory, not only because the South continued to lag behind the national average on most measures of achievement and well-being, but because a bitter sectional conflict developed over the civil rights movement. The emergence of civil rights for black Americans as a national issue, the Truman administration's sponsorship of a broad equal-rights reform program, and the epochal 1954 school desegregation decision in *Brown* v. *Board of Education* led to a southern rebellion against the national Democratic party and a regional pattern of political defiance and resistance to federal intervention in race relations in the southern states. This sectional intransigence was aptly labeled "Massive Resistance." The attitudes of northern and southern whites became steadily more polarized, although the interaction of North and South was not invariably hostile. Interregional understanding was evident in the increasing competitiveness of presidential Republicanism in the South, in the strength of the conservative coalition in Congress, and in the reluctance of northern business interests to offend the South.

Even so, by 1960 the accelerating pace of the civil rights movement was beginning to concentrate the nation's attention and energies on the South's sectional defiance and the possibility of its reconstruction. The Second Reconstruction brought the most momentous sectional clash in twentieth-century American history and transformed the politics and society of the South. The civil rights revolution owed a great deal to the pressure exerted by outside leaders, organizations, and public opinion. But the two most influential figures in the Second Reconstruction—Martin Luther King, Jr., and Lyndon B. Johnson—were both southerners, and the role of indigenous protesters and reformers was vital to the success of the movement. Another point is also important: many northern and western whites sympathized with racial conservatives in the South, and the decline of the civil rights movement was in considerable part a consequence of the mounting disaffection of white northerners, particularly as the struggle moved out of the South and as urban riots and racial violence erupted in other regions. Ironically, a reform endeavor that had begun with the South as the prime target ended by shifting to other regions and provoking responses similar to those of white southerners.

The convergence of North and South in the half-century following World War II was nowhere more apparent than in the economic development and diversification, industrialization and urbanization, dynamic new middle class, and rising income and consumer-oriented life-style of southerners in this period. Yet these changes were accompanied by new sectional conflicts, such as the one resulting from the energetic campaigns by southern promoters to "sell the South" to northern industrialists and investors. Northerners also complained about federal defense allocations and revenue and appropriations policies that seemed to favor the South and Southwest. When they organized to reverse this discrimination and to create training and research facilities to make themselves more competitive, southerners employed similar tactics. Meanwhile, the rise of the Sunbelt and the decline of the old industrial centers in the Northeast and Midwest raised the confidence and morale of the South and brought it a more favorable image in other regions.

Equally compelling was the South's political transformation in the postwar decades. At the heart of this alteration was the disruption of the Solid South and the emergence of a competitive politics in the southern states. The process began in the 1930s, but its overt unfolding came after the war with the southern revolt against the national Democratic party, the use of a "southern strategy" by Republicans, and the approval of the Voting Rights Act of 1965 and other federal policies that removed formidable institutional supports from the old political system. The result was an enlarged electorate in the South, an increasingly competitive Republican party, and a recomposition of the Democratic party on the basis of black-white coalitions. A new party system replaced the old one-party organization, and southern politics, while retaining much of its familiar style and distinctive cultural context, was more fully integrated into the national party system than ever before. Furthermore, the South played a large part in the rejuvenation of the Republican party after the upheaval of the 1960s and in the GOP's success in presidential elections on the basis of a conservative ideology. The contemporary South, a recent study emphasizes, may well be the most important region in the United States "in terms of establishing the partisan direction of presidential politics."[9]

As time passed, it became more difficult to distinguish the South from other parts of the nation. Regional differences remained, such as the South's political conservatism and strong opposition to labor unions, but most of these were differences of degree rather than of kind. Vocation and profession, business enterprise, the arrangement of cities, demographic and social characteristics, the powerful role of the media, and other aspects of contemporary society reflected the erosion of regional variations and the growing homogenization of American life. The process of Americanization produced more subtle changes as well. The images and stereotypes in the North-South dialogue lost much of their sting, and nonsoutherners seemed more prepared to accept southerners on equal terms. Northerners grew less inclined, in David M. Potter's words, to equate "northernism with nationalism and southernism with sectionalism."[10] The Southernization of America was also having its effect—through the migration of people north and south, through the export of southern music and literature, through the widespread appeal of evangelical religion. Still, southern distinctiveness did not entirely disappear. Southerners—black and white—continued to place more emphasis than other Americans on place and locality,

9. Earl Black and Merle Black, *The Vital South: How Presidents Are Elected* (Cambridge, Mass., 1992), p. 344.
10. David M. Potter, "The Historian's Use of Nationalism and Vice Versa," *American Historical Review* 67 (July 1962): 941.

family, and tradition. Their religious beliefs and practices, their tendency toward violence, and the distinguished and distinctive literature produced by
their novelists and poets also continued to set them apart within their own
country.

In terms of *la longue durée*, the South and the North have undergone an extraordinary convergence since the end of Reconstruction—in their objective
conditions, behavior, and basic attitudes. The process has not followed a
straight line or moved at a steady pace; it has waxed and waned through the
years. One is reminded of what John Egerton describes as a South "evolving, a
different and familiar place in constant motion, like a painting in progress."[11]
This was also true of sectional conflict. The bitter divisions of secession, war,
and Reconstruction became less virulent by the turn of the century, but intersectional condemnation and recrimination erupted from time to time, as in the
1920s and 1960s. Also, efforts to protect regional interests gave rise to recurrent
conflict and controversy: over the autonomy of the South's system of racial segregation, control of the Democratic party, domination of Congress, and the
economic struggle between the northern industrial core and the southern and
western periphery. Yet neither North nor South was ever truly united; neither
ever spoke with a single voice. This encouraged interregional compromise, accommodation, and alliances in an effort to enhance the position of various economic, ideological, and political interests in each section. This transregional cooperation took many forms over the years: the mutual concessions of the
northern and southern wings of the Democratic party, the alliance between
northeastern Democrats and New South Redeemers in the post-Reconstruction period, the community of interests between South and West on agrarian
reform and Bryan Democracy, the New Deal Democratic coalition, the conservative coalition between southern Democrats and northern Republicans in
Congress after 1937, the cooperation of northern and western congressional
leaders on agricultural policy in the 1930s and after, and the coalescence of
northern and western voters in support of conservative Republicans in presidential elections beginning in 1964.

The interaction of North and South, and more generally of regions with
well-defined interests, constitutes an essential part of American history, in the
twentieth century as well as the nineteenth. As Vann Woodward once noted,
"The South has been almost as essential to the North and North to the South in
the shaping of national character and mythology as the Afro-American to
Southern-American and vice versa."[12] The reciprocal effects of this regional
interaction reveal an important aspect of the national experience. For a long
time the South was a region at odds, its role in the nation circumscribed, its
example almost never emulated. Yet, however it may have been perceived by
contemporaries, the region was never outside our national history. Without the
South, Carl N. Degler argues, "the history of the United States would have

11. John Egerton, *Shades of Gray: Dispatches From the Modern South* (Baton Rouge, La., 1991), p. 5.
12. C. Vann Woodward, *American Counterpoint: Slavery and Racism in the North-South Dialogue* (Boston, 1971), p. 6.

been quite different." Rather than seeing the South as the adversary of the nation, Degler has urged historians to show how the region shaped the values and the history of the United States. At times, the South reinforced or reflected values held in common with the rest of the country; at other times it modified the way in which the North would have gone had the South not existed; and on other occasions southern influence established a pattern followed by the nation.[13] Thus the interplay of the South, the North, and the nation represents a rich and instructive theme in modern American history. It offers a useful geographical perspective and organizational approach in understanding our national history. This pattern of regional interaction illuminates much of the nation's conflict and tension, its efforts to reconcile divergent interests, and its struggles to realize its historic ideals. The odyssey of the South as a region at odds is a story that is meaningful in the larger context of American history.

13. See Carl N. Degler, "Thesis, Antithesis, Synthesis: The South, the North, and the Nation," *Journal of Southern History* 53 (February 1987): 3–18.

Bibliographical Note

Readers can identify the sources on which this study rests in the notes that accompany the text. These references reveal two important aspects of my research: the dynamic character of southern historiography and my reliance on the extensive writings devoted to the twentieth-century South. The scope and volume of the scholarly and popular writings on the American South are suggested in several of the chapters in John B. Boles and Evelyn Thomas Nolen, eds., *Interpreting Southern History: Historiographical Essays in Honor of Sanford W. Higginbotham* (Baton Rouge, La., 1987); in Merle Black, John Shelton Reed, James C. Cobb, and Charles Reagan Wilson, eds., *Perspectives on the American South*, 6 vols. (New York, 1981–1994), a repository of interdisciplinary articles on the historical and contemporary South; and in the *Journal of Southern History*'s annual bibliography of periodical articles on the region. I am indebted to the hundreds of historians, social scientists, journalists, and others whose contributions have facilitated my own study.

No one who sets out to write a book about the modern South can be unaware of the profound influence of three magisterial works in shaping our understanding of the field: C. Vann Woodward's *Origins of the New South, 1877–1913* (Baton Rouge, La., 1951); George Brown Tindall's *The Emergence of the New South, 1913–1945* (Baton Rouge, La., 1967); and V. O. Key's *Southern Politics in State and Nation* (New York, 1949). These volumes provide an incomparable portrait of the South between the end of Reconstruction and the middle of the twentieth century. They are notable for their comprehensive coverage, original concepts, and valuable interpretive themes. Several other large-scale studies of the modern South complement and extend the volumes by Woodward, Tindall, and Key. Among the best of these are Richard Franklin Bensel, *Sectionalism and American Political Development, 1880–1980* (Madison, Wis., 1984), a study based on an analysis of roll call votes in the House of Representatives; Earl Black and Merle Black, *Politics and Society in the South* (Cambridge, Mass., 1987), on the new southern politics; and Edward L. Ayers, *The Promise of the New South: Life After Reconstruction* (New York, 1992), a fresh and vivid reappraisal of the southern experience in the late nineteenth century. I have also benefited from the themes developed in C. Vann Woodward, *American Counterpoint: Slavery and Racism in the North-South Dialogue* (Boston, 1971); Jack Temple Kirby, *Media-Made Dixie: The South in the American Imagination* (Baton Rouge, La., 1978); Richard

343

N. Current, *Northernizing the South* (Athens, Ga., 1983); and Carl N. Degler, "Thesis, Antithesis, Synthesis: The South, the North, and the Nation," *Journal of Southern History* 53 (February 1987): 3–18.

A number of documentary works throw revealing light on the South in national affairs, notably Elting E. Morison et al., eds., *The Letters of Theodore Roosevelt*, 8 vols. (Cambridge, Mass., 1951–1954); Arthur S. Link and associates, eds., *The Papers of Woodrow Wilson*, vols. 1–69 (Princeton, N.J., 1966–1994); Louis R. Harlan and others, eds., *The Booker T. Washington Papers*, 14 vols. (Urbana, Ill., 1972–1989); and *The Public Papers of the Presidents of the United States* (Washington, D.C., 1961–). I have consulted the Gallup, Roper, and Harris polls for northern and southern attitudes on certain issues. While my research for this study did not entail extensive work in newspapers and manuscript collections, earlier research undertakings enabled me to make considerable use of such sources in this volume.

Index